ELINOR VERVILLE, Ph.D.

BEHAVIOR PROBLEMS OF CHILDREN

W. B. SAUNDERS COMPANY
Philadelphia and London

W. B. Saunders Company: West Washington Square
Philadelphia, Pa. 19105

12 Dyott Street
London W.C.1

Reprinted June, 1968

BEHAVIOR PROBLEMS OF CHILDREN

To George
and
Ann, Tom, and Barbara

who, in infinite ways, aided
in the production of this book

PREFACE

The function of clinical psychology is not only that of understanding and assisting with human adjustment difficulties but also of minimizing the need for such service by establishing effective programs for the prevention of emotional and behavior problems. An obvious preventive measure is the elimination in children of such problems which, left alone to flourish, inevitably produce the withdrawal or aggression of the chronic neurotic or psychotic adult.

Surveys indicate that the training of clinical psychologists to evaluate and deal with the behavior problems of children has been neglected. In many community guidance clinics, children are given only cursory attention; and university faculties, clinic directors, and clinical psychologists themselves deplore this gap in training. Until a major effort is made to resolve children's problems, there will be no significant reduction in the incidence of emotional disorders for the entire population. Even the psychologist who plans to work exclusively with adults will find his knowledge incomplete if he knows nothing of children's behavior problems, because the adult he tries to help is tied to habit patterns acquired as a child.

With a hint from academicians that not enough is known about clinical child psychology to teach the subject, this text was written to assemble and synthesize the facts, insights, and conclusions garnered by many persons working with children and their problems. The book is divided into six parts. The first part is concerned with the determinants of behavior, both objective and interpersonal, in identification of the concrete characteristics and experiences of the child which direct his actions. Motivation for parental mismanagement is discussed, and correlations are drawn between the child's daily life and the development of deviate behavior.

The next three parts of the book deal respectively with the pre-

v

school child, the elementary school child, and the adolescent. The first section of each part is devoted to a description of behavior typical of the normal child. This description is not a catalogue of development, but a sketch of recognized processes of change in every child which disturb parental expectations and evoke anxiety, irritation, and emotionally charged reactions from adults. It is hoped that this discussion will provide both a clearer visualization of the daily occurrences in ordinary homes and an enduring awareness that unusual or mysterious events seldom are the basis for creation of a setting in which conflict and misunderstanding between parent and child develop.

The second section of each part is devoted to behavior problems. Similar forms of deviate behavior are discussed at each age level, because these hold different meanings and respond to different management according to a child's chronological age. Some clinicians regard behavior problems in themselves as of little significance, serving only to herald the existence of basic feelings of loneliness, fear, or failure. In dismissing them as minor aspects of more critical difficulties, however, they fail to recognize that the deviate behavior contributes to increased tension in an already unhappy situation. Stealing, thumb-sucking, enuresis, and stuttering are behaviors which are disturbing to both parents and child. When a symptom can be eliminated, a reason for contention also vanishes, and both parent and child are bolstered in self-respect from their joint conquest of an irritating problem.

The fifth part of the book is concerned with the characteristics, problems, and training of the handicapped child. The clinical psychologist frequently is held responsible for assisting in planning for the handicapped, and in some communities he must instigate public concern and guide parents in rearing such children.

The sixth part consists of case histories, assembled as a unit to provide greater continuity in the text and to permit the student to examine in detail the information they contain. The behavior problems of a child are not limited in scope or etiology, and therefore every case history illustrates many facets of commonly encountered difficulties.

Many persons have assisted in many ways in the writing of this book. Dr. Paul Benton read the entire manuscript, and his suggestions for emphasis, interpretation, and organization were invaluable. Dr. Richard Pasewark, Mr. Robert Bassham, Dr. Lillian Whitmore, and Mrs. Berneice Fort read parts of the manuscript and offered pertinent suggestions for clarification. Dr. Pasewark and Mr. Dolph Hess gave special assistance with reference materials; and Dr. Benton, Dr. Raymond Bice, Dr. Ned Papania, and Mrs. Arthur Pongratz loaned source materials from their private libraries. Mrs. Kenneth Buchholtz, Mrs. Wilbur Fletcher, Mrs. James Glassco, and Mrs. G. J. Wiloth devoted time and effort to recording daily events in the lives of their families.

To the hundreds of children with whom I have been acquainted, both in the neighborhood and in the clinic; to their parents and teachers; and to my colleagues, I owe the continually renewed and broadened knowledge which affords new discernment and affirms old convictions.

The wiles and woes of children, their generosity, and their fortitude contain lessons for us all, but the rearing of a child is a lonely affair. Parents do not have access to comforting reminders that much of a child's distressing behavior is normal, nor do they often receive encouragement and assurance that their methods of rearing the child are adequate. Teachers also must work alone in educating the children entrusted to them, and their attempts to accomplish their task are thwarted by children's behavior which they misunderstand and cannot alter. The parent's plea for aid in defining the goals of child rearing and his request for specific suggestions for implementing these goals should not be ignored, nor should teachers be left to devise whatever methods they can to curb or overlook the behavior of pupils unwilling or unable to learn. The knowledge of the clinical psychologist is available for the use of adults who are intelligently concerned with the child's welfare. With it, they can assure his developing to maturity as a considerate and self-respecting individual.

ELINOR VERVILLE

CONTENTS

Part III
THE ELEMENTARY SCHOOL CHILD

Part IV
THE ADOLESCENT

Part I

BEHAVIOR DETERMINANTS

Chapter 1

Introduction

During the past 50 years there has been an ever-broadening accumulation of knowledge about children, and efforts devoted to understanding and improving child behavior never before have been so concentrated. Committees studying the causes of juvenile delinquency are formed by local, state, and national groups. Parents are besieged with child care articles and books. Teachers are instructed in the emotional needs of children, and school guidance counselors are standard staff members in many cities. Community mental health clinics and child guidance centers are prevalent; and increasing numbers of social workers, psychologists, and psychiatrists offer private assistance.

Despite all of this concern, knowledge, and effort, few adults confronted with a child who behaves ineffectually or obstreperously can identify accurately the reasons for his actions, nor do they know how to revise them. Adults meet the difficulty with anger or guilt; and after abortive efforts to punish the child, to reason with him, or to conciliate him, they resign themselves to an inevitable permanency of the deviate behavior. Sometimes, if they find the child's actions too unpleasant to live with, they rid themselves of the burden by banishing the child: The school expels him; the parents send him to boarding school; the professional worker hospitalizes him; and the judge remands him to his parents, ordering the child to obey them.

An examination of the history of the interest in child behavior and of the attitudes, theories, and practices which have developed offers clues to the perplexing problem of why parents have become immobilized and professional workers confused in the management of the individual child.

1

STUDY OF THE CHILD

The first stirring of interest in discovering what the child was really like came at the turn of the century. Early observations consisted of biographical reports of the daily lives of infants and small children[58] and of adult reminiscences about their own childhoods. These were followed by the questionnaire, with its formal and detailed inquiry into childhood experiences and attitudes.[14] Alfred Binct,[8] reporting in 1908 on his direct sampling and chronological placement of children's abilities with explicit tasks, was the first person to use the experimental method with children.

Since these beginnings, hundreds of investigators have studied everything from prenatal conditioning[53] to morality in children.[33] Developmental observations identified differences in ability and behavior between children of various ages.[24, 60, 68] Emotional reactions were observed, experimentally induced, and extinguished.[31] Children's drawings,[21] musical aptitude,[67] vocabularies,[38, 62] motor skills,[26] social development,[11] and reasoning ability[50] were examined. All of these studies contributed vast new knowledge about the child's abilities and their orderly change with maturation and engendered both an appreciation of the child's capacities and a previously unrecognized awareness that age imposes limitations on behavioral control. These ideas combined to accord the child a status he had not previously enjoyed and an excuse for inadequacies. He was both respected for his capabilities and forgiven for his limitations.

The first university-sponsored nursery schools were associated with the careful studies of the 1920's, which were primarily concerned with the child's social adjustment and the establishment of habit routines. Because of the existence of the schools, students could observe the same children in the same setting over a period of many months. During this time the occurrence, development, and modification of specific problems could be recorded, and correlations with parental rearing practices and attitudes could be affirmed.

Parent guidance books summarizing the findings of these investigations began to appear in the 1930's, and the specter of the child guidance expert loomed, to be greeted with mixed feelings by parents. They were relieved to learn that there were answers to their questions and that knowledge was available which presumably would guarantee the trouble-free rearing of their children. However, their relief was tinged with resentment by the implication that their actions were to blame for the child's misbehavior, and their daily contacts with the child were shadowed by the fear of committing drastic errors.

No longer considering themselves capable of independent decisions, parents obeyed precepts of child rearing which were incompletely explained and understood. They were informed that punishment can produce strong negative emotions in the child, so they abandoned punishment completely. They were taught that the child depends on them for support and comfort, so they provided needlessly prolonged service and protection.[4, 37] They were told that the child's feelings must be respected, so they were attentive to these and excused his behavior. Practicing what they believed was preached, parents became increasingly bewildered as the child failed to develop in self-control and consideration for others. Mothers who felt helpless and who were unwilling to assume responsibility for the child's faulty development began leaving their homes to work. They substituted gifts of clothing, toys, and commercial entertainment for companionship and conversation; and they renounced their positions as mentors by arranging for their children's lives to be supervised by sitters, scout leaders, dancing instructors, and recreation directors.

About this same time, social workers became interested in the characteristics of the juvenile delinquent, who had appeared in court and about whom a decision had to be made. Histories of individual delinquent children were compiled, and these reports were followed by numerous studies of the traits of delinquents and statistical reports of their activities.[25, 28, 37] These histories and studies led to the investigation of all varieties of deviate behavior and emotion. Such symptoms as stuttering, obesity, nightmares, stealing, sexual misconduct, school phobia, enuresis, cheating, lying, and disobedience were studied; and children's feelings of aggression, hostility, and anxiety were examined objectively.[5]

This work provided evidence that antisocial and abnormal behaviors were end results of multiple environmental and training influences operating in an unfavorable emotional climate, and thus the evidence suggested that the child was not responsible for his actions. Alerted to this knowledge, judges began to feel uncertain about the wisdom of punishing the delinquent child; teachers adopted a *laissez-faire* policy for the nonproductive student; and clinicians promulgated the child's viewpoint and counseled patience. Behavior problems were permitted to continue with no serious attempt being made to curb them by any method.

ASSISTANCE FOR THE CHILD

As more was learned about children, people became concerned about those who were neglected physically, educationally, or emotionally by their parents or by the community, and they sought to better the lot of the ill-treated child.

Social agencies began to work with families, and children were taken by the courts from homes where they were abused. A child removed from his home to an orphanage, however, was often "lost." Little or no information accompanied him to the institution, and seldom was there any contact by either the placement agency or his family in the years that followed. Usually he remained at the orphanage until he was 18 years old, daily hoping that he would be returned to his family and never fully cognizant of why he was there or who was responsible for him.

To replace the impersonal atmosphere and limited attention available to the child at a state orphanage, the use of foster homes for the placement of children separated from their parents became common and still is considered preferable to institutionalization for most children. In some foster homes, if a neglected child is placed during his pre-school years, he can achieve both emotional stability and intellectual growth and find a valid substitute family in his foster relatives. In other homes, or if the child is older when he is removed from his parents, he is unable to tolerate the separation, and his behavior continues so troublesome that foster parents request his removal. The child suffers once again from being banished. Knowing that foster home placements are not always successful, judges increasingly hesitate to terminate parental rights; and social workers, juvenile counselors, and public health nurses now make a determined effort to rehabilitate the home before resorting to removal of the child.[1]

Care and retraining for children with physical and intellectual handicaps have expanded steadily. Schools for blind and deaf children are available in most states, and larger cities provide classes within the public school system for them. Special classes for moderately retarded and trainable children are growing in numbers, and sheltered community workshops afford useful work for adolescent retarded children. Cerebral palsied and orthopedically handicapped children are treated regularly at hospitals staffed with speech, physical, and occupational therapists.*

The most concerted effort to deal with children's behavior problems exists in the hundreds of child guidance clinics now available in many moderate-sized cities. The prototype of such centers was Thom's Boston Habit Clinic, established in 1921 to assist parents in learning how to handle the problems they encountered in rearing their children. Today, child guidance clinics are supported jointly by federal, state, and local governments, with supplementary income from Community Chest contributions and fees. They are staffed by child psychiatrists, psychologists, and social workers. Parents in the middle to high socioeconomic levels utilize the clinics most,[55] with children of low-income families appearing there only under duress of the courts. Waiting lists are lengthy, prompt help is rare, and when it finally is obtained, it may not appear practical or efficacious in resolving the difficulty.[56] Traditionally, child guidance clinic staff members work individually with parent and child over a period of many months; and parents often are unable to endure the

---

* See Part V, The Handicapped Child.

weekly probing of their own motives or the mystery of their child's play therapy sessions.

The Influence of Theory

Some of the difficulty in understanding a child's maladaptive behavior and assisting him in revising it has developed from the adherence by professional workers to intriguing, but narrow, theories. Tried over the years and found wanting, these theories have nevertheless been retained by many clinicians and counselors as absolute tenets, thus blinding them to the need to obtain exact, complete information about the child and to devise appropriate retraining techniques. There are four theories about children which have been prominent for many years and which still direct the interpretation and management of behavior problems by both professional workers and parents. The theories are not mutually exclusive and there is an historical relationship among them, but proponents of each principle tend to relate all phenomena of child development to the single belief they consider most significant.

Psychoanalytic theory, from its inception in 1893, and continuing until the present time, has offered systematic analyses of motivations for specific abnormalities in greater number than any other school of thought. Useful concepts of interfamilial emotion, regressive behavior, and motivation developing from forgotten experiences originate from psychoanalytic theory.[12, 29] The use of Freud's basic tenets of infantile sexuality in the therapy of children, however, has led its practitioners to ascribe sexual significance to such diverse behavior as fear of cars, temper tantrums, and refusal to eat, and to interpret the symptom in sexual terms to the child.[17, 34, 36] Such interpretations not only produce anxiety for the child and his parents but obscure valid reasons for the difficulty and postpone its solution.

Watson's theory of behaviorism appeared 25 years later, after the experimental demonstrations of conditioned learning by Pavlov and Bekhterev.[19, 29, 65] Watson insisted that any child could acquire any desired traits and abilities if he were reared by specified techniques. He also stressed the need for training in independence, and he deplored nurturing the child. His emphasis on the values of achievement has endured, and his staunch support for thoughtful training as well as his optimistic view of human potentiality are useful to clinicians.

Behaviorism implies, however, that there is an ideal way to meet each of the problems encountered in the 18 years during which a child is reared. It also implies that parents will be able to adhere consistently to ideal training methods. These are unrealistic concepts in that they ignore the certainty that unpredictable responses will occur as parent and child interact, each according to his own distinctive needs and characteristics. Behaviorism also fails to recognize that there are ramifications of learning associated with the primary intended response. Parents can train an infant to feel hunger only at regular intervals by disregarding his hunger cry except prior to set feeding times, but he may be learning simultaneously to refrain from expressing his needs and to develop a habit of subservience.

Emerging from the rejection of both of these theories as providing complete answers to questions of child development was the recognition that the child was not a repository for innate evil which must somehow be submerged or sublimated, nor was he a lump of clay ready for shaping. He was acknowledged to be an individual with needs, capabilities, and rights.[54] It was believed that the child's own viewpoint was essential to the correct assessment of his behavior and that the protection of his feelings was mandatory. Adults need to be continually aware that the child is reacting both emotionally and rationally to his own behavior and to the behavior of others toward him, and they need to recognize that childhood is not a state which automatically cancels the individual's right to fairness and consideration. These ideas, however, have been distorted into the principle that a child has the right to do or say anything he wishes and that respect for his feelings is the chief consideration in any conflict. Clinicians, in their zeal to guard the child from emotional insult, limit their efforts in coping with his behavior problems to observation, conversation, and conciliation. Parents adhering to this concept excuse themselves from opposing, or even directing, the child. The child, whose judgment is immature and whose interests are self-centered and short-sighted, succeeds in avoiding responsibility and regulation and becomes increasingly anxious and unrestrained in his behavior.

Investigations of the last 20 years support the theory that many behavior problems arise because of the way parent and child respond to one another. It is essential that a parent manage his child from a base of affection and intelligent concern for him, but this truth has been distorted into an assertion that all misbehavior of the child occurs because he is rejected by the parent.[40] Although children with behavior problems seldom are regarded fondly by their harassed parents, the assumption that the adult's distaste for the miscreant child precipitated the trouble is not valid for most families. The helplessness and anger which the adult feels toward the child reflect his conviction that he has failed as a parent, a conviction which has grown out of hundreds of unpleasant encounters. Clinicians convinced that parental dislike is the reason for the problem turn their attention from the child and the present to the parent and his past, and in so doing they by-pass the existing difficulties and provide no solution for them.

Each of these fragmental theories has merit, but none is complete;

and adherence to any one of them exclusively leads to errors in understanding and revising the child's deviate behavior.

BEHAVIOR DETERMINANTS

Bandura and Walters[4] observed that deviate behavior is the result of widely varying antecedent consequences which produce different responses in different individuals. A given environmental background or a consistent kind of rearing will produce certain behavior deviations in one child, other deviations in another child, and no unusual behavior at all in a third child. These findings suggest that a thorough, precise, and complete identification of every factor influencing behavior in a given child seldom is made.

To determine why a child behaves as he does, every aspect of his life must be studied. His physical, intellectual, and emotional assets and liabilities can be assessed objectively by formal examination and correlated with observations and information from his physician and teachers. The clinician can discover from the child's parents how much responsibility the child discharges or evades; the kind and frequency of punishment given him; and how much protection he seeks, obtains, or has thrust upon him. His eating and sleeping habits need to be known, and whether they are associated with irregularity or emotional strain. The frequency and nature of the child's daily contacts with other children, both within and without the family, are important. The pressures he experiences in physical, social, and intellectual areas can be judged from his behavior, and whom he tries to please and whether he is successful can be learned. He will say what he thinks of himself—that he is babyish, afraid, stupid, bad, lazy, or disliked—and his evaluation will fit the facts of his life. Knowing these facts provides an accurate picture of the child, but it is necessary to know also how these facts relate to the overt, unwanted behavior which is hindering the child's maturation.

Physical and intellectual endowment define a child's potentiality, and yearly growth sharpens his abilities and broadens his interests. Within this framework, the básic determinant of the child's behavior is learning,[57] and adults concerned with him need to discover what the child has learned which is causing him to misbehave.

From his earliest days the child learns that his actions affect those of his parents; and from their actions he draws conclusions about their attitude toward him—conclusions which may not be correct, but upon which some of his behavior is based. As an infant, if he cries and always is given immediate attention, he learns to cry automatically at any slight discomfort or disappointment. As a pre-school child, if he complains, resists, or makes demands and obtains solicitude or concession by such actions, he learns how to manage his parents. As an elementary school child, if he receives censure for everything he does, he learns that he is displeasing and inept. As an adolescent, if he is held to no requirements of courtesy, obedience, or obligation, he learns that he is entitled to unfettered self-indulgence.

What he learns from his parents' actions and from his own in hundreds of different situations becomes stabilized into habitual, enduring ways of behaving. Longitudinal studies reveal that the child shows consistency in activity level, adaptability, intensity of reactions, responsiveness, mood quality, and distractibility from pre-school days to adulthood.[9] Behavior becomes fixed because it provides the child with the comfort of familiarity. Altered behavior, even though the change is socially approved and urged by others, involves risks, uncertainty, and a feeling of isolation for the child because he cannot predict its effect.

Parental behavior toward the child also stabilizes rapidly, initiated by early reactions of worry, ingratiation, helplessness, dominance, or indifference to the infant and repeated in numerous contacts. Parents reporting difficulty in rearing the child discover, when they observe themselves carefully, that they never speak to him except to criticize or that inevitably they grant every wish the child expresses. Their actions are consistent and predictable to the child, but they themselves have never noticed that their behavior toward him is automatic, rather than thoughtful and adaptive.

In recognizing that certain habitual actions of the parent and of the child are creating problems, the clinician then needs to identify those factors in the child's life which elicit and perpetuate these actions. These determinants of behavior can be classified as objective, and therefore not subject to extensive alteration, or as interpersonal and thus controllable.

Objective Determinants

Objective determinants of the child's behavior include his individual characteristics and those of his family structure. His intelligence, physical status, ordinal position in the family, its size, and his sex direct many facets of behavior. If he is a twin, a stepchild, an adopted child, or an illegitimate child, he is influenced in certain ways. The neighborhood in which he lives and the children available to him there affect his development. The values held by his parents direct his own attitudes and actions, and the presence of relatives in his home or near it alters his behavior. His teachers and the kind of educational experience he has, the socioeconomic status of his family, and his church affiliation not only contribute to the child's estimation of others, but also present him with un-sought challenges and labels.

These individual, familial, and sociological determinants of behavior can be altered to no significant degree; yet their influence should be known so that compensating measures can be adopted to counteract inherent hazards.

Interpersonal Determinants

Interpersonal determinants are those factors related to the care and training of the child by the adults responsible for him. The adults' inter-pretation of their task in rearing him is significant in his development. The child welcomes and responds to favorable attention and to concern for his physical welfare; he requires discipline, training in responsibility, and practice in social interaction; he deserves honorable and honest treatment. Without attention and concern for his needs, he is lonely and irritable. Without practice in self-control, meeting obligations, and con-tacts with peers, he is unproductive and immature. Without respect, he becomes vengeful and deteriorates intellectually and emotionally.

Interpersonal determinants are described as fixation of immaturity, neglect, unbalanced social experience, fatigue, rejection of responsibility, distortion of parental role, damaged self-respect, excessive punishment, and freedom to defy and attack. In the life of every child with behavior problems, one or more of these conditions is operant, and its elimination or minimization produces improved behavior in the child.

BEHAVIOR REVISION

Behavior problems of the child do not vanish spontaneously; indeed, they become more firmly entrenched as time passes. As long as they exist, they constitute irritants to adults and affect their attitudes toward the child; they characterize the child to himself and to others; they are evidence of failure; and they can lead to punishment and ostracism by society. As an adult, an individual must function equably and usefully as a member of his own culture, respect the rights of others, and behave so that he merits the trust of those who depend upon him.[43] A child whose behavior problems are ignored cannot achieve this maturity. He will continue in attitudes and actions which always have caused him difficulty and which are even more inappropriate in adulthood than in childhood.

Deviate behavior persists because it is rewarded. Some rewards are obvious: Misbehavior is reënforced when it provides attention or acclaim from other people or when it leads to the acquisition of possessions or freedom which would not be obtainable otherwise. Other rewards of undesirable behavior are more subtle and may not be apparent to adults puzzled by a child's protracted troublesomeness. The thrill of mastering others or the ease of continued self-indulgence, automatic retreat, or avoidance of effort can be pleasures too satisfying to relinquish.[14] If undesirable behavior is to be changed, its rewards must be replaced with the rewards of appropriate actions: self-control and self-respect.

Attitude and action are intermingled in the production of undesirable behavior. Although most clinicians consider negative attitudes to be responsible for unwanted actions, the reverse relationship also holds: Unworthy actions cause distressed feelings. Mothers who scream at their children feel guilty and ashamed; the child who does not work in school is disappointed in himself and angry at others who do better. Conversely, any individual who meets his daily responsibilities and who solves his problems rationally is content with himself and tolerant of others. He has no need to deceive, hurt, or rebel.

Working directly on new ways of behaving, rather than attempting to change attitudes, improves disturbing situations in a minimum of time and with little concomitant emotion of guilt and anxiety. Marital difficulties disappear when each partner begins to behave differently toward the other. The hesitant individual loses his uncertainty as he practices making decisions. Institutions for the retarded and psychiatric hospitals operate increasingly on the principle that activity is needed to subordinate self-concern or arouse dormant initiative in patients.[2, 39, 56]

In the revision of a child's behavior, the parents, by virtue of their position as the child's most valued and continuous models, are the most significant of all the adults who deal with him. Not only are their actions with him critical, but their behavior toward other persons, including each other, furnishes a pattern which he inevitably imitates. Unfortunately, the parental behavior he selects to imitate may not be that which is most mature but that which is least controlled and worthy. If the adults' anti-social or immature behavior remains the same, the child's actions will continue to reflect what he observes.[13] This immutable fact is not re-iterated to imply that parents deserve or benefit from criticism.[34] They, too, have burdens to bear, not the least of which is the child himself, and his contribution to their feelings of ineptitude and discouragement is great. Adults as well as children, however, can learn new ways of be-having,[30] and as they do, the child copies the more reasonable and thoughtful models they provide him.

Parents and teachers also can train the child to modify undesirable behavior by utilizing reward to strengthen wanted actions and punish-ment to weaken unwanted ones. They can apply known learning prin-ciples of conditioning, extinction, generalization, practice, discrimination, and social imitation to the instruction of the child in acceptable behavior. The use of such techniques is suggested in the discussions of specific behavior problems and indicated by the procedures described in the case histories.*

Every child's life is a patchwork: Success and affection are interspersed with gloom, failure, and loneliness. No child is ever treated with complete consistency, perfect fairness, impeccable judgment, and invariable understanding. A child grows to adulthood either supported by competence, control, and good will or mired in self-pity and self-concern. The direction of his development is determined by whether constructive or defeating experiences are predominant in his daily life.

REFERENCES

1. Abramovitz, A. B., ed.: *Emotional Factors in Public Health Nursing.* Madison, The University of Wisconsin Press, 1961.
2. Anker, J., and Walsh, R.: Group psychotherapy, a special activity program, and group structure in the treatment of chronic schizophrenics. *J. Consult. Psychol.,* 1961, *25* (6), 476–481.
3. Bandura, A.: Psychotherapy as a learning process. *Psychol. Bull.,* 1961, *58,* 143–159.
4. Bandura, A., and Walters, R. H.: *Social Learning and Personality Development.* New York, Holt, Rinehart and Winston, 1963, pp. 30, 34, 40, 70, 226–253.
5. Bender, L.: *Aggression, Hostility and Anxiety in Children.* Springfield, Ill., Charles C Thomas, 1953.
6. Benne, K. D.: Deliberate changing as the facilitation of growth. *In* Bennis, W. G., Benne, K. D., and Chin, R., eds.: *The Planning of Change.* New York, Holt, Rinehart and Winston, 1961, p. 231.
7. Bettelheim, B.: *Love Is Not Enough.* Glencoe, Ill., The Free Press, 1950, p. 27.
8. Binet, A., and Simon, T.: Le développement de l'intelligence chez les enfants. *L'Année Psychologique,* 1908, *14,* 1–94.
9. Birch, H. G., Thomas, A., Chess, S., and Hertsig, M. E.: Individuality in the development of children. *Developm. Med. Child Neurol.,* 1962, *4,* 370–379.
10. Blake, J. A.: Comprehension versus motivation in child behavior. *Understanding the Child,* 1955, *24,* 77–79.
11. Bridges, K. M. B.: A study of social development in early infancy. *Child Developm.,* 1933, *4,* 36–49.
12. Brill, A. A.: *The Basic Writings of Sigmund Freud.* New York, The Modern Library, Random House, Inc., 1938, pp. 580–603.
13. Brim, O. G., Jr.: Methods of educating parents and their evaluation. *In* Caplan, G., ed.: *Prevention of Mental Disorders in Children.* New York, Basic Books, Inc., 1961, pp. 124–125.
14. Brooks, F. D.: *Child Psychology.* New York, Houghton Mifflin Co., 1937, pp. 4–17.
15. Brower, D.: Child psychology: A look at tomorrow. *J. Genet. Psychol.,* 1963, *102,* 45–50.
16. Bruch, H., and Rosenkotter, L.: Psychotherapeutic aspects of teaching emotionally disturbed children. *Psychiat. Quart.,* 1960, *34,* 648–657.
17. Burlingham, D., Goldberger, A., and Lussier, A.: Simultaneous analysis of mother and child. *Psychoanal. Stud. Child,* 1955, *10,* 165 186.
18. Cameron, N.: *The Psychology of Behavior Disorders.* Cambridge, Mass., Houghton Mifflin Co., 1947, p. 16.

---

* See Section Two in Parts II, III, and IV. See also Part VI.

19. Dashiell, J. F.: *Fundamentals of General Psychology.* Cambridge, Mass., Houghton Mifflin Co., 1937, pp. 169–172.
20. Eisenberg, L.: School phobia: A study in the communication of anxiety. *In* Trapp, E. P., and Himelstein, P., eds.: *Readings on the Exceptional Child.* New York, Appleton-Century-Crofts, 1962, pp. 629–639.
21. Eng, H.: *The Psychology of Children's Drawings: From the First Stroke to the Colored Drawing.* London, Kegal Paul, Trench, Trubner, 1941.
22. Felix, R. H., *In* Caplan, G., ed.: *Prevention of Mental Disorders in Children.* New York, Basic Books, Inc., 1961, p. viii.
23. Garfield, S. L.: *Introduction to Clinical Psychology.* New York, The Macmillan Co., 1957, pp. 372–373.
24. Gesell, A.: *Infancy and Human Growth.* New York, The Macmillan Co., 1928.
25. Glueck, S., and Glueck, E. T.: *One Thousand Juvenile Delinquents.* Cambridge, Mass., Harvard University Press, 1934.
26. Goodenough, F. L., and Brian, C. R.: Certain factors underlying the acquisition of motor skills by preschool children. *J. Exper. Psychol.,* 1929, *12,* 127–155.
27. Haring, N. G., and Phillips, E. L.: *Educating the Emotionally Disturbed Child.* New York, McGraw-Hill Book Co., 1962, p. 188.
28. Healy, W.: *The Individual Delinquent.* Boston, Little, Brown and Co., 1920, pp. 24–29.
29. Heidbreder, E.: *Seven Psychologies.* New York, The Century Co., 1933, pp. 247–260, 385–400.
30. Jersild, A. T.: *Child Psychology,* Ed. 4. New York, Prentice-Hall, Inc., 1954, p. 591.
31. Jones, H. E.: The retention of conditioned emotional reactions in infancy. *J. Genet. Psychol.,* 1930, *37,* 485–498.
32. Jones, V.: Character development in children—an objective approach. *In* Carmichael, L., ed.: *Manual of Child Psychology.* New York, John Wiley and Sons, 1946, pp. 725–726.
33. Jones, V.: Ideas of right and wrong among teachers and children. *Teachers College Record,* 1929, *30,* 529–541.
34. Kanner, L.: *Child Psychiatry.* Springfield, Ill., Charles C Thomas, 1957, pp. 11, 103–107.
35. Kitano, H. H.: Adjustment of problem and nonproblem children to specific situations: A study in role theory. *Child Developm.,* 1962, *33,* 229–233.
36. Klein, M.: *The Psychoanalysis of Children.* New York, Grove Press, 1932.
37. Kvaraceus, W. C.: *The Community and the Delinquent.* Yonkers-on-Hudson, N. Y., World Book Co., 1954, p. 95.
38. McCarthy, D. A.: *The Language Development of the Preschool Child.* Minneapolis, University of Minnesota Press, 1930.
39. McCormick, E.: New hope for darkened minds. *Reader's Digest,* March, 1962, pp. 139–143. Condensed from *Today's Health,* March, 1962.
40. Mandler, G.: Parent and child in the development of the Oedipus complex. *J. Nerv. Ment. Dis.,* 1963, *136,* 227–235.
41. Miller, J.: *Unconsciousness.* New York, John Wiley and Sons, 1942.
42. Mowrer, O. H.: *Learning Theory and Behavior.* New York, John Wiley and Sons, 1960, pp. 216–217.
43. Mowrer, O. H.: What is normal behavior? *In* Pennington, L. A., and Berg, I. A., eds.: *An Introduction to Clinical Psychology.* New York, The Ronald Press Co., 1948, p. 45.
44. Murray, H. A.: Studies of stressful interpersonal disputations. *Amer. Psychol.,* 1963, *18* (1), 28.
45. Mussen, P. H., and Conger, J. J.: *Child Development and Personality.* New York, Harper and Bros., 1956, p. 542.
46. Pavlov, I. P.: *Conditioned Reflexes.* London, Oxford University Press, 1927.
47. Peck, R. F., and Havighurst, R. J.: *The Psychology of Character Development.* New York, John Wiley and Sons, 1960, pp. 124–125.
48. Phillips, E. L., and Haring, N. G.: Results from special techniques for teaching emotionally disturbed children. *Except. Child,* 1959, *26,* 64–67.

49. Phillips, E. L., Wiener, D. N., and Haring, N. G.: *Discipline, Achievement and Mental Health.* Englewood Cliffs, N. J., Prentice-Hall, Inc., 1960, pp. 94–95.
50. Piaget, J.: *Judgement and Reasoning in the Child.* New York, Harcourt, Brace and Co., 1928.
51. Pratt, E. C., Nelson, A. K., and Sun, K. H.: *The Behavior of the Newborn Infant.* Columbus, Ohio State University Press, 1930.
52. Rabin, A. I.: The maternal deprivation hypothesis revisited. *The Israel Annals of Psychiatry and Related Disciplines,* 1963, *1,* 189–200.
53. Ray, W. S.: A preliminary report on a study of fetal conditioning. *Child Developm.,* 1932, *3,* 175–177.
54. Ribble, M.: *The Rights of Infants.* New York, Columbia University Press, 1943.
55. Roach, J. L., Gurrslin, O., and Hunt, R. G.: Some social-psychological characteristics of a child guidance clinic caseload. *J. Consult. Psychol.,* 1958, *22,* 183–186.
56. Russo, S.: Adaptations in behavioural therapy with children. *Behavior Research and Therapy,* 1964, *2* (1), 43–47.
57. Schaefer, E. S., and Bayley, N.: Maternal behavior, child behavior, and their intercorrelations from infancy through adolescence. *Monogr. Soc. Res. Child Developm.,* 1963, *28* (87).
58. Sears, R. R.: Experimental analysis of psychoanalytic phenomena. *In* Hunt, J. McV., ed.: *Personality and the Behavior Disorders.* New York, The Ronald Press Co., 1944, vol. 1, p. 329.
59. Shinn, M. W.: *Notes on the Development of a Child: I.* University of California Publications of Education, 1893, vol. 1.
60. Shirley, M. M.: *The First Two Years.* Minneapolis, University of Minnesota Press, 1933.
61. Slater, P. E.: Parental behavior and the personality of the child. *J. Genet. Psychol.,* 1962, *101,* 53–68.
62. Smith, M. E.: An investigation of the development of the sentence and the extent of vocabulary in young children. Iowa City, University of Iowa, 1926.
63. Terman, L. M.: *Genetic Studies of Genius.* Stanford, Calif., Stanford University Press, 1925, vol. 1.
64. Thompson, G. G.: *Child Psychology.* Cambridge, Mass., Houghton Mifflin Co., 1952, p. 289.
65. Watson, J.: *Psychological Care of Infant and Child.* New York, W. W. Norton and Co., 1928.
66. Watson, J. B., and Rayner, R.: Conditioned emotional reactions. *J. Exper. Psychol.,* 1920, *3,* 1–14.
67. Williams, H. M., et al.: *The Measurement of Musical Development.* Iowa City, University of Iowa, 1932.
68. Wilson, C. A., et al.: *The Merrill-Palmer Standards of Physical and Mental Growth.* Detroit, Merrill-Palmer School, 1930.
69. Yarrow, M. R.: Problems of methods in parent-child research. *Child Developm.,* 1963, *34,* 215–226.

Section One

OBJECTIVE DETERMINANTS

Chapter 2

The Individual and the Family

The child learns to live first as a member of his own family and only later as a member of the larger communities of neighborhood, school, and church. He brings his individual assets and liabilities to the family— contributing, disturbing, pleasing, and discouraging his parents and siblings, while they interact with him similarly. If he is well integrated into his family, he is more successful in all of his endeavors.[11]

The integration of the child into his family is influenced negatively or positively by behavior determined partially by differences of sex, intelligence, and physical status. The family structure, including its size, the ordinal position of the child, and whether he is an only child, a twin, a stepchild, an adopted or illegitimate child, prejudices parental behavior and the child's concept of himself. Special characteristics of the family, such as the presence of relatives, the family's established values and customs, and its race and nationality, have their effect.

INDIVIDUAL DIFFERENCES

Sex

The sex of the child preordains him to manifest certain abilities and liabilities, and directs him toward explicit modes of behavior. Girls mature physically and emotionally at an earlier age than boys.[1] When they enter kindergarten, girls play more readily with other children and relate more easily to the group than do boys.[3] Kindergarten and early elementary school boys show more severe personality difficulties than girls of the same age,[31] and 70 per cent of admissions to child guidance clinics are boys.[32]

A girl absorbs a feeling of importance because at an early age she is able to identify with her mother, on whom all members of the family rely for care, comfort, and direction.[27, 30] In contrast, a young boy has limited awareness of his father's worth to the family. He seldom observes his father at work, and he is dependent on his mother to care for him. Knowing that he is unlike her and yet not cognizant of basic differences between the sexes, he has no well-defined, continuous model to imitate and he is less assured in his behavior.

Changes occur with age, however, and during the later elementary years girls show more personality problems than boys, are less independent, and feel less adequate.[2] Because she becomes increasingly concerned about the impression she makes on others, a girl loses some of her former confidence. Her interests at this time include masculine as well as feminine diversions,[36] and she displays a mixture of traits typical of both sexes. A boy, during these years, is permitted increasing freedom and begins to feel proud of the fact that he is male. His acquisition of typically male behavior is difficult, nevertheless, because he still lacks an adequate model, still is supervised by women, and finds the demands of the male role both conflicting and rigid.[16] Fear of failing to measure up as a member of the male sex produces anxiety and insecurity in a boy.

During adolescence, a girl, preparing for emancipation from her family, increasingly interprets a woman's work as unimportant, confining drudgery, and she places a high value on the freedom and public acclaim which males retain during adulthood. If she tends to reject a woman's traditional role, she often finds herself in conflict with her mother and disturbed about the fact that she is female. An adolescent boy is expected to control his emotions and to behave responsibly, but if he has failed to acquire masculine traits because of insufficient association or lack of rapport with his father, he cannot behave in valid masculine ways and resorts instead to experimenting with aggressive actions such as smoking, drinking, stealing, vandalism, insolence, and disobedience.

Adults expect different behavior from girls than from boys. They are less disturbed about rowdy, rude behavior in boys than in girls, and they find it more difficult to limit the misbehavior of boys. Freer to act on his own initiative, a boy consistently demonstrates less self-control and more determined resistance to rules than does a girl. Parents require a son to defend himself, but they protect a daughter from others' attacks, even if these attacks are retaliatory. A boy who is unwilling or unable to act aggressively feels isolated from the male world and may be scorned by both parents and peers, but a girl who behaves aggressively is disliked because her actions are considered inappropriate.

Boys find school achievement more difficult than girls do, because boys' higher metabolic rate makes them restless at the confinement school necessitates, their fine muscle coördination is poor and contributes to inefficient reading and writing, and their resistance to direction leads to clashes with their teachers.

Special problems exist for the child who is the only one of his sex in a family with several children. A girl reared only with brothers imitates them in activities and interests; she resents being a girl. If she is overprotected by her brothers, she learns to demand special consideration from others because of her sex. A boy reared in a family of girls often is victimized by his sisters. They bestow inordinate amounts of direction and control on him and superciliously inform him of his gross errors in dress, behavior, and speech. If he wishes their approval, he must acquire feminine characteristics and learn to be quiet, obedient, and clean; and he may grow up resentful of all girls and women.

Intelligence

Children in the same family usually perform differently in school and comparison of grades is inevitable. A child unable to achieve as well in school as his siblings often develops a permanent concept of himself as intellectually inferior.

Parental expectations may not coincide with the child's school performance. Parents of superior intelligence, devoted to the benefits of education, are keenly disappointed in the child who has only average ability and who offers no prospect of ever becoming a source of pride to them for academic achievement or professional excellence.[8]

If the child is dull intellectually but has the physical appearance of a normal child, his parents may goad him incessantly, insisting on his remaining in regular classes and participating in the activities of children of his chronological age. This child, never commended for anything he does because his associates are always superior to him, becomes depressed and anxious.

The more severely retarded child may attend special classes where he can achieve appropriately, but he still must face the competition of his siblings and of neighbor children in play, and often he will be left out and left behind.

A child of superior intelligence born into a family in which education has never been valued must struggle against parental disparagement of scholarship or his parents' refusal to permit him to remain in school. Or he may be regarded with awe by his parents, who permit him to behave irresponsibly because he is a "genius."

Physical Status

The child whose illnesses and accidents are infrequent and mild develops at a normal rate without interruptions and unpredictable setbacks. Superior strength and coördination afford the child assets in games and physical competition with other children, increasing his self-esteem.[9] Early-maturing adolescents are more stable emotionally and better accepted by their peers than are late-maturing boys and girls.

The child who is ill often or who suffers repeated accidents becomes discouraged and may feel that he is singled out for bad luck. Accustomed to isolation, restrictions, and overconcern, he deteriorates intellectually, socially, and physically. Hospitalization can be a traumatic experience for the child and should be avoided when possible.[6] The child who is hospitalized for lengthy periods of time or on repeated occasions becomes accustomed to being cared for and leading a regulated life, and he loses initiative. Disturbance because of hospitalization is greatest if the child is between seven months and three years of age.[44]

Prematurity may have lasting effects which permeate the child's development and set a negative attitude toward himself. Both physical and intellectual deficit and dysfunction have been noted in children born prematurely, with some of the defects attributable in part to inhibitive restraint of the children by their overconcerned parents.[7, 26] Wortis *et al.*[42] confirmed the deleterious effects of prematurity, and suggested that, inasmuch as premature children are born more frequently to parents of lower economic levels, such factors as insufficient prenatal care, family disorganization, inadequate food, and poor hygiene contribute to the child's unhealthy development.

Minimal brain damage, often undetected by parents and teachers, causes impulsivity, distractibility, and perceptual abnormalities. The child exhibits many behavior and learning problems, which are unresponsive to the usual retraining methods.[12, 20] Unsuccessful and untaught, the brain-damaged child is censured by adults and peers alike, and develops feelings of loneliness and oppression.

More obvious physical deficiencies, such as crippling, harelip, or strabismus, invite attention from friends and strangers. Comments may be derogatory or sympathetic, but all tend to single out the child as deficient and different. Such characteristics as protruding teeth, prominent ears, obesity, heavy freckling, or under- or overaverage height cause the child to feel inferior and peculiar.[33]

FAMILY STRUCTURE

Size

The child who is one of four or more children inevitably receives little direct attention from his parents. He not only feels unnoticed but may also grow up with too little control and guidance. He seeks the attention he does not receive, looking for special favors or tending to drift, with sporadic flare-ups of attention-getting troublemaking.

He is with his siblings more than he is with his parents, and their strenuous competition and stern treatment can be unpleasant. He may be engaged in a running and bitter battle with another sibling which endures for years. If he is younger, his supervision usually is delegated to an older child, who directs, protects, educates, and dazzles in determined fashion, often prolonging dependence in his ward.[35]

Hawkes et al.[17] believed that children from smaller families fared better than those from larger ones. Vuyk,[40] in a study of 85 children, reported on characteristics of siblings in the two-child family. Unless there is a marked age difference between siblings, the older of two brothers typically is seclusive, anxious, introverted, and has a serious attitude toward life—in contrast to the younger brother, who is extraverted and optimistic. Boys are not as jealous of younger sisters as they are of younger brothers. Older sisters tend to show a discouraged and less active attitude than younger sisters.

Ordinal Position

Koch[23] observed that the effect of ordinal position varies according to the sex of the siblings, and this observation seems to be borne out in the descriptions by Vuyk.[40] Nevertheless, most investigators concur in concluding that the oldest and youngest children in the family are subject to unusual influences.[25, 37]

Phillips[32] reported that 73 per cent of the boys and 85 per cent of the girls referred to children's clinics for behavior problems are firstborn children. Overconcerned with the first child, parents demand perfection of him because they themselves wish to succeed in their new roles. They feel their way, fearful of making mistakes, and because every parental experience occurs initially with this child, they manage him more emotionally than they do his younger siblings. When other children are born, the oldest child is elevated to near-adult status. He is expected to look after the younger children and to be tolerant of their faults and provocations. A dispute between the children is considered to be the oldest child's fault, and he is held responsible for his siblings' actions. Because he is expected to show maturity, he does imitate adult behavior more readily than his younger siblings will when they reach his age.[28]

The youngest child in the family is often the most irresponsible. His mother postpones teaching him to care for himself because she has more time to do things for him and because she clings to his need for her. Parents automatically rebuke older children for any physical or verbal attack on the youngest child, and he assumes from this that he merits no criticism and is free to act as he chooses. Admiring his older siblings, he deliberately annoys and provokes them to gain their attention, knowing that if their retaliation becomes unpleasant, adult reinforcements are available.

He develops feelings of inferiority, however, as he discovers that his knowledge and abilities are never equal to those of his siblings,[37] and he learns less because he is not required to take responsibility at as early an age as were the older children. Although he needs his turn at chores, the other children work so efficiently that his help is neither asked nor required. Often he is reared without adequate discipline because his parents, after years of battling with older children, have lost the persistence necessary to enforce their orders.

The middle child or children sometimes are considered neglected, receiving neither the concentrated, erratic training of the oldest child or the favored attention and indulgence of the youngest. The behavior of middle children may be directed either toward pleasing the parents and offering little resistance to them, or toward personal achievement, which provides its own recognition. Cohen[10] stated that the second child is more intelligent, humorous, and fun loving, and less neurotic and introverted than his older sibling.

The Only Child

Many parents of one child bemoan their miniature family and inevitably give the child excessive attention. Everything the child does and says is noticed, reacted to, and considered of great import; and his rearing becomes a complex and burdensome process to his parents. They tire of his company, but they may feel guilty about leaving him out; and when their concern forces them always to take him along wherever they go, they never escape the responsibilities of parenthood, and one or both may resent the child's intrusion.

The child himself, faced with managing two adults, often attempts to do so with vehement demands and some anxiety. He feels abused, no matter how reasonably he is treated, because he never hears his parents criticize or direct a sibling, and as the odd member of the family, he feels lonely.

Twins

Fascinated with and stimulated by a constant companion, the twin experiences problems because of his uninterrupted association with one sibling. As small children, twins tend to isolate themselves from other children and do not learn to adapt to their peers. They remain content to communicate only with each other in a private jargon, and they defy parental orders with equanimity because their actions delight each other even when they earn parental censure.

Like-sexed twins show marked similarities during the first year of life in cognitive, motor, and personality development,[13] and the constant process of identifying with each other on the basis of similar emotional experiences keeps identical twins "identical" despite differences acquired later.[5]

An inherent competition exists as twins are admired and then compared. Friends and even parents will prefer one to the other; and there will be differences in appearance, energy, intelligence, physical skill, and leadership which will be noted by everyone. Boy and girl twins frequently experience a reversal in traditional sexual roles, because the girl matures more rapidly and assumes dominance over her twin.

Twins ordinarily mature with less difficulty if they are not dressed alike, placed in the same classes, given the same toys and lessons, and treated as though they were separate halves of one individual. To avoid excessive mutual dependence, the unique traits and abilities of each should be emphasized and opportunities provided for them to develop apart from each other in their contacts outside the home.

The Stepchild

Bowerman and Irish[4] reported that adolescents living with steprelatives showed more stress and ambivalence and a lower degree of family cohesiveness than those in normally constituted homes. Stepdaughters manifested more extreme reactions than stepsons, and the presence of a stepparent adversely affected the child's adjustment to his natural parent.

The older the child is when a stepparent joins the family, the more difficult the situation becomes. Horrocks[18] observed that the older child brings to the new family well-established personal characteristics and motivations. He considers the stepparent an intruder who is competing actively with him for the affection of his remaining parent, and he causes trouble for the stepparent. The stepparent, on the other hand, may resent the child, whom he cannot win and who is visible evidence of his spouse's former affectionate ties. The role of the stepmother, because of her greater concern with acceptance by and direction of the children, is more difficult than the role of the stepfather.[4]

The Adopted Child

Some couples adopt children because they cannot produce their own; others adopt out of pity, a desire to be charitable, or a need to cement a wavering marriage or provide a companion for an only child. The reason for adoption influences parental attitude toward the child and the degree to which the child is considered a true member of the family. Kirk[22] observed that the adoptive parent attempts to fill an incongruous role in trying to make the child an integral unit in the family and yet aid him to develop autonomy. As the adopted child reaches adolescence, he identifies with his natural parents and attempts to rejoin them. If he cannot do this, he imitates their known behavior in a determined effort to establish hereditary roots for himself.

Adoptive parents have all the fears, worries, and hopes of natural parents and many also feel a heavy obligation to the child entrusted to their care. An oppressive sense of duty may cause laxity in rearing and a tendency to treat the child as a guest, if the parents fear that showing displeasure implies rejection. Or, in unrelenting vigilance to rear the child well, the parents are overly strict and tolerate no opposition or initiative in the child.

The ghost of heredity is always present, and some adoptive parents promptly consider every failure or misbehavior of the child as evidence of his natural instability or inadequacy. They punish him with tales of his drunken father or promiscuous mother, and they absolve themselves of responsibility for his problems by crediting his natural parents with creating these problems when they created him.

Even in a family in which he is loved and well reared, the adopted child has many moments of loneliness. He is certain that his natural parents did not want him, and no amount of reassurance by his adoptive parents that they appreciate him can ease the fact of his initial abandonment by those who should have cared for him. Adoptive parents who tell the story as though the natural parents reluctantly gave up the child so that he might have a better home than they could provide help him to believe that his welfare is the concern of both sets of parents.

The Illegitimate Child

The illegitimate child, whether adopted or reared by his natural mother, believes that his existence is a mistake and his arrival was a calamity to his parents. As he reaches adolescence and understands the illegality of the conception, the child believes that he himself is guilty of immorality.

Podolsky[34] noted that the illegitimate child finds it difficult to love others because he has not been given love. He feels inferior, insecure, isolated, and rejected; and he develops feelings of jealousy toward other children whose birth was not so unwelcome. He also considers adults to be frauds, preaching at and scolding their children but violating the rules of decency themselves. He concludes that immorality and expediency are correct, and he imitates the worst behavior of his elders. Illegitimate girls are drawn toward repeating the sexual misconduct of their natural mothers, in identification with them.

The illegitimate child needs assistance in developing independence and self-esteem, in assimilating disappointment, and in concerning himself with others.[34]

CHARACTERISTICS OF THE FAMILY

Relatives

Children seldom are aware of tension between their parents and the relatives who contribute to or interfere with child rearing, but the presence of relatives alters not only parental practices but attitudes toward the child.

Grandmothers living with the family may be in charge of the children while both parents work, but when all of the adults are home, contradictory opinions about management keep the children uncertain of their own behavior and maneuvering for advantages. One grandmother sympathetically put her arm around her grandson and patted his shoulder whenever his parents scolded him, thus cancelling the effect of their reprimands and weakening his respect for them.

Many a young mother, unsure of her ability to rear her child, concurs quickly with a negative comment of the grandmother, and the child receives a double dose of criticism for behavior which might otherwise have gone unnoticed. Or the opposite reaction occurs, and a critical grandmother arouses defensiveness in a parent, who then permits obstreperous behavior which he normally would have curtailed.

Jealousy of grandparents who woo the child with gifts and affection is common, and parents are angered by a grandparent's blatant favoritism of one child over the others. The presence of extra adults in the family contributes to temper outbursts in the child; and more direction, stimulation, and interpersonal difficulties occur as the number of adults in the family increases. In the history of morose, angry children there is often a record of an early stay in the home of grandparents.

Younger siblings of the parents who live with the family often complicate the relationship between husband and wife. A wife's bachelor brother sometimes is regarded by her as being better to the children than their father is, and she elevates her brother's status above that of her husband by catering to his preferences and seeking his companionship. Some unsettled younger relatives, living temporarily with their married siblings after leaving or being sent away from home, are jealous and abusive of the children. Their actions are uncorrected by the parents because of their concern for the plight of the displaced young person.

Sometimes relatives do not share the same roof, but live so near to one another that they spend inordinate amounts of time together, shutting out other persons and becoming uninterested in assuming the ordinary responsibilities of neighborliness. A child, content with the close relationship he has with cousins and the constant acceptability he receives from adult relatives, avoids the challenge of finding a place for himself among his peers and maintains a dependent attitude toward adults outside the family, expecting approval without effort.

Values and Customs

Each family has its own values which determine its customs and emphases in living.

If parental prestige is based on impressing neighbors and friends with elaborate possessions, the children seek others' acclaim in the same way. On the other hand, if the parents set cautious limits on the sums they spend for necessities and if they rarely indulge in luxuries, their children may grow up restive about economic security.

Taking part in many social activities, belonging to the country club, associating with only the "best" people, and being popular are of prime concern to some parents; and the child learns to value popularity so greatly that he becomes overdependent on the moods and opinions of others and, as he grows older, he dedicates himself to social exhibition and exploitation. Other parents are so seclusive that they avoid contacts with everyone, and the children learn that they do not need other people, or even that others hold nothing but ill will toward them.

Educational achievement is an essential of life to some families; others consider higher education an expression of snobbery. The child's own attitude toward education parallels his parents' attitude and affects his vocational choices.

The investment of vast amounts of time and effort in promoting a given cause or excelling in a certain skill are of great importance to some parents. Their devotion to the attainment of a single goal is passed on to their children, and sometimes it is accompanied by defensiveness and the abuse of persons less enthusiastic than they.

Parental recreation may consist of solitary hobbies or reading, television and spectator sports, active participation in dramatics, sports, choirs, and study groups, or repeated nights of party-going and giving, with late hours and heavy drinking. In adopting the recreational preferences of their parents, children find their satisfactions with or without people, in achievement or in empathy, and by means of broadened or restricted stimulation.

Race and Nationality

The Mexican or Puerto Rican child, the Negro, the Oriental, or the Jewish child reared in a community in which he is a member of a racial minority group faces difficult problems. Although young children are not prejudiced against those of other races without instruction by their elders, some ethnic cleavage is observable in their play choices[24] until more frequent association minimizes their awareness of differences in appearance.

Because of the circular effect of inadequate education and low economic status of the parents, Negro children and those of Spanish and Italian descent find much academic instruction incomprehensible. Their lack of stimulation at home and their subsequent failure to develop both skills and initiative contribute to lowered scores on intelligence tests.[1] School failure sharpens the child's feeling of inferiority and hopelessness, and his inadequacy, coupled with the rejection he experiences, keeps him on guard against real or implied insult.

Old World families customarily supervise their children strictly and delegate authority over girls to their brothers, which leads to problems during adolescence. Young people dependent on peer acceptance also are embarrassed if one or both parents cannot speak English.

Many young people of minority groups accept the verdict of the majority that they are inferior, and consequently they feel free to violate laws and behave irresponsibly. Some become depressed, others isolate themselves, and a few seek to change their status by high achievement. Jewish children utilize this latter solution. They are imbued with the desire to acquire knowledge and fortified by pride in their heritage taught by parents devoted to them and to their training.

The assimilation or isolation of ethnic groups within a community is related to the number of families involved and to the minority group's tendency to limit its associations. A single Chinese, Jewish, or Negro family in a community often is accepted fully by other families; but if several families of a minority racial or national group live in a neighborhood, they seek out each other for companionship and then are ostracized by the majority.

REFERENCES

1. Anastasi, A.: *Differential Psychology*. New York, The Macmillan Co., 1937, pp. 386–443, 481–515.
2. Bledsoe, J. C.: Sex differences in mental health analysis scores of elementary pupils. *J. Consult. Psychol.*, 1961, 25 (4), 364–365.
3. Blomart, J.: Attitudes maternelles et réactions à l'entrée au jardin d'enfants (Maternal attitudes and reactions to entering kindergarten). *Acta Psychologica* (*Amsterdam*), 1963, 21, 75–97.
4. Bowerman, C. E., and Irish, D. P.: Some relationships of stepchildren to their parents. *Marriage Fam. Liv.*, 1962, 24, 113–121.
5. Burlingham, D.: *Twins: A Study of Three Pairs of Identical Twins*. New York, International Universities Press, 1952.
6. Capes, M.: The child in the hospital. *Ment. Hyg.* (*N. Y.*), 1956, 40, 107–157.

7. Caplan, H., Bibace, R., and Rabinovitch, M. S.: Paranatal stress, cognitive organization and ego function: A controlled follow-up study of children born prematurely. *J. Child Psychiatr.*, 1963, *2*, 434–450.
8. Child, I. L., and Bacon, M. K.: Cultural pressures and achievement motivation. *In* Hoch, P. H., and Zubin, J.: *Psychopathology of Childhood.* New York, Grune and Stratton, Inc., 1955, pp. 166–176.
9. Clarke, H., and Clarke, D. H.: Relationship between level of aspiration and selected physical factors of boys aged nine years. *Res. Quart. Amer. Assn. Hlth., Phys. Educ. Recr.*, 1961, *32*, 12–19.
10. Cohen, F.: Psychological characteristics of the second child as compared with the first. *Indian J. Psychol.*, 1951, *26*, 79–84.
11. Copper, J. B., and Lewis, J. H.: Parent evaluation as related to social ideology and academic achievement. *J. Genet. Psychol.*, 1962, *101*, 135–143.
12. Fish, B.: The study of motor development in infancy and its relationship to psychological functioning. *Amer. J. Psychiatr.*, 1961, *117*, 1113–1118.
13. Freedman, D. G., and Keller, B.: Inheritance of behavior in infants. *Science*, 1963, *140* (3563), 196–198.
14. Goodenough, F. L., and Leahy, A. M.: The effect of certain family relationships upon the development of personality. *J. Genet. Psychol.*, 1927, *34*, 45–71.
15. Haring, N. G., and Phillips, E. L.: *Educating Emotionally Disturbed Children.* New York, McGraw-Hill Book Co., 1962, p. 157.
16. Hartley, R. E.: Sex-role pressures and the socialization of the male child. *Psychol. Rep.*, 1959, *5*, 457–468.
17. Hawkes, G. R., Burchinal, L., and Gardner, B.: Size of family and adjustment of children. *Marriage Fam. Liv.*, 1958, *20*, 65–68.
18. Horrocks, J. E.: *The Psychology of Adolescence*, Ed. 2. Boston, Houghton Mifflin Co., pp. 104–105.
19. Jersild, A. T.: Emotional development. *In* Carmichael, L., ed.: *Manual of Child Psychology.* New York, John Wiley and Sons, 1946, p. 771.
20. Kann, J.: Central nervous system disturbance and the behavior problem child. *Z. Kinderpsychiat.*, 1957, *24*, 161–176.
21. Kanner, L.: *Child Psychiatry.* Springfield, Ill., Charles C Thomas, 1948, p. 53.
22. Kirk, H. D.: A dilemma of adoptive parenthood: Incongruous role obligations. *Marriage Fam. Liv.*, 1959, *21*, 316–328.
23. Koch, H. L.: Attitudes of young children toward their peers as related to certain characteristics of their siblings. *Psychol. Monogr.*, 1956, *70* (426).
24. Lambert, W. E., and Taguchi, Y.: Ethnic cleavage among young children. *J. Abnorm. Soc. Psychol.*, 1956, *53*, 380–382.
25. Lehrman, N. S.: Anarchy, dictatorship, and democracy within the family, a biosocial hierarchy. *Psychiatr. Quart.*, 1962, *36*, 455–474.
26. Lubchenco, L. O., Horner, F. A., Reed, L. H., Hix, I. E., Jr., Metcalf, D., Cohig, R., Elliott, H. C., and Bourg, M.: Sequelae of premature birth. *Amer. J. Dis. Child.*, 1963, *106*, 101–115.
27. Lynn, D.: A note on sex differences in the development of masculine and feminine identification. *Psychol. Rev.*, 1959, *66*, 126–135.
28. McDavid, J. W.: Imitative behavior in preschool children. *Psychol. Monogr.*, 1959, *73* (486).
29. Mussen, P. H., and Conger, J. J.: *Child Development and Personality.* New York, Harper and Bros., 1956, pp. 319–321.
30. Parsons, T.: Age and sex in the social structure of the United States. *In* Kluckhohn, C., Murray, H. A., and Schneider, D., eds.: *Personality in Nature, Society, and Culture.* New York, Alfred A. Knopf, 1956, p. 364.
31. Peterson, D.: Behavior problems of middle childhood. *J. Consult. Psychol.*, 1961, *25* (3), 205–209.
32. Phillips, E. L.: Cultural vs. intrapsychic factors in childhood behavior problem referrals. *J. Clin. Psychol.*, 1956, *12*, 400–401.
33. Podolsky, E.: How the child reacts to his physical defects. *Ment. Hyg. (N. Y.)*, 1953, *37*, 581–584.

34. Podolsky, E.: The emotional problems of the illegitimate child. *Arch. Pediat.*, 1953, *70*, 401–403.
35. Rosenbaum, M.: Psychological effects on the child raised by an older sibling. *Amer. J. Orthopsychiat.*, 1963, *33*, 515–520.
36. Rosenberg, B. G., and Sutton-Smith, B.: A revised conception of masculine-feminine differences in play activities. *J. Genet. Psychol.*, 1960, *96*, 165–170.
37. Schmid, P.: Über die Stellung des Kindes in der Geschwisterreine (About the position of the child in the series of siblings). *Heilpädag. Werkbl.*, 1954, *23*, 149–156.
38. Sontag, L. W.: Some psychosomatic aspects of childhood. *In* Kluckhohn, C., Murray, H. A., and Schneider, D., eds.: *Personality in Nature, Society, and Culture*. New York, Alfred A. Knopf, 1956, pp. 494–497.
39. Stark, S.: Symptom und Geschwisterposition im Spiegel einer Verhaltungsbeobachtung (Symptom and sibling constellation in the mirror of an observation of behavior). *Prax. Kinderpsychol., Kinderpsychiat.*, 1962, *11*, 177–187.
40. Vuyk, R.: *Das Kind in der Zweikinderfamilie* (The child in the two-child family). Stuttgart, Germany, Hans Huber, 1959.
41. Wiener, G., Rider, R. V., and Oppel, W.: Some correlates of IQ change in children. *Child Developm.*, 1963, *34*, 61–67.
42. Wortis, H., Heimer, C. B., Braine, M., Redlo, M., and Rue, R.: Growing up in Brooklyn: The early history of the premature child. *Amer. J. Orthopsychiat.*, 1963, *33*, 535–539.
43. Wright, L.: A study of special abilities in identical twins. *J. Genet. Psychol.*, 1961, *99*, 245–251.
44. Yarrow, L. J.: Separation from parents during early childhood. *In* Hoffman, M. L., and Hoffman, L. W., eds.: *Review of Child Development Research*. New York, Russell Sage Foundation, 1964, vol. 1, pp. 89–136.

Chapter 3

Sociological Factors

The neighborhood, the school, and the church enhance or diminish the child's prestige and self-confidence and aid in the determination of his basic values and motivations.[19] The manner in which sociological factors influence the child's behavior is inextricably intertwined with the family's reasons for choosing a given neighborhood, school, or church; and it is difficult to isolate the degree of influence exerted specifically by these environments, which are selected as complements to that provided by the family itself.[13] Studies indicate, however, that differences in such diverse areas as intelligence, identity, self-esteem, achievement, and antisocial behavior are related in some degree to sociological factors.

THE NEIGHBORHOOD

Socioeconomic Status

The direct influence of socioeconomic status on a child's intelligence and language skill and on his ability to profit from education has been repeatedly observed.[10, 11, 12] Pre-school children living in homes in which toys, books, and conversation are rare now are being enrolled in nursery schools designed to encourage verbalization and expose them to objects and ideas they have not known previously. The marked improvement in receptivity and initiative displayed by children given these kinds of stimulation confirms the depressing effects of sterile environment on learning ability.

Parental behavior and attitudes vary with socioeconomic status.

27

Working-class fathers tend to remain more aloof from their children at all ages, believing that child rearing is a woman's task. Middle-class fathers play a more active role.[14] Middle-class mothers emphasize achievement in their children's training and avoid physical punishment. Working-class mothers use physical punishment, but are more conscientious about nursing their babies than are middle-class mothers.[16] Social class influences the attitudes parents take toward their children's school grades.

The personal traits and problems of the children are related to the differentiating attitudes and behavior of parents of various socioeconomic levels. Most investigators report that children of lower socioeconomic status display emotional and behavior problems with greater frequency than do children of higher status.[4, 6, 22] Mitchell[18] administered the California Test of Personality to fifth and seventh grade pupils. He found that a significantly higher proportion of those of low economic status than of higher economic status reported economic worries and feelings of rejection; exhibited aggression, insecurity, anxiety, and psychosomatic disorders; and displayed strong desires for independence and new experiences. Stronger feelings of aggression and competitiveness are evidenced by lower-class children,[17] who place a lower value on conformity to adult standards and conventional modes of conduct than do middle-class children. Kvaraceus[15] and Pope[21] observed that low economic status contributes to delinquency as an adolescent seeks to obtain possessions which his parents cannot supply or to escape from a crowded, unattractive home where he is unsupervised and unoccupied for long periods of time.

Lower-class children show greater concern with status and achievement than those of higher classes.[23] The occupational prestige of fathers is evaluated by children less in terms of income than according to the working conditions and the education required. As children grow older, they accord most prestige to occupations which command authority,[25] and adolescents often hide the fact that their fathers are truck drivers, brick layers, or bartenders, even though they may be devoted to them as individuals.

Neighbors

The neighbors, unchosen, play a major part in the happiness of the entire family by irritating its individual members or providing them with support and diversion. Neighbors may be friendly or distant. Some drop in uninvited several times each day; others criticize, quarrel, and object to the children's activities. In some neighborhoods everyone works and no one is acquainted. A neighborhood may contain few children or only those of inappropriate ages for play, or it may be overrun with a hundred or more children in a single block. Contacts with neighbors and their children alter the behavior of parents and children with each other.

Permanency of the Home

Motility of families is more common today than ever before and is contributing to increased deliquency.[1, 15] Frequent moving need not be detrimental to a child if the family is cohesive; in fact, sometimes it can be helpful in establishing independence and versatility and in increasing practical knowledge. If the moves are made because of the father's work instability, however, the child suffers from impermanency and uncertainty.

With every move, the child must make a place for himself in the neighborhood and at school. He may do so aggressively, or he may retreat and avoid other children. If he anticipates moving frequently, he has little incentive to learn responsibility or to achieve in school, because he seldom remains long enough in one place to receive recognition for his efforts. His own personality and the degree of interaction between him and his parents determine his ability to cope successfully with his family's motility.[24]

THE SCHOOL

Introduction to School

Kindergarten attendance is not compulsory and many school systems have insufficient funds with which to provide kindergarten experience. The child who does not attend kindergarten is thrust from the complete freedom of all-day play into sedentary pursuits for five hours a day. He must attend closely, obey the instructions of a strange adult, and do so while ignoring the appearance and antics of a roomful of unknown and challenging children. Tired, distracted, afraid, and lonely during his first year at school, he learns little and dislikes attending. A year of kindergarten prepares him for formal instruction by accustoming him gradually to working, playing, and learning with a group under a teacher's direction, and he is better able to tolerate the demands of first grade.

Many children begin school at too early an age and are permanently disadvantaged. In some states a child must be six years old by mid-September to enter first grade, but in other states a child who will not be six until mid-January is accepted in the fall. A mother who is tired of having her child at home and who observes his restlessness insists that he will be bored with school or oversized if he must wait another year, and she maneuvers to enroll him early. A child younger than his class-mates often fails to learn to read and cannot keep up in independent work. He develops habits of indolence and feelings of failure which persist throughout his school years, attitudes which would not have occurred had he been the oldest, rather than the youngest, member of his class.

Size and Organization

In a small school, the influence of siblings over the younger child continues, and he finds it more difficult to establish himself independently. His misbehavior at school is broadcast, and anonymity for disapproved actions is impossible.

The child who is a member of a small class receives more individual attention from his teacher and is less hesitant to seek help when he needs it. If he is taught in a large class, however, he must be able to learn with little direct assistance from his teacher, or he will be left behind.

In some schools, even in the first grade, pupils are placed in the platoon system where they are assigned one teacher for basic subjects and spend either the morning or afternoon journeying from one classroom to another for instruction in special subjects. Most young children need the security of one room and one teacher, and without these they dread school and fail to learn. Their teachers, burdened with large classes meeting for brief periods, have no time to assist the child who is failing.

Curricular Emphases

Less than half of all young people finishing high school continue their education, and yet graduation requirements are based on the assumption that all students are college-bound. The young person who plans to find work after high school is not prepared to do so: He has no marketable skills, and often his complete disinterest in the nuances of English grammar, the pronunciation of foreign languages, the dates of historical events, and the symbols of chemical elements have resulted in his developing habits of ignoring work assignments—habits which prepare him poorly for employment.

Homework is increasing steadily in most school systems. The elementary school child, who should be free to play in the afternoon and get to bed early at night, often has assigned homework which prevents both. The junior or senior high school student will receive low grades if he does not do his homework, regardless of his knowledge of the subject. A conscientious student spends all of his spare time completing the extra work; and the adolescent who keeps up his grades, goes out with friends, and participates in extracurricular activities rides a merry-go-round which leaves him little time for sleep, chores, and his own interests.

THE CHURCH

Restriction and Isolation

The influence of the church increases as the child grows older, becomes more aware of religious differences, and is more thoroughly indoctrinated with the beliefs of his own church.[7, 8]

When his church's rules, customs, and holidays are not the same as those followed by most of the children he knows, the child will feel different from others. If he attends a parochial school, he is physically isolated from neighborhood friends for several hours daily. Catholics, Mormons, and Jews have prescribed regulations of diet and worship. Children attend religious classes daily in some churches, with a subsequent drain on their time and energy. Jewish children and members of the Seventh Day Adventist church refrain from work and ordinary activities on Saturdays instead of Sundays.

The Christian Scientist child sometimes is denied needed medical care and may feel bewildered and guilty by the treatment of lay practitioners when he is ill. Children whose parents are members of fundamentalist churches become the center of conflict when routinely required immunizations are opposed by parents. They become the center of public and emotional attention in the church when they are visited by trouble. Controversies concerning the flag salute and school prayers arise from religious rules which restrict loyalties and forbid participation in worship not conducted by the church.

The adolescent, struggling with changing religious convictions, may feel that his religion causes him to appear inferior to others or that it prejudices them against him. Or he may believe that because he is a member of a certain faith he is superior to others and that they are self-centered and sinful. Evangelistic requirements of his church or its fostering ideas of male superiority can result in his attempted domination of or interference with others, as well as his indifference to their needs or rights.

Obedience and Guilt

Churches with prescribed rules for acceptable conduct require unquestioning obedience to these dictates. If church officials possess the power to forgive disobedience and exact penance, the offender who complies with their requirements absolves himself from ultimate responsibility for his behavior. If he is completely committed to accepting the regulation and the punishment of the church, he feels less guilt about anything he may do, and he makes less effort to improve undesirable behavior.

More often, however, the child to whom religious beliefs are important feels guilty and afraid. Fundamentalist churches preach the old-time religion that all men are sinners and that eternal punishment will be the fate of the unsaved. The young child believes firmly that these doctrines are true, and when he misbehaves, he worries excessively about the consequences.

Adolescents typically repudiate early religious convictions and many begin to avoid church attendance as an expression of independence and maturity. They sometimes feel guilty about their rejection of religion, fearing that they are violating moral codes or flaunting cultural standards. If they abandon a religious affiliation to which their parents are devoted, the adults are angered, concerned, and humiliated.

Inspirational Effect of the Church

When the church achieves its true purpose, children and young people are strengthened in self-control and selflessness.

The moral teaching of the church reënforces parental instruction and tempers the child's tendency to dismiss parental precepts as old fashioned. Knowing that the weight of the church is behind his own moral concepts, the adolescent is better able to resist his overwhelming need to conform with the activities of his peers at times when these activities are ill advised.

Regular attendance at well-organized and well-taught church school classes can promote a child's feeling of worthiness. As a member of a group dedicated to concern for others and to ethical conduct, his own ideals are strengthened. Respite from pressures and problems is provided by church worship, with its experience of beauty in song and ritual and the submergence of self. Prayer offers a child or young person unique attention and the conviction that he does not bear his burdens unaided.

REFERENCES

1. Bennett, I.: *Delinquent and Neurotic Children*. New York, Basic Books, Inc., 1960.
2. Boehm, L.: The development of conscience: A comparison of upper middle class academically gifted children attending Catholic and Jewish parochial schools. *J. Soc. Psychol.*, 1963, 59, 101–110.
3. Buhler, C.: School as a phase of human life. *Education*, 1952, 73, 219–222.
4. Burchinal, L., Gardner, B., and Hawkes, G. R.: Children's personality adjustment and the socio-economic status of their families. *J. Genet. Psychol.*, 1958, 92, 149–159.

5. Campbell, W. J.: The influence of sociocultural environment on the progress of children at the secondary school level. *Aust. J. Psychol.*, 1955, *7*, 140–146.

6. Drucker, A. J., and Remmers, H. H.: Environmental determinant of basic difficulty problems. *J. Abnorm. Soc. Psychol.*, 1952, *47*, 379–381.

7. Elkind, D.: The child's conception of his religious denomination: II. The Catholic child. *J. Genet. Psychol.*, 1962, *101*, 185–193.

8. Elkind, D.: The child's conception of his religious denomination: I. The Jewish child. *J. Genet. Psychol.*, 1961, *99*, 209–225.

9. Haller, A. O., and Thomas, S.: Personality correlates of the socio-economic status of adolescent males. *Sociometry*, 1962, *25*, 398–404.

10. Hindley, C. B.: Social class influences on the development of ability in the first five years. *In* Nielson, G., ed.: *Proceedings of the XIV International Congress of Applied Psychology. Vol. 3, Child and Education.* Copenhagen, Munksgaard, 1962, pp. 29–41.

11. Jackson, W. S.: Housing and pupil growth and development. *J. Educ. Sociol.*, 1955, *28*, 370–380.

12. John, V. P.: The intellectual development of slum children: Some preliminary findings. *Amer. J. Orthopsychiat.*, 1963, *33*, 813–822.

13. Klineberg, O.: Cultural factors in personality adjustment of children. *Amer. J. Orthopsychiat.*, 1953, *23*, 465–471.

14. Kohn, M. L., and Carroll, E. E.: Social class and the allocation of parental responsibilities. *Sociometry*, 1960, *23*, 372–392.

15. Kvaraceus, W. C.: *The Community and the Delinquent.* Yonkers-on-Hudson, N. Y., The World Book Co., 1954, pp. 99–100, 237.

16. McGuire, C.: Family life in lower and middle class homes. *Marriage Fam. Liv.*, 1952, *14*, 1–6.

17. McKee, J. P., and Leader, F.: The relationship of socio-economic status and aggression to the competitive behavior of pre-school children. *Child Developm.*, 1955, *26*, 135–142.

18. Mitchell, J. V., Jr.: The identification of items in the California Test of Personality that differentiate between subjects of high and low socio-economic status at the fifth and seventh grade levels. *J. Educ. Res.*, 1957, *51*, 241–250.

19. Opler, M. K.: The influence of ethnic and class sub-cultures on child care. *Soc. Probl.*, 1955, *3*, 12–21.

20. Patel, A. S.: Family adjustment and economic status as related to some character traits in children. *Educ. Psychol., Rev., Baroda*, 1961, *1*, 85–91.

21. Pope, B.: Socio-economic contrasts in children's peer culture prestige values. *Genet. Psychol. Monogr.*, 1953, *48*, 157–220.

22. Sewell, W. H.: Social class and childhood personality. *Sociometry*, 1961, *24*, 340–356.

23. Sewell, W. H., and Haller, A. O.: Factors in the relationship between social status and the personality adjustment of the child. *Amer. Sociol. Rev.*, 1959, *24*, 511–520.

24. Switzer, R. E., Hirschberg, J. C., Myers, L., Gray, E., Evers, N. H., and Forman, R.: The effect of family moves on children. *Ment. Hyg.* (*N. Y.*), 1961, *45*, 528–536.

25. Weinstein, E. A.: Weights assigned by children to criteria of prestige. *Sociometry*, 1956, *19*, 126–132.

26. Werner, E.: Milieu differences in social competence. *J. Genet. Psychol.*, 1957, *91*, 239–249.

INTERPERSONAL DETERMINANTS

Chapter 4

Fixation of Immaturity

\

The newborn infant is dependent on his parents to care for him physically, to make him comfortable, to soothe him, and to protect him from harm. Necessary and important as these functions are to the neonate, they must not be continued indefinitely or the child fails to develop his capacity to care for himself.

The child first asserts his independence before the end of his first year, testing parental willingness to placate him,[29] and normally he relinquishes his dependence on adults and turns to his peers during his preschool years.[30] The child who does not abandon dependency but retains immature characteristics will experience a limited and unsatisfying developmental period and will reach adulthood with his intellectual, social, and emotional potential unrealized. His awkward efforts to cloak himself with the appearance of maturity may include seriously deviate behavior.

FIXATION OF IMMATURITY

Immaturity is fixated in the child by prolonged, unnecessary care; by the immediate availability of the parent to assist and comfort; and by restriction of the child's associations and freedom of action. All of these practices are attempts by the parent to shield the child from stress.

Prolonged Care

An overprotective mother, continuing close supervision of daily routines for years or actually executing them herself, convinces her child

34

that he is incapable of doing anything for himself, and he soon ceases to try to do so. Levy[17] described typical care of this kind. One mother helped her 13-year-old son to dress; another buttered bread and fetched drinks for her 12-year-old; still another punished her 13-year-old boy by putting him to bed in the afternoon, just as she had done since he was a pre-schooler. A divorced and working mother stated that the one thing she could do for her nine- and ten-year-old son and daughter was to brush their teeth for them each night. The chauffeuring service provided children for their daily trips to and from school evidences adults' belief in the tenderness of the child and assures his underdevelopment in physical strength, speed, and endurance.[26]

Permitting the child to sleep with his parents on request confirms his conviction that he is helpless and needs protection. Parental direction of the child's eating is continued from birth to adulthood in some families. A protective mother may accompany her older child to the bathroom, checking on the thoroughness of the wiping and completing the job if it has been carelessly done. She addresses her adolescent son or daughter as "Junior" or "Cooky" and fusses over them and at them, just as she did when they were four years old. She makes their beds, cleans their rooms, cares for their clothing, prepares favored foods, and tucks them in bed when they complain of *malaise*.*

Parental Availability

Parents fixate immaturity in the child when they are available on demand to succor or cheer him. With maturity, a child develops the capacity to wait, but when parents respond immediately to the older child's request for entertainment, assistance, or sympathy, they imply that he is incapable of enduring delay. The child whose parents rush to his aid learns that he need not attempt new and difficult tasks because his parents will rescue him from the discomforts associated with effort or patience. They ease his way by managing his homework for him, waiting on him, and providing him with ample funds to pay for his hobbies and recreation.

Restriction of Contacts and Freedom of Action

To protect the child from undesirable influence, unwarranted abuse, and unknown dangers, the parent limits the child's associations with others and refuses him permission to seek new experiences independently. Restriction of association may be achieved deviously, by teaching the child that others do not wish him well and should be avoided, as well

---

* See Case 1, Wallace J., p. 495.

as by direct prohibition. An overprotective mother scolds, chases, or spanks other children who mistreat her child, and eventually she eliminates all of his acquaintances, thus succeeding not only in protecting him from the onslaughts of his peers but also in retaining for herself his exclusive companionship and affection. Criticizing the child's teachers prevents him from developing attachments to them and also excuses his failures at school.

Making certain that the child rarely is unsupervised guarantees that he will not attempt to leave his parent when he is old enough to do so. The mother who drives her child to school, escorts him to the shopping center, accompanies him to swimming class and remains for the lesson, joins him at an afternoon matinée, and seldom permits him to play with other children ensures his complete dependence on her protection and his conviction that he cannot manage alone.

PARENTAL MOTIVATION

Overprotective parents are motivated by a failure to understand the value of stress in the child's growth, by a desire to mold the child into a perfect testimonial of their excellence as parents, by long-standing habits of domination, or by a need to bind the child in a close relationship of affection, appreciation, and companionship.

The Value of Stress

Many parents believe that protecting the child from frustration or criticism will cause him to develop into a cheerful, happy, and considerate person. No individual experiences life without stress, however, and each must develop the ability to meet challenge and to conquer difficulty. Such development is possible only with repeated practice in facing difficult situations and managing adequate solutions.

Withdrawal of support can lead to greater independence. Hartup[7] presented two learning tasks to two matched groups of four-and-a-half-year-old children. Prior to assignment of these tasks, children in one group were nurtured for five minutes and then left alone for five minutes; children in the other group were nurtured for ten minutes. Girls and those boys recognized as being consistently dependent who were members of the interrupted nurture group showed greater speed in learning the tasks than did the children presented with the tasks after receiving prolonged attention. Although Hartup stated that these children's prompt learning demonstrated their need to regain the attention of adults, it is significant that they did so by continuing the independence of action initiated by the withdrawal of nurture, rather than by resorting to pleas for help or excuses to avoid the tasks.

Murphy[23] emphasized that adults need to learn more about what a child can do for himself, rather than considering only what they can do for him, and that creative consequences result from coping with stress and crisis. The mastery of difficulties can produce optimism in the child and a greater capacity for both struggle and achievement.

Perfectionistic Aims

Many parents are overwhelmed with the weight of the task of child rearing. Convinced that their management of the child is the sole cause of his every display of temper, incompetence, or misbehavior, they feel guilty and uncomfortable when things do not go smoothly and when pleasant relationships are interrupted. It is important to them to rear a perfect child, and therefore they ignore any evidence of fault in him. They guard against putting him in situations in which he may misbehave or fail. They conciliate him, serve him, and substitute for him in order to avoid the embarrassment of witnessing imperfection in him.

Habitual Domination

Levy[17] found that the overprotective mothers he studied were highly responsible women who always had been competent. Many of them were accustomed, as children, not only to caring for themselves but also to caring for their younger siblings. Dominating their own children was natural for them, and they supervised and directed with a capability too powerful for the child to resist.

Need for a Dependent Relationship

An adult who is unsure of himself may use his position as a parent as an opportunity to control completely another individual. He discovers that he can teach his child to suppress rebellious behavior if censure is severe and prompt and if proper actions are rewarded with affectionate approval. The child subordinates his own wishes to those of the parent and in return receives protection, companionship, and service.

Either parent who fails to find the affection and admiration he expects from his spouse may turn all of his attention to the child, binding the child in a close dependency which compensates for the missing satisfactions in the marriage.

PERSONALITY AND BEHAVIOR CORRELATES
OF IMMATURITY

The immature child fails to achieve in school and work and is over-cerned with himself. Because he never becomes socialized, he is aggres-

sive in infantile ways and holds himself innocent of blame for his behavior. Set apart from his peers, he loses his capacity for emotional
contact, and withdrawal or unfamiliar stress may lead to complete intellectual and emotional deterioration.

Achievement Failure

The immature child is noted for his lack of achievement. In school,
he fails to learn to read, and he never acquires the ability to persist with
schoolwork. Accustomed to his parents' intercession and convinced that
he is incapable of mastering difficult tasks, he believes that he is exempt
from requirements of work, self-discipline, and coöperation.

Self-concern

The child's custom of focusing on his own desires and his own in-
effectuality leads to retention of erratic habit behavior. Night fears and
enuresis endure into adolescence, and food demands and eating peculiarities persist.

Psychophysiological complaints are frequent in the immature child,
who thereby demonstrates his habit of directing his attention to himself
and his intolerance for discomfort or pain. He welcomes the sympathy
and concern of his parents, and illness also serves to excuse him from
participation and effort.*

Socialization Failure

The dependent child substitutes his parent for his peers and never
learns to compete with or appreciate the members of his own generation.[9, 15] Even during the pre-school years, the dependent child is unpopular with his age-mates. A small girl who hangs on adults, openly
asking for affection, or a boy who repeatedly requests adult help is indicating a preference for the comforts of adult companionship, and other
children dislike and disdain him for this.[18, 19]

Kagan and Moss[15] reported that a girl's excessive dependence on
her parents during preadolescence is prognostic of a strong, continuing
need for an emotionally supporting relationship with them when she is
an adult. Horwitz[10] studied 13- and 14-year-old children rejected by their
peers and found that overdependence on adults was a common characteristic.

As the child becomes older, he becomes increasingly less adept than
his peers in social intercourse and in independent, responsible behavior.

---

* See Case 3, Neal R., p. 497.

Because he feels inferior to them and is aware of their contempt,[14] he retreats to his home where his parents will care for and direct him.*

Infantile Aggression

The immature, dependent child, knowing that he is not as competent as his peers and is scorned by them, develops strong feelings of aggression, which he expresses in sadistic actions, either open or disguised.[6, 20] He resents his parents for their failure to permit him to develop his capacities and to gain independence from them, but inept and fearful, he cannot dissociate himself from their domination and protection. Ashamed of himself, hating both his parents and his peers, he attacks others. Premeditated vandalism, arson, sexual attacks, and brutality toward animals, strangers, or rejecting acquaintances are identical in purpose with the small child's use of weapons or fists to express his anger or enforce his will.

Ideas of Innocence

Permitted to be irresponsible from an early age, the immature person never considers any of the difficulties in which he finds himself to be his fault. He is expert at blaming others' selfish motives or ignorant behavior for his troubles, and he complains that others misbehave more than he and are not punished. An injured attitude of being unfairly chastised for inconsequential actions is characteristic of delinquent adolescents.

Mowrer[24, 25] warned that self-centered and irresponsible behavior of emotionally disturbed persons is better considered sin than sickness and that excusing harmful actions only confirms the immature individual's belief that he is innocent of offense.

Loss of Emotional Contact

The immature child is skilled in imitating the manners and modes of social behavior known to win approval from adults, and when he is with them he talks calmly, displays deference and courtesy, and exchanges sophisticated comments. He is merely performing, however, in a detached and manneristic way, and his contact is tenuous and artificial, rather than real.

Unable to reach others naturally, the child becomes increasingly detached and inept in social communication.[20] As he withdraws and broods over his insufficiency and his rejection by others, he is subject

---

* See Case 2, Bill C., p. 496.

to complete intellectual and emotional deterioration. The demands of adulthood for responsibility and selflessness are totally beyond the immature individual's ability to meet, and stress caused by the imminence of adulthood may precipitate psychosis in the highly dependent older adolescent.[20]

REFERENCES

1. Beller, F. K.: Dependence and independence in young children. *J. Genet. Psychol.*, 1955, *87*, 25–35.
2. Brammer, L. M., and Shostrom, E. L.: *Therapeutic Psychology.* Englewood Cliffs, N. J., Prentice-Hall, Inc., 1960, p. 392.
3. Brody, S.: Preventive intervention in current problems of early childhood. *In* Caplan, G., ed.: *Prevention of Mental Disorders in Children.* New York, Basic Books, Inc., 1961, p. 185.
4. Cameron, N.: *The Psychology of Behavior Disorders.* Cambridge, Mass., Houghton Mifflin Co., 1947, p. 175.
5. Centers, R., and Centers, L.: Social character types and beliefs about child rearing. *Child Developm.*, 1963, *34*, 69–78.
6. de la Vega, G.: On booklearning. *J. Hillside Hosp.*, 1956, *5*, 433–440.
7. Hartup, W. W.: Nurturance and nurturance-withdrawal in relation to the dependency behavior of pre-school children. *Child Developm.*, 1958, *29*, 191–201.
8. Hartup, W. W., and Keller, E. D.: Nurturance in pre-school children and its relation to dependency. *Child Developm.*, 1960, *31*, 681–689.
9. Heathers, G.: Emotional dependence and independence in nursery school play. *J. Genet. Psychol.*, 1955, *87*, 37–57.
10. Horwitz, A.: Nearim mevodadim behevrot noar (Rejected boys in youth groups). *Megamot*, 1958, *9*, 103–123.
11. Hurlock, E.: *Child Development.* New York, McGraw-Hill Book Co., 1950, pp. 518–520.
12. Ikeda, N.: A comparison of physical fitness of children in Iowa, U. S. A. and Tokyo, Japan. *Res. Quart. Amer. Assn. Hlth., Phys. Educ. Recr.*, 1962, *33*, 541–552.
13. Johnson, F. L.: Responsibility. *Bull. Inst. Child Stud.* (*Toronto*), 1955, *17*, 1–4.
14. Kagan, J., and Moss, H. A.: The stability of passive and dependent behavior from childhood through adulthood. *Child Developm.*, 1960, *31*, 577–591.
15. Kagan, J., and Moss, H. A.: *Birth to Maturity.* New York, John Wiley and Sons, 1962, pp. 58, 67, 225–226.
16. Kanner, L.: *Child Psychiatry.* Springfield, Ill., Charles C Thomas, 1948, pp. 126–129.
17. Levy, D.: *Maternal Overprotection.* New York, Columbia University Press, 1943, pp. 16, 28, 40, 53, 72, 101, 124, 135, 150.
18. McCandless, B. R.: *Children and Adolescents.* New York, Holt, Rinehart and Winston, 1961, p. 326.
19. McCandless, B. R., Bilous, C. B., and Bennett, H. L.: Peer popularity and dependence on adults in pre-school age socialization. *Child Developm.*, 1961, *32*, 511–518.
20. McCord, W., McCord, J., and Verden, P.: Familial and behavioral correlates of dependency in male children. *Child Developm.*, 1962, *33*, 313–326.
21. Marshall, H. R., and McCandless, B. R.: Relationships between dependence on adults and social acceptance by peers. *Child Developm.*, 1957, *28*, 413–419.
22. Miller, D. R., and Swanson, G.: *The Changing American Parent.* New York, John Wiley and Sons, 1958, p. 224.

23. Murphy, L.: Preventive implications of development in the pre-school years. *In* Caplan, G., ed.: *Prevention of Mental Disorders in Children.* New York, Basic Books, Inc., 1961, pp. 220–221.
24. Mowrer, O. H.: Sin, the Lesser of Two Evils. Unpublished manuscript.
25. Mowrer, O. H.: Some constructive features of the concept of sin. *J. Counsel. Psychol.,* 1960, 7, 185–188.
26. Rarick, G. L., and Reddan, W.: Youth fitness and health. *Rev. Educ. Res.,* 1962, 32, 515–529.
27. Rattner, L.: A study of excessive dependency in mother-son relationships. *Amer. J. Individ. Psychol.,* 1956, 12, 171–176.
28. Stendler, C. B.: Critical periods in socialization and overdependency. *Child Developm.,* 1952, 23, 3–12.
29. Stendler, C. B.: Possible causes of overdependency in young children. *Child Developm.,* 1954, 25, 125–146.
30. Stith, M., and Connor, R.: Dependency and helpfulness in young children. *Child Developm.,* 1962, 33, 15–20.

Chapter 5

Neglect

The parent who neglects his child does so by his failure to involve himself in the child's life, and thus the parent subordinates the child to a position of inconsequence and abandons him to rear himself. Neglect of the child is not the province solely of the irresponsible parent: It occurs also among conscientious adults, unaware of the child's need for their attention and overly concerned with other endeavors. A parent who demonstrates his interest in his child increases the child's self-esteem[18] and social awareness;[24] a parent unconcerned with his child imperils the child's personal security.[2, 12, 14]

NEGLECT

A child is neglected when his parent fails to provide him with adequate physical care, gives him no personal attention, or demonstrates disinterest in him as a person.

Inadequate Care

Welfare department case files tell many sorry stories of children left in an unheated apartment without food, adequate clothing, or bedding; or turned out to roam the streets when they were unwanted at home. These children, in acute physical need, often are placed in orphanages or foster homes to ensure at least minimum physical care.

In other homes, gross neglect is not as apparent; but there are children from middle- and upper-class homes who subsist on dry cereal and sandwiches which they prepare themselves. In these homes, the mother seldom cooks an adequate meal, nor does she attempt to provide the child with clean and mended clothing. She permits and even encourages the child to absent himself from home all day and sometimes until late at night. He is free to spend his time at a neighbor's house, to wander through stores, or to sit in a movie theater for hours. His mother neither knows nor cares where he is and what he is doing.

Inattention

Lack of personal attention may be initiated during infancy, when the baby is isolated in his crib, away from the other members of the family. He lives alone, and as he grows older, his need for stimulation, affection, and communication is ignored. His attempts to gain attention from his parents are rebuffed. He is never questioned about what he does or what he thinks, and he is not included in parental plans. His care is delegated to others, and even though the child exhibits many learning and behavior problems, the parents remain indifferent to these signs of trouble.

Disinterest in the Child

The parent who is disinterested in his child refuses to share his time, experiences, or ideas with him. He feels that playing with the child is demeaning, and he considers the child's conversation dull, his abilities limited, and his expression of emotion unpleasant. Such a parent regards the child as an expected requisite of marriage but not as an individual in his own right. Knowing nothing of the child's successes, dreams, or burdens, the parent treats him as a possession to manipulate or parade or as a nuisance to consign to others for training.

PARENTAL MOTIVATION

A parent's neglect of his child is motivated by fatigue, self-concern, or feelings of inadequacy as a parent.

Fatigue

Many young couples have three or four babies in rapid succession, and their care imposes several years of 18-hour days on the mother. Six hours each day are required to care for a newborn infant, and a mother who must care for a baby and also dress, feed, train, watch, and bathe one or more crying and resisting runabouts becomes exhausted. Postpartum depression and episodes of infanticide and suicide by distraught young mothers attest to the extreme demands made on their energy.

Mothers whose children are all in school and whose housework has decreased to six hours daily sometimes conclude that they are not being useful, and they feel obligated to serve any cause for which their help is solicited. Their lives become an harassed succession of unrelated meetings, telephone calls, chauffeuring, baking, fund-raising, and interruptions.

Fathers also become overinvolved with extra work and community activities, either from a sense of duty or a desire to win acclaim. Leading lives crowded with extra work, they neglect their own children. The father of two young boys known for their disrespect and unruly behavior in church was a deacon and church school superintendent who spent every spare minute at church work. The father of a lazy and untrustworthy 14-year-old boy had worked long hours for many years with Little League baseball. A 16-year-old boy who committed suicide, after repeatedly threatening to do so, had a father who was a prominent lay official for the Boy Scouts.

In addition to managing their homes and undertaking civic responsibilities, many mothers are employed regularly. The United States Department of Labor reported that 6,561,000 mothers of children under 17 years of age were working either full or part time in 1959, and 2,474,000 of these mothers had children under five years. A year later the number of working mothers with children had increased to 7,080,000.[21, 22] According to the National Manpower Council, 40 per cent of the mothers of school age children are working. Deleterious effects on the children are reported, particularly for younger children and for those whose mothers dislike working.[9, 10, 15]

Parents who have obligated themselves to others and exhausted their own time and freedom feel burdened and fatigued, and the child's attempts to gain their attention become an added irritation.

Self-concern

Some parents, accustomed to pleasing themselves rather than to sharing with and helping those dependent on them, consider the child a nuisance and a bore. They believe themselves superior to him and feel that any prolonged contact with him is degrading. Avoiding his company, they devote themselves to social activities with adults or to seeking the rewards inherent in more recognized achievements than child rearing.

The emotionally disturbed or alcoholic parent neglects his child because of his absorption with himself and his indulgent compensations for his problems.

Feelings of Parental Inadequacy

Sometimes a parent believes that he is unnecessary to the child. He is ill-at-ease when he talks or plays with him, feeling that the child finds him unstimulating or incompetent. If the child expresses his feelings and opinions forcefully, an uncertain parent may believe that the child is wiser than he, and the adult begins to avoid contacts with the child to protect himself from feeling inadequate.

An uncertain adult may also avoid his responsibility for caring for the child by convincing himself that parental attention makes the child dependent. Preferring not to hear the child's tales of woe and defeat or to wrestle with his problems, the parent sends him away when he seeks comfort or counsel, and the child is convinced that his parent is indifferent to him.

PERSONALITY AND BEHAVIOR CORRELATES
OF NEGLECT

The neglected child is anxious, and his anxiety leads to irresponsible behavior and intellectual deterioration. He is resentful of the treatment accorded him, and he retaliates with aggressive or troublesome behavior. Often he is lonely, withdrawn, and depressed.[4]

Anxiety

When parents are not available to rear the child or are too busy, weary, or indifferent to attend to his behavior, he is subjected to the unpredictable and inconsistent directions and wishes of a series of adults or older siblings, or he is left to his own devices and receives no direction from anyone. When he does not know how to behave in order to satisfy his current mentor, he becomes anxious. If he must fend for himself, he is frightened and acts impulsively and thoughtlessly.[3] He seeks to force attention from his indifferent parent. He cries at length when he is distressed; he expresses his affection endlessly and demands similar assurance from his parents; he may develop nightmares and senseless fears; and he runs to adults for help or sympathy whenever he is mistreated or rebuffed. Often he distracts himself by constant talking and restless activity, or he continually seeks his parents' attention by hovering near them, interfering in their activities, and misbehaving in minor but annoying ways. His anxiety impedes his intellectual development, and his verbal and manual skills are retarded.[20]

Resentment

As he becomes older, the child is aware that his parents choose those contacts and activities they prefer. Sometimes a mother bluntly states that she cannot bear to stay home with her children; at other times the child assumes that a choice is made because of the parents' total engross-ment with other activities. Resenting being shunted aside, the child at-tacks sitters, siblings, peers, and parents; destroys possessions; steals; or is grossly disobedient or annoying. Believing that his parents care nothing for him and restricted in his contacts with them to clashes over routines, he is convinced that they dislike him.*

Both because he has no adequate direction and because he is angry over his parents' indifference, the child behaves in increasingly chaotic and inappropriate ways.[3] He is irresponsible about completing school work, discharging home duties, and keeping promises. Left alone for hours daily when he is older, he soon experiments with stealing, sex adventures, and running away. Many parents become aware of their adolescent's long-pursued delinquencies for the first time when he finally is apprehended by the police.

Decreased Capacity for Personal Relationships

When a child becomes convinced that he is regarded by his parents as dispensable, he defends himself against being hurt similarly by others.[5] He avoids close relationships,[23] especially with adults, although he may seek a facsimile of them among his peers. Unsure of his acceptance by others, he often becomes subservient to all wishes of his peers, regard-less of their nature, and a girl may attempt to create the image of a close relationship by sexual promiscuity or by an early marriage.

Sometimes the child becomes attached to possessions as a substitute for people, and he devotes himself to collecting or to stealing articles he does not need.

A child who is convinced that no one is interested in him becomes progressively withdrawn,† and if his feeling of being alone becomes acute at a time of crisis or severe disappointment, he may attempt suicide.

REFERENCES

1. Ackerman, N. W.: Disturbances of mothering and criteria for treatment. *Amer. J. Orthopsychiat.*, 1956, *26*, 252–263.
2. Appel, G.: Les effets de la privation de soins maternels sur le développement de l'enfant (The effects of deprivation of maternal care on the development of the child). *Cah. Pedag.*, 1954, *13*, 171–185.
3. Aubry, J.: Les formes graves de carence de soins maternels (Serious manifestations due to absence of maternal care). *Evolut. Psychiat.*, 1955, *1*, 1–32.

---

* See Case 16, Loretta K., p. 507.
† See Case 15, Paul G., p. 507.

4. Bowlby, J.: Mother-child separation. *In* Soddy, K.: *Mental Health and Infant Development.* New York, Basic Books, Inc., 1956, vol. 1, pp. 117–122.
5. Bowlby, J.: Some pathological processes set in train by early mother-child separation. *J. Ment. Sci.*, 1954, *99*, 265–272.
6. Fanshel, D., and Maas, H. S.: Factorial dimensions of the characteristics of children in placement and their families. *Child Developm.*, 1962, *33*, 123–144.
7. Gewirtz, J. L.: Three determinants of attention-seeking in young children. *Monogr. Soc. Res. Child Developm.*, 1954, *19*, (2).
8. Glaser, K., and Eisenberg, L.: Maternal deprivation. *Pediatrics*, 1956, *18*, 626–642.
9. Glueck, S., and Glueck, E.: Working mothers and delinquency. *Ment. Hyg. (N. Y.)*, 1957, *41*, 327–352.
10. Hoffman, L. W.: Effects of maternal employment on the child. *Child Developm.*, 1961, *32*, 187–197.
11. Lajewski, H. C.: *Child Care Arrangements of Full-Time Working Mothers.* Children's Bureau Publication No. 378, 1959.
12. Litwinski, L.: Les névroses de séparation d'origine infantile et l'autoprotection (Neuroses of separation of infantile origin and autoprotection). *Enfance*, 1952, *5*, 250–261.
13. McCord, J., McCord, W., and Thurber, E.: Effects of maternal employment on lower-class boys. *J. Abnorm. Soc. Psychol.*, 1963, *67*, 177–182.
14. National Manpower Council: *Work in the Lives of Married Women: Proceedings of a Conference on Woman-power.* New York, Columbia Univer. Press, 1958.
15. Powell, K. S.: Maternal employment in relation to family life. *Marriage Fam. Liv.*, 1961, *23*, 350–355.
16. Rabin, A. I.: The maternal deprivation hypothesis revisited. *Israel Anns. Psychiatr. Rel. Discp.*, 1963, *1*, 189–200.
17. Rautman, E., and Rautman, A.: Every child needs four sets of parents. *J. Child Psychiat.*, 1951, *2*, 221–228.
18. Rosenberg, M.: Parental interest and children's self-conceptions. *Sociometry*, 1963, *26*, 35–49.
19. Roudinesco, J.: Severe maternal deprivation and personality development in early childhood. *Underst. Child*, 1952, *21*, 104–108.
20. Schenk-Danzinger, C.: Social difficulties of children who were deprived of maternal care in early childhood. *Vita Hum. Basel*, 1961, *4*, 229–241.
21. Schiffman, J.: *Marital and Family Characteristics of Workers, March, 1960.* Special Labor Force Report, No. 13. Bureau of Labor Statistics, United States Department of Labor.
22. Schiffman, J.: *Marital and Family Characteristics of Workers, March, 1961.* Special Labor Force Report, No. 20. Bureau of Labor Statistics, United States Department of Labor.
23. Schraml, W.: Zum Problem der frunen Mutter-Kind-Trennung (Concerning the problem of early mother-child separation). *Prax. Kinderpsychol., Kinderpsychiat.*, 1954, *3*, 243–249.
24. Slater, P. E.: Parental behavior and the personality of the child. *J. Genet. Psychol.*, 1962, *101*, 53–68.

Chapter 6

Unbalanced
Social Experience

Readiness for social interaction is inherent in most children, but techniques of achieving adequate relationships with others must be acquired through practice.[30] Peer contacts provide for the utilization and revision of the child's motor skills, his capacity for verbal expression, and his moral standards.[7] When he plays, the child comprehends and controls more of his world,[24] and with his peers he can display emotion more freely and with less danger of rejection than he can with adults.[28] The kind of social experience he has is a major influence in his development of attitudes of tolerance, adaptability, dominance, trustfulness, deceptiveness, dependence, indifference, and self-acceptance.

Social attributes of the child which appear at the pre-school level persist for years. Kagan and Moss[17, 18] reported that passivity during the first three years correlated with timidity in social situations during the early elementary period, and that inhibition and apprehension with peers during the six-to-ten-year period were predictive of social anxiety in adults for both sexes. Physical aggression toward peers remained a stable trait for the first ten years of life, and competitiveness, dominance, and indirect aggression were stable from three to 14 years of age. The early appearance and constancy of characteristic social reactions suggest that a child's basic tendency toward passivity or aggression combines with his early experiences in interpersonal relations with both adults and peers to establish strong habitual responses to others.

A child whose associations with his peers are rare, warped by constant contact with children younger, older, or of the opposite sex, or sub-

ject to the interference of siblings or parents fails to acquire social behavior appropriate for his age and sex. His relationships with others
remain inept, uneasy, and unsatisfying.

UNBALANCED SOCIAL EXPERIENCE

Absence of Playmates

Some elementary school children never play with their classmates.
They stand aside on the playground at recess time, and at home they
play by themselves. Often they are not unhappy as spectators, because
they are quiet, unaggressive children who cannot compete successfully
with their rowdy, impetuous peers. Social development cannot occur in
the absence of social contacts, however, because it is a gradual process
which requires the acquisition of new ways of behaving as the child
matures. The one-year-old plays adjacent to another child but in general
ignores his existence. The two-year-old grabs toys and pushes other
children in an initial acknowledgment of their presence. The older pre-
school child controls some of his physical aggressiveness and begins to
learn coöperation in play.[30] Empathy with peers increases during the
elementary school years, and in the later years of this period a cleavage
between the sexes in interests and play activities occurs. During adolescence, the relationships between the sexes and the interests of each sex
change in predictable ways. Continuing peer associations are needed to
ensure normal social growth, and the child who does not have these
associations interprets peer behavior incorrectly and retains immature
ways of responding to others.

Younger Playmates

A child finds relief from the competition which peers offer when he
plays occasionally with younger children, whom he can dominate. If he
always plays with younger children, however, he has no skill for adapting to his own age-group. When he attempts to utilize his well-learned
and successful techniques of coercion on them, he is scorned and isolated
for his overbearing manner.

The child who plays with younger children most of the time also
remains immature in his interests and behavior, because his younger playmates cannot participate effectively in play which is appropriate for him.[1]
At a time when his classmates are engaged in bike-riding expeditions and
group sports, he will be occupying himself with hide-and-seek, and both
his independence and the development of his skills suffer.

Older Playmates

Constant association with older children sets a pattern of submission and inferiority in a child which leaves him ill-equipped to hold his own with his age-mates. A child is proud of being accepted as a playmate by an older child, but this pride dissipates as he discovers that his customary dependent and imitative manner makes him a lackluster companion for children his own age.

Older children tend not only to dominate but to abuse younger playmates, ridiculing and reviling their awkwardness and ignorance. An eight-year-old boy, stuttering badly, completely avoided children of his own age. He was preoccupied with finding approval but convinced that he did not merit it. Both as test and punishment, he attached himself to older boys, who treated him roughly and mocked his stutter.

The child who has no one but an older child with whom to associate will suffer frequent rebuffs of his invitations to play. The older child is more attracted to playmates whose interests are similar to his own and whose skills he respects, and his rejection can lead the younger child to enduring anxiety about the reaction of others to any initiation of social contact.

Playmates of the Opposite Sex

Boys and girls share activities appropriate to both sexes throughout the pre-school period and well into elementary school years. Sex differences in play preferences appear early, however, and the sex-role content of boys' play activities between three and six years is an accurate predictor of their sex-role interests as adults.[18] Pre-school girls already show a strong interest in people, a trait characteristic of their sex throughout their lives.

A boy associating only with a group of girls usually will spend his time playing house or school, and a girl who plays with a group of boys will participate in mock gun battles, football, and wrestling matches. Although none of these activities is undesirable for either sex, the child whose play consists solely of that more typical of the opposite sex fails to acquire and develop play interests and skills appropriate to his own.

Play deficiencies cause difficulty for the child as he reaches the later elementary years, when the members of each sex rely heavily on peer companionship and also tend to isolate themselves from the opposite sex.[31] Children of this age who engage in activities typical of the opposite sex are anxious and uncertain, and they exhibit a variety of behavior problem.[32]

Interference With Friendships

Intrusion by Siblings. Fascinated small siblings will play a submissive role if they are allowed to remain during older children's play; but if they are ordered to leave, they refuse and effectively halt the activity by seizing toys, asking questions, and demanding attention and favors. Older children without playmates interfere in younger siblings' play in the same fashion by criticizing and appropriating toys, thus producing angry reactions which interrupt the playing. If the age difference between siblings is slight, an older sibling may entice away the friend of the younger and then not permit him to join the new twosome. Such interference, if it is common, results in a child's having no friends with whom he can play normally, and he is deprived of needed association with his peers.

Domination by Parents. A child whose social experience is dominated by his parents never learns how to associate freely with his peers. He is not permitted to play as he chooses with friends he prefers. His friends are chosen for him from among those considered desirable by his parents, and frequently both large parties and private visits are planned for him without consideration for his preferences. The parents always are present when other children visit, and it is the parents who direct the activities and provide the entertainment. When the child's social contacts consist only of staged performances, instituted and conducted by his parents, his relations with other children are tenuous and joyless.

PARENTAL MOTIVATION

Unbalanced social experience may be the accidental result of parental unawareness that the nature of early peer contacts significantly influences the child's social development. Initial parental indifference to distorted play associations may continue in succeeding years or may change to overconcern with social behavior.

Indifference

The earliest associations of the child set a pattern of social growth or retardation. The pre-school child who has no suitable playmates becomes the elementary school child who finds his friends among the outcasts and who avoids or attacks most of his peers. As he continues to feel different from and inferior to others, he seeks solace, as an adolescent, in a sweetheart of demonstrated immaturity or questionable morality. Parental concern about these later undesirable associations often is tardy in appearing.

Overconcern

A parent's indifference to the nature of the pre-schooler's social contacts may change to embarrassment as the child grows older and attracts no friends at all. Social acceptability is important to most adults, and the parent whose child has no companions may resort to constant urging of the child to mingle with his peers. As he exhorts the child to greater sociability, the parent shows his disappointment in the child and adds to the child's unhappiness.

Parents who dominate the child's social life are overconcerned with social acceptability. They are dependent on others' opinions, and they seek status for themselves through the child. By directing the social appearance which the child presents, they believe they achieve social recognition for the family.

Socially isolated parents with rigid, negative attitudes toward others refuse to permit the child to associate with peers of his own choice. Because they are suspicious of others' influence on him or good intentions toward him, they limit his contacts to the few persons of whom they approve. Often these are their own adult friends, who resemble them in their feelings about other people.[2]

Parents who are overprotective do not permit the child to mingle with his peers and to manage himself without them. Because they cannot bear mistreatment of the child, they cannot tolerate the quarreling, selfishness, and rejection which normally occur in play. They terminate the play, often with abuse of the offending child. Nor can such parents accept the child's attachment to and support of companions other than themselves, and gradually they sever all of his social relationships.[*]

PERSONALITY AND BEHAVIOR CORRELATES OF UNBALANCED SOCIAL EXPERIENCE

When a child does not have satisfying relationships with his peers, he develops feelings of inferiority, isolation, and self-concern; and serious behavior problems may be associated with these feelings.

Feelings of Inferiority

No one teaches a child more about living than his peers do. If he cheats, they loudly and insultingly expose him. If he brags, they top his brag. If he cries, whines, and complains, they label him "baby." They repudiate immaturity and deception, but they forgive quickly and renew broken friendships with a spontaneity and a faith in future reliability never shown by adults. Even though a child suffers from the rebuffs and challenges of his age-mates, if they continue to play with him and listen to his ideas, he knows that they consider him competent and acceptable.

---

[*] See Chapter 4, "Fixation of Immaturity."

The child who rarely associates with his peers neither tests his own acceptability nor learns to adapt to others' variable treatment, and he thinks of himself as less capable and desirable than they are. Because he spends no time with them, he also is convinced that they are thoroughly confident of their own abilities and secure in the complete acceptance of their fellows, and his own shortcomings seem overwhelming by comparison. If his faults appear too monumental to him, he will cease to try to use the abilities he has, and he may devote increasing amounts of time to brooding over his defects.*

Feeling inferior to his peers, he is unhappy when he is with them, and he tends to withdraw from social contacts whenever he can and show his discomfort during unavoidable associations. Symptoms such as excessive crying or stuttering may accompany withdrawal, and social isolation may lead to the rigid, fearful attitudes on which compulsiveness depends. Adolescents find that they can escape both from the need to respond normally to others and from the awareness of their own unhappy assessment of themselves by overindulgence in alcohol or drugs.

Feelings of Isolation

The child who is inept in peer relationships avoids associating with his fellows, and his choice of isolation leads them to ignore or reject him because he is unresponsive to their overtures and because they believe that he considers himself superior to them.[28] As he increasingly confines his social contacts to adult members of his own family, his desire and opportunity for peer associations diminish.[18] While he confines himself to the familiarity of home and family, his peers progress toward emancipation from their parents, aided by their identification with each other, and the social differences between the isolate and his agemates increase.

The child who lives apart from his own generation tends to underscore his isolation by direct action, such as being truant from school in disavowal of his assigned place with his peers. An isolated child also finds it difficult to achieve valid sexual identity because of his limited contact with members of his own sex and generation. In failing to acquire the definitive traits of his own sex, he becomes even more isolated as his appearance, interests, and behavior become those of an amorphous hybrid.

Self-concern

The child who must withstand the irritations and failures of peer association feels sorry for himself at times, but he is concerned with

---

* See Case 4, Harriet L., p. 498.

others' activities and ideas rather than solely with his own. He does not dwell only on his own thoughts, work only on his own plans, or ally himself only with adults for protection and comfort. If he does, his interests and attitudes narrow, and he fails to have those experiences with peers which he needs to supplement adult approval or disapproval.[21]

A knowledge of the infinite variety of ways in which peers live and think teaches the child that there is no single, obligatory mode of life, and his tolerance broadens, as do his concepts of what is necessary and what is possible. He also discovers that his peers have problems and troubles, some of which are more serious than his own, and this information makes him less self-centered. Without the contacts which provide this awareness of others, the child becomes self-righteous, rigid, and self-pitying. Even though he initiated and maintains separation from his peers, he interprets his isolation as rejection, resents being excluded, and dislikes and distrusts others.

The child who is concerned only with himself has frequent psychophysiological complaints, and these serve to excuse him from participation in peer activities. If he resents his peers, he may attack them; often he succeeds in doing so without exposing himself to the contact of a counterattack: A younger child hits and runs, and an adolescent starts gossip about others. Attacks may be made against persons who are unknown to the child, and vandalism, arson, assault, and theft frequently are instigated by the individual's feeling of being unneeded and unwanted. The adolescent who directs his concern exclusively to himself and withdraws from contacts with others is unable to compare his opinions and conclusions with those ideas held by other people. Gradually he may develop delusions, and these can lead eventually to deterioration in thinking, loss of self-control, or suicide.

REFERENCES

1. Amatora, M.: Interests of pre-adolescent boys and girls. *Genet. Psychol. Monogr.*, 1960, *61*, 77–113.
2. Bandura, A., and Walters, R. H.: *Social Learning and Personality Development.* New York, Holt, Rinehart and Winston, 1963, p. 100.
3. Bowerman, C. E., and Kinch, J. W.: Changes in family and peer orientation of children between the fourth and tenth grades. *Soc. Forces*, 1959, 37, 206–211.
4. Brooks, F. D., and Shaffer, L. F.: *Child Psychology.* Cambridge, Mass., Houghton Mifflin Co., 1937, pp. 374–377.
5. Cameron, N.: *The Psychology of Behavior Disorders.* Cambridge, Mass., Houghton Mifflin Co., 1947, pp. 44–45.
6. Campbell, W. J.: Preferences of children for others of the same or opposite sex. *Aust. J. Psychol.*, 1955, 7, 45–51.
7. Chateau, J.: *L'enfant et le jeu* (*The Child and Play*). Paris, Editions du Scarabée, 1954.
8. Commoss, H. H.: Some characteristics related to social isolation of second grade children. *J. Educ. Psychol.*, 1962, 53, 38–42.

9. D'Evelyn, K. E.: *Meeting Children's Emotional Needs.* Englewood Cliffs, N. J., Prentice-Hall, Inc., 1957, pp. 13–14, 22, 73.
10. Dymond, R. F., Hughes, A. S., and Raabe, V. L.: Measurable changes in empathy with age. *J. Consult. Psychol.,* 1952, *16,* 202–206.
11. Gold, H. A.: The importance of ideology in sociometric evaluation of leadership. *Group Psychother.,* 1962, *15,* 224–230.
12. Goodenough, E. W.: Interest in persons as an aspect of sex difference in early years. *Genet. Psychol. Monogr.,* 1957, *55,* 287–323.
13. Höhn, E.: Sociometric studies on the adjustment process of displaced persons. *Int. Soc. Sci. Bull.,* 1955, *7,* 22–29.
14. Horrocks, J. E.: *The Psychology of Adolescence,* Ed. 2. Cambridge, Mass., Houghton Mifflin Co., 1962, pp. 123–124.
15. Horrocks, J. E., and Buker, M. E.: A study of the friendship fluctuations of preadolescents. *J. Genet. Psychol.,* 1951, *78,* 131–144.
16. Hubbell, A.: Two-persons role-playing for guidance in social readjustment. *Group Psychother.,* 1954, *7,* 249–254.
17. Jersild, A. T.: *Child Psychology,* Ed. 4. Englewood Cliffs, N. J., Prentice-Hall, Inc., 1954, p. 195.
18. Kagan, J., and Moss, H. A.: *Birth to Maturity.* New York, John Wiley and Sons, 1962, pp. 66, 79, 87–89, 93–94, 169, 174, 266.
19. Kanous, L. E., and Cohn, T. S.: Relation between heterosexual friendship choices and socioeconomic level. *Child Developm.,* 1962, *33,* 251–255.
20. Lantz, H. R.: Number of childhood friends as reported in the life histories of a psychiatrically diagnosed group of 1000. *Marriage Fam. Liv.,* 1956, *18,* 107–108.
21. McGuire, C.: Family and age-mates in personality formation. *Marriage Fam. Liv.,* 1953, *15,* 17–23.
22. Meister, A.: Perception and acceptance of power relations in children. *Group Psychother.,* 1956, *9,* 153–163.
23. Mensh, I. N., Kantor, M. B., Domke, H. R., Gildea, M. C.-L., and Glidewell, J. C.: Children's behavior symptoms and their relationships to school adjustment, sex, and social class. *J. Soc. Issues,* 1959, *15,* 8–15.
24. Millichamp, D. A.: Another look at play. *Bull. Inst. Child Stud. (Toronto),* 1953, *15,* 1–13.
25. Morrison, I. E., and Perry, I. F.: Acceptance of overage children by their classmates. *Elem. Sch. J.,* 1956, *56,* 217–220.
26. Rogers, D.: *The Psychology of Adolescence.* New York, Appleton-Century-Crofts, 1962, pp. 116, 398–399.
27. Shugart, G.: The play history: Its application and significance. *J. Psychiat. Soc. Wk.,* 1955, *24,* 204–209.
28. Sorokin, P. A., and Gove, D. S.: Notes on the friendly and antagonistic behavior of nursery school children. *In* Sorokin, P. A.: *Explorations in Altruistic Love and Behavior.* Boston, Beacon Press, 1950, pp. 295–300.
29. Spock, B.: *Baby and Child Care.* New York, Pocket Books, Inc., 1957, pp. 388–389.
30. Stott, L. H., and Ball, R. S.: Consistency and change in ascendance-submission in the social interaction of children. *Child Developm.,* 1957, *28,* 259–272.
31. Sutton, R. S.: An appraisal of certain aspects of children's social behavior. *J. Teacher Educ.,* 1962, *13,* 30–34.
32. Sutton-Smith, B., and Rosenberg, B. G.: Manifest anxiety and game preferences in children. *Child Developm.,* 1960, *31,* 307–311.
33. Sutton-Smith, B., Rosenberg, B. G., and Morgan, E. F., Jr.: Development of sex differences in play choices during preadolescence. *Child Developm.,* 1963, *34,* 119–126.
34. Wang, J. D.: The relationship between children's play interests and their mental ability. *J. Genet. Psychol.,* 1958, *93,* 119–131.
35. Wilkins, W. L.: Social peers and parents. *Education,* 1952, *73,* 234–237.

Chapter 7

Fatigue

Prevention of fatigue is a fundamental but widely disregarded way in which parents can avert behavior problems in their children. Bleckmann[1] noted that 57 ten-year-old children referred to clinics suffered from being forced to exceed their physical, as well as their intellectual and emotional, limits. A child needs protection from overstimulation and from a daily schedule so full that he has no time to be alone, to play as he chooses, or to create and experiment with his own ideas.

FATIGUE

Lack of Sleep

Children are expert at resisting bedtime, and many parents avoid nightly arguments by convincing themselves that children always take as much sleep as they need. It is not uncommon for pre-school children to stay up as late as their parents do, and adolescents slowly work away at studies, hobbies, or hair curlers two hours after their parents have retired.

Spock[9] stated that pre-school children should be in bed 12 hours each night, supplemented by a nap or rest during the day. The early elementary school child relinquishes his daytime rest, but he still needs 12 hours of sleep at night. By the time the child is nine years old, he requires only 11 hours at night, and when he starts junior high school, ten hours. The 15-year-old, still growing, needs nine hours of rest at night.

Few children receive this much rest, and even those with set bed-

56

times frequently are deprived of them by attendance at evening functions. Children are taken to movies, concerts, plays, sporting events, and church and school programs. In some families evening visits to relatives or friends are made several times weekly.

School Requirements

Even nursery school attendance produces fatigue effects in preschool children, whose energy is depleted rapidly as they meet the challenges and requirements of unfamiliar children and adults away from home.

The elementary school child spends a minimum of five hours each day in class, where he must think, observe, remember, produce new ideas, listen, and exercise close control over his muscles. He must do these things in the presence of his peers, who try to better his performance and who are quick to snicker at his errors. The quantity of information which must be learned at every school level is increasing steadily, and new methods of teaching basic subjects demand more attentiveness to detail than ever before. Homework requirements for the adolescent sometimes are so monumental that he spends ten or more hours daily at academic work.

Activities and Lessons

Multitudes of activities and organizations exist for children, and although their variety and availability are laudable, the practice of requiring the child to participate in all of them is not. Junior choir rehearsals, dancing lessons, piano lessons, scouting, and baton-twirling are routine. Sewing classes, charm classes, dramatics classes, and art classes are all scheduled for the child, regardless of his interest or need. Summer vacation vanishes with weeks of organized baseball and summer school courses. The child is continually harassed by a timetable, and his freedom not only is usurped but is replaced with added hours of adult supervision and instruction.

Overstimulation

Television. Few children escape the fascinating and exhausting adventures of television, but both pre-school and older children tire from sitting still for long hours and failing to exercise outdoors. Staying up late at night to watch one show after another, they not only lose sleep but go to bed remembering scenes of hatred, greed, and sudden death which prolong their wakefulness.

Air Force physicians examining children from three to 12 years of age for the cause of their symptoms of nervousness, continuous fatigue, headaches, loss of sleep, stomach aches and occasional vomiting, discovered that the children spent from three to six hours watching television every weekday and from six to ten hours on Saturdays and Sundays. Totally abstaining from television viewing eliminated the symptoms within two to three weeks, and restricting the children's viewing to two hours daily removed symptoms in five or six weeks.[11]

Social Activities. A premature bustle of social life is tiring children. Little girls celebrate their birthdays with hotel luncheons, complete with imitation cocktails; dancing parties are given for ten-year-old children; sororities bid for members among 12-year-old girls, and formal dresses with corsages from escorts are expected attire at their spring dances.

The hours spent in such stilted recreation, filled less with fun than with worry over making a *faux pas,* produce more tension and fatigue for the child.

PARENTAL MOTIVATION

Parents' perpetuation of fatigue reactions in the child seldom is motivated by a desire to harm him; on the contrary, the reasons often are intertwined with parental interest in his welfare. Indifference, identification, the need to conform, and a desire for family unity all obscure the adults' awareness of the effects of fatigue.

Indifference

Many parents are both unaware of and indifferent to the child's need for protection from fatigue. Only a small proportion of parents is concerned about the effect of television on their children,[3] and these are the better-educated parents, who not only limit television watching but consistently insist on an appropriate bedtime.[8]

The parents' own desire for distraction and entertainment often takes precedence over the child's need for rest. Weary of being confined at home, mothers take every opportunity to go shopping, pay visits, or attend movies; and the child goes along because this is the most expedient procedure for simultaneously getting away from home and providing for the child's supervision.

Identification

Parents inevitably live again through their children, and adults who most diligently burden their children with extra lessons freely express their own regret at not having received similar training. They envision the child as a graceful dancer, a star athlete, and an accomplished performer in foreign language, art, or music. They pridefully anticipate the applause which will be accorded them as the parents of a trained and talented child. Their disappointment when the child fumbles the ball, fails to earn ranks in youth organizations, and begs to quit piano lessons does not dismay them for long, and they try again in other areas. Thrusting the child into inappropriate social ventures results from the parent's desire to identify with a mature, poised, attractive, and popular member of a recognized social set; and the parent is too impatient for this pleasure to wait until the child is old enough to acquire valid social competence.

Conformity

Parents seldom think for themselves or have the courage to manage their children differently from other parents in the community. When it is the custom for children to take piano and dancing lessons, participate in Little League, and accompany their parents to evening meetings and performances, parents who question the value of these activities for their own child still follow the pattern. They are not confident of the correctness of their own beliefs, and they fear that they will be considered different from other parents or miserly in not providing the child with the advantages his peers have.

Family Unity

Some parents announce proudly that they never go anywhere without their children, and they do not. But the children lose needed sleep when the adults play cards or go to evening movies. Others maintain that watching television together is an activity which unifies the family. Parents' viewing habits parallel those of their children,[12] and adults cannot justify restricting the child's television when they derive so much pleasure themselves from watching. These parents often believe that they are depriving the child if they go anywhere without him, and they cannot understand the child's preference, as he grows older, for avoiding family visits to relatives or for joining his friends at a drive-in movie instead of remaining home with his parents to watch television.

PERSONALITY AND BEHAVIOR CORRELATES OF FATIGUE

The fatigued child achieves at an inferior level, and his actions are imitative, rather than spontaneous or original. He reacts to pressure with avoidance and negativism, and he may regress to earlier forms of behavior.

Inferior Achievement

A tired child is unable to utilize his capacity for growth and development. He is inattentive at school and cannot concentrate on instruction or complete school requirements adequately.

When the child's free time is consumed by extra activities or television, homework is put aside and he gains less from his courses.[8] He also has little opportunity to use his intelligence in investigating or creating, and consequently his intellectual ability decreases.

Imitative Behavior

Pre-school children watching slapstick comedy on television tenaciously repeat the aggressive actions and insulting verbal expressions they have observed, and clinical evidence on 200 older children confirms the effect on their behavior of viewing violence on television.[13]

Children engaged in imitative athletic activities, such as Little League baseball or organized football at the elementary school level, acquire the mannerisms and values of adult competitiveness years before they are ready for them; and their own freedom to play when and as they choose, adapting to situations as they occur, is sacrificed to playing a minor role which fits into an adult's concept of sport.

Similar privation occurs in social learning when children are prematurely introduced to adult social behavior. They act an artificial, mandatory role during the years when they most need to learn empathy, tolerance, and concern for others and when they need to engage in independent activity and share experiences and plans with friends.

A child prematurely introduced to adult social customs exhausts these possibilities for diversion at an early age, and during adolescence he will experiment with such activities as drinking and sexual intercourse, the only remaining adult practices he has not sampled.*

Avoidance and Negativism

The fatigued child, weary of constant adult coercion and continually aware of failing to measure up in a wide variety of learning and competitive situations, demonstrates his complete rejection of this way of life by refusing to participate in the adults' plans for him. With persistent negativism, he evidences his need for privacy, peace, and self-determination. His refusals are not confined to activities he does not choose for himself but spread to include all requests made of him by adults, and he balks at any order or requirement, whether or not it is reasonable.[1] Temper tantrums, irritability, and rudeness are common in the tired child.[10]

---

* See Case 5, Eddie A., p. 499.

Regression

Fatigue and exhaustion cause earlier forms of behavior to reappear and self-control and self-discipline to be lost. When fatigue is extreme, the individual becomes completely unaware of the effects of his behavior on others and oblivious to previously learned social requirements for acceptable conduct.

The deleterious effect of fatigue on the ability of an individual to function is confirmed by the successful use of continuous sleep as treatment for restoring emotional control to anxious and disturbed adults. Kutin[4] reported that 31 schizophrenic patients, whose illnesses had endured for over three years, were treated with a combination of aminasine therapy and continuous sleep, resulting in discharge from the hospital of 24 persons in this group.

The tired, overstimulated child is inattentive and shows a lowered tolerance for disappointments and frustrations. His sleeping and eating habits are disturbed, and he cries uncontrollably, clings to his parents, and reverts to thumb-sucking and enuresis. Anxiety is an outgrowth of excessive television viewing or unrelenting competitiveness, and stomach aches and headaches are traceable to combined fatigue and fear reactions.

REFERENCES

1. Bleckmann, K. H.: Ueberforderte Kinder (Children who are under too much pressure). *Prax. Kinderpsychol., Kinderpsychiat.*, 1957, *6*, 273–277.
2. Eron, L. D.: Relationship of TV viewing habits and aggressive behavior in children. *J. Abnorm. Soc. Psychol.*, 1963, *67*, 193–196.
3. Hess, R. D., and Goldman, H.: Parents' views of the effect of television on their children. *Child Developm.*, 1962, *33*, 411–426.
4. Kutin, V. P.: Lechenie bol'nykh schizofreniei dlitel'nym nepreryvnym snom s odnovremennym primoncniom aminazina (The treatment of schizophrenics with uninterrupted sleep and simultaneous application of aminasine). *Zh. Nevropat. Psikhiat.*, 1961, *61*, 228–234.
5. Merrill, I. R.: Broadcast viewing and listening by children. *Publ. Opin. Quart.*, 1961, *25*, 263–276.
6. Noshpitz, J. D., and Spielman, P.: Diagnosis: Study of the differential characteristics of hyper-aggressive children. *Amer. J. Orthopsychiat.*, 1961, *31*, 111–112.
7. Scott, L. F.: A study of children's TV interests. *Calif. J. Educ. Res.*, 1953, *4*, 162–164.
8. Scott, L. F.: Relationships between elementary school children and television. *J. Educ. Res.*, 1958, *52*, 134–137.
9. Spock, B.: *Baby and Child Care.* New York, Pocket Books, Inc., 1957, pp. 318–319.
10. Thom, D. A.: *Everyday Problems of the Everyday Child.* New York, Appleton-Century, 1934, p. 79.
11. Those Tired Children. *Time*, 1964, *84* (19), 76.
12. Witty, P., and Kinsella, P.: Children and the electronic Pied Piper. *Education*, 1959, *80*, 48–56.
13. Wertham, F.: The scientific study of mass media effects. *Amer. J. Psychiatr.*, 1962, *119*, 306–311.

Chapter 8

Rejection
of Responsibility

The lazy child is not a happy one. The child who consistently succeeds in avoiding or refusing responsibility finds that his freedom soon palls and that he is left behind while others learn, contribute, achieve, mature, and attain independence. Constructive experiences are needed by children to develop strength for coping with both normal and special stress.[7]

Successful achievement with tasks suited to his ability provides the child with merited self-satisfaction and predisposes him to success with later tasks.[5, 8] A strong desire for both maturity and independence is inherent in children, and these attributes are acquired by the child who is given responsibility and who meets it well.[3, 9, 10, 25] The child who practices responsibility by completing his work and school requirements and who earns and spends money realistically will become an adult who works efficiently, without self-pity, and who manages his income sensibly.

Although children normally resist adult efforts to require responsibility of them, evading work whenever they can, they do so less often when they have repeated experiences with work and thus become more skilled and successful at doing what is expected of them. Keister and Updegraff[16] demonstrated that even young children can be trained to approach difficult tasks without rebellion, refusal, or excitement. In individual sessions over a period of 16 weeks, 12 pre-school children who had sulked, cried, given up, or retreated after failing two problems, one a puzzle and the other demanding great physical strength, were presented similar tasks of gradually increasing difficulty. No assistance was given the child, but he was praised for his independence at completing the tasks. In a final test with a difficult problem, these children showed no exaggerated emotional responses. Their behavior contrasted with an untrained group who faced the final problem with the same excitement and rebellion they had shown initially.

REJECTION OF RESPONSIBILITY

Rejection of responsibility occurs in the child who remains inexperienced in working at home, studying at school, and earning and spending money appropriately.

Home Responsibilities

The pre-school child plays at working. His toys are imitation tools of those used by his parents, and he delights in mixing up a cake, mowing the lawn, and carrying in the milk. As he grows older, his horizons broaden to activities and companions outside of his home, and his enthusiasm for helping wanes. The school age child complains loudly of being abused when he is requested to make his bed or carry out the trash. The adolescent objects more subtly, regretfully informing his mother that he wishes he could wash the dinner dishes but that his teachers have assigned homework which will take all of his time.

Failure to require the child to meet home responsibilities is characteristic of parents of lower socioeconomic status, both of whom are working and away from home much of the time. When they are home, they are too tired to enforce their requests for help, or they may have no established routine for accomplishing the necessary work. Children from low income families find it difficult to see value in work, because they know that their parents work hard but that the family's living standard does not improve.[18]

When the child repeatedly succeeds in evading chores, he adopts the attitude that work at home is not his responsibility, and soon he believes that his parents have no right to ask for his help.*

Schoolwork

Sontag and Kagan[26] found that the child's motivation to master intellectual tasks develops during the first five school years and that high levels of achievement at this time are correlated with later adult achievement.

---

* See Case 6, Albert B., p. 499.

The child who feels no responsibility for completing schoolwork spends his study time in idle scribbling, gazing out the window, or conversing with or directing others who try to work. He never manages to persevere long enough to complete an assignment. His teacher may scold and threaten, but if she does not insist, the child remains indifferent to class requirements.

When his low grades reflect his idleness, he informs his parents that the teacher does not explain well, that he is tired from other school requirements, or that the work is too difficult. An even more effective excuse is his assertion that he already knows everything the teacher assigns and that repeating it is a waste of time. Parents who believe that the child is intelligent frequently agree with his explanation of his failures and berate the school for failing to keep him interested. Because they are not required to do their work, many gifted children never summon up the self-discipline and effort demanded by study.[18] One third of the boys and girls identified by Terman as having superior intelligence failed college work.[27]

A child can ignore homework just as resolutely as he does classroom assignments. Too often, parental desire for his success leads the adults to do the child's work for him. They look up articles in the encyclopedia for him, rewrite his themes, and solve his math problems. The child concludes that homework is not his responsibility, and he loses all interest in studying by himself.

Money Management

Practice in the realistic use of money aids the child in developing responsibility. The child who does not earn his money but who receives it as a gift, either on a regular basis or whenever he requests it, is never satisfied with the amount. He persistently wheedles more from his parents, and if they refuse him, he is angry and abusive. The child who is paid stated amounts for regular chores learns that money must be earned and that it is not bestowed either by whim or obligation. The child who earns his money appreciates the tangible evidence that his work is worth-while, and he feels more mature and independent.

The child learns to manage money well by practice in doing so.[9, 10, 19] If he is not required to use his money for multiple purposes, he believes that it is intended solely for pleasure. Adolescent girls given charge accounts at expensive clothing stores or boys permitted to spend earnings from part-time work in whatever way they choose develop the grievous habit of indulging their every desire for entertainment and possessions. The child who is required to use money he has earned not only for pleasure but also for giving, saving, and buying necessities, learns to select and reject wisely, to share his money, and to plan for future needs.[25]

ADULT MOTIVATION

Teachers share with parents the obligation to teach children to accept responsibility. Adults who fail in this task are those who wish to avoid conflict with the child, who are impatient with his ineptitude, or who have erroneous concepts concerning the purpose of money.

Avoidance of Conflict

Adults become weary of giving and enforcing directions to reluctant, resisting children, and they tend to retreat when the child procrastinates or refuses. They rationalize their failure to insist on compliance by accepting his promises or excuses as valid, and they convince themselves of his sincerity and good intentions. Teachers avoid direct conflict with the idle child by considering themselves obligated to devote all of their time and effort to the entire class. In doing so, they abandon the child who requires more direction and control than the average pupil and who cannot succeed in school without this. Both teachers and parents shrug off the child's resistance with the comforting theory that either he will develop responsibility or he will suffer the consequences. Suffer he does, both then and later, because adults acceded to his desire for ease rather than requiring him to complete assigned tasks.

Ineptitude of the Child

Adults justify their failure to insist on a child's helping with home duties or producing correct papers at school by concluding that he is incapable of doing so. Careless and unconcerned, awkward and unobservant, the child produces work which creates acute feelings of discouragement and hopelessness in adults.

A mother knows that household tasks are done better and more quickly if she does them herself. She feels only despair when she views the mess her child makes in creating a batch of inedible cookies. The dried soap on the rims of glasses, the still-greasy frying pan, and the egg left on the fork tines all convince the dishpan tutor that she has a hopeless pupil and that not only are time and effort wasted, but retaining the child on the job clearly is unsanitary.

The teacher similarly becomes convinced that the child cannot write more adequately, follow directions more carefully, or ever be relied upon to complete an assignment, and she ceases her efforts to require improved performance from him. The parent, trapped into assuming responsibility for the child's homework, convinces himself that the child cannot complete it satisfactorily without his help.

Erroneous Concepts of Money

Failure to use money to teach the child responsibility is based on erroneous concepts of its purpose. To some parents, money represents bestowing or withholding approval, and it is not granted to a child unless he deserves it by behaving in approved ways.

Other parents believe that it is their duty to provide for the child, and they gain pleasure from buying everything he needs or might want. If they provide extravagantly, they assume that the child will reward them with gratitude and affection. A few parents cannot permit the child to manage his own money because their supplying his needs is evidence that they are necessary to him.

Many parents object to paying a child for home chores, claiming that work at home is an obligation the child owes as a member of the family. Although this viewpoint is laudable philosophy, in actual practice it rarely results in the child's assisting regularly and willingly with chores. Instead, there are battles whenever he is asked to help, and eventually the parents retreat and cease to request anything of him.

Some parents express concern that a child paid for chores will demand payment whenever he is asked to do anything, and it is true that "How much is it worth?" is an automatic response to many requests for assistance. This response is a delaying, bargaining tactic used both by children accustomed to payment for work and by those who are never paid for it. It is more common as the child becomes aware of the possibilities for earning money and acquires needs or desires which he wishes to satisfy. Children who earn enough money by their work to meet their needs, however, ordinarily are more generous with their time and more inclined to assist others spontaneously and gratuitously than are children who feel abused by being forced to work without compensation or who cannot count on a regular income. The child should not be paid for work which involves only the care of his own possessions, such as making his bed, cleaning his room, polishing his shoes, or pressing his clothes. Distinguishing in this way between the beneficiaries of his efforts aids him in accepting the fact that all work does not carry a monetary reward.

PERSONALITY AND BEHAVIOR CORRELATES OF REJECTION OF RESPONSIBILITY

The child who rejects responsibility and in so doing fails in personal achievement suffers from feelings of inadequacy and uselessness, from a constriction of activity, and from repressed intellectual and emotional expression. Socially isolated from his peers and resentful of adults, his indolence increases and his immaturity may lead to open aggression. Sometimes he attempts to compensate for his lack of achievement by simulating adulthood with obsequious manners, by engaging in premature sexual adventures, or by quitting school.

Feelings of Inadequacy and Uselessness

Baldwin[2] considered achievement to be an internalized value with antecedents similar to those of conscience. The child who fails to complete assigned tasks is contemptuous of himself because he can anticipate a loss in respect from others.

The child who does not study falls behind his classmates in both knowledge and self-discipline, and he becomes convinced that he is inadequate and unintelligent. Failure to require home responsibilities of him also suggests to him that he is considered useless, and some parents tell the child that his help is only an annoyance. The child who fails to learn that he can provide for his financial needs by his own efforts grows to adulthood believing that he is incapable of supporting himself.

The child removed from responsibility, either because of his own unwillingness to exert himself or because of parental impatience with his inefficiency, accepts the adults' verdict that nothing can be expected of him and he ceases to try. Believing himself to be incompetent, he restricts himself to participation in those activities in which he is reasonably certain he can succeed, and much potential achievement is lost as the child refuses to attempt the acquisition of new skills. He may also restrict himself in expressing emotion, either because he fears disapproval or because he feels himself unworthy of the right to indicate his feelings.[15, 30]

Social Isolation and Aggression

Children who fulfill their obligations continue to grow both in personal independence and in broadened, constructive interests.[13] The child who has been permitted to reject his responsibilities is no match for his peers, and he resents their competency. Increasingly, he isolates himself from them, failing to conform to the social norms of the group and being unconcerned about its welfare.[13]

The child resents not only his peers but also adults, whom he blames for permitting him to evade responsibility. Their indulgence of his refusals to work evokes his disrespect and scorn, and he directs these attitudes toward all persons in authority. Walsh[30] reported that children of average or better intelligence who were underachieving in school believed that everyone was too critical of them, and their reactions to people were evasive and negativistic. The irresponsible child is disgruntled and dissatisfied, and regardless of the ease of his daily life, he feels and acts exploited.[6]

He irritates adults deliberately by purposely careless work and persistent failure to fulfill his promises. Believing that he is not obligated to conform to any requirement, the irresponsible child indulges himself in cheating, stealing, lying, and disobedience.[23]

Simulated Adulthood

In his total failure to achieve, the irresponsible child has developed no assets to assist him in meeting the challenges and difficulties he inevitably encounters, and he disguises his inadequacies by simulating adulthood. Adults with whom he has only casual contact describe him as pleasant, courteous, and respectful. He seeks commendation and acceptance by a faithful mimicry of the social proprieties of maturity and with facile compliments for all.

The boy or girl who feels inadequate and isolated from his peers may devote himself to the vigorous pursuit of members of the opposite sex. Successful flirting, dating, and petting help to assure him that he is admirable and attractive. Although dating is of little real interest to boys and to many girls before the age of 15 years, the child who seeks esteem in this way acquires boy or girl friends and engages in moderate to excessive sexual behavior during the later elementary and early adolescent years. A girl attempting to play a mature role by attracting sexual attention may run away from home with a boy or man, and sometimes concludes the drama in logical fashion by marrying a virtual stranger when she is only 14 or 15 years old.

In a major effort to leap the gap between childhood and adulthood, the irresponsible adolescent rejects school as inappropriate for him. He leaves to seek a job which will provide him with a paycheck, proof to himself that he is mature. If he does find work, however, he does not continue with it long. Complaining that it is too hard, that the pay is too little, and that his fellow workers dislike him, he soon returns to his customary dependence on his parents for financial support.

REFERENCES

1. Ackerman, N. W.: Preventive implications of family research. *In* Caplan, G., ed.: *Prevention of Mental Disorders in Children.* New York, Basic Books, Inc., 1961, p. 150.
2. Baldwin, A. L.: Pride and shame in children. *Newsltr. Div. Develpm. Psychol., Amer. Psychol. Assn.,* 1959, Fall.
3. Cox, F. N.: An assessment of the achievement behavior system in children. *Child Developm.,* 1962, *33,* 907–916.

4. Crandall, V. J., and Rabson, A.: Children's repetition choices in an intellectual achievement situation following success and failure. *J. Genet. Psychol.*, 1960, 97, 161–168.
5. D'Evelyn, K. E.: *Meeting Children's Emotional Needs.* Englewood Cliffs, N. J., Prentice-Hall, Inc., 1957, p. 9.
6. Erikson, E. H.: Growth and crises of the "healthy personality." *In* Kluckhohn, C., Murray, H. A., and Schneider, D. M., eds.: *Personality in Nature, Society, and Culture.* New York, Alfred A. Knopf, 1956, p. 213.
7. Felix, R. H. *In* Caplan, G., ed.: *Prevention of Mental Disorders in Children.* New York, Basic Books, Inc., 1961, p. viii.
8. Fink, M. B.: Self concept as it relates to academic underachievement. *Calif. J. Educ. Res.*, 1962, 13, 57–62.
9. Foster, C. J.: *Developing Responsibility in Children.* Chicago, Science Research Associates, 1953.
10. Foster, N.: The child and his money. *Bull. Inst. Child Stud.* (*Toronto*), 1953, 15, 14–17.
11. Haring, N. G., and Phillips, E. L.: *Educating Emotionally Disturbed Children.* New York, McGraw-Hill Book Co., 1962, pp. 9–10.
12. Harris, D. B., Rose, A. M., Clark, K. E., and Valasek, F.: Personality differences between responsible and less responsible children. *J. Genet. Psychol.*, 1955, 87, 103–109.
13. Harris, I. D.: *Emotional Blocks to Learning.* New York, Free Press of Glencoe, 1961.
14. Horrocks, J. E.: *The Psychology of Adolescence*, Ed. 2. Boston, Houghton Mifflin Co., 1962, pp. 3, 507–508.
15. Kahn, D., and Baumann, D.: De quelques difficultés d'adaptation recontrées chez des adolescents orphelins éléves en collectivité (Social adaptation difficulties observed in adolescents educated in orphanages). *Enfance*, 1954, 7, 89–96.
16. Keister, M. E., and Updegraff, R.: A study of children's reactions to failure and an experimental attempt to modify them. *Child Developm.*, 1937, 8, 241–248.
17. Lucas, C. M., and Horrocks, J. E.: An experimental approach to the analysis of adolescent needs. *Child Developm.*, 1960, 31, 479–487.
18. McCandless, B. R.: *Children and Adolescents.* New York, Holt, Rinehart and Winston, 1961, pp. 204, 403, 460–466.
19. Marshall, H. R., and Magruder, L.: Relations between parent money education practices and children's knowledge and use of money. *Child Developm.*, 1960, 31, 253–284.
20. Miller, D. R., and Swanson, G.: *The Changing American Parent.* New York, John Wiley and Sons, 1958, p. 223.
21. Mussen, P., and Conger, J. J.: *Child Development and Personality.* New York, Harper and Bros., 1956, pp. 151, 382–383, 455.
22. Pasquasy, R.: L'indaptation scolaire (Inadaptation in school). *Bull. Orient. Scol. Profess.*, 1961, 10, 1–11.
23. Peck, R. F., and Havighurst, R. J.: *The Psychology of Character Development.* New York, John Wiley and Sons, 1960, p. 151.
24. Phillips, E. L., Wiener, D. N., and Haring, N. G.: *Discipline, Achievement, and Mental Health.* Englewood Cliffs, N. J., Prentice-Hall, Inc., 1960, pp. 32, 184–185.
25. Rogers, C. R.: *Clinical Treatment of the Problem Child.* Cambridge, Mass., Houghton Mifflin Co., 1939, pp. 129, 284.
26. Sontag, L. W., and Kagan, J.: The emergence of intellectual achievement motives. *Amer. J. Orthopsychiat.*, 1963, 33, 532–535.
27. Terman, L. M., and Oden, M. H.: *Genetic Studies of Genius: IV. The Gifted Child Grows Up.* Stanford, Calif., Stanford University Press, 1947.
28. Thompson, G. G.: *Child Psychology.* Cambridge, Mass., Houghton Mifflin Co., 1952, p. 177.
29. Wall, W. D.: Les facteurs sociaux et affectifs dans le retard scolaire (Social and emotional factors in school backwardness). *Enfance*, 1954, 7, 119–129.
30. Walsh, A. M.: *Self Concepts of Bright Boys with Learning Difficulties.* New York, Bureau of Publications, Teachers College, Columbia University, 1956.
31. Wertheim, J., and Mednick, S. A.: The achievement motive and field independence. *J. Consult. Psychol.*, 1958, 22, 38.

Chapter 9

Distortion
of Parental Role

The principal means by which a child learns how to act is the imitation of his like-sexed parent. Idealized concepts of typically distinguishing characteristics between mothers and fathers are held even by young children. Mothers are considered more helpful, more protective, and more generous than fathers; fathers are considered more competent and punitive than mothers. Boys at the early elementary level already evidence ambivalent attitudes toward their mothers and are beginning to identify with their fathers.[11, 26, 44] When the like-sexed parent does not fulfill his expected role in attitude, behavior, or function, the child does not acquire acceptable and satisfying modes of action. He may pattern his behavior after that of the opposite-sexed parent or any chance model he encounters.[22]

Distortion of parental role occurs in any one of five forms: (1) reversal of mother-father roles; (2) absence of a parent; (3) reversal of parent-child roles; (4) identification of spouse and child; and (5) parental assumption of peer status with the child. Severe abnormalities appear in the child reared under these conditions because the role distortions involve the persons on whom the child is most dependent and because the distortions endure throughout his developmental years.

REVERSAL OF MOTHER-FATHER ROLES

Traditionally assigned the child rearing role and of necessity normally assuming it, the mother is with the child more than the father is, and it is she who devises most of the plans and rules for the child's rearing and feels responsible for his development. Young children recognize that their mothers exert more control over them than their fathers, both directly and indirectly.[11]

In fulfilling her obligations as a parent, the mother may assume a dominant position in the family and replace the father as its head, rejecting his attempts to balance her child-rearing views and methods with his own. She may repudiate his criticism of her techniques or her results, or she may react angrily in defense of the child when the father attempts to correct him or to require more independence and courage from him. She may extend her dominance to assume duties normally reserved to the male, such as managing the money, filing the income tax, and undertaking her husband's home chores. By wheedling, petulance, or ultimatums, she manages to make the final decision in all disputed matters.

If the mother is employed, traditional sexual roles become even less distinct[18] as the child concludes that the father's importance to the family is minimal because his efforts are insufficient to meet its financial needs. The working mother, seldom home and too tired and busy to supervise, train, and comfort the child, is indifferent to or irritable with him.

Effectively displaced as a disciplinarian and reduced to a subservient position in the family, the father may adopt attitudes and behavior which are characteristically feminine. Accepting the mother's complaint that she is overburdened, he dons an apron to hang out the laundry, cook the dinner, wash the dishes, and put the children to bed. He may be the parent who expresses sympathy and demonstrates patience with the child, in contrast to the demanding and difficult-to-please mother.

ABSENCE OF A PARENT

The Fatherless Home

Divorces are increasing, and many families are composed of only mother and children. The mother must rear the child alone, often while working full time; and her contacts with him are colored by fatigue, worry, loneliness, and resentment. The younger the child, the less he is concerned about the absence of his father,[41] but as he becomes older, his loyalties are divided, and he is anxious about what Despert aptly describes as the "uncertain, the unexpressed, and the unexpressible."[10]

In the absence of his father, the child can only guess how a man behaves, and his guess is based in part on the opinion of men and of his father he acquires from his mother. The divorcee who tries to spare her child by concealing her feelings about his father and his transgressions paints a vague picture of him, tinged with rosy overtones which contribute to the child's bewilderment about why he is deprived of his parent. If the mother describes the father as a selfish, incompetent black-guard, she compels the child to choose her as the desirable and wronged parent. When he does so, the child is afraid to criticize or rebel for fear that she will desert him, and he feels disloyal when he thinks of his father with longing and sympathy.

As well as the increasingly common middle- or upper-class family devoid of a father because of divorce, there are large numbers of lower-class families which are headed by women alone. Sometimes several women relatives without husbands live together, so that a child is reared not only by his mother, but also by an aunt and a grandmother, each of whom has minor children. It has been estimated that in the larger urban cities, from 25 to 50 per cent of lower-class families are so constituted. In such matriarchal homes, the normal role of a male is further obscured by the child's observation that the men who visit his mother and women relatives assume the rights and pleasures of husbands without the responsibilities.

The Motherless Home

Some children are reared without mothers because of desertion, prolonged illness, or death. When there is no mother in the home, the functions of the father as provider, organizer, and director of the family are strengthened, and severe emotional disturbance of the child seldom occurs because a father rears his family alone.[13]

Problems develop, however, because the child must adapt to a succession of mother substitutes: sitters, housekeepers, or women relatives, each of whom requires different kinds of behavior from him. Actions ignored by one may produce severe punishment from another, and the child is unable to learn behavior which is acceptable consistently. The attitude of the mother substitutes toward him is as variable as their standards for his behavior. One pities him, another treats him abusively as a castoff, and still another considers him a heavy responsibility and burdens him with her own uncertainty about rearing him. The changing succession of caretakers keeps him anxious and constantly aware of impermanency and rootlessness, and if the mother has deserted, the possibility of her return makes him resistive to his present situation because it may be altered at any time.*

Ostracism of the Parent

Even though both parents are living in the home, the child may experience the near-total loss of one because of his ostracism by the other.

When the mother ostracizes the father, she dismisses him as a significant person by ignoring his wishes, interrupting and contradicting

---

* See Case 7, Irene B., p. 500.

him when he speaks, degrading his ability and earning power, engaging in many activities without him, and monopolizing all of the child's time and attention. She considers everything the father does to be wrong and views him as an irritant, a meddler, a bully, or a fool, an attitude which she effectively transmits to the child.[42]

The father, averse to battling with the mother, withdraws from all contact with her and the child. He refrains from comment when the child is boisterous or rude to his mother or to visitors. He says and does nothing when the child's misbehavior or low grades are reported to him. Mother and child form a closed unit within the family, and the mother finds all of her satisfactions in the child, whom she grooms and trains devotedly.

In other families, it is the mother who is relegated to insignificance. The father criticizes her ability as a homemaker, countermands her orders to the child, or humiliates her and destroys her authority by siding with the child against her in disagreements. He urges disobedience to the mother's requests, fails to show her attention and courtesy, plans all of his recreation without her, and abuses her verbally or physically. The mother becomes increasingly uncertain of herself, and she is ineffective and vacillating with the child.

REVERSAL OF THE PARENT-CHILD ROLES

A mother who considers herself unable to meet the demands made on her by her family and by society leans on the child for support and care in a reversal of the usual relationship. She receives from the child the attention, service, and consideration which normally she provides for him, and she rewards him with fervent expressions of gratitude and praise for his dependability.

One mother, convinced of her utter uselessness to her busy and successful husband, began to drink heavily. Her 12-year-old daughter got the younger children up in the morning, fed them, and sent them to school; she took breakfast to her mother in bed and inquired solicitously about her mother's health. An 11-year-old boy, after the suicide of his stepfather, assumed complete responsibility for his younger brother and shepherded his mother through the day. He foraged for extra food for the family, prepared meals, and made certain his mother got up in the morning so that she could get to work on time.

IDENTIFICATION OF SPOUSE AND CHILD

An adult completely dependent on his spouse for affection, concern, and security finds it difficult to criticize him or even to assert his rights n they are violated. Convinced of his own worthlessness, he cannot tolerate even unintentional slights by his spouse, let alone criticism or scorn. Usually he is ashamed of his helplessness, but he does nothing to alter it and he resents the self-assurance of his mate.

Lacking the courage to attack his spouse, the parent substitutes the child as the target of his anger and attains the double satisfaction of exerting power and hurting the spouse's object of affection. One father, an habitual drunkard who periodically deserted his family, treated his children cruelly when he was home. He required them to sit silently on the sofa for hours, beat them for neglecting to put away their toys, and was particularly abusive to the oldest girl, who at the age of eight already assumed heavy responsibilities in helping her mother.

PARENTAL ASSUMPTION OF PEER STATUS

Instead of exemplifying maturity in their own behavior and fulfilling their obligation to train the child, some parents place themselves on a par with him, seeking to woo his friendship and approval by acting as he does and by sharing his viewpoints.

The parent of a younger child may attempt to maintain a comradely relationship by good-naturedly jeering at him and seldom taking seriously his requests for help or advice. He labels the child with an odd nickname or addresses him as "pest" or "lame-brain," not intending to be uncomplimentary but only to imitate the casual insults exchanged between friends. Such inappropriate communication perplexes and annoys the child, who cannot understand why the adult acts as he does.

The parent with adolescent children, anticipating their desertion and also apprehensive of his promotion to the status of elder, clings energetically to a display of youthfulness. He dresses in the latest adolescent fashion, expresses himself in the current adolescent jargon, enthusiastically endorses adolescent singing idols, and agrees vehemently with all criticism of his own generation.

There is increasing evidence that much delinquent behavior of children results from its tacit encouragement by parents who gain pleasure from their children's thwarting of authority and breaking of conventions. In some cases, parents join in law violation with their children[23] or are the first to demonstrate it. A father driving a group of boys and girls to a church youth convention exceeded the speed limit during most of the trip and proudly pointed out to his young passengers how ably he outwitted the police. Other parents express satisfaction with the child's antisocial behavior or minimize its seriousness. Johnson[25] observed that a parent communicates his sanction of misbehavior by rapt attention when the child recites his misdeeds or by eager questioning for details. He gives indirect approval when his reproof is mild and unconvincing or when he confuses the issue by making involved ethical distinctions between behavior considered acceptable under certain conditions and the same behavior disapproved under other conditions. Misbehavior directed by the parent, such as telling the child to lie or to strike another child, provides him with both permission and incentive to act in these ways indefinitely. ✗

Sexual delinquencies of adolescents frequently result from over-attention to sex on the part of parents who are concerned with their own sexual attractiveness. They direct the child's attention to sex by constant discussion and by stimulating their children sexually. Bettelheim[4] reported several instances of boys whose mothers laughed at erections occurring during dressing or bathing, told the child lewd jokes, or handled his penis. Some mothers regularly permit their sons to sleep with them during late childhood and adolescence, accompany them to the bathroom, bathe and massage them, dress and undress in their presence and require the same display of nudity from them. Some adolescent drinking and sex parties are sponsored by a parent of a participant, and the ultimate adoption of peer status is sexual tutelage by incestuous relations.

PARENTAL MOTIVATION

Emotional immaturity and the need to excel or dominate motivate parents to deviate from their appropriate roles as mentors for their children.

Emotional Immaturity

Jealousy. A young husband often is unsure of himself and of his ability to provide for a family, and the advent of a child prompts powerful feelings of self-pity and jealousy in the father. Craving his wife's dependence on him and her total affection, he witnesses her new competence and her new love, and he resents the child's disruption of the original relationship. In retaliation, he undermines his wife by constant criticism or punishes the child in order to hurt the mother.*

Hostility. A father angered by his wife's isolating him from the family or assigning him an inferior role in the child's life becomes bitter and hostile. He withdraws from contact with the child, refrains from enforcing regulations, and declines to involve himself in extricating mother and child when matters go amiss.[40]

Hostility is not always caused by the actions of the spouse, but instead it may be an expression of attitudes learned during childhood.

---

* See Case 8, Milton R., p. 501.

If a husband or wife believes that all members of the opposite sex are inferior, selfish, or unreliable, he treats his spouse as though he or she possessed these characteristics.

Overdependence. The adult who requires solicitude and care from the child lacks confidence in his own ability and is overdependent on others' attention and concern. He continually seeks evidence that others regard him affectionately, and often his helplessness results in the permanent bondage of the child. The parent who acts as a peer of the child does so because of his need for the child's approval and acceptance.

Gratification in Rebellion. Exemplification of legal and moral violations and encouraging the child toward similar delinquencies testifies that the parent retains childish habits of defiance. Attacking or ignoring the child in order to hurt or thwart the spouse demonstrates the adult's pleasure in rebelling against actual or implied direction of his behavior by anyone.

Need to Excel or Dominate

Some adults need to believe themselves superior to others in knowledge, judgment, and competency. If they are unrecognized as superior in the community, they seek to demonstrate superiority at home. Adults who ridicule and abuse their spouses or use their children to satisfy their own emotional needs for power are indicating their need for recognition of their abilities. Lu[33] found that parents who assume domineering roles in their families are those who were in conflict with their own parents, particularly with their mothers, and who as adults adopted arbitrary attitudes of self-righteousness forbidden them as children.

Many women seek prestige as they attempt to excel as mothers, becoming domineering with their families in trying to rear perfect children.

PERSONALITY AND BEHAVIOR CORRELATES OF DISTORTION OF PARENTAL ROLE

A child reared by an atypical parent suffers from sex-role confusion and social deviation. These disturbances lead to aggressive behavior, depression, and anxiety and may end eventually in intellectual and emotional disintegration.

Sex-role Confusion

Strong sex-role identification is a basic index of personal adequacy and emotional stability for both boys and girls.[16, 38] The child imitates his like-sexed parent if that parent is available and admirable. If either in reality or through ostracism the like-sexed parent is absent, if parental roles are reversed, if parent-child roles are reversed, or if the parent acts as a peer, the child has no model to imitate.

McCord *et al.*[36] found that sons of working mothers evidenced decreased respect for their fathers' status, and those boys whose fathers were absent from the home identified in behavior and attitude with their mothers.[37] Bender and Grugett[3] stated that homosexual patterns in children are traceable to the children's inability to identify with their own sex because of having been reared by a domineering, homosexual parent of the same sex, because of experiencing inadequacy or absence of the opposite-sexed parent, because of growing up in the absence of the like-sexed parent, or because of hating or fearing the like-sexed parent.

A boy reared in a family in which the mother rules and the father plays a subordinate or maternal role tends to be effeminate. Female traits are those with which he is most familiar and the feminine sex appears to be the more important. Overly courteous with adults, he is lost in association with normally-reared boys of his own age. He begins to avoid contacts with them and may adopt a moralistic disdain for such male preoccupations as smoking, drinking, swearing, telling smutty stories, and petting. To achieve a semblance of manhood, however, and to satisfy his curiosity, he may secretly delve into pornographic literature and imagine himself as a romantic figure. If his self-control is poor and his need to prove his manhood becomes overwhelming, he may attempt rape.

A girl reared in a home without a father or in one in which he is degraded may develop male characteristics. She seeks to become self-sufficient and thus rejects any need for a man's care, an attitude derived from her mother's emphasizing masculine weakness and unreliability or from imitation of the capable, authoritarian behavior of her mother. She apes men in her dress and appearance, competes aggressively with them in sports and work, and may become the aggressor in homosexual acts. Usually she is lonely, in the realization that she differs from both sexes, and if she marries, she finds it difficult to feel at ease with neighbor women and tends to consider herself a complete failure.

Social Deviation

The child who finds no acceptable sex model in his home differs from his peers in behavior and attitudes. He is unacceptable to them,[9] and when they taunt him, he reacts defensively. As he retreats from or becomes aggressive toward his peers, his isolation increases and his aversion to others stabilizes.

His distrust of people and his hostility toward others originate not only in his atypical sexual characteristics but also in his feeling of having been betrayed by parents who did not play their expected roles.[5] Hostility toward inadequate parents was found in tests given by Linton *et al.*[32] to 69 children from a metropolitan slum area. Daughters were hostile toward fathers who failed to provide adequately for the family; sons displaced the hostility they felt toward their fathers onto a younger sibling.

Animosity toward others is taught directly by the parent who degrades his spouse or unrestrictedly condemns all members of the opposite sex. The child adopts his parent's mannerisms of superiority and censure of others, characteristics which alienate him from both peers and adults.*

Parents who act as peers to their children earn their scorn and disgust for failure to behave as mature adults. The child, disappointed in his parents and feeling alone, assumes a superior attitude toward them. He points out their faults, ridicules them, and quarrels and fights with them as though they were his siblings.

The child of divorced parents also feels betrayed, believing that his parents selfishly separated for insufficient reason and deserted him by so doing. When the absent parent is idealized or is readily accessible to the child, his acceptance of the divorce is more difficult.[14] If he cannot accept the dissolution of the family as reasonable or excusable, he believes that no one is trustworthy or responsible.

Degrading and mistrusting others, the child forms attitudes which are rigid, suspicious, and accusatory, and he guards himself from close and dependent relationships by holding himself aloof from contacts.

Aggression

The child who does not develop the typical traits of his sex and who is isolated from his peers and distrustful of others easily explodes into aggressive activity. Delinquent adolescent boys frequently are found to have been reared without fathers or to hold their fathers in disrepute.[31, 37] Boys dominated by their mothers rebel,[3] and aggressive behavior is known to appear in boys whose mothers work full time and whose families are disorganized.[21] Boys and girls taught by fathers to ignore their mothers become undisciplined, aggressive, and self-centered.

Children who identify with an absent or rejected parent known for his unreliability act aggressively in confirmation of their belief that they are like the despised adult. They fear inheritance of his characteristics but invite reproof and condemnation in testing their theory.

Divorced mothers rearing a child alone usually report serious trouble when the child enters junior high school. At that age, he first becomes aware of the inconsistency between the ethical pronouncements of adults and their own behavior, and he is both bewildered and indignant in the

---

* See Case 9, Bernard K., p. 502.

realization that a double standard exists for the two generations. He also ponders the implications of marital disharmony and broods over adult infidelity and capriciousness. He believes himself to have been victimized by parental whim, and if his mother dates other men, this appears to him usurpation of his right to her sole attention. Her obvious repudiation of his father seems both unfeeling and immoral. Added to this newly acquired condemnation of his mother is his normal need at adolescence for freedom from control. He exaggerates independence into aggression, using his concept of his mother as a suitable peg on which to hang his disobedience, arrogance, irresponsibility, and temper and believing he has a right to please himself because his parents pleased themselves.

Depression

When the child is reared without an adequate and typical parent, he often is lonely and depressed.[39] His self-respect must be based on the approval of an admired parent, and when the parent proves unworthy, the parent's expression of satisfaction with the child is valueless because the child considers his parent's judgment to be inferior.

The child who must replace his parents in assuming the adult's home duties and responsibility for younger children bears his burden without complaint, but he fears that he may not be equal to the task. He is sad and unresponsive, and he seldom finds it easy to laugh or to enjoy himself. Frequently he is disappointed in himself and perplexed by his failures.

The child of divorced parents may believe that he is somehow responsible for the dissolution of the marriage; and if he recalls arguments about his management, he is convinced that he was the focus of parental difficulties. If he was too young to be aware of disputes about him or if they did not even occur, he still cannot remain aloof from parental quarreling and accusations. He must take sides, but he takes both sides, and when his parents do not become reconciled, he feels the guilt of failure. He also believes that his existence is a mistake, because if it is right that his parents should never have married, it is wrong for him to have been born; and he experiences some of the feeling of isolation, worthlessness, and depression of the illegitimate child[14] and becomes nonassertive and ineffective.[21] Because there are unavoidable clashes with the parent who rears him, he may reject this parent in favor of the absent parent. If he does, he eliminates both parents and in effect rears himself.

Anxiety

The child who believes himself alone, without parents on whom he can rely, becomes anxious and tense. He is irritable with others and preoccupied and inattentive in school, and these behaviors further isolate him. A child also becomes anxious if he is led by his parents into delinquencies and sexual experimentation as adults seek to maintain peer status with him. The child is bewildered by the discrepancy between his parents' example and society's teachings, and he is distressed and worried as he complies with parental desires.

Anxiety develops in boys from feelings of worthlessness and uncertainty about the adequacy and appropriateness of masculine behavior, and a lifelong dependence on women may be fostered in the absence of an adequate father model. Anxiety is expressed in ineffectual performance and limited initiative and determination. The boy who worries about masculinity is overconcerned about himself, avoids situations which involve hardship or disapproval, cannot make decisions or fulfill commitments, and daydreams much of the time. He may marry early, expecting to receive from his wife the same care his mother provided.

Intellectual and Emotional Disintegration

Psychotic children whose morbid adjustment is known to have been poor come from homes in which the mother is dominant and in which there is great conflict between the parents.[12, 15] The child who is unable to behave consistently as a member of his own sex, who becomes a social isolate, who develops feelings of suspicion toward others, and who is beset by depression and anxiety loses the ability to think, act, and feel rationally.

If he has been identified with the spouse by an immature parent, he is bewildered and frightened by the unpredictable overreaction to his minor errors and by the unwarranted attacks made on him by an adult on whom he depends for affection. He lives in apprehension of severe censure and brutal punishment and with the knowledge that he cannot protect himself. Increasingly vague in thinking and action because of his overwhelming fear and unable to plan, follow instructions, or anticipate consequences, he loses the ability to direct his own behavior, and his actions become expedient and aimless.

REFERENCES

1. Ackerman, N. W.: Preventive implications of family research. *In* Caplan, G., ed.: *Prevention of Mental Disorders in Children.* New York, Basic Books, Inc., 1961, pp. 155–156.
2. Becker, W. C., Peterson, D. R., Hellmer, L. A., Shoemaker, D. J., and Quay, H. C.: Factors in parental behavior and personality as related to problem behavior in children. *J. Consult. Psychol.,* 1959, 23, 107–118.
3. Bender, L., and Grugett, A. E., Jr.: A follow-up report on children who had atypical sexual experience. *Amer. J. Orthopsychiat.,* 1952, 22, 825–837.

4. Bettelheim, B.: *Love Is Not Enough*. Glencoe, Ill., The Free Press, 1950, pp. 316–317.
5. Bowlby, J.: Mother-child separation. *In* Soddy, K., ed.: *Mental Health and Infant Development, Vol. I. Papers and Discussions*. New York, Basic Books, Inc., 1956, p. 117.
6. Cameron, N.: *The Psychology of Behavior Disorders*. Cambridge, Mass., Houghton Mifflin Co., 1947, p. 33.
7. Cameron, N., and Magaret, A.: *Behavior Pathology*. Cambridge, Mass., Houghton Mifflin Co., 1951, pp. 102–103.
8. Carek, D. J., Hendrickson, W. J., and Holmes, D.: Delinquency addiction in parents. *Arch. Gen. Psychiat.*, 1961, *4*, 357–362.
9. Cox, F. N.: An assessment of children's attitudes towards parent figures. *Child Developm.*, 1962, *33*, 821–830.
10. Despert, J. L.: *Children of Divorce*. Garden City, N. Y., Doubleday and Co., 1953.
11. Droppleman, L. F., and Schaefer, E. S.: Boys' and girls' reports of maternal and paternal behavior. *J. Abnorm. Soc. Psychol.*, 1963, *67*, 648–654.
12. Farina, A.: Patterns of role dominance and conflict in parents of schizophrenic patients. *J. Abnorm. Soc. Psychol.*, 1960, *61*, 31–38.
13. Frumkin, R. M.: Childhood supervision and mental disorders. *Alpha Kappa Deltan*, 1953, *24*, 8–10.
14. Gardner, G. E.: Separation of the parents and the emotional life of the child. *Ment. Hyg. (N. Y.)*, 1956, *40*, 53–64.
15. Garmezy, N., Farina, A., and Rodnick, E.: Direct study of child-parent interactions: I. The structured situational test. A method for studying family interaction in schizophrenia. *Amer. J. Orthopsychiat.*, 1960, *30*, 445–452.
16. Gray, S. W.: Perceived similarity to parents and adjustment. *Child Developm.*, 1959, *30*, 91–107.
17. Hartley, R. E.: Sex-role pressures and the socialization of the male child. *Psychol. Rep.*, 1959, *5*, 457–468.
18. Hartley, R. E., and Klein, A.: Sex-role concepts among elementary-school-age girls. *Marriage Fam. Liv.*, 1959, *21*, 59–64.
19. Heuyer, G.: Le rôle de la réaction d'opposition dans la formation du caractère chez l'enfant (The role of the opposition reaction in the formation of child character). *Criança Portug.*, 1951–1952, *11*, 27–44.
20. Hilgard, J. R., Newman, M., and Fisk, F.: Strength of adult ego following childhood bereavement. *Amer. J. Orthopsychiat.*, 1960, *30*, 788–798.
21. Hoffman, L. W.: Effects of maternal employment on the child. *Child Developm.*, 1961, *32*, 187–197.
22. Holmes, M. H.: The child's need for identification. *Ment. Hlth. (Lond.)*, 1951, *10*, 64–65.
23. Horrocks, J. E.: *The Psychology of Adolescence*, Ed. 2. Cambridge, Mass., Houghton Mifflin Co., 1962, pp. 269–270.
24. Jersild, A. T.: *Child Psychology*, Ed. 4. New York, Prentice-Hall, Inc., 1954, p. 528.
25. Johnson, A. M.: Juvenile delinquency. *In* Arieti, S., ed.: *American Handbook of Psychiatry*. New York, Basic Books, Inc., 1959, pp. 845–848.
26. Kagan, J., and Lemkin, J.: The child's differential perception of parental attributes. *J. Abnorm. Soc. Psychol.*, 1960, *61*, 440–447.
27. Kanner, L.: *Child Psychiatry*, Ed. 3. Springfield, Ill., Charles C Thomas, 1957, pp. 155–156.
28. Keeler, W. R.: Children's reaction to the death of a parent. *In* Hoch, P. H., and Zubin, J., eds.: *Depression*. New York, Grune and Stratton, Inc., 1954, pp. 109–120.
    Zubin, J.: *Depression*. 109–120.
29. Koch, M. B.: Anxiety in preschool children from broken homes. *Merrill-Palmer Quart.*, 1961, *7*, 225–231.
30. Kohn, M. L., and Carroll, E. E.: Social class and the allocation of parental responsibilities. *Sociometry*, 1960, *23*, 372–392.
31. Kvaraceus, W. C., and Miller, W. B.: *Delinquent Behavior*. Washington, D. C., National Education Association, 1959, pp. 94–98.

32. Linton, H., Berle, B. B., Grossi, M., and Jackson, E.: Reactions of children within family groups as measured by the Bene Anthony Tests. *J. Ment. Sci.*, 1961, *107*, 308–325.
33. Lu, Y.: Parent-child relationship and marital roles. *Amer. Sociol. Rev.*, 1952, *17*, 357–361.
34. Lynn, D.: A note on sex differences in the development of masculine and feminine identification. *Psychol. Rev.*, 1959, *66*, 126–135.
35. McCandless, B. R.: *Children and Adolescents.* New York, Holt, Rinehart and Winston, 1961, pp. 331–332.
36. McCord, J., McCord, W., and Thurber, E.: Effects of maternal employment on lower-class boys. *J. Abnorm. Soc. Psychol.*, 1963, *67*, 177–182.
37. McCord, J., McCord, W., and Thurber, E.: Some effects of paternal absence on male children. *J. Abnorm. Soc. Psychol.*, 1962, *64*, 361–369.
38. Mussen, P.: Some antecedents and consequents of masculine sex-typing in adolescent boys. *Psychol. Monogr.*, 1961, *75* (506).
39. Mussen, P. H., Young, H. B., Gaddini, R., and Morante, L.: The influence of father-son relationships on adolescent personality and attitudes. *J. Child Psychol. Psychiat.*, 1963, *4*, 3–16.
40. Plotsky, H., and Shereshefsky, P.: An isolation pattern in fathers of emotionally disturbed children. *Amer. J. Orthopsychiat.*, 1960, *30*, 780–787.
41. Rouman, J.: School children's problems as related to parental factors. *Calif. J. Educ. Res.*, 1955, *6*, 110–117.
42. Thom, D. A.: *Everyday Problems of the Everyday Child.* New York, Appleton-Century, 1934, pp. 47–48.
43. Thompson, G. G.: *Child Psychology.* Cambridge, Mass., Houghton Mifflin Co., 1952, p. 577.
44. Ucko, L. E., and Moore, T.: Parental roles as seen by young children in doll play. *Vita Humana*, 1964, *6*, 213–242.
45. Wechsler, H., and Funkenstein, D. H.: The family as a determinant of conflict in self-perceptions. *Psychol. Rep.*, 1960, *7*, 143–149.
46. Winder, C. L., and Rau, L.: Parental attitudes associated with social deviance in preadolescent boys. *J. Abnorm. Soc. Psychol.*, 1962, *64*, 418–424.

Chapter **10**

Damaged Self-respect

Damaged self-respect is a prime characteristic of every maladjusted, neurotic, or psychotic individual. The disturbed person believes that he has made some serious error or has failed in his duty and that he is incompetent, peculiar, and worthless.

A child's opinion of himself is based on his parent's opinion of him,[12] and he must have parental confirmation of his worth in order to achieve self-respect.[1, 8, 14] Delinquent and psychotic children typically have parents who do not express acceptance and approval, and the children believe themselves to be unloved and undesirable.[7, 10, 25] Parents demonstrate lack of respect for the child by disparaging, deceiving, and degrading him. They do not always intend to convey rejection of the child by their actions, but the child's adjustment is based on his perception of his relationship to the family,[26] and if his parents behave toward him in these ways, he is convinced that they regard him as undeserving of better treatment.

DAMAGED SELF-RESPECT

Disparagement

Parents disparage the worth of the child when they restrict his activities because they consider him lacking in judgment and ability or when they dominate him by taking the initiative and acting for him in situations which he should manage alone.[17]

Some children always are refused permission to experiment with original ideas or to complete their own plans. The parents inform the child that his projects are ridiculous and doomed to failure, and he soon concludes that any ideas or opinions he has are inferior. Unable to try out what he has conceived, he fails to learn and cannot improve initially faulty concepts.[11]

Parents also disparage a child when they cannot accept his immaturity and his need for time to practice. Instead, they constantly reject his work as inadequate, revising and improving on his efforts.

Many parents demean the child by hastening to his assistance whenever he is faced with a new or difficult situation. If he remains awkward and silent at an adult's question or a peer's challenge, his parent answers for him or tells him what to do. The child learns from his parent's intercession that he is considered incompetent to manage alone.

Deception

There is much in the world that a young child does not understand and little that he can control, and he fears the unknown and the unfamiliar. He needs support in determining truth, and he trusts his parents to give him accurate information and to protect him from unknown dangers and from uncertainty.

There are parents who regularly deceive their child, and by failing to respond to his trust of them, they imply that he is unworthy of honorable treatment. Many a child has been led to the hospital door for a tonsillectomy after being earnestly told by his mother that she is taking him for a pleasant visit with his grandmother. Parents slip away from home without informing the child of their intention to leave him, and they glibly make promises which they fail to keep.

The adopted child who first learns of his parentage from outsiders or the child who is told by others about an impending birth, his father's new job, or a relative's penitentiary sentence feels deceived by his parents and believes they did not value him enough to include him in the private concerns of the family, even though they granted outsiders this privilege.

Degradation

Parents degrade a child by treating him discourteously,[28] invading his privacy, and publicizing his inadequacies and failures.

A child is taught not to interrupt, to listen and answer when someone speaks to him, to refrain from insistence on having his own way, to request assistance rather than demand it, and to express appreciation to others for their attention and help. Knowing that he is expected to act in these ways toward others, he is at first baffled and then indignant about the gross disregard of these same edicts by his own parents in their treatment of him. He discovers that he is not entitled to the courtesy which he is required to extend to others and that there is an immense difference between the way his parents treat him and the way they treat everyone else.

Invasion of the child's privacy implies distrust of his intentions, his truthfulness, or his competency and denies him the right to exclusive possession of his own thoughts and experiences. Some parents pick up the extension phone when their adolescent is making plans with his friends, read his diaries, rummage through his wastebasket and books for notes, and open his mail without apology. They telephone both his adult leaders and his friends to check on the veracity of information he gives about his plans.* Parents who discuss the child in his presence, making plans for him and airing his problems with both strangers and relatives, humiliate him with the implication that neither his feelings nor his opinions are important. When they criticize him, punish him, or order him about in the presence of others, they degrade him.

PARENTAL MOTIVATION

Parents damage the child's self-respect unwittingly more often than deliberately, and they seldom find it difficult to devise a cogent argument for the propriety of their actions. Their motivations for disparaging, deceiving, and degrading the child originate from their own fear of the child's emotion, from self-concern, and from projection of guilt.

Fear of the Child's Emotion

Many deceptions of parents are traceable to their own consternation over a child's outbursts of anger or fear in unpleasant situations. Not knowing how to help the child control emotion or understand potentially traumatic events, they gain a temporary reprieve by lying. Although their deception compounds their difficulties with the child, they are unconcerned about future problems in their zeal to avoid present ones.

Self-concern

Self-concern is reflected by parents who are discourteous to the child and refuse him respect. Parents who need to dominate and control their children, leading their lives for them by directing their actions and supervising all of their affairs, are overly concerned with the impression

---

* See Case 10, Tony J., p. 503.

the child makes on others.[3] They are unable to tolerate evidence that the child is inadequate and weak, and they hide his ineptitude by replacing his behavior with their own.

A parent evidences self-interest when he refuses to permit the child to experiment with his own ideas because these ideas are disrupting and inconvenient or when he is unwilling to tolerate delay and inefficiency by granting the child freedom and time to learn how to work competently.

Some parents, clinging to the superiority they consider inherent in adulthood, are proud of themselves when they deceive the child.[13] Indifferent to the immorality of empty promises or complex falsehoods, they consider the child dull-witted when he believes them and scorn him for his trust.

Projection of Guilt

Parents who damage their child's self-respect are those who have none for themselves. They believe that they have failed as marital partners, as parents, or in adherence to recognized standards of ethical behavior, and they attack the child as they believe they deserve to be attacked.[19, 23] When the marriage is unhappy and a parent no longer has the love and respect of his spouse, the child becomes a symbol of distasteful, unwanted bondage, and the adult deliberately disparages him.

If the child fails in school or behaves in ways which are embarrassing to the parent, he is evidencing the adult's failure as a parent. Disliking him for revealing this failure, the parent believes that the child returns his dislike and is deliberately misbehaving. When the adult becomes convinced that a battle has begun between himself and the child, he feels that any kind of attack is warranted, and distrusting the child and his motives, he degrades the child in every way that he can.

Guilt of the parent over his own misconduct causes him to seize on any indication of similar misbehavior in the child. Parents who are most restrictive and suspicious of the child and who justify their invasion of his privacy are those whose lives have been less than exemplary. They express convincingly their own wish that someone had prevented them from engaging in unacceptable behavior when they were young, and they tell themselves that everything they do in degrading the child is for his benefit.

PERSONALITY AND BEHAVIOR CORRELATES
OF DAMAGED SELF-RESPECT

The child who is disparaged, deceived, or degraded by the adults in whom he most trusts suffers severe damage to his self-respect. He feels inferior and fails to achieve, and he withdraws from contacts with others. He may turn to revenge in retaliation for the hurt inflicted on him or he may play the part assigned him by distrusting parents. His conviction that he is unworthy of respect causes anxiety and fearfulness.

Feelings of Inferiority

The child whose parents have staved off unpleasantries by interceding for him or who have ridiculed his ideas and not permitted him to increase his skills by practice believes that he is incapable of meeting any challenge. He is immobilized and panic stricken at the prospect of any new experience. He has few original ideas and no confidence in their worth or in his ability to utilize them. Accustomed to his parent's thinking and acting for him, he does little or nothing by himself, and because he remains passive, his belief that he is inferior is strengthened. He has difficulty achieving in school, both because he has no confidence in his ability and because he shields himself from contacts and effort. Uncertain and preoccupied, he is inattentive and he cannot concentrate or remember.

Withdrawal

Convinced that he is less able and acceptable than others, the child withdraws from contact with them. He has not been accepted or treated fairly by his own parents, and therefore he is certain that all associations with others are unpleasant and to be avoided. He believes himself to be peculiar and undeserving, and he dreads being with people, finds it difficult to learn from others, and cannot accept others' friendship and regard as genuine. He may take refuge in consistent failure to see or hear others, and he may appear to be unaware of their existence.[6, 15] Or, to ward off contacts, he resorts to excessive, constant talking in the presence of others. Sometimes he continues a solitary torrent of words even when no one else is near, and by this device he avoids contemplating the contempt he believes his parents feel for him.

The degraded child who is isolated and who turns his attention toward himself exhibits numerous physiological difficulties, such as sleep disturbances, headaches, motor retardation, and eating problems.[27]

Feelings of Revenge

The child who is treated disrespectfully by his parents despises and hates them.[5, 20] He resents being humiliated and deceived by those on whom he relies for support, approval, and honesty; and he seeks revenge by hurting others as he has been hurt.

The adolescent who has learned to hate makes calculated, vicious attacks on others. He is more likely to attack alone, rather than in association with peers in gangs.[16] As an adult, he often expresses his hatred of others by capturing the trust of innocent persons and bilking them of their money. He considers himself shrewd and enterprising,[15] and he gains some shred of self-respect by laughing at others' gullibility as his parents once laughed at his.

Adoption of Assigned Role

With an appropriate sense of fitness, the child adopts the role assigned him. If his parents falsely brand him as evil and unworthy and if he receives no commendation for desirable behavior, he believes he has earned the right to indulge in the behavior of which he has been accused.

When a father labels his son a liar, the boy will begin to lie deliberately and constantly, and designating a young child a thief for one offense ensures his stealing again. A set of parents who habitually maintained promiscuous relations with their friends' husbands and wives upbraided their 13-year-old daughter for staying out late one night with an older boy, telling her that she was a whore and a tramp. Innocent of wrongdoing then, despite her parents' example, she quickly became promiscuous and eventually ran away with a boy several years her senior.

Anxiety and Fearfulness

The child whose self-respect is damaged is excessively anxious and fearful.[19] He is subject to nightmares, he fears separation from his parents, and he worries about potential harm to himself when he learns of remote world crises or disasters. His fearfulness originates not only from having lost adult support but also from being unable to predict accurately the outcome of any event. Knowing that he cannot rely on his parents to interpret situations or to describe the future truthfully and believing himself to be incompetent, the child becomes frantic with fear of the unknown.[4]

REFERENCES

1. Ausubel, D. P., Balthazar, E. E., Rosenthal, I., Blackman, L. S., Schpoont, S. H., and Welkowitz, J.: Perceived parent attitudes as determinants of children's ego structure. *Child Developm.*, 1954, *25*, 173–183.
2. Becker, W. C., Peterson, D. R., Luria, Z., Shoemaker, D. J., and Hellmer, L. A.: Relations of factors derived from parent-interview ratings to behavior problems of five-year-olds. *Child Developm.*, 1962, *33*, 509–535.
3. Block, J.: Personality characteristics associated with fathers' attitudes toward child-rearing. *Child Developm.*, 1955, *26*, 41–48.
4. Cameron, N., and Magaret, A.: *Behavior Pathology.* Cambridge, Mass., Houghton Mifflin Co., 1951, p. 292.

5. De Moragas, J.: Conséquences psychiques chez l'enfant repoussé (Psychic sequelae in the rejected child). *Z. Kinderpsychiat.*, 1958, *25*, 49–52.
6. Despert, J. L.: Some considerations relating to the genesis of autistic behavior in children. *Amer. J. Orthopsychiat.*, 1951, *21*, 335–350.
7. Donnelly, E. M.: The quantitative analysis of parent behavior toward psychotic children and their siblings. *Genet. Psychol. Monogr.*, 1960, *62*, 331–376.
8. Drewry, H. H.: Emotional needs of children. *Except. Child.*, 1955, *21*, 178–180.
9. Frank, L. K.: Working toward healthy personality. *In* Senn, M. J. E., ed.: *Problems of Infancy and Childhood.* New York, Josiah Macy Foundation, 1951.
10. Friedman, A.: A wayward child, unloved. *Nerv. Child*, 1955, *11*, 57–59.
11. Gropko, M. F.: How can parents tell? *Bull. Inst. Child Stud.* (*Toronto*), 1953, *15*, 4–6.
12. Helper, M. M.: Parental evaluations of children and children's self-evaluations. *J. Abnorm. Soc. Psychol.*, 1958, *56*, 190–194.
13. Hoffman, L. W., Rosen, S., and Lippitt, R.: Coercizioni dei parenti, autonomia dei ragazzi e ruolo dei ragazzi nella scuola (Parental coercion, autonomy of boys and their role in school). *Riv. Psicol. Soc.*, 1960, *7*, 197–204.
14. Jayasuriya, J. E.: Psychological needs of children. *J. Educ. and Psychol.*, 1950, *8*, 60–68.
15. Jersild, A. T.: *Child Psychology*, Ed. 4. Englewood Cliffs, N. J., Prentice-Hall, Inc., 1954, pp. 598–602.
16. Lewis, H.: Unsatisfactory parents and psychological disorder in their children. *Eugen. Rev.*, 1955, *47*, 153–162.
17. Liber, B.: Elusive mental cases; parents and children. *N. Y. St. J. Med.*, 1951, *51*, 1939–1942.
18. Lipsitt, L. P.: A self-concept scale for children and its relationship to the children's form of the Manifest Anxiety Scale. *Child Developm.*, 1958, *29*, 463–472.
19. McDonald, R. L.: Intrafamilial conflict and emotional disturbance. *J. Genet. Psychol.*, 1962, *101*, 201–208.
20. Martin, P. O.: Unwanted children. *Teach. Coll. Rec.*, 1955, *57*, 189–195.
21. Martin, W. E.: Learning theory and identification: III. The development of values in children. *J. Genet. Psychol.*, 1954, *84*, 211–217.
22. Mussen, P.: Some antecedents and consequents of masculine sex-typing in adolescent boys. *Psychol. Monogr.*, 1961, *75* (506).
23. Porter, B. M.: The relationship between marital adjustment and parental acceptance of children. *J. Home Econ.*, 1955, *47*, 157–164.
24. Rogers, C. R.: *Clinical Treatment of the Problem Child.* Cambridge, Mass., Houghton Mifflin Co., 1939, pp. 91, 147.
25. Schulman, R. E., Shoemaker, D. J., and Moelis, I.: Laboratory measurement of parental behavior. *J. Consult. Psychol.*, 1962, *26*, 109–114.
26. Serot, N., and Teevan, R. C.: Perception of the parent-child relationship and its relation to child adjustment. *Child Developm.*, 1961, *32*, 373–378.
27. Sperling, M.: Equivalents of depression in children. *J. Hillside Hosp.*, 1959, *8*, 138–148.
28. Thom, D. A.: *Everyday Problems of the Everyday Child.* New York, Appleton-Century, 1934, pp. 45–46, 193–194.

Chapter 11

Excessive Punishment

All children require discipline if they are to achieve self-control; and punishment, in its many forms, inevitably is a principal enforcing agent of adult requirements. Punishment includes expressions of disapproval ranging from a disappointed glance to a severe beating and deprivations ranging from averted attention to weeks of confinement. Opportunities to punish the child excessively are many, and the training of any child to acquire the multifarious socialized behaviors expected of him would appear to be an impossible task. Parents participating in a home survey of discipline by Cutts and Moseley[16] identified 132 separate children's actions of which they disapproved.

Punishment is intended to teach the child to inhibit undesired responses,[6] and the strength and kind of punishment which is needed to accomplish this result vary with the child, the act, and the significance of the behavior to the parent. When punishment serves to intimidate the child or to provide an outlet for adult aggression, it fails in its intended purpose,[4, 18] and the child develops personality and behavior problems as a direct result of the punishment. The disturbed child frequently has parents who are authoritative and hostile and who demonstrate these characteristics in their management of him.[1, 24, 29, 32] The child is punished excessively if he is physically abused, if he is subjected to severe and continual criticism, or if deprivation is overly harsh for the offense committed.

EXCESSIVE PUNISHMENT

Physical Abuse

To many physicians, small children's multiple fractures, including those of the skull, have become so familiar that they are labeled "the

90

battered-child syndrome." A University of Colorado team, headed by Dr. C. Henry Kempe, checked the records of 71 hospitals and found 302 battered-child cases in one year. Thirty-three of these children died, and 85 suffered brain damage.[7] Belt buckles, switches, fists, and hammers are used to beat children. Their hands are held over fire, and they are smothered with pillows and plastic bags. They are chained to furniture, kicked, and burned with cigarettes.

The American Humane Association investigated 662 cases of child beating reported by newspapers in 1962. The ages of the children ranged from infancy through 17 years, but 90 per cent of those involved were under ten years of age and 56 per cent were under four years of age. Fathers were responsible for 38 per cent of the injuries inflicted and mothers for 29 per cent, with grandparents, sitters, and mothers' boy friends also guilty of child abuse. One out of four of these children died, with the youngest age group experiencing the highest death rate.[31]

Severe Criticism

Parents punish excessively when they convey their disapproval of the child with an unending torrent of scolding, sarcasm, and exasperated criticism, either shouted angrily or expressed as pained disappointment.

Jersild[21] described the life of the child who hears nothing but criticism from his parents. Impossible standards of errorless behavior are demanded of him; his every move is stopped short with "Don't!" and the splendid achievements, willing obedience, and cheerful forbearance of other children are recited, applauded, and contrasted with his own performance. His innumerable failures—neglecting to tie his shoelaces, to sing on key, to use his napkin, to get 100 on every school paper, to speak up, to keep quiet, to share his popcorn and his bicycle with playmates, to clean his nails, to read good books—all are noticed and peevishly pointed out to him. One mother recorded a daily total of 200 instances of criticism, correction, and direction she had bestowed on her 11-year-old son.

Bettelheim[10] noted that the routine daily activities of eating, washing, playing, using the toilet, and going to bed assume great consequence in personality formation because their performance repeatedly is associated with pleasing or displeasing the parents and sets the tone for all discipline of the child.

Harsh Deprivation

Penalties which are overly severe for the offense committed constitute excessive punishment of the child.[30] Thom[34] noted that punishment often is administered not only to penalize for the offense but also to serve as a deterrent to its repetition. A parent who is angry and disappointed at a child's disobedience or who is frantic with concern if the child has endangered himself punishes with a ferocity intended to "teach him a lesson he'll never forget!"

A 12-year-old boy who brought home a poor report card was punished for six weeks by being prohibited from viewing television or leaving his home except to attend school. The parents of a ten-year-old admitted that they attached so many penalties to various offenses that the child never succeeded in working his way clear of the accumulated restrictions. A 17-year-old boy, anticipating his parents' typically severe penalties for disobedience, involved himself in a serious automobile accident in his haste to arrive home before the deadline set by his father.

PARENTAL MOTIVATION

Parents who punish excessively sometimes are motivated by concern for the child, but they also act unjustly because of social pressure, identification with the child, self-concern, or low self-esteem.

Social Pressure

Many parents, uncertain about the wisdom of their decisions or even their right to make them but convinced that they alone are responsible for every misbehavior of the child, react out of proportion to the seriousness of the misconduct. Needing to impress other adults with a well-behaved child, the parent who receives a complaining telephone call from another parent may inflict severe penalties on his child which are unwarranted by the incident reported.

Parent-teacher conferences, in which the child's behavior and ability are discussed in detail, keep parents alert to the impression the child is making on others. The hesitation of parents to seek aid for a disturbed child reflects their feeling of guilt for the problems he presents and their aversion to being confronted with accusations of mismanagement. Parents overdependent on others' opinions tend to punish severely in an effort to force improved behavior in the child.

Faulty and incomplete knowledge about how the average child behaves contributes to parental overconcern and subsequent excessive punishment. A mother who observes the courtesy of young visitors is led to believe that most children are obedient, polite, generous, and mannerly. She knows that her own child quarrels and is slovenly, resists her reasonable commands, and resents his sibling. Convinced that she has a steadily disintegrating situation with which to deal, she deals with it as forcefully as she can.

Identification With the Child

Excessive punishment of the child occurs when a parent identifies with him and considers every fault and mistake of the child to be his own. The parent, certain that he could not exhibit these defects nor commit these errors, feels that he must eliminate these evidences of inadequacy in the child immediately and permanently.

The consistent tendency of children to view the parent of the same sex as more dominant and punitive evidences the stricter behavioral standards imposed by the parent in identification with the child of his own sex.[22]

Self-concern

Adults endure many conflicts, frustrations, and disappointments, some of which are inescapable and unalterable. Worried and unhappy, they express their despair and anger by punishing the child.[36]

A father faced with bills he cannot pay, tied to work he dislikes, or victimized by his wife's tongue-lashing does not show patience and wisdom in disciplining his child. A mother, lonely and confined to home and children, must endlessly face emergencies, make decisions, and be subjected to the demands and opposition of the child. If she feels unappreciated and overwhelmed, she shrieks at a child who causes her more work or concern. Poverty and inadequate housing, with no hope of economic improvement, also lead adults to vent their dissatisfaction in excessive punishment of the child.[12]

Many adults do not express self-pity audibly, but in assuming an autocratic position over their children, they indicate their feeling of being unfairly burdened and their conclusion that they are entitled to suffer no inconvenience, embarrassment, or disturbance because of the child.[28]

Low Self-esteem

Excessive punishment of children is common among parents who feel inadequate.[27, 37] Considering themselves to be social or economic failures, they seek superiority by treating their children brutally or by responding rigidly and punitively to every indication of inadequacy in the child.[20]

Sometimes low parental esteem originates from the adult's guilt over his own immoral or socially unacceptable practices, but at times it develops from his feeling of having failed as a parent. The dislike of parents for the child they must bring to a guidance clinic results in part from this evidence that they have been unable to rear the child so that assistance was unnecessary. The parent who has failed to achieve personally punishes the child for the child's failings with the forcefulness and anger he feels about his own.

PERSONALITY AND BEHAVIOR CORRELATES OF
EXCESSIVE PUNISHMENT

The child who is punished excessively develops feelings of worthlessness, and he may become subservient or socially distant. Frequently he is hostile and aggressive toward others.

Feelings of Worthlessness

Thompson[35] observed that a child seeks social approval from his parents, teachers, and peers; and if he does not secure it, he underrates his effectiveness and personal value. The parent who punishes excessively informs the child in this way that he disapproves of him and considers him worthless. Convinced that his parents' low estimation of his worth is accurate, the child turns some of his resentment of his punitive parent against himself.[19]

A child punished severely for every unwanted action cannot distinguish between inconsequential lapses in correct conduct and critical misbehavior. He relinquishes his responsibility to acquire self-control, deferring to parental power, and his behavior becomes increasingly unpredictable and uninhibited when his parents are not nearby to direct him.[15, 33] Behaving impulsively, he is inattentive and indifferent, not only to the effect on others of his behavior or to the consequences of his acts but even to stimuli which ordinarily serve as warning reminders. The accident-prone child often has rigid, punitive parents whose disapproval has made him uncertain in his management of himself.

Subservience

The child who feels himself to be incapable of acceptable or admirable behavior may become subservient. The young child seeks constant evidence of adult approval.[3] Soon he leaves initiative to others,[9] and his own intellectual striving dulls.

Anderson and Anderson[2] observed that subservience develops when the individual's integrity and his right to think and act for himself are attacked and when he reaches the conclusion that he has nothing to gain by opposing those who dominate him.* They warn that the submissive

---

* See Case 11, Ruth M., p. 503.

individual atrophies and disintegrates, increasing the distance between himself and others by his failure to act independently.

Sexual deviations were found by Hartogs[17] to occur in persons with a history of severe, brutal punishment by parents. Of the cases reported, 92 per cent had been severely beaten by one or both parents, and the victims had felt that this punishment was deserved. The sexual deviates had received limited affection from their parents, and they had become both masochistic and passive.

Social Isolation

A child who believes himself to be worthless and who becomes passive and subservient in his behavior isolates himself from his peers. Because he fails to associate with them, he loses the opportunity to learn from them how to behave independently, and he is unable to replace parental disapproval with peer acceptance.

The adolescent who is disappointed in himself is reluctant to expose himself to the repeated denunciations or exhortations of more competent persons. He hides both from personal contacts and from the necessity to exert the effort to prove himself able, and he discovers that drugs or alcohol transport him from a reality he finds too unpleasant to face.

Not only does the harshly reared child avoid his peers, but eventually he rejects them as well. He learns attitudes of authoritarianism and prejudice from his parents,[27] and these attitudes are fostered and stabilized by his unsatisfying contacts with his peers. Peck and Havighurst[28] stated that the child of severe, autocratic parents develops an "irrational-conscientious" character, evaluating every act of others in accordance with his own standards of morality. Rigid in his judgments and severe in his condemnations, but unable to attack directly, he substitutes an ethic which enables him to wound and scorn others.

Aggression

The child who condemns others in imitation of and in retaliation for negative parental attitudes may show direct hostility by attacking others.[5, 8, 13, 26] Young children hit, bite, scratch, and throw objects at both peers and parents. The older child learns to inhibit overt expressions of hostility toward the punitive parent,[6] but he retaliates for the treatment he receives by behaving aggressively toward peers and other adults with whom he comes in contact, whether or not he has cause. The severely punished child frequently shows cruelty toward animals, venting his anger on something which cannot harm him. He is easily aroused to anger, and overreacts to minor unpleasantries with revengeful ideas and actions.

REFERENCES

1. Abbe, A. E.: Maternal attitudes toward children and their relationship to the diagnostic category of the child. *J. Genet. Psychol.*, 1958, *92*, 167–173.
2. Anderson, G. L., and Anderson, H. H.: Behavior problems of children. *In* Pennington, L. A., and Berg, I. A., eds.: *An Introduction to Clinical Psychology.* New York, The Ronald Press Co., 1948, pp. 79–86.
3. Ayer, M. E., and Bernreuter, R. G.: A study of the relationship between discipline and personality traits in little children. *J. Genet. Psychol.*, 1937, *50*, 165–170.
4. Bakwin, R., and Bakwin, H.: Discipline in children. *J. Pediat.*, 1951, *39*, 632–634.
5. Bandura, A., Ross, D., and Ross, S. A.: Transmission through imitation of aggressive models. *J. Abnorm. Soc. Psychol.*, 1961, *63*, 575–582.
6. Bandura, A., and Walters, R. H.: *Social Learning and Personality Development.* New York, Holt, Rinehart and Winston, 1963, pp. 15, 130.
7. Battered-child syndrome. *Time*, 1962, *80* (3), 60.
8. Becker, W. C.: Consequences of different kinds of parental discipline. *In* Hoffman, M. L., and Hoffman, L. W., eds.: *Review of Child Development Research.* New York, Russell Sage Foundation, 1964, vol. 1, pp. 169–208.
9. Becker, W. C., Peterson, D. R., Luria, Z., Shoemaker, D. J., and Hellmer, L. A.: Relations of factors derived from parent-interview ratings to behavior problems of five-year-olds. *Child Developm.*, 1962, *33*, 509–535.
10. Bettelheim, B.: *Love Is Not Enough.* Glencoe, Ill., The Free Press, 1950, p. 6.
11. Brammer, L. M., and Shostrom, E. L.: *Therapeutic Psychology.* Englewood Cliffs, N. J., Prentice-Hall, Inc., 1960, pp. 352–353.
12. Chesser, E.: *Cruelty to Children.* New York, Philosophical Library, 1952.
13. Chorost, S. B.: Parental child-rearing attitudes and their correlates in adolescent hostility. *Genet. Psychol. Monogr.*, 1962, *66*, 49–90.
14. Crandall, V.: Reinforcement effects of adult reactions and nonreactions on children's achievement expectations. *Child Developm.*, 1963, *34*, 335–354.
15. Crandall, V. J., Orleans, S., Preston, A., and Rabson, A.: The development of social compliance in young children. *Child Developm.*, 1958, *29*, 429–443.
16. Cutts, N. E., and Moseley, N.: *Better Home Discipline.* New York, Appleton-Century-Crofts, 1952.
17. Hartogs, R.: Discipline in the early life of sex-delinquents and sex criminals. *Nerv. Child*, 1951, *9*, 167–173.
18. Havighurst, R. J.: The functions of successful discipline. *Underst. Child*, 1952, *21*, 35–38.
19. Helper, M. M.: Parental evaluations of children and children's self-evaluations. *J. Abnorm. Soc. Psychol.*, 1958, *56*, 190–194.
20. Hoffman, L. W., Rosen, S., and Lippitt, R.: Coercizioni dei parenti, autonomia dei ragazzi e ruolo dei ragazzi nella scuola (Parental coercion, autonomy of boys and their role in school). *Riv. Psicol. Soc.*, 1960, *7*, 197–204.
21. Jersild, A. T.: *Child Psychology*, Ed. 4. Englewood Cliffs, N. J., Prentice-Hall, Inc., 1954, p. 358.
22. Kagan, J.: The child's perception of the parent. *J. Abnorm. Soc. Psychol.*, 1956, *53*, 257–258.
23. Kanner, L.: *Child Psychiatry*, Ed. 3. Springfield, Ill., Charles C Thomas, 1957, pp. 127–128.
24. Kearsley, R., Snider, M., Richie, R., Crawford, J. D., and Talbot, N. B.: Study of relations between psychologic environment and child behavior. *Amer. J. Dis. Child.*, 1962, *104*, 12–20.
25. Keyserlingk, H.: Kindermisshandlungen—Ihre Ursachen und Folgen (Mistreatment of children—their causes and consequences). *Psychiat. Neurol. Med. Psychol. (Berlin)*, 1950, *2*, 151–154.
26. Lafore, G. G.: *Practices of Parents in Dealing with Preschool Children.* New York, Columbia University, 1945.
27. McCandless, B.: *Children and Adolescents.* New York, Holt, Rinehart and Winston, 1961, p. 402.

28. Peck, R. F., and Havighurst, R. J.: *The Psychology of Character Development*. New York, John Wiley and Sons, 1960, pp. 3–10, 110–117, 191.
29. Peterson, D. R., Becker, W. C., Hellmer, L. A., Shoemaker, D. J., and Quay, H. C.: Parental attitudes and child adjustment. *Child Developm.*, 1959, *30*, 119–130.
30. Phillips, E. L., Wiener, D. N., and Haring, N. G.: *Discipline, Achievement, and Mental Health*. Englewood Cliffs, N. J., Prentice-Hall, Inc., 1960, p. 15.
31. Rickard, R.: Groups ask broader law on child beating. *Tulsa World*, May 10, 1964.
32. Schulman, R. E., Shoemaker, D. J., and Moelis, I.: Laboratory measurement of parental behavior. *J. Consult. Psychol.*, 1962, *26*, 109–114.
33. Slater, P. E.: Parental behavior and the personality of the child. *J. Genet. Psychol.*, 1962, *101*, 53–68.
34. Thom, D. A.: *Everyday Problems of the Everyday Child*. New York, Appleton-Century, 1934, p. 128.
35. Thompson, G. G.: *Child Psychology*. Cambridge, Mass., Houghton Mifflin Co., 1952, pp. 520–521.
36. Vogel, E. F.: The marital relationship of parents of emotionally disturbed children: Polarization and isolation. *Psychiatry*, 1960, *23*, 1–12.
37. Winder, C. L., and Rau, L.: Parental attitudes associated with social deviance in preadolescent boys. *J. Abnorm. Soc. Psychol.*, 1962, *64*, 418–424.

Chapter 12

Freedom to
Defy and Attack

In tragic contrast to excessive punishment of the child is the complete abandonment of his discipline, which leaves him free to defy authority and attack others. The child learns self-control only if he first learns to accede to the control of adults who are responsible for him.[4, 24] Discipline, by establishing standards of behavior and requiring suitable effort, prompts the child toward mastery of self-determined goals,[31] provides him with security,[14] and assures him self-respecting maturity[12] as he adapts himself to the moral and social conformity required of him as a member of society.[17]

Aggressive and self-centered behavior which is not curtailed becomes habitual and is retained as the individual's sole mode of reaction.[13, 29, 33] Moral behavior is learned from the anticipation of external punishment,[2] and if parents ignore, reward, defend, or encourage undesirable behavior, it continues.

FREEDOM TO DEFY AND ATTACK

Permitting Misbehavior

The parent who relies on moralizing and gentle reproof to alter misbehavior discovers that these tactics are ineffective. The child who attacks a parent by name-calling, hitting, or kicking and learns that he will be neither stopped nor punished takes malicious advantage of the adult's passivity and attacks him more frequently and more viciously.*

The child who pretends he does not hear parental requests or who procrastinates with promises and discovers that the parent does not insist on compliance concludes that adult requests need not be obeyed. Free to please himself rather than his parent, the child does so.

Rewarding Misbehavior

The child whose misbehavior is rewarded has an overwhelming incentive to continue it and none at all to inhibit it. A mother expressed bewilderment at the laziness of her 13-year-old daughter, who was expected to wash the dishes and clean the bathroom after her parents left for work but who seldom made even a cursory attempt to do either. The girl was paid weekly for helping out in this way, and she received the money whether or not she did the work. Her defiance of her parents' instructions was rewarded with both ease and cash.

Parents who assume the penalties resulting from the child's misbehavior are rewarding it. A boy who breaks school windows on a week-end spree and who learns that his father will pay for the damage and expect nothing from him but respectful silence during the parental lecture soon will indulge in other acts of vandalism. Some parents, in sympathy for a child apprehended by police, reward him with concern and respect for his encounter with society's legal machinery; some even add gifts intended to compensate him for his ordeal. One father bought his son an expensive sports car soon after his release from jail on a charge of stealing.

A parent who obeys his child's orders is rewarding him for rudeness, and he fixates the child's technique for acquiring adult service. When angry objections of the child to his parents' plans or behavior result in the adults' altering their intentions and actions, the child learns that he can influence and control them without concession or courtesy on his part.

Defending Misbehavior

If misbehavior is minimized in importance or defended by parents, the child learns that not only is it condoned, it is justified.

A neighbor who complains about the child's trampling on his flower beds is told that the child is too young to know better. A playmate who reports the child's assault automatically is considered to have invited it by provoking him. A teacher who describes the child as lazy is answered with the retort that he is bored by the work assigned or that the instruction is inadequate.

---

* See Case 12, Doris F., p. 504.

The child who fails to follow directions to clean his room or help out with chores is excused from obedience by parental judgment that he is too busy with other activities, too tired from late hours and long school days, too old to order about, or too concerned with more important matters. When parents defend misbehavior, the child continues it without guilt.

Encouraging Misbehavior

Misbehavior is not only excused by some parents but encouraged. A teacher, neighbor, or court official who reports misbehavior of the child is vilified by the parent and accused of prejudice, antagonism, and improper action which instigated the child's behavior. When the child's attack on one parent is approved and justified by the other, defiance and abuse of the scorned parent are established as permanent modes of behavior. A parent who joins the child in aggression by teaching him that others wish him ill and are deserving of attack supports misbehavior and encourages its repetition.

PARENTAL MOTIVATION

Feelings of uncertainty and failure, waning endurance, protection of the child's feelings, and need for the child's approval are parental motivations for permitting the child freedom to defy authority and to attack others.

Feelings of Uncertainty and Failure

Faced with living proof of parental failure in the form of a misbehaving, dominating child, an uncertain adult retreats in confusion, not knowing how to gain control and immobilized by feelings of guilt. IIe withdraws from conflict with the child and avoids encounters with him. An insecure mother may literally abandon responsibility for the child's training, taking a full-time job and turning over the child's care to someone else.

Napier[26] reported that mothers unable to control their pre-school children had experienced stormy relationships with their own parents and held a poor opinion of themselves as mothers and as women. They had made unfortunate marriages, often with men whose drinking or aggressiveness they had mistaken for masculine strength. Unsure of themselves, they could not distinguish between major and minor misbehavior, react consistently, or insist on respect and obedience.

An ineffectual and overpermissive father negates his role as principal authority within the family and as the representative of external society. His reluctance to discipline the child may develop from his being dominated by the mother, who has convinced him that his function is to understand the child rather than to criticize him.

Waning Endurance

A child possesses inordinate amounts of perseverance. He can pursue a request for hours or even days if necessary, and he persists for years in any annoying or disapproved kind of behavior which he has adopted. Children experiment with so many different kinds of undesirable behavior that a parent wearies of constantly attempting to oppose the child's steady refusal to change his actions. Eventually, the parent no longer requires the child to obey, his corrections become hesitant, and his requests are converted to pleas. Discipline is notably lax for the youngest children or children born to parents who have already reared an earlier family.

Protection of the Child's Feelings

A mother who identifies with the child or attempts to follow modern precepts of child rearing may sharply rebuke her husband for scolding or disciplining the child. She empathizes with the child and feels hurt as she believes he is hurt by criticism, and she is certain that any punishment is damaging to his self-confidence. Sometimes a father is overly sympathetic toward the child, in remembrance of abuse he suffered from his parents or in the conviction that the child's mother is too demanding, and he tries to spare the child from unpleasantness by failing to correct him or to require him to exert himself.

Need for the Child's Approval

A parent often has a strong need to gain his child's approval. This is particularly true with the first child, whose arrival brings wonder and delight but also overwhelming feelings of inadequacy. A mother of a pre-school child wants him to feel the same joy in her companionship that she does in his, and any conflict between them threatens her feeling of camaraderie. Anxious and worried when the relationship is disrupted, the mother submits to the child's wishes in order to preserve a semblance of friendliness. Her desire to please the child and to merit his approval is obvious in the hesitancy with which she makes requests of him, and the child quickly learns that he need only glower to produce his mother's abject retreat.

A parent who finds no acceptance and affection from his spouse may become dependent on the child to provide this esteem. He seeks the child's approval by supporting him in everything he does, by requiring nothing of him, and by never correcting his behavior, wistfully indicating to concerned teachers or probation officers his belief that the child likes him.

PERSONALITY AND BEHAVIOR CORRELATES OF FREEDOM TO DEFY AND ATTACK

 ⍺ The child who does not learn obedience to authority and control of his impulses to hurt others fails to achieve his potential and lives with anxiety. His actions become increasingly antisocial and amoral.

⍺ Underachievement

The undisciplined child finds it nearly impossible to complete school assignments because he is unaccustomed to the pursuit of distasteful tasks. He is also unaccustomed to conforming, and his refusal to complete his work is in part a refusal to accept authority.

Because he does not work, either at school or at home, he learns less and develops fewer skills than he would with consistent practice. He tends to drift, and he cannot bring himself to engage in any task which he anticipates will cost him undue effort or lead to failure.

Anxiety

The child whose parents have abandoned control feels real fright at bearing complete responsibility for his behavior. When he dominates the adults who should be caring for and protecting him, he knows that he alone makes the decisions regarding himself, and he recognizes his limitations in judgment and knowledge.

Spivack[32] studied 64 hospitalized disturbed adolescents and found them to be more desirous of external controls than normal adolescents. He interpreted their rebellious behavior as a confused search for self-definition and for standards of conduct which they might follow. The desire for control is evident in the progressive gravity of aggressive behavior in the undisciplined child, who seeks to force parental action by transgressions so extreme they cannot be overlooked or condoned. He believes that his parents do not care enough about him to ensure his learning approved behavior, and when his misdeeds produce only averted glances, he engages in increasingly vicious crimes in a desperate attempt to find the control his parents refuse to provide.*

---

* See Case 13, Randy J., p. 505.

Sometimes the child's anxiety over his lack of direction, combined with his strong impulse toward aggressive action, results in his devoting all of his energy to excelling in a single area, such as athletics, and earning esteem in this way. Similar motivation impels a girl of low frustration-tolerance and driving aggressiveness to devote herself to excellence in intellectual pursuits, often those associated with masculine interests.[22]

Antisocial Behavior

✗ Aggressive, antisocial behavior is the only kind the child knows, and conformity, obedience, and consideration are traits foreign to him because he has never practiced them. Indeed, he may despise these characteristics because he has witnessed his parents' subservience to his domination, and their passivity has not served him well. Permitted to defy authority and to attack others, the child rebels continually against parents, teachers, peers, and society, and reacts aggressively whenever he is faced with discipline or even criticism. ✗

Kagan and Moss[22] reported that elementary school boys who displayed dominating and rage reactions, aggression toward their mothers, and low frustration-tolerance were, as adults, quick to retaliate for real or imagined abuse. The delinquent adolescent commonly has a father who has subtracted himself from the family as its traditional symbol of authority and a mother who is exceptionally lenient.[15]

Amorality

The child who is free to defy and attack does not acquire moral concepts of behavior. These concepts are based on others' rights, and he is concerned only with his own. He obtains what he wants with as little personal expenditure as possible, and he behaves morally only when he chooses to do so. He is accustomed to support from others without the need to contribute obedience and love or to sacrifice himself. He can sustain continuity in neither effort nor ambition, and his behavior is impulsive and irresponsible.[11] He is convinced that nothing he does is wrong and that neither codes of conduct nor regulations apply to him.[20]

The amoral individual's bland persistence in misbehavior is based on his conviction that what he does really does not matter to anyone. He behaves as he has since infancy, in whatever manner inclination moves him. He is practiced only in defiance of authority and in harming others, and self-control is an ability he has never acquired.

REFERENCES

1. Abbe, A. E.: Maternal attitudes toward children and their relationship to the diagnostic category of the child. *J. Genet. Psychol.*, 1958, 92, 167–173.

2. Aronfreed, J.: The nature, variety, and social patterning of moral responses to transgression. *J. Abnorm. Soc. Psychol.*, 1961, *63*, 223–240.
3. Bernhardt, K. S.: A philosophy of discipline. *Bull. Inst. Child Stud.* (*Toronto*), 1959, *21*, 2–6.
4. Bernhardt, K. S.: How permissive are you? *Bull. Inst. Child Stud.* (*Toronto*), 1956, *18*, 1–6.
5. Bettelheim, B.: *Love Is Not Enough.* Glencoe, Ill., The Free Press, 1950, pp. 4–5.
6. Bronfenbrener, U.: The changing American child: A speculative analysis. *J. Soc. Issues*, 1961, *17*, 6–17.
7. Cameron, N., and Magaret, A.: *Behavior Pathology.* Cambridge, Mass., Houghton Mifflin Co., 1951, pp. 192–193.
8. Cleckley, H. M.: Psychopathic states. *In* Arieti, S., ed.: *American Handbook of Psychiatry.* New York, Basic Books, Inc., 1959, pp. 572–573.
9. Colm, H.: Help and guidance as discipline for pre-adolescents. *Nerv. Child,* 1951, *9*, 131–138.
10. D'Evelyn, K. E.: *Meeting Children's Emotional Needs.* Englewood Cliffs, N. J., Prentice-Hall, Inc., 1957, pp. 25–26.
11. Dorcus, R. M., and Shaffer, G. W.: *Textbook of Abnormal Psychology,* Ed. 3. Baltimore, The Williams and Wilkins Co., 1945, pp. 420–422.
12. DuBois, F. S.: The security of discipline. *Ment. Hyg.* (*N. Y.*), 1952, *36*, 353–372.
13. Feshback, S.: The catharsis hypotheses and some consequences of interaction with aggressive and neutral play objects. *J. Pers.,* 1956, *24*, 449–462.
14. Geisel, J. B.: Discipline viewed as a developmental need of the child. *Nerv. Child,* 1951, *9*, 115–121.
15. Glueck, S., and Glueck, E. T.: *Unraveling Juvenile Delinquency.* New York, Commonwealth Foundation, 1950.
16. Haring, N. G., and Phillips, E. L.: *Educating Emotionally Disturbed Children.* New York, McGraw-Hill Book Co., 1962, p. 5.
17. Havighurst, R. J.: The functions of successful discipline. *Underst. Child,* 1952, *21*, 35–38.
18. Hoffman, M. L.: Child rearing practices and moral development: Generalizations from empirical research. *Child Developm.,* 1963, *34*, 295–318.
19. Jersild, A. T.: *Child Psychology,* Ed. 4. Englewood Cliffs, N. J., Prentice-Hall, Inc., 1954, pp. 88–89.
20. Jessner, L., and Kaplan, S.: "Discipline" as a problem in psychotherapy with children. *Nerv. Child,* 1951, *9*, 147–155.
21. Jones, V.: Character Development in Children—An Objective Approach. *In* Carmichael, L., ed.: *Manual of Child Psychology.* New York, John Wiley and Sons, 1946, pp. 725–726.
22. Kagan, J., and Moss, H. A.: *Birth to Maturity.* New York, John Wiley and Sons, 1962, pp. 95, 200.
23. Levy, D. M.: Psychopathic behavior in infants and children: A critical survey of the existing concepts. Round Table, 1950. The deprived and the indulged forms of psychopathic personality. *Amer. J. Orthopsychiat.,* 1951, *21*, 250–254.
24. Lourie, N. V.: Discipline: A consistent, non-punitive concept. *Child Welfare,* 1951, *30*, 3–6.
25. Mussen, P. H., and Conger, J. J.: *Child Development and Personality.* New York, Harper and Bros., 1956, p. 440.
26. Napier, M. M.: On mothers being unable to control their preschool children. *Smith Coll. Stud. Soc. Wk.,* 1958, *28*, 151–156.
27. Peck, R. F., and Havighurst, R. J.: *The Psychology of Character Development.* New York, John Wiley and Sons, 1960, pp. 3–10, 110–117, 197.
28. Peterson, D. R., Becker, W. C., Hellmer, L. A., Shoemaker, D. J., and Quay, H. C.: Parental attitudes and child adjustment. *Child Developm.,* 1959, *30*, 119–130.
29. Phillips, E. L., Wiener, D. N., and Haring, N. G.: *Discipline, Achievement, and Mental Health.* Englewood Cliffs, N. J., Prentice-Hall, Inc., 1960, pp. 10–11, 65–66.

30. Sánchez-Hidalgo, E.: La psicología de la crianza. VIII: La necesidad de disciplina (The psychology of rearing. VIII: The need for discipline). *Rev. Asoc. Maestros P. R.*, 1956, *15*, 86–87, 102.
31. Settlage, C. F.: The values of limits in child rearing. *Children*, 1958, *5*, 175–178.
32. Spivack, G.: Child-rearing attitudes of emotionally disturbed adolescents. *J. Consult. Psychol.*, *21* (2), 178.
33. Thom, D. A.: *Everyday Problems of the Everyday Child.* New York, Appleton-Century, 1934, pp. 25–26, 118–119.

Part II

THE PRE-SCHOOL CHILD

Chapter 13

Introduction

The events of the pre-school years are of the greatest significance in determining the child's achievement, adaptability, sex-role identification, competitiveness, and maturity of behavior throughout his entire developmental period and adulthood.[4] From infancy until he begins school, the child undergoes the most conspicuous changes in appearance, physical competence, communicative skill, coping ability,[7] independence, and socialization which he will ever effect within a single five-year period. He is converted from a completely helpless individual into a person who can care for many of his daily needs, influence and predict the behavior of others, leave his home and mingle with his peers, and perform hundreds of specific skills.

During these five years his development is orderly, and his abilities and reactions are related closely to his chronological age.[8] Often he appears illogical in what he does, however, because he is confronted continually with the need to act, even though his experience is meager and his knowledge unsound. His behavior is inconsistent with his announced intentions because these are stated tentatively and forgotten immediately. His choices are erratic and contradictory because he does not feel strongly about them.[9] His responses are fluid and easily altered[3] because he rarely is certain that his behavior is adequate or correct. The child's instability gradually diminishes, however, and he fixates on behavior which has proved rewarding for his purposes, using a successful technique not only in those situations for which it is appropriate, but in many other social settings where it may not be appropriate.[2]

The parent, in order to rear his child successfully, must continually adapt his own management to the orderly development and increasing competency of the child, while still maintaining consistency in providing the care and training requisite for satisfaction of the broad human needs of social acceptability, personal accomplishment, adherence to moral standards, and self-respect. Few parents discharge this formidable task with ease or complete success. The provocations of the child, supplemented by the adults' concern about their experiences as parents, intensify their difficulties.

PROVOCATIONS OF THE CHILD

A clinician trained in identifying parental mishandling must guard against assigning total blame for a child's behavior problems to the parents' ignorance, willfulness, or emotional needs. The child himself, with his moods, unpredictability, and frequent testing and abuse of his parent, adds large doses of irritation to the relationship.

Constant Association

The pre-school child needs a regulated life at home and minimal separation from his mother, and their forced companionship is inevitable. This prolonged contact, annoying in itself, results also in magnification of the child's imperfections and faults. When a mother witnesses hundreds of incidents of thumb-sucking, whining, and toy-throwing, she is convinced that both she and her child are failing and she becomes impatient and angry.

Unruly Emotion

Because he is young and relatively helpless, the pre-school child's emotion is violent and frantic. His screams are intense and wild; his hitting, biting, and scratching are determined and painful; his fearfulness is heart rending. Such tumultuous emotion appears to an adult to be totally unsuited for the event which elicited it. Its occurrence can create anxiety in the parent, who may respond by imitating the child's emotional excess or by retreating in confusion.

Physical Care

The physical care of a young child drains energy from his mother. Dressing, bathing, feeding, and protecting a pre-school child takes hours of time. Lifting and carrying a 20-pound baby, pinning on a diaper while he rolls and scrambles, and pushing a suddenly limp hand into a mitten or flailing feet into boots requires unflagging strength. Dozens of paper scraps, kitchen utensils, and toys are strewn daily over the house. After every feeding, applesauce and cereal must be scrubbed off the floor and high chair, and a mother's back aches from leaning over a low crib to change sheets and from carrying heavy containers of soiled diapers. Extra surprises come often. One mother grimly tackled the task of removing quantities of melted grease from the hair and clothing of a sick child on whose head a can of drippings had been bestowed by a sympathetic two-year-old physician. Exhaustion causes a mother to remain irritated with the child and despairing over the work he necessitates.

Recurrent Teaching Demands

Within a five-year time span, the child must learn how to drink from a cup, handle a spoon and then a fork, and eat adult food. He must learn to use the toilet for elimination, and he must learn to dress himself, including the manipulation of buttons and zippers. He must pick up his toys, say "Please" and "Thank you," and run errands on request. He must refrain from hitting and biting others, keep out of the street, and not wander away from home; and he must not touch electric outlets, hot stoves, and unsteady lamps. As the mother attempts to instruct the child in all of these accomplishments, she suffers repeated discouragement as the child learns slowly, resists loudly, and fails often.

Independence of the Child

The parent's tolerance of the demands imposed on him for care and training of the child is reënforced by pleasure in the child's dependence on him for affection and wise guidance. Even during pre-school years, however, the child becomes increasingly independent of his parents,[10] and his repudiating actions lead to resentment in the adults.

As he experiments in independence, he rejects his parents with both verbal and physical abuse. As he devotes himself to his playmates, imitating their mannerisms and quoting their statements, he indicates that neither his parents' companionship nor their precepts are indispensable. In convincing himself and others that he and his wishes are important, he fights openly with his siblings and his peers. He subtly dominates his parents and evades their directions[6] by interrupting their conversations, hiding unwanted bread crusts behind the sofa, dawdling, and reappearing repeatedly after being put to bed. As he tries out one method after another of proving that he is a person of consequence, his parents react with annoyance and belittling, anger and coercion, or deflection of his most vexatious techniques by not permitting them to succeed.

A Typical Day

The fatigue, frustration, and dismay inherent in a life shared with pre-schoolers is illustrated by the following account of a typical day with them. The events as they occurred were recorded by a mother of four small children. Helen is seven years old and attends a special school for retarded children; Laura is five, and in kindergarten; Frank is three-and-a-half years old; and Martin is 16 months.

6:30 A.M.   Frank comes in and wakes me up.

7:15   Get Helen and Laura out of bed and send to bathroom. Get Martin up and change him. Serve breakfast to all. Get after all to start eating. Help Helen eat so she will make it in time. Give Helen her pills and Frank his medicine. Send Helen to the bathroom to brush her teeth and wash.

7:40   Helen still not in the bathroom. Put her there and put toothpaste on her brush. Laura comes out to ask what she should wear. Martin spills his juice and breaks the glass. Laura comes back to see if the clothes she has picked out are all right. Helen still hasn't brushed her teeth. Martin throws dish of cereal on the floor. Wash Martin and take him away from the table. Drag Helen out of bed, take her to bathroom, and help her brush her teeth and wash. Frank comes to find out what he should wear. Helen asks if she can take paste to school; answer is "no"; she continues to pester and beg to take paste. Frank back asking what else he should wear and then disagrees with what I tell him. Send Helen to bedroom to dress. Take Martin off the middle of the kitchen table. He has spilled the sugar bowl. Send Helen back to her room to dress. Helen starts asking again for paste to take to school. Frank lost the mate to his sock; help him find it—also get knot out of his shoe.

8:00   Tell Helen to get her pajamas off. Tie Frank's shoe. Laura asks to play in the basement. Went after her to lock the gate. Helen has her slip on backwards. Comes out to show me her new socks. We discussed how hard the new socks would be to put on. Send her back to finish dressing. Helen has her sock on wrong, so turn it around for her. Took Martin in to dress him but Laura and Frank have the Lincoln logs all over the floor and I can't get in the room. Send Helen in to put her shoes on. Finally got in the bedroom and dressed Martin. Frank asked for gum, got mad and cried when I said no. Turned Helen's slip around and braided her hair. She fought having it done so had to rebraid part of it. Helen pestered some more about taking paste to school. Spanked her and told her to get her shoes on. Fixed Laura's hair. Frank informed me that if I didn't give him gum that he wouldn't like me any more.

8:30   Helen's shoes still not on. Put her shoes on for her, also her dress, and gave her a hanky. Martin threw an ashtray—spanked his hands. Frank kicked Martin in the head, tipped the hassock over. Refused to set it back up unless I give him some gum. Spanked him and put him in his room. Helen steps on my sore foot. Frank comes out of his room, pushes Martin over, and sits on him. Send Frank back to his room. Helen and Laura get in fight while I am trying to comfort Martin. Helen starts to cry that she doesn't want to go to school and that if she has to go, she wants her dad to take her. Goes into kitchen and throws some pencils on the floor and tears up my notes. Martin throws a temper tantrum because I won't let him go to the basement with me. Put Martin's sweater on him. Load everyone in the car and start for Helen's school. Laura and Frank argue all the way. Martin stands up in car seat and tries to shift gears.

9:00   Arrived at Helen's school and Helen cried and didn't want to go in. Walked with her to the door. Martin screamed because I left him in the car. Laura and Frank argued all the way back home. Martin tried to climb in my lap for a few hugs and kisses. Arrived home, put Martin outside to play, and Laura and Frank went to the basement.

9:30   Martin wanted in and begged for cracker. Laura and Frank came upstairs to see what Martin had and why they couldn't have one too. Wouldn't unlock the gate for them, so Frank crawled over gate. Sent them back down to play. Laura came back up to show me the picture she drew. Frank came up and crawled over the gate and asked for chalk. Martin took all the pots and pans out of the cupboard. I put them back; he got into them again and threw the lids down the basement stairs. Martin begged for another cracker and threw a tantrum when I said no. Laura came up to show me her numbers she had written. Martin begged again for cracker—gave him a drink, changed his diaper, and put him to bed. Frank went into bedroom to get toys; I went back to settle Martin down. Frank went back for another toy; I went in again and settled Martin down.

10:00   Frank asked for something to eat. Laura came up to see what Frank was getting that she wasn't. Gave them some rolls and they fought over the crumbs and frosting. Frank won and Laura cried. Frank asked where the rolls came from and Laura tried to tell him; so Frank got mad because Laura was talking all the time: He hit her. Next he wanted a button pin he had yesterday, and a search began. He found it on a high chest of drawers. Pushing over the rocking chair, he climbed up on it to get the button on the chest. He fell over with the rocking chair.

10:30   Laura came upstairs to show me an old toy she had found. Frank came up asking for something to eat. Wanted to know

why he couldn't have anything, called me an old meany, and
said he would die if I didn't give him some candy—then I
would be sorry and cry. Made himself cry thinking about it,
so I sat down and had a talk with him.

12:00   Martin wakes up. Change his diaper and give the family
lunch. Frank asks for second helpings. Martin crams too
much food in and chokes on it. Called Frank back to the
table to finish eating and drink his milk. Martin throws his
spoon and some food on the floor. Frank climbs on his chair
and knocks his chin on it. Frank and Martin have a bread-
throwing contest.

12:30 P.M.   Send Laura to her room to dress for school. Tell her to stop
playing with Martin and get busy. Told Frank to stop play-
ing in bathroom and get out. Frank left bathroom door open
and Martin went in and played in toilet, getting water all
over the floor. Frank wants to invite friend in to play. Button
and tie Laura's dress. Caught Frank trying to choke Martin;
rescued Martin from Frank. Frank wants to go barefooted.
When I said no, he sat on Martin. Send Frank to pick up
his room. Combed Laura's hair. Frank takes toy away from
Martin and steps on him. Throws Lincoln logs. Martin tries
to open door to dishwasher and gets burned. Put Martin
outside to play in back yard. Frank wants out front but can't
open door. I let him out. Frank is back and wants out back
door.

1:00   Frank tries to put Martin on swing and Martin falls off.
Frank back in the house. Martin wants in—take his cap and
jacket off. Martin unrolls the oilcloth. Give Martin a drink;
let Frank's friend in the house. Give them some candy and
gum. Frank doesn't like his candy and fusses for something
else. Frank left bathroom door open and Martin got in and
splashed water all over the floor. Gave Martin a drink and
some crackers, changed his diaper, and put him down for a
nap. Frank fell off back steps into window well and got
stuck. Boys left the water running all over the patio and got
themselves wet. Frank heard a fire engine and was afraid of
it: I calmed him down. Woke up Martin, changed his diaper,
put on his jacket, put both boys in car, and went to pick up
Helen from school.

3:00   Helen brought a water painting she had made; told me that
the other kids called her slobber mouth; started to cry and
tore up the painting. Arrived home. Frank's friend came
back to play. Helen had a bloody nose. Frank and Helen
fought. Took Martin off coffee table; gave him drink and
cracker. Laura came home from school and told me about her
day. Laura's friend comes over to play. Frank and friend
want to go upstairs. Helen gets naughty and friend wants
to go upstairs. Took Martin off the kitchen cupboards.
Frank's friend unchained the dog. Helen's nose starts to
bleed again.

4:00   Helen took Laura's jump rope; Laura took it away from
                Helen. Helen hit Laura's friend. Frank got on the high swing
                and couldn't get down. Frank got hit in the head with a
                swing. Took Martin off kitchen table; told Frank and friend
                to turn the water off outside and leave it off. Sent Frank in
                to clean up his room; he refused, so spanked him. Frank was
                angry and pushed Martin out of his room and shut the door
                on Martin's fingers.

5:00   Sat down to eat. Martin spilled milk, threw food, and hit
                Frank with spoon.

5:30   Frank falls off hassock and hits Martin in the head. Helen
                and Laura fight over book and tear it. Frank hits Martin and
                pushes him down. Frank and Laura get magazines out to
                look at: Martin grabs and tears new magazine. Helen falls
                and hits head on corner of rocking chair. Martin falls off
                davenport. Helen trips over rug and hurts her arm. Martin
                hits Frank with play hammer. Frank hits Martin back. Laura
                and Frank wrestle on the floor. Laura gets hurt and comes
                crying about it. Martin back on davenport and pushes lamp
                off end table. Martin throws ashtray on the floor. Helen walks
                into door and hurts her eye.

7:00   Put Martin in pajamas and put him to bed. Send Helen,
                Laura, and Frank in to put on pajamas. Send Helen back to
                her room—she hasn't put pajamas on yet. Send Helen in to
                pick up her clothes. Give Helen her pills and Frank his medi-
                cine. Send all three to the bathroom and put them to bed.

10:00   Helen is up. Take her to bathroom and put her back to bed.

THE CONCERNS OF PARENTHOOD

Although the care of the child and contacts with him are sufficiently
disruptive of the parent's natural affection for him, other aspects of parenthood also concern an adult and affect the manner in which he reacts to
the child.

Deficiency in the Child

Some children are blessed with curly hair, symmetrical features, a
sturdy body, and large brown eyes. Others start life with misshapen ears,
protruding teeth, crossed eyes, runny noses, and stringy hair. Despite
huge meals, they are thin and pale and appear to be badly neglected, and
a sensitive parent is embarrassed by his child's unprepossessing appearance.

If the child is slow at walking, talking, or achieving dryness, anxious parents may consider him retarded, and they feel ashamed of him and are apprehensive about negative comments from others.

As soon as a child begins to associate with other children, he endures some bad moments, but often his parent endures more. He gauges the child's popularity and self-confidence in his contacts with other children and values him accordingly.

Faulty Rearing

Disappointment in himself disturbs a parent as much as disappointment in the child. A conscientious parent worries continually about making errors in decisions and management and judges himself after every contact with the child. Concern with correct rearing can lead to overreactions. Parents who worry about spoiling the child may let him cry too long, fail to protect him from older children, or require decisions and independent action of him before he is equipped to undertake them. A parent unduly frightened by the first "No!" the child delivers responds with severe punishment and unvarying insistence on the child's capitulation in every dispute.

Other parents, alert to an occasional temper tantrum, bad dream, wet bed, or display of shyness, believe that they have a "problem child," and they blame themselves for creating insecurity in the child. Unsure parents avoid all conflict with the child, permitting him to do as he chooses when he announces that he is not sleepy at bedtime or that he prefers playing to eating when he is called to dinner.

Disappointment in Parenthood

Parents experience frequent disappointments in child rearing. The child often shows that he dislikes them, and he rarely appreciates what they do for him. The child's assertion that he prefers one parent to another, his annoying or hurting his sibling, and his refusal to coöperate with his parents' efforts to rear him well are distressing to parents who hold an idealistic concept of family harmony. Their distress can lead to avoidance of the child and to feelings of hopelessness.

Dutiful parents overextend themselves to accommodate the child. A mother plays with or reads to the child long after she has become bored or needs to attend to other matters. She permits him to "help" each time the dishes are washed or baking is done—even though his assistance interferes with her efficiency, creates added work, and affords her no relief from his presence. The parent who is a slave to the child's whims resents his demands even while acceding to them and concludes that parenthood requires excessive sacrifice. If the parent yearns for his lost freedom, he will dominate and coerce the child in certain areas while placating him in others, and the inconsistency leaves both parent and child uncertain and dissatisfied with each other.

REFERENCES

1. Anderson, H. H., and Anderson, G.: Personality development in infancy and the preschool years. *Rev. Educ. Res.*, 1958, *28*, 410–421.
2. Bandura, A., and Walters, R.: *Social Learning and Personality Development.* New York, Holt, Rinehart and Winston, 1963, p. 21.
3. Gesell, A.: *The First Five Years of Life.* New York, Harper and Bros., 1940, p. 6.
4. Kagan, J., and Moss, H. A.: *Birth to Maturity.* New York, John Wiley and Sons, 1962, pp. 79, 123, 169, 276.
5. Martin, M. H.: Some reactions of pre-school children to discipline. *Nerv. Child,* 1951, *9*, 125–130.
6. Müller, A.: Über die Entwicklung des Leistungs-Anspruchsniveaus (On the development of a level of aspiration). *Z. Psychol.*, 1958, *162*, 238–253.
7. Murphy, L. B.: Coping devices and defense mechanisms in relation to autonomous ego functions. *Bull. Menninger Clin.*, 1960, *24*, 144–153.
8. Smith, D. B., and Roth, R. M.: Problem-solving behavior of preschool children in a spontaneous setting. *J. Genet. Psychol.*, 1960, *97*, 129–143.
9. Stewart, B. R.: Developmental differences in the stability of object preferences and conflict behavior. *Child Developm.*, 1958, *29*, 9–18.
10. Stith, M., and Connor, R.: Dependency and helpfulness in young children. *Child Developm.*, 1962, *33*, 15–20.

Section One

CHARACTERISTIC BEHAVIOR

Chapter 14

Early Pre-school Years

The birth of the first baby plunges parents into a round of peaks of elation and depths of depression. Pride is offset by fatigue, delight by disgust, and confidence by discouragement.

Engineering the creation of a live, amazingly tiny but continually changing and responding human being surpasses all previous achievements. A mother's initial pride fades, however, as she tires from holding the infant for hours of daily feedings; laundering endless piles of clothing, diapers, and bedding; and leading a life of interrupted sleep, meals, and leisure. It has been estimated that there are 3000 separate feeding contacts between child and mother within the first two years of the child's life, and total contacts number in the tens of thousands.[7]

As a mother touches her baby's soft cheek and plays with his miniature fingers, she feels devoted to him and willingly dedicates herself to his care. His sweetness alternates, however, with the production of smelly excretions on innumerable diapers; and his burping often results in his depositing half-digested milk on his fresh clothes, clean sheets, or mother's dress.

A mother is smugly satisfied when she has bathed, fed, changed, and bedded down her baby and he peacefully falls asleep. Sometimes, however, after all the preparations finally are accomplished, the result is not sleep but frantic crying. The mother's confidence is shattered, and in the first few weeks of caring for her child she weeps often with exhaustion and discouragement.

The contrasting mood swings of new parents make them vulnerable to overreaction and overconcern about events which normally occur in the development of every child.

118

INFANCY

Crying, sleeping, feeding, and resistance provide opportunities for conflict or mismanagement during the baby's first year.

Crying

Hunger, illness, indigestion, fatigue, and occasionally even an open safety pin can cause excessive crying during the first weeks of the baby's life.[14] The hypertonic infant is overresponsive to stimulation and frets sporadically. Colic causes several consecutive hours of daily crying, usually at the same time each day and seldom responsive to soothing efforts. Although early crying and rage reactions are not related to later behavior of a similar nature in the child,[9] a crying baby causes his mother to feel helpless, guilty, incompetent, and uncertain in her feelings and behavior toward him.[14]

By the time the baby is six weeks old, his digestion, elimination, and breathing are better regulated by his nervous system, and he outgrows his early tension and discomfort. His crying is reduced to a bearable minimum. If the parents, in attempting to soothe him, have been accustomed to picking him up whenever he cried and if they continue to do so when he is older, he begins to expect prompt attention for crying. He cries whenever he is awake and alone, and he screams in rage when attention is not immediate and constant. He becomes less dependent on his own resources and less tolerant of frustration, and he learns to control his parents by crying.

Sleeping

Early domination of parents by the infant is associated with his successful disruption of sleeping routines. Once in his crib, the baby announces his aversion to rest with an ear-piercing howl which convinces his anxious parents that he must be in pain. After examination reveals no obvious difficulty, they leave him again, but the baby persists in his objections and the adults conclude that he is not tired. Taking him from his bed, they amuse him until he finally becomes exhausted and falls asleep, sometimes an hour or more past their own bedtime. If this procedure becomes habitual, the infant's sleep is erratic and insufficient, and he is irritable and dissatisfied.

As he becomes older, the child requires less sleep than formerly, and he is awake and with his mother for more hours during the day. If he has learned how to evade regular bedtimes, the association between mother and child is prolonged, and the mother wearies of being subjected to his demands for her attention.

Feeding

A mother is concerned about whether the baby is getting enough to eat, and her vacillation about breast feeding often is related to her inability to determine how many ounces the baby consumes. Her decision that the infant must finish every drop in his bottle conflicts with his easy habit of falling asleep at the beginning of a feeding and sets the stage for authority disputes which extend into other areas.

Later, when solid food is first put into the baby's mouth, parental indecision or conflict may develop from the baby's response. A child's usual reaction to solid food is to shove it out of his mouth with his tongue, sometimes deliberately, but more often because muscle coördination is undeveloped and he has had no experience in swallowing anything but liquids. If his behavior is considered by his mother as a refusal and if her belief that she is being opposed apparently is confirmed by the baby's later rejection of some new foods, an enduring battle may begin over whether the child will eat what has been prepared for him.

Most babies hold and nibble on crackers at around six months of age, and a little later they dip their fingers into their food and lick them. As early as ten months, a baby may engage in a tussle with his mother for possession of the spoon with which she is feeding him, and if she gives it to him, he tries to feed himself.[14] He has small success at first and usually turns the spoon upside down and spills its contents over himself. He flings food on the floor because he is uncoördinated or because it is fun, and if his messiness and awkwardness are too much for his mother, she refuses to permit him to feed himself. Defeated in his masterful attempt to manage independently, the child learns to wait docilely for his mother to attend to his needs.

Resistance

After the age of six months, the baby is no longer the placid, malleable infant he once was. He escapes the cup, the diaper, and the bonnet with adroit maneuvering, and he shows his displeasure by screaming and kicking. Sometimes a resisting, angry baby approaching a year in age holds his breath until he literally turns blue. A mother frightened by the child's fury ceases her efforts to enforce her wishes, and the child adopts violent emotion as an automatic opposition reaction. Breath-holding increases in frequency during the next year.[10]

Parents sometimes are alarmed by the child's resistance to contacts with strangers. A normal infant of nine or ten months shows his distrust and fearfulness by sucking his thumb, hiding his head, and even sobbing when outsiders approach him.[15] His parents are distressed by his failure to show friendliness, ashamed of his bad manners, and concerned that he always will be shy.

THE ONE-YEAR-OLD

As the infant celebrates his first birthday by digging into the cake with his fist, he also celebrates a turning point in his life. No longer is he considered entirely helpless and lovable by his parents. During this second year, they start a regime of training which continually interferes with what he would prefer to do and which results in disapproval and punishment he has not experienced previously.

The one-year-old uses eating and sleeping routines to demonstrate his autonomy. His new freedom to explore endangers him and annoys his mother. Toilet training, with its opportunities for daily conflict and disturbance, is introduced. The child's emotional reactions begin to approximate those of adults, and because these reactions appear more appropriate than formerly, parental response to them becomes more complex.

Opposition to Routines

Even the child whose early sleep habits were well established now begins to show his unwillingness to settle down. He is more aware of people and of his own increasing skills, and he greatly enjoys utilizing both. He stands in his crib and calls loudly for his mother at naptime, and she eventually resorts to lying down with him to induce him to sleep,[15] thus teaching him that he need not conform to necessary routines without adult concessions. When he discovers how to climb out of bed and nonchalantly and unexpectedly puts in an appearance, his mother's first reaction is admiration for his prowess. Her second reaction is dismay because she can no longer keep him confined to his crib. In desperation, she may lock his door or strap him in bed, or she may give up, permitting him to sleep when and where he chooses, night or day.

Three times daily, meals provide the setting for trouble between mother and child. Disastrous self-feeding practice periods with spoon and cup continue; and, bored with meals, the child enlivens them by standing up in his high chair and splashing food with his spoon. He stops eating after a few bites and successfully resists his mother's attempts to force feed him. If he is at the family table, he reaches for the jelly dish, demands drinks of coffee, and loudly insists on sampling the barbequed spareribs and garlic bread his father is eating, while he steadily drops overboard the chopped chicken and mashed potatoes his mother has prepared for him. He enjoys the commotion he causes and the control he exercises. His mother's desperation at failing to get into him the vitamins and vegetables he requires mounts with every meal, and her efforts to direct his eating become increasingly frenzied.

Exploration

As soon as a baby can get around by himself, he causes unending trouble for his parents and exposes himself to danger.[10, 18] The toddler can wander far away from home before he is missed. He can unscrew lids and consume the contents of medicine bottles and jars of cleaning fluids, turn on electric fans and stoves, tip a pan of boiling water over himself, and choke on small buttons and beads. He digs into wastebaskets and cuts himself on opened cans; and he climbs up the front of tall chests which topple over on him. Accidents are the most frequent cause of death in children under six years of age. Falls, poisoning, burns, suffocation, and the inhalation and ingestion of food and other materials are the common causes of these deaths.[6]

Because the child is free to explore and experiment and because he constantly does so, his mother cannot let him out of her sight. She must continually anticipate accidents, arrange safeguards to prevent them,[2] and attempt to teach the child safety. If she teaches by scolding and spanking, she punishes all day long, and the mother's vexation is matched by the child's determination, so that the two are battling each other for hours every day. The mother becomes convinced that her child is willful, disobedient, and uncontrollable.

Toilet Training

Few teaching chores produce as much antagonism between tutor and pupil as does toilet training, often because it is introduced before the child is physiologically capable of controlling elimination. Because the child fails more often than he succeeds, his performance leads his mother to respond with discouragement and punishment. When training continues for many months, both child and mother become steadily more angry and disappointed with each other and with themselves, producing attitudes which permeate their other contacts and endure long after training finally has been accomplished.

Appropriate Emotion

The infant's emotional expressions of delight or rage are undifferentiated and nonspecific, but the one-year-old reminds his parents of their own feelings with his unaffected but appropriate emotional reactions. He entertains for an audience by repeating performances at which others have laughed; and his expressions of fear, anger, affection, anxiety, and sympathy are congruent with the situation evoking them.[4]

His emotional reactions appear reasonable to observant parents, who understand his objections to their requirements and appreciate his desire for pleasure and acclaim. They welcome this evidence that he has human motivations because they can empathize with him more now than when he was an infant. Understanding his emotion, however, they feel greater guilt in opposing him and become confused about whether to follow their own convictions or to acknowledge the rectitude of the child's desires. If their indecision persists, they fail to provide either protection or discipline for the child.

THE TWO-YEAR-OLD

The independence of thought and action which appeared when the child was one year old is augmented by new possibilities for conflict as he reaches two years of age. His negativism achieves heroic proportions. He absorbs excitement, and the overstimulation tires him and makes him irritable. He begins to associate with other children, and this causes problems for his parents. He oscillates between dependence and independence, and his unpredictability perplexes and disturbs his parents.

Negativism

Most parents have heard that two is the age for refusals and temper, and they brace themselves for an onslaught of opposition. Although the child's refusals increase during this year as he objects to routines and commands and also resists social pressures,[7] severe tantrums are less common than they will be a year later.[10]

Kanner[10] counselled parents to consider a child's verbal refusal to comply with their requests as a healthy sign of development, an indication of the child's belief in his right to independence and self-respect. Criticizing, opposing, and competing with others requires courage, and the child's ability to practice negativism at home enables him to resist playmates' attempts to dominate him. Parents can conduct necessary routines without arguing, pleading, involved explanations, or severe punishment merely by failing to hear and respond to the child's verbal refusals. A rebelling small child can be carried wherever he must go and started at what he must do without comment or anger from his parent.

Overexcitement

A two-year-old often is tired and irritable because he is curious and busy continually. He responds to every stimulus and cannot inhibit his activity in order to rest when he should. As he observes and experiences more, he also becomes more fearful. Television cartoons with sudden close-ups, rapidly moving figures, and scenes of danger frighten him. Older children tell him stories of ghosts in the basement and bears in the bushes which keep him awake at night. Even the playful growling of his father, wrestling with him for fun, seems realistically ferocious.

Langford[11] suggested that the exhausting physical pace two-year-olds maintain should be interrupted periodically throughout the day with quiet play, story telling, and listening to records, and the hour before bedtime should be kept free from excitement. Without this parental supervision of activity, fatigue-based conflicts increase.

Social Difficulties

When the child reaches two years of age, his parents begin to assume the referee's chores and endure the humiliation and anger incident to his contacts with other children. A two-year-old bites or is bitten by his peers; small visitors grab toys; older children use him as a doll or help themselves to his toys, laugh at him, and run him out of his own yard.

By the end of this year, his ability to manage the onslaughts of other children will determine his acceptability to them and his pleasure in associating with them. If he is flexible in his reactions and can retain their companionship while still asserting his rights, he usually welcomes his contacts with other children.[12] If he is overly aggressive or isolates himself and does not participate in other children's activities, he will be rejected by them.[13] These initial social reactions persist during the first ten years of the child's life.[9]

The parent witnessing the two-year-old's ineptness at social contacts may be disappointed in him and may scold, force, or defend the child in attempts to alter his behavior. Uncertain about how much interference or guidance he should give when the child is with other children, the parent becomes angered and discouraged by problems arising from social encounters.

Oscillating Dependency

At one moment a two-year-old is obdurate in his refusals, braving any punishment in insistence on his rights. At the next, he is running to his mother's arms, bawling loudly over a playmate's unfriendly push or his own inability to open a door. Although he likes to play outdoors by himself, he must reassure himself often that his mother is nearby.

His behavior vacillates unpredictably between dependence and independence, but because he appears self-sufficient at times, his immature actions convince his parents that he is regressing. To prevent this supposed regression, the parents react strongly to dependent behavior and punish, ridicule, or repudiate the child when he seeks protection and support. Maturity is not achieved instantaneously, however, and dependent behavior, reflecting the child's natural immaturity and self-concern, will continue predominant for years.

REFERENCES

1. Anderson, H. H., and Anderson, G.: Personality development in infancy and the preschool years. *Rev. Educ. Res.*, 1958, *28*, 410–421.
2. Dietrich, H. F.: Accident prevention in childhood. *Crippled Child*, 1955, *32*, 10–15, 28–29.
3. Franus, E.: Reakcje oporu i gneiwu malego dziecka (Reactions of resistance and anger in a small child). *Zes. Nauk. Uniw. Jagiellońskiego Psychol. Pedag.*, 1957, *1*, 137–163.
4. Gesell, A.: *The First Five Years of Life.* New York, Harper and Bros., 1940, pp. 26, 28, 33, 40, 45.
5. Hurlock, E. B.: *Child Development.* New York, McGraw-Hill Book Co., 1950, p. 294.
6. Jacobziner, H.: Accidents a major child health problem. *J. Pediat.*, 1955, *46*, 419–436.
7. Jersild, A. T.: *Child Psychology*, Ed. 4. New York, Prentice-Hall, Inc., 1954, pp. 79, 151, 769.
8. Jersild, A. T.: Emotional development. *In* Carmichael, L., ed.: *Manual of Child Psychology.* New York, John Wiley and Sons, 1946, pp. 769–770.
9. Kagan, J., and Moss, H. A.: *Birth to Maturity.* New York, John Wiley and Sons, 1962, pp. 79, 87–89, 276.
10. Kanner, L.: *Child Psychiatry*, Ed. 3. Springfield, Ill., Charles C Thomas, 1957, pp. 42, 45.
11. Langford, L. M.: *Guidance of the Young Child.* New York, John Wiley and Sons, 1960, pp. 46–47.
12. Müller, A.: Über die Entwicklung des Leistungs-Anspruchsniveaus (On the development of a level of aspiration). *Z. Psychol.*, 1958, *162*, 238–253.
13. Murphy, L. B.: Coping devices and defense mechanisms in relation to autonomous ego functions. *Bull. Menninger Clin.*, 1960, *24*, 144–153.
14. Sorokin, P. A., and Gove, D. S.: Notes on the friendly and antagonistic behavior of nursery school children. *In* Sorokin, P. A., ed.: *Explorations in Altruistic Love and Behavior.* Boston, Beacon Press, 1950, pp. 295–300.
15. Spock, B.: *Baby and Child Care.* New York, Pocket Books, Inc., 1957, pp. 175–187, 261–280, 306–312.
16. Thom, D. A.: *Everyday Problems of the Everyday Child.* New York, Appleton-Century, 1934, p. 74.

Chapter 15

Later Pre-school Years

Parents are misled into thinking of the older pre-school child as a miniature adult. His behavior is purposeful, his vocabulary and conversation are impressive, and he no longer looks like a baby. Because they expect maturity from him, they are ashamed of him when his independence and self-control are deficient, annoyed when his behavior does not conform to the social proprieties, and angered by his inept interaction with others.

They react to their disappointment with extra efforts to force more mature behavior or with protection which restricts the need for mature behavior. Their dissatisfaction with the child and their extreme methods of managing him are unfortunate at this time, because it is during the later pre-school years that the child acquires set ways of responding to other people and of meeting challenges, and his parents become fixated in their concept of him and their methods of rearing him.

THE THREE-YEAR-OLD

The three-year-old annoys his parents with his continual talking, and he regresses in previously learned habits. His emotional reactions are immature and self-centered, and there are daily disputes between him and his parents over the management of his possessions.

Continuous Talking

Gratified by his ability to communicate and curious about everything, the three-year-old is a garrulous talker.[2] During his entire waking day, he refrains from talking for only 19 minutes, and his longest period of silence is four minutes. His vocabulary nearly doubles during this year, reaching 1600 words, and he never stops exercising his new verbal skill.[5]

Much of his conversation takes the form of questions. These are not always valid requests for information, but they are used to gain attention from a busy mother or to elicit the respect implied in a considered answer. Sometimes the unending flow of "Why?" substitutes for the real questions which puzzle and worry the child, such as the reasons for sex differences, family arguments, death, and deformity.

Regression in Habits

With three years of rapid habit learning behind him, the young child reaches a plateau where he rests on his laurels and demonstrates a casual disdain for conformity. He uses his spoon when a fork is more appropriate, he crawls on the floor instead of walking or running, and he fails in previously acquired bladder and bowel control. Strong negative reactions from parents are common when the child behaves in these ways, and he defends himself by persevering in the behavior. He guilelessly continues to use his spoon or crawl until he is scolded, and he insists that he is not responsible for the puddle on the floor: His big brother or the lady visitor must have made it.[9]

Parents who accept temporary regressions as an indication that the child now is concentrating on less well-learned achievements, such as adequacy in speech and competency in social contacts, are less inclined to regard this behavior as completely inappropriate or to be concerned about its permanency.

Infantile Emotion

Just as the child is losing his babyish appearance and helpless ways, he develops a whole new set of fears and worries.[6] He refuses to enter a dark room alone, and he screams when a dog approaches. He sobs and clings to his mother if he spies a worm or notices a moving crane. He declines to try the swing or the slide, and he runs crying from the edge of the lake when his father tries to coax him in. His embarrassed parents tell him with exasperation and disgust that he is behaving like a baby.

If he has acquired a younger sibling by this time, the three-year-old shows his jealousy by hurting the baby and informing his mother that she may return him to the hospital or by adopting infantile habits of sucking on a bottle, wetting himself, crying, and being generally annoying and troublesome.[9] His aggressive or immature behavior seems completely unnecessary to his busy mother, who thinks of him as capable and independent and who does not welcome expressions of jealousy which add to her burdens.

Tantrums used on a trial basis by the two-year-old now appear with greater frequency.[11] His anger reflects sturdier courage and greater certainty of his own desires. He is more persistent because his independence is developing steadily,[12] and his enlarging contacts with other children increase the incidence of conflicts, annoyances, and rebuffs he encounters and provide him with more practice in self-assertion.

His parents consider his fearfulness, jealousy, and anger to be immature, and they expect more, rather than less, emotional control from him as he grows older. Not only is his temper understandable, but his fearfulness and jealousy are also natural. Because he is older, he observes more closely and can anticipate dangers to which he previously was oblivious; and when a new baby forces him to share his parents' time, attention, and affection, he believes that his position in the family has been downgraded.[18]

Management of Possessions

To the three-year-old, tidiness is incomprehensible and picking up toys is an interminable task to be avoided. His mother, trying to prepare dinner, must maneuver around his trucks and balls which have been left on the kitchen floor; his father wades through blocks and inadvertently crushes plastic toys in the living room; books, dolls, wagon, and tricycle are left out in the rain and ruined. His father roars at the disorder and carelessness; his mother pleads and scolds but is perplexed by how much help she should give the child in putting away his toys and how neat she should require him to be.

Similar disturbances occur daily over the child's scattering his clothing and dressing himself. He regularly loses one mitten and one shoe, and he can be counted on to kick his soiled clothing under the bed. Getting himself dressed is an infinitely tedious process, concluded by the child's presenting himself to his mother with most of his clothes on backwards. He rages at the difficulty he experiences, and his mother is torn between permitting him to manage alone or keeping order by continuing to be responsible for his clothes and dressing.

THE FOUR-YEAR-OLD

Kanner[11] spoke of the child's entering communal socialization at the age of four, when he begins to relinquish his inward attention to himself and to the immediate members of his family. As he moves out into the world, he sometimes attempts to direct it single-handed, but he takes with him the strength and familiarity of his home by conversing often about *his* parents, siblings, house, room, and possessions.

The new problems he presents to his parents are related to his increased encounters with a challenging and cool society. Difficulties center on his playmates, his restlessness, his aggressiveness, and his indecency.

Playmates

The four-year-old plays with both boys and girls but prefers a child of his own sex.[10] He spends more time with one child than another, and paired friendships can be long lasting and exclusive. His imitation of his best friend's swagger, off-color vocabulary, shoulder shrug, stutter, or belligerent stare discomfits his parents, who abhor the mannerism of the other child and feel their own is defiled by associating with him.

A mother aware of the need of her child for companions may find herself serving as an unpaid baby-sitter as indifferent or thoughtless parents turn their children loose to roam the neighborhood and spend their waking hours where they choose. Trouble between playmates is always arising. The young visitor complains to the mother that he is not allowed to have a toy he wants, and she must decide whether to take sides and if so, whose side to take.

If she is concerned about her child's social acceptability, the mother arranges, dominates, and eases social contacts for him, often causing the child to regard himself as an unnecessary third party to an association existing for the benefit of his mother and his peers. Sometimes the child is playing with others all day long, and he becomes tired and irritable from overstimulation.

At four years of age, the child is old enough to learn to coöperate with other children,[7] and if parental mismanagement of early peer contacts interferes with his learning to do so, he is handicapped socially both then and later.

Restlessness

Uncertain of themselves but committed to winning their friends' admiration, four-year-olds move at a whirlwind pace. They noisily chase each other, scream, jump on the furniture, giggle, laugh, and shout. They whirl around with their eyes closed until they fall, put on dancing acts, make faces, and crawl and growl like animals, working themselves up to a feverish pitch of hilarity.[6] Excessive activity can result in destruction of property and even in injury to the child, who is inattentive and impulsive during such performances.[16] He requires parental control and direction to ward off fatigue and tension developing from such a constant effort to entertain other children and to act as though he is having a good time.

Thompson[19] reported that two equated groups of four-year-olds were compared after being handled in different ways by teachers. In one group, the teachers were understanding and interested but permitted the children to plan their own activities, helping them only when specifically requested to do so. In the other, the teachers were friendly and coöperative, maintained considerable personal contact with the children, guided their activities, and spontaneously gave them help and information. After eight months, children in the second group participated more actively in social relationships than the others; and they were also less hostile, rejecting, persecuting, threatening, and destructive than the children left to their own devices.

Aggressiveness

Bullying and cruelty are natural reactions of the four-year-old.[11] He hits, pushes, shoves, grabs, and orders other children about as though he is irrevocably determined to have his own way in everything. He may try out this kind of aggression on his parents, although more often he wisely confines himself to verbal attacks. His behavior worries his parents, and they consider him both unpleasant and undisciplined.

His playmates, however, are trying as he does to demonstrate their own importance, and his life is harsh. Often he finds himself disdainfully left behind while two friends run off together, and his ability to ride his tricycle or to build a complicated sand castle is compared unfavorably by his hard-competing peers with their own.

The child's aggressive response to adult criticism or command often occurs after numerous unpleasant experiences at play. The child feels that this final insult to his dignity must be answered if he is not to run a poor last in every encounter.

Indecency

Associated with the four-year-old's aggressiveness is his lack of decorum and his abandonment of the proprieties. As he asserts his right to do as he chooses, he experiments with indecency. Four-year-olds urinate outdoors, more often than not in the presence of playmates, and sometimes display their genitals to each other. Children who have never seen the genitals of those of the opposite sex undress each other for examination. Masturbation may appear to be habitual because of the frequency with which the child grabs his genitals when he is worried or uncertain. In his verbal attacks on others, the child uses words he associates with elimination, and he repeats curses and obscenities that he has heard adults use.

Most parents react with shock and severe punishment for the child who behaves in these ways, failing to realize that the four-year-old's indecency is a facet of his aggressive independence, rather than evidence of abnormal sexual interest.

THE FIVE-YEAR-OLD

The accumulation of all that the child has learned from the time of birth is crystallized in the behavior of the five-year-old. By this time, he is more like himself than he is like other children his age, and his dependency on his family has decreased markedly.[17]

The following brief summaries of psychological examinations made of children to determine their readiness to enter kindergarten confirm the distinctive characteristics of individual five-year-olds.

Charles R. Average intelligence; siblings, aged 13, 12, 3. Good motor coordination, distractable, unsure of himself, would not try, speech difficult to understand. Mother is dominant, resentful of the freedom other mothers have, unconcerned about child's needs.

Sally M. Average intelligence; sibling, aged 2. Says she can't do things, then brags about how she can build a better castle or work stiff clay. Supercilious with examiner, but afraid away from mother. Mother is timid, kept child close to home, avoided tears by sneaking away from the clinic during child's examination.

Ronald A. Average intelligence; siblings, aged 17, 4, 3, 2. Docile, conforming, afraid to get dirty, verbally facile. He sometimes has nightmares and is enuretic. Mother is domineering with husband and neighbors, suspicious, discontented, and uses a paddle to force the children to eat.

Sarah C. Average intelligence; many siblings, all older. Alert, active, talks and hums, points out how pretty the things are which she makes, is eager, tries everything and is unconcerned about results, responds in exaggerated fashion, dramatizing herself and enjoying her performance. Mother is calm, seems to understand the child.

Larry D. Average intelligence; sibling, aged 3. Refuses suggestions for play, discontented, asks constant meaningless questions, vaguely expresses fears and feelings of inadequacy. Attacked his mother with a paint brush when she laughed at his false claim that he had a sister. Mother identifies with younger brother, punishes Larry more, forcing him to remain at the table until he eats.

Teresa M. Dull intelligence; sibling, aged 9 months. Unhappy, quiet, patiently continues tasks she is failing to accomplish, rare but negative verbalization. Mother avoids punishment, but her interest in child's activities is artificial, and the child ignores her.

John H. Average intelligence; no siblings. Negativistic, refused to follow suggestions, demanding and selfish. Mother gives him money and presents, dresses him, takes him visiting at night and permits him to stay up until parents retire. John throws stones at other children, is rude to adults and blames his imaginary playmate for these actions. The mother is ineffectual, the father disapproving.

Parents of the five-year-old are concerned if early difficulties with eating, sleeping, training, and insecurity have not been solved. The attitudes of persons outside the family toward the child now cause more problems because of their greater involvement with him. School attendance now confronts the family.

Persistence of Problems

Parents unsuccessful at solving problems which have endured over several years are discouraged and angry. Three times a day and each day of every year there may be a battle over the child's eating habits. If the child was a night wanderer at an early age or did not settle down to sleep without repeated demands on his parents, he may still be up half the night, and both he and his parents are irritable and unpredictable because of fatigue. Many five-year-olds are enuretic, and washing a daily allotment of wet sheets and underwear for a child of this age angers his mother, who feels sentenced to a distasteful and unnecessary task. Immature, insecure behavior in a five-year-old is a continuance of dependency reactions acquired at an earlier age.[9] Solitary play, clinging to adults, fearful crying, requesting help with tasks which other children perform by themselves, whining, and demanding special treatment seem inappropriate to the parents of a five-year-old.

The patient parent, at one time distressed by his child's unhappiness, can recognize no gains from his years of understanding tolerance. The impatient parent, long disgusted, becomes increasingly abusive and forceful as the child's early undesirable habits persist unchanged.

Relationships With Others

The five-year-old is sensitive to social situations and aware of status, and he feels some sense of shame when he does not fulfill his own or others' expectations.[6] His parents also are exposed increasingly to repercussions from the child's enlarged relationships with others.

Both children and adults evaluate his behavior and seek to revise it. His playmates complain about him or abuse him. Relatives' comments and concern sharpen. Neighbors may object to the child's behavior or discipline him. Nursery school and church school teachers may make casual observations which disturb parents. The child's loyalty to his playmates and his devotion to his teachers threaten the parents' position as prime recipients of his admiration.

The observations, reactions, and interference of others irritate and worry parents. They respond by acceding unwillingly to suggestions, rejecting them regardless of their merit, unwisely defending the child, or resentfully punishing him for any action which subjects them to outside criticism.

School Attendance

Now and for many years, the child must stand comparison with his peers as he begins to attend school. Because the pre-school child's playmates were limited to those in his immediate neighborhood, any comparisons the parents made were colored by their knowledge of conditions in individual families and tempered by the conviction that his companions were atypical. In school, however, placed with a group of unselected children of like chronological age, the child's deficiencies are apparent immediately and cannot be ignored. Parents may be notified by the teacher that the young scholar will not sing with the group and cannot draw a recognizable picture. They may be told that he sucks his thumb, grabs equipment, hides under the teacher's desk, does not know his address, cries when disciplined, or refuses to do his share at cleanup time.

The five-year-old may have to be convinced by his parents each day that he should go to school. When he pleads that he does not want to attend because he is tired or he has no fun or the teacher does not like him, his parents vacillate between accepting his excuses or forcing him to attend, uncertain which procedure is more harmful.

Concerned about his ability to manage without them, parents worry that other children will ignore or hurt him or that his teacher's criticism will damage his self-confidence and his pleasure in school. They expand his normal trepidation with their own, effusively assuring him that his teacher loves him and that school is a delightful place, thus arousing his suspicions that school attendance is a devious, adult plot to get rid of him and force him into unpleasant activities.

Although the child will encounter new conflicts and different challenges as he becomes older, the foundation for his response to his parents, to other people, and to frustration and defeat is established during these first six years. His behavior is predictable and his predominant characteristics are evident in many areas of his life. Parental attitudes about the child and methods of managing him also are established firmly by this time, and barring deliberate or traumatic interference, acquired modes of reaction of both parents and child will remain essentially the same for many years.

REFERENCES

1. Bandura, A., and Walters, R.: *Social Learning and Personality Development.* New York, Holt, Rinehart and Winston, 1963.
2. Bereiter, C.: Fluency abilities in preschool children. *J. Genet. Psychol.,* 1961, *98,* 47–48.

3. Brooks, F. D.: *Child Psychology*. Boston, Houghton Mifflin Co., 1937, p. 187.
4. Caldwell, B. M.: The effects of infant care. *In* Hoffman, M. L., and Hoffman, L. W., eds.: *Review of Child Development Research*, New York, Russell Sage Foundation, 1964, vol. 1, pp. 9–87.
5. Curti, M. W.: *Child Psychology*. New York, Longmans, Green and Co., 1938, p. 264.
6. Gesell, A., and Ilg, F. L.: *Infant and Child in the Culture of Today*. New York, Harper and Bros., 1943, p. 345.
7. Gottschaldt, K., and Frühauf-Ziegler, C.: Über die Entwicklung der Zusammenarbeit im Kleinkindalter (On the development of coöperative behavior in young children). *Z. Psychol.*, 1958, *162*, 254–278.
8. Hurlock, E. B.: *Child Development*. New York, McGraw-Hill Book Co., 1950, p. 590.
9. Jersild, A. T.: *Child Psychology*, Ed. 4. New York, Prentice-Hall, Inc., 1954, pp. 121, 136, 774–777.
10. Kagan, J., and Moss, H. A.: *Birth to Maturity*. New York, John Wiley and Sons, 1962, pp. 93–94, 123, 169.
11. Kanner, L.: *Child Psychiatry*, Ed. 3. Springfield, Ill., Charles C Thomas, 1957, pp. 43, 45.
12. Müller, A.: Über die Entwicklung des Leistungs-Anspruchsniveaus (On the development of a level of aspiration). *Z. Psychol.*, 1958, *162*, 238–253.
13. Mussen, P. H., and Conger, J. J.: *Child Development and Personality*. New York, Harper and Bros., 1956, pp. 297–298.
14. Sears, P. S., and Levin, H.: Levels of aspiration in pre-school children. *Child Developm.*, 1957, *28*, 317–326.
15. Spock, B.: *Baby and Child Care*. New York, Pocket Books, Inc., 1957, pp. 365–382.
16. Stewart, B. R.: Developmental differences in the stability of object preferences and conflict behavior. *Child Developm.*, 1958, *29*, 9–18.
17. Stith, M., and Connor, R.: Dependency and helpfulness in young children. *Child Developm.*, 1962, *33*, 15–20.
18. Thom, D. A.: *Everyday Problems of the Everyday Child*. New York, Appleton-Century, 1934, pp. 168, 183, 213.
19. Thompson, G. G.: The social and emotional development of preschool children under two types of educational program. *Psychol. Monogr.*, 1944, *56* (5).
20. Trapp, E. P., and Kausler, D. H.: Dominance attitudes in parents and adult avoidance behavior in young children. *Child Developm.*, 1958, *29*, 507–513.

Section Two

BEHAVIOR PROBLEMS

Chapter 16

Eating Problems

In a study of 100 normal young children, Foster and Anderson[7] found that feeding difficulties were encountered more frequently than any other single problem. A peak was reached at three years of age, but eating continued to be a problem with 25 per cent of these children until they reached six years. Among children brought to child guidance clinics for a variety of behavior disorders, 75 per cent also caused concern because of eating. Problems arise in connection with weaning, food refusal, dawdling, vomiting, and pica.

WEANING

Learning to feed himself, to relinquish his bottle, and to shift from liquids to strained food and then to table food are developmental hurdles for the child, and each can create balking and tears. If the child's weaning is delayed or managed either with severity or indecision, not only does he become frustrated[13] but his health and general development may be impaired.* Retaining infantile dependency in feeding causes him to respond immaturely in other areas of living. This behavior subjects him to ridicule, and he becomes defensive and resentful of peers and adults alike.

A one-year-old child cannot resist feeding himself with a spoon,[5, 12] and if he is allowed to practice alone, his skill increases quickly. Near the end of a meal, when he tires, his efforts can be supplemented by

---

* See Case 14, Bobby R., 506.

his mother.[15] He also can learn at an early age to manage a small glass if he is allowed to use one daily.

The child who clings to liquids or to strained foods should have solid food, limited in quantity and variety, offered at every meal. Crackers and cookies, which he can handle himself, aid his transition to solid food. A child who cries for a bottle long past the usual weaning age should be refused each time he asks, rather than occasionally being permitted to have one. If he knows that he may succeed in his demands, his attachment is prolonged and the persistence of his requests increases. Langdon[9] suggested that the child himself help dispose of bottles he no longer needs. A new toy to take to bed is a useful substitute for a night bottle.

FOOD REFUSAL

Food refusal occurs more commonly in children from homes where food is plentiful and appetites are satiated,[17] and problems often begin between one and two years of age.[15] At this time, the child's need for food normally decreases, and a shrinking intake alarms parents. They are unaware that although a healthy infant triples his weight during his first year of life, he gains only one third of this amount during his second year. Many pre-school children eat well at only one meal each day, and this meal usually is at noon.

The one-year-old frequently is promoted from solitary feeding to the family table, and the unaccustomed activity and conversation distract him from eating.[10] If he hears or sees his parents express aversion to any food, he imitates their behavior, broadening its scope.[1] Fatigue, illness, or insufficient exercise can cause him to be disinterested in food,[6] and every child experiences a normal variation in appetite from meal to meal and day to day. A young child learns to liven his day by exciting his parents with food refusals, and with innate skill he provokes them to wrath by asking for something to eat ten minutes after the conclusion of a meal he refused to touch.

Many parents attempt to compel eating because they are concerned about the child's health,[13] his resistance to their wishes, and the cost and effort involved in food preparation. In some families, every mealtime consists of an angry tirade of orders and threats.[3] A few children routinely remain at the table two hours after a meal is over, under sentence to clean their plates before they can leave. Others are required to consume the uneaten remains of the previous meal before starting the new one. Belts and paddles are conspicuously displayed and sometimes used. A child bullied into eating three times every day dreads mealtimes. He loses all appetite for food, as fear and anger inhibit the normal functioning of digestive glands and muscles.[1]

To reverse a child's consistent refusal of food, the negative attitudes he has acquired toward it must be eliminated. Overstimulation and parental urging can be prevented if the child eats alone and is permitted to leave the table when he decides he is finished.[4, 5, 6, 19] Quantities should be small, finger foods should be common, and food he prefers should be served exclusively for a time, even if this means peanut butter sandwiches for breakfast, lunch, and dinner. Nonnutritious, filling foods he may enjoy, such as huge pieces of cake, soft drinks, and potato chips, are not mealtime fare, however. Straight-handled, small silverware, dishes with straight sides, and small plastic glasses make eating easy to manage.[19]

Sometimes parents try to solve a child's food refusal by giving him nothing to eat except at meals. Because of his tension at that time, however, he is not hungry, and if he is not permitted to eat when he is relaxed, his appetite decreases steadily and he loses all desire for food. In contrast, other parents let a finicky eater help himself to food all day long, and he never is hungry at mealtime.

When a child seldom wants food at mealtime, he should eat between meals, although what he eats, and to some extent when he eats, can be controlled.[4, 10, 19] He can have fruit juice and a cracker or plain cooky regularly at midmorning and midafternoon; and a dish containing small portions of raw fruits and vegetables can be kept in the refrigerator and the child can be allowed to help himself at any time, even immediately after a regular meal is over. In this way neither his appetite nor his food consumption is eliminated completely, and he retains choice but not complete control over every aspect of eating.

A mother can decrease her tendency to urge or to force eating if she substitutes foods of equivalent nutritive value for those temporarily refused, such as fruits for vegetables and bread for cereals. Keeping a daily record of everything the child eats assures her that he is receiving nourishment despite mealtime refusals.[19]

DAWDLING

The dawdling child exasperates his parents, who finish an entire meal while he takes two or three bites, holding each one in his mouth for long minutes without attempting to chew and swallow it. Many young children, tired from play or not yet fully awake in the morning, daydream through a meal, unable to summon the energy to feed themselves. Sometimes a child eats slowly as an aftermath of prolonged refusal to eat and lack of interest in food. Or he may be too busy to eat because he is trying to hold the attention of his assembled parents and siblings

by talking, arguing, or annoying them. Occasionally a child stalls at mealtime to avoid what will come at its conclusion: naptime, bedtime, cleaning up his room, or having to sit on the toilet.[4] Slow eaters sometimes
are children who were not allowed to feed themselves when they wished
to do so and who ceased to take responsibility for eating.[5] The one-
year-old, testing his mother, delays his eating by playing with his food
and using his high chair for acrobatics.

Dawdling will be prolonged if the parents, after urging and threats
have proved useless, feed the child themselves,[2] because he learns to
wait for their assistance. The small child will pay attention to his meal
if his playing is considered a signal that he is finished and he is removed
from his high chair when he starts to climb or throw food.[15] The older
child who dawdles should eat alone. He should be given small quantities
of preferred foods which he can handle easily. Calling him in from outdoor play at least 30 minutes before mealtime calms him so that he is
not excited when his food is ready.[1] If he is drowsy in the morning, his
breakfast can be delayed until he has been awake for an hour. Limiting
eating time to 30 or 40 minutes and then removing his food without
comment teaches him that if he wants his meal he must eat it with
reasonable dispatch.[19]

VOMITING

Illness usually is and should be a parent's first thought when a child
vomits. However, if vomiting occurs without other indications of illness,
with regularity, and only in certain situations, then probably it is being
induced by the child, who has learned that it effectively produces anxiety
in his parents.[8]

Vomiting may be precipitated the first time by physiological factors.
When a child is forced to eat something he does not like, he tends to
gag, and the choking, aided by tense stomach muscles, causes regurgita-
tion of food. A child who is furiously angry and crying hard vomits because his muscles and glands are diffusely overactive. If the child notices
that vomiting produces parental concern and accession to his wishes,
he uses it automatically when he is thwarted. His mother submits to
prevent his making himself "sick with disappointment."

When a relationship between vomiting and parental control is apparent, adults must not permit vomiting to win arguments. They need
to refrain from showing sympathy and to enlist the child's aid in cleaning up. If vomiting occurs only at mealtime, it provides clear evidence
that force and food are incompatible and that reasonable methods are
needed to alter the child's eating habits.

PICA

Pica, a craving for unnatural foods, presents a problem in the management of some pre-school children. Most small children at some time consume substances never meant for humans, and there are few who do not sample sand or chew on grass, twigs, and leaves. When a baby's gums are tingling from erupting teeth, he gnaws on crib rails and furniture, absorbing both paint and wood in unusual quantities.

Besides these common kinds of experimentation, children have been known to eat nearly every inedible substance imaginable, sometimes with gusto. Among the substances eaten by 30 children described by Kanner[8] were dirt, rags, splinters, ashes, plaster, match heads, shoestrings, hair, rubber, coal, stones, toys, buttons, clothing, soap, thread, paper, sticks, bugs, feces, polish, and oilcloth. Most of these children were two or three years old, and many were retarded. Inadequate diet and neglect were related to the persistence of their pica.

Pica can have serious physical consequences, such as constipation, anemia, and intestinal obstruction from accumulated hair, rags, and thread in the colon. Lead encephalopathy produces severe abnormalities in behavior and development.[8, 14]

More nutritious food should be given the child with pica, and inedible substances should be cleaned up or kept out of his reach. He must be closely supervised so that he can be restrained from consuming forbidden matter and offered food instead. Playing with the child each day provides him with the personal attention he often has lacked.

REFERENCES

1. Aldrich, C. A.: Appetites in babies. In *The Mother's Encyclopedia*, New York, The Parents' Institute, Inc., 1933, vol. 1, pp. 67–72.
2. Alschuler, R. H.: Habit training. In *The Mother's Encyclopedia*, New York, The Parents' Institute, Inc., 1933, vol. 2, pp. 342–344.
3. Blanton, S., and Blanton, M.: *Child Guidance*. New York, The Century Co., 1927, pp. 38–53.
4. Breckenridge, M., and Murphy, M.: *Growth and Development of the Young Child*, Ed. 6. Philadelphia, W. B. Saunders Co., 1958, pp. 239, 244, 246.
5. Edge, P.: *Child Care and Management*. London, Faber and Faber Ltd., 1962, pp. 106–107.
6. Faegre, M. L., and Anderson, J. E.: *Child Care and Training*, Ed. 4. Minneapolis, University of Minnesota Press, 1937, pp. 129–141.
7. Foster, J. C., and Anderson, J. E.: *The Young Child and His Parents. A Study of One Hundred Cases*, Ed. 2. Institute of Child Welfare Monograph Series No. 1. Minneapolis, University of Minnesota Press, 1930.
8. Kanner, L.: *Child Psychiatry*, Ed. 3. Springfield, Ill., Charles C Thomas, 1957, pp. 470–477, 487–492.
9. Langdon, G.: Weaning the baby. In *The Mother's Encyclopedia*. New York, The Parents' Institute, Inc., 1933, vol. 4, pp. 892–896.

10. Langford, L. M.: *Guidance of the Young Child*. New York, John Wiley and Sons, 1960, pp. 206–222.
11. Lapin, J. H.: Common errors in infant feeding. *J. Pediat.*, 1954, *45*, 583–589.
12. Peck, L.: *Child Psychology*. Boston, D. C. Heath and Co., 1953, p. 51.
13. Sears, R. R., Maccoby, E. E., and Levin, H.: *Patterns of Child Rearing*. Evanston, Ill., Row, Peterson and Co., 1957, pp. 92–93.
14. Smith, H. D., Baehner, R. L., Carney, T., and Majors, W. J.: The sequelae of pica with and without lead poisoning. *Amer. J. Dis. Child.*, 1963, *105*, 609–616.
15. Spock, B.: *Baby and Child Care*. New York, Pocket Books, Inc., 1957, pp. 188, 278, 299–302.
16. Stimson, P. M.: Feeding problems. In *The Mother's Encyclopedia*, New York, The Parents' Institute, Inc., 1933, vol. 2, pp. 291–296.
17. Teagarden, F. M.: *Child Psychology for Professional Workers*. New York, Prentice-Hall, Inc., 1940, pp. 177–181.
18. Thompson, J. McK.: Survey of the literature on psychological aspects of eating in infancy and early childhood. *Psychol. Serv. Center J.*, 1950, *3*, 203–226.
19. Verville, E.: What to do when your child refuses to eat. *Parents' Magazine, 27* (5), 42.

Chapter *17*

Sleeping Problems

Prompt solution of sleep disturbances is essential[4] because lack of rest creates irritability and decreased tolerance in the child, because daily unresolved battles over sleeping habits produce ill feeling between parents and child, and because the success of the child in controlling his parents by resisting their desire that he rest makes him anxious about their ability to care for him. Parents themselves develop anxiety, anger, and guilt feelings when they fail to solve the child's problems with sleep.[6]

Resistance to sleeping and night wandering are common problems in the pre-school child.[13]

RESISTANCE TO SLEEPING

Early in the child's life, his parents discover that he does not conform to their expectation of round-the-clock eating and sleeping. Within two or three months, however, wakefulness caused by incoördinated functioning of the infant's physiological processes disappears, and the baby settles into a sleep routine adequate for his needs. If parents retain their anxiety about the child's sleep beyond this adjustment period and continue to pick him up whenever he cries, he becomes tense, tired, and wakeful because he is not left alone long enough to compose himself for sleep.

Any child over two years of age, tired or not, can postpone sleep for two or three hours after he is put to bed.[12] Young children cry in pitiful whimpers or indignant screams; older ones repeatedly summon their parents with requests for drinks, conversation, or trips to the bathroom.

The child resists bedtime because he does not like to be excluded from parental activities;[2] and, prevented from joining the adults in the living room, he arranges for them to visit him in his bedroom.

A pre-school child may resist sleep because he is afraid of the dark or worried about his parents' leaving him. Unprepared for a sitter, small children have wakened to find their parents gone and a stranger with them, and they have shown their fear of sleeping for many weeks afterward.[12]

Failure to maintain a regular time for going to bed guarantees that the child will protest every night. Because of occasional or frequent success with pleas to postpone bedtime, a late nap or none at all, or evening shopping trips or visits, the child is variously put to bed as early as 6 o'clock or as late as midnight.

A child may be too tense and excited to feel drowsy at bedtime because he has been wrestling with his father,[10] company has arrived, older children are arguing or playing, or he has been absorbed in watching television. When his parents are impatient and hasty about bedtime routines, he is resistive to sleep.[9] Letting a child stay up late as a reward or sending him to bed as punishment adds to the natural attractiveness of avoiding bed. Listening to his parents discuss their late hours or restless sleep provides him with a model for his own sleep habits.[3]

A child may refuse to sleep unless his mother lies down with him or unless he is allowed to sleep in his parents' bed with them. One tiny mother climbed into her pre-schooler's crib each afternoon to coax him to nap. A child permitted to sleep with his mother when the father is out of town often continues to do so into adolescence. Other children move into the parents' bed after they have wet their own, have been wakened by storms, or have become lonely at night. Although parents' amiability suffers the next day because of the child's kicking and crowding, most of them believe that the child really needs to be with them and that they would be unkind and selfish if they refused him.

Arguments about bedtime and schemes to postpone sleep should not continue. The child needs his rest, and the parents need time away from him for each other and their own interests. Both the infant and the older child learn that crying or calling out does not work if the parents do not respond.[11] Bedtime routine should provide for all of the child's needs, and after saying goodnight, the parents must be as resolute about refusing to answer the child's calls as he is persistent about making them. Most small children left alone fall asleep within 20 minutes after they go to bed.[3] Bedtime should be the same every night,[2, 3, 9] as should afternoon naps or rests, and these need to be terminated early enough to protect night sleep. Pre-school children should neither be taken out at night nor kept up when the family has company.

The hour before bedtime should be used for relaxing, with time provided for a long bath, conversation, and stories.[8, 12] The child is free to decide when he is ready for sleep if he is permitted to have a bed toy with which he can play quietly, but resting is assured by his parents' adherence to a regular bedtime.

Deliberately changing routines in slight ways enables the child to sleep despite differences in the procedure and the supervisor. The father should help the child prepare for bed once or twice a week so that he can go to bed on time when his mother is gone for the evening. A sitter can put an infant to bed while the mother is nearby. Parents going out at night must always tell the child when they are leaving and when they will return,[8] and if possible the child should have some time to talk and play with the sitter.

The child who cannot sleep unless he is with his parents needs to find comfort in his own bed and courage within himself. The only cure is to cease permitting him to join his parents in their bed. The child accustomed to napping only when his mother sleeps with him can be allowed to rest, rather than be required to sleep. If he is fearful during a storm, he should be returned to his own bed, but the parent's sitting near him until he falls asleep again is reassuring.[12]

NIGHT WANDERING

Leaving his bed and prowling the house at night is a habit which the child develops early and which can persist for years. The two-year-old who has learned how to climb out of his crib delights in practicing his new skill and does so repeatedly. If his appearance in the living room is greeted more with admiration than censure, he correctly concludes that both he and his parents are benefited by his joining them. When getting up at night offers shared fun and special attention, it becomes the expected and preferred behavior.

Having learned that getting up is permissible, the child may do so after his parents have gone to sleep. One three-year-old regularly left his bed, turned on the light, looked at magazines, emptied ashtrays, tidied up the living room, and then returned to bed. Other children are not so handy at amusing themselves in the dead of night, and they get their parents up to read or play with them.

Related to night wandering is a small child's habit of getting up early in the morning and roaming the neighborhood. A four-year-old climbed into a neighbor's car, released the brake, and involved himself in a slight accident before returning home to his sleeping family.

The child who has learned to leave his bed whenever he is awake does not get enough rest, and his fatigue affects all of his behavior. To teach him that he must remain in bed, he should be returned there promptly each time he leaves. Spock[12] suggested tying a net over the top of the crib during the period when the child is experimenting with climbing out, providing this does not make him fearful or angry. Once he learns to get out of his crib, however, little is gained by leaving him in it, and changing him to a youth bed eliminates his need to climb and gives him more space in which to move around.

Regular and sufficient attention and fun during the day with both playmates and parents decrease the child's need to seek diversion at night.

REFERENCES

1. Anthony, J.: An experimental approach to the psychopathology of childhood: Sleep disturbances. *Brit. J. Med. Psychol.*, 1959, *32*, 19–37.
2. Blanton, S., and Blanton, M.: *Child Guidance.* New York, The Century Co., 1927, pp. 71–76.
3. Faegre, M. L., and Anderson, J. E.: *Child Care and Training*, Ed. 8. Minneapolis, University of Minnesota Press, 1958, Chapter 9.
4. Fischle-Carl, H.: Ein Beitrag zur Kasuistik schlafgestörter Kinder (A contribution to case histories of children with sleep disturbances). *Prax. Kinderpsychol., Kinderpsychiat.*, 1955, *4*, 37–40.
5. Gesell, A., and Ilg, F. L.: *Infant and Child in the Culture of Today.* New York, Harper and Bros., 1943, pp. 182, 303.
6. Hirschberg, J. C.: Parental anxieties accompanying sleep disturbance in young children. *Bull. Menninger Clin.*, 1957, *21*, 129–139.
7. Illingworth, R. S.: Sleep problems in the first three years. *Brit. Med. J.*, 1951, *1*, 722–728.
8. Langdon, G.: Sleep routine. In *The Mother's Encyclopedia*, New York, The Parents' Institute, Inc., 1933, vol. 4, pp. 764–773.
9. Langford, L. M.: *Guidance of the Young Child.* New York, John Wiley and Sons, 1960, pp. 187–199.
10. Peck, L.: *Child Psychology.* Boston, D. C. Heath and Co., 1954, p. 54.
11. Rogers, R. R.: Crying. In *The Mother's Encyclopedia*, New York, The Parents' Institute, Inc., 1933, vol. 1, p. 184.
12. Spock, B.: *Baby and Child Care.* New York, Pocket Books, Inc., 1957, pp. 164, 182, 186–187, 273, 351.
13. Wyss, R.: Schlafstörungen bei Kindern (Disturbances of sleep in children). *Heilpädag. Werkbl.*, 1957, *26*, 194–197.

Chapter **18**

Problems of Elimination

Permanent uncertainties and antagonisms between mother and child have developed from problems with elimination. Toilet training is an arduous process, resulting in months of interminable interruptions of the mother's activities with hasty trips to the bathroom. The child fails unpredictably and often, and his failures disappoint or anger his mother, whose feelings about her unsuccessful teaching permeate her behavior with him in other situations.

Bowel training usually is introduced when the child can sit alone steadily, at about nine months of age, and the mother places him on the toilet whenever she observes by his straining that a movement is imminent.[25] The child's playing with his feces or adorning his bed or the wall with it is no indication of depravity. He uses fecal matter just as he does clay or mud, and prevention requires only snug diapering for the infant and prompt emptying of the chamber after an older child's defecation.[11]

When a child is between 15 and 18 months old and can hold urine for as long as two hours, he can be taken to the toilet routinely after naps and at two-hour intervals through the day. He begins to take responsibility himself for getting to the bathroom when he is able to use a word to signal his need to urinate.

Children learn to stay dry at night without any effort on their parents' part to train them. Spock[25] pointed out that most children are dry at night spontaneously between two and three years, and one in every 100 is dry by 12 months. Less urine is produced when the child is quiet, and the bladder's capacity is not reached as quickly at night. Because their nervous systems mature more rapidly, girls are more apt learners than

145

boys at all stages of training,[4] and boys have continuing problems with controlling elimination much more frequently than girls.

Complete training requires closely coördinated interaction of a child's nerves and muscles. The child must learn to recognize the sensations of a full bladder or bowel, retain the contents until he reaches the toilet, and then relax the muscles he has held in contraction.[25] Such control takes time and attention, and parents who expect instantaneous learning erroneously attribute the child's unusual behavior during training to a desire to dupe them or to his deliberate refusal to practice what he is taught.

The young child undergoing training often signals after he has urinated instead of before, proudly announcing "Tinkle!" as he points to the puddle he has just made. His discouraged mother does not understand that his associating a word with urination, even though the order is reversed, indicates that he is learning something about what she is trying to teach him. Prior signalling is possible only when he associates the word with the pressure of a full bladder and also is able to retain urine until he reaches the bathroom.

A mother also feels victimized when, after rushing the child to the bathroom on his urgent signal, nothing happens. She finally gives up and takes him off the toilet, and he then immediately wets all over his clothes and the floor. No matter how the situation appears, the child was not trying to fool or anger her. Tense with expectancy that success was near, he could not release his contracted muscles, but off the toilet and the excitement over, his muscles relaxed spontaneously.

Besides these common misunderstandings and disappointments of the training process, there are more enduring problems associated with elimination. These are enuresis, encopresis, regression in training, and constipation.

ENURESIS

Enuresis is involuntary micturition after the age of three years, although nocturnal wetting in boys is not considered unusual until after the age of four years. Powell[19] stated that 15 per cent of all children are enuretic, and over two thirds of these are boys.[11, 25] Greater frequency occurs among children referred to guidance clinics, and for this population percentages ranging from 26 per cent to 50 per cent have been reported, with the highest frequency among the youngest children.[11, 14] Kanner[11] observed that 30 per cent of the children he studied were enuretic both day and night, 63 per cent wet nocturnally only, and 7 per cent diurnally only. Half of the group wet daily.

In determining the reasons for a child's enuresis, physical abnormalities should not be overlooked, and every enuretic child should be examined by his physician for bladder or urine irregularities.

A child who wets himself during the day often is excited and pre-occupied or reluctant to leave his play, and he worries that his friends will disappear while he is in the bathroom. Some children have developed unpleasant associations with the bathroom because of unhappy experiences there or fear of the flushing toilet. Others obviously know that wetting is impending: They jump around, hold onto their genitals, and cross or squeeze their legs together. They loudly insist that they do not need to go to the bathroom and seem unperturbed by accidents. These children are enuretic as an expression of generalized resistance to parental wishes.

The child who wets his bed has been described as one who feels isolated and rejected.[3, 5] He neither competes satisfyingly with his peers nor has a close relationship with his parents and siblings. Sibling rivalry is sometimes a factor,[19] with enuresis utilized by the child to gain his parents' attention, unfavorable though it may be.[11]

Many enuretic boys are overly dependent on their mothers, who carefully direct everything they do and fail to provide them with opportunities to play with boys their own age. Sometimes nocturnal enuresis appears first when a boy starts to kindergarten and receives daily and humiliating doses of aggression from other children, with whom he feels inadequate and strange. Enuretic girls tend to be masculine, competitive, and disdainful of femininity; and they seem to be trying to accomplish more than they can manage. Feeling different from other girls, but unable to compete successfully with boys, they are lonesome and dissatisfied with themselves. The inadequate and lonely child, who prefers undisturbed comfort and habitually retreats from unpleasantries, assures himself of uninterrupted sleep by relieving the unpleasant sensation of bladder pressure with as little effort as possible.[15]

Rigid training procedures and punitive attitudes lead to enuresis. The child who fails to respond to training in accordance with parental expectations and who elicits the adults' anger and severe punishment is frightened by their violent reaction and his control diminishes.[6, 20] Some children lie awake for hours at night, fearful of wetting the bed if they fall asleep.

Other parents are tolerant of or indifferent to wetting, telling the child that he has inherited weak kidneys or making no attempt to keep clean bedding and night clothes on the child. One small child was bedded down in the hall on a pile of old blankets reeking with urine from his nightly wettings. If the child imitates his parents in ignoring his enuresis, it persists for years.

Many enuretic children gain control spontaneously as maturity increases, and they are praised for success.[23] Persistent enuresis, however, emphasizes to the child that he is immature, usually creates negative feelings between him and his parents, and leads to the development of other neurotic symptoms.[27] Consequently, early eradication of the problem is needed.

Therapy for the enuretic child in the past has included such measures as surgery, the use of mechanical devices, drugs, diet control, bed rest, and hypnosis.[11] Severe punishment and shaming are common motivating techniques.[3, 19]

Less emotional methods of solving the problem have been directed toward keeping scant amounts of urine in the bladder by restricting fluid intake before bedtime and by getting the child up during the night to use the bathroom. Although the avoidance of an excessive accumulation of urine is reasonable, taking the child to the bathroom at night only confirms his opinion of his general inadequacy and also permits him to vacate his responsibility for solving the problem.

An enuretic child learns to attend appropriately to bladder stimulation only when he holds himself accountable for overcoming the difficulty. He needs to know that other children have the same problem but learn to conquer it.[2, 11] A chart on which dry nights can be indicated encourages and rewards him, and a prize for five dry nights gives him incentive to become alert to toileting requirements.

A boy feels more capable if he is given increased responsibility in all areas of living. Daily chores, relaxation of directions and supervision by his mother, and friendly association with his father build his self-confidence.[25] His contacts with other boys his age away from home should be increased. An enuretic girl can learn to enjoy feminine activities. Mixing up cookies, splashing in dishwater, and helping her mother hang up clothes and vacuum the rug are fun and can help her to become closer to her mother. Playing regularly with other girls lessens her feeling of being an outcast.

Conditioning techniques have proved successful in retraining enuretics. Mowrer and Mowrer[16] found that children between the ages of three and 13 years achieved dryness within four to eight weeks when conditioned to wake and go to the bathroom on hearing a bell. The bell was wired to ring as soon as a few drops of urine wet the mat on which the child slept. Providing the child with a flashlight or leaving a dim light on in the bathroom helps him get about at night independently.

Some pediatricians recommend giving the enuretic child extra amounts of fluid during the day and instructing him to retain urine as long as possible. This practice serves to alert him more often to the feeling of pressure of a full bladder and also increases his retentive ability. Holding greater amounts of fluid may stretch the capacity of an unusually small bladder and enable it to store more urine than formerly.

The child who wets in the daytime needs retraining, and he should go to the toilet every two hours, although his verdict concerning whether he can or cannot urinate should be accepted after five minutes. The mother should keep out of the bathroom, and if the child is afraid of the toilet's flushing, she can take care of this after he has left. When the child shows that he needs to go to the bathroom, his parents should insist on his doing so, assuring him that whoever is playing with him will be there when he returns.

ENCOPRESIS

Encopresis is persistent soiling by a child over two years of age. Sometimes encopresis can be attributed to failure to learn bowel control because of low intelligence or parental neglect of training.[1] Spasms or constriction of the anal sphincter may cause soiling. Lempp[13] found brain damage and subsequent weak cortical control in encopretic children. Pick[18] considered constipation to be three times more common as a cause of encopresis than psychogenic factors are. When a constipated child has had a painfully hard movement and does not wish to risk another, he avoids going to the bathroom, and fecal matter finally is expelled when it can no longer be retained.[11]

Soiling has been interpreted as an expression of resistance to parents, and encopresis frequently follows coercive bowel training.[1] Garrard and Richmond[8] stated that the encopretic children they studied were conforming and obedient but seemed immature and did not get along with other children.

Some small children avoid the toilet because they fear the flushing or dislike the bathroom, and they defecate when they must wherever they happen to be, often hiding the feces to avoid punishment.[11] A busy child, reluctant to interrupt his play, believes he can hold a bowel movement, delays going to the bathroom too long, and eventually soils himself.

Shaming and threatening the child, requiring him to wash the soiled clothing, dosing him with medicines and vitamins, and punishing him severely have all been used by parents of encopretic children in attempts to solve the problem.

Consistent retraining is more effective. The child needs to become aware of the sensation of a full bowel, to regain voluntary muscle control, and to go to the bathroom promptly on signal from bowel muscles. Reacquiring this sequence necessitates practice, and using time taken from more attractive activities focuses the child's attention on what he is to learn. The encopretic child should sit on the toilet for ten minutes twice daily and attempt to move his bowels, but he should not be scolded for failure nor kept there longer than the set time.

If soiling continues at the same rate after this routine has been maintained for two weeks, then the child can be required to try three or four times each day in the same way. If handled encouragingly, rather than punitively, practice in evacuating on the toilet enables the child to attend to bowel muscle contractions, and concomitantly decreases constipation when it is a contributing cause. The child learns that failure to defecate in the toilet on his own initiative results in regular interruption of his play.

This kind of retraining does not parallel the child's experience when he is punished for soiling by being forced to remain on the toilet for increasingly lengthy periods of time. Anger and resentment over this parental injustice will provoke him to prolong his soiling from spite, when originally this factor did not contribute to the problem.

REGRESSION IN TRAINING

Occasional accidents and failures in training during the pre-school years are to be expected, but sometimes a child who has shown good control lapses into repeated daily failures.

Perfect control of elimination requires close attention to bodily sensations, and often the child's regression appears because he considers knowledge of toilet use to be accomplished, and he turns his attention to new achievements. His attention also wanes when toilet supervision becomes more lax or when his eating and sleeping routines are disrupted temporarily because his mother is too busy to give him accustomed care. This latter situation occurs when the family moves or visits relatives or when an illness in the family claims the mother's time.

Anxiety distracts the child. He may be so frightened by an unfamiliar sitter that he cannot confide his need to go to the bathroom, or the adult may not understand his signal word. Fears related to parental quarreling or aggressive playmates keep a child tense and unobservant to bladder pressure.

Regression in a child's toilet habits at the time a new baby arrives is a familiar story, but it is caused as often by changes in routine and the abrupt deterioration in parental attention as it is by imitation of the baby. Training introduced because a baby is anticipated may be ill timed for the maturity of the child, and having been established only precariously, it cannot be maintained without close supervision.

An overexcited or tired child often wets or soils himself. A small child cannot maintain consistent control when he is surrounded constantly by other children and adults, is taken to late movies, watches frightening television programs, or receives insufficient sleep.

The regressing child needs regularity of routine, consistency of attention, and a reduction in exciting or anxiety-arousing situations. His regular mealtime and bedtime schedules should be observed, regardless of where he is, and the mother should not become so involved in conversation or her own activities that she fails to heed signs that the child needs to go to the bathroom or forgets to follow his usual toileting routine.

Regression which is not traceable to temporary changes or which occurs in a child who is not overly stimulated nor subjected to a variable routine is an indication that he needs to begin again. Training should be reintroduced, and the child should be sent or taken to the toilet at two-hour intervals to accustom him once more to its use.

CONSTIPATION

Constipation in a child often is reported when none exists. Many mothers believe that failure of the child to have a movement each day is abnormal. A breast-fed baby, however, has fewer movements than a bottle-fed baby, and often the breast-fed baby evacuates only every other day, a habit which may continue when he becomes older.

If a child's movements are irregular and the mother tends to be a strict or protective person, she does not accept the normality of the child's evacuation pattern and becomes so concerned that she decides to take charge of managing the bowels herself.[11, 12] She requires the child to sit on the toilet for hours, and she administers suppositories, enemas, and laxatives daily to induce a movement. One mother reported emotional and tiring two-hour periods spent every day in the bathroom with her three-year-old daughter, during which pleading, medicine, and entertainment were employed without effect. Artificial inducement of movements, instead of ensuring regularity of bowel function, reduces muscle tone and decreases the ability of the child to evacuate independently and voluntarily.

Constipation also develops in the small child who is too busy to go to the bathroom and habitually ignores the sensation of contracting bowel muscles. When there is no response to contractions, they cease, and fecal material is retained for long periods of time. Because of the retention, the movement is large, painful, and time consuming, and the child postpones this unpleasant task as long as possible, thus setting up a cycle which perpetuates constipation.

Information about normal irregularity can be given a mother to reassure her that a child does not suffer if he misses a daily movement. Enemas, suppositories, and laxatives should be used only under a physician's direction and in an orderly reduction until they are no longer administered. The child can drink more water and have mildly laxative foods such as prunes or molasses, which help soften fecal masses. These steps are reasonable substitutes for the specific and unusual efforts directed toward deliberately moving the bowels regardless of readiness or need.

If since infancy the child has had his bowel movements at a fairly regular time during the day, encouraging him to continue to try to do so takes advantage of his body's natural rhythm and ensures that time is provided for him to evacuate. If the child does not have a movement at this time, it is unimportant, providing that he understands that he should go to the bathroom promptly whenever he needs to do so. If there is no preferred time of evacuation and constipation is severe, daily ten-minute sessions alone after breakfast and dinner help to direct the child's attention to bowel function.

REFERENCES

1. Anthony, E. J.: An experimental approach to the psychopathology of childhood: Encopresis. *Brit. J. Med. Psychol.*, 1957, *30*, 146–175.
2. Blanton, S., and Blanton, M.: *Child Guidance.* New York, The Century Co., 1927, pp. 65–66.
3. Bostock, J.: Enuresis and toilet training. *Med. J. Aust.*, 1951, 2, 110–113.
4. Breckenridge, M., and Murphy, M.: *Growth and Development of the Young Child,* Ed. 7. Philadelphia, W. B. Saunders Co., 1963.
5. Decurtins, F.: Bettnässen in psychiatrischer Sicht (Bedwetting from the psychiatric point of view). *Heilpädag. Werkbl.*, 1957, *26*, 197–201.
6. Faegre, M. L., and Anderson, J. E.: *Child Care and Training,* Ed. 8. Minneapolis, University of Minnesota Press, 1958.
7. Galton, L.: What's normal for your child? *Family Circle,* September, 1963, 99.
8. Garrard, S. D., and Richmond, J. B.: Psychogenic megacolon manifested by fecal soiling. *Pediatrics,* 1952, *10,* 474–483.
9. Gesell, A., and Ilg, F. L.: *Infant and Child in the Culture of Today.* New York, Harper and Bros., 1943, p. 321.
10. Jones, H. G.: Specific conditioning treatment of enuresis nocturna. *Cerebral Palsy Bull.,* 1961, *3,* 227–236.
11. Kanner, L.: *Child Psychiatry,* Ed. 3. Springfield, Ill., Charles C Thomas, 1957, pp. 410–416, 439–452.
12. Langford, L. M.: *Guidance of the Young Child.* New York, John Wiley and Sons, 1960, p. 160. .
13. Lempp, R.: Zur Ätiologie des kindlichen Einstuhlens (The etiology of fecal soiling in children). *Z. Psychother. Med. Psychol.,* 1956, 6, 206–218.
14. Levy, D.: *Maternal Overprotection.* New York, Columbia University Press, 1943, p. 188.
15. Meyerhardt, O.: Al hamekhanizm shel hartavat layla (On the mechanism of enuresis nocturna). *Harefuah,* 1957, *52,* 258–260.
16. Mowrer, O. H., and Mowrer, W. M.: Enuresis—a method for its study and treatment. *Amer. J. Orthopsychiat.,* 1938, 8, 436–459.
17. Müller, E.: Zur Behandlung der Bettnässer in den Erziehungsheimen für Schwererziehbare (On treatment of enuretics in institutions for children with behavior problems). *Heilpädag. Werkbl.,* 1957, *26,* 202–205.
18. Pick, W.: Fecal soiling due to paradoxic constipation. *Amer. J. Dis. Children,* 1963, *105,* 229–233.
19. Powell, N. B.: Urinary incontinence in children. *Arch. Pediat.,* 1951, *68,* 151–157.
20. Probst, E.: Sauberkeit und Bettnässen (Cleanliness and bedwetting). *Heilpädag. Werkbl.,* 1957, *26,* 205–211.

21. Richter, H.: Beobachtungen an 14 Kindern mit chronisher Obstipation (Observations of 14 children with chronic constipation). *Psyche (Heidel.)*, 1958, *12*, 291–308.
22. Salfield, D. F.: Enuresis: addenda after two-and-a-half years. *Z. Kinderpsychiat.*, 1956, *23*, 107–111.
23. Salfield, D. F.: Enuresis—with special consideration of the nocturnal type encountered in children. *Z. Kinderpsychiat.*, 1954, *21*, 1–8.
24. Segall, A.: Report of a constipated child with fecal withholding. *Amer. J. Orthopsychiat.*, 1957, *27*, 823–829.
25. Spock, B.: *Baby and Child Care*. New York, Pocket Books, Inc., 1957, pp. 246–260. 503–507.
26. Thom, D. A.: *Everyday Problems of the Everyday Child*. New York, Appleton-Century, 1934, p. 96.
27. Werczberger, A.: Zur Katamnase der Enuresis Nocturna (Concerning the catamnesis of nocturnal enuresis). *Prax. Kinderpsychol., Kinderpsychiat.*, 1959, *8*, 42–52.

Chapter 19

Manipulative
Motor Habits

Head-banging and rocking, thumb-sucking, masturbation, hair-pulling, and tics are manipulative motor habits of the pre-school child which cause parents concern. These forms of behavior are less accessible to correction by retraining than are problems with eating, sleeping, and elimination, and parents feel frustrated by their inability to rid the child of them. Parents are embarrassed by the unfavorable comments these habits attract, and they are troubled by the belief that these habits indicate immaturity or acute tension in the child.

HEAD-BANGING AND ROCKING

Lourie[15] reported that 15 to 20 per cent of an unselected group of young children was found to engage in head-banging, rocking, or swaying —the onset of these activities being from two months to two years of age and ceasing by the age of three years. DeLissovoy[4] studied 22 boys and ten girls with a mean age of 26.6 months who were habitual head-bangers. Most of the children rocked or banged their heads prior to sleeping, and they rocked on their hands and knees and from sitting, prone, standing, and kneeling positions.

Rhythmical movement and monotonous sound patterns soothe the newborn infant, whose nervous system overresponds to minor stimulation, and the deep slumber of infants in swaying car beds on long trips is reminiscent of that of babies in earlier times whose cradles had treadles so that they could be rocked to sleep. The baby who rocks himself obtains similar soothing, and the habit persists as a preliminary inducement to sleep. Rhythmical movements also have been attributed to the child's

154

need for comfort during weaning[8] and have been associated with restrictive rearing practices.[2]

Physical disorders can contribute to initiation and perpetuation of the habit.[17] DeLissovoy[5] matched a head-banging group of 11 boys and four girls, aged ten to 42 months, with a similar group of control children. He discovered that there was a significantly higher incidence of otitis media among the head-bangers, and suggested that the habit was motivated by a need to gain distraction or relief from pain.

A physician should determine if there is infection or nervous system damage which is contributing to head-banging or rocking and which requires treatment. Holding and rocking a baby or small child some of the time when he is awake decreases his need to soothe himself. If he continues head-banging and rocking after he is three years old, more rest or more diversion, whichever is appropriate for him, will weaken the habit.

THUMB-SUCKING

In a study of 2650 infants selected consecutively from a pediatric practice, Traisman and Traisman[20] found that approximately 46 per cent sucked their thumbs or fingers. Although these investigators observed no sex difference in incidence, Honzik and McKee,[12] in a smaller group of 21-month-old children they studied, found thumb-sucking to occur in 33 per cent of the girls, as compared to 21 per cent of the boys.

The infant's need to suck is strongest in the first three or four months of life, and the sucking habit persists after this time in combination with situations and with objects other than food.[19] A child may put himself to sleep by simultaneously sucking his thumb and stroking his check with a favorite blanket. As a toddler, he keeps his blanket with him, dragging it behind him and sucking his thumb. Between 18 and 21 months of age, when the young child is watching other children at play, thumb-sucking is common.[10] As the child becomes more active, there is less daytime sucking, although it remains associated with sleep. The pattern is the same for most children, with spontaneous remission of sucking at three, four, or five years.

Inadequate sucking activity during feeding time, especially during the first six months, has been found to be related to the severity and duration of thumb-sucking,[9, 21] and a higher percentage of slow eaters has been found among thumb-suckers.[20] Parents who continually scold and shame the child prolong the habit,[18] and not infrequently a child is admonished by complete strangers for sucking his thumb.

Parents worry about lasting damage to teeth and facial appearance when a child sucks vigorously, but most dentists claim that permanent damage does not occur if sucking stops prior to eruption of the permanent teeth. Children with malocclusion caused by structural anomalies are more adversely affected by thumb-sucking than are those whose oral structure is good.[18]

Early substitution of a pacifier for the baby's thumb accustoms him to rely on it rather than his thumb for sucking satisfaction, and the pacifier need not accompany him away from home.[19] A pacifier puts no pressure on the jaw or roof of the mouth, and most children give it up between one and two years of age. Thumb-sucking provides the double pleasure of stimulation to both mouth and thumb, and because the thumb is always available, an established habit of sucking is difficult to end.

Mechanical arm restraints and bitter-tasting liquids painted on the thumbs sometimes condition a child to stop sucking. Because these methods are punishing and forcing, however, many children return immediately to sucking when the restraints are removed, and some learn to relish the bitter medicine used.

The one- or two-year-old who sucks constantly can be kept busier with a variety of play objects and with helping his mother with her work. If a child is still sucking frequently when he reaches four years, however, he should be taught to overcome it so that he is not exposed to teasing when he starts school.

Parents training a child to stop thumb-sucking are asking him to give up a habit which is dear to him. The sacrifice is easier if a new pleasure is substituted for the old. Promising magnificent rewards (such as an expensive doll or a new swing set) if the child refrains from thumb-sucking for six months is useless, because no small child can terminate a satisfying and fixed habit abruptly and permanently. The child can learn to refrain from sucking if he is rewarded repeatedly and often for his attention and effort. Four or five hours of successful abstention can be recognized with a penny, and five pennies can be exchanged for ice cream or candy. If rewards are frequent and encouraging, the inevitable lapses are disappointing rather than disastrous.

Bedtime sucking may persist for several years, but need not cause great concern if the child has abandoned daytime sucking. Sometimes when the child's favorite blanket finally has worn to a two-inch scrap, night sucking disappears along with the blanket.

A child often sucks his thumb while watching television or when his mother reads to him. Turning off the television or stopping the reading momentarily teach him voluntary control, because interruption of the entertainment signals him to remove his thumb, and in time he remembers by himself to refrain from sucking.[1]

MASTURBATION

Parents rarely remain calm when a child handles his genitals. They slap his hand, scold him severely, and threaten him with dire results from his act. A one-year-old child seated on the toilet explores his genitals as curiously as he examines his toes. By the time he is two, he knows that urination is geographically related to the genital area, and he is interested in what happens there. His genitals, always covered unless he is dressing, bathing, or using the toilet, are more fascinating than his knees or his nose, which he has available for study and prodding at any time. A three-year-old may hold on to his genitals as though he were worried.[19] He is now aware of sex differences between boys and girls and is perplexed by what he may believe is mutilation in girls. By four years, he grabs his genitals when he is excited, often because he needs to go to the bathroom and is trying to keep from wetting himself. More than half of all children who masturbate begin to do so before they are five years old.[6]

Children sometimes accidentally discover the pleasant sensation of genital manipulation and then stimulate themselves deliberately, either manually or by squeezing their thighs together or rubbing on pillows placed between their legs. Little girls have inserted beads or buttons into their vaginas. Masturbation also can originate from the irritation of tight clothing or from an infection of the genitals which causes itching or burning.[14] Small children often do not dry thoroughly after urinating and chapping results.

Parents of a masturbating child need to determine first if there is irritation from clothing or infection which can be remedied. A curious baby can be distracted from his exploration with a toy, and if his clothing is replaced promptly, genital handling is minimized. When he reaches three years of age, he needs a simple and reassuring explanation of physical sex differences, and if he masturbates frequently, either deliberately or inattentively, he should be told firmly each time he does so that this is impolite and must not be done. Shaming and false threats frighten him needlessly, but routine insistence on refraining from genital play usually is effective with the pre-school child.

HAIR-PULLING

Hair-pulling, or trichotillomania, is considered a more serious manipulatory habit than those previously discussed.[14] A child who pulls out his own hair hurts himself, and he does this because he feels angry and defeated. He is a child who witnesses and is subjected to violence and emotional erraticism, and he has learned to control others with temper.

Alicia P., age 4, of superior intelligence, sucked her thumb and simultaneously pulled out her hair by the handfuls. Her temper was violent, and she called her mother names and hit her. She acted toward children in the same way. The mother displayed severe temper herself and vacillated between impetuous punishment of Alicia and coddling. She did little to correct Alicia's abuse of her, permitting the child to express every angry feeling she had. She herself was an example of extreme emotionality and lack of self-discipline, which the child imitated with increasing anxiety.

Sometimes a child begins to pluck at his hair because of irritating inflammation or infection of the scalp; or in aimless activity he winds his hair around his finger, progressing to hard pulling which leaves bald spots. Girls tend to pull out hair more than do boys because girls have more to grasp. Huber[13] described a four-year-old boy who had torn out his hair for two years, while both awake and asleep, and who was found to have petit mal epilepsy. His hair-pulling was considered stereotyped behavior associated with the epilepsy.

To help calm a child who pulls out his hair, parental anger and extreme emotion must cease. The child's own emotional displays should be stopped quickly, and he should be taught to obey reasonable parental requests. When his parents are able to control him, the child develops self-control and his anxiety decreases. Small girls hesitate to damage their hair when it has been beautified with a short cut and curl and when colored bows and barrettes are added. A child's head should not be shaved for punishment or prevention of hair-pulling unless infection makes this mandatory. If a child looks worse than he did before, he pretends he does not care and yanks away with more determination than ever when the hair starts to grow.

TICS

Tics are persistent, involuntary movements restricted to small groups of muscles. Eye-blinking, dry coughing, clearing the throat, and sniffing have been observed in pre-school children over the age of two years, although not as frequently as in older children.[19] In one group studied, 15 per cent of children between the ages of two and four years were tiqueurs, but the rate dropped to 5 per cent for four- and five-year-olds.[14]

Tics occur several times daily and may last over a period of weeks or months. One tic may be replaced or supplemented by another during this time.[19] Tics of throat clearing or coughing begin in a child who has had a cold, and shrugging or shaking can be traced originally to ill-fitting clothing. Chronic sinusitis leads to blinking, nose-twitching, and mouth-jerking.[3]

The child who is conscientious and sensitive to criticism is most likely to develop tics, and their appearance coincides with periods in his life when he is subjected to excessive criticism or is aware that he is failing frequently. Suppressing his irritability and anger, he shows his increased tension in involuntary muscle contractions.[14, 19]

Physical examination and treatment of any localized disturbance is the first step in aiding the tiqueur. The child's tension should be relieved by ignoring his transgressions and acknowledging his achievements. If he is too busy, either with parental activities or his own, a simpler schedule with extra rest and time to himself is needed.

REFERENCES

1. Baer, D. M.: Laboratory control of thumbsucking by withdrawal and representation of reinforcement. *J. Exp. Anal. Behav.*, 1962, 5, 525–528.
2. Bethell, M. F.: Restriction and habits in children. *Z. Kinderpsychiat.*, 1958, 25, 264–269.
3. Brown, E. E.: Tics (habit spasms) secondary to sinusitis. *Arch. Pediat.*, 1957, 74, 39–46.
4. DeLissovoy, V.: Head banging in early childhood. *Child Developm.*, 1962, 33, 43–56.
5. DeLissovoy, V.: Head banging in early childhood: A suggested cause. *J. Genet. Psychol.*, 1963, 102, 109–114.
6. Dennis, W.: The adolescent. *In* Carmichael, L., ed.: *Manual of Child Psychology*. New York, John Wiley and Sons, 1946, pp. 646–647.
7. Faegre, M. L., and Anderson, J. E.: *Child Care and Training*, Ed. 8. Minneapolis, University of Minnesota Press, 1958.
8. FitzHerbert, J.: Some further observations on head-banging and allied behaviour. *J. Ment. Sci.*, 1952, 98, 330–333.
9. Gandler, A. L.: Nature and implications of thumb-sucking; a review. *Arch. Pediat.*, 1952, 69, 291–295.
10. Gesell, A., and Ilg, F.: *Infant and Child in the Culture of Today*. New York, Harper and Bros., 1943, pp. 306–307, 344, 345.
11. Haring, N. G., and Phillips, E. L.: *Educating Emotionally Disturbed Children*. New York, McGraw-Hill Book Co., 1962, pp. 158–159.
12. Honzik, M. P., and McKee, J. P.: Sex difference in thumbsucking. *J. Pediat.*, 1962, 61, 726–732.
13. Huber, E. G.: Trichotillomanie als Leerlaufmechanismus (Trichotillomania as stereotyped activity). *Z. Psychother. Med. Psychol.*, 1959, 9, 77–81.
14. Kanner, L.: *Child Psychiatry*, Ed. 3. Springfield, Ill., Charles C Thomas, 1957, pp. 424–428, 557–558, 580.
15. Lourie, R. S.: The role of rhythmic patterns in childhood. *Amer. J. Psychiatr.*, 1949, 105, 653–660.
16. Overholser, W., and Richmond, W. V.: *Handbook of Psychiatry*. Philadelphia, J. B. Lippincott Co., 1947, p. 226.
17. Schachter, M.: Étude sur les rythmes du jour ou du sommeil chez l'enfant: spasmus nutans, tic de salaam, jactatio capitis nocturna (Study of diurnal and nocturnal rhythms in the child: spasmus nutans, salaam tics, jactatio capitis nocturna). *Encéphale*, 1954, 43, 173–191.
18. Sillman, J. H.: Thumb-sucking and the oral structures. *J. Pediat.*, 1951, 39, 424–430.
19. Spock, B.: *Baby and Child Care*. New York, Pocket Books, Inc., 1957, pp. 205–217, 368–369, 391.
20. Traisman, A. S., and Traisman, H. S.: Thumb- and finger-sucking: A study of 2,650 infants and children. *J. Pediat.*, 1958, 53, 566–572.
21. Yarrow, L. J.: The relationship between nutritive sucking experiences in infancy and non-nutritive sucking in childhood. *J. Genet. Psychol.*, 1954, 84, 149–162.

Chapter 20

Problems With Play

Much of the child's self-concept evolves from the attitudes his peers hold toward him.[2] Close friendships, even between two-year-olds, develop from similarities in interests and personalities,[6] but because small children are restricted to the playmates available in their immediate neighborhoods, their contacts with peers may be unsatisfying and warping. Such social experiences create self-concepts which predispose the child to rigid or inappropriate responses to others.

Gratifying peer associations result in diminished dependence on adults, less isolated activity, and increased helpfulness and coöperativeness.[10, 23, 24] As the child tries to alter both persons and environments to suit himself during the later pre-school years, he develops personal defense mechanisms,[20] and if these are varied and flexible, he emerges from encounters with other children with increased confidence.[19] Girls, even at an early age, are more concerned about the impression they make and are more empathic than boys. Girls are rated more likable by their peers, even though actual choices of playmates reveal no distinction between the sexes in either popularity or participation in playing.[15]

The child's initial entrance into any group is accompanied by a lack of feeling for its members and its activities; gradually his interest quickens and he participates some of the time with group members; finally, he and his peers are cohesive: They make plans, help each other, and work together.[4] Time is needed to achieve true group feeling, and because of this the child varies in his submissiveness or aggressiveness in different groups and at different times.[3] Children considered shy and withdrawn in nursery school one year become confident leaders the next; and some who approach a group aggressively later retreat, demonstrating their need

160

for time to develop real communication with peers. A child with nursery school experience seems to regress in sociability and lose his adaptability and self-confidence when he begins kindergarten,[18] but this occurs because he must undergo the process of identification each time he joins a new group. As he becomes older and more experienced, the time required for coalescence decreases.[1]

Interfering with the pre-school child's achieving close identification with his peers are a restriction in playmates, exhausting play, the child's own aggressiveness or submissiveness, and his creation of imaginary playmates.

RESTRICTION IN PLAYMATES

Isolation of the pre-school child from his peers makes him dependent on adults,[17] insecure socially,[10] and sometimes aggressive.[9] A child may have no playmates because he lives in a remote area or in a neighborhood in which there are no other children. Not infrequently, however, playmates are available, but parents and grandparents subordinate the child's needs and interests to their own, monopolizing his time and serving as his only companions. Because he is included in their activities and conversation, the child learns how to be pleasing to adults: He jokes, performs, displays an impressive vocabulary, and is obsequiously courteous, but these social techniques seem pompous to other children.

A child who plays with only one friend is better off than the child who plays with no one, but his exclusive social life denies him breadth of experience. When the child has a variety of playmates, each will treat him differently, challenge his adaptability, and stimulate him with new ideas. The child accustomed to a single friend fears losing him, and he guards against this loss by rebuffing any other child who tries to join them. Leaning too heavily on one individual for approval and companionship, he isolates himself from others.

Because of the accidental constituency of neighborhood families, a pre-school girl may have only boys with whom to play, or a young boy may be limited to feminine companionship. These limitations are not important before the age of three years, but by this time a child prefers play companions of his own sex;[14] and his identification with his own sex, which is based partly on play activities, begins to crystallize.[12] Four-year-old boys reject the imitation life toys with which they played happily at an earlier age,[18, 22] and they also become more restless and tend to engage in solitary play more than girls, who appreciatively share activities and conversation.

A child without playmates or a child restricted to one close companion or to playmates of the opposite sex needs to attend nursery school two or three times weekly. Playing normally with different children of his own sex ensures his steady growth in adapting to others, adopting his appropriate sex-role, and acquiring a feeling of belonging to his own generation.

EXHAUSTING PLAY

Some neighborhoods house dozens of children, and it is not uncommon for a pre-school child to be outside playing with throngs of children for long hours every day. Overtired and excited, he is never calm enough to eat or sleep well, and his contacts with children are fraught with competitiveness and fatigue.

There are mothers who believe a child's social skills improve the more he plays with other children, and they permit their pre-schoolers to wander around the neighborhood all day and into the evening, stopping to play where they choose and coming home only to eat and sleep. These children feel abandoned and often attach themselves to the mothers, rather than to the children, of the families they visit.

Other parents mistakenly believe that a child must fend for himself, regardless of the odds, and they insist that he join any group of playing children. Turned out of the house to be victimized by older or brutal children, a pre-schooler equipped with neither courage nor skill to rebel against commands or to resist abuse learns to hate and fear all children, and he avoids them whenever he can.

A young child should play with other children no longer than an hour at a time, and two consecutive hours are sufficient for the older pre-school child. Playing should alternate between homes, and times of arrival and departure should be specific and convenient for the supervising mother. Playmates should be children of similar chronological age, predominantly of the same sex, and the playing of small children should be protected from interference by older ones.

AGGRESSIVENESS

Inevitably there is conflict and disagreement as children play.[22] Tolerance of others' unwanted actions does not develop for years, and the younger the child, the more direct is his attack on those who displease him. Most children's quarrels terminate spontaneously, however, without residual ill feeling.[21]

A two-year-old grabs, hits, and pushes when he is with other children. This is his way of acknowledging their existence, which he did not do when he was younger. Most children of this age exchange one blow and retreat to the safety of adult protection. The three- or four-year-old attacks from a distance, and instead of pushing or hitting, he calls names or throws any handy object at his opponent. Aggressiveness increases through the age of five years, as the child demonstrates increasing courage and greater persistence.[18]

When a child is always aggressive, however, attacking with slight or no provocation, his behavior is caused by factors other than age. Kagan and Moss[12] reported that dominance, competitiveness, and physical aggression toward peers observed in three-year-old children remained stable until the later adolescent years. An overly aggressive child may have learned physical violence from being punished severely by his parents or from being dominated and criticized by older siblings. Unable to retaliate against them, he hurts other children. A kindergarten child scolded by his teacher walked over to a classmate and kicked him hard, later acknowledging that he was angry at the teacher but kicked the child because the child was smaller.

Sometimes a child is encouraged in aggressiveness by a father who urges him to stand up for himself and teaches him that others take advantage of weakness. A five-year-old, thus instructed, smashed his fist into the face of a little girl he had not seen for six months. At the time of their previous meeting she had damaged a toy of his, and remembering, he revenged himself.

The child who plays often with older children who pepper him with orders and require him to do things their way may be aggressive with children his own age and with younger ones. He imitates his older companions and at the same time relieves the frustration he experiences in always being treated as an insignificant person.

Prolonged, unprovoked aggression against other children should be checked. It isolates the child from his peers, who dislike and fear him,[21] and he fixates on the single method of force as his only technique for establishing a relationship. When the child hurts another without cause, he should be required to apologize and the play should be terminated temporarily if the act is repeated. The aggressive child should not be banned from playing with other children, but varying his playmates reduces the stability of his dominating behavior,[5] and including him as a member of a small, supervised play group is helpful in teaching him other ways of relating to peers.[8] As he abandons hitting and pushing, he becomes for a time more dependent on adults and substitutes complaints for his former aggression. His tales of woe merit token sympathy, accompanied by praise for refraining from striking another child. Scolding him for whining, dismissing his hurt feelings as unimportant, or failing to recognize his improved self-control will send him back to using his fists.

Physical abuse, excessive criticism, and incitement to aggression by members of his own family, as well as play contacts with older, domineering children, should cease.

SUBMISSIVENESS

More disturbing to some parents than an aggressive child is a submissive one. A mother becomes furious when her little girl stands quietly, puzzled and unhappy, after her doll is seized by another child. A father denounces his small son for willingly handing over anything his playmates ask for and doing whatever they tell him to do. Parents are jealous, angry, and pitying if their child wails or screams when his playmates desert him for other friends.

Even though a young child is ready to associate with his peers, he still must learn to be socially interactive and communicative with them,[24] and a child who seeks other children has more opportunity to learn this than does one who feels no need to initiate contacts.[6] Passivity during a child's first three years leads to timidity in social situations, avoidance of sports, and withdrawal from peer group activity to solitary play during the elementary school years.[12] The submissive child is rejected by his peers, who find nothing in him to admire or to interest them.[21]

Failure to assert his rights is natural in the child who has neither witnessed nor suffered abuse from others, and he is more bewildered than angered by the first such aggression he encounters. Parents who anticipate the child's needs without waiting for him to express them or who overdirect him teach him to rely on parental action rather than his own initiative, and he learns to do nothing he has not been instructed to do. Active, protective interference of the parent in the child's contacts with playmates and suppression of his autonomous behavior produce lasting social uneasiness in both boys and girls.[12]

To increase the self-confidence and nurture the initiative of the submissive child, parents must avoid interfering when the child has difficulties with playmates, and they must respond to his reports about these difficulties only with their approval for him to use whatever courage and indignation he can muster to meet his problem. If the child has been overdirected by adults, they need to stand aside and wait for him to manage by himself. They should permit him to try out his own ideas unhampered by their prohibitions and warnings.

Training in play skills and practice in social contacts increase a child's confidence. Jack[11] trained submissive children in techniques of making block designs, solving puzzles, and recalling stories, and demonstrated a significant change in their self-assurance with other children. Small play groups composed of children less certain or younger than the submissive child afford him opportunities to be superior.[6, 8] If his constant companion is a bullying child, this association should end.[22]

IMAGINARY PLAYMATES

The peak age for invention of imaginary playmates is three and a half years, and they usually are the creation of children of superior intelligence, especially girls, who have no siblings or friends.[13]

An imaginary playmate affords great pleasure to a child because he can control his "friend" and arrange for both his coöperation and admiration. Sometimes a child requests his parents to supply toys or treats for his imaginary playmate, but his thoughtfulness somehow seems to result in final benefit to himself. Often the make-believe friend is a scapegoat whom the child blames for his own misbehavior,[25] and rigid parental standards sometimes are the basis for this practice.[22]

No harm is done when a child creates an imaginary playmate, and he usually disappears when the child starts to school and exchanges his private world for the real one. Opportunities for him to play with children his own age should be arranged long before this, however. Parents need not act as though they believe the imaginary friend actually exists, but neither should they ridicule the child's play. If they do, they may force him to resort furtively to the satisfactions of fancied companionship.

REFERENCES

1. Allen, G. B., and Masling, J.: An evaluation of the effects of nursery school training on children in the kindergarten, first and second grades. *J. Educ. Res.*, 1957, *51*, 285–296.
2. Axline, V.: Observing children at play. *Teach. Coll. Rec.*, 1951, *52*, 358–363.
3. Curti, M. W.: *Child Psychology*. New York, Longmans, Green and Co., 1938, p. 378.
4. Friedmann, A.: Observations in a play group of young children. *Indiv. Psychol. Bull.*, 1951, *9*, 25–30.
5. Gellert, E.: The effect of changes in group composition on the behavior of young children. *Brit. J. Soc. Clin. Psychol.*, 1962, *1*, 168–181.
6. Goodenough, F. L.: *Developmental Psychology*. New York, D. Appleton-Century Co., 1945, pp. 312–317.
7. Gottschaldt, K., and Frühauf-Ziegler, C.: Über die Entwicklung der Zusammenarbeit im Kleinkindalter (On the development of coöperative behavior in young children). *Z. Psychol.*, 1958, *162*, 254–278.
8. Hartley, R. E., Frank, L. K., and Goldenson, R. M.: *Understanding Children's Play*. New York, Columbia University Press, 1952.
9. Hartup, W. W., and Himeno, Y.: Social isolation vs. interaction with adults in relation to aggression in preschool children. *J. Abnorm. Soc. Psychol.*, 1959, *59*, 17–22.
10. Heathers, G.: Emotional dependence and independence in nursery school play. *J. Genet. Psychol.*, 1955, *87*, 37–57.
11. Jack, L. M.: An experimental study of ascendant behavior in preschool children. *Univ. of Iowa Stud. Child Welfare*, 1934, *9* (3).

. Kagan, J., and Moss, H. A.: *Birth to Maturity.* New York, John Wiley and Sons, 1962, pp. 79, 87, 93–94, 160, 169, 225–226, 276.

13. Langford, L.: *Guidance of the Young Child.* New York, John Wiley and Sons, 1960, pp. 236–237.

14. McCandless, B. R., and Hoyt, J. M.: Sex, ethnicity, and play preferences of pre-school children. *J. Abnorm. Soc. Psychol.,* 1961, *62,* 683–685.

15. McCandless, B. R., and Marshall, H.: Sex differences in children. *Child Developm.,* 1957, *28,* 421–425.

16. McKee, J. P., and Leader, F.: The relationship of socio-economic status and aggression to the competitive behavior of pre-school children. *Child Developm.,* 1955, *26,* 135–142.

17. Marshall, H. R., and McCandless, B. R.: Relationships between dependence on adults and social acceptance by peers. *Child Developm.,* 1957, *28,* 413–419.

18. Murphy, L.: Childhood experience in relation to personality development. *In* Hunt, J. McV., ed.: *Personality and the Behavior Disorders.* New York, The Ronald Press Co., 1944, vol. 2, pp. 672–674.

19. Murphy, L.: Coping devices and defense mechanisms in relation to autonomous ego functions. *Bull. Menninger Clin.,* 1960, *24,* 144–153.

20. Norsworthy, N., and Whitley, M. T.: *The Psychology of Childhood.* New York, The Macmillan Co., 1925, p. 281.

21. Sorokin, P. A., and Gove, D. S.: Notes on the friendly and antagonistic behavior of nursery school children. *In* Sorokin, P. A., ed.: *Explorations in Altruistic Love and Behavior.* Boston, Beacon Press, 1950, pp. 295–300.

22. Spock, B.: *Baby and Child Care.* New York, Pocket Books, Inc., 1960, pp. 307, 309–311, 312, 362.

23. Stith, M., and Connor, R.: Dependency and helpfulness in young children. *Child Developm.,* 1962, *33,* 15–20.

24. Stott, L. H., and Ball, R. S.: Consistency and change in ascendance-submission in in the social interaction of children. *Child Developm.,* 1957, *28,* 259–272.

25. Teagarden, F. M.: *Child Psychology for Professional Workers.* New York, Prentice-Hall, Inc., 1940, p. 247.

26. Zazzo, R., and Jullien, C.: Contribution à la psychologie differentielle des sexes au niveau pré-scolaire (Differential psychology of the sexes at the preschool level). *Enfance,* 1954, *7,* 12–23.

Chapter *21*

Speech Disorders

Speech and personality intertwine and mutually influence each other. Children so young that they still play alone or on a parallel basis are better liked by other children if they talk freely.[11] The pre-school child who speaks effectively gains in self-esteem, knowledge, and sociability.

Emerging from noncommunicative isolation, the small child who uses words understood by others gains allies and servants he did not have before. Parents admire and obey him when he speaks, and his pride in himself is indicated by his delight at listening to his own voice as he repeats the same word over and over and dots his conversation with his name and "I," "me," and "mine." He resolutely captures others' attention by talking constantly during meals, and with urgent and interminable questions he effectively diverts his mother from her work or conversation with someone else.

As he talks, he instructs himself in known requirements or prohibitions, and he assumes verbal roles while playing with dolls or toy animals. This usage of speech strengthens ideas, information, and feelings which would not be as meaningful or permanent if they were unexpressed. He absorbs both facts and attitudes, and he learns to recall and to attend when he tells others of his experiences and hears about theirs.

Speech acquires unpleasant connotations for the child when it conveys others' negative attitudes. Angry denunciations of parents and hostile taunts of playmates are unwelcome communications. If a parent speaks to a child only to give him orders, speech represents little but authority. When parents do not listen or respond to the child's talking, their noncommunication attests to their disinterest in him.[20]

167

Speech evolves in an orderly, predictable way. McCarthy[12] stated that only after eating and breathing functions are well established does the infant begin to coo and babble and that language development appears to await both the child's postural control and his acquisition of some psychological integrity. Infants' babbling sounds include every nuance to be found in languages spoken all over the world: German gutterals, French nasals, and Scottish burring have all been identified in their vocalizations. The most difficult individual sounds the child must master are *l* and *r,* and sometimes these are omitted for years.

Malrieu[14] emphasized that after six months of age the infant's ability to attend to stimuli and to respond to people is imperative for the development of language. At this age, the baby normally produces the same sound repeatedly, and when his parents hear his "ba-ba-ba-ba," they hand him a ball and call it by name. In this way, they help him sort out sounds and relate them to objects continually and naturally, and as they pronounce words singly, point, and explain their words with action, the child grasps meanings long before he can put together sounds and reproduce what he hears.

Most one-year-olds can use three or four words appropriately, and sentences consisting of at least two words are common for the two-year-old, half of whose vocabulary is nouns. From this stage the child advances at a remarkable rate. He forms compound sentences, acquires new verbs, and adds adjectives and adverbs. By five years of age, he quotes others, tells of his experiences, and expresses his wishes with a vocabulary of over 2000 words.[6]

Speech disorders in the pre-school child reflect disruption of the methodical sequence of language development. They include retarded speech and mutism, articulation disability, and stuttering.

RETARDED SPEECH AND MUTISM

The child whose speaking is retarded or who is mute suffers from physical, intellectual, situational, or emotional abnormalities. Fluency can be well defined at an early age, but fluency is possible only if individual and environmental factors are conducive to communication.[4, 24]

A child's failure to speak or to understand spoken instructions may be the first indication of deafness. Unrecognized deafness leads to early disability in communication which isolates the child and predisposes him to avoid people.

Brain damage, either congenital or acquired, may cause aphasia, the impairment of understanding or expression of language. A congenitally aphasic child may also have partial deafness for higher sound frequencies, and this contributes to his difficulty in learning to speak. Speech activity in the congenitally aphasic child sometimes accelerates at the age of four or five years. Acquired aphasia can occur either from accidental injury to the brain or as a residual effect of brain infection from an illness, such as encephalitis. The child usually recovers his original speaking ability in a few weeks, although complete restoration has been known to take as long as two years.[3]

The child of low intelligence is slow in beginning to talk and progresses through each speech development stage at a later age than does a child of average ability.[8, 9, 22]

Jerry L., I.Q. 45, was brought for examination by his parents when he was four years old. They described his extreme fearfulness and his inability to play, but their chief complaint was that he did not talk.

When his insistent father repeatedly coached him to say "My name is Jerry," he could produce only "Muh-uh-uh-duh."

An attractive, obedient child, eager to please his parents and showing no gross motor defects, Jerry was unable to perform the simple tasks appropriate for his age, whether or not they required language facility. Despite his normal appearance, he was seriously retarded.

The speech retardation of the child placed in an institution at an early age is well known, and delayed speech is not uncommon in a young child hospitalized for lengthy periods. In both situations, the child's physical needs are attended to efficiently without his request, and there is neither opportunity nor necessity for speaking.

Twins are slower than single children to talk to other people.[8] They develop their own means of communicating with each other, using sounds not understood by their parents or siblings, and they receive sufficient pleasure from this relationship that they have little desire to contact others verbally.

A bilingual home confuses a child who is learning to talk. Smith[19] found that monolingual pre-school children used a greater variety of words than bilingual children, and the handicap of the latter was related to the extent to which they heard two languages with equal frequency.

A child's home environment may not be conducive to communication.[10] In some families, there is little conversation, with meals eaten in silence and the child's feeding, dressing, and training managed with few words. In impoverished homes, where possessions are few and activities are stereotyped and limited, the child's speech is retarded because his interest is not stimulated.[23] Nursery classes associated with public schools are being established to provide broader experience for underprivileged pre-school children in order that their ability to respond will be adequate when they reach school age.

Some children remain silent in resistance to emotional pressures. They may have been forced to talk to obtain what they want, criticized for mispronunciations, and coached in correct speaking by zealous, perfectionistic parents.[13] Peckarsky,[16] comparing the mothers of 52 speech-retarded children with those of normal controls, found the former to be critical and rigid. The atmosphere in these homes was tense, and routine activities were poorly organized. Many speech-retarded children seem infantile, and overprotection and parental anxiety are contributing factors which have been noted by several investigators.[2, 9, 13] A child may remain mute in order to gain attention or to reduce his own fear of contacts with others or of participation in joint activity.[17]

The child who does not talk adequately by the age of three years needs a hearing examination. If he is deaf, special training in lip reading and sound formation should not be delayed. If the child is aphasic, but there is no accompanying intellectual deficit, he can be trained to use language in a school for the deaf, where he practices with sounds and their meanings.

A child's intelligence can be checked by testing at a child guidance clinic or by special arrangement with the schools. Testing often relieves parents' dread that the child is defective, but if he is retarded, the parents should know as soon as possible to spare them prolonged uncertainty and enable them to plan suitable training.

Specific situational factors such as hospitalization, twin talk, bilingual practices, or limited stimulation for speech at home can be altered enough to make broader communication possible.

If the child is being pressured by his parents to speak and is criticized when he does or is having his needs anxiously anticipated, his parents can be encouraged to ease their demands and maintain a calmer and more orderly home, permitting the child greater freedom to use initiative.

Contact with normally talking children helps the speech-retarded or mute child.[21] If he plays regularly with a child who is friendly and does not dominate him, he cannot long refrain from communicating with him, and gradually he will express himself to other persons as well.

ARTICULATION DISABILITY

Indistinct articulation results from a child's substitution or omission of sounds in words, making him difficult to understand and leading to ridicule from other children. Blanton[5] reported that twice as many boys as girls have speech defects—except for lisping, the inability to sound sibilants. Common substitutions are *th* for *s, sh, z,* and *ch,* resulting in the child's saying *dith* for *dish; t* or *d* for *g, k,* and *x,* which produces *tan* for *can* and *dood* for *good;* and *w* for *l* and *r,* so that the child says *woad* for *road.*

Hearing defects contribute to a child's inability to pronounce words correctly. Because he is unable to distinguish one sound from others, he retains early modes of speech. Structural defects may occur in any of the organs contributing to speech clarity: size or shape of the tongue and poor control of its movement, size of the uvula, arch of the palate, cleft palate, large tonsils, protruding teeth, diseases and deformities of the nose or larynx—all interfere with clarity of sound.[22]

A child may imitate siblings or parents who enunciate incorrectly, because their pronunciation is that with which he is most familiar.[9] Occasionally parents use baby talk with the child when he is long past the initial learning period, and they encourage him to continue lisping by fondly quoting his mispronunciations to their friends.

Sometimes a child starts school speaking so poorly that his teacher cannot understand what he is saying, but in discussing his speech with his mother, the teacher discovers that the parents were unaware of any difficulty. Having learned to understand him, they literally forgot that his speech differed from others' and made no attempt to train him in more accurate speech.

Many children who continue to speak indistinctly are demonstrating infantile feelings.[9] Most pre-schoolers revert to immature expression when they feel hurt, ill-treated, or jealous. The child who considers himself a long-suffering victim of life's trials attempts to appear helpless in order to gain sympathy or service from his parents. He retains articulatory defects as characteristic features of inadequacy and irresponsibility.

Physical defects interfering with articulation often can be remedied, at least partially. Some operations may have to be postponed until a child is older, and occasionally a series of operations is required.

Special speech training for the pre-school child is rarely necessary or desirable. Too often it merely emphasizes speaking errors and makes the child so worried and self-conscious that he avoids talking. Parents can steer the child toward better articulation by selecting one habitually mispronounced word, and each time the child says it incorrectly, they can pronounce it clearly and have him repeat it once. After this word is mastered, another may be selected for practice. All members of the family can exercise care in their own enunciation.

A child demonstrating his feelings of inadequacy in his speech needs more self-confidence. Increased experience with other children of his age develops his self-respect. He should be taught the skills needed to manage his own dressing and toileting, and he should be expected to help with simple daily chores.

STUTTERING

The majority of stutterers begin speaking hesitantly and repetitively before they are five years old,[1] and the problem is first evident between two and three years of age, when the child is working diligently to perfect his speech.[21] Left-handed children more frequently are stutterers than right-handed children; four to ten times as many boys as girls are stutterers; and a familial tendency has been verified.[9] Mixed cerebral dominance formerly was considered a primary cause for stuttering. The stuttering of the pre-school child, however, usually can be traced to situational and emotional pressures leading to tension readily reflected in his amorphous speech.

A young child, in trying to remember the word he wants to say next, repeats 40 or 50 times in every 1000 words he speaks. Overanxious parents seize on his repetition, label it stuttering to themselves and to the child, and immediately begin a program of requiring the child to slow down, take a deep breath, and start over. Soon he begins to feel that each time he attempts to talk there is doubt concerning whether he will be able to produce the words he needs. His anticipation of trouble causes vocal muscles to tense, and he stutters.

In their urgency to catch the fleeting attention of a busy parent who is walking away, looking in another direction, or concentrating on other things, many young children try to talk too hastily, and stuttering results.

Frightening events such as storms, separation from parents, moving, and accidents have all precipitated stuttering in small children. The child's fear does not disappear when the incident is over but remains pervasive, interfering with the fine coördination of muscles and nerves required for facile speech.

An anxious child, uncertain of parental love, fears communicating with his parents because their response may be rejecting. His hesitation appears in the words he uses as he dubiously tries to make contact with them.[1]

Speech therapy for pre-school stutterers has been found ineffective,[18] and nine out of ten children outgrow stuttering in a few months.[21] Parental response is critical in eliminating or prolonging the small child's stuttering. Adults help if they disregard the child's repetitive speech and give him their complete attention whenever he speaks. The child is less tense if frightening situations, overtalking, and excitement are avoided. Quiet companionship with his mother helps a stuttering child, and listening to music or making things together is preferable to reading or playing competitive games. Lowering standards, avoiding criticism, and letting the child have his way in nonessential matters help him feel that he need not battle through every contact with his parents. He also needs time to run and play outside daily in order to relax tense muscles and distract him from his worries.[21]

REFERENCES

1. Barbara, D. A.: Stuttering. *In* Arieti, S., ed.: *American Handbook of Psychiatry,* New York, Basic Books, Inc., 1959, vol. 1, pp. 954–959.

2. Beckey, R. E.: A study of certain factors related to the retardation of speech. *J. Speech Dis.*, 1942, *7*, 223–249.
3. Benton, A. L.: Aphasia in children. *In* Trapp, E. P., and Himelstein, P., eds.: *Readings on the Exceptional Child.* New York, Appleton-Century-Crofts, 1962, pp. 450–455.
4. Bereiter, C.: Fluency abilities in preschool children. *J. Genet. Psychol.*, 1961, *98*, 47–48.
5. Blanton, S.: Speech disorders. *Ment. Hyg.* (*N. Y.*), 1929, *13*, 740–753.
6. Brooks, F. D.: *Child Psychology.* Boston, Houghton Mifflin Co., 1937, pp. 188–189.
7. Goodstein, L. D.: The functional speech disorders and personality: a survey of the literature. *In* Trapp, E. P., and Himelstein, P., eds.: *Readings on the Exceptional Child.* New York, Appleton-Century-Crofts, 1962, p. 404.
8. Hurlock, E. B.: *Child Development.* New York, McGraw-Hill, 1950, pp. 242–246.
9. Kanner, L.: *Child Psychiatry*, Ed. 3. Springfield, Ill., Charles C Thomas, 1957, pp. 510–526.
10. Kowalski, S.: *Rozwój mowy i myślenia dziecka* (*The Development of Speech and Thinking in Socio-educational Situations in Kindergarten*). Warsaw, Poland, Panstwowe Wydawnictwo Naukowe, 1962.
11. Langford, L. M.: *Guidance of the Young Child.* New York, John Wiley and Sons, 1960, pp. 130–142.
12. McCarthy, D.: Language development. *Monogr. Soc. Res. Child Developm.*, 1960, *25* (77), 5–14.
13. McCarthy, D.: Language development in children. *In* Carmichael, L., ed.: *Manual of Child Psychology.* New York, John Wiley and Sons, 1946, pp. 514–515, 549.
14. Malrieu, P.: Vie sociale et prélangage dans la première année (Social life and prelanguage in the first year). *J. Psychol. Norm. Pathol.*, 1962, *59*, 139–165.
15. Overholser, W., and Richmond, W.: *Handbook of Psychiatry.* Philadelphia, J. B. Lippincott Co., 1947, pp. 230–231.
16. Peckarsky, A. K.: Maternal attitudes towards children with psychogenically delayed speech. Ph.D. thesis, New York University, 1953.
17. Reed, G. F.: Elective mutism in children: A re-appraisal. *J. Child Psychol. Psychiat.*, 1963, *4*, 99–107.
18. Ross, M. M.: Stuttering and the pre-school child. *Smith Coll. Stud. Soc. Wk.*, 1950, *21*, 23–54.
19. Smith, M. E.: Word variety as a measure of bilingualism in preschool children. *J. Genet. Psychol.*, 1957, *90*, 143–150.
20. Spiegel, R.: Specific problems of communication in psychiatric conditions. *In* Arieti, S., ed.: *American Handbook of Psychiatry*, New York, Basic Books, Inc., 1959, vol. 1, pp. 924–926.
21. Spock, B.: *Baby and Child Care.* New York, Pocket Books, Inc., 1957, pp. 236–238, 354–456.
22. Teagarden, F. M.: *Child Psychology for Professional Workers.* New York, Prentice-Hall, Inc., 1940, pp. 570–576.
23. Tyborowska, K.: W sprawie roli dzialania i mowy w mysleniu dzieci prezedszkolnych (On the role of action and speech in thinking of preschool children). *Studia Psychol.*, 1956, *1*, 110–126.
24. Yakubovkaya, K. L.: Some peculiarities in the development of speech understanding among 2 year olds in infant's homes. *Pediatria*, 1963, *6*, 30–35.

Chapter **22**

Withdrawal Reactions

Withdrawal from difficult situations is natural and appropriate in a young, inexperienced child. The pre-school child is inadequate in size, skill, and knowledge, and for these reasons he evaluates potential danger differently than his parents do. Moriarty[10] found that a child's ability to cope with new and perplexing experiences is associated with his capacity to relate socially, his positive self-feeling, his ability to express himself, and his motor facility. Few young children possess these traits in dependable quantities.

Withdrawal reactions often are obvious attempts at flight: The child frantically hides his arm behind his back when the nurse approaches with her needle, or he disappears behind the drapes when strange adults enter the living room. Sometimes he does not hide literally but instead assumes an identity which relieves him of responsibility for adequate behavior.[2] A three-year-old girl, accompanying her parents to a company picnic, caught sight of the crowd of adults and children just ahead and immediately stuck a finger in her mouth, turned her feet inward, and proceeded pigeon-toed as slowly as possible toward the formidable gathering. She looked and acted like a retarded child from whom no response need be expected. Other children become frenzied when they are frightened: They run, shout, pull at their parents, knock ashtrays off tables, slam doors, and jump on the furniture. This inappropriate behavior, unrecognized as a withdrawal reaction, often produces strong countermeasures from parents.[17]

Most pre-school children display their inability to cope with annoying or overwhelming events by crying or showing fear. Lying, regression, or autism are even more determined methods of retreating from un-

174

pleasantries, and these reactions trouble or anger parents, who sometimes conclude that the child is attempting to outwit them. Undertones of resistance are detectable in these latter forms of withdrawal, and if they develop into fixed modes of adjustment, they are used to dominate others as well as to avoid or alter unwelcome situations.

CRYING

Crying is noisy, is difficult to stop, and can anger an immature parent so greatly that he beats the child to silence him. Beatings for crying have resulted in the deaths of small children.

A child whose customary reaction to unpleasantness is to cry will do so when other children leave him or argue with him, when his parents go out for the evening, when he is denied a request, when he is afraid, when routines must be maintained, when he is scolded, and at any and all times when life is disagreeable. His tears indicate uncertainty about his resourcefulness and safety, and they express feelings of loneliness, helplessness, and self-pity.

If the child succeeds in turning the parent's attention from the action required by the situation to his own unhappiness, crying becomes firmly implanted as an automatic response to displeasure. Prolonged sympathy and explanation for a crying child do not help him learn other ways of meeting defeat. The parent can stop the child's crying if he neither sees nor hears it but instead begins some new activity which requires the child's participation. If no reference to the child's crying is made and he is diverted from his unhappiness, he learns to cease crying spontaneously and eventually withholds tears over minor disappointments.

FEAR

By 18 months or two years of age, real and persistent fears have developed for many children. One of the most common fears in a child of this age is his anxiety about his parents' leaving him with a sitter or at a nursery. Sometimes the child screams so loudly each time his parents attempt to leave that they give up and never go anywhere without him.

Unexpected stimulation is fear producing. A small girl walking outdoors with her mother suddenly began to cling to her and cry fearfully. Her abrupt fearfulness was explained when the mother discovered that the child had noticed her own moving shadow as they walked along, and the unpredictable movements of this dark object had frightened her. Fearfulness has been reported in two-year-olds watching television cartoons in which the figures move suddenly and there are unexpected close-ups of contorted faces.

When he is from three to five years of age, the child becomes more aware of his surroundings and consequently more cognizant of his inability to protect himself from objects and situations he does not fully understand. He is afraid of doctors, dogs, the dark, possible accidents or injuries, storms, and death for himself or his parents.[3, 4, 6, 15]

Fears mushroom when a small child is separated from his family.[8, 14] When his mother is away for a visit or in the hospital for a few days, a child may become so afraid during her absence that after she returns he will not let her out of his sight for weeks. Experience with frightening objects produces fear reactions.[3] A barking dog, the wailing sirens of fire engines and ambulances, the crack of thunder and the brilliance of lightning, or a death in the family or neighborhood all frighten a small child. Because his knowledge is limited, a pre-school child anticipates danger when none exists. He screams at the prospect of wading into a lake, he worries about a small bug he spies, and he peoples the dark with nonexistent ogres and animals. He is literal, and some fears arise because a child misinterprets an adult's casual comment.

"Be careful!" a father jokingly warned his small daughter on a blustery day. "The wind might blow you away."

For many months afterward this child showed fear whenever she was outside and the wind was blowing.

Forcing or shaming a frightened child will not eradicate his fear.[7] For the younger child, protection from the feared situation or object is best. A child frightened by television cartoons should not watch them, and one who fears the dark can have a dim light in his room and his door left ajar. If he is afraid during a storm, his mother's sitting with him is reassuring. Fearfulness which has generalized from his mother's temporary absence or the family's moving is relieved by more personal attention and by his parents' remaining at home more than usual for several weeks.

The older pre-school child can be accustomed gradually to the thing he fears.[1, 6, 7] A train, regularly thundering by the child's house, can be observed first from a distance, and later the child will gain courage to approach nearer to watch. If he is afraid when left in a nursery or with a sitter, his mother's initial absences should be brief—only 15 minutes at first, with the time lengthened gradually.

Parents unintentionally induce or prolong fears. Permitting a small child to take his toy gun to bed with him as protection against the imaginary animals he sees only makes him more certain that they really are there. Telling of frightening experiences, letting a young child listen to older siblings' ghost stories, or setting an example of fear during storms or prior to dental visits ensures the small child's acquisition of many worries.

Explanation and minimizing the danger has proved to be of little help in real fear-producing situations, but it is the only usable method to help a child who anticipates harm. Encouraging a child to talk about his ideas of death or injury or to ask questions about deformed or strange-acting people he sees enables parents to reassure him and give him some positive information.[16]

Permanent resolution of fear is achieved by teaching the child skills so that he can manage better by himself.[7] The child who learns to pump no longer fears the swaying swing, and the child who learns to greet an approaching dog feels less fear. Informing the child about procedures at the doctor's or dentist's office and telling him how he should behave there gives him enough advance knowledge to keep him from complete disintegration. When a child is always afraid or uncertain around people, instructing him in what he is to do prior to making visits, or assigning him useful tasks to perform when visitors come provides direction for his behavior and leaves less range for uncertainty and panic.

LYING

Some parents consider lying the most heinous crime of all, and they angrily tell a deceptive child, "I'd rather raise a thief than a liar!"

Many confuse their children by informing them that they are not being punished for the offense they have committed but for lying about being responsible for it.

Adults' own sense of verity is not this strict, however. Parents solemnly teach the child about Santa Claus and the Easter bunny, and they embroider tales of daily events with ingenious trappings designed to represent themselves to others as extraordinarily clever or unjustly martyred. Adult falsehoods are more deliberate and purposeful than are the untruths of a pre-school child.[8] Confused easily and often between what is true and real and what is storied or make-believe and finding that others disregard the distinction, he rarely pays close attention to what he says. The younger the child, the less deliberate is his lying, and he is so guileless that he readily identifies himself as the sought-for culprit if led to do so.

"Show me how you spilled the sugar" produces a quick demonstration rather than a denial of guilt.

Sometimes factual elaboration reflects only a child's lively imagination and his desire to attract attention or admiration.[14] A three-year-old's vivid story of an elephant in the back yard does not merit condemnation of the child for lying. Some children, learning that their tales produce a startling reaction in their parents, make up ever more dramatic stories to witness parental alarm. Others need to feel important, and they recite aloud their daydreams of adventure and conquest.

The more experienced child, who knows that punishment follows misbehavior, will deny his misdeeds and even attribute them to others to save himself.[8] Lying is a natural, protective reaction and should not be considered unusual in a young child. Parents who feel their trust in the child has been irrevocably destroyed when he deceives them forget that self-protection is an automatic reaction of most human beings.

For the child who occasionally invents mild tales, a parent need only recognize aloud that the story is just that. If the child continually tells extravagant stories to achieve status, his parents and older siblings need to give him their attention when he speaks or suggests doing something with them. Sometimes his life is overstimulating, with too much activity or too many ghost and fairy stories, and he needs more quiet and less excitement.[14] On the other hand, he may be lonely and bored, and if so, different and stimulating experiences will counter his tendency to invent them.

A child who admits his misdeeds, even after first denying them, should be praised for doing so. He thus can salvage some measure of pride and parental approval from an unhappy situation, even though he still must be punished. Punishment for misbehavior should never be so severe that it is dreaded with real reason and its cruelty forces the child to lie.

Parents who habitually exaggerate, tell white lies, or fail to give accurate information to the child need to practice greater truthfulness. The child imitates deception and sees no reason for a double standard.

REGRESSION

Regressing to less mature forms of behavior is a common reaction of an unhappy pre-school child. Infantile actions express his feeling of helplessness and his desire for the protection and comfort which was his in former years.[2] A regressing child may forget his toilet training, cry over incidents which he formerly accepted equably, suck his thumb, whine, and complain. If he has acquired a new baby sibling and cannot tolerate his parents' averted time and attention, he demands a bottle and diapers for himself. When he finds himself in a situation in which he does not know how to act or cannot anticipate how others will act toward him, he reverts to screaming and hiding, behavior which is now inappropriate for his age. This behavior may occur when he must start nursery school or kindergarten, face a roomful of adults, or join a crowd of exuberant children at a birthday party. Sometimes he is overstimulated by being with playmates or adults continually and not getting enough rest, and to escape the demands made on him, he acts the part of an infant.

A pre-school child should be prepared for all new experiences. An expectant older sibling should be given an accurate description of a new-born infant, and he also should be told that the care of the baby will necessitate a decrease in the attention he has been receiving from his parents. When the child is to join a group of other children or adults at school or at a party, he needs to be told what to expect from them and what he is to do. Because it. ۷. 37 (437) Child Psy.

With misplaced sympathy, parents sometimes permit a regressing child to continue immature behavior for months. Acting immaturely only prolongs the child's helplessness and increases his anxiety. He knows that bottles and diapers are not appropriate for him, and he worries about his parents' allowing him to behave like an infant when he is not one. Lapsed toilet habits, excessive thumb-sucking, and easy crying need not continue if parents devote some attention to retraining the child in previously-acquired, more suitable ways of acting. The child's desire to relinquish his maturity is reduced if his parents play with him alone, at times take him with them unaccompanied by younger siblings, and give him added responsibility and freedom.

If the child is regressing because of overstimulation, his daily life should be more orderly and less challenging. Playing with other children can be curtailed, and his association with adults can be limited temporarily to his parents.

AUTISM

Kanner[8] reported in 1943 on 11 children who withdrew from human contact during the first year of life, and many other autistic children have been described since then. The autistic child pays no attention to people and often is mute. He plays alone for hours, and angrily rejects attempts to interrupt his play or remove his toys. He does so by pushing away the reaching hand, seldom even looking at the person to whom the hand belongs. He is content with objects, and compulsiveness is evident in his irritated disturbance when his toys or furniture is re-arranged.

The autistic child appears to be self-sufficient and happier when left alone. Because he seldom speaks, he often is credited with hidden wis-dom, and an older child impresses adults by reciting lengthy memorized passages or a series of numbers and by remembering long-past events. Some autistic children communicate only by parroting phrases used by their parents, and their use of words is essentially meaningless. Vaillant[19] stated that impaired language development, hereditarily determined, may be a contributing cause to the child's extreme withdrawal. The communicative failure, easy irritability, and need for restricted stimula-tion suggest central nervous system damage.[12] The child unable to rely on his own consistency of response to given stimuli is continually startled and maintains his security only by a major reduction in the amount of stimulation to which he must react.*

Phillips[11] pointed out that autistic children are predominantly first-born boys. He suggested that the parental dilemma of setting controls for the child versus permitting freedom of action is more acute for a first son and that the adults' resulting indecisiveness causes the child to develop strong assertiveness. Although he becomes increasingly unsure of his ability to assume full responsibility for his actions, the child is committed to doing so, and he retreats to the protection of a limited and controllable environment.

Trapp and Kausler[1] studied 16 children aged three to five years and reported that pre-school children avoid adult contacts if their parents are either overcontrolling or lax with them or if there is wide discrepancy in dominance between the two parents.

Diagnosis of autism is difficult because a child's failure to react to the approaches of other persons suggests deafness or retardation. Thorough physical, intellectual, and observational examination of a withdrawing, unresponding child is required. Inconsistency in performance, with evidence of occasional normality, provides the best clue that the child is autistic, rather than retarded or hard of hearing.[11]

Formerly it was believed that the autistic child needed long-term treatment in a children's psychiatric hospital and that his condition would remain relatively stable. This pessimistic viewpoint represents acceptance of the child's version of solution to a problem, whereas adult control and direction of the child's behavior are mandatory if it is to change.

Lovatt[9] described the placement of pre-school autistic children in a nursery where each had a private playroom and his own teacher for two hours a day, four days a week. The child's teacher initially followed his lead, but eventually she began to structure playing and impose limits on activities. Gradually, the child was moved for short periods into the regular nursery with normally-playing children. All of these autistic children were able to enter regular kindergarten at five or six years of age, and although some adjusted poorly at first, several were doing well by the time they reached second or third grade.

Steady efforts to break through the autistic child's resistance should be made. Whether he wants it or not, he should have the daily companionship of his mother for playing, and he should be given physical affection, even though his rejection may limit this to only a brief contact at first. Stories and music should be shared with him, and if everyone else is doing something together, he should not be permitted to isolate himself by refusing to eat with the family or by going off by

---

* See Chapter 46, "Cerebral Dysfunction."

himself. Having another child play daily with him can entice responsiveness from him which eludes adult efforts.

REFERENCES

1. Bentler, P. M.: An infant's phobia treated with reciprocal inhibition therapy. *J. Child Psychol. Psychiat.*, 1962, *3*, 185–189.
2. Cameron, N.: *The Psychology of Behavior Disorders.* Cambridge, Mass., Houghton Mifflin Co., 1947, pp. 170, 174.
3. Gesell, A., and Ilg, F. L.: *The Child from Five to Ten.* New York, Harper and Bros., 1946, pp. 112–113.
4. Hagman, E. R.: A study of fears of children of preschool age. *J. Exp. Educ.*, 1932, *1*, 110–130.
5. Hurlock, E.: *Child Development.* New York, McGraw-Hill Book Co., 1950, p. 264.
6. Jersild, A. T.: Emotional development. *In* Carmichael, L., ed.: *Manual of Child Psychology.* New York, John Wiley and Sons, 1946, pp. 762, 767–768.
7. Jersild, A. T., and Holmes, F. B.: Methods of overcoming children's fears. *J. Psychol.*, 1935, *1*, 75–104.
8. Kanner, L.: *Child Psychiatry*, Ed. 3. Springfield, Ill., Charles C Thomas, 1957, pp. 83, 691–695, 739–742.
9. Lovatt, M.: Autistic children in a day nursery. *Children*, 9 (3), 103–108.
10. Moriarty, A. E.: Coping patterns of preschool children in response to intelligence test demands. *Genet. Psychol. Monogr.*, 1961, *64*, 3–127.
11. Phillips, E. L.: Contributions to a learning-theory account of childhood autism. *In* Trapp, E. P., and Himelstein, P., eds.: *Readings on the Exceptional Child.* New York, Appleton-Century-Crofts, 1962, pp. 602–609.
12. Rimland, B.: *Infantile Autism.* New York, Appleton-Century-Crofts, 1964.
13. Rothenberg, M.: The strange story of Jonny. *Reader's Digest*, 77 (464), 75–80.
14. Spock, B.: *Baby and Child Care.* New York, Pocket Books, Inc., 1957, pp. 348, 362–366.
15. Teagarden, F.: *Child Psychology for Professional Workers.* New York, Prentice-Hall, Inc., 1940, p. 329.
16. Thom, D. A.: *Everyday Problems of the Everyday Child.* New York, Appleton-Century, 1934, pp. 152–153.
17. Thompson, G.: *Child Psychology.* Cambridge, Mass., Houghton Mifflin Co., 1952, pp. 289–303.
18. Trapp, E. P., and Kausler, D. H.: Dominance attitudes in parents and adult avoidance behavior in young children. *Child Developm.*, 1958, *29*, 507–513.
19. Vaillant, G. E.: Twins discordant for early infantile autism. *Arch. Gen. Psychiat.*, 1963, *9*, 163–167.

Chapter 23

Aggressive Reactions

Aggressive reactions of the pre-school child notify others that he is a person, not a possession, a plaything, or a doormat. The younger pre-school child, equipped with fists and feet but not with reason or authority, normally is aggressive when he is frustrated. If direct aggression increases during the later pre-school years, however, early modes of reaction are being prolonged unduly and identification of the cause is needed.

Absence of the father from the home increases the aggressiveness of young boys,[18] and lower economic status, with its attendant emotional and economic privations, is related to aggressiveness. Physiological and neurological disabilities sustain irritability and incite aggressive reactions.[4, 17] Laboratory experiments and observation of doll play indicate that aggression in these restricted situations increases when it has been suggested or witnessed,[14] especially if the aggressor is not punished.[2] There is a high incidence of early and continuing aggression in institutionalized children.[3, 4, 8]

Young boys are more aggressive than girls, tending to attack physically in contrast to the girls' more devious methods of insulting others or appropriating their friends and toys.[9, 15, 18] Common aggressive reactions of the pre-school child are negativism, destructiveness, stealing, running away, and attacks based on jealousy and anger.

NEGATIVISM

By the time he is a year old, a baby effectively opposes his parents' wishes, batting away the proffered spoon and blandly ignoring admoni-

182

tions to leave lamp cords alone. Between two and three years, the child appears to do nothing but rebel, and he automatically responds to every parental request with opposition.

Negativism is a natural expression of the child's growing independence and his need to decide things for himself. Heroic efforts to overcome resistance are unnecessary, because time lessens the desire to oppose every parental suggestion and edict. Hurrying, scolding, and forcing a negativistic child pressures him into more vigorous opposition. Sometimes parents become frightened by the child's negativism, meekly accept his refusals, and thus set a pattern of pacification which perpetuates his rebellion.

As he grows older, his negativism diminishes spontaneously if his parents have not made issues of such matters as toilet performance, eating, talking plainly, and cleanliness but still have required conformity to regulations necessary for his health and safety. The child resists less during these early years if his parents are not hesitant in their requests, if daily routines are conducted with minimum discussion, and if only one parent at a time manages him.[19] Ignoring the child's frequent "No" and "I won't" conserves time and energy. His refusals require neither recognition nor comment, and responding to them with explanation, justification, capitulation, or argument only spurs him to increased rebellion.[12]

DESTRUCTIVENESS

A pre-school child can be depended on to crayon on the wallpaper, cut a jagged hole in his bedspread, rip a boot, or dent a table with a mallet blow at least once each week. Much of his destructiveness is idle experimentation: He uses whatever he has in his hand on the nearest available object, and the unnatural combination causes unfortunate results. Sometimes he tries out an old technique on an unknown object. Three pre-schoolers vigorously kicked a sack of cement mix stored in a garage. They soon had a large hole torn in it, and clouds of cement dust rose to settle thickly over everything. Cleaning up the children took hours, and the garage never again was completely free of cement particles.

Haste, thoughtlessness, and lack of dexterity cause the young child to pull off buttons, drop dishes, overwind springs on toys, tear pages in books, and trample flower beds; and his inability to anticipate the destruction which will result from his uninhibited actions persists for several years.[12]

Some destructiveness is deliberate, especially in the older pre-school child. He may angrily tear his room apart when he is banished for misbehavior, or with less noisy vindictiveness, he may smear paste on the wall or cut his curtains to shreds.

Pre-school children, inadvertently or purposely, do cause damage;

and therefore the use of inexpensive furnishings, clothing, and toys during these years is sensible. Uncluttered rooms minimize destructiveness, and objects kept out of reach except when they are being used cannot be taken apart, stepped on, or torn up. Paste, scissors, crayons, and paints can be issued for use only under supervision, and frequent checking on small children's play reduces the possibility of grand destructive sprees.

The older child or the one who destroys intentionally should attempt to repair the damage he has done. He will not succeed completely or even adequately, but he does learn that destructiveness carries a penalty, and he is able to exercise greater care with possessions sooner than he would otherwise.

STEALING

The child under three years of age does not steal when he takes something, because he has no ethical concept of stealing.[12] Although he may understand that there are things he is not to touch, the reasons for the prohibition are ill defined, and he takes whatever he sees that attracts him if he is not prevented from doing so. If he is accustomed to helping himself to his siblings' toys, he calmly picks up to take home the truck which belongs to the child he is visiting, and it takes many thwartings of similar appropriations for him to learn the difference between *mine* and *thine,* and that *thine* is taboo.

The older child who helps himself to money has some understanding that it is not his to take, but he is concentrating only on the candy or gum he can buy with it. Sometimes he does not comprehend the value of money itself. Teagarden[20] told of a four-year-old girl who bought candy with pennies taken from a visitor's purse, and when she was reprimanded, she insisted that pennies were not money. Each evening her father had selected all the pennies from his collection of change and had given them to her, and she believed that pennies were useless to adults. Another small girl raided her mother's sewing box and offered, unsuccessfully, the buttons she had obtained to the ice cream vendor in exchange for a cone.

A child may take some of his mother's costume jewelry and hide it away in his room to admire later. He does the same thing with an older sibling's toy or book, and occasionally he arrives home from a shopping trip with an unpaid-for item in his pocket. He takes things because he wants them, and he knows that requesting them chances a denial. His guilt is limited to a vague uneasiness, and the carelessness with which he hides his plunder testifies to his belief that his action was unimportant.

He will take others' possessions repeatedly if they are allowed to take his. If his younger brother plays with his toys whenever he chooses, his older sister borrows his crayons without asking, or his mother uses his mittens for another child, he will not honor others' property rights because he has none of his own.

Branding a pre-school child a thief mystifies him, because ownership standards are confusing and because he is too immature to understand how he has offended. To teach him to ask for what he wants, every possible request should be granted while he is learning so that he does not conclude that taking is more practical than asking. His opportunity to take things is restricted if money and the fascinating possessions of siblings are kept out of sight. Parents should protect and respect the property rights of children and should teach each child to ask permission before using anything belonging to another. Furthermore, if permission is denied, the parent must not nullify his protection by shaming or coaxing the child into reversing his decision.

The child quickly learns that money is exchanged for things he wants, but he will not help himself to others' money if he has some of his own to handle and spend. He can be given money to pay the clerk for toys or clothes, and if he is allowed to work for small sums, he can learn that money is earned before it is spent. A child who has taken something from a store must return it and apologize, and the article should not be bought for him to keep, lest he conclude that the way to get something is to take it.

RUNNING AWAY

Left unsupervised, any child old enough to walk will wander off. He has no awareness of the dangers involved and finds it pleasant to explore the world by himself, just as earlier he explored the contents of wastebaskets and drawers. As he discovers what can be obtained in certain places, he heads for the house of the lady who gives him cookies or pays a visit to the park with a fish pond. One mother reported that her four-year-old son had twice set off by himself on his tricycle, to be brought back hours later after he had crossed several heavily travelled streets. A three-year-old girl made a habit of walking two miles to a shopping center three or four times each week.

Although running away originates from simple curiosity, some young travelers quickly adopt it as a regular practice, leaving home without asking permission or even telling their parents. A child continues to wander if he is not supervised closely and stopped when he leaves or if he hears no objection when he announces he is going somewhere. If he is free to roam the neighborhood at will, he becomes accustomed to leaving home rather than staying there.

He can be taught not to run away if he is well supervised and consistently trained to receive permission before leaving. A two-year-old child must be watched closely, and although he is capable of playing outdoors alone, his mother must observe him continually so that as soon as he leaves the yard, she can retrieve him. The three- or four-year-old who purposely leaves whenever he can without asking permission should be penalized by being required to remain indoors unless his mother is with him outside. A few days of oversupervision will usually convince him to obtain permission to leave home rather than suffer the humiliation of public mothering when he plays outdoors.

When a child wants to visit a friend, his mother should determine whether this is convenient for the other family and she should set a time for his return home, so that there is never an "out-of-sight, out-of-mind" relationship between parent and child and so that he always has adult supervision. A young child cannot be allowed to go alone to public places or to travel any considerable distance from home by himself because he has neither the judgment nor the experience to manage himself in traffic or in strange places among strange adults. A parent must accompany him when he leaves his own neighborhood.

RESPONSES TO JEALOUSY

Jealousy between siblings is nearly inevitable, but its deleterious effects have been stressed so zealously that many parents with a new baby think of nothing but the sad fate of the first-born. They feel helpless to stop the older child when he abuses the baby, and they try to make him feel better by making slighting remarks about the infant. These adult reactions seem unnatural to him, and he is wise enough to wonder if his parents betray him in similar fashion. Parents can guard against excessive jealousy in an older child, but they do not need to believe that all unhappiness is disastrous and must be avoided; children are emotionally sturdier than this.

Jealousy is most common in the oldest child, both because he has had undivided parental attention and because the family constellation changes completely with the arrival of a second child. A one-year-old rarely realizes that he has been superseded; but a two-year-old, still needing his mother for both care and protection, may act belligerently toward her and the baby.

Jealousy shows itself in many ways. The child may protest uneasily and continually that he loves the baby, or he may regress to infant behavior himself. If he is aggressive, however, his actions clearly announce his feelings.[19] The four-year-old intentionally hurts the baby by squeezing him as hard as he can under the guise of affection. Pre-school children have been known to tip over the carriages of infant siblings, throw them out the window, and attack them with scissors, knives, and matches. Far from giving the jealous child relief, his hurting the baby only makes him feel more unworthy, and all of his behavior becomes increasingly destructive, flighty, uncontrollable, and anger-motivated.

A younger child becomes jealous of an older sibling who receives more solicitude and deference from parents than he. Because of adult uncertainty in handling the first child, he may succeed in misbehaving without punishment or in getting what he wants by demanding it, whereas the younger child, reared more sensibly, does not obtain these advantages and interprets them as favoritism based on preference.

A small child sometimes is jealous of his parents.[12] When they embrace, he quickly joins them, hugging his father around the legs and demanding a kiss from his mother. Most such reactions are bids for attention and for reassurance that he is not being excluded from their affection.

Jealousy rarely is preventable, but it need not be extreme. Accurate and explicit preparation should be given a pre-school child who is to have a new sibling. He should see a new-born baby if possible, so that he does not mistakenly assume from his parents' promise of a playmate that a brother or sister his own size is being provided for his pleasure. He should know that a baby cries, that his mother must spend time caring for the baby, and that he also can assist in the baby's care. Necessary changes in beds or rooms should be made several months in advance of the baby's arrival. If the older child is to attend nursery school, he should begin long before the baby comes.[19] He should be well acquainted with whoever is to care for him while his mother is in the hospital, and his own daily life should be changed as little as possible after the baby's birth.

The older child must not be permitted to abuse the baby. Usually he will give some sign or even announce his intention of hurting him before he tries to do so, and although the parent can acknowledge the child's occasional distaste for the baby, he must firmly tell the child that he will not be allowed to hurt the baby. Parents who exhort the child to love the baby at times when he shows his dislike anger the child and burden him with guilt. The fear that he compares unfavorably to the newcomer is the real root of his hatred. Parents need to pay attention to him when he wants to talk or demonstrate a skill, give him physical affection, and play with him alone. When visitors come to admire the baby, the older child who is directed in giving special help to the guests is assured of receiving attention and praise from them which maintains his self-esteem.

Jealousy often does not develop until a baby becomes old enough to walk and then help himself to the older child's possessions. These should be protected from a marauding toddler by a hook on the door or a lock on the toy chest.[19] If they are not, the older child will hit or spank the younger, and the punishment he subsequently receives for his justifiable revenge deepens his hatred for the baby and convinces him that the younger child is favored.

ANGER REACTIONS

Jersild[10] emphasized that anger in a child serves a useful purpose if it calls attention to an irritant which should be corrected. If someone is abusing or taking advantage of the child, his anger is a healthy reaction. Anger is not helpful, however, when it is unsuited to the occasion, when it is directed at blameless persons or objects, or when it results only in added difficulty for the child.

In Goodenough's[7] study of anger in pre-school children, she observed that boys have more outbursts than girls and that the highest number of tantrums occurs at 18 months, followed by a sharp decline in frequency. Many factors appear to precipitate tantrums: the number of adults in the family; the number of older siblings; visitors; critical, anxious, nagging adults; inconsistent discipline; and such health conditions as illness, hunger, constipation, and fatigue.

Restraint of the small child's freedom to experiment or to complete purposeful actions leads to impetuous anger. Lack of maternal affection and nurturance of the infant and small child are conducive to increased anger reactions, both then and continuing as the child grows older.[3] Parents who explode easily themselves serve as models for the child.[12]

The infant first shows temper by holding his breath, sometimes until he turns blue. As he grows older, he uses his whole body to express anger: He hits his head against the wall or floor and kicks, pounds, and screams. The two-year-old strikes the person who angers him, but an older pre-school child more cautiously relies on verbal abuse or throwing something at his tormentor. Although some name-calling occurs at nearly every pre-school age, it is much more frequent when a child is four years old. By then he has outgrown his earlier spontaneous reactions of grabbing and hitting, but he is keenly aware of his status with other people and wants his rights respected. He often does not know the meaning of the terms he uses, but he adopts them in imitation of angry peers or adults or after hearing them on television.

When a child is angry several times each day, living becomes increasingly difficult for both him and his mother. Constant tantrums frighten or anger her and weaken her ability to manage him. They are rewarding to the child if they succeed in giving him attention, solicitude, or control.*

Observation of patterns of anger in a child aids in identification of

---

* See Case 15, Ralph T., p. 507.

causes which can be removed, such as overstimulation and fatigue, parental haste and forcing, inadequate personal attention, or playing with dominating children.

Rewarding a tantrum by granting the child's wish guarantees that he will scream with rage the next time he is denied something he wants. Embarrassing public outbursts require special parental fortitude in resisting the child's demands, and a knowledgeable child is noisiest when visitors are present.

When the child is furiously angry, he may need parental help to stop, and without it he continues to scream and kick until he is exhausted. Picking up the small child and tossing him in the air interrupts his tantrum. He cannot continue to thresh about or pound his head on space, and his angry screaming changes to laughter as parental cheerfulness erases his awareness of what angered him.

When he is too heavy or too big for physical handling, he is better off alone in his room, or he can be sent to the car if he has a tantrum at the grocery store.[19] This technique separates him from the source of his anger, and he no longer has anyone to fight or maneuver. Parent and child gain time to recover composure; and explanation, discussion, or compromise of their conflicting desires is more profitable when both are calm.

If name-calling or hitting is automatic, frequent, and used for attack as well as in requital, some measure of control is needed. The child who attacks his parent verbally or physically should be rebuked and, if older, required to apologize—although his justification for anger should be determined. Parents need to make certain also that they are not setting an example of attacking behavior by calling the child a baby, a nuisance, or a bad boy or by spanking him frequently and severely.

REFERENCES

1. Ammons, C. H., and Ammons, R. B.: Aggression in doll-play: interviews of two- to six-year-old white males. *J. Genet. Psychol.*, 1953, *82*, 205–213.
2. Bandura, A., Ross, D., and Ross, S. A.: Vicarious reinforcement and imitative learning. *J. Abnorm. Soc. Psychol.*, 1963, *67*, 601–607.
3. Bandura, A., and Walters, R. H.: *Adolescent Aggression.* New York, The Ronald Press Co., 1959, p. 39.
4. Bender, L.: *Aggression, Hostility, and Anxiety in Children.* Springfield, Ill., Charles C Thomas, 1953, pp. 38, 39.
5. D'Evelyn, K. E.: *Meeting Children's Emotional Needs.* Englewood Cliffs, N. J., Prentice-Hall, Inc., 1957, pp. 122–123.
6. Franus, E.: Reakcje oporu i gneiwu malego dziecka (Reactions of resistance and anger in a small child). *Zes. Nauk. Uniw. Jagiellonskiego Psychol. Pedag.*, 1957, *1*, 137–163.
7. Goodenough, F. L.: *Anger in Young Children.* Minneapolis, University of Minnesota Press, 1931.
8. Gordon, J. E., and Cohn, F.: Effect of fantasy arousal of affiliation drive on doll play aggression. *J. Abnorm. Soc. Psychol., 1963, 66,* 301–307.

 9. Hartup, W. W., and Himeno, Y.: Social isolation vs. interaction with adults in relation to aggression in preschool children. *J. Abnorm. Soc. Psychol.,* 1959, *59,* 17–22.
10. Jersild, A. T.: *Child Psychology,* Ed. 4. New York, Prentice-Hall, Inc., 1954, pp. 391–392.
11. Jersild, A. T.: Emotional development. *In* Carmichael, L., ed.: *Manual of Child Psychology.* New York, John Wiley and Sons, 1946, p. 771.
12. Kanner, L.: *Child Psychiatry,* Ed. 3. Springfield, Ill., Charles C Thomas, 1957, pp. 42, 596–602, 605–607, 697, 709–710.
13. Landreth, C.: Factors associated with crying in young children in the nursery school and the home. *Child Developm.,* 1941, *12,* 81–97.
14. Larder, D. L.: Effect of aggressive story content on nonverbal play behavior. *Psychol. Rep.,* 1962, *11,* 14.
15. McKee, J. P., and Leader, F.: The relationship of socio-economic status and aggression to the competitive behavior of pre-school children. *Child Developm.,* 1955, *26,* 135–142.
16. Otis, N. B., and McCandless, B.: Responses to repeated frustrations of young children differentiated according to need area. *J. Abnorm. Soc. Psychol.,* 1955, *50,* 349–353.
17. Paulson, G.: Breath holding spells: a fatal case. *Developm. Med. Child Neurol.,* 1963, *5,* 246–251.
18. Sears, P. S.: Doll play aggression in normal young children: influence of sex, age, sibling status, father's absence. *Psychol. Monogr.,* 1951, *65.*
19. Spock, B.: *Baby and Child Care.* New York, Pocket Books, Inc., 1957, pp. 330–335, 338–346, 353–354, 396.
20. Teagarden, F. M.: *Child Psychology for Professional Workers.* New York, Prentice-Hall, Inc., 1940, p. 484.
21. Thom, D. A.: *Everyday Problems of the Everyday Child.* New York, Appleton-Century, 1934, p. 136.
22. Thompson, G. G.: *Child Psychology.* Cambridge, Mass., Houghton Mifflin Co., 1952, p. 317.

Part III

THE ELEMENTARY SCHOOL CHILD

Chapter 24

Introduction

During the busy, kaleidoscopic years from six to 12, the child changes from a lovable, innocent, dependent possession to a person in his own right, one who has ideas and achievements to his credit and who has suffered disappointments and rebuffs. He establishes his ability or inability to utilize his capacities, to discharge responsibility, and to adapt himself to the requirements and challenges of others, behavior which he demonstrates in various ways and in different settings.

His parents are forced to new adaptations because of the reactions of the child to unfamiliar requirements and to the motivations imposed by his own maturing. Former methods of managing him no longer are assured of success, and parents are bewildered by the child's new behavior and are uncertain of their obligation toward him. Misunderstandings between parent and child are common, and each is disappointed in the other frequently. Nevertheless, the elementary school child is highly dependent on his parents for affection and approval, and he needs them to direct and train him in responsible, moral actions, as well as to protect him from impulsive and exhausting behavior.

THE ELEMENTARY CHILD'S DEVELOPMENT

Adoption of Sexual Role

Even the pre-school child is not a contented neuter, for by three years of age differences between the sexes are evident in play, choice of companions, verbal ability, test performance, and sociability.[2, 3, 7] The pre-school child's sexual identification fluctuates, however, and does not influence all of his activity.

On the other hand, the child entering school is constantly reminded that there are two distinct sexes and that there is one group to which he does not belong. Play at recess seldom consists of united, coöperative endeavors between boys and girls, but instead it takes the form of chasing contests between groups of each sex. Boys' lines and girls' lines are formed at the door when the bell rings, and spelling and arithmetic matches are set between the sexes. There is the unique existence of two separate bathrooms, and each child steals a quick glance at the forbidden facilities when a door is momentarily ajar.

As time goes on, dissimilarities increase in play interests and preferences, and as boys and girls diverge in their activities, they are less familiar with and sympathetic to the attitudes of the opposite sex. During the later elementary years, each sex claims superiority for itself, with the girls disdaining the rough, careless boys and the boys ridiculing the girls for their silliness and their airs.

Joining His Generation

Before he reaches the age of six years, the child begins his shift from dependence on adults to assertion of his rights with his peers and limited reliance on them for companionship and acceptance—providing he has had an opportunity to play regularly with other children.[6] If he has not or if his contacts with children have been unsatisfying or unpleasant, as a kindergartener he can outdistance his mother in a race back home after she delivers him at the classroom door. He wants no part of a harried life with peers away from his home and family.

By the time he reaches 12 years, all of this has changed. His keenest pleasure is found in leaving home and going out with friends. His parents still are important to him, but he is not dependent on them to provide inordinate reassurance or to intercede for him. His teacher no longer is a substitute mother, but is evaluated accurately as a member of the adult generation. The child's happiness depends greatly on the reactions of his peers to him, and parental acceptance does not substitute completely for theirs.

Acquisition of Self-concept

The pre-school child knows what he wants and tries to get it any way he can. His attempts to please or displease his parents are direct and to the point, and he does not care how he impresses others.

Between six and 12 years, however, because he examines his actions in terms of others' standards, he acquires a concept of himself as a certain kind of person. He thinks of himself as usually capable or inept, welcomed by his peers or rejected by them, and approved or disapproved by his parents. If he is not hampered by firmly established habits of dependency or self-centeredness, he works hard to be successful, and the outcome of every endeavor or personal contact is of greater concern to him than to anyone else. He reacts to his own performance with increased confidence in himself and renewed determination to do well, or he reacts with discouragement, followed by retreat or rebellion. If he judges himself a failure, he ceases to try, and his actions become increasingly imitative[1] and retain characteristics of immaturity.

LIFE WITH THE ELEMENTARY SCHOOL CHILD

The erratic swings of the elementary child from responsibility to pettiness, from thoughtfulness to resentment, and from pride to frantic concern are illustrated in these descriptions of episodes from two days in the lives of ten- and 11-year-old girls, Janice and Martha, the older children in a family of four. The two younger brothers, Billy and Jimmy, are five and four years old.

JANICE—AGE 10

Friday: 7:30—Still in bed and cannot understand why she's not tired at night but is tired in the morning. First one to breakfast table and then tries to clear table while rest of siblings are still eating. This causes some heated words and she grumblingly puts food back on table. Tries to get done what she can and leave kitchen before Jimmy is through so she won't have to do his dishes. Wonders aloud what she'd do with all her time if she didn't have so much work to do.

At noon, lunch conversation is about the "spoiled" kids in our block, about school, about how other kids get to stay up much later at night, etc.

Home from school at 3:40. Excited and mad about boy with a stick whom she saw knock robin from nest. Went into room to read. Mother calls and reminds her of upstairs bathroom. (She's added the job of cleaning sink and mirror as she works for her Girl Scout housekeeping badge.) Mother asks her to baby-sit brothers while she goes to grocery. . . . At 4:15 mother reminds Janice of her Girl Scout cookies. She stops playing ball with her brothers with a shrug, comes in for the cookies and order blank, and leaves. In a few minutes she's back. "Mother, I don't have the right kind. I'm in real trouble." Sounds worried—voice is shrill and face flushed. She counts undelivered orders and boxes. "I need seven boxes and I have six. I'll have to pay for that out of my own money." She is near tears. She counts again. "What'll I do?" Her voice rises with each sentence. She doesn't wait for an answer and goes over the orders again. Looks up dismayed. Phones cookie mother for Girl Scouts but no answer. Decides to deliver the cookies she can and leaves. Is back in 15 minutes.

No one was home where she went. Phones again. Still no answer. Mother goes over order with her and error is discovered: right number of boxes but two of the wrong kind.

After supper Janice practiced piano. Playing took on added flourish when neighbor girl, Betty, age 9, arrived. They talked about demands of piano teacher. Mother reminds Janice to finish practicing. . . . Mother asks if Janice has everything ready for tomorrow's 4-mile hike with her scout troop. Janice says she doesn't know if she's going: She might be too tired. Mother talks of keeping your word, other people who have changed plans to accommodate this hike, etc. (Piano lesson time is involved.) Janice leaves porch mad! Comes back in ten minutes with knapsack packed, a big smile on her face. "I've decided to go." Phones her piano teacher and confirms change of time. Asks for wieners, etc. for tomorrow's lunch. The cupboards are bare so mother and Janice walk to the grocery. Janice chatters all the way—about hiking and getting in shape for the World's Fair and about tornadoes, as the wind gets stronger. On the walk home, Janice grabs mother's hand and mother responds with affectionate words and praise. Janice says, "I like me, too. I really do. I can't help it." (Until this year, Janice had always said she hated herself.)

Saturday: Awakened by mother at 8:15. Dresses quietly and eats a good breakfast. Conversation about tornado that destroyed home in Michigan. She seems to be putting herself into that family's place and feels bad. By the time she leaves at 8:50 she is bubbling with energy and anticipation of her day.

3:45—Janice returns, tired and dirty. Lies in living room chair to tell about her day. "It was 3½ miles. Mrs. Bishop didn't see why our patrol didn't win first prize for our campfire. It was really the best one." Proceeds to tell what was wrong with the others and how their own was made. Mother suggested that Janice relax in a nice, warm tub. "Can I get my hair wet, too?" After 1½ hours, mother tells Janice that it's almost supper time. . . . She reluctantly agrees to do dishes and then practice piano. Watches her sister and friend bounce balls outside. Reads a story to Jimmy and tucks him into bed. Reads to herself until bedtime.

MARTHA—AGE 11

Friday: 7:30—is getting dressed and has made bed when mother looks in open door of dark room to see if the girls are up. Comes late to breakfast and quarrels with Billy about kicking under the table. Practices piano and goes off to school. . . . At noon she hurries into her room to read a library book, *Madame Curie,* hoping she won't be asked to make lunch.

3:40—opens front door, bangs it closed. She is crying to herself. Sits on the stairs and buries her head in her arms. Mother sits on step with arm around her for a few seconds until crying subsides. In response to mother's question she looks up, still crying. "A boy pulled off my scarf—I gave his bike a *little* push and he kicked me." She puts her hand to her groin. Mother says she is sorry and talks about getting mad and how hard it is to get even without getting hurt more. Martha says, "He was younger than me." (Martha seldom cries so this is quite an experience.) Her sister, who followed her in the door by a minute, offers sympathy. Martha picks up her school books. "I did the arithmetic the old way so I have to do it over. Mr. Jones (teacher) explained squaring numbers this morning while I was gone." . . . Asks if she should bike or walk to dentist because it looks like rain. Mother says it's up to her and she leaves, walking. Arrives 15 minutes late. After stitches are removed, she takes her certificate for bravery given by the dentist to the drug store for a free ice cream cone. When she returns home, her dad is there and they go to the basement workbench where Martha has started a science project. He shows her how to paint the inside of the box containing it. She is called to supper in the middle of her painting and returns to it after supper. Neighbor girl, Betty, comes in and watches Martha paint. She is quite impressed and asks if Martha helped paint our house. Martha says she was just a baby then.

Saturday: Reads in bed until called for breakfast at 9:30. Eats with her dad and then he takes her and friend to junior choir practice at church two miles away. . . . returns from choir and tells mother details about new choir robes. Starts doing breakfast dishes. Helps four-year-old brother who comes in crying. Washes cut and puts on Band-Aid. In a few minutes she is verbally fighting and slapping him. Mother intervenes and Martha leaves the room. In a few minutes she is calling Jimmy who runs to her saying "I'm sorry." They play a game in Jimmy's room. . . . Mother asks for Martha's help in preparing lunch so mother can sew. Martha reluctantly agrees and opens a can of soup for herself, mother, and dad. Sister is eating on hike and brothers are at a birthday party. After lunch mother asks Martha to clean kitchen and bedrooms for 25 cents. Martha does a good job but keeps being interrupted when brothers return, and visits with parents as they go in and out. She goes outside to watch her dad repair the car. Offers advice to mother in altering dresses. Practices piano. Takes another dental slip for ice cream cone as she leaves to walk the mile to her lesson. . . . Home after 5. Helps Billy put together and fly the airplane he brought home from party. At supper, she talks about meeting and visiting with our friend, a Negro, who was among many downtown soliciting for NAACP.

After supper she talks Janice into doing the dishes since she had done them at breakfast and lunch. Is happy not to *have* to do dishes or practice piano and goes outside and bounces ball against the house with a girl friend until bedtime, when she's called in to wash her hair and take a bath. Is affectionate with her parents and seems to feel very happy as she visits with them before climbing into bed.

ADAPTATIONS OF PARENTS

Uncertainty and Insecurity

The inevitable changes in the child's behavior during the elementary years and the need to manage many minor crises combine to invade parental certainty and security in rearing the child.

Adults sometimes react to their decreased self-confidence by abdicating from parenthood. They enroll the child in every kind of extra lesson and organized activity, winter and summer, and thus minimize the time during which they must be responsible for him. A few mothers cannot cope with their children's disturbing presence for even a few hours daily, and they habitually take to their beds shortly before the children are due home from school. They win obedience and quiet from them because of their purported ill health, and they successfully avoid the normal pains of child rearing.

Other parents, unable to accept the altered status now allotted them, battle with the child. They are determined that he will obey and that he will learn to read or dance or play the piano, and they approach him with a grim expression and a ready switch. Their uncertainty leads them to rigid domination of the child and prevents his behaving in unpredictable ways.

Many uncertain parents flounder their way through the days, weeping over the child's actions, their own failures, and the loss of the child's affection and dependence. They are forbearing and understanding, permitting the child to abuse them and to shirk responsibility. Occasionally they rebel at the child's insubordination and laziness and flare at him violently, producing temporary improvement in his behavior but leaving them feeling guilty about having criticized him.

Uncertainty and insecurity are natural when parents meet new problems in a child whom they thought they knew well and who could be influenced by his devotion to them. To restore their self-confidence, they need to be aware of the effect on the child of the changes and pressures he is experiencing, and they must not credit the appearance of difficulties solely to their own inadequacies.

Deficiencies of the Child

The deficiencies of the elementary school child are on public exhibition. His grades, his athletic skill, and his popularity are known to many people, and his parents beam or cringe accordingly.

Their own self-esteem is inextricably entwined in the child's performance, and when his behavior or learning ability initiates a stream of unpleasant contacts between home and school, the child becomes the focus of trouble between parents and teachers. A boy's ease with or avoidance of sports is important in determining his father's attitude toward him. A mother who unrealistically compares her daughter with the most gregarious children she observes is disappointed when her child is not sought after or remains silent in peer groups.

When parents feel acutely embarrassed by the child's deficiencies, they may resort to constant scolding, dwelling on every weakness and failure of the child, and never recognizing successful achievements. Sometimes they react by excusing his failures or by arranging situations designed to protect him from exposure to challenge. Other parents act for the child, completing his schoolwork and conversing with his friends, thus obscuring awareness of inadequacy.

Loss of the Child

The pre-school child is under parental direction continually. His parents order his life and require him to behave as they wish. His dependence on their goodwill and affection is complete, and both he and they know that they are indispensable to him. When a child starts to school, this begins to change, and the loss of both parental control and of the child's dependency increases each year.

The teacher now is responsible for the child's guidance, instruction, and discipline for many hours each day, and she fulfills her obligation in her own way, regardless of the desires of the parents. Friends become the child's preferred companions, and the days when his fun centered solely in family activities are over. Rivalry and resentment can develop in parents as the child shuts them out by forming clubs with his peers and by insisting that their ideas excel those of his parents. When he argues about a rule's being unfair because they are the only parents who impose it, they are angered by his critical comparison.

Some parents withdraw from the child as he appears to do from them, but they do so in jealousy and never attempt to regain his companionship and trust. Others refuse to be relegated to a less favored status, and by one method or another they chase away the child's new friends and undermine his belief in others' ideas. Some accept the inevitability of the child's expanding contacts, but they maintain a director's position by choosing his friends and subjecting him to educational and social experiences they consider beneficial.

With his decreasing need to rely on his parents for direction and acceptance, the child may rebel against stringent rules and total control which he did not dispute when he was younger. His defiance startles and angers his parents, who recall him hazily at an earlier age as a charming and obedient child. Now he forgets instructions, ignores commands, and glibly informs the sitter that his parents permit him to watch the late show on television.

Parents expecting trustworthy and conscientious behavior from the child because he is older believe something is seriously wrong when he honors neither his word nor their instructions. Many parents cease trying to enforce their requirements. They do for him what he fails to do by himself: making his bed, picking up his clothes, and cleaning up the disorder he creates—always with a headshake and a deep sigh. Other parents lecture, scold, and punish endlessly, achieving only limited change in the child's behavior and convincing him that they dislike and disapprove of him.

The child's rebellion against parental rules is an inevitable corollary of the independence he must demonstrate at school, and slavish obedience at home is no longer possible for him when he must manage by himself for hours each day.

The child of this age does not reject his parents, even though they feel that he does. He needs them most of the time, relies on their judgment and information, and follows their directions when he is sure they mean them. He has embarked on a new and difficult life, much of which he must live without them. He ponders experiences he has with other people, recalling fears and disappointments of the day but remembering triumphs as well. These occurrences and the recollection of them influence the way he behaves at home.

He is preoccupied with new concerns and with assimilating and governing the complicating events of his life. He takes his parents for granted, expecting from them the same casual attitude he now has toward matters of slight importance, such as tooth-brushing and sibling disputes. He needs his parents, however, not only to restrict and direct his behavior when it is harmful but also to encourage him and to express their confidence and pride in him. Their opinion of him retains its prime significance in influencing his behavior.

REFERENCES

1. Bandura, A., and Walters, R. H.: *Social Learning and Personality Development.* New York, Holt, Rinehart and Winston, 1963, p. 85.
2. Brown, D.: Masculinity-femininity development in children. *J. Consult. Psychol.,* 1957, *21* (3), 197–202.
3. Brown, D.: Sex-role preference in young children. *Psychol. Monogr.,* 1956, *70* (421).
4. Commoss, H. H.: Some characteristics related to social isolation of second grade children. *J. Educ. Psychol.,* 1962, *53,* 38–42.
5. Crandall, V. J., and Rabson, A.: Children's repetition choices in an intellectual achievement situation following success and failure. *J. Genet. Psychol.,* 1960, *97,* 161–168.
6. Heathers, G.: Emotional dependence and independence in nursery school play. *J. Genet. Psychol.,* 1955, *87,* 37–57.
7. Kagan, J., and Moss, H. A.: *Birth to Maturity.* New York, John Wiley and Sons, 1962, p. 169.
8. Sontag, L. W., and Kagan, J.: The emergence of intellectual achievement motives. *Amer. J. Orthopsychiat.,* 1963, *33,* 532–535.
9. Spock, B.: *Baby and Child Care.* New York, Pocket Books, Inc., 1957, pp. 385–386.
10. Thompson, G. G.: *Child Psychology.* Cambridge, Mass., Houghton Mifflin Co., 1952, p. 131.

CHARACTERISTIC BEHAVIOR

Chapter 25

Early Elementary Years

Mother and child finally arrive at a destination they have long anticipated: regular school attendance. He proudly joins the older children who disappear from the neighborhood daily, and his mother welcomes an intermission in his care. Each is soon disappointed. The mother discovers that her child is changing for the worse, and she blames the school. The neophyte student discovers that school means sitting, being quiet, paying attention, and completing assignments—a far cry from the lazy freedom to which he has been accustomed.

Grapko[5] considered the six-to-eight-year-old child to have three basic needs: achievement, autonomy, and recognition by his peer group. The degree of effort he expends in attempting to fulfill these needs establishes habits which endure for years. Kagan and Moss[7] found that such behavior as passive withdrawal from stressful situations, dependency on the family, ease of arousing anger, involvement in intellectual mastery, social interaction anxiety, and sexual behavior patterns evident during the six-to-ten-year period appear as related behavior in adulthood.

THE SIX-YEAR-OLD

Parents are not entirely in error when they attribute the changed behavior of the six-year-old to the effect of school attendance. The child's daily experience of competition with his peers and his independence from his mother impel him to utilize forms of behavior which before were unnecessary. Because of school, he often is tired, lonely, defiant, and angry, and he appears to be an ethical chameleon.

Fatigue and Loneliness

The six-year-old is a tired child. For the first time in his life, he is required to be away from home and follow directions of adults other than his parents for five or six hours each day. Time is needed to develop endurance, and few six-year-olds feel rested during the school week. A few days after starting school, the child tends to isolate himself, playing listlessly and sleeping poorly.[9] School days are difficult, and before the day even begins he relives the fatigue he feels at its end, and his dawdling through dressing and eating exasperates his clock-conscious mother. When long hours at school are followed by a late bedtime, the child becomes exhausted and he shows his fatigue in irritability and forgetfulness. Saturdays he is a changed child, and he bounds from bed at 6 o'clock in the morning, dresses quickly, and courteously lets his mother sleep while he prowls around the kitchen accommodating his ravenous appetite.

Even though they do become tired, many six-year-olds enjoy schoolwork and their contacts with other children. Others, however, dread every school day. They are wary of their classmates and lonesome for their mothers and their homes, especially if a younger sibling is left behind to enjoy privately all of the toys and all of the attention. The child who finds school too unpleasant may beg every morning to stay home, insisting that the teacher does not like him or that he is abused by his classmates.

Defiance and Anger

The six-year-old astounds his mother with an angry outburst when she mildly tells him, as he walks in the door after school, to change his clothes. Worn out when he reaches home, he is thinking of little else except that he can relax, and he cannot tolerate one more order after his hours of laboring under adult instructions. Sometimes he rebels at his mother's greeting him with a command because he is pleased with himself for managing so well during the day. If he has learned some new words, answered a question correctly, been chosen first for a tug of war, and in general conducted himself admirably, he feels like a conquering hero, and to be subjected to orders as though he were a small child insults his dignity.

Irritation with parental control is normal for the six-year-old, and the child who never exhibits it is one who is retreating from meeting his new obligations. A conforming, nonaggressive attitude toward his mother and other adults during the early school years has been found related to the repression of anger and the inhibition of aggression in adolescence and early adulthood.[7]

Contradictory Ethical Behavior

The six-year-old perplexes and worries his parents by his contradictory ethical behavior, which appears to range from prudishness to callousness and impropriety. Announcing to his parent or teacher that another child has broken a rule is his trademark, and adults worry that the child will become a permanent informer. Their fear is groundless, however, because the six-year-old is trying to demonstrate only that he knows right from wrong, and he does so by recognizing and reporting misbehavior. He is not so concerned that a guilty child be punished as he is with earning approbation from adults. His increased attention to misbehavior in others also serves as moral self-coaching which guards him from impetuous actions.

In contrast to his devotion to correct behavior in others are his jokes at the dinner table, which reflect interests and inclinations his parents consider improper.

They include such sallies as: "What's the button that doesn't button? . . . A belly button!"

"What are the smelliest letters in the alphabet? . . . P. U.!"

"Why did the little moron put his father in the refrigerator? . . . He wanted cold pop!"

The adult's more sophisticated concepts of propriety for children are unknown to the six-year-old. His dabbling with forbidden topics seems to him both interesting and funny, and it is a bond which unites him with his peers. His tale-bearing, which proves that he recognizes the existence of a universally-accepted set of rules for behavior, is a significant step in his ethical development.

THE SEVEN-YEAR-OLD

The seven-year-old has become more accustomed to his daily life, although he still resents the appropriation of his freedom. He illustrates his growing confidence in himself by his careless disregard of parental requirements for neatness and correct manners. He is subjected increasingly to competition and challenge, and if he fails more than he succeeds, he responds with depression, aggression, or withdrawal.

Carelessness

He is constantly in trouble because of his lack of neatness. He trails his coat, gloves, cap, and mittens all over the house when he arrives from school. His dirty socks are flung in the wastebasket; library books are lost among his toys; and the clothing, empty cereal boxes, used tissues, and comics under his bed would fill a large suitcase.

At the table his parents scarcely can watch him eat. He shovels in huge mouthfuls, grabs for the butter at the far end of the table, spills food out of his mouth, knocks over his milk glass, and insists that he has washed his hands when they are covered with grime.[12]

Not only is he careless with his possessions and grubby at eating and washing, but his intellectual interests deteriorate. He becomes an avid comic book reader, just when his parents expect that education will develop him into an erudite individual. He goes through a dozen comics each month[8] and much prefers them to the library books his parents select for him.

His daily life is studded with nagging reminders as his parents see their vision of a conscientious, mannerly, thoughtful child disappearing rapidly. When he is away from home, however, his calm conversation and courteous requests delight the adults; and at school he is capable of offering information and considering ideas which demonstrate that his intellectual capabilities are expanding constantly.

Competition and Challenge

Many extracurricular activities are started when the child is seven, and these can complicate his life and harass him by exposing him to constant competition and challenge.

Junior groups of Scouts and Campfire Girls are organized for second graders, and membership in these means a weekly afternoon away from home. Even though he regrets the loss of his play time, the child enjoys the group if he usually is successful at the activities planned and has fun. If he is held to a rigid schedule of complex handiwork or if the children rule the leader and the meeting degenerates into a free-for-all, he dislikes the organization and protests continuing.

Piano lessons are introduced at seven years, and these consume more of the child's play time, as well as necessitating daily practice. His painfully slow translation of printed musical notes to the keyboard rarely affords him either pleasure or pride. Some instructors grade the child weekly on his performance, and he resists the added pressure by objecting to practice and begging to quit his lessons.

A girl taking ballet lessons must execute difficult exercises and acrobatics. If she is awkward, makes mistakes, falls, or is corrected often, she feels foolish and discouraged. In class, she must obey adult direction, keep quiet, and try to perform well. Her efforts often are graded and she is assigned exercises to practice during the week.

Boys participating in Little League baseball for the first time are the lowliest members of the team. They spend hours at practice and at games. Most of the time, they are confined to the bench or subjected to the jeers and anger of teammates and coach when they make errors.

The seven-year-old, faced with increased challenge, is also afflicted with a strong need to win at games and to excel in any competition. Losing, either as a member of a group or as an individual, angers and saddens him, and he rails or cries at the outcome, blaming his competitors for unfair tactics or advantages. To his parents he seems self-centered and sensitive, and they are concerned not only by the severity of his reaction to failure but by his strenuous efforts to win, which often include cheating and lying.

Reactions to Failure

The seven-year-old is confronted daily with evidence of his success or failure socially, academically, and athletically, and he assesses himself in comparison with his peers. If his classmates read more fluently than he and contribute information the teacher requests when he cannot or if his teacher scolds him often for laziness, talking, or bullying, he knows he is failing at school.

The child's opinion of himself is closely related to his academic achievement, especially for boys,[3] and a child who is aware of frequent failure at school tends to think of himself as inferior, rejected, and isolated. He defends himself by excessive compliance with others' directions, by negativism and aggression, or by evading instructions.

Extracurricular activities, which test him in social and athletic endeavors, may confirm his inadequacies and burden him further. He demonstrates his resentment of forced participation in them by evasion and rebellion which keep him in conflict with his parents. They react to his failures and resistance by pleas, lectures, punishment, conferences with teachers, and disappointment. The child's dissatisfaction with himself is compounded by their disapproval, and his reactions to their criticism become increasingly explosive.

THE EIGHT-YEAR-OLD

During the next year, the buffeted child begins to establish a base of self-confidence. He accepts the inevitability of school, he chooses some children for friends and rejects others, and he displays a new bravado in situations which test or try him.

Acceptance of School

After two full years, plus kindergarten, daily school attendance no longer seems strange to the child. Even if he is unhappy at school, he has graduated from his conviction that he should not have to go if he does not wish to. He knows he must, and he is now so familiar with school routine that he does not object to it, although he still may complain about his teacher or the work he is assigned.

He feels superior to kindergarteners and first graders, and he enjoys playing school with them and directing them in arithmetic and reading. He points out to them how demanding his own studies are and warns them about the difficult time they can expect in third grade. He poses questions to younger children which they cannot answer, and he ridicules them for their ignorance.

Spelldowns, arithmetic duels, speed tests, and flash card contests are regular events in his classroom, and if he is able, he gains in self-esteem in these public comparisons with his peers. Conversely, if he is slow to respond, afraid to speak first, or has not learned thoroughly, his poor showing crystallizes his low opinion of himself. His evaluation of his ability influences his willingness to exert the effort required for learning.[11]

Choice of Friends

When he was younger, the child believed he must be acceptable to everyone, and he cried when another child, even a disagreeable one, deserted him to play with someone else. At school, he tried to win popularity by whatever social technique was most familiar to him. If he did not attract attention from his peers, he retreated to solitude, convinced that they did not like him.

At eight, however, the child's confidence in himself is strengthened, and he no longer feels he must please everyone. He begins to pick and choose among the children and selects a few, whom he admires and from whom he usually receives approval, to be his best friends. Any act of rejection or unkind comment from one of these trusted companions represents betrayal and causes deep hurt. Sometimes a child admires another who does not choose him for a friend, and he seeks to win his approval with gifts, even stealing to provide them.

As well as acquiring a few close friends for himself, the eight-year-old voices his dislike for children he has discarded. He is critical and abusive of some children, particularly those who have no friends and are seldom in the teacher's favor. He joins a group attack on another child with alacrity, feeling little guilt and stoutly insisting that the child deserves such treatment because he really is fat, stupid, quarrelsome, or dirty. If adults explain the need for friendliness toward an unpopular child, however, he is easily convinced of the correctness of considerate behavior and readily reverses himself, especially if his classmates also cease their abuse of that child.

Many children select a child of the opposite sex to admire, partly because of the coy encouragement of adults. This honor is bestowed by the majority of girls on one boy and by the boys on only a few girls. The favored children are those who are comely, academically successful, and unhesitant about expressing their ideas and directing others.

Bravado

The eight-year-old wades in up to his chin as he attempts to conquer the challenges which confront him. He battles as an equal with his older siblings, and he hesitates only briefly before delivering the un-complimentary remark or sanctimonious reproof which is certain to elicit irate words or deeds from them.

His desire to appear completely self-sufficient aids him in an expert pretense at being unmoved by adult scoldings, and he listens in stony silence to sentences imposed for misbehavior, as well as proclaiming "That didn't hurt!" as a dignified finale to a spanking. His barely re-pressed tears and the tense laughter accompanying this manifest uncon-cern suggest that his indifference is a brave performance intended to disguise his misery.

He experiments with his newly-acquired assertiveness by entertain-ing all audiences. He plays the piano loudly, does acrobatics, tells and reads jokes to everyone, and grandly defies parental orders in the pres-ence of his friends. He imitates adult actions and conversation and seeks to place himself on a comradely level with them. Girls of this age, fully aware that they are acting, dismay their mothers by flinging their arms around boys and smothering them with kisses.

Their attempts to establish rapport with adults lead them to frank observations previously reserved for peers.

One eight-year-old girl, a dinner guest at a friend's home, heard the hostess say laughingly, "I thought I put some nuts in this cake, but I certainly can't find any."

"I can't find any nuts either, Mrs. Miller," said the child. "But I can sure find a burned place on the bottom!"

The free-speaking and acting eight-year-old is unaware of the incongruity or poor judgment reflected by his behavior. He seeks only to imitate the casual actions of his elders, now permissible by virtue of his budding self-respect. He feels that he no longer merits treatment as a child because he does not feel like one, and his many achievements establish some validity to his belief.

During these early elementary years, the child has separated himself from his home and has become involved in daily competition with his peers in significant social and academic endeavors. He has progressed from his initial distaste for the necessity to compete and achieve to an acceptance of the challenges his life presents, and he has acquired a degree of self-respect as a competent person.

REFERENCES

1. Ausubel, D. P.: *Theory and Problems of Child Development.* New York, Grune and Stratton, Inc., 1958, pp. 299, 351, 357.
2. Brooks, F. D.: *Child Psychology.* Cambridge, Mass., Houghton Mifflin Co., 1937, p. 376.
3. Fink, M. B.: Self concept as it relates to academic underachievement. *Calif. J. Educ. Res.,* 1962, *13,* 57–62.
4. Gesell, A., and Ilg, F. L.: *The Child from Five to Ten.* New York, Harper and Bros., 1946, pp. 92, 102, 106, 109, 144–146, 166, 173, 179.
5. Grapko, M. F.: The early school years. *Bull. Instit. Child Stud.* (*Toronto*), 1963, *25,* 1–14.
6. Harrison, H. K.: An investigation of transfer from children's expectations of mothers to children's expectations of teachers. *Psychol. Newsltr.* (N.Y.U.), 1956, 7, 107–120.
7. Kagan, J., and Moss, H. A.: *Birth to Maturity.* New York, John Wiley and Sons, 1962, pp. 154, 174, 266.
8. Kvaraceus, W. C.: *The Community and the Delinquent.* Yonkers-on-Hudson, New York, The World Book Co., 1954, pp. 351–352.
9. Müller, R.: Eine Socialpsychologische Untersuchung an Schulanfängern (A social-psychological study of first-graders). *Psychol. Beitr.,* 1953, *1,* 227–263.
10. Murphy, L. B.: Childhood experience in relation to personality development. *In* Hunt, J. McV., ed.: *Personality and the Behavior Disorders.* New York, The Ronald Press Co., 1944, vol. 2, p. 678.
11. Phillips, A. S.: Self concepts in children. *Educ. Res.,* 1964, *6,* 104–109.
12. Spock, B.: *Baby and Child Care.* New York, Pocket Books, Inc., 1957, pp. 386–387.
13. Walsh, A. M.: Self concepts of bright boys with learning difficulties. New York, Teachers College, Columbia University, 1956.

Chapter 26

Later Elementary Years

Almost imperceptibly the little child disappears about the time he reaches fourth grade, and a new and more mature individual emerges. Teachers observe a confidence and purposefulness in the nine-year-old which was only an unstable fragment of the blustering eight-year-old's personality. Even his parents, who see him daily, notice that he looks older and that he is beginning to enjoy separating himself from the family in his interests and activities.

During the later elementary years, the child increasingly acts and thinks independently. He sheds his need to conform to others' ideas and instead develops his own standards and opinions. Although these are still based essentially on his parents' concepts, he does not hesitate to question or oppose them, and he pays more attention than formerly to his peers' beliefs. He evaluates other people more realistically, and he emphasizes the isolation and self-responsibility which independence entails by evaluating himself as well.

During these three years, he also turns into an explorer. He is free to leave his home and to investigate new places and try new experiences. He also explores with ideas, not only questioning what he is told but also imagining grandeur and wisdom for himself, creating original languages, new versions of history, and elaborate tales based on anything he sees. He devotes himself to interests he selects and spends hours at hobbies, sports, or studies which intrigue him. As he acquires new ideas, he acquires new heroes, and he adopts for his inspiration someone outside his family who suits his idea of perfection.

Exploration fascinates him and independence satisfies him, but he also is engaged in continuous self-testing, much of which is by choice but not all of which results in greater appreciation of himself. He tries himself in contacts with his peers, in the acquisition of lasting skills in certain areas, and in attempting a wide variety of activities in which he has never participated before. He sets certain standards of achievement for himself academically, and because his skill is often inferior to his desire for success, he is dissatisfied and unhappy. In general, however, the child who establishes himself securely as a capable and acceptable individual has many moments of pride in himself and camaraderie with both peers and adults during these three years.

THE NINE-YEAR-OLD

The nine-year-old approaches a clearer division in sex roles, and he accepts his prescribed place, strengthening his choice by leaning more heavily for companionship on members of his own sex than ever before. He is aware of his arrival at a new level of independence, and this leads him to set high standards of performance in order to establish a respected place for himself.

Acceptance of Sex Role

Only now does the child begin to identify himself consistently with his own sex. A girl becomes anxious about her appearance, storming over an unruly strand of hair and glooming at herself in the mirror. She complains that all the other girls are prettier than she and that her clothes are unstylish. A boy, in squalid contrast, wears his underwear for a week and exits from the bathtub without touching either soap or washcloth.

Recess playtime no longer consists of chasing games between boys and girls. The boys go off by themselves to play football and baseball. The girls play Fox and Geese and Red Rover; or they pair off to play jacks, swing, climb on bars, or exchange secrets. Neighborhood friends of different sexes have less fun together. A girl finds that her former boy playmate jeers when she misses at bat and never hesitates to tackle her hard in a football game. He scorns her invitation to play house or school, although he may be an interested spectator while two girls talk and act for their paper doll families.

A girl or boy may admire a child of the opposite sex, not because they share common interests but because he is a successful member of his own group. Sometimes each sex treats the other derisively, but this behavior seldom is based on real contempt. It represents instead the child's overvaluation of his own sex, fortifying his identification with it.[2] Girls initiate criticism of boys, and the boys' antagonism is imitative and retaliatory.[12]

Extensive supervision by women at home, school, and in extra-curricular activities is customary for elementary boys, and their limited contact with adult males makes accurate imitation of masculine behavior difficult.[13] Rigid demands are made of boys to demonstrate dominance, skill, strength, and daring.[14] A boy must deny his need for comforting and concern, and he must not cry when he is lonely or abused. He must face up to aggression, even when he is badly frightened. He must accept every invitation to participate in every activity, even though he is the least skilled of the group. Such persistent courage is not easy to dredge up, and each failure signifies to the boy that he is not as manly as he is expected to be.

A girl slips easily from dependent child to dependent woman, because she is not held to the same standard of emotional self-control as a boy, nor is she censured for avoiding challenge. She must inhibit physical aggressiveness, however, and pay attention to deportment and to the proportion of time she spends playing exclusively with boys.

Children who do not adopt their appropriate sex roles are worried and unhappy. Rosenberg et al.[22] found that femininity in boys in the fourth, fifth, and sixth grades is associated with anxiety and impulsiveness, and masculinity in girls of this age produces anxiety and is related to conflict between the girls and their parents.

Expanded Peer Association

In his accepted role as a boy or girl, the child must find others like himself to strengthen his ability to behave appropriately. His friends begin to replace his parents, both as companions and as arbiters of what is proper in speech, dress, and manners. He learns from them, sympathizes with them, and modifies his behavior according to their treatment of him. He thinks highly of his peers as a group and defends them if they are criticized by adults.[12] The child who is uneasy with peers usually has been subjected to overprotection and suppression of his autonomy.[14]

Rules govern most play with peers for the nine-year-old. These are original rules rather than conventional, and cheating or ignoring agreed-upon rules is greeted with loud denunciation. Clubs and gangs are customary.[8] They formalize peer associations and provide both certainty of contacts and acceptance for the child. They are attractive also because they are off limits to adults, and the children do as they choose without direction or ridicule from parents or teachers. When a club is formed, the members choose a name, elect officers, and establish a few rules, but activities are haphazard and usually the group evaporates after a few meetings. Boys, who often spend some time building a clubhouse, achieve more cohesion in purpose and activity than do girls, and boys continue longer as a group.[5]

High Standards

The nine-year-old is beginning to think of himself as a person of independence and importance, and he seeks to maintain this pleasant feeling. He manages this in part by increased self-direction, and he conscientiously obeys his own orders. Gesell and Ilg[10] speak of him as being self-motivated for the first time.

He is inexperienced in self-direction, however, and he seeks structure and control of his efforts by establishing systems for maintaining order. He makes lists of his possessions and his plans, and these enable him to capture and act on his ideas. His addiction to regulation is apparent even when his activity is aimless, as he requires himself to avoid stepping on cracks in the sidewalk or to touch every third board of the fence he is passing.[23] Devoted to rules for himself, he also imposes them on others, and his door is plastered with signs informing his siblings when and under what conditions they may enter his room.

His orderliness and his obedience to rules convince him that there are absolutes to be observed, and he requires perfection in himself. Because he is so determined to do everything correctly, he is upset and disappointed when he does not. He cannot tolerate failure in himself, and he is furious at minor errors in a letter he is composing or a fault in his finished project. He gives up only momentarily, however, and later he will try again.

THE TEN-YEAR-OLD

As a ten-year-old the child continues to test himself in many activities, and his determination to be first and best is heightened. He develops special interests and spends hours on hobbies or in practicing any work or play activity which appeals to him. Many of these interests are sex linked and further stabilize his sex-role consistency. They also permit him to acquire new skills and new knowledge independent of the direction or formal instruction of adults.

His parents are demoted from their position on the summit of authority and wisdom, and he chooses heroes from among adults outside his family. Because he is able to recognize achievement and independence in himself, he attains solid self-respect, and he repudiates parental solicitude as inappropriate and demeaning.

Special Interests

Boys and girls diverge increasingly in the ways in which they spend their leisure time.[7] Boys play football, basketball, and baseball, and each wants to be a star player in the most important position on the team. A boy is dissatisfied if he considers his assignment unimportant, and he may stop playing.[5]

Girls spend less time playing mother to their dolls and instead act out with paper dolls the eventful daily experiences of large families they create. Dramatization delights them, and they devote hours to practicing and presenting shows to child and adult audiences.[19] A girl also enjoys playing outdoors, where she skates, rides her bike, and joins boys or girls in group play of all kinds. She seldom initiates group games, however, and is content to play by herself or with one other girl. Because she is not involved in regular competitive play, her life is more placid and satisfying than is a boy's.

The child of either sex, however, confines himself to activities he prefers, and if he is inept at group play, he retreats to stamp-collecting, model-making, cooking, sewing, reading, gardening, drawing, building, or printing a neighborhood newspaper. These solitary activities are not subject to peer appraisal and he chooses those at which he is successful. Parents may become concerned about the child's overemphasizing one interest or limiting his association with peers. There may also be conflict over his forgetting to complete chores or homework because of his absorption in his hobby, and parents may deplore the money spent on stamp collections or the chaos resulting from rock-collecting or scooter-building.

Dethroning His Parents

A ten-year-old listens to his teacher's factual presentations, reads about unknown places and new customs, learns a modern way of checking fractions, hears his peers' reports of their parents' convictions, and makes the accurate and startling discovery that his parents do not know everything. Unfortunately, he sometimes assumes also that his parents know nothing, and he begins to reject everything they say as incorrect. He is equipped to argue with his parents because of his daily acquisition of knowledge, and he outdistances them easily in areas unrelated to their work or interests. Some of his objections to their ideas and rules are made intentionally to determine whether there are reasonable bases for their philosophies and ethical standards.[15]

In divesting his parents of their superior status, he transfers his admiration to another adult, an idealized hero whom he would like to resemble. This hero may be a prominent historical figure about whom he has read, such as Florence Nightingale or Davy Crockett; a fictional character who solves mysteries and conquers adversity; or an older neighbor or relative, a teacher, or a Scout leader who is admired for his skills and social ease. Usually such hero worship increases the child's self-control, generosity, and conformity, although occasionally it leads to overcriticism of parents.

As he becomes convinced that he need not rely exclusively on his parents, the child finds a substitute for their guidance in his peers. Although he does not accept their moral concepts as conclusive, he nevertheless welcomes them and deliberately seeks them.[24] In his final decision about his own behavior, he usually acts according to his parents' viewpoints, but his conclusion is based to some extent on his evaluation of the divergent beliefs expressed by peers and adults.

Acquisition of Self-respect

The child is increasingly free to visit new places and engage in a wide variety of activities without parental supervision. He is exposed to new ideas so that he is induced to think independently, and he selects and completes many difficult tasks on his own initiative. The strength of his desire to succeed with what he undertakes is related to his feeling of independence.[25]

In veering away from parental domination, he continues to seek new experiences and new achievements of his own with greater confidence than formerly. He is allowed to go with his friends some distance from home, wandering through dime stores and stopping for cokes. He may take his bike and lunch to explore the countryside for several hours with a friend. To get completely away from the adults who usually supervise his actions and plan his days is a cherished privilege, and this freedom contributes to his ability to manage alone.

He experiments not only in where he goes and what he does but also in what he says. His verbal contacts are more pertinent and socialized than ever before, both with adults and friends.[20] He keeps on tap a supply of puzzles and riddles with which he can thwart adults and older siblings. He jokes with others but now recognizes the difference between banter and insults, and his sense of humor, which includes laughing at himself, marks him as a person of some sophistication.

On receiving his report card, a ten-year-old boy commented to his teacher with a grin, "I'm sure glad I brought my ink eraser along today!"

A fifth grade class with a teacher named Miss Ness labelled themselves "The Unteachables."* Nicknames are standard and are deliberately uncomplimentary. Thomas is addressed as "Too-mouse"; Michael changes to "Mitch," then to "Itch," and finally to "Scratch"; and a boy named Andy Eaton must answer to "Ant-eater."

---

* After a television program, "The Untouchables," starring Elliot Ness.

Because of his soundly-based self-respect, the ten-year-old is keenly embarrassed both for himself and for his parent when he is treated with less esteem than he merits. He avoids being kissed by his mother, and he walks beside her in public only if he is under the impression that he is escorting her. If his older brother chases away an aggressive playmate, the ten-year-old is abashed, not grateful, at the protection given him. If his mother plans entertainment for his "little friends" or his father sends him to bed for misbehavior, he is grossly insulted by the implication that he is so young that he requires constant help and close discipline.

THE ELEVEN-YEAR-OLD

Physical changes complicate the eleven-year-old's reactions to others and to himself. His detachment from parents and siblings increases steadily, and he affirms the separation by sharp disapproval of them. He believes his conscience is the product of his own thinking, and he acts as he sees fit. The lives of people he does not know interest him, and he is genuinely concerned about significant social problems.

Physical Changes

Social, intellectual, and emotional maturity progress in relationship to the child's biological growth. If his physical development parallels that of his peers or does not deviate from it to an extreme degree, he is not as concerned by changes as he is if he precedes or lags behind his friends in growth.[16]

Preceding the onset of menstruation, girls experience glandular changes which make them touchy and moody. They cry easily, resent correction, and appear to be miserable most of the time. Boys may be concerned about their height. A few 11-year-olds have made great gains in size, and a boy whose head reaches to his friend's shoulder begins to have misgivings about himself. Because there are marked individual differences at this period, the child is not as worried about growth as he will be a year or two later, but he is aware that his body is changing and he reorients his thinking about himself.

Disapproval of Family

The obnoxious young brother vividly portrayed in the Sunday comics is no hypothetical character. He is an 11-year-old boy who announces to his sister's boy friend, loudly enough so she can hear, that she isn't ready yet because she's still struggling into her girdle. He ridicules and embarrasses her because he considers her an alien creature who has rejected the younger generation's alliance and deserted him by adopting adult manners, actions, and thoughts. He is uneasy and disappointed at being left out and left behind.

He feels the same isolated strangeness when he sees his parents kissing or holding hands and, knowing that he can no longer join them in displaying mutual affection, he comments with a loud and disgusted "Mush!" Unable to visualize himself as ever acquiring the interests and habits of the adult world, he disparages them in defense of his familiar and hard-won position of importance with his contemporaries.

Not only does he scorn his elders, he also deprecates his younger siblings.[15] His own superiority affords him security, and he contemptuously corrects the information offered by a younger sibling, roars his disapproval of cheating at games, and complains to his parents about the younger child's getting by with slovenly bed-making and dish-washing. He makes himself unpopular with everyone at home, and thus his separation from his family is less difficult for him.

Obedience and Morality

His criticism of the members of his family and their subsequent disapproval of him isolate him and lead him to justify his behaving as he chooses, rather than as his parents wish. His mother tells him to shovel the snow off the sidewalk, and although he intends to do so, usually he gets to it only after his mother has descended on him irately two hours later. He is cautioned repeatedly about leaving his father's tools out in the yard, but he never remembers to bring them in.

Restless and inattentive, he feels little guilt about his actions and is unhappy only at the unpleasantness he must endure when his shortcomings are pointed out to him.[15] His parents believe that he is disobedient, lazy, and thoughtless, which he is—although not deliberately or revengefully. He leads the life he prefers, does what interests him, and uses his time for himself. Parental demands strike him as singularly unimportant and he treats them accordingly.

The 11-year-old is completely aware of the difference between moral and immoral behavior and of his obligation to conform to recognized ethical standards.[3, 11] His allegiance is to his own conscience, however, and not to adult rules. If he believes that an act is wrong, he avoids it; and if he fails to do so, he feels great guilt and hopes for discovery and punishment.

Concern for Others

His concern for persons other than the immediate members of his family is aroused. He discusses thoughtfully the plight of the Negro, and he wonders why Communist citizens cannot choose their leaders. He talks politics, inquiring how Democrats and Republicans differ and debating the implications of adhering to party lines in voting. He is curious about who is responsible for wars, and he does not understand why poverty and millionaires exist simultaneously. He can understand, if he is taught, the motivations of individuals who commit cruel or criminal acts.[17] He is momentarily appalled by the living conditions of the underprivileged when he accompanies his Scout group to deliver Christmas presents to a poor family, and he empathizes with the children.[9]

Although he does not dwell on these problems, he is serious when he does consider them, and he has ideas for improving matters. His conscience, which does not bind him to rigid personal behavior, is broadening to include an awareness of significant social problems which pose questions of fairness and equality.

During the later elementary years, the child's tentative, uncertain, initial effort to establish himself as an individual changes to assertive independence. His achievements in academic learning and social interaction, his acquisition of varied skills, and his expansion of convictions and concepts are accomplished with mingled joy and pain, but they result in his attainment of self-confident independence.

REFERENCES

1. Ausubel, D. P.: *Theory and Problems of Child Development.* New York, Grune and Stratton, Inc., 1958, pp. 390, 394, 448, 468.
2. Bjerstedt, A.: A double-directed analysis of preference motivations and other pal-description statements: studies in socio-perceptual selectivity. *Acta Psychologica* (Amsterdam), 1955, *11,* 257–268.
3. Boehm, L., and Naas, M. L.: Social class differences in conscience development. *Child Developm.,* 1962, *33,* 565–574.
4. Bowerman, C. E., and Kinch, J. W.: Changes in family and peer orientation of children between the fourth and tenth grades. *Soc. Forces,* 1959, *37,* 206–211.
5. Brooks, F. D.: *Child Psychology.* Cambridge, Mass., Houghton Mifflin Co., 1937, pp. 347–349, 375.
6. Brown, D.: Masculinity-femininity development in children. *J. Consult. Psychol.,* 1957, *21*(3), 197–202.
7. Campbell, W. J.: Preferences of children for others of the same or opposite sex. *Aust. J. Psychol.,* 1955, *7,* 45–51.
8. Crane, A. R.: The development of moral values in children: IV. Preadolescent gangs and the moral development of children. *Brit. J. Educ. Psychol.,* 1958, *28,* 201–208.
9. Dymond, R. F., Hughes, A. S., and Raabe, V. L.: Measurable changes in empathy with age. *J. Consult. Psychol.,* 1952, *16,* 202–206.
10. Gesell, A., and Ilg, F. L.: *The Child from Five to Ten.* New York, Harper and Bros., 1946, pp. 89, 192–193, 208, 214.
11. Griffiths, W.: *Behavior Difficulties of Children as Perceived and Judged by Parents, Teachers, and Children Themselves.* Minneapolis, University of Minnesota Press, 1952.

12. Harris, D. B., and Sing, C. T.: Children's attitudes toward peers and parents as revealed by sentence completion. *Child Developm.*, 1957, *28*, 401–411.
13. Hartley, R. E.: Sex-role pressures and the socialization of the male child. *Psychol. Rep.*, 1959, *5*, 457–468.
14. Kagan, J., and Moss, H. A.: *Birth to Maturity.* New York, John Wiley and Sons, 1962, pp. 58, 139, 225–226.
15. Kanner, L.: *Child Psychiatry,* Ed. 3. Springfield, Ill., Charles C Thomas, 1957, p. 45.
16. Krogman, W. M.: Biological growth as it may affect pupil's success. *Merrill-Palmer Quart.*, 1955, *1*, 90–98.
17. Levitt, E. E.: Punitiveness and "causality" in grade school children. *J. Educ. Psychol.*, 1955, *46*, 494–498.
18. Mussen, P., Conger, J., and Kagan, J.: *Child Development and Personality,* Ed. 2. New York, Harper and Row, 1956, pp. 360, 370, 374.
19. Norsworthy, N., and Whitley, M. T.: *The Psychology of Childhood.* New York, The Macmillan Co., 1925, pp. 292–294, 302.
20. Phillips, E. L., Wiener, D. N., and Haring, N. G.: *Discipline, Achievement and Mental Health.* Englewood Cliffs, N. J., Prentice-Hall, Inc., 1960, p. 151.
21. Rosenberg, B. G., and Sutton-Smith, B.: A revised conception of masculine-feminine differences in play activities. *J. Genet. Psychol.*, 1960, *96*, 165–170.
22. Rosenberg, B. G., Sutton-Smith, B., and Morgan, E.: The use of opposite sex scales as a measure of psychosexual deviancy. *J. Consult. Psychol.*, 1961, *25*(3), 221–225.
23. Spock, B.: *Baby and Child Care.* New York, Pocket Books, Inc., 1957, pp. 386–391.
24. Sutton, R. S.: An appraisal of certain aspects of children's social behavior. *J. Teacher Educ.*, 1962, *13*, 30–34.
25. Wertheim, J., and Mednick, S. A.: The achievement motive and field independence. *J. Consult. Psychol.*, 1958, *22*, 38.

Section Two

BEHAVIOR PROBLEMS

Chapter 27

Habit Problems: Eating and Sleeping

Eating and sleeping habits ordinarily stabilize during the pre-school years, except for deviations attributable to temporarily distressing situations. Significant disturbance is indicated if there are continuing or new problems in the smooth functioning of these basic activities during the elementary years.[3]

Difficulties may be caused by indifference of the parents to the child's need for adequate physical care, by overstimulation or fatigue which interferes with orderly habit maintenance, by the use of eating and sleeping requirements as a test of dominance by parent and child, or by anxiety arising from home or school conflicts and worries.

EATING

Early eating problems to which parents have contributed by forcing, coddling, or overconcern will continue when the child is older.* Eating habits also are disturbed by new emotional pressures stemming from school attendance and daily competition with peers. Food refusal, obesity, vomiting, and a different form of pica may occur during the elementary years.

---

* See Chapter 16, "Eating Problems."

Food Refusal

Most lackadaisical eaters show a sudden spurt of appetite at six or seven years of age. The normal child of this age regards mealtime as merely a break in a busy day and no longer uses it as a battleground to liven dull hours. Increased demands on energy stimulate appetite, and the child wastes little time in eating, often gulping down a meal in five minutes so that he can return to his interrupted activities. The child who retains a poor appetite during these years opposes the natural tendency of his age toward increased and rapid food consumption.

Kanner[7] described undereaters as more alert, aggressive, communicative, and congenial than overeaters. Moreover, he found undereaters better able to resist parental pressure. When the child's eating is of constant concern to his mother, her fussing increases his determination to resist her wishes. The child's appetite disappears when he is worried or tired, and an older child may refuse his dinner because he habitually indulges in milk shakes and potato chips at a short order stand en route home from school. Other children have been initiated into the vexations of orthodontia, and for them eating is difficult and sometimes painful. Illness reduces appetite, and elementary school children are prone to sickness during their first two years of school attendance.

Wheedling or forcing food works against the child's natural increase in appetite and disguises emotional and physical distress which the parent otherwise would notice. Small servings, increased gradually and limited at first to food the child likes, overcome habitual mealtime refusals. An after-school snack takes advantage of the child's keenest hunger and increases his interest in food generally. The child with a poor appetite should play outside when school is over, but to counteract fatigue resulting from hard playing, a younger child should be called in 30 minutes before dinner is ready. If this practice makes him feel either abused or overprotected, his mother can arrange to need his help in setting the table.

Obesity

Many children between the ages of seven and 12 years retain a moderate amount of fat which disappears as the child reaches adolescence.[10] The obese child, however, overeats to such a degree that he finds it difficult to get around and impossible to keep up with his peers in running games and sports. Increasingly isolated, he commences an unhappy cycle of eating to solace his distress, gaining more weight and diminishing his opportunities to live with and like his own generation.*

---

* See Case 18, Henry P., p. 509.

Obese children are characterized by emotional dependence, passivity, isolation, and personal insecurity. Many are enuretic, and their interests are narrow.[7] Ostergaard[8] reported that overeating was precipitated by a specific traumatic event in 16 of 58 observed cases.

Overeating may develop around seven years of age, as a child attempts to replace his parents with friends. If he fails, he is lonely, and he treats himself to food as consolation. The child worried about school failure or displeasing his parents may also compensate with food for his unhappy life.[7]

Maternal overprotection has been identified as a contributing cause to obesity in children, sometimes as a disguised reversal of rejection.[4] Iversen et al.[5] noted that mothers of obese children had experienced childhoods devoid of love. Overprotective mothers demonstrate their need for response from others by their emotional lability, manifested by helpless crying and impulsive punishment of the child. The family atmosphere is uncertain and laden with clinging solicitude and the dramatic expression of hurt feelings. Overfeeding the child sometimes represents the mother's attempt to atone for punishment which she later regrets.[7]

Other investigators credit constitutional tendencies and a family pattern of abnormal food intake, combined with inactivity, for a child's obesity.[2, 6, 9, 11, 12] Huge quantities of food always are available to the child and he acquires the habit of excessive eating by imitation, encouragement, and pressure from parents. Some parents defend the child's eating habits and consider his size an indication that he is healthy and well nourished.

If the parents can be convinced that obesity harms the child, his overeating can be curtailed. Food sufficient for only one moderate helping should be prepared at mealtime, and unneeded food should not be available. Candy, nuts, soft drinks, cake, pie, cookies, and ice cream should appear only in limited quantities. One mother, tentatively trying to help her two obese children lose weight, reported proudly that she now bought only a quart of ice cream, rather than a half-gallon, for their dinner dessert.

A calorie count can be started with a record of the child's normal caloric intake each day during a week of unrestricted eating. Each succeeding week, a daily reduction of 100 calories can be made, so that the child's appetite decreases gradually along with his food consumption. If he keeps the record himself, he will be more interested in and honest about food limitation, and if other overweight members of the family join in the program, he will not feel resentful. A child giving up food, even gradually, needs extra pleasures to replace it, and arranging for more excursions, peer contacts, parental attention, and praise than usual during this period helps him fret less about his deprivation.

Vomiting

The pre-school child's deliberately induced vomiting disappears as he becomes older. A healthy elementary school child who is unable to retain food usually is tense and fearful.

Many young children are so concerned about going to school that they cannot eat breakfast, and if forced to do so, they lose it on the way or even in the classroom.[10] An older child may vomit before a public performance in a school play or a piano recital or after becoming overly excited or fatigued at play. Moving to a new city or starting in at a new school often creates tension which causes vomiting over a period of several weeks.

Persistent vomiting requires a physical examination, and if the child is found to be in good health, the situations which are frightening him should be identified. Helping him become more familiar with them reduces his disturbance. Such experiences cannot always be avoided or easily conquered, however, and if the child's inevitable reaction is vomiting, the parent's contribution may be only to see that his stomach is not overloaded with food. With age and experience, the child will overcome his fears.

Pica

Elementary school children sometimes consume large quantities of unusual substances, more often liquids than solids, and frequently they experience no ill effects. One ten-year-old girl ate and drank huge amounts of medicine, reportedly without any serious subsequent illness; another ten-year-old girl drank an entire bottle of vinegar. These girls also ate excessively, although neither was overweight.

This behavior is not comparable to the pica of the pre-school child, who experiments from curiosity or undernourishment. Older children punish themselves in this way or use themselves as substitutes for parents they believe to be deserving of punishment. Both of the girls described above had witnessed violent arguments between the parents which led to irrational anger displaced onto the child, and in both families, the child was vaguely aware of infidelity on the part of one or both parents.

Deliberate and drastic self-harm warns parents of serious disturbance in the child. The child needs increased physical affection and attention, and anger directed against him and against the other parent should be curtailed. As the family tension decreases and the child is able to regain some trust in his parents, he should be encouraged to talk about his worries and ask questions, even though these are embarrassing or accusatory. The parents need to settle their differences and provide assurance to the child that the family is not disintegrating.

SLEEPING

Many sleeping problems of the school-age child are retained as poor habits founded in earlier years.* Others develop because the older child is more aware of events which lead to insecurity or possible violence. He also has a greater verbal capacity than before, so that when he is alone and in the dark, he dwells on frightening experiences. Persistent sleep disturbances require attention because a child cannot learn in school, compete adequately with peers, or cope with his problems when he is exhausted from insufficient rest. Common difficulties are resistance to bedtime; resistance to sleep; and nightmares, night terrors, and somnambulism.

Resistance to Bedtime

Some children turn every night into a contest when bedtime is announced. They suddenly remember homework which must be done or embark on projects which they insist cannot be interrupted. One ten-year-old girl invented an imaginary school assignment, due the following day, and prevailed on her father to help her with it for over an hour past her bedtime. The child may turn bedtime into a test of parental affection, crying in self-pity and accusing his parents of wanting to be rid of him. Many children demand the right to stay up as late as any sibling, regardless of age, and charge favoritism if they are refused.

Some children resist bedtime because they are afraid of the dark, a fear which appears sporadically throughout the elementary years, triggered by recent frightening experiences. Others associate nighttime with fear because they are left by themselves when their parents go out. A child whose father has threatened to leave the family or whose mother is seldom home when he arrives from school worries about their disappearing when he is asleep, and he delays bedtime so that he can keep his parents in sight longer.

The child who is overexcited at bedtime, whose parents have shown little concern about bedtime regularity, or who is punished by being sent to bed resists going to bed because staying up is more attractive.

To teach a child to go to bed without delaying each night, parents should establish a regular bedtime at the beginning of each school year, and it should be observed faithfully. If a later bedtime is permitted on weekends, this time also should be set, and it should be later only by minutes, not hours. Children of six and seven still need a parent for conversation and stories, and the association makes bedtime

---

* See Chapter 17, "Sleeping Problems."

more welcome. As soon as a child can tell time, he should be responsible for starting to bed without a reminder, with the understanding that failure to heed the clock one night results in an earlier bedtime the next. If a child is afraid of the dark or worried about his parents' leaving, his bedroom door can be left open and a night light provided. A sitter should stay with the child when his parents are away at night.

Resistance to Sleep

A child may go to bed willingly only because he does not plan to stay there. He gets up for a drink of water and lingers in front of the television set, sipping slowly. He remembers that he failed to brush his teeth, or he discovers that he needs to have a bowel movement.* Night wandering continues if it was the child's custom during pre-school years.

Older elementary children claim that they lie awake for hours or do not sleep at all. Although they sleep more than they report, they do keep themselves awake pondering the events of the day or their fears for the future. Siblings sharing a room often keep each other awake with animated conversations or arguments.

To ensure a child's learning to remain in bed, his parents must refuse him permission to get up, checking to make certain that his needs have been met before he goes to bed. A child who habitually needs to have a bowel movement at night has accustomed himself to do so and should choose another time during the day for elimination. The night wanderer should be returned promptly to his own bed, but the child resisting sleep in this way is demonstrating a need for regular parental attention during the day.

The child who mulls over his problems in the dark needs to communicate more with his parents, and if one of them talks over the day's happenings for a few minutes with him each night after he is in bed, the child is reassured by the parent's awareness of his difficulties.

Siblings interfering with each other's sleep can be controlled better by automatic signalling than by irate parents. A timer which buzzes after five or ten minutes can indicate that talking is to cease, with a violator penalized by an extra chore the next day.

Nightmares, Night Terrors, and Somnambulism

Kanner[7] defined nightmares, night terrors, and somnambulism as fear manifestations occurring during sleep. The experience of the child differs in several respects with each.

The nightmare is a frightening dream from which the child awakes

---

* See Case 19, Barbara N., p. 510.

by himself. Usually he recalls the content of his dream, and he knows where he is and what happened. The dream itself lasts only a minute or two, although the child may stay wakeful as he recalls and recounts it to his parents.

The night terror is a frightening dream which may last 15 or 20 minutes, during which time the child cannot be wakened or calmed. He does not recognize persons or objects in the room, includes them as part of the dream, and hallucinates dream objects into the room. He shows extreme fear in his facial expression, perspires, jumps up, and runs about the room, crying and clutching at his parents for protection from an hallucinated attacker. The child falls asleep peacefully when the dream is over and remembers nothing of the episode the next day.

Somnambulism is related to night terror in that the child does not wake from sleep nor is he aware of what he does. There is total amnesia for a night terror, but sometimes the child remembers his actions in sleepwalking as though they were part of a dream. The somnambulist's movements are slow and deliberate. Usually the child's eyes are open, but his gait is unsteady and he is unresponsive to any stimulation which is not part of the dream content. Occasionally he comes to some harm because he leaves the house too scantily clad on a cold night or wanders into traffic.

Helen D., age ten, a child of superior intelligence, walked in her sleep and had nightmares. She made frequent trips to the bathroom after going to bed each night. She had often been left alone at night by her parents and had been badly frightened on several such occasions. At the father's insistence, her mother worked most of the time, and when younger, Helen had been cared for by a series of sitters. By the time she was seven, she was staying by herself at home after school until her parents returned.

The parents were encouraged to provide a sitter when they went out at night, and it was recommended that the mother stop work, which she wished to do, so that she would be at home when Helen returned from school. The child's fearfulness gradually decreased.

Fear stems from a feeling of inability to ignore or to overcome problems or from reactions of shock at times of unexpected violence or danger. Identification of the specific fears troubling the child and assisting him in overcoming them is necessary if night fearfulness is to be eliminated. Overstimulation should be curbed: Television shows should be monitored and disturbing ones banned, heavily competitive daily activities should be decreased, and anger of the parents toward each other and toward the child should be minimized.

The somnambulistic child needs retraining in learning to remain in bed. Helen's frequent getting up to visit the bathroom served to reassure her of her parents' presence, but it also conditioned her to leave her bed whenever she felt anxious. If the child is taught to stay in bed when he is awake, the possibility that he will get up when he is asleep is lessened. Safeguards must be provided for a sleepwalking child to prevent his leaving the house at night and endangering himself.

REFERENCES

1. Anthony, J.: An experimental approach to the psychopathology of childhood: Sleep disturbances. *Brit. J. Med. Psychol.*, 1959, *32*, 19–37.
2. Burchinal, L. G., and Eppright, E. S.: Test of the psychogenic theory of obesity for a sample of rural girls. *Amer. J. Clin. Nutr.*, 1959, *7*, 288–294.
3. Fischle-Carl, H.: Ein Beitrag zur Kasuistik schlafgestörter Kinder (A contribution to case histories of children with sleep disturbances). *Prax. Kinderpsychol., Kinderpsychiat.*, 1955, *4*, 37–40.
4. Iversen, T.: Psychogenic obesity in children. I. *Acta Paediatr.* (*Stockh.*), 1953, *42*, 8–19.
5. Iversen, T., Juel-Nielsen, N., Quaade, F., Tolstrup, K., and Ostergaard, L.: Psychogenic obesity in children with special reference to Hilde Bruch's theory. *Acta Paediatr.* (*Stockh.*), 1952, *41*, 574–576.
6. Juel-Nielsen, N.: On psychogenic obesity in children. II. *Acta Paediatr.* (*Stockh.*), 1953, *42*, 130–146.
7. Kanner, L.: *Child Psychiatry*, Ed. 3. Springfield, Ill., Charles C Thomas, 1957, pp. 473–474, 481–482, 496–505.
8. Ostergaard, L.: On psychogenic obesity in children. V. *Acta Paediatr.* (*Stockh.*), 1954, *43*, 507–521.
9. Quaade, F.: On psychogenic obesity in children. III. *Acta Paediatr.* (*Stockh.*), 1953, *42*, 191–205.
10. Spock, B.: *Baby and Child Care*. New York, Pocket Books, Inc., 1957, pp. 318, 409, 433–435.
11. Stuart, H. C.: Obesity in childhood. *Quart. Rev. Pediat.*, 1955, *10*, 131–145.
12. Tolstrup, K.: On psychogenic obesity in children. IV. *Acta Paediatr.* (*Stockh.*), 1953, *42*, 289–304.
13. Vogl, M.: Neurotische Schlafstorungen im Kindesalter (Neurotic sleep disturbances in childhood). *Prax. Kinderpsychol., Kinderpsychiat.*, 1955, *4*, 33–37.

Chapter 28

Peer Maladjustments

Popularity is valued by some parents above a child's reliability, generosity, or morality. The adults identify closely with the child in his social successes or failures; their own opinion of him is swayed by the opinions of his peers; and they strive constantly to improve his acceptability.

Their uneasy concern is futile, for there is no predetermined, fixed, ideal, or consistent social development pattern for any child. Social skills must be learned by trial and error and in repeated contacts with other persons. A child's ability to empathize with others is related to their acceptance of him,[29] develops only with age,[9] and appears more certainly in girls than in boys.[7] Thompson[26] pointed out that friendship is a nebulous concept which varies from a parasitic relationship with another person to universal acceptance which may be neither sought nor consciously attained.

A child's behavior with others differs according to the group and his abilities in varying situations. He may lead his church school class in knowledge and alertness, but scarcely be noticed in discussions at school. He may be exuberant and dominant with a best friend, but passive and withdrawn in a group. He may show courtesy and consideration toward older children or adults, but pinch and hit younger children. The presence of his parents may make him more or less communicative with peers than he otherwise is.

His social contacts do not always contribute to his happiness or his moral stability. His friendship with another child may be close and constant, but unwanted; he may become a member of a gang engaged in predatory and antisocial acts;[5] or he may be the target of jeers and hoots every time he plays with his peers. He is tested, betrayed, rejected, and tempted. Inevitably, he tries new activities he knows are wrong, choosing to please his friends rather than obey his parents.

Troublesome and painful though his peer associations are, they lead to independence of behavior and individual acquisition of values, and they force emotional weaning from parents. The child begins to identify strongly with his peers as soon as he accepts the finality of regular school attendance, and the treatment his classmates give him influences his morale daily.[8] Few children, faced repeatedly with defeats and disappointments in their contacts with peers, consider themselves well liked. Those who are accepted most consistently are children of proven ability, either intellectual or physical,[3] who combine these assets with friendliness and enthusiasm.[18]

Although peer associations never proceed with complete smoothness and satisfaction, some children repel others by their behavior most of the time, and soon their contacts are limited and warping. The disliked child, unable to suit his peers, associates with other unpopular children, but his friendships are not lasting,[12] and his social ineptitude increases in contrast to the growing tolerance and self-assurance of children with broad contacts. His initial difficulty originates from a paucity of early associations; limited verbal or motor abilities; or the development of belligerent, dependent, or self-protective behavior toward others, acquired from early experiences with both children and adults.[28]

Peer maladjustments include belligerence, dependency, opposite-sex friendships, and rejection of friends.

BELLIGERENCE

Belligerence toward peers may be mild or severe. A child uncertain of himself tries to dominate his playmates by insisting on one game rather than another, by establishing all the rules, and by banishing unwanted children. The blatantly belligerent child seeks to hurt others, whether or not he is provoked and whether or not an irritation was deliberate or unintended. Frequently he limits his attacks to younger children or to girls, or fearful of retaliation, he throws rocks from behind a tree or waits until others have gone before he destroys a fort they have made.

He may act this way in imitation and revenge because he is punished severely or criticized constantly at home or because one parent behaves this way toward the other. Sometimes he has retained belligerence as a social technique because of his success at dominating his parents with threats, hitting, and anger. If he is inexperienced in playing with other children, his first contacts are reminiscent of a two-year-old's, and he pushes and grabs because he has not learned to expect and deal with the challenges of his peers, and he fears them. The socially immature child is especially susceptible to imitating aggressive behavior. Eron[10] noted that third grade boys considered aggressive by their peers preferred violent television programs to other kinds, a finding which suggests that they were convinced that belligerence was both acceptable and rewarding. Erratic, unpredictable treatment by parents produces a belligerent child. A child is in constant turmoil when he is loved, protected, and awarded excessive sympathy at times but punished inordinately for minor faults at other times. Unable to learn how to please, his attempts to form relationships with others are defensive and tinged with apprehension that he will be rebuffed.*

Other children find a belligerent child unpleasant and offensive, and if he habitually hurts others, they fear and avoid him. His opportunities to learn more acceptable behavior diminish as his contacts with his peers become steadily limited in frequency and variety.

DEPENDENCY

An enduring conviction that he is unwelcome and unattractive may develop in the child who overvalues the importance of pleasing others. Some children are uncomfortable when they do not control the attention and influence the behavior of peers, and they do so by enticing giggles with clowning, acrobatic performances, loud singing, or expansive rule-breaking. Usually they are children who have been repulsed at an early age by older playmates or siblings or who have been rewarded with adults' admiration when they performed or were mischievous.

A child dependent on others' approval may attach himself solely to playmates younger or older than he, thus providing himself with a social situation tailored to his liking, either for dominance or submission, and enabling him to avoid the demands of adaptability required by association with equals.

It is more comfortable for a child to limit himself to one close friend than to mingle with many peers because he can assume that he is preferred by another, and he also has available a confidant and companion who can be relied upon to behave predictably most of the time. Such a close and limiting contact, however, stifles the child's facility in adjustment to all of his peers. One of a pair of friends will

---

* See Case 20, Betty R., p. 511.

dominate the other, a steady relationship which does not answer the purpose of social development. The child who habitually permits himself to be dominated suppresses his natural resistance to unfair or ill-advised actions, fails to utilize his potential ability to make decisions, and acquires the habit of being easily persuaded by others.[21]

All limiting contacts, or those requiring great effort to maintain, develop feelings of inferiority in the child and eventual resentment of others.

OPPOSITE-SEX FRIENDSHIPS

The early elementary child plays with both boys and girls although interests, modes of play, and skills diverge increasingly each year. By the beginning of the fourth grade, boys' interests narrow, becoming increasingly mature and masculine. Girls retain some childish interests but broaden their activities to include both dramatic play and group sports and exploratory activities.[25] A boy unable to shift to masculine interests at this time tends to associate with girls and to avoid his male peers. His aversion to boys' companionship subjects him to the revilement of peers of both sexes and of adults as well.

Abner T., age 11, a boy of superior intelligence, associated only with girls at school and at home and resisted all attempts of adults to get him to play with boys. The other boys teased him, and he reacted with complete avoidance whenever possible, even to the extent of walking three miles home after school rather than riding the bus. When he could not escape from the boys' taunting, he swore at them and fought furiously.

Grover B., age ten, of average intelligence, played almost exclusively with a neighbor girl, dressing dolls and playing house. After even brief contacts with boys, he came home to rest, saying that he was tired. Fearful of all physical activity, he retreated into helplessness whenever he was faced with it.

A girl who develops the limited interests of the male at this age and who associates exclusively with boys often finds herself alone, both then and in the future.

Shirley W., 11 years old, of average intelligence, played football and basketball with the boys, often rounding them up to play and sometimes excelling them, much to their embarrassment. She wore boys' jeans for play and sometimes to school, and she was rough with boys and girls alike. As she grew older, she was disciplined frequently by school authorities for disturbances in class and failure to obey rules.

Each of these children had rejected his own sex and adopted the other, with the result that he became an outsider and a misfit. Unacceptable to the opposite sex and unable to behave as a member of his own, retreat and rebellion were inevitable.

REJECTION OF FRIENDS

When children reach the fourth grade, close friendships increase and the number of isolated children also increases.[23] The children left to themselves are those who do not verbalize easily or whose behavior is immature or antagonistic.

If a child does not join others at school and lives in a neighborhood devoid of playmates, he remains alone much of the time. Because he is accustomed to solitary pursuits, he is comfortable by himself; and when another child does ask him to play, he replies that he cannot and returns to his reading, building, experimenting, or collecting. On the school playground, he joins a teacher and spends recess time talking with her. If other children approach him then, he suspects they plan to trick or embarrass him, and he warily turns down their invitation to play.

The solitary child is not necessarily unhappy, and his learning to find pleasure in private activities is a valued ability which contrasts with the restlessness of the child who cannot bear being alone. The child who has no contacts with his peers, however, feels that he is different from them and less desirable than they are. His deliberate avoidance reflects his need for them to accept him with unreserved eagerness, a standard which is unrealistically high. He needs to abandon his conviction that he has the right to isolate himself constantly. Even though he does so because he is uneasy and afraid, repeated repulsion of others' advances leads to their avoiding him, and he begins to dislike his peers because they ignore him.

TRAINING IN SOCIAL ADJUSTMENT

Children who are maladjusted in their relationships with peers can be assisted by increasing their skills and the frequency of their contacts with others.

Kubie[17] suggested individual assistance for the physically awkward child whose poor performance in sports can isolate him from the majority of peer activities. Extra practice in basic school subjects and family discussion of current events and issues increase a child's ability to participate in the classroom.

Association with other children in small groups benefits the withdrawn child, the belligerent child, and the child whose contacts are limited. Boy Scouts, Girl Scouts and Campfire Girls are open to all children and provide regular opportunities to share in work and play with peers of the same sex. Morris et al.,[20] studying 54 persons designated as shy and withdrawn 16 to 27 years earlier, reported that two thirds were adjusting satisfactory, one third was marginally adjusted, and only two persons in the group were seriously disturbed. The best-adjusted individuals of the 54 persons studied were those who engaged regularly in group recreation.

The nonadapting child selects companions who are similarly unpopular, but these are preferable to none at all. He gains some feeling of acceptability by being with any peer, and prolonged arguing or frequent aggression can be minimized if the contacts between socially inept children are limited in duration but not in frequency.

Parents who regularly provide for small parties with a variety of child guests or who invite for dinner families with children of appropriate age and sex broaden contacts for the child whose associations are limited. The child without any friends can begin by inviting one other desired companion to accompany him on family outings.

The belligerent child's behavior will change only if he has other models and new reasons for acting differently toward others, and this requires revision of parental attitudes and behavior toward him.

A teacher can assist children in accepting each other by organizing small, flexible groups for study and by planning within the larger class, thus giving each child the opportunity to become better acquainted with every other child.[16] Pairing children for projects also leads to greater respect and tolerance of each child for others.

REFERENCES

1. Bandura, A., Ross, D., and Ross, S. A.: Imitation of film-mediated aggressive models. *J. Abnorm. Soc. Psychol.*, 1963, *66*, 3–11.
2. Brooks, F. D.: *Child Psychology.* Boston, Houghton Mifflin Co., 1937, p. 381.
3. Clarke, H. H., and Greene, W. H.: Relationships between personal-social measures applied to 10-year-old boys. *Res. Quart. Amer. Ass. Hlth., Phys. Educ. Recr.*, 1963, *34*, 288–298.
4. Commoss, H. H.: Some characteristics related to social isolation of second grade children. *J. Educ. Psychol.*, 1962, *53*, 38–42.
5. Crane, A. R.: The development of moral values in children: IV. Preadolescent gangs and the moral development of children. *Brit. J. Educ. Psychol.*, 1958, *28*, 201–208.
6. Curti, M. W.: *Child Psychology*, Ed. 2. New York, Longmans, Green and Co., 1938, p. 387.
7. DeJung, J. E., and Meyer, W. J.: Expected reciprocity: Grade trends and correlates. *Child Developm.*, 1963, *34*, 127–139.
8. D'Evelyn, K. E.: *Meeting Children's Emotional Needs.* Englewood Cliffs, N. J., Prentice-Hall, Inc., 1957, pp. 13–14, 22.
9. Dymond, R. F., Hughes, A. S., and Raabe, V. L.: Measureable changes in empathy with age. *J. Consult. Psychol.*, 1952, *16*, 202–206.
10. Eron, L. D.: Relationship of TV viewing habits and aggressive behavior in children. *J. Abnorm. Soc. Psychol.*, 1963, *67*, 193–196.
11. Goodenough, F. L.: *Developmental Psychology*, Ed. 2. New York, D. Appleton-Century Co., 1945, p. 433.
12. Haiker, F.: Ausehen und Beliebheitsgrad in der Volkschule (Appearance and degree of popularity in public school). *Psychol. Rdsch.*, *195*(1), 285–290.

13. Hartley, R. E.: Sex-role pressures and the socialization of the male child. *Psychol. Rep.*, 1959, *5*, 457–468.
14. Horrocks, J. E., and Buker, M. E.: A study of the friendship fluctuations of pre-adolescents. *J. Genet. Psychol.*, 1951, *78*, 131–144.
15. Jersild, A. T.: *Child Psychology*, Ed. 4. New York, Prentice-Hall, Inc., 1954, p. 195.
16. Kinney, E. E.: A study of peer group social acceptability at the fifth grade level in a public school. *J. Educ. Res.*, 1953, *47*, 57–64.
17. Kubie, L. S.: Competitive sports and the awkward child. *Child Study*, 1954, *31*, 10–15.
18. Laughlin, F.: The peer status of sixth and seventh grade children. New York, Teachers College, Columbia University, 1954.
19. Luck, J. M.: A study of peer relationships. *Group*, 1955, *17*, 13–20.
20. Morris, D. P., Soroker, E., and Burruss, G.: Follow-up studies of shy, withdrawn children—I. Evaluation of later adjustment. *Amer. J. Orthopsychiat.*, 1954, *24*, 743–754.
21. Roland, A.: Persuasibility in young children as a function of aggressive motivation and aggression conflict. *J. Abnorm. Soc. Psychol.*, 1963, *66*, 454–461.
22. Spock, B.: *Baby and Child Care*. New York, Pocket Books, Inc., 1957, p. 389.
23. Strang, R.: *An Introduction to Child Study*. New York, The Macmillan Co., 1938, p. 480.
24. Sutton, R. S.: An appraisal of certain aspects of children's social behavior. *J. Teacher Educ.*, 1962, *13*, 30–34.
25. Sutton-Smith, B., Rosenberg, B. G., and Morgan, E. F., Jr.: Development of sex differences in play choices during preadolescence. *Child Developm.*, 1963, *34*, 119–126.
26. Thompson, G.: *Child Psychology*, Ed. 2. Boston, Houghton Mifflin Co., 1962, pp. 485–487.
27. Wilkins, W. L.: Social peers and parents. *Education*, 1952, *73*, 234–237.
28. Winder, C. L., and Rau, L.: Parental attitudes associated with social deviance in preadolescent boys. *J. Abnorm. Soc. Psychol.*, 1962, *64*, 418–424.
29. Zelen, S. L.: The relationship of peer acceptance, acceptance of others and self-acceptance. *Proc. Iowa Acad. Sci.*, 1954, *61*, 446–449.

Chapter 29

Psychophysiological Disturbances

Psychophysiological disturbances were found in 40 per cent of 7000 children seen in a pediatric clinic population.[45] Health problems distress both parent and child and complicate already tense and difficult situations. The child suffers discomfort or pain which increases his irritability and unhappiness; and if his parents react to his illness or malfunction as though it were a disaster or if they feel guilty or blame the child for the inconvenience he causes, the conflicts or fears which precipitated the reaction persist and spread.[22]

Sontag[47] suggested that children whose energy level is lower than normal have less vitality and resistance and therefore are predisposed to adopt illness or physical disturbance as a defensive measure. The child less able to compensate for or disregard family difficulties by identifying with persons outside of the home makes a passive adjustment to restriction or anxiety in this way. Mohr *et al.*[33] concluded that children who develop psychophysiological symptoms are those who are exposed to inadequate mothering care during the first year of life, a period when any noxious physical or psychological stimulus impedes functional growth and integration.

The child's adoption of physical disturbance as an expression of anxiety or tension may serve him purposefully.[37] Cameron[13] noted that a child learns quickly to enjoy the oversolicitude which illness often brings, and physical complaints shield him from demanding and unpleasant tasks. A child uses illness as a domineering technique when he forces extra care and attention from a mother who ordinarily is indifferent or demanding.

Illness reactions do not always bring relief or pleasure to the child, and there is an element of self-punishment in them. The child who is convinced by adult harshness that he is behaving badly, whether or not this is true, develops physical difficulties and tends to believe that he is justly punished by suffering. Teachers who met regularly to learn about the emotional needs of children and who presumably were more responsive to them, demonstrated a 96 per cent decrease in frequency and acuteness of psychophysiological symptoms in their pupils, as compared to a 50 per cent decrease in the pupils of a control group of teachers during the same period of time.[16]

Common psychophysiological disturbances of elementary school children are headaches, stomach aches and ulcers, accident proneness, manipulative motor habits (including nail-biting, thumb-sucking, and tics), asthma, and problems of elimination, such as enuresis, encopresis, and constipation. It cannot be assumed that all children with these kinds of difficulties are responding to emotional pressures. Any child suffering chronically from physical malfunction should be under a physician's care. Emotional or physical aspects of illness, separately or jointly, can cause psychic or somatic disturbances or both, and treatment should be directed toward improving both conditions.[3] A child with malaise or pain cannot cope even with ordinary daily problems, and he should be assisted in maintaining good health.

HEADACHES

Kanner[23] pointed out that there is scarcely any physical illness which is not accompanied by headache, so that the frequency of this complaint is not surprising.

A child may develop a headache when he has exercised too vigorously or when his food intake is insufficient to give him the energy he needs. A child who has inadequate time to himself and is kept on the run with school, chores, and extra lessons and meetings may have frequent headaches.[10] A mother who acquires a headache which prevents her from preparing dinner is an inspiring model for the child who lacks the knowledge required for a test or the courage demanded by a party. Severe denunciation of a child makes him taut with anxiety, and tensed muscles lead to headaches.* Tension appears also when the child feels that he is failing in what is expected of him.

Migraine headaches occurred in 4 per cent of a group of children studied by Macoun.[29] These headaches are characterized by their sudden

---

* See Case 11, Ruth M., p. 503.

onset, acute pain, and vomiting. Immediate relief usually follows the vomiting. Migraine headaches have been related to familial tendencies and also have been considered an epileptic equivalent or an indication of cerebral lesion. Emotional tension is a precipitating factor, but reduction of tension seldom succeeds in complete elimination of the headaches.

If headaches occur frequently but physical examination reveals no abnormality, the child's daily life should be freed of tension, with demands and requirements reduced and perfectionistic standards forgotten. The child should have more rest and freedom to try his own ideas and to explore by himself and with friends. If he has difficulty with school requirements, his learning ability and academic problems should be evaluated so that he can be given the appropriate placement or assistance he needs.

To minimize the possibility of a child's learning to use headaches as a technique of avoidance or retreat or as a device for gaining sympathy, he should be encouraged to continue his studies or chores, rather than be permitted to avoid them, and parents who advertise their own headaches must set the example. Medication prescribed by a physician can be given to relieve pain.

STOMACH ACHES AND ULCERS

A stomach ache is a common and painful complaint of tense children. It is often associated with forced feeding or critical attention to manners and food consumption at mealtime, and it can lead to vomiting. It is sometimes used by children to escape a distasteful task and is effective because parents worry that something is seriously wrong with the child.

Abdominal pain or pain in the colon may indicate the presence of ulcers, a condition being diagnosed with increasing frequency in children. Chapman et al.[14] studied five children with duodenal ulcers and concluded that they had unmet needs for emotional security and affection, as well as difficulty in asserting themselves. These children were passive in manner but inwardly frantic because they were unsuccessful in their search for evidence of affection from their parents. Taboroff and Brown[51] also noted in children with peptic ulcers the presence of real or felt danger of losing the mother. Mohr et al.[33] related the threat to security to a traumatic experience of separation or grossly inadequate maternal care occurring during the child's first year of life and reënforced by further withdrawal of maternal care during the succeeding pre-school years. Reca and Raskovsky[41] studied six children with duodenal ulcers and found that all had authoritarian families in which spontaneous affection did not exist and in which there was no outlet for a child's antagonistic feelings. In these families there was also extraordinary concern with diets and digestive disorders. Some children with ulcers give evidence, not of passivity, but of hyperactivity and expressions of anger, in family atmospheres characterized by tumultuous emotion and hostility between parents and child.*

The child with stomach aches or ulcers is in pain, and diet and medication should be prescribed to ease it. Affection, control, and calmness from parents are reënforcements to the child's security which relieve his anxiety. Parents can learn techniques for managing routines and recurring problems which aid them in maintaining a more stable and confident relationship with the child, and they can regain their appreciation of him as an individual by talking and playing with him each day.

ACCIDENT PRONENESS

The early years of some children's lives are marked by a series of crises caused by illness and accidents. These children constantly visit the doctor for medication or are hospitalized for mending, and they rarely are seen without bandages, crutches, or a cast. Although most illnesses and accidents appear to be unrelated, close study suggests that habitual living and behavior patterns cause accidents and even illness to be more probable for some children than for others. Marcus et al.[30] compared a group of accident-prone children, aged six to ten, with a group of enuretic children and a group of symptom-free children. They found that the accident-prone children had as many emotional problems as the enuretic children and also that they were more active, even before birth, than children in the other two groups. Their parents were anxious, insecure, and nonassertive. Hospitalized accident-prone children have been reported to establish pleasant, but superficial, relationships with adults.[25]

Insecure parents alternate between unpredictable, severe criticism and punishment of the child and casual disregard of his actions. They warn against but do not prevent the child's engaging in dangerous behavior. Never taught to ride his bicycle safely, the child speeds into the street in complete disregard of traffic and his own riding skill. Forgotten when he is not physically present, he climbs roofs, plays at hanging himself, and collects and uses broken glass or rusty nails. He plays outside in freezing weather without a coat, races for hours under the hot sun, wades knee-deep in sewers running with water, and finishes a half-eaten candy bar he spies in the alley. Uncertain and

---

* See Case 21, Nelson P., p. 512.

anxious, he acts impulsively and observes carelessly, and his experiments with danger are tinged with aggression felt toward his parents and their inconsistency.[24]

Parents must prohibit specific actions which involve potential danger and must enforce their prohibitions. Instruction and supervision in handling tools, knives, and power equipment are necessary, and safety in traffic must be taught. As the child learns to obey instructions, he gradually is able to judge the risk involved in various deeds, and he acts more thoughtfully when he is alone. Parents who practice their basic responsibility of ensuring safety for the child gain a better understanding of their role, and severe censure and punishment resulting from an accumulation of disappointments in their management of the child will diminish.

MANIPULATIVE MOTOR HABITS

The overcontrolled child expresses his tension in manipulative motor habits such as nail-biting, thumb-sucking, or tics. Trying hard to please others, he is afraid that he will fail to do so. He is overdependent on adult direction and therefore shows no originality, initiative, or breadth of effort. He chooses familiar tasks and works hard only when he is in the mood. He finds little pleasure in achievement because his labors are intended only to satisfy others.[19]

Nail-biting

Birch[6] reported that 51 per cent of a group of 4000 children were nail-biters, 17 per cent to a severe degree. The frequency of nail-biting was greater for boys than for girls, and there was a steady increase in incidence until 12 years of age, after which there was a gradual cessation. The symptom has been reported to appear more frequently in first and last born children than in middle children.[44]

A child who bites his nails continually is indicating his tension and anxiety, and he usually shows other signs of motor restlessness. He often sleeps poorly, cannot sit still, displays tics, sucks his thumb, or picks his nose.[23] His restlessness is a response to overexpectation on the part of parents, who criticize and scold for minor failures, overdirect the child, and burden him with extra lessons and organized activities. He is given little freedom to act as he chooses and do what he likes, and he is seldom credited for a completely satisfactory performance.

To minimize nail-biting, the child must be relieved of harassment. Nonessential activities and duties can be eliminated, and standards of excellence can be made more realistic. Encouragement, praise, and freedom reduce tension and enable the child to perform more capably and spontaneously.

Thumb-sucking

The child who continues thumb-sucking into the elementary school years feels isolated from his peers and earns their rejection by his obtrusive display of immaturity. The thumb-sucking elementary school child has been described as regressive, unsociable, and showing low frustration tolerance.[32] He behaves like the small child he feels that he is, denying his responsibility for compliance and achievement and avoiding his peers.*

The child who publicly sucks his thumb at this age needs to be given greater responsibility and practical instruction in how to do what is required of him. Frequent rewards for refraining from thumb-sucking direct his attention to the habit, and provide him with an incentive for abandoning it. A ten-year-old boy, who had sucked his thumb all his life and remained indifferent to the teasing of his siblings and the scolding of his parents, stopped within two weeks after he was rewarded with a nickel for each half day of restraint.

Tics

Tics occur more commonly at the elementary school age than at any other time and have been reported in about 25 per cent of children between the ages of seven and 12 years. Head-shaking or nodding, blinking, grimacing, clearing the throat, coughing, or jerking the shoulders, arms, or legs are common forms.[23]

Tics can be acquired in imitation of another child's or adult's habit. They may originate as efforts to shrug away binding clothing or ill-fitting glasses. Tics of coughing and throat-clearing may be residuals of a cold. A specific irritating, distressing, or frightening event may precipitate tics. An accumulation of mishaps, failures, or disapproving comments by parents eventually becomes too much for an over-conscientious child to bear and he develops a tic.†[28] Occasionally, postencephalitic tics occur, traceable to brain lesions, and Brown[11] reported cessation of tics of blinking, nose-twitching, and mouth-jerking in children treated for previously undiagnosed chronic sinusitis.

Severe tics of long duration can be eliminated by bringing them under voluntary control, a technique especially effective with the older elementary child, who is aware of his tics and embarrassed by them. Daily sessions of deliberate practice of the tic change the stimulus cue

---

* See Case 12, Doris F., p. 504; Case 14, Bobby R., p. 506; Case 20, Betty R., p. 511.
† See Case 9, Bernard K., p. 502.

from one unknown to the child to one of instruction originating with him, and self-direction eventually replaces the unidentifiable stimulus and eliminates the involuntary muscle action. Lórand[28] used rhythmical and inhibitional gymnastic exercises in teaching the child attention to and control of his muscle movements.

Removing physical irritations or incapacities sometimes is necessary, and more rest and less stimulation can be provided. A child suffering from tics responds well to praise and approval, and he will be helped by a more relaxed attitude toward both the defeats and successes he experiences.

ASTHMA

Asthma is an allergy of the bronchial tubes to an irritating substance which causes them to swell and secrete a thick mucus. This narrows the air passages so that breathing is difficult, and the child coughs and wheezes. A younger child usually is sensitive to particular kinds of foods and an older child to substances floating in the air.[48] Tests can be made to determine what substances are irritating, although such factors as climate, season, and temperature also contribute to the difficulty.

There are disagreements about the role of personality and of emotional stress in aggravating asthmatic attacks. Kanner[23] characterized the asthmatic child as one who is anxious about his own ability to get along and who demands protection from his parents but who still strongly desires to dominate them. Mussen et al.[36] and Alcock[2] reported that parents of asthmatic children are overcontrolling, and a high level of emotional tension exists in the home. Living under these conditions, the child fails to express the fear, anger, or aggression he feels, and an asthmatic attack substitutes for this release. DeQueiroz and Straus[15] studied 40 asthmatic children and noted that a variety of factors is influential. Strong emotion precipitated attacks, but the child often had other kinds of personality and behavior difficulties, such as a poor attitude toward school and excessive reactions of either dependency or aggression at home. Saul[43] noted the precipitating effects of sudden emotion but considered the asthmatic child overdependent on his parents in reaction to their solicitous treatment of him.

Harris and Shure,[20] in a study of teachers' records of the emotional behavior of asthmatic and nonasthmatic children, concluded that no specific personality pattern was evident in either group and that asthmatic children did not demonstrate any intensification of disturbed behavior. Bostock[8] stated that if the child's crying rhythm is disrupted during infancy by maternal rejection or by prolonged, unalleviated discomfort, the irregular crying later is transformed into irregular breathing. Holmgren and Kraepelien[21] reported that one third of the asthmatic children they studied had abnormal electroencephalograph records, and Rhodes[42] attributed the swift and violent alternations of personality expression in allergic children to metabolic fluctuations.

The fear of having an attack while playing hard often keeps the asthmatic child isolated from other children, and he unwillingly remains apart, resenting the constant companionship of his parents and both disliking and pitying himself because of his handicap. When he does have an attack, he is both miserable and frightened.

Identification and removal of irritating substances are basic steps in relieving the asthmatic child. When his breathing is difficult, he should be kept warm and in bed, with extra moisture in the room. An attack rarely is as dangerous as it seems, and parents should hide obvious concern, which only frightens the child and leads to more severe coughing.[48] If the child is occupied with reading or games while in bed, he pays less attention to his breathing.

He should be permitted and encouraged to play with other children and allowed the freedom to make his own decisions and manage his own affairs whenever this is feasible. Parental pressures and overconcern about the child should be decreased.

ELIMINATION PROBLEMS

Problems with elimination are considered disgraceful in a child old enough to attend school. A mother sometimes bases her complete opinion of the child's worth on his ability to urinate or defecate in the proper place; a father scorns and punishes the child who does not show control; and siblings tease him unmercifully. Public errors produce much giggling and shocked discussion by his peers. Through all of these attempts to shame him, the guilty child remains stoic. He appears to have become accustomed to ridicule, punishment, and ostracism, and indifferent to improvement. He denies wetting his bed and quickly makes it before his mother can check in order to avoid a lecture or punishment, but he knows no way to become more attentive to elimination habits and he feels little need to do so.

Enuresis

Diurnal wetting of a school-age child often is caused by excitement or uncontrollable laughter during play, when the bladder involuntarily relaxes its usual tension. Sometimes the child wets because he has waited too long to empty a full bladder, and at school he may be embarassed to ask permission to leave the room or be afraid of the strange toilet facilities.

Most excited or forgetful wetting vanishes as the child grows older and is more self-controlled around other children. When a young child fears the school bathroom, he can urinate at home in the morning and at noon, and if he is self-conscious about asking to leave the classroom, usually his teacher will permit him to go to the toilet without a public request.

Nocturnal enuresis is much more common, troublesome, and habitual; and early parental attitudes about it seldom change. If parents were sympathetic with or indifferent to the bed-wetting of the child as a pre-schooler, usually they feel the same way when he is older. Those who punished and shamed the enuretic pre-school child become even more disturbed when their censure fails and the habit continues. They require the child to wash his sheets and hang them outdoors; they talk about his "problem" to every visitor in his presence; and they scream names at him each time they discover he has wet. One nine-year-old boy was handed a glass of amber liquid by his mother and ordered to drink it, after being told it was urine she had wrung out of his bedsheet. He calmly identified it as tea.

The enuretic boy usually is a child who remains dependent on the protection of his parents. He is uncertain of himself with other boys, and when he is with them he demands special favors and privileges and does not accept group standards. He feels inferior and guilty, and he is angry, resentful, and jealous.[49] Enuretic girls retain boys' interests longer than usual and feel uncomfortable around other girls. They do not get along well with their mothers, and they resent domestic duties or any of the customary restrictions on behavior required by their sex.[48]

Early, rigid toilet training is associated with enuresis.[9] When this has occurred, the child reacts to the parent's overemphasis on achieving dryness with the twin attitudes of abdication of his responsibility for correct performance and of resistance to compliance under pressure. The child learns to feel justified in the helplessness and irresponsibility he has adopted. Chronically enuretic children admit that they sometimes waken before wetting but dislike leaving the comfort of a warm bed to go to the bathroom.

Immaturity of the nervous system has been suggested by Gunnarson and Melin[18] as a contributing factor. They found a greater frequency of abnormal electroencephalograph records in children who had never attained dryness than in those enuretics who had remained dry for a year or more before reverting to wetting. The existence of central nervous system damage, however, cannot be considered solely responsible for continued failure to establish control of elimination.

The same methods appropriate for retraining the enuretic pre-school child are applicable to the elementary school child.* If responsi-

---

* See Chapter 18, "Problems of Elimination," p. 148.

bility for maintaining dryness is shifted from parent to child, if his effort in attending to body signals is rewarded, and if he gains in self-confidence, the enuresis will disappear.

Encopresis

A child who soils himself can expect severe reprimands, punishment, and exile from indignant and horrified adults. His peers also shun him and regard him as peculiar. Encopresis in the pre-school child can be attributed to many situational and experiential factors, such as fear of the toilet, lack of time or privacy, previously painful movements, absorption in play, or inadequacy of training.

Few of these reasons are significant in the soiling of an elementary school child. His act nearly always is aggressive, motivated by anger and the determination to punish others and please himself.[1] Sometimes he is angry at his parents or teachers, and at other times he is disappointed in himself because he accomplishes little or does not get along with his peers. He projects his anger at himself onto others, whose lives seem so much more satisfying than his own. Kanner[23] reported that of 25 encopretic children with normal or superior intelligence, 18 had marked scholastic difficulties.*

Lempp[26] suggested that encopretic children have a history of brain damage, but inasmuch as retarded children with varying degrees of organic deficit can be trained to adequate bowel control, the contribution of organic destruction to encopresis in the average child must be considered indirect. It does establish impulsive behavior patterns which lead to disapproval and rejection of the child, and these may produce anxiety, anger, and subsequent retaliatory soiling.

The encopretic child can disturb others by soiling whenever he chooses, but the problem is managed more easily if parents assume that the soiling is beyond the child's control. It then becomes reasonable to retrain him by requiring him to attempt to have a movement on the toilet at a regular time each day and to clean up the mess he makes when he does soil himself. Taking logical action of this kind seems more natural to the child than if his parents are overwhelmed completely by such a major infraction of accepted behavior. Minimal rules also provide parents with a substitute for angry tirades, proof that the child has succeeded in annoying.

The parents' real task is to make it possible for the child to tell them why he is angry. If he is being ignored, restricted, or punished continually at home or if he is friendless and feels ignorant at school, these situations need to be changed. A child who is reasonably content

---

* See Case 22, Kenneth J., p. 512.

with himself and who is treated fairly by others does not remain continuously angry.

CONSTIPATION

Constipation may develop for the first time when a child starts school and his time schedule does not permit him to move his bowels when he is accustomed to doing so. He learns to inhibit his response to bowel pressure, and it claims increasingly less of his attention. He no longer has as much time to use the bathroom as he did when he was at home all day, and he dislikes interrupting exciting activities because he has less opportunity for them than previously. A tense and worried child, troubled with the demands of school and home, may develop a spastic colon.[5] Tight muscles cause the movement to be small and painful, and the child avoids evacuation because it hurts him. Many children constipated during pre-school years are still subjected to daily administration of enemas, suppositories, and laxatives, and natural muscle tonus has disappeared.

The tense child needs a calmer, more reassuring daily life, with adequate time to rest and play and with less rigid standards to meet. Retraining methods similar to those used for the pre-school child are effective with the older child.*

REFERENCES

1. Albrecht, H., and Hoffmann, H.: Encopresis im Kindesalter (Encopresis in childhood). *Nervenarzt*, 1950, *21*, 271–281.
2. Alcock, T.: Some personality characteristics of asthmatic children. *Brit. J. Med. Psychol.*, 1960, *33*, 133–141.
3. Andersen, O.: Psychosomatic disease in childhood. *Acta Paediatr.* (*Stockh.*), 1951, *40* (83), 37–43.
4. Baller, W., and Schalock, H.: Conditioned response treatment of enuresis. *Except. Child.*, 1956, *22*, 233–236, 247–248.
5. Bell, A. I., and Levine, M. I.: The psychologic aspects of pediatric practice. I: Causes and treatment of chronic constipation. *Pediatrics*, 1954, *14*, 259–266.
6. Birch, L. B.: The incidence of nail biting among school children. *Brit. J. Educ. Psychol.*, 1955, *25*, 123–128.
7. Boncour, G. P.: Les tics chez l'écolier et leur interprétation. *Progrès Médical*, 1910, *26*, 445.
8. Bostock, J.: Asthma: a synthesis involving primitive speech, organism, and insecurity. *J. Ment. Sci.*, 1956, *102*, 559–575.
9. Bostock, J.: Enuresis and toilet training. *Med. J. Aust.*, 1951, *2*, 110–113.
10. Bourdier, P.: La céphalée de l'enfant ou contribution à l'étude des états prémorbides de l'enfance (Headache in the child: A contribution to the study of premorbid states in childhood). *Rev. Franc. Psychanal.*, 1962, *26*, 633, 654.

---

* See Chapter 18, "Problems of Elimination," pp. 151–152.

11. Brown, E. E.: Tics (habit spasms) secondary to sinusitis. *Arch. Pediat.*, 1957, *74*, 39–46.

12. Buck, C. W., and Laughton, K. B.: Family patterns of illness. The effect of psychoneurosis in the parent upon illness in the child. *Acta Psychiat. Neurol.* (*Scand.*), 1959, *34*, 165–175.

13. Cameron, N.: *The Psychology of Behavior Disorders*. Boston, Houghton Mifflin Co., 1947, pp. 212, 240–243.

14. Chapman, A. H., Loeb, D. G., and Young, J. B.: A psychosomatic study of five children with duodenal ulcer. *J. Pediat.*, 1956, *48*, 248–261.

15. DeQueiroz, A. M., and Straus, A.: Contribuicos psicologicos a clinica da crianca asmatica (Psychological aspects in asthmatic children). *Rev. Psicol. Norm. Patol.*, São Paulo, 1958, *4*, 83–94.

16. Fleming, R. S.: Psychosomatic illness and emotional needs. *Educ. Leadership*, 1951, *9*, 119–123.

17. Forres, H.: Emotional dangers to children in hospitals. *Ment. Hlth.* (*Lond.*), 1953, *12*, 58–62.

18. Gunnarson, S., and Melin, K. A.: The electroencephalogram in enuresis. *Acta Paediatr.* (*Stockh.*), 1951, *40*, 496–501.

19. Haring, N. G., and Phillips, E. L.: *Educating Emotionally Disturbed Children*. New York, McGraw-Hill Book Co., 1962, pp. 158–159.

20. Harris, M. C., and Shure, N.: A study of behavior patterns in asthmatic children. *J. Allergy*, 1956, *27*, 312–313.

21. Holmgren, B., and Kraepelien, S.: Electroencephalographic studies of asthmatic children. *Acta Paediatr.* (*Stockh.*), 1953, *42*, 432–441.

22. Johnson, R.: How parents' attitudes affect children's illnesses. *Bull. Inst. Child Stud.* (*Toronto*), 1955, *17*, 5–8.

23. Kanner, L.: *Child Psychiatry*, Ed. 3. Springfield, Ill., Charles C Thomas, 1957, pp. 377–382, 399, 408, 410–433, 439–440, 551–556.

24. Krall, V.: Personality characteristics of accident repeating children. *J. Abnorm. Soc. Psychol.*, 1953, *48*, 99–107.

25. Langford, W. S., Gilder, R., Wilking, V., Genn, M. M., and Sherrill, H.: Pilot study of childhood accident; preliminary report. *Pediatrics*, 1953, *11*, 405–415.

26. Lempp, R.: Zur Ätiologie des kindlichen Einstuhlens (The etiology of fecal soiling in children). *Z. Psychother. Med. Psychol.* 1956, *6*, 206–218.

27. Levy, D.: *Maternal Overprotection*. New York, Columbia University Press, 1943, p. 188.

28. Lórand, B.: Les tics nerveux des enfants (Nervous tics of children). *Paediat. Danub.*, 1949, *6*, 203–230.

29. Macoun, S.: Migraine in school children. *Developm. Med. Child Neurol.*, 1963, *5*, 62–63.

30. Marcus, I. M., Wilson, W., Kruft, I., Swander, D., Southerland, F., and Schulhofer, E.: An interdisciplinary approach to accident patterns in children. *Monogr. Soc. Res. Child Developm.*, 1960, *25*(76).

31. Martin, B., and Kubly, D.: Results of treatment of enuresis by a conditioned response method. *J. Consult. Psychol.*, 1955, *19*, 71–73.

32. Miyamoto, M.: Jido no yubi shaburi no kenkyū (A study of finger sucking of children). *Jap. J. Educ. Psychol.*, 1958, *6*, 21–27, 62–63.

33. Mohr, G. J., Richmond, J. B., Garner, A. M., and Eddy, E. J.: A program for the study of children with psychosomatic disorders. *In* Caplan, G., ed.: *Emotional Problems of Early Childhood*. New York, Basic Books, Inc., 1955, pp. 251–268.

34. Müller, E.: Zur Behandlung der Bettnässer in den Erziehungsheimen für Schwerezienbare (On treatment of enuretics in institutions for children with behavior problems). *Heilpädag. Werkbl.*, 1957, *26*, 202–205.

35. Munn, N. L.: Learning in children. *In* Carmichael, L., ed.: *Manual of Child Psychology*. New York, John Wiley and Sons, 1946, p. 380.

36. Mussen, P., Conger, J., and Kagan, J., *Child Development and Personality*, Ed. 2. New York, Harper and Row, 1956, pp. 397–398.

37. Oller, O. B.: Understanding and management of psychosomatic problems in children. *Amer. J. Individ. Psychol.*, 1952, *53*, 10, 175–181.

38. Overholser, W., and Richmond, W. V.: *Handbook of Psychiatry*. Philadelphia, J. B. Lippincott Co., 1947, p. 226.
39. Palermo, D. S.: Thumbsucking: a learned response. *Pediatrics*, 1956, *17*, 392–399.
40. Powell, N. B.: Urinary incontinence in children. *Arch. Pediat.*, 1951, *68*, 151–157.
41. Reca, T., and Raskovsky, C.: Ulcera duodenal en la infancia (Duodenal ulcer in the child). *Acta Neuropsiquiát.* (*Argent.*), 1955, *1*, 342–356.
42. Rhodes, I. G.: Allergic causes of emotional disturbances in children. *Nerv. Child*, 1952, *9*, 369–377.
43. Saul, L. J.: Physiological effects of emotional tension. *In* Hunt, J. McV., ed.: *Personality and the Behavior Disorders*. New York, The Ronald Press Co., 1944, vol. 1, p. 286.
44. Schachter, M., and Chatenet, H.: Recherches et confrontation de deux enquêtes sur l'onychophagie infantile (Research and a comparison of two inquiries on infantile onychophagia). *Progr. Méd., Paris.*, 1951, *79*, 87–88.
45. Scull, A. J.: The challenge of the "well child." *Calif. Med.*, 1952, *77*, 285–292.
46. Shaffer, L. F.: *The Psychology of Adjustment*. Boston, Houghton Mifflin Co., 1936, p. 270.
47. Sontag, L. W.: Some psychosomatic aspects of childhood. *In* Kluckhohn, C., Murray, H. A., and Schneider, D., eds.: *Personality in Nature, Society, and Culture*. New York, Alfred A. Knopf, 1956, pp. 494–497.
48. Spock, B.: *Baby and Child Care*. New York, Pocket Books, Inc., 1957, pp. 391–392, 477, 503–506.
49. Stokvis-Warnaar, J., and Stokvis, B.: Psychodrama of enuresis nocturna in boys. *Group Psychother.*, 1962, *15*, 285–303.
50. Swartz, H.: *The Allergic Child*. New York, Coward-McCann, 1954.
51. Taboroff, L. H., and Brown, W. H.: A study of the personality patterns of children and adolescents with the peptic ulcer syndrome. *Amer. J. Orthopsychiat.*, 1954, *24*, 602–610.
52. Thom, D. A.: *Everyday Problems of the Everyday Child*. New York, Appleton-Century, 1934, p. 96.
53. Vignec, A. J., Moser, A., and Julia, J. F.: Treatment of chronic enuresis, poor weight gain, and poor appetite in institutional children. *Arch. Pediat.*, 1957, *74*, 119–130.
54. Walton, D.: Experimental psychology and the treatment of a ticqueur. *J. Child Psychol. Psychiat.*, 1961, *2*, 148–155.
55. Yates, A. J.: The application of learning theory to the treatment of tics. *J. Abnorm. Soc. Psychol.*, 1958, *56*, 175–182.

Chapter 30

Speech Disorders

Speech disorders in the elementary school child complicate his learning and subject him to ridicule. His difficulties with communication or in the use of written and oral symbols can lead to social and intellectual isolation. Problems encountered with speech are articulation disorders, stuttering, aphasia, and excessive talking.

ARTICULATION DISORDERS

Van Hattum[29] stated that speech fluency and clear articulation are not fully developed until the child reaches eight years of age but, nevertheless, any school child who still lisps or is unable to pronounce certain sounds is teased for his baby talk, and there are snickers when he reads aloud.

Environmental, emotional, and physical factors, including partial deafness, have been found to contribute to retention of articulatory difficulties. Mange[16] compared 35 children who misarticulated *r* with a matched group of normally-speaking children, and he discovered less ability to discriminate pitch in the children who did not speak clearly. Dickson[8] studied 60 children, half of whom had outgrown articulation defects spontaneously and half of whom had not. He found that those retaining speech inadequacies were inferior in gross motor tasks and that their mothers were immature and unstable; both are conditions which tend to retard development in the child. Behavior and learning problems often are associated with speech defects.

Articulation difficulties in children of this age usually are restricted to only a few sounds. Parents can train the child by choosing two or three words he consistently mispronounces and having him repeat them correctly when he errs, proceeding to other misarticulated words after he has mastered these. McCarthy[17] stated that children with articulatory defects respond well to increased practice in speaking, combined with renewed self-confidence from greater independence and broader social contacts.

In many schools a speech therapist is available to work with children in small groups for limited periods of time. The therapist tries to increase the child's ability to distinguish between sounds and to develop his control in the accurate production of sounds. Games, stories, exercises, songs, watching the therapist's mouth as she speaks, and observing his own mouth movements in a mirror are all methods used to teach correct articulation.

In larger cities speech clinics associated with universities or hospitals are common, and individual instruction can be given a child whose difficulty persists. Teaching the parent how to train the child to distinguish between sounds is considered preferable at times to professional tutelage.[33]

STUTTERING

There is one stutterer in every 100 children attending school.[12, 24] Stuttering may be continued from the pre-school period,* may reoccur after an earlier disappearance, or may develop for the first time during the early elementary school years. During this period the child is subjected to special stress in leaving home, working independently, suffering indignity and rebuff from his peers, and fitting himself into a day packed with activity and demands.[24] A tense child, especially one who is perfectionistic and believes he is not doing well, shows his insecurity in his hesitant speech.†

Several investigators have reported that stutterers are shy and self-conscious, are insecure, are inadequately socialized, have strong needs for affection, and possess parents who are overprotective and dominant.[2, 3, 11, 19, 20] Consistent attitudes of rejection of the child and persistent dissatisfaction with him have been noted in parents of school-age stutterers.[7] Other writers, summarizing many studies of child stutterers, have concluded that there is no single characteristic personality pattern.

The stuttering child meets ridicule wherever he turns. Stutterers are portrayed as laughable on television and in comics. People who listen to the child's disturbed speech are discomfited or impatient, and they either

---

* See Chapter 21, "Speech Disorders," pp. 171–172.
† See Case 23, Charles S., p. 513.

order him to hurry up and finish what he is trying to say or they complete his sentences for him, thus emphasizing his inadequacy and their strong reaction to it.

The more the child notices his stuttering, the more he tenses and struggles to get the words out. His voice may increase in pitch or intensity until he nearly sings or shouts when he speaks. He tries to get the word out by sheer force, pressing hard to shove the air past his tight lips and tongue. In his effort, he may stamp a foot, jerk his head, or hit himself, and these extraneous movements become associated with speaking the difficult word. He then interprets the movements as necessary preliminaries to speaking, and he precedes his attempts to speak with contortions of these kinds.[30]

Once the child becomes afraid of error, he notices repetitions or hesitations in his speech, and he pauses. He may start over, half-heartedly, but he tends to retreat into silence. He wants to communicate, but he is afraid he will stutter, and his voluntary silence makes him more miserable than ever.

The child remembers situations and words which disconcert him, and he builds up a private list of sounds he cannot get out and speech situations he cannot handle. His fear grows each time he encounters them. If he avoids them, he becomes even more afraid. If he tries and fails, he becomes discouraged and retreat is more possible next time. Inevitably focusing on the feared sound or word, he tenses and stutters, and he becomes increasingly less able to manage speaking.[33]

The child who stutters only at times of tension and who is not concerned by his hesitant speech should be given the same management suggested for the pre-school child.* The child aware of his difficulty and becoming increasingly tense and fearful should be under the care of a speech therapist. Stuttering children are best retrained in groups, and this lessens the child's conviction that he is odd and inferior. Varied techniques are used by therapists, depending on the age of the child and the ramifications of the problem. One aim is to help the child lose his fear of particular words or letters, and this is sometimes done by repeated practice in speaking or reading the feared sounds. Negative practice, in which the child deliberately stutters before a mirror, can bring speech under voluntary control.

Parents of stutterers sometimes feel helpless and guilty because of the persistence of the problem and the conflicting advice they have received. They may be afraid to punish the child for misbehavior for fear of aggravating the stuttering, but they are angered by their self-imposed restraint. The parents' regular conferences with the child's speech therapist provide opportunities for gaining valid information, create renewed confidence in their ability to help the child, and present tech-

---

* See Chapter 21, "Speech Disorders," p. 172.

niques for establishing a more understanding relationship with him.[33] Discussing problems and management methods with the parents of other stuttering children frequently enables some parents to relax their standards for exceptionally mature behavior in their own child.

APHASIA

Aphasia is the inability to understand or to express language as the result of injury to the brain. *Sensory aphasia* is the failure to understand language: Inability to understand oral language is known as *word deafness*, and inability to understand written language is termed *word blindness* or *alexia. Motor aphasia* is inability to express language, and disturbances in writing are known as *agraphia*.

Aphasia may be congenital or acquired from infection or accident to the brain. Cerebral lesions or lack of cortical development may appear congenitally. Lesions ordinarily are found in the left hemisphere, which is dominant for speech regardless of handedness. The nearer the lesion is to the junction of the parietal, occipital, and temporal lobes, the greater is the disturbance of reading and writing. When the posterior superior temporal region is involved, the individual tends to show more difficulty in comprehending speech. Perseveration and problems with naming are observed in nearly all cases of aphasia. In word blindness, perception is variable, and a child sometimes can read when the letters are enlarged, even though there is no loss of visual acuity.[25] Occasionally the child shows a sudden spurt in language development at four or five years, but usually he is less responsive to treatment than the child with acquired aphasia.[4]

Acquired aphasia may result from encephalitis, high fever, a blow on the head, or a fall resulting in damage to the brain. At onset the child is nearly mute and has little understanding of speech. As the condition stabilizes, he is able to identify objects or pictures of them when they are named for him, and then he can repeat short sequences of digits and words. Later, he will be able to name many common objects with occasional blocking or misnaming, and he will be able to converse haltingly. Eventually he will be able to follow simple oral directions and finally more complicated ones. Recovery may occur within a few weeks, but it has been known to range from a few days to two years.[4]

Other physiological defects and disabilities contribute to the disorder. Ewing[10] and Benton[4] stated that a consistent hearing loss for the higher sound frequencies is found in aphasic children, and Penfield and Roberts[25] reported that none of the word-deaf aphasics they studied had intact hearing. Monsees[21] considered aphasia to be related to a disorder in temporal perception, either auditory or visual. West[31] believed that reduced auditory memory span was a factor in a child's faulty perception of word meanings.

Diagnosis of aphasia is difficult, and the child's verbal impairment often is interpreted as deafness, as retardation, or as symptomatic of autism or psychosis.[14, 22]

Aphasia frequently is overlooked as the basis for a child's inability to learn to read or write, and the child is accused of being inattentive or of deliberately trying to ridicule, by a refusal to learn, those who are teaching him. As he attempts to make sense of instructions or to copy symbols he perceives incorrectly, he is baffled by his inability to match other children's quick responding and he is convinced that he is stupid. He has frequent temper tantrums because of his frustrated efforts to understand the communications of others and because of the constant rebukes he receives from adults unaware of his difficulty. He is characteristically tense, resistive, and withdrawn.*

Special education is mandatory for the aphasic child during his early school years.[22] If the disturbance is not severe and his teacher understands the handicaps aphasia imposes, the child can be retained in a regular class, providing the teacher can give him detailed instructions and individual help.

When this is not possible and if there is no special class in the school system for brain-damaged children, he should be enrolled in a school for deaf children. Although he may or may not have a hearing handicap, methods used to teach the deaf help him. He learns to recognize and use sounds with their associated meanings, and he can learn to lip read, which assists him if his hearing acuity is severely limited. The use of varied colors to identify syllables in words, distinctive backgrounds for letters and numbers, and motor reënforcement through tracing and outlining all have proved successful with the aphasic child.[15] After several years of special teaching, the child will be able to return to a regular classroom.

Parents of an aphasic child need to explain carefully what they mean when they give him instructions. They should encourage the child to talk, rather than retreat into silence, and they should gradually correct his word usage and understanding by helping him write and define words he habitually confuses.

EXCESSIVE TALKING

Some children are never silent. They begin a barrage of comments, criticisms, suggestions, and questions as soon as they are out of bed in the morning, and at school they talk ceaselessly to the teacher until she

---

* See Case 24, Leo P., p. 514.

orders them to keep quiet. Even then they are able to refrain from speaking for only brief periods. During the dinner hour, they monopolize the conversation, interrupt their parents' discussions with extraneous questions, and are still talking and singing to themselves in bed after the lights are out.

Overtalkative children are anxious about events they do not understand, worried about trouble at home, or unsure of their own acceptability. They continually force recognition and seek to establish contact with others by talking. Uninterrupted verbalization also screens serious worries, and the child successfully avoids thinking about them by occupying himself with speaking.

An elementary school child may ask questions continually, not caring about the answers but attempting to capture an indifferent parent's attention this way. Like the pre-school child, he may ask questions about many subjects, trying to find courage to slip in the one question which really troubles him. He may revert to infantile tactics with repeated, plaintive questions about whether his mother really loves him. Excessive talkers often bear feelings of guilt based on their own behavior or their feelings about their parents.

The overtalkative child should be required to remain quiet some of the time. At school this can be accomplished by isolating him from the classroom when he cannot inhibit talking, and at home he can be sent to his room to read or play alone for a specified period. If the child repeatedly interrupts at dinner, he should be required to remain silent for five minutes. The talkative child restimulates himself the longer he continues, and imposed quiet helps him gain self-control and learn not to fear his own thoughts.

The child who talks excessively has unsolved problems which require solutions and questions which require answers. If parents reserve time to spend with the child daily, he soon becomes certain that he can have the parent's attention regularly, and eventually a perplexed or troubled child will confide his worries to his parent.

REFERENCES

1. Barbara, D. A.: Stuttering. *In* Arieti, S., ed.: *American Handbook of Psychiatry.* New York, Basic Books, Inc., 1959, vol. 1, pp. 952–963.
2. Bender, J. F.: *The Personality Structure of Stuttering.* New York, Pitman Pub. Corp., 1939.
3. Bender, J. F.: The prophylaxis of stuttering. *Nerv. Child,* 1943, 2, 181–198.
4. Benton, A. L.: Aphasia in children. *In* Trapp, E. P., and Himelstein, P., eds.: *Readings on the Exceptional Child.* New York, Appleton-Century-Crofts, 1962, pp. 450–455.
5. Chapman, M. E.: *Self-inventory: Group Therapy for Those Who Stutter,* Ed. 3. Minneapolis, Minn., Burgess Pub. Co., 1959.

6. Clark, R. M., and Snyder, M.: Group therapy for parents of pre-adolescent stutterers. *Group Psychother.*, 1955, *8*, 226–231.
7. D'Evelyn, K. E.: *Meeting Children's Emotional Needs.* Englewood Cliffs, N. J., Prentice-Hall, Inc., 1957, pp. 111–112.
8. Dickson, S.: Differences between children who spontaneously outgrow and children who retain functional articulation errors. *J. Speech Hear. Res.*, 1962, *5* (3), 263–271.
9. Elkan, D.: Development of an aphasic child: a case study. *Volta Rev.*, 1955, *57*, 71–72.
10. Ewing, A. W. G.: *Aphasia in Children.* London, Oxford University Press, 1930.
11. Goodstein, L. D.: Functional speech disorders and personality: A survey of the literature. *In* Trapp, E. P., and Himelstein, P., eds.: *Readings on the Exceptional Child.* New York, Appleton-Century-Crofts, 1962, p. 406.
12. Hurlock, E.: *Child Development.* New York, McGraw-Hill Book Co., 1950, pp. 234–235.
13. Kanner, L.: *Child Psychiatry,* Ed. 3. Springfield, Ill., Charles C Thomas, 1957, pp. 520–541.
14. Karlin, I. W.: Aphasias in children. *Amer. J. Dis. Child.*, 1954, *87*, 752–767.
15. Kleffner, F. R.: Teaching aphasic children. *Education*, 1959, *79*, 413–418.
16. McCarthy, D.: Language development in children. *In* Carmichael, L., ed.: *Manual of Child Psychology.* New York, John Wiley and Sons, 1946, pp. 514–515.
17. Mange, C. V.: Relationships between selected auditory perceptual factors and articulation ability. *J. Speech Hear. Res.*, 1960, *3*, 67–74.
18. Miles, T. R.: Two cases of developmental aphasia. *J. Child Psychol. Psychiat.*, 1961, *2*, 48–70.
19. Moncur, J. P.: Environmental factors differentiating stuttering children from non-stuttering children. *Speech Monogr.*, 1951, *18*, 312–325.
20. Moncur, J. P.: Parental domination in stuttering. *J. Speech Hear. Dis.*, 1952, *17*, 155–165.
21. Monsees, E. K.: Aphasia in children. *J. Speech Hear. Dis.*, 1961, *26*, 83–86.
22. Myklebust, H.: Aphasia in children. *Except. Child*, 1952, *19*, 9–14.
23. Myklebust, H. R., and Boshes, B.: Psychoneurological learning disorders in children. *Arch. Pediat.* (*N. Y.*), 1960, *77*, 247–256.
24. Overholser, W., and Richmond, W.: *Handbook of Psychiatry.* Philadelphia, J. B. Lippincott Co., 1947, pp. 230–231.
25. Penfield, W., and Roberts, L.: *Speech and Brain-Mechanisms.* Princeton, N. J., Princeton University Press, 1959, pp. 72–78, 102.
26. Sheehan, J. G.: Projective studies of stuttering. *In* Trapp, E. P., and Himelstein, P., eds.: *Readings on the Exceptional Child.* New York, Appleton-Century-Crofts, 1962, p. 421.
27. Strauss, A. A.: Aphasia in children. *Amer. J. Phys. Med.*, 1954, *33*, 93–99.
28. Teagarden, F. M.: *Child Psychology for Professional Workers.* New York, Prentice-Hall, Inc., 1940, pp. 576–578.
29. Van Hattum, R. J.: Speech grows too. *N. Y. State Educ.*, 1955, *43*, 184–185, 221.
30. Van Riper, C.: *Stuttering.* Chicago, The National Society for Crippled Children, 1948, pp. 26, 30, 32, 39–41, 45.
31. West, R.: *The Rehabilitation of Speech.* New York, Harper and Bros., 1947, pp. 238, 383–385, 467–503.
32. Wood, N. E.: Decision making: Childhood aphasia. *ASHA*, 1963, *5*, 571–575.
33. Wyatt, G. L., and Herzan, H. M.: Therapy with stuttering children and their mothers. *Amer. J. Orthopsychiat.*, 1962, *32* (4), 645–659.

Chapter 31

School Problems

The problems associated with school attendance represent the single most common cause for which children are referred to clinics,[34] and school difficulties have been noted as prominent in 45 per cent of the children referred for a variety of personality and behavior disturbances.[12]

For 12 years or longer, schoolwork is the child's chief daily occupation, one which mirrors with fidelity his industry, obedience, initiative, and adaptability. At school he develops habits of working with others and competing against them—habits which will endure into adulthood.[43] If he performs successfully with relative ease and if he usually can overcome failure by increased effort, he grows in self-confidence and self-respect.[9] If he does not, he is ashamed, perplexed, and angry.

Despite the singular importance of the school in setting behavior habits, the child's difficulties there are overlooked and neglected by clinicians and educators alike. Misconceptions have accumulated because of insufficient communication between clinicians and school personnel.

Some clinicians scarcely seem to be aware of the child's school life. They dismiss it from attention and soothe troubled parents with the assurance that some children are "slow developers," and given time, the child will blossom into the alert, conscientious student they want him to be.[34]

The teacher, working alone and responsible for the child for five hours daily, has no access to the clinician's objective insight into the child's irritating nonconformity.[19] She tries to get the child to achieve more and to behave better by appealing to his pride and offering him friendship, and when this does not help, she feels rebuffed by the child and discouraged by her failure.[14] Antagonism and frustration mount between teacher and child, and soon the teacher ceases her attempts to assist the child in revising his actions.

Brain-damaged and emotionally disturbed children comprise 10 per cent of the school population, but the school is blocked in its ability to help them because extra rooms and staff members are not available for the specialized teaching and small classes these children require. Sometimes a determined, ingenious teacher, willing to give individual instruction and able to isolate the distractable or distracting child during the school day, can bring him to adequate performance, both behaviorally and academically,[14, 39] but such teachers are rare and seldom encouraged by their fellow staff members or even by the child's parents.

Problems associated with school develop in three areas: (1) learning difficulties, including underachievement, perfectionism, and reading and arithmetic disability; (2) behavior disturbances, such as attention-seeking, restlessness, and negativism and disobedience; and (3) active avoidance of school, as evidenced by school phobia and truancy.*

LEARNING DIFFICULTIES

Underachievement

There are children in every classroom who idle away the time allotted for completing seatwork by daydreaming or wandering about the room visiting. They never start work without an individual command from the teacher, and they seldom finish it without repeated prodding.†

The lackadaisical child may be suffering from physical illness or deficit. His vision or hearing may be impaired, or he may be so tired from lack of sleep or rushing to lessons and activities after school that he rests whenever he is free to do so.[21] Lantz[25] reported that a survey of third graders showed numerous minor but cumulative illnesses which contributed to their low energy at school. Cardiac, respiratory, and glandular malfunction were noted, as well as poor nutrition and a low maturation rate in some children.

Undetected brain damage makes class work incomprehensible to a few children. Letter and number symbols are perceived inaccurately and erratically; sounds are misinterpreted or indistinguishable from each other; and restlessness and a short attention span combine to make successful learning impossible. Because he cannot understand what is ex-

---

* In the discussion of school problems which follows, inadequate intelligence is assumed not to be a contributing factor. The special characteristics and needs of the retarded child are described in Chapter 45.

† See Case 19, Barbara N., p. 510.

pected of him, the brain-damaged child soon ceases to try to do his work and promptly is branded as lazy or rebellious by his parents and teacher.[26]

The dependent, self-conscious child does not exert himself to do schoolwork.[15, 29, 31, 45] If his mother makes his bed, picks up his clothes and toys, takes him in the car to school, and does his homework, he is untrained in independence and cannot work without direction. Furthermore, he feels no obligation to do so because he has never been required to manage unpleasant or difficult tasks. The child who anticipates that he will fail at schoolwork will not attempt it.[20]

A child may spend his time in school entertaining himself if he has been coerced as a pre-schooler into working at academic tasks.[21] An ambitious mother may conduct daily instruction periods, during which she requires the young child to color precisely, learn the alphabet, count, and submit to flash card drills. When he finally arrives in the classroom, he is satiated with learning tasks and rebels against them.

If coerciveness has extended into all areas of his life, school presents an opportunity to the overdirected child to resist adult orders. He is more successful at evading instructions there because his busy teacher cannot supervise him closely or force him to work.

Some children are inattentive and indifferent at school because they are preoccupied with problems at home.[15] Writing a column of numbers seems unimportant to a child who is wondering what his mother and baby sister are doing in his absence, who anxiously recalls his parents' angry argument of the previous evening, or who feels alone and miserable because of his mother's constant censure.*

The degree of motivation to master tasks which can be observed in a child during his first five years of school is an accurate predictor of his achievement efforts as an adult,[37] and prompt evaluation of the causes for underachievement is needed so that remedial aid can be provided. A thorough medical examination should be made to rule out or uncover physical defects. Adequate sleep, food, and time for free play should be assured the child. Parents need to trust the child's abilities more and hover over him less, teaching him to be responsible for caring for his possessions, helping with work at home, and getting himself to school on time. Demanding and critical parents should use more reasonable corrective methods.

The teacher can determine whether the child has difficulty understanding word or number concepts or perceiving symbols accurately. If he does, he will need individual teaching and extra practice.[33] The parents can be enlisted to help, with the teacher directing drills and instruction.

Haring and Phillips[14] described teaching techniques which proved

---

* See Case 20, Betty R., p. 511.

effective with both emotionally disturbed and brain-damaged children, some of whom were three years retarded in academic achievement. The children, placed in a classroom limited to ten or 12 pupils, were able to return to regular classes within one to three years, and at that time they were achieving normally.

In the special class, group activity was restricted and interruptions during work periods were minimal: Recess was postponed until work was completed. Private study booths were built into the classroom so that a child could do his work without distraction. He was given only one task at a time, and his work was scored immediately and the grade recorded. If he did not understand the work, his teacher helped him complete it and revised his next assignment so that it was suited to his current knowledge. Every assignment had to be completed each day. If the child played during work time, he forfeited his freedom at recess, the noon hour, or after school; or he was required to finish his academic work while the rest of the class enjoyed art, singing, or games in the afternoon. Noting which school activity the child most preferred, the teacher gave him the choice of sacrificing it for the privilege of idleness during working hours. Praise for prompt and thorough work encouraged the child to continue his efforts.[10]

As the child learned to work and stimultaneously acquired more knowledge, his assignments gradually were lengthened. His newly established work habits were strengthened by both his increasing knowledge and his pride in successful achievement.

Perfectionism

Some children consider school to be detestable drudgery. Trying to do everything perfectly, they spend wearying amounts of time checking their work again and again to make certain everything is correct.[21, 38] During tests, they become so tense that they cannot recall what they have learned,[36] and they cry or become angry when they do not make the best grade in the class.*

The natural state of a child is haphazardness and carelessness, and the perfectionistic child is one who has been taught to require high standards of himself. Usually he lives in a home where excellence is demanded of everyone; and his critical, correct parents point out endlessly the advantages of superior knowledge, manners, possessions, and appearance. Impropriety and mistakes are received with cold disapproval and exhortations to the child to improve himself.

The teacher can help the perfectionistic child to achieve appropriately with less effort and concern. When assigning a theme, she can specify that spelling must be accurate, but punctuation will not be

---

* See Case 23, Charles S., p. 513.

graded on that particular paper. Speed tests, which increase tension, can be curtailed; and the perfectionistic child will benefit from shorter assignments for a time, so that he is able to succeed without extraordinary effort. If weekly tests are given in certain subjects, the practice of omitting the two lowest scores in calculating a midsemester grade is a comfort to all pupils and of special assistance to the perfectionistic child.

Parents can reverse their attitudes if they understand that overconcern hinders learning by slowing performance. They can praise good work and ignore errors, give the child greater freedom to play as he chooses, permit him to get away from home with his friends, and avoid critical attention to manners and dress.

Reading Disability

Reading is the most common area of learning difficulty for the child, as well as the most crucial for his entire education. It has been estimated that 12 per cent of all school children read so far below their expected level that they require special assistance,[27] and of this group, 84 to 94 per cent are boys.[21] Despite average or superior intelligence, the poor reader has a low sight vocabulary, does not know the sounds of individual letters, shows reversal tendencies, and is restless and distractable.[3] Reading disability is related to brain damage and to emotional patterns of dependency and resistance.[21, 22, 26, 34]

Brain damage may produce disturbances in verbal understanding, perception, and attention. The child cannot understand the meaning of words he hears or sees. He fails to recognize inconsistencies in his own statements, his memory is defective, and what he learns with painstaking toil one day is completely forgotten the next.[34] He may be unable to equate symbols with sounds or to equate symbols and sounds with words. He cannot inhibit responses to extraneous stimulation: He looks for the pencil he hears drop and he puzzles about the noises from a radiator. Restless and inattentive, he misses large segments of instruction. Perception is distorted and the child sees letters or numbers reversed, or he separates each symbol into discrete parts and is unable to visualize it as a single configuration.[39] He may reverse directions, reading from right to left, and if he does, *was* becomes *saw* and *on* becomes *no*.[26, 27] He remembers the distinctive appearance of a long word and surprises adults by reading it easily, although he consistently fails to read short, simple words, all of which appear the same to him.

Reading disability occurs in children without demonstrable organic damage. Nonreaders have been characterized as insecure, resistant, and less adaptable socially.[21] They are dependent children with little self-confidence. Accustomed to relying on others, they are uninterested in expending the effort which learning demands, and they would prefer to remain at home where little is expected of them. By refusing to learn, they underline their determination to disassociate themselves from school.

Prompt and continuing aid should be given each child with a reading disability, and every elementary school teacher should be equipped to give remedial instruction. If the time of a trained remedial teacher is limited, it should be utilized for instruction of classroom teachers in recognizing and dealing with reading problems; and if this help is not available, the teacher can study remedial reading techniques herself and train defective readers individually or in small groups.

The Initial Teaching Alphabet, developed in Great Britain by Sir James Pitman, is an innovation for teaching reading which has proved effective with both normal and retarded readers. Ordinarily the 44 distinct sound units of English are spelled in 2000 different ways, but the ITA consists of 44 characters, each of which represents a single sound in the English language so that what a child sees in print corresponds more closely to what he hears in sound. A group of seven-year-old slow readers, unable to read more than three words, attained normal reading levels within eight weeks after beginning ITA training. They were able to change later from ITA reading to conventional reading after two hours of instruction, and average readers accomplish the changeover in minutes.[42]

Some schools have adopted the Joplin plan, in which all children in the fourth, fifth, and sixth grades are grouped according to reading ability and spend an hour daily in reading class.[28] This systems permits continued teaching for poor readers in the upper grades, the level at which individualized reading instruction usually is abandoned.

The brain-damaged child must have special training, and few communities provide the necessary instruction within the public school system.* The aphasic child may have to be enrolled in a school for the deaf, and the child with less severe problems may have to be taught privately. The brain-damaged child who receives the special attention he requires during the early elementary years can return to a regular classroom by the age of ten.[23]

The child who chooses not to learn to read needs to practice self-reliance and independent action by getting himself dressed and to school, by helping with daily chores at home, and by being permitted to try out his own ideas whenever possible. As his parents express their confidence in his ability in these ways, he becomes more eager to learn and more certain that he can succeed. Sending home a short written or oral assignment for the child to prepare for his parents enlists their support for his efforts. He should read orally at home for 15 minutes

---

* See Chapter 46, "Cerebral Dysfunction," pp. 460–463.

daily, selecting his own material. His selections will seem too simple to his parents, but the purpose of daily reading is to acquire fluency, and a child forced always to struggle with difficult words continues to dislike and avoid reading.

Arithmetic Disability

Low grades in arithmetic can plague a child who is successful in verbal subjects. He may read well, enjoy giving oral reports, and be able to contribute information on any subject the teacher mentions, and yet he may make many errors in arithmetic. Arithmetic requires close attention to detail and the willingness to devote time to memorizing meaningless combinations, and some alert, quick children are reluctant to slow their learning pace. They are baffled by the discovery that a glance at multiplication tables is insufficient to master them. Emotionally disturbed children perform poorly in arithmetic because they cannot muster the necessary self-discipline and attentiveness required for accuracy.[5]

Difficulties occur when a child works too quickly and a single erroneous calculation makes an entire problem wrong, when absence from school results in imperfect learning of new procedures, or when the child applies numerical concepts in an original manner. Some children panic when they are given speed tests in number combination drills, and for years they dread arithmetic because of its association with unpleasant pressure. A child with organic defect may not be able to manage the symbolism of written numbers or even of pictured objects.

The child's specific arithmetical defects can be identified by his teacher, and remedial work can be conducted at home under parental supervision. The child who cannot understand symbols can learn by counting, adding and subtracting pennies or blocks, and then translating each solved problem into written numbers. If he is weak in remembering combinations, he should drill daily with flash cards. If he continually fails because of a single error on a long problem, he can be required to check his work and locate mistakes.

Using arithmetic makes it seem more sensible to expend effort on it. The child can figure how much change he should receive after a purchase; add up total costs for produce, meats, and groceries from figures on the register tape; and have his own money to allocate for different purposes. Games involving sums of numbers improve his addition skill effortlessly.

New techniques of teaching mathematics which originated at the college level have sifted downward through senior high school, junior high school, and now are used in many elementary schools. The "new math" is based on manipulations necessary for solving problems with computing machines and is intended to aid pupils in understanding the relationships between numbers. The techniques permit greater freedom in using numbers in varied ways and require the mastery of a new and complex vocabulary. An elementary school child must understand what is meant by *multiple* and *sequence* in order to follow the directions in his workbook. He must learn how to make an *expanded notation,* and he must remember the difference between a *standard numeral* and a *cardinal number,* besides deciding whether a number is *commutative, associative,* or *distributive.* A child unable to absorb modern mathematics instruction should be held responsible only for traditional combinations and methods of problem solution.

BEHAVIOR DISTURBANCES

Attention-seeking

Attention-seeking behavior may take any one of several forms. A child may play the clown, entertaining his classmates by making faces and funny noises, climbing on his desk, throwing paper wads, playing jokes on the teacher, and tapping each child on the head with his pencil as he swaggers down the aisle. Or he may disengage himself from his peers and look to his teacher for attention, plying her with tales of his prowess, tattling on his classmates, and asking innumerable questions about assignments.

His behavior advertises his feeling of uncertainty in the classroom. Usually his inappropriate actions are matched by poor academic performance, caused in part by his interrupting his work to seek the reassurance of others' admiration or interest.

Teachers deplore childish, disrupting behavior, even when they understand the need which produces it, and they often ridicule and reject a child who acts this way. Such a response to his efforts, understandable though it is, usually results only in alteration of the form of his distracting activity.

To decrease the child's feeling of unimportance and to curtail unwanted behavior, he can be given an overabundance of opportunities for legitimate attention and prestige. He should be assigned oral reports, be appointed chairman of a committee, and be called on repeatedly to recite. His self-distracting habits need curbing so that he can complete his work and replace his need for attention with real achievement. Minor, isolated attention-seeking behavior ordinarily is best ignored by a teacher, but that which is gross, continuous, and disturbing should not be allowed to continue. Every classroom should have a screened area where a child can be sent to work alone when he is overstimulated and unable to inhibit action.[14]

Examination of the child's home life will reveal the circumstances which result in his feeling uncertain and inadequate, and parents can help him to achieve greater maturity and self-confidence by altering their attitudes and training.

Restlessness

[A teacher is baffled and frustrated by the child who busily gets to work on request but whose diligence lasts only momentarily.] Then he is up and about the room, and by the time he is ordered to his seat, he has forgotten completely what he is supposed to be doing. He darts from one task to another, never completing any.

Many children who behave this way are burdened with serious home problems or convictions of inadequacy, and they distract themselves from thinking by ceaseless activity.* These children not only find it difficult to sit still but also talk or sing to themselves constantly, ask questions and comment on others' performances, and fidget with pencils and books whenever they must remain in their seats.†

Brain-damaged children, attracted to stimuli unnoticed by their classmates, typically show restlessness and variable attentiveness. They are constantly on the move, prowling and investigating, worried and apprehensive, and unresponsive for long to the teacher's requests for them to attend to their work.

A restless, distractable child should be isolated in the classroom. Working in a screened area, he is shielded from extraneous stimulation and can attend to assigned tasks for longer periods. He should be given only one assignment at a time, and he should be required to complete it correctly before receiving another.[14] Instructions should be clear and specific,[6] and the child should write them to forestall his requesting the teacher to repeat them.

At home, the restless child should be provided regularly with time and attention from his parents so that he can ask them the questions which trouble him and gain reassurance and support. The brain-damaged child requires a simple, routine schedule which permits him extra rest and a minimum of stimulation. He needs many opportunities to ask questions of his parents and to secure their approval, and he benefits from firm direction.

Negativism and Disobedience

Some children calmly or belligerently refuse to do school assignments. [A teacher, angered and frustrated by the refusal and unable to influence the child, often assumes that the child refuses to work because he dislikes her.[14]]More often, however, the child is not angry at his

---

* See Case 17, Paul G., p. 508.
† See Case 25, Willard K., p. 515.

teacher but at other people, including himself. His siblings or playmates may belittle and tease him continually, or his parents imply by their actions that they care little about him. Trodden on by others, he asserts himself when he is certain of succeeding.*

Negativism may be the child's usual reaction to any request with which he prefers not to comply, well learned from parental indulgence of his wishes.[2] Parents may support a child in his refusal to do school-work: They believe him when he claims that he already knows everything being taught and that completing assignments is a waste of time, or they agree that the work is too difficult and it is unreasonable to require it of him. Parents teach a child irresponsibility for school assignments when they do homework for him and vouch for his having finished work when he did not. If parents excuse every difficulty the child has at school by blaming the prejudice of the teacher, the indifference of the principal, the inadequacy of instruction, or the absurdity of rules, they provide the child with solid support for opposing any requirement of his teacher.[38]

The habitually disobedient child, who not only refuses to do his work but also breaks rules or attacks teachers, acts from strong motivation to rebel. Few elementary children dare to challenge the authority of the school, and the child who does is one who has experienced violence, neglect, and rejection. He detects threats and rejection in situations where none exists, and he strikes out in anger and fear.

Teacher and parents can coöperate to help the negativistic or disobedient child. Parents should insist on the child's completing assignments, regardless of how reasonable his objections may appear. Academic progress is impossible without self-discipline, and a child should learn to do what is asked of him, rather than consider himself entitled to special treatment.[33] Parents who meet a child's criticism of his teacher with a firm statement of support for her as the person best qualified to instruct him can deflect his stratagem for evading work; and a teacher who comments to a belligerent pupil that his parents expect him to do his schoolwork has allied on one side all of the important adults in his life.

A teacher needs to anticipate that sometimes a child will refuse to work, and she must decide in advance what to say and do so that she is not left helpless by opposition. Permitting the child to choose between completing his work during the time provided or sacrificing more desirable time later eventually convinces him that he cannot permanently avoid it.

The aggressively disobedient child antagonizes his teacher and principal, and if his parents defend his actions, both objectivity and real concern for the child's welfare are required for school officials to deal nonemotionally with him.[19, 35] Much inconsistency and angry management of the recalcitrant child can be avoided if school rules are few and

---

* See Case 22, Kenneth J., p. 512.

are explicitly stated and explained to pupils both at the beginning of the year and as often later as necessary. Teachers and principal together should establish uniform school procedures for dealing with offenses. Penalties should be set in advance, known to the children, and consistently applied. Otherwise, a teacher unprepared for disobedience responds erratically or ineffectually or resorts to the time-honored expression of helplessness by sending the child to the principal's office. Fixed disciplinary procedures also circumvent the unusual and degrading punishments imposed by an occasional teacher who uses her pupils to satisfy her own emotional needs.

Class rules for behavior can be established by the children themselves, who conform more readily under self-discipline and accept the judgment of peers with more grace than they do that of adults.

The disobedient child who receives nothing but angry censure and punishment from school officials knows they dislike him, and his behavior worsens. His teacher and principal should attempt to counteract their own negative feelings by giving the child audible credit for every commendable action and academic achievement. Recognition of his worth softens his antagonism and halts rebellion.[35]

Parents must discover why the usually troubled or angry child is disturbed, and they must provide the reassurance or altered treatment he needs.

AVOIDANCE OF SCHOOL

School Phobia

School phobia appears suddenly and dramatically. The child cries, trembles, and pleads to stay home, adding to the mystery of his behavior by shaking his head and insisting he does not know why he is afraid.[38] This statement is more truthful than the reason he will produce if adults demand that he explain his resistance to school attendance.[11]

In most cases of school phobia, a precipitating incident can be identified. There is a new baby at home, or the child has suffered a recent illness or accident and feels less self-sufficient than before. If he became ill or was hurt at school, he dreads returning to the scene of the trouble, fearing that the incident will be repeated.[38]

Hersov[17] studied 50 cases of school phobia and found that the children, though timid and fearful at school, were willful and demanding at home. They dominated their mothers, who were overprotective of them, and their fathers were inadequate and passive. This is the family picture observed by most investigators, who point out that the child's real fear is of being separated from his mother, from whom he receives great comfort and over whom he exerts control, and these are satisfactions he does not find at school.[7, 8, 9, 11, 34] Inbred family constellations, with each parent dependent on his own parents and neither able to establish a mature marital relationship, were noted by Talbot.[40]

The child who develops a school phobia often is one who does average or better schoolwork, but he tends to isolate himself from his classmates and he derives little pleasure from his accomplishments. He fears others' discovery of his weaknesses and is acutely embarrassed by any mistake or mishap. If he is permitted to remain away from school, he is relaxed and happy, busying himself with many projects, including his studies, and even cheerfully helping his mother with her housework.

The longer the child's return to school is delayed, the more difficult it becomes for him to give up his pleasant existence at home for one in which he is lonely and uncertain.[11, 44] Delay also retards his instruction, and each day's absence gives him added reason to resist returning because now he is certain that his lack of knowledge will embarrass him before his classmates.

For these reasons, he needs to be sent back to school immediately, but he need not be forced to rejoin his class. Instead, he can be permitted to spend the day in the principal's office and complete his work there. More often than not, after a few days, or perhaps weeks, he becomes bored with solitude and his courage returns. When he reënters the class, his teacher should avoid giving him special attention and should call on him to recite only when she is certain he can do so successfully.

The child can learn to feel more comfortable at school and less concerned about himself if his teacher pairs him with each classmate in turn for drills, planning, and oral reading. In this way he becomes better acquainted with his peers, and they with him. At home, the father should assume greater direction and control of the child, with the mother agreeing to defer to the father's edicts. Mother and child can disentangle themselves from each other if each becomes involved in separate activities with other people outside of the home. The mother can learn to resist the child's demands if definite rules are established which are never subject to compromise and if she never makes a request of the child which she does not intend to enforce.

Truancy

The truant child often has sound reasons for avoiding school. Such factors as failing to understand or succeed with schoolwork, being the largest or smallest in the class, or being forced to wear ragged clothing all single him out for unfavorable comparison.[41] A child may find subject matter dull and useless, or he may wish to escape the strict discipline and scoldings which are daily events for him in school.[24]

Emotional difficulties contribute to truancy. If there is trouble at home, the child symbolically runs away from it by first running away from school. Sometimes he truants in revenge against indifferent, restricting, or rejecting parents, and he delights in their anxiety and anger over his behavior.[41]

Truanting is encouraged unwittingly by many parents who disparage the school and the instruction offered. Others minimize the need for regular attendance by taking their children out of school, either to assist them at home or to accompany them on trips.

Hersov[16] found that truants were members of large families in which discipline was inconsistent. As infants many of these children had been cared for by persons other than their own mothers, and during their elementary school years their fathers were no longer living at home. In general, they were poor students, who found little satisfaction at school and who were unaccustomed to regulated lives.

Other delinquencies develop from truancy.[41] The truant child must remain out of sight during school hours and somehow occupy his time. He may steal money for a movie ticket or take a bicycle so that he can keep moving. Fearing punishment when his truancy is discovered, he is often so afraid to return home that he hides out long after the school day is over.

The truant child needs attention as promptly as does the child who is afraid of school. A routine morning check with parents on absentee children is a growing practice in most schools, and this enables the truant to be detected quickly and a search started.

If a child can state his reasons for truanting, these should be investigated and changes should be made. Although the elementary school curriculum is not subject to alteration, the child who finds his work dull and his teacher unpleasant can be tried in a different classroom. Daily individual instruction, enabling him to compete adequately with his classmates and given by a sensible, friendly teacher, can draw him to school. The child who participates in school-sponsored nonacademic activities such as intramural athletics and the school choir or the child who assists with the school store or in the office identifies with the school through service.

A visiting teacher can determine why a child is kept out of school by his parents and can assist in his return. When the child truants, he should make up missed work, both to lessen his pleasure in avoiding school and to guard against his falling behind in his classwork.

REFERENCES

1. Anastasi, A.: *Differential Psychology*. New York, The Macmillan Co., 1937, pp. 417, 422.
2. Averill, L. A.: *Mental Hygiene for the Classroom Teacher*. New York, Pitman Pub. Corp., 1939, pp. 88–103.

3. Barbe, W., Williams, T., and Ganaway, V.: Types of difficulties encountered by 80 children receiving instruction at a reading clinic. *J. Educ. Res.*, 1958, *51*, 437–443.
4. Bettelheim, B.: *Love Is Not Enough.* Glencoe, Ill., The Free Press, 1950, p. 140.
5. Bower, E. M.: Comparison of the characteristics of identified emotionally disturbed children with other children in classes. *In* Trapp, E. P., and Himelstein, P., eds.: *Readings on the Exceptional Child.* New York, Appleton-Century-Crofts, 1962, pp. 610–629.
6. Bruch, H., and Rosenkotter, L.: Psychotherapeutic aspects of teaching emotionally disturbed children. *Psychiat. Quart.*, 1960, *34*, 648–657.
7. Chazan, M.: School phobia. *Brit. J. Educ. Psychol.*, 1962, *32*(3), 209–217.
8. Davidson, S.: School phobia as a manifestation of family disturbance: Its structure and treatment. *J. Child. Psychol. Psychiat.*, 1961, *1*, 270–287.
9. D'Evelyn, K. E.: *Meeting Children's Emotional Needs.* Prentice-Hall, Inc., Englewood Cliffs, N. J., 1957, pp. 9, 83.
10. Dinkmeyer, D., and Dreikurs, R.: *Encouraging Children to Learn: The Encouragement Process.* Englewood Cliffs, N. J., Prentice-Hall, Inc., 1963.
11. Eisenberg, L.: School phobia: A study in the communication of anxiety. *In* Trapp, E. P., and Himelstein, P., eds.: *Readings on the Exceptional Child.* New York, Appleton-Century-Crofts, 1962, pp. 629–639.
12. Gilbert, G. M.: A survey of referral problems in metropolitan child guidance centers. *J. Clin. Psychol.*, 1957, *13*, 37–42.
13. Grimes, J. W., and Allinsmith, W.: Compulsivity, anxiety, and school achievement. *Merrill-Palmer Quart.*, 1961, *7*, 247–269.
14. Haring, N. G., and Phillips, E. L.: *Educating Emotionally Disturbed Children.* New York, McGraw-Hill Book Co., 1962, pp. 9–10, 59, 132–143.
15. Harris, I. D.: *Emotional Blocks to Learning.* New York, Free Press of Glencoe, 1961.
16. Hersov, L. A.: Persistent non-attendance at school. *J. Child Psychol. Psychiat.*, 1960, *1*, 130–136.
17. Hersov, L. A.: Refusal to go to school. *J. Child Psychol. Psychiat.*, 1960, *1*, 137–145.
18. Hurlock, E. B.: The psychology of incentives. *J. Soc. Psychol.*, 1931, *2*, 261–290.
19. Jersild, A.: *Child Psychology*, Ed. 4. Englewood Cliffs, N. J., Prentice-Hall, Inc., 1954, p. 258.
20. Kagan, J., and Moss, H. A.: *Birth to Maturity.* New York, John Wiley and Sons, 1962, p. 272.
21. Kanner, L.: *Child Psychiatry*, Ed. 3. Springfield, Ill., Charles C Thomas, 1957, pp. 559–577.
22. Kinsbourne, M., and Warrington, E. K.: Developmental factors in reading and writing backwardness. *Brit. J. Psychol.*, 1963, *54* (2), 145–156.
23. Kleffner, F. R.: Teaching aphasic children. *Education*, 1959, *79*, 413–418.
24. Kvaraceus, W. C.: *The Community and the Delinquent.* Yonkers-on-Hudson, New York, The World Book Co., 1954, p. 265.
25. Lantz, B.: Children's learning, personality and physiological interactions: a progress report. *Calif. J. Educ. Res.*, 1956, *7*, 153–158.
26. Lawrence, M. M.: Minimal brain injury in child psychiatry. *Comprehen. Psychiat.*, 1960, *1*, 360–369.
27. Monroe, M.: *Children Who Cannot Read.* Chicago, Univ. of Chicago Press, 1932.
28. Morgan, E. F., Jr., and Stucker, G. R.: The Joplin plan of reading vs. a traditional method. *J. Educ. Psychol.*, 1960, *51*, 69–73.
29. Nel, B. F., and Sonnekus, M. C. H.: Psigiese beelde van kinders met leermoeilikhede (Psychic patterns of children with learning difficulties). *Opvoedkund. Stud.*, 1963, No. 33.
30. Nessel, M. A.: Short term treatment of learning difficulty in a child. *USAF SAM Tech. Doc. Rep.*, 1963, No. 63–5.
31. Pasquasy, R.: L'inadaptation scolaire (Inadaptation in school). *Bull. Orient. Scol. Profess.*, 1961, *10*, 1–11.
32. Phillips, E. L., and Haring, N. G.: Results from special techniques for teaching emotionally disturbed children. *Except. Child*, 1959, *26*, 64–67.

33. Phillips, E. L., Wiener, D. N., and Haring, N. G.: *Discipline, Achievement, and Mental Health.* Englewood Cliffs, N. J., Prentice-Hall, Inc., 1960, pp. 24, 140.
34. Rabinovitch, R. D.: Reading and learning disabilities. *In* Arieti, S., ed.: *American Handbook of Psychiatry.* New York, Basic Books, Inc., 1959, vol. 1, pp. 857–869.
35. Rogers, C. R.: *Clinical Treatment of the Problem Child.* Cambridge, Mass., Houghton Mifflin Co., 1939, p. 235.
36. Sarason, S. B., Davidson, K., Lighthall, F., and Waite, R.: Classroom observations of high and low anxious children. *Child Developm.,* 1958, *29,* 287–295.
37. Sontag, L. W., and Kagan, J.: The emergence of intellectual achievement motives. *Amer. J. Orthopsychiat.,* 1963, *33,* 532–535.
38. Spock, B.: *Baby and Child Care.* New York, Pocket Books, Inc., 1957, pp. 406–410.
39. Strauss, A. A., and Lehtinen, L. E.: *Psychopathology and Education of the Brain-Injured Child.* New York, Grune and Stratton, Inc., 1947.
40. Talbot, M.: Panic in school phobia. *Amer. J. Orthopsychiat.,* 1957, *27,* 286–295.
41. Teagarden, F. M.: *Child Psychology for Professional Workers.* New York, Prentice-Hall, Inc., 1940, pp. 448–449, 453–456.
42. The initial teaching alphabet. *Time, 83* (4), 52.
43. Thom, D. A.: *Everyday Problems of the Everyday Child.* New York, Appleton-Century, 1934, pp. 16–17.
44. Waldfogel, S., and Gardner, G. E.: Intervention in crises as a method of primary prevention. *In* Caplan, G., ed.: *Prevention of Mental Disorders in Children.* New York, Basic Books, Inc., 1961, p. 308.

Chapter 32

Sex Problems

Despite evidence that sexual morality is waning, in individual cases the old taboos still hold, and censure for deviant or public sexual behavior is severe. The authority of social convention offers protection to the child in guiding him toward control of sexual actions so that he does not use them as symptomatic outlets for tension, as expedient devices for either social acceptability or personal retaliation, or as substitutes for affection of which he has been deprived.

Sex problems of the elementary school child include inspection, masturbation, heterosexual activity, and sexual molestation.

INSPECTION

Inspection of the genitalia of members of the opposite sex is a common practice of young children. By the age of six years, a boy who has been told about but has never seen the unusual construction of the female is consumed with curiosity.[5] Girls seldom initiate examination of boys, but they are not unwilling to participate in joint inspection. Children manage to look each other over when they play doctor and take rectal temperatures, and a boy and girl will visit the bathroom together and learn from doing so. A boy will undress a girl to inspect her,[7] and occasionally he entices away from her home a small girl whom he does not know, because he is uncertain how a girl playmate will react if he attempts to examine her.

The child's curiosity is natural, but by six or seven years children are self-conscious about nudity, and mutual inspection at this age is considered improper by both participants.[5] A child's need to obtain information in any way he can should be prevented. If he has reached elementary school age without ever seeing a nude child of the opposite sex, it should be arranged for him to observe infants of both sexes during bathing and changing. Sometimes parents, in attempting to educate the child to sex differences, overemphasize nudity, exposing the child to their own bodies daily and permitting him to wander around the home unclothed. This practice can be an overly constant and powerful stimulus which tends to preoccupy the child with anatomical sexual distinctions. Although excited prohibition of the child's ever viewing the unclothed parent of the opposite sex is equally detrimental, increasing modesty among members of the family is appropriate as the child grows older.

The child who has been found inspecting another must be told that it is not permissible to undress other children nor to show his genitals to them. He should apologize to the child involved, but punishment is not helpful and he should be invited to ask questions about sex differences.

MASTURBATION

Masturbation is a less frequent problem in the elementary school child than in either the pre-school child or adolescent.[12] Accurate figures of incidence in the six-to-12-year age group are difficult to obtain because most surveys consist of adults' imperfect recollection of earlier masturbation, and the data from child guidance clinics are based on incomplete inquiry and selected populations.[4, 7] From the information available, a reasonable estimate is that by the end of the elementary school years, half of all children have engaged in masturbation, the majority of them as pre-schoolers.

Kanner[7] differentiated three methods of masturbation: automasturbation, mutual masturbation, and psychic masturbation. In automasturbation, the child stimulates his genitals manually or digitally, or he rubs against objects. Mutual masturbation occurs among young boys when one member of a group demonstrates the act and leads the others to stimulate each other. A group attains cohesiveness by regularly meeting for masturbatory indulgence, and gangs originating on this basis sometimes expand their activities to include stealing and vandalism. Psychic masturbation is attainment of orgasm through fantasy or visual excitation and is rare in children of this age. It is possible only after manually-induced orgasm or the witnessing of others' sexual activity.

In most children masturbation is of no greater significance than nail-biting.[7, 12] It represents restlessness caused by tension, and the child often is unaware of his action until someone calls his attention to it. Sometimes masturbation first begins because tight clothing, itching or chapped skin, pinworms, or phimosis irritate the genital area.[7] The child scratches or touches the affected area and in so doing may discover new sensations which he then elicits deliberately because they are pleasurable.

Masturbation which is continued for solitary pleasure or used as a social ticket is a more serious matter than casual and incidental genital handling. It preoccupies and isolates the child and acclimates him to sexual response in an inappropriate setting.

Severely scolding and frightening the masturbating child remains the prevailing treatment used by parents. Many of them still believe that the child weakens himself intellectually, physically, and morally by masturbation and that he can drive himself to insanity.[7, 13] They warn the child that people can tell by looking at him that he is evil and self-destructive, but burdening him with deep fear and guilt creates a more critical and enduring problem than the masturbation itself.[6, 12]

A child's masturbation should not be ignored, however, as it occasionally is by parents too shocked or helpless to express their opinions firmly.* The child will be subjected to criticism and ostracism by his teachers and schoolmates if he continues. He needs to be told that handling his genitals is discourteous and impermissible, and he should be stopped whenever he does so. If he is unaware of masturbation, he can be taught to inhibit it by associating it with a signal, such as a nonsense word known only to child and parent, to be spoken when the child is observed masturbating. If tight clothing or skin irritation cause genital discomfort, these conditions can be remedied.

Gang masturbation seldom is discovered by parents and usually breaks up only when boys drift off individually into other associations. If it is discovered, however, parents should refrain from tormenting the child with name-calling or severe punishment. They should try to understand the strong group pressure which induced the child's compliance. They need to reëmphasize their own and society's disapproval of this behavior and to assist the child in finding other companions and better supervised activities.

HETEROSEXUAL ACTIVITY

Heterosexual practices are unusual in elementary school children.

---

* An 11-year-old boy of borderline intelligence regularly ordered his mother out of the bedroom where he lay masturbating. "Go away! I'm having fun!" he announced. She obeyed him.

They range from tentative exploration between the sexes to complete intercourse, which may occur in groups.

A child may engage in heterosexual experimentation because his attention has been focused on sex.[14] A mother who fondles, bathes, and dresses a boy of elementary school age shows her excessive interest in his body,[3] and children stimulated this way have been known to explore their mothers' breasts and genitalia, sometimes while the mother sleeps but occasionally with her delighted awareness.

Witnessing the sexual behavior of adults instigates imitation in children,[2] and many children sleep in the same room, or even the same bed, with their parents. Others note the frequency with which male visitors of their divorced mothers stay overnight, and they soon discover why.

A few children are introduced to sexual intercourse by an older child or adult, and they seek out partners for private sex play. A child familiarized with sexual actions in these ways may consider them a substitute for the love and attention he fails to receive from his parents, although involvement with the sex object is uncommon in the elementary school child.*

Group heterosexual activities develop when children are unsupervised. There are sexual exchanges between all members of the group, and they meet regularly for this purpose.

The sexually delinquent child needs close supervision, and cessation of sexual stimulation at home is mandatory. Parents who are concerned about the sexual actions of their children are able to revise their own habits, but many are indifferent to the child's welfare and preoccupied sexually themselves. If there can be no change at home, the child will require a foster home to provide the supervision he needs and to afford him opportunities to obtain satisfactions in other ways.

MOLESTATION

A number of children witness adult sexual aberrations and at times are the victims of them. Landis[9] reported that one third of the college students he questioned had had one or more experiences with sexual deviates. Eighty per cent of the boys' experiences were with homosexuals; over 50 per cent of the girls' experiences were with exhibitionists, and 25 per cent involved sexual fondling by adults. The ages of these students when the events occurred are unknown, but no serious traumatic effect was observed.

Bender and Grugett[2] reported an investigation of the adult adjust-

---

* See Case 26, Laura K., p. 516.

ment of ten girls and four boys who between the ages of five and 12 years had been involved over a prolonged period of time in sex activity with adults, ranging from sexual fondling to intercourse. At the time the molestation was discovered, none of the children showed great guilt or anxiety, and as adults they established normal homes and made a satisfactory adjustment.

The molested children did not consider the behavior sexual in the usual sense. No significant emotional relation was expressed by the acts, and because they were initiated by adults, the acts never became the responsibility of the child. Innately and through instruction, a child trusts adult decisions and accedes to adult direction even when he does not understand it, and these children felt little guilt about their behavior because it had been obedient.

A child's participation in sexual acts represents to him an imitation of adulthood,[8] and he feels some sense of privilege to be chosen to engage in behavior normally reserved for adults. The molested child has been described as often conversing and behaving in coy, seductive ways, but to him romantic expression is only imitative dramatization and he acts as adults have taught him to act.

Some children spontaneously report sexual molestation,[11] but there are many instances when a child has delayed telling his parents for a year or more after an incident has occurred. He fears punishment and publicity for both himself and the molester, who sometimes is an adult known and trusted by his parents. Once reported, the occurrence should be discussed with the child, who should be absolved of blame and given instructions for eluding a similar future situation. The child will be confused by his discovery that adults are not always trustworthy and honorable with children, and he needs an explanation which enables him to understand that adults differ in their ability to behave in accordance with accepted standards. If the adult molester is a relative of the child's family, the parents must insist on his obtaining psychiatric aid and must supervise children carefully so that they are never alone with him.

REFERENCES

1. Bakwin, H.: Disturbed sexual behavior in children and adolescents. *J. Pediat.*, 1955, *46*, 729–730.
2. Bender, L., and Grugett, A. E., Jr.: A follow-up report on children who had atypical sexual experience. *Amer. J. Orthopsychiat.*, 1952, *22*, 825–837.
3. Bettelheim, B.: *Love Is Not Enough.* Glencoe, Ill., The Free Press, 1950, pp. 316–317.
4. Dennis, W.: The adolescent. *In* Carmichael, L., ed.: *Manual of Child Psychology.* New York, John Wiley and Sons, 1946, pp. 646–647.
5. Gesell, A., and Ilg, F.: *The Child From Five to Ten.* New York, Harper and Bros., 1946, p. 116.

6. Healy, W.: *The Individual Delinquent*. Boston, Little, Brown and Co., 1915, p. 407.
7. Kanner, L.: *Child Psychiatry*, Ed. 3. Springfield, Ill., Charles C Thomas, 1957, pp. 580–583, 586–587.
8. Lafon, M. R., Trivas, J., and Pouget, R.: Aspects psychologiques des attentats sexuels sur les enfants et les adolescents (Psychological aspects of sexual crime among children and adolescents). *Ann. Méd.-Psychol.*, 1958, *2*, 865–896.
9. Landis, J. T.: Experiences of 500 children with adult sexual deviation. *Psychiat. Quart. Suppl.*, 1956, *30*, 91–109.
10. Litin, E. M., Giffin, M. E., and Johnson, A. M.: Parental influences in unusual sexual behavior in children. *Psychoanal. Quart.*, 1956, *25*, 37–55.
11. Schlif, E.: Beiträge zur Kinderpsychologie. *1:* Zur Frage, ob Kinder an ihnen begangene Sittlichkeitsverbrechen verheimlichen oder spontan melden (Contributions to child psychology. 1: To the question, whether children conceal or spontaneously report sexual crimes against them). *Psychiat. Neurol. Med. Psychol. (Leipzig)*, 1952, *4*, 336–339.
12. Spock, B.: *Baby and Child Care*. New York, Pocket Books, Inc., 1957, pp. 370–371, 520.
13. Teagarden, F. M.: *Child Psychology for Professional Workers*. New York, Prentice-Hall, Inc., 1940, p. 367.
14. Weiss, J., Rogers, E., Darwin, M. R., and Dutton, C. E.: A study of girl sex victims. *Psychiat. Quart.*, 1955, *29*, 1–27.

Chapter 33

Withdrawal Reactions

Withdrawal reactions range from mild shyness in specific situations to deliberate and continual rejection of contact with others. They are expressions of a child's feelings of helplessness and his refusal to involve himself in situations which could lead to disparagement or which demand effort. Although withdrawal reactions are protective, they are also self-punitive because they sustain immaturity in the child and provide no resolution of his difficulties. Single events may precipitate withdrawal, or generalized avoidant reactions may be adopted by the child at an early age as his typical response to unpleasantrics.

Excessive crying and seclusiveness express the child's desire to retreat and to avoid responding. Anxiety and fear reactions of the child produce his temporary or persistent immobilization and prevent him from making adaptive responses not only to the fear-producing stimulus but sometimes to all stimuli. Childhood psychosis is a catastrophic withdrawal reaction in which the child, incapable of adequate response, insulates himself from the encroachment of stimulation by insensitivity to sight, sound, motion, or touch.

EXCESSIVE CRYING

Crying remains common in the younger elementary child, but he cries for cause more than he did as a pre-schooler. He cries when he is hurt, he cries in frustration and anger, and he cries in penitence. As the child

275

grows older, he cries less, scorning tears as babyish and not permitting behavior in himself which he rebukes in younger children. He is able to refrain from crying in public sooner than he can from crying at home. Excessive crying as a reaction to distress deepens the child's feelings of helplessness and fixates his resistance to more mature responding.

The younger child who cries frequently or the older one who cries at school or in the presence of playmates may be tired from a lack of sleep, a crowded schedule, or the struggle for unattainable standards of excellence. Exhaustion lowers his tolerance for disturbing situations and his ability to manage them. Another child may cry in self-pity over every disappointment or requirement. If he has been placated and consoled by devoted parents and sheltered from hardship and responsibility, he joins them in believing that he should never suffer denial or unhappiness.

The fatigued child needs a revision in the daily demands made of him. The immature, immobile child needs assistance in acquiring a degree of self-control,[49] and he will cease his crying more quickly if no attention is paid to his tears. To complaints of mistreatment by peers or teachers, parents can respond with moderate sympathy and an explanation of the unhappy truth that such difficulties are the lot of all. Training the tearful child to greater responsibility and proficiency in a variety of commonly required skills bolsters his confidence and broadens his adaptability.

SECLUSIVENESS

The child who isolates himself physically from others is determined to avoid situations which frighten or displease him. The seclusive child not only remains alone but also resents any interruption of his daydreaming or his play, and he avoids physical activity. He has few interests, and these become increasingly regressive. He flies into a rage or collapses in sobs when he is criticized or when he interprets a chance comment as critical.[32] Instead of learning more about people and the world as he grows older, he retreats into a private life, uninterested in what happens around him.*

Sometimes a child isolates himself because he never has privacy and quiet or because he is overtired from activity and stimulation. The overdirected or coerced child seeks self-direction and tranquillity in seclusion.† Every child envies others' superior accomplishments and resents the scornful comments of more able peers. When he is overconcerned about real or imagined inferiorities, the child seeks to avoid

---

* See Case 7, Irene B., p. 500.
† See Case 27, Raymond K., p. 517.

comparisons by refusing to do his schoolwork or to participate in games with peers. If secluding himself becomes his usual response to challenge, however, he habituates himself to a solitary state of eminence and self-direction, and increasingly he becomes disinclined to exert the effort needed to mingle and compete with others. Withdrawal originating from fear of failure can lead to self-righteousness and feelings of superiority, as the child convinces himself that his preoccupations are of more value than the work or play of his peers.

Parents should interfere with the isolation of the seclusive child by joining him to talk and play and by instituting regular family excursions and games. They need to review their standards for neatness, correctness, and conformity, and to simplify the life of the child if it has become too busy. More association with peers should be arranged, and the child should be assisted in increasing his knowledge and skills in many areas.

Teachers can help the withdrawn child by developing his self-confidence through success with schoolwork, arranging more contacts with his classmates, seeing to it that he feels at home and useful in the classroom, and eliminating class tension by refraining from harshness and anger.[31]

ANXIETY AND FEAR

Anxiety

Anxious children are labelled "nervous" by parents and teachers. They sleep restlessly, and when awake they are overexcitable, tense, and anticipative of personal tragedy.* In school they cannot sit still, and they chew on pencils and clothing, repeatedly leave their seats, and interrupt others' work.

Some children, more often girls than boys, have acute anxiety attacks, which last from a few minutes to half an hour. During an attack, the child perspires heavily, his pulse rate increases, he feels smothered, and he is afraid that he is dying. He may complain about pain near his heart, stomach aches, or dizziness. Attacks may occur several times a week or even several times during the day. They usually take place in the evening or after the child has gone to bed, and they are precipitated by a frightening event, such as a death in the family, hospitalization of the child, or extreme fear of school failure or of strangers.[32]

Persistent anxiety in the elementary school child is an unreduced emotional state of fear caused by the child's inability to find security or consistent acceptance.[9] If his parents behave unpredictably toward him, alternating extreme affection with unwarranted punishment, he tensely

---

* See Case 17, Paul G., p. 508.

awaits impetuous emotional scenes, not knowing what action or comment will trigger them. If they tease and mock him, deceive and embarrass him, or treat him with tenderness when he has earned a reprimand, he recognizes their dishonesty and unreliability and feels panicky and alone.* If his parents disagree over how to manage him, he feels guilty and uncertain of his behavior. If they quarrel violently over any issue he fears losing one or both of them, and unable to choose between them, he is ashamed and worried.

A child imitates anxious behavior. A father who worries audibly about his ability to pay the family bills will have a son who is concerned about many minor problems. A mother who cautions and warns her child constantly creates visions of disaster which keep him miserably tense. Unhappy parents or teachers who plunge from one task to another or who talk loudly or constantly are models on which the child patterns his own behavior.

A child suffering from anxiety attacks responds well to a physician's statement that there is nothing physically wrong with him.[32] If the precipitating fear can be identified, reassurance and explanation also help the child overcome his fright.

The child who is anxious because his parents are erratic, deceptive, or worrisome will not change until they do. The overstimulated or pressured child should have his daily living simplified and balanced.[5]

Children in the upper elementary grades find life less vexing when they have some understanding of how and why people behave as they do.[36] Such knowledge helps a child accept his teacher's pressure as resulting from her own unresolved conflicts, and an explanation of the bases for his parents' behavior relieves generalized anxiety. When he becomes able to manage reasonably well by himself and does not depend wholly on adults for security and consistency, he is less anxious.

Fear

Specific fears do not necessarily produce generalized anxiety, but they may distress the child so greatly that he is temporarily immobilized. A fear which originally was justified and reasonable may endure for days or weeks, preoccupying the child and causing agitation, sleeplessness, and loss of appetite. Sometimes a fearful child even becomes inattentive to elimination and regresses to a state of near helplessness.[32]

New fears are created for the child when he begins school. He cannot escape some unpleasantries there, and he is measured continually against others and plagued by fears of failure and public humiliation if he always knows less than his classmates or is subjected to frequent scoldings or punishment by his teacher.

---

* See Case 28, Calvin M., p. 518.

Fear of death is common in the younger elementary child, who increasingly is exposed to it, both in real life and in stories. Fear of the dark is rearoused when the child has been frightened by a television program or a barking dog and remembers these experiences when he is alone in bed. Thunder and lightning frighten most children who are wakened by them.[32] Older boys who witness or participate in fights are afraid of being physically hurt.

Eight-year-olds wrote these summaries of fear-producing events.

THE WRECK

When I was five years old I had a wreck. Heres the story; One day I was crossing the street. Then a boy came real fast on his bike. He hit me and I rolled to the gutter. I cut my hand on a pop bottle. It was cut real bad. I had to go to the hospital. I was afraid, but not when my mom was there. That day I had to have an operation to get the glass out. I was afraid. After the operation I felt sick. I got to go home after a few hours. I felt a lot better. Now I am afraid of other people who ride bikes near me.

I'M AFRAID OF WATER

I'm afraid of water because water gets in my nose. And because I got dunked under the water. So now I'm afraid of water. And I never tried to swim. So thats why I'm afraid of water.

THE T.V. SHOW

One night before I went to bed I watched a TV show about space monsters. When I was asleep I had a dream. I was dreaming that I was the little girl that was being chased. They caught me. Then they killed me. I woke up and found it was just a dream. But still I am afraid to go to bed because I am afraid I will have another dream.

MICKEY

My neighbors got a new dog that was very big and they named him Mickey. He was not going to play because he did not know us. Their Aunt was the one who knew Mickey and he did not want to leave her. Now I was coming from a party and Linda ran up to me and said we have our new dog and he is very big. But Linda dragged me down to her house and there sat Mickey. I got at the back of Linda and I said how come he is SO big and Linda said that is the way his bones grow. But I was so in fright I could not say a word. Then I went up to Mickey and patted him and said you are a nice dog Mickey.

THE BOAT

One summer day we went on a boat ride with our friend. Jim said that Merrydale would be the best place to go boating. When we got there I said I think this will be fun. But when I got into the boat I was afraid the boat might tip over. Mother said not to be afraid. I asked how to help it. Mother said just to forget that were even on a boat. Just look at the lovely things. So I did and I forgot all about it.

THE DARK

I'm afraid of the dark because one night when I was in bed my sister snuck down the stairs and came in the back door and scared me half to death. Another time when I was in bed my brother was in the furnace room. I got up to get a glass of water. Then my brother jumped out of the furnace room and scared me. Now whenever I go to bed I'm afraid all night.

Children of this age also fear dangers they have never experienced. A surge of fearfulness appeared in children attending a school which held several air raid drills during a two-week period. The children began to ask many questions about the imminence of raids and the evil intent of the enemy, even though there was no war; and their worry was expressed in their dreams and spread to include fear of the dark and of separation from their parents. Witches, ghosts, kidnappers, and burglars are all feared by the elementary school child, even though he has had no contact with any of these.

General fearfulness is more prevalent in the anxious child than in one who ordinarily remains reasonably calm, and measures which reduce anxiety are needed to assist him in reacting less acutely to frightening events.[32]

A specific fear which tends to persist or reappear can be rendered less disturbing to the child if parents acknowledge that it is natural, rather than ridicule it. When the child has been frightened, everything that happened should be discussed with him. He may seek even a second or third review of the event. After this much discussion, however, he should be diverted from talking about it, because repeatedly recalling it reënforces the associated emotions. Fear is extinguished more quickly if the child promptly is placed again in the setting of the fear-producing experience. After a car accident, he should be taken on a series of short, uneventful journeys in the car; or after swallowing too much water while swimming, he should reënter the water soon and often, though with adequate instruction for self-protection.

A child afraid in the dark can have his door ajar, a flashlight avail- able, or a string attached to the light pull and tied to his bed so that he can examine his room whenever he is worried. If storms frighten him, he should remain in his own bed, but he can count the seconds between lightning and thunder and estimate their distance from him, and he can learn what causes storms. Knowledge strengthens his courage and provides substitute responses for fearfulness.

Skill in managing a feared situation banishes fright. The child afraid of water can begin swimming lessons, and one afraid of dogs can train a puppy to obedience. The child worried over school failure needs extra practice with his lessons; or if his learning ability is limited, he should enter a special class. If his teacher is cross and frightens him, she can be invited home for dinner, and the special acquaintance will reduce his dread of her.

Fears of ghosts and burglars can be discussed and the facts can be presented to the child, but only maturity rids him of these worries. Parents can avoid glooming about the possibility of war, the national debt, the high cost of living, the death rate from cancer, the illnesses of relatives or themselves, the crash of an airplane, and the misdeeds of juvenile delinquents. Their complaints and hopeless attitude convince the child that trouble exists and harm is inevitable.

CHILDHOOD PSYCHOSIS

Childhood psychosis is a controversial subject, with some investigators denying its existence and others categorizing it as equivalent to adult schizophrenia.[25] Some have reported manic-depressive psychosis in children; others maintain that severe affective psychosis does not occur in either elementary age children or adolescents. Most agree that childhood psychosis is a manifestation of pervasive, gross deficit in ego functioning and in adaptability.[19, 27]

A psychotic child is identified by symptoms of seclusiveness and fantasy, inappropriate affect, abnormal reactions to common stimuli, and extreme difficulty in communication.* These symptoms approximate some of those typical of the adult schizophrenic. However, the psychotic child seldom evidences hallucinations or delusions, and his problems with reality seem to develop from illusions and misinterpretations of the stimuli which attract him, rather than from the creation of an individualized world of his own.[28]

Bender and Helme[7] observed that psychosis affects all major areas of function in the child, as contrasted to the concentration of symptoms in single areas characteristic of neurotic children and of those with primary behavior disorders. The psychotic child is totally incapable of competent reaction most of the time.

He is asocial and avoids human relationships.[46] Norman[37] observed 25 psychotic children and stated that although some showed nearly com-

---

* See Case 26, Laura K., p. 516.

plete avoidance of humans, others sought at least physical contact with
them. These children did not communicate with others by speech, vision,
or audition, however, and they displayed a marked lack of affect.

The child uses fantasy in an unsuccessful effort to cope with conflict,[22] and his fantasy productions are extreme, irrational, and indicate
a degeneration of awareness. They reflect anxiety, rather than a normal
child's wishful thinking.[42] The psychotic child's capacity to tolerate conflict has been observed to fluctuate greatly within a single hour. He is
fearful, and he shows a high vulnerability to both external and internal
stimulation.[22] He is startled by or suspicious of ordinary objects, sounds,
and comments. He considers it impossible for him to complete any task,
and on projective tests he expresses his fear of annihilation.[23]

Difficulties in the child's understanding and communication are
severe and constitute a major barrier to aiding him.[22] Universal speech
difficulties have been reported in psychotic children,[46] and mutism was
the end result in one group of unimproved psychotic children.[17] The
autistic pre-school child's ability to communicate is a major prognostic
indicator of his final adjustment.[33]

In a follow-up study of school children seen at a clinic for emotional disturbance, Frazee[24] compared the characteristics of those who
later became schizophrenic with those who did not. The former had
displayed more symptoms of temper, shyness, disinterest, seclusiveness,
daydreaming, poor social relations, and vacillation between extremes of
behavior. They also were handicapped by disturbed sleep, malnourish-
ment, and frequent illness.

The etiology of childhood psychosis is nonspecific,[27] and its development is attributed to the interaction of debilitating constitutional, environmental, and organic factors.[34]

There is strong evidence that organic and physiological deficits
occur in the psychotic child and that these defects cause distortion of
both perception and response in a variable and unpredictable fashion.[29]
Bender[4] considered physiological crisis, at birth or at the time of severe
illness or accident, to be the precipitating cause of psychosis, but she
believed the course of the illness is dependent on maturational lag at
the embryonic level in all areas in which biological and psychological behavior are integrated. She considered the child's emotional problems to
be related to his experiencing disturbance in homeostatic control of body
functions, respiratory patterns, speech and language development, and
perceptions of all kinds, including gravity and space. These physical
distortions provoke primitive, inadequate responses in the child which
are disturbing, unsatisfying, and ineffectual.[6]

Confirmation of disturbance in orientation was offered by Colbert
et al.[16] using rotational tests to compare 43 psychotic children with 18
children who showed behavior problems and with 32 normal children.

The latter two groups gave responses similar to those of normal adults; but most of the psychotic children displayed markedly depressed or absent vestibular responses, with the degree of hypoactivity greatest for the youngest children.

Broader physiological defects were noted by Berkowitz,[8] who compared 43 psychotic children in motor activity, visual perception, memory function, and laterality. Significant differences were found between the two groups, and the extent of deficiency in the psychophysiological performance of the psychotic children was related to the severity of the disorder.

Organic deficit has been identified by many investigators.[1, 3] Pasamanick and Knobloch,[39] studying early responses of infants who later developed psychosis, concluded that psychotic and autistic children were exposed to significantly more precursors of brain injury than were normal children, and they found early neurological signs, such as difficulty with sucking, in the disturbed children. Abnormal birth delivery was reported in 21 of 25 psychotic children studied by Cameron.[13] Neural defects which result in inadequate reception of touch, pain, temperature, and vibration sensations delay the child's formation of an accurate body image.[21] Norman[38] reported that the psychotic child attends more closely to the perceptual properties of objects than to their use. Because the psychotic child is unable to grasp the essentials of size, shape, and the relationship of parts instantaneously and surely, he cannot acquire stable and accurate concepts of objects and their functions.

The proponents of physiological and organic deficit as the prime cause for development of psychotic behavior agree that environmental factors and family climate interact mutually with physiological disturbance in the child and can precipitate the appearance of psychosis or prolong its effects.[2, 6, 29]

Cameron[13] reported that the mothers of psychotic children he studied were rigid, restrictive, punitive, and impersonal and that premature and overstimulating educational drive was evident in their training of the child. In this group of children, behavior anomalies had been reported as early as eight months, and in half of the cases a traumatic incident was related to the final illness, which first appeared between the ages of two and four years. Other investigators have described mothers of psychotic children as being closely identified with and overprotective of them,[46] overpossessive, anxious, and domineering.[15] In other studies, parents have been found to be obsessive,[17] rejecting, and cruel. Some were psychotic, others were burdened with conflict, and many were separated or divorced.[24]

The psychotic child also has been considered the victim of isolation and poverty of stimulation at home.[40] Donnelly[20] reported that the psychotic child is less accepted as an individual and as a member of the family than his siblings are and that his parents show little understanding of his capacities and needs, direct more emotional and impulsive behavior toward him, and remain aloof in their relationship with him. This emotionally-oriented, driving, erratic, yet distant parental attitude toward the child may not have precipitated the psychosis, but instead it might have evolved from the parents' early failure to establish a normal relationship with the child. Because of his perceptual distortions and communicative disabilities, the child responds with resistance and rejection to parental attempts at affection and contact and continues these inappropriate and unpredictable reactions. The parents, in their failure to reach and teach the child and their conviction that they are unnecessary to him, feel both guilt and an increased determination to succeed, but their behavior with the child is tinged with overtones of resentment because of his unresponsiveness.

Treatment of the psychotic child has often meant hospitalization and long-term therapy, directed most productively toward training in academic achievement, normal affective response, and acquisition of a stable body image. Outpatient treatment in child guidance clinics, which can combine concomitant aid for parents and utilize various community resources, is often more effective within a shorter period of time. Bender[4] reported on the spontaneous improvement in a psychotic child who was being treated, not for emotional disturbance, but for reading disability. Early and thorough diagnostic evaluation of the child is needed to identify all contributing factors and to provide individualized treatment for every physiological, psychological, and environmental deficit.[45]

Prognosis for the psychotic child varies according to the severity and character of deficiencies and the extent of retraining which is possible. Kanner and Eisenberg[33] noted that the severity of maladjustment in 42 adolescents who were autistic as younger children was directly related to the severity of language dysfunction during their pre-school years, but in general the treatment they had received had been ineffectual. Burns[12] found that children with withdrawal tendencies and feelings of unreality during their elementary school years adjusted eventually with greater success than did children considered hypersensitive and feminine during this period. In a follow-up study of 129 children earlier diagnosed as suffering from infantile psychosis, Brown[10] reported that 59 per cent of the children, by the age of nine years or older, were competing adequately with their peers in academic achievement.

REFERENCES

1. Anderson, C.: Organic factors predisposing to schizophrenia. *Nerv. Child*, 1952, *10*, 36–42.
2. Baer, P. E.: Problems in the differential diagnosis of brain damage and childhood schizophrenia. *Amer. J. Orthopsychiat.*, 1961, *31*, 728–737.

3. Bakwin, H.: Early development of children with schizophrenia. *J. Pediat.*, 1953, *43*, 217–219.

4. Bender, L.: Childhood schizophrenia. *Psychiat. Quart.*, 1953, *27*, 663–681.

5. Bender, L.: Current techniques in the management of the anxious child. *Amer. J. Psychother.*, 1961, *15*, 341–347.

6. Bender, L.: Twenty years of clinical research on schizophrenic children, with special reference to those under six years of age. *In* Caplan, G., ed.: *Emotional Problems of Early Childhood.* New York, Basic Books, Inc., 1955, pp. 503–515.

7. Bender, L., and Helme, W. H.: A quantitative test of theory and diagnostic indicators of childhood schizophrenia. *AMA Arch. Neurol. Psychiat.*, 1953, *70*, 413–427.

8. Berkowitz, P. H.: Some psychophysical aspects of mental illness in children. *Genet. Psychol. Monogr.*, 1961, *63*, 103–148.

9. Brooks, F. D.: *Child Psychology.* Boston, Houghton Mifflin Co., 1937, pp. 466–467.

10. Brown, J. L.: Follow-up of children with atypical development (infantile psychosis). *Amer. J. Orthopsychiat.*, 1963, *33*, 855–861.

11. Buhler, C.: The diagnostic problem in childhood schizophrenia. *Nerv. Child*, 1952, *10*, 60–62.

12. Burns, C.: Pre-schizophrenic symptoms in pre-adolescents' withdrawal and sensitivity. *Nerv. Child*, 1952, *10*, 120–128.

13. Cameron, K.: A group of twenty-five psychotic children. *Z. Kinderpsychiat.*, 1958, *25*, 117–122.

14. Chess, S., and Rubin, E.: Treatment of schizophrenic children in a child guidance clinic. *Nerv. Child*, 1952, *10*, 167–178.

15. Clardy, E. R.: A study of the development and course of schizophrenia in children. *Psychiat. Quart.*, 1951, *25*, 81–90.

16. Colbert, E. G., Koegler, R. R., and Markham, C. H.: Vestibular dysfunction in childhood schizophrenia. *AMA Arch. Gen. Psychiat.*, 1959, *1*, 600–617.

17. Creak, M.: Psychoses in childhood. *J. Ment. Sci.*, 1951, *97*, 545–554.

18. Creak, M., and Ini, S.: Families of psychotic children. *J. Child Psychol. Psychiat.*, 1960, *1*, 156–175.

19. Despert, J. L.: Differential diagnosis between obsessive-compulsive neurosis and schizophrenia in children. *In* Hoch, P. H., and Zubin, J., eds.: *Psychopathology of Childhood.* New York, Grune and Stratton, Inc., 1955, pp. 240–253.

20. Donnelly, E. M.: The quantitative analysis of parent behavior toward psychotic children and their siblings. *Genet. Psychol. Monogr.*, 1960, *62*, 331–376.

21. Eickhoff, L. F. W.: The aetiology of schizophrenia in childhood. *J. Ment. Sci.*, 1952, *98*, 229–234.

22. Ekstein, R., and Wallerstein, J.: Observations on the psychology of borderline and psychotic children. *Psychoanal. Stud. Child*, 1954, *9*, 344–372.

23. Engel, M.: Psychological testing of borderline psychotic children. *Arch. Gen. Psychiat.*, 1963, *8*, 425–434.

24. Frazee, H. E.: Children who later became schizophrenic. *Smith Coll. Stud. Soc. Wk.*, 1953, *23*, 125–149.

25. Friedman, S. W.: Diagnostic criteria in childhood schizophrenia. A review of some major trends in the literature. *Bull. Menninger Clin.*, 1954, *18*, 41–51.

26. Gesell, A., and Ilg, F. L.: *The Child From Five to Ten.* New York, Harper and Bros., 1946, pp. 112–113.

27. Goldfarb, W., Braunstein, P., and Scholl, H.: An approach to the investigation of childhood schizophrenia: The speech of schizophrenic children and their mothers. *Amer. J. Orthopsychiat.*, 1959, *29*, 481–490.

28. Grage, H.: Zur Differntialdiagnose der endogenen Psychosen des Kindesalters (To the differential diagnosis of the endogenous psychoses in childhood). *Psychiat. Neurol. Med. Psychol. (Leipzig)*, 1953, *5*, 29–34.

29. Hendrickson, W. J.: Etiology in childhood schizophrenia. *Nerv. Child*, 1952, *10*, 9–18.

30. Jersild, A. T.: Emotional development. *In* Carmichael, L., ed.: *Manual of Child Psychology.* New York, John Wiley and Sons, 1946, pp. 762, 767–768.

31. Johnson, O. G.: The teacher and the withdrawn child. *Ment. Hyg. (N. Y.)*, 1956, *40*, 529–534.

32. Kanner, L.: *Child Psychiatry*, Ed. 3. Springfield, Ill., Charles C Thomas, 1957, pp. 608–623, 693–694, 731.

33. Kanner, L., and Eisenberg, L.: Notes on follow-up studies of autistic children. *In* Hoch, P. H., and Zubin, J.: *Psychopathology of Childhood*. New York, Grune and Stratton, Inc., 1955, pp. 227–239.

34. Kornfeld, M.: The development of schizophrenic symptoms in young children. *Nerv. Child*, 1952, *10*, 112–119.

35. Lebovici, S., and Diatkine, R.: Essai d'approache do la notion de prépsychose en psychiatrie infantile (Essay on the approach to the idea of prepsychosis in child psychiatry). *Bulletin de Psychologie*, 1963, *17*, 20–23.

36. Muuss, R.: The relationship between "causal" orientation, anxiety, and insecurity in elementary school children. *J. Educ. Psychol.*, 1960, *51*, 122–129.

37. Norman, E.: Affect and withdrawal in schizophrenic children. *Brit. J. Med. Psychol.*, 1955, *28*, 1–18.

38. Norman, E.: Reality relationships of schizophrenic children. *Brit. J. Med. Psychol.*, 1954, 27, 126–141.

39. Pasamanick, B., and Knobloch, H.: Early feeding and birth difficulties in childhood schizophrenia: An explanatory note. *J. Psychol.*, 1963, *56,* 73–77.

40. Prick, J. J. G., and Calon, P. J. A.: Problèmes autour de l'aphasie, de la surdité psychique et de la dyslexie; une contribution à la psychiatrie infantile (Problems about aphasia, psychic deafness and dyslexia; a contribution to child psychiatry). *Folia Psychiat. Neerl.*, 1951, *54*, 112–123.

41. Richards, J. E.: Techniques used in a school program for children emerging from early infantile autism. *Except. Children*, 1963, *29*, 348–357.

42. Saito, Y.: A psychopathological study of day-dreaming in early childhood schizophrenia. *Jap. J. Child Psychiat.*, 1960, *1*, 13–31.

43. Sarason, S. B., Davidson, K., Lighthall, F., and Waite, R.: Classroom observations of high and low anxious children. *Child Developm.*, 1958, *29*, 287–295.

44. Schmideberg, M.: Sincerity. *Amer. J. Psychother.*, 1958, *12*, 297–299.

45. Silver, A. A.: Management of children with schizophrenia. *Amer. J. Psychother.*, 1955, *9*, 196–215.

46. Slimp, E.: Life experiences of schizophrenic children. *Smith Coll. Stud. Soc. Wk.*, 1951, *21*, 103–122.

47. Spock, B.: *Baby and Child Care*. New York, Pocket Books, Inc., 1957, p. 363.

48. Strang, R.: *An Introduction to Child Study*. New York, The Macmillan Co., 1938, pp. 523, 524.

49. Teagarden, F. M.: *Child Psychology for Professional Workers*. New York, Prentice-Hall, Inc., 1940, pp. 322–330.

50. Thom, D. A.: *Everyday Problems of the Everyday Child*. New York, Appleton-Century, 1934, pp. 152–153.

51. Thompson, G. G.: *Child Psychology*. Cambridge, Mass., Houghton Mifflin Co., 1952, p. 289.

52. Whiles, W. H.: The nervous or "highly-strung" child. *Med. Press*, 1951, *113*, 362–365.

Chapter 34

Aggressive Reactions

With the discovery that the problems of the withdrawn child were being ignored, there arose a sequential opinion that the problems of the aggressive child were not as serious as had been thought. A theory developed that children should be permitted to rid themselves of aggressive feelings by aggressive actions, and in doing so, they gained in emotional health. This viewpoint disregards the need of the individual to exhibit increasing maturity in all of his behavior as he grows older. A child who continues from pre-school days to adulthood to take revenge on others, to lose self control, and to justify his own antisocial and self-centered actions is not emotionally healthy. He is instead a social isolate, who never attains self-respect or merits the respect of others.

In a study of the later behavior of 551 children seen 28 years earlier at a child guidance clinic, those classed as extraverts had engaged in proportionately more delinquencies and criminal actions, both as adolescents and adults, than children considered introverted.[17] Clinicians have learned that children permitted to "act out" aggressive feelings remain unsatisfied and more impulsive than those taught to keep their behavior within acceptable boundaries.[6] Children themselves condone aggressive actions in their peers only when they are justifiably provoked, and they strongly condemn indirect, secretive retaliation.[13]

Normal aggression stems from a child's need to feel important and to dominate others, and it also occurs as an inept effort to make contact with peers or parents.[16] The aggression of siblings toward each other is more usual than not, and it provides practice for the child in self-assertion

287

within a setting of greater tolerance for aggression than is available elsewhere. The child who belittles a younger brother does not ridicule a classmate unless everyone else does; and he is more impudent with his parents than he dares to be with school officials because encounters with teachers always end in punishment and humiliation, never in prestige and victory.

The child who always is aggressive, attacking all adults and peers with blind impartiality and little judgment, is motivated by factors other than a natural desire for recognition and dominance. His aggression originates in strong feelings of anger or jealousy, which produce direct reactions of temper tantrums and retaliation at the time of provoking incidents and also become pervasive, leading him to suspect and resent nonprovoking individuals.

Anger develops in a child who is coerced and criticized by his parents,[9] severely punished, or consistently denied both his wishes and his rights. When he reacts aggressively the parents isolate him from the family and threaten him with military or reform school. Acute antagonism between parent and child can develop to a peak as the child becomes continually angered by the arbitrary and rejecting treatment of the adults.*

Jealousy is inevitable between siblings who must share parents and possessions, but it need not develop into bitter hatred. A parent cannot avoid behaving differently toward each child because of differences in the child's sex, age, health, popularity, conformity, and success at endeavors valued by the adult. A child who is unsure of himself broods over differences between himself and his siblings[19] and believes that his parents are disappointed in him and could get along very well without him. Afraid and angry, he attacks the sibling who appears to be preferred and shows defiance and aggression toward everyone else.†

Mishandling of the child perpetuates aggressive behavior. Permitting a child's rage reactions to gain advantages for him fixates their continuance and assures the child's remaining self-centered all of his life. Parents sometimes are both fascinated and horrified by a child's persistent stealing or bullying. They convince themselves that he is motivated by hidden, uncontrollable forces which they are powerless to combat, and they make no effort to interfere with his behavior. Other parents gain vicarious satisfaction from the child's aggressiveness, admiring him for behaving as they themselves lack the courage to behave and encouraging him to continue by keeping misbehavior secret or by minimizing and defending it if it becomes public.[10, 11]

Bender[2] pointed out that the behavior of large numbers of hyperactive, aggressive children is caused by organic and constitutional defects.

---

* See Case 29, Catherine P., 518.
† See Case 30, Gregory L., p. 519.

Less inhibited and more active from birth than others, they soon are engaged in continual clashes with adults who can neither anticipate their actions nor succeed in efforts to teach and control them. The brain-damaged child does not achieve real understanding with his parents, and because he is anxious and lonely, he believes that everyone is against him and that he must protect himself.*

Mild aggression is evident when the child resists adults by negativism or disobedience. Stronger aggression appears as the child attempts to influence or direct adult behavior by lying, stealing, or running away. Extreme aggression involves revenge and harm to others and includes fighting and cruelty, destructiveness and vandalism, and fire-setting.

NEGATIVISM AND DISOBEDIENCE

Negativism

The finality of a child's refusal to comply with requests baffles adults. Calm but unreachable, he remains unmoved by the agitation his refusal excites. He may act this way at home but not at school, or *vice versa;* he may be more negativistic with one parent than the other; or he may oppose directions more at certain times of the day than at others.

Negativism usually occurs if adults interrupt the child when he is engaged in an enjoyable activity. His tractability varies with the strength of his desire to continue what he is doing and with his knowledge of the reactions of the adults involved to a refusal. Sometimes, once having taken a stand, pride will not permit him to reverse himself, and he may persist in refusing a simple request to hang up his coat, even after receiving a severe whipping for noncompliance.

Physical changes can be responsible for negativism. Preadolescent girls who seem unreasonably stubborn to their parents often are experiencing the glandular changes preceding menstrual onset which make them irritable and sensitive over a period of several months.[8]

Fatigue and accumulated pressures induce negativism. When a child has followed his teacher's instructions at school all day and has had little say about activities with his peers, his need to speak for himself and do as he chooses is paramount, and he is adamant in refusals at home. Insufficient sleep and excessive demands on his time and energy leave him irritable and uninterested in pleasing his elders with obedience.

Some children refuse parental requests because the requests occur too frequently and are both inconsiderate and unnecessary. A child rightly resents being asked to leave his play to fetch his mother her scissors, when she could get them more readily herself. Adult requests

---

* See Chapter 46, "Cerebral Dysfunction," pp. 452–458.

made rudely are resented and refused for similar reasons.

Children often are negativistic because they fear they will perform poorly. They refuse to play in a piano recital, fix a running toilet, or give a report at school because they anticipate failure.

Because the child conceals his anger or fear, showing no violent emotion and giving no reason for refusal, his opposition appears inexplicable to adults and more difficult to combat.[23] When negativism has become more habitual than logical, the child can be taught compliance with reasonable and courteous requests by permitting him the dignity of choice. An adult refused compliance by a child should state, in one sentence, why the request is necessary. This alone induces most children to yield, because the conflict has been placed in the realm of reason rather than of will. If it does not, then an alternative choice is given the child. He may choose not to set the table for dinner, but if so, he is also choosing to miss the meal. Compliance with requests deserves the courtesy of adult thanks, and appreciation eases the child's displeasure at being interrupted in his own pursuits or pressured against his own desires.

Disobedience

No child's curiosity and pleasure always are subordinated to parental instructions,[25] and parents should not regard occasional disobedience as evidence that the child is devoid of filial loyalty and is basically untrustworthy.

Children who disobey more often than not, however, do so defiantly and purposefully. Negativism is an open refusal and challenge to the adult. Evasive disobedience, in which the child promises to obey but does not or claims he did not hear the direction, is more subtle and avoids an open clash. The child who not only fails to comply but does exactly the opposite of what he is told is indulging in a grand gesture of contempt—asked to close the front door he has left ajar, he marches over to it and flings it wide open.[12]

Permissiveness is the most common reason for recurrent disobedience. The child has learned that he can disobey when he chooses without penalty. His mother retreats when he says "I won't!" She believes him when he claims he did not hear; and although she scolds when he defiantly throws open the door, she closes it herself, feeling vaguely guilty at having provoked him.

Inconsistency in enforcing rules induces disobedience. Although at times every parent forgets his own instructions or lacks sufficient energy to enforce them, if required conformity usually is a matter of conjecture, the child always attempts to evade directions.

A younger child characteristically repeats a forbidden act immediately after being punished for it, and this behavior bewilders and discourages his mother. His motive for doing so is less likely to be defiance than uncertainty about whether this prohibition is permanent or is merely a parental whim of the moment, and he seeks information by inducing parental reaction to the same behavior.

The child who lives under too many rules deliberately disobeys some of them. If he must be quiet, neat, and respectful at home and at school, he will slop through mud puddles, throw rocks at dogs, and delay his arrival at either destination as long as possible. In similar and sensible rebellion, he refuses to obey an order to approach the lady guest whom he knows will grab and squeeze him.

He will disobey most of the time if his mother defends him when his father attempts to punish him for misbehavior or if his father countermands his mother's orders or ridicules her.

When a child is irresponsible and actively disobedient most of the time, parents must unite to teach him obedience. Each must reënforce the authority of the other, and if there are extenuating circumstances, the child, not the parent, should plead his cause. Two or three necessary rules should be established which the parents enforce without exception, and the child should be informed of the penalty for disobedience. Penalties should not consist of severe deprivation or punishment, but they should be unpleasant enough so that the child prefers to avoid them. When he consistently obeys these few rules, one or two more can be added and the same absolute enforcement procedures used.

A parent accustomed to acceding to a child's opposition must learn never to give an order he cannot enforce. A mother busy getting dinner should not choose that time to tell her habitually disobedient child to clean up his room. Before making a request, the parent must ask himself if he has both the time and energy to insist on compliance, and if not, the request should be withheld. All requests should be made courteously, rather than belligerently, and obedience should be commended.

LYING

The lying of the elementary school child is more deliberate than that of the pre-school child. The older child knows reality from fiction, and he also knows that lying is disapproved. When he lies, he usually has a reason which makes sense to him, but lying can become habitual and can be used to deceive others solely for the satisfaction that deception brings.

Kanner[12] listed three reasons for a child's lying. Most distressing to parents, but most reasonable to the child, is the lie he tells to protect himself. Astounded adults cannot understand why a child continues to claim innocence when he has been caught in the act, and they resent his lying because they interpret it as an attempt to dupe them. The child, however, denies his guilt because he seeks to banish the entire matter from existence and to postpone or avoid the consequences of his actions.

A child lies in imitation of adults, who are noted for their maintaining the amenities with shading and reversal of the truth. Younger elementary children, in keeping secrets and protecting other children, tell many social lies of this kind, and girls do this more than boys.[23]

A child lies to gain attention and prestige, boasting that he was first on a test he barely passed or claiming that he has a color television set in his room. He also tells falsehoods about other children in order to get them into trouble. He has limited self-confidence, and he tries by lying to construct an image of himself as a person of importance and authority.

The child who lies habitually, casually, and glibly is not enticed into lying by the needs of the situation. He lies in order to delude and influence others, and his fanciful tales or flat misstatements enhance his feeling of superiority. He often is described as a "charmer," and he flatters adults as easily and scornfully as he convinces them of his sincerity in everything he tells them. Usually he is a child who has been successful at evading adult requirements all of his life, and he retains well-learned techniques of deceiving and influencing others.

The child who lies to protect himself should be helped to confess his misdeeds. When he does not, his lies either burden his conscience or teach him that he can escape punishment for misbehavior. Persistent questioning of the child should produce the truth, and he should be commended for admitting guilt. He must receive whatever punishment is customary for his offense, but this should be neither extreme nor inappropriate.

Social lies told by young children to protect each other can develop into automatic deception of both peers and adults. Such lies should be identified by parents and the child cautioned either to tell the truth or, if he prefers, to decline to say anything at all. The child who lies to increase his self-esteem needs real achievement to counteract his need for pretense. He will respond to daily praise from his parents, increased responsibilities and trust, and practice to improve his skill at studies or play. A child who lies constantly, making up stories and never keeping promises, needs close supervision and direction. His statements should be checked promptly for their accuracy, and he must be required to conform to established rules.

STEALING

The elementary school child who takes what does not belong to him knows that this is wrong, although his feelings of guilt may not be acute nor his efforts to conceal his crime determined. Most children indulge at least once in the casual appropriation of candy or a balloon from a store. Stealing which is more frequent or purposeful originates from three sources: The child is satisfying a need; he has received either tacit or direct approval of stealing; or he attacks his parents in this way, either trying to embarrass them or to force them to give him greater recognition and control.

Some children need the things they steal or want them so badly and hopelessly that they take them. Bicycles are stolen for this reason, as are pens or mittens. A child also needs friends, and he steals in order to get money or gifts to give other children, with his deed well advertised by the delighted beneficiaries.

The need for affection withheld by parents impels a child to acquire possessions as a substitute. If he believes that his parents never think of him or need him, he picks up trinkets and toys in the dime store, accumulating a large store of treasures which afford him some consolation.

Some children, with a moderate amount of attention and affection, want more. They are envious of the concern parents show over a sick baby or a brother with low grades, and they decide to do something which will produce attention for themselves. These children neither hide what they have stolen nor change their ways after scolding or punishment.

Older elementary children may be involved with gangs which require their members to steal, and they do so under threat of banishment from the group. Even if a child decides he would rather not remain a member when he discovers the rules, usually he conforms to avoid the others' taunts.

A child who is a member of a family with lax ethical standards imitates what he sees and hears. He listens when his father laughs uproariously as his older brother produces a watch he "found" in his pocket, and he remembers his mother's assertion that the smart person is the one who can put something over on someone else. He steals with a clear conscience and the certainty of family admiration.

Taking others' possessions is encouraged when property rights are not protected at home. If a child's clothes and toys are used at will by other members of the family, he also appropriates theirs. At school, he helps himself to other children's paper and pencils and brings home classroom supplies without feeling guilty, because he is accustomed to taking what he wants without permission.

Parents condone stealing when they permit the child to keep what he takes and fail to punish him. A mother, too embarrassed to go with the child to the store to return a stolen article or to admit to a neighbor that the child helped himself to money during a visit there, will tearfully extract a promise from the child that he will never steal again and will then permit him to keep what he took. He seldom waits long before repeating such a satisfactory action.

Some children steal in anger. They resent peers who ignore and scorn them, and they steal costly clothing, musical instruments, or books from them to cause trouble with their parents. A child jealous of a sibling or friend may steal a valued possession from him and destroy it. Sometimes a child steals to embarrass his parents, an effective technique when their moral standards are high and they are well regarded in the community.*

The child who is permitted to do whatever he likes with no more than a wistful reprimand steals deliberately and persistently in an effort to force his parents to control him. He tries to shock them into action because he is convinced that their indifference to his behavior reflects their disinterest in him.

The child's parents must teach him that stealing is never permissible, regardless of need or provocation, and the child always should be required to return a stolen article, to confess, and to apologize. Public admission of guilt seriously embarrasses him, and if he is certain that stealing results in this kind of reckoning, he refrains from it.

The child who steals from need should have it fulfilled in other ways. Even acquiring a bicycle is not an impossibility for an indigent child if he is willing to work to earn it. Friends, affection, attention, and membership in clubs all can be attained in ways not dependent on theft. Forced sharing and casual appropriation of others' possessions at home must cease if the child is to acquire a concept of property rights. When stealing is fostered by the example of other members of the family, the best appeal to the child is an explanation of the punishment demanded by the law and an attempt to educate him to an understanding of peoples' rights. Aggressive stealing signals more critical trouble, and the reasons for it should be identified so that rearing procedures can be evaluated and altered.

RUNNING AWAY

Few children grow up without contemplating running away from home, and many do so. A child runs away because he is angry at injustice and has convinced himself that his family enjoys making him miserable. He feels sorry for himself, but he also hopes that his leaving will impress his parents with his value to them and result in contrition on their part. Leventhal[14] compared 27 runaway boys and 15 runaway girls between the ages of five and 16 years with a control group, and he reported that those who had left home were children who exerted little influence on others and were themselves overly concerned about being dominated.

---

* See Case 31, Rex A., p. 520.

Some children disappear repeatedly, and their parents seldom know where they are or when they will return. The child allowed to wander off at the age of two or three years continues to do so. He lingers at school, talking to the custodian or to teachers; he strays far off his route on the way home, pausing to ask questions of adults and to play with children he sees. Often he stops in for a visit with adults he knows, and he is welcomed with cookies and flattering attention.*

Without telling his parents, a child may walk several miles to visit a friend or relative, or he may ride his bicycle even further. If he has the fare, he rides the bus to all areas of the city and may take an occasional trip out of town. He does not hesitate to ask directions or favors of adults, and he manages to get along in strange territory with surprising ease. Children from poorer homes, whose parents are away at work all day and whose supervision is left to older siblings, are adept in finding their way and locating food in places they have never been before. With nothing and no one at home to attract them, they seek adventure in new contacts and new places.[24]

If a child has not developed a pattern of absenting himself from home but suddenly begins to do so, he is indicating extreme fear. His fear may be based on such frightening episodes as violent and unpredictable treatment from an alcoholic or psychotic parent. Moreover, if a parent is or has been seriously ill and death is imminent or if there has been talk of divorce between the parents, the child avoids his home, afraid that his parent will be gone when he arrives there.†

Persistent wandering of long duration can be stopped only by close attention to the child and circumvention of his leaving. Neighbors and friends he customarily visits can be asked to send him home and notify his mother of his whereabouts. Home will seem more welcoming to him if he can count on his mother's always being there and being available for extra attention when school is over. It may be necessary for her to meet him at school and accompany him home until he can come home promptly without an escort. The child who wanders miles from home in a determined effort to avoid fear-producing experiences at home needs close supervision and an examination and adjustment of his problems.

FIGHTING AND CRUELTY

Fighting

Many boys, by carefully planning their routes to school and failing to show up in the vacant lot as promised, manage to get through their elementary school years without a single fight. Others, however, are

---

* See Case 18, Henry P., p. 509.
† See Case 32, Peter C., p. 520.

roughed up occasionally and some are involved in fights several times weekly. Girls also fight—kicking, pulling hair, and scratching other girls with whom they are angry. Many fights are not really desired by either antagonist, but once begun they are continued as required evidence of courage.[18]

Fights start when one child taunts or hits another, either good-naturedly or aggressively. If the teased child accepts the act as friendly and responds in kind, he establishes himself as a good sport and seldom is bothered. If he reacts belligerently or fearfully, believing that he is being singled out for abuse because he is disliked, the shoving and tentative hitting increase and develop into a serious fight.

The aggressive child instigates fights with others, usually preying on younger children. He interferes in their disputes and "straightens them out," shoves them aside as he walks by, or stuffs their books or caps into mailboxes. A child behaving this way has been subjected to erratic, emotion-ridden treatment at home and may have been brutally punished by his parents. He retaliates for abuse in safer settings.

Verbal fights are a trademark of some children. They insult their peers, laughing derisively at any mistake and disparaging every proudly related achievement. The child who attacks verbally is lonely and believes himself to be different from other children, either because he has had little opportunity to associate with them or because he is over-protected at home. He tends to feel out of place, inferior, and helpless, and he tries to bolster his self-esteem by depreciating others.

Some boys do not bully young children or insult their classmates, but they fight unfairly, resorting to pinching and kicking when supposedly they are wrestling or fighting for fun with friends. They are immature, overly frightened by fighting, and afraid of being hurt.

The child who fights excessively, either verbally or physically, needs assistance in understanding his peers and associating more with them. He should know that their taunting is testing, and he should practice returning what they offer without being offended. Praise and responsibility from adults increase his self-esteem, and added opportunities to spend time with a few friends who like him and with whom he can enjoy himself help him to relax with all of his peers.

If an aggressive child is being severely punished at home or treated unfairly, the parents must learn other methods of management and acquire a greater awareness of the child's dependence on them for affection, attention, and approval. To help him acquire a degree of self-control, a child who fights unfairly or bullies younger children should be required to apologize and make amends.

Cruelty

Pre-school children hurt and frighten animals unwittingly when they pick them up by one leg, pull their tails, or ride or chase them. These are not deliberate attempts to hurt and are not comparable to the abuse inflicted on animals by an elementary school child who knows what he is doing and intends to do it. Older children have been known to fling animals against walls, dunk them in wet cement, set them afire, or wring their necks. The child wants to injure or kill, and he does so with all the energy he can bring to bear.

The cruel child lives in a home steeped in violence. Adults argue, accuse, scream, and struggle with fists or weapons. The child is fought over with extreme emotion and is severely beaten or punished in unusual and cruel ways by one or both parents. Little attention is paid to what he does or where he goes. His cruelty results from his imitation of his parents' actions, and it becomes increasingly violent as his fright, loneliness, and anger overwhelm him.

Some studies of cruel children indicate that many of them are victims of organic disorder, which further hampers self-control and lessens the possibility of their learning to inhibit impulsive and revengeful behavior.

Kanner[12] stated that institutionalization seemed to be the only solution for children like this, and certainly the care, control, and regularity of living available in institutions are major ingredients missing from their lives. The attempt to alter home conditions should be made first, however, in recognition of the fact that any child responds to care and control from his parents more readily and permanently than he does to that offered by strangers.

DESTRUCTIVENESS AND VANDALISM

Destructiveness

The elementary school child does not seem much more concerned than the pre-school child about caring for his possessions. Both boys and girls come home from school with their jackets torn and the buttons ripped off. They pull threads out of their bedspreads, break down the backs of shoes, poke holes in the tablecloth with their forks, swing on towel racks and light fixtures, scratch their names with pins on the furniture, and run through the flower beds. Most of this destructiveness comes from a continuation of childish clumsiness, haste, exuberance, and idle experimentation. Not yet responsible for the provision of material possessions, children are unaware of the work needed to repair damage and of the cost of replacements.

Destruction can be deliberate, and an angry child vents his wrath on objects, smashing a doll's head or pulling off its legs. A braver child who smarts from punishment will destroy, secretly or openly, something which belongs to his parents. A child who destroys his own possessions is condemning and punishing himself. He acts as though he believes he does not deserve to own anything, but his self-abuse is also a desperate move to force pity and reacceptance from his parents.

A nine-year-old boy of average intelligence had always earned poor grades in school, because of both immaturity and erratic management at home. When his younger sister started school and soon began bringing home superior marks, he systematically cut holes in the expensive clothing his parents bought him.

Whether or not destruction is deliberate, the child should make a restorative attempt. Inadvertent breakage should be followed by an apology and cleaning up, and anything deliberately destroyed should be repaired or paid for by the child. A child's destructiveness should not elicit further anger from parents and isolation from the family because this confirms his fear of rejection, and his destructiveness will become more determined.

Vandalism

Vandalism in the elementary school child ordinarily occurs in groups, is unpremeditated, and is considered a great lark by the perpetrators. Seldom does the child anticipate either discovery or punishment, and he rarely has any real concept of the damage he does. Vandalism occurs during group exploration of unoccupied houses or of those under construction, although some children break into homes when the owners are away.

Two boys, aged eight and nine years, readily admitted their responsibility for vandalizing an unoccupied house and appeared to be completely unconcerned about what they had done. They had set four fires, rammed holes through walls with a two-by-four, ripped linoleum table tops, pulled light fixtures from the walls, broken windows, and torn off a screen door. They used kitchen drawers for firewood, damaged the furnace, broke off the shower pipe, and battered the hot water tank.

Sometimes group or paired vandalism is proposed by a child who has been angered by rejection or humiliation, and his target is chosen deliberately for revenge. The depth of guilt feeling in young vandals seems to be related to the degree to which their actions are directed against known persons. Greater pleasure is experienced in vandalizing property which is public or which belongs to someone the child does not know, because there is no personal involvement.[27]

All acts of vandalism should necessitate apology and restitution by the child. Revengeful vandalism indicates gross immaturity, and a review and revision of rearing practices is needed so that the child can attain greater self-respect and self-control.

FIRE-SETTING

Most young children have been cautioned for years about the danger of fire, and only extreme hostility and anxiety lead them to indulge in such a hazardous action. A child who sets a fire usually becomes frightened and immediately attempts to put it out.

Bender[2] studied a group of children, six to eight years old, who had set fires in and around their own homes. The fires seldom had caused serious damage. All of the children had physical or learning handicaps and had engaged in other kinds of aggressive behavior, such as running away or stealing. All of them had nightmares in which they dreamed of the devil and of ghosts. They had experimented with masturbation or sodomy. These children were highly jealous of one or more members of their own families and had felt repudiated by their favorite parent.

Fire-setting shocks parents, but their reaction to it often permits its continuance. They convince themselves that fire holds a fascination for the child which must not be thwarted; so they permit him to start fires in their presence. An anxious, uncontrolled child, however, is incapable of fine distinctions between permitted and nonpermitted forms of the same action, and if he is allowed to start fires in his parents' presence, he will start them in their absence. To inhibit fire-setting, the parents must make it unmistakably clear that the child may not start fires at any time. Matches should not be available to him and he should not be left alone at home. Identification of the factors which have precipitated the child's aggressive feelings is necessary, and inequities should be adjusted.

REFERENCES

1. Bandura, A.: Punishment revisited. *J. Consult. Psychol.*, 1962, *26* (4), 298–301.
2. Bender, L.: *Aggression, Hostility, and Anxiety in Children.* Springfield, Ill., Charles C Thomas, 1953, pp. 38–39, 137.
3. Boardman, W. K.: Rusty: a brief behavior disorder. *J. Consult. Psychol.*, 1962, *26* (4), 293–297.
4. Eron, L. D.: Relationship of TV viewing habits and aggressive behavior in children. *J. Abnorm. Soc. Psychol.*, 1963, *67*, 193–196.
5. Gesell, A., and Ilg, F.: *The Child From Five to Ten.* New York, Harper and Bros., 1946, p. 216.
6. Haring, N. G., and Phillips, E. L.: *Educating Emotionally Disturbed Children.* New York, McGraw-Hill Book Co., 1962, p. 141.
7. Hoffman, L. W., Rosen, S., and Lippitt, R.: Parental coerciveness, child autonomy, and child's role at school. *Sociometry*, 1960, *23*, 15–22.

8. Hurlock, E.: *Child Development*. New York, McGraw-Hill Book Co., 1950, p. 315.

9. Jersild, A. T.: *Child Psychology*, Ed. 4. New York, Prentice-Hall, Inc., 1954, pp. 202–203, 391–392.

10. Johnson, A. M.: Juvenile delinquency. *In* Arieti, S., ed.: *American Handbook of Psychiatry*. New York, Basic Books, Inc., 1959, vol. 1, pp. 846–847.

11. Johnson, A. M., and Szurek, S. A.: The genesis of antisocial acting out in children and adults. *Psychoanal. Quart.*, 1952, *21*, 323–343.

12. Kanner, L.: *Child Psychiatry*, Ed. 3. Springfield, Ill., Charles C Thomas, 1957, pp. 88, 596–602, 687–690, 695–711, 716–719.

13. Lesser, G. S.: The relationships between various forms of aggression and popularity among lower-class children. *J. Educ. Psychol.*, 1959, *50*, 20–25.

14. Leventhal, T.: Control problems in runaway children. *Arch. Gen. Psychiat.*, 1963, *9*, 122–128.

15. McCord, J., McCord, W., and Thurber, E.: Some effects of paternal absence on male children. *J. Abnorm. Soc. Psychol.*, 1962, *64*, 361–369.

16. Mandel, R.: *Die Aggressivitat bei Schulern* (Aggressiveness in school boys). Bern, Switzerland, Hans Huber, 1959.

17. Michael, C. M.: Follow-up studies of introverted children. III. Relative incidence of criminal behavior. *J. Crim. Law Criminol.*, 1956, *47*, 414–422.

18. Norsworthy, N., and Whitley, M. T.: *The Psychology of Childhood*. New York, The Macmillan Co., 1925, pp. 292–294.

19. Podolsky, E.: *The Jealous Child*. New York, Philosophical Library, 1954.

20. Rexford, E. N.: Some meanings of aggressive behavior in children. *Ann. Amer. Acad. Pol. Soc. Sci.*, 1959, *322*, 10–18.

21. Roland, A.: Persuasibility in young children as a function of aggressive motivation and aggression conflict. *J. Abnorm. Soc. Psychol.*, 1963, *66*, 454–461.

22. Shaffer, L.: *The Psychology of Adjustment*. Cambridge, Mass., Houghton Mifflin Co., 1936, pp. 185–186, 318, 511.

23. Strang, R.: *An Introduction to Child Study*. New York, The Macmillan Co., 1938, pp. 392–393, 520–521, 526–527, 532.

24. Teagarden, F. M.: *Child Psychology for Professional Workers*. New York, Prentice-Hall, Inc., 1940, pp. 323, 336–337, 380, 484–489, 508.

25. Thom, D. A.: *Everyday Problems of the Everyday Child*. New York, Appleton-Century, 1934, pp. 136, 245.

26. Wylie, H. L., and Delgado, R. A.: A pattern of mother-son relationship involving the absence of the father. *Amer. J. Orthopsychiat.*, 1959, *29*, 644–649.

27. Wyss, R.: Zum kindlichen Vandalismus (Vandalism in children). *Z. Kinderpsychiat.*, 1954, *21*, 190–196.

Part IV

THE
ADOLESCENT

Chapter 35

Introduction

Parents endure their child's adolescent years with alternating feelings of fortitude, despair, resignation, or pride. Extreme conflict between parent and child is not inevitable, but earlier problems predispose toward conflict,[3] and the perpetuation of the child's earlier attitudes and behavior or of the parent's habits of managing and evaluating him causes difficulty.[1, 4] Parents sometimes believe the child's need of them fades rapidly during the adolescent years. On the contrary, it is their attentiveness to training him in responsibility and granting him increasing independence which determines whether he achieves self-confident emancipation.[6] If they fail to provide him with practice in responsible freedom, he reaches the day of departure from home frightened by his insufficiencies and resentful of his parents' omissions in rearing.

Adolescent behavior disconcerts and disappoints parents because they are unprepared for the inconsistency inherent in the child's half-grown state. Both adolescent and parent somehow must manage to switch roles according to the requirements of the moment. At times, they are equals; but on other occasions the old relationship of parent and child is mandatory.

Not only must the parent adapt himself to the unpredictable needs of the child, but he must adjust to contradictions in the child's behavior which startle him and appear inappropriate in an adolescent. Because of his physical appearance, the adolescent deludes adults into thinking of him as mature. Some 13-year-old boys are 6 feet tall; and many eighth grade girls, well developed, hair piled on their heads, and wearing lipstick and high heels, cannot be distinguished from high school seniors.[5] The adolescent surprises and pleases his parents by his consideration for older people, his poise with both friends and adults, his thoughtful conclusion about a moral problem, his forbearance and skill with younger children, and his use of fact and logic in arguing a variety of subjects. His loyalty to his friends is the culmination of years of parental teaching in showing concern and forgiveness, and he even demonstrates that the lesson has been overlearned by defending the thief, the runaway, the liar, and the alcoholic among his peers, permitting them to use him in selfless dedication to their rights and their welfare.

Considerate and thoughtful behavior of these kinds, as well as his physical appearance, imply that he is mature, and therefore his failures in knowledge and skills and his lapses in responsibility and concern for others appear inexplicable. On the day following an integrated, reasonable display of commendable thought and action, the adolescent departs for school leaving a heap of clothes on the floor and an unmade bed; and on returning home he dissolves in tears or explodes in anger at everyone in the family because someone at school snubbed him.[9, 16, 20] In contrast to his consideration for others is his relentless criticism of his parents' ideas and behavior and his insatiable demands for clothes and late hours, privacy and service. His inconsistency indicates only that he is, as usual, in a state of growth and that his behavior must consist of an assortment of actions typical of many ages. His ability to act as an adult even occasionally is evidence that he is maturing appropriately.

Parent and child also suffer mixed feelings about the young person's steady development and inevitable departure from home. His parents are proud of his achievements and increasing self-discipline, but they regret the end of their usefulness to him and the end of an era in their lives. The adolescent delights in freedom from parental supervision and acceptance by his peers, but he regrets the forfeiture of parental care and concern. Unfortunately, the joy or regrets attendant to his maturing seldom coincide in parents and adolescent. When the parents attempt to retain the young person's dependence on them, he strains for freedom; when he seeks their sympathy and defense, they exhort him to "grow up and act like a man."[20] These contradictions in behavior and attitudes inevitably produce unexpected, unwelcome reactions on the part of both parent and child.

THE ADOLESCENT'S DAMAGED SECURITY

In addition to the uncertainty associated with the unpredictability of his own and his parents' behavior, the adolescent encounters a series of events which damage his feelings of security.

His self-confidence is invaded as he is embarrassed by pimples, upset by social deficiencies, and depressed by school failure.[7, 15, 20] His disregard of rules and lack of courtesy to teachers at school; his grandiose, false claims of experience he has never had; his reckless driving; his experimentation with smoking, drinking, and love-making; and his desperate need for money and what it buys all advertise his lost self-confidence.

His convictions vacillate, and no longer is he certain of the validity of moral distinctions and religious beliefs.[7, 19] Wherever he goes, he has companions who by example, encouragement, and reason convince him that any kind of behavior can be proper.[18] His religious concepts deteriorate, and in abandoning childish beliefs, he unconditionally rejects all religious faith.[10, 14] Uncertain of his ethics and unaware of immutable truths, the adolescent is dissatisfied and disquieted by his own behavior, regardless of what it is.

Total dependence on his parents is no longer possible. He becomes aware only gradually that in time he must depend solely on himself for the care his parents always have provided.[19] Where he lives, how he manages to feed and clothe himself, and what work he does rests with him, and he feels unequal to undertaking this responsibility. As the image of the family vanishes and the young person realizes that he can no longer rely on his parents as protectors, he may be acutely lonely. The adolescent who cannot bear to lose his dependency retreats from the world of his peers, but shows his self-concern by increasing indecisiveness and anxiety.[14]

Peers subject him to critical analysis, and his freedom to act as he chooses is curtailed by the force of their opinions. Their capricious, rigid standards are those of a generation now seeking to establish itself as worthy of respect, but it is important to him to be acknowledged as one of them, and he tries to please by accepting their judgments as correct.

PARENTAL ADAPTATIONS

Not only is the adolescent's security weakened, but he also is required to transfer it from its former base in his family to a new foundation of confidence in himself. His efforts to achieve this confidence wound his parents, both as mentors and as persons. Their adaptations are vital and difficult. They must endure an increasing loss of obedience, respect, and companionship in their relationship with the child. They must tolerate new demands and irritants, and they live with constant anxiety about his future.

In adopting the standards and behavior of his own generation and in seeking new experiences for himself, the adolescent will deviate from the prohibitions and rules set by his parents.[15] Their former techniques for exacting obedience—physical control, approval, uncritical acceptance, and appeals to personal loyalty—are inappropriate for the adolescent, who cannot be restrained and will not be wooed.[1] Some parents, anticipating a dread reckoning for the disobedient adolescent, try to tighten their control, imposing strict rules governing minutiae of the young person's life and attaching severe penalties for slight infractions. Even parents who are willing to listen, ready to compromise, and able to set fair penalties find that the adolescent disobeys their direct orders and well-understood prohibitions.

The considerate parents of two sons, Joe, aged 17, and Ray, aged 16, reported on episodes which strained their endurance:

Believe me, the bigger the kids, the bigger the problems. Our latest fracas was: Joe felt the pinch of not enough gas money, because of an on-coming date with his girl friend. Do you think he would walk to school for two weeks to save gas? Oh, no—but he and another fellow did go out and siphon some gas from a construction truck. Luckily, some people saw them and called the sheriff. They were not caught stealing, but just reported, and the sheriff called us. Well, this really shook us up, but good! So Bob [the father] spent a lot of time several Saturdays, contacting the people involved, taking the boys around, seeing that they apologized and offered to work out the price of the gas. We are hoping this has been a good lesson. Now, I'm sure that Joe has some way of justifying this to himself: "Old-fashioned parents, stingy with allowance, don't understand the needs of kids nowadays." To us—pure and simple spoiled, self-centered thoughtlessness.

Ray came home from an Explorer Scout swim: cost, 35 cents for him. He knelt down in front of Bob (time, 9:30 p.m.). He had cut his head on the diving board while trying to do a fancy dive in the last minute before closing time. So we had to call a doctor, take him to the hospital, and get it sewn up. Cost: hospital, $9.50; doctor, $20.00. Eleven o'clock before we got home —just because he wanted to show off the last minute.

Some days they make no demands at all. Other days we can't work fast enough to make them happy.

The adolescent also denies his parents respect, and he assumes a new stance of superiority over them.[7] He freely criticizes his mother's cooking and appearance as well as his father's language and ideas, and he does so with the earnest sincerity of favoring them with suggestions which will help them overcome their defects. He interprets the innocent questions and ordinary directions of parents, assuming their accustomed role, as prying and bossing, and he attacks them abusively for both their actions and their motives.

These comments were made by a conscientious, intelligent mother of four children. Betty Lou was the oldest, a senior in high school.

As a self-conscious parent I'd love to believe that adolescents may be demanding and obnoxious without any provocation. The truth is that more times than not I go to bed wondering just what I did to bring on the torrent of sassy retorts and scornful upbraidings. And I feel all mixed up—half sympathetic with the child because I realize that I occasionally do treat her like a ten-year-old and half MAD that any child should talk to her parent that way and think she can get away with it.

Take last Saturday. Betty Lou works from 9 till 12 playing the piano at a ballet studio. It takes her a good hour to get home on the bus and she had not arrived when I had to leave. So when I got home at 2:30 and found her at the kitchen table munching a late lunch, all breezy and friendly I said, "Hi, kid. What time did *you* get home?" She dressed me down with a dirty look and scolded, "Why do you have to check up on me every minute?" "Oh no, honey," sez I, "I'm just interested is all." To which she added in a wounded tone, "Well, I wish you'd just leave me alone."

And the other evening when she got in at 11:00, I bestirred myself in bed just enough to say "Hi! Don't forget to turn off the driveway light." She snarled, "Well, don't I always? Gee, Mom!"

And on and on. I can understand better even as I type it out that her snippy responses are because I question her—conversationally and maternally, I think—and she interprets this as a slur on her adequacy. On the subject of college she flatly stated that she would stay out a year and work rather than live at home. "Just get me outa here!" she has reiterated.

Sometimes a parent cannot tolerate evidence that his child no longer values him, and he attempts to force the child to acknowledge his superiority. He is condescending and belittling with the young person, and he scolds and scorns him, imposes extreme penalties and unfair rules, or delivers an ultimatum that the child either demonstrate respect and obedience or leave home.

The adolescent's recreational pursuits are now equal to, but separate from, those of his parents, and for some adults the pain of being last choice is accompanied by envy of the exciting life the young person enjoys. A mother compares her daughter's handsome, attentive boy friends with her own paunchy, balding mate. A father sees his eager son flattering and delighting a bevy of beautiful young girls and feels he does not appreciate nor deserve such good fortune.[2, 20] The days of family games and foolishness are over. The young people have chosen more suitable companions, and their parents must endure not only rejection but also the regular display of their attractive replacements.

Parents must suffer the adolescent's awkwardness and live with his noise.[18] He bangs doors and drops pans, and he plays the same dissonant, tuneless record interminably. His friends take possession of the house with loud singing, laughing, and horseplay—tracking in mud, breaking furniture, and consuming many dollars' worth of food and drink. Gone are the parents' relaxing evenings alone after a hard day's work. Now there is a succession of disturbances as the adolescent seeks help with his homework, talks endlessly on the telephone, complains about one thing and demands another, and always outlasts his parents in getting to bed. His transportation requirements are endless: He needs a ride to the bowling alley or swimming pool, to football games and night activities at school; he must get to the library and to the young people's meeting at church; and he must be taken to parties and movies. All of his demands are expressed with an urgency which overwhelms his parents and leaves them feeling uncertain and guilty about their decisions.[8, 15]

As the adolescent nears the time when he will leave home, parents suffer many anxieties related to choices he is making and to his adequacy in managing by himself. The young person who restricts himself to a steady in dating worries his parents, even if they approve of his selection. A mother deplores and envies the influence which a young girl has with a son she can neither win nor order to compliance with her wishes. A father is concerned that his son may lose sight of vocational objectives because his interest in his girl friend erases every intention but that of marriage. Both parents worry that early marriage will burden their children with work and responsibilities they are too young to bear.

When parents disapprove of the adolescent's choice, their anxiety is acute. They anticipate misery for a son who marries a selfish, domineering, lazy girl, and they foresee heartbreak for a daughter who marries an undisciplined, irresponsible boy. To some parents no choice is ever right, and they examine any potential mate critically and negatively, eventually succeeding in driving the normally rebellious adolescent to settle hastily on the least desirable possibility.

Parents who are concerned about the adolescent's post-high school vocational plans may dictate them for him. In asserting his independence from their direction, he tends to reject everything they propose, regardless of its wisdom.[4] If they have failed through the years to accustom him to working and to providing for some of his needs, he may feel little obligation to continue his education or to seek employment.[11] Many an adolescent, unsure of his interests and uninformed about vocations, tries one idea after another and wastes much time and money in a series of aborted, disappointing training efforts.[19]

When parents are overanxious about the adolescent's future and dread its arrival, they sometimes find comfort in making life pleasant for the young person. They try not to harass and worry him, and they keep family problems to themselves, making certain that he has everything he wants.[19] The years speed by too quickly for them, and they hide their foreboding even from themselves by maintaining a placid and pleasant relationship with him.

The six years of adolescence are blended into indistinguishable units of growth and change, and the reactions of the young person cannot be related definitively to specific years. Therefore, the adolescent's experiences are described as they pertain to his school, his social contacts, his decisions, his self-evaluation, and his relations with his parents.

There are broad differences in the purposefulness and emotional responses of boys and girls, and these are indicated according to their effect on the behavior of the adolescent in each of the areas discussed. The problems and strivings of the two sexes are not unlike, but they are encountered at an earlier age in girls, and often they have been solved or reconciled while boys still are struggling with them.

The behavior problems of adolescents assume greater significance and are less amenable to alteration than were similar problems appearing at the pre-school and elementary levels of development.

REFERENCES

1. Ausubel, D. P.: *Theory and Problems of Adolescent Development*. New York, Grune and Stratton, Inc., 1954, pp. 224, 226–227, 229, 235–236, 250, 341–343, 437.
2. Bernard, H. W.: *Adolescent Development in American Culture*. Yonkers-on-Hudson, New York, The World Book Co., 1957, pp. 72–78, 188–189.
3. Bowerman, C. E., and Kinch, J. W.: Changes in family and peer orientation of children between the fourth and tenth grades. *Soc. Forces*, 1959, 37, 206–211.
4. Conklin, E. S.: *Principles of Adolescent Psychology*. New York, Henry Holt and Co., 1935, pp. 253, 333–341.
5. Davis, K.: Adolescence and the social structure. *In* Seidman, J., ed.: *The Adolescent*. New York, The Dryden Press, 1953, pp. 42–48.
6. Dimock, H. S.: *Rediscovering the Adolescent*. New York, Association Press, 1937, p. 151.
7. Gardner, G. E.: Psychiatric problems of adolescence. *In* Arieti, S., ed.: *American Handbook of Psychiatry*. New York, Basic Books, Inc., 1959, vol. 1, pp. 870–871.
8. Garrison, K. C.: *The Psychology of Adolescence*. New York, Prentice-Hall, Inc., 1934, pp. 101, 113, 138, 165.
9. Hall, G. S.: *Adolescence*. New York, Appleton and Co., 1904, vol. 2, pp. 75–94.
10. Horrocks, J. E.: *The Psychology of Adolescence*, Ed. 2. Boston, Houghton Mifflin Co., 1962, pp. 25–26, 96–97, 104–105.
11. Landis, P. H.: *Adolescence and Youth*. New York, McGraw-Hill Book Co., 1945, pp. 177, 179, 236, 335.
12. Midcentury White House Conference on Children and Youth: The course of healthy personality development. *In* Seidman, J., ed.: *The Adolescent*. New York, The Dryden Press, 1953, pp. 204–218.
13. Rogers, D.: *The Psychology of Adolescence*. New York, Appleton-Century-Crofts, 1962, p. 14.
14. Spivack, G.: Child-rearing attitudes of emotionally disturbed adolescents. *J. Consult. Psychol.*, 1957, 21 (2), 178.
15. Staton, T. F.: *Dynamics of Adolescent Adjustment*. New York, The Macmillan Co., 1963, pp. 76, 81, 181, 183, 242.
16. Strang, R.: *An Introduction to Child Study*. New York, The Macmillan Co., 1938, p. 585.
17. Symonds, P.: Development of the ego and of the self. *In* Seidman, J., ed.: *The Adolescent*. New York, The Dryden Press, 1953.
18. Thom, D. A.: *Normal Youth and Its Everyday Problems*. New York, D. Appleton-Century Co., Inc., 1932, pp. 26, 269.
19. Zachry, C. B.: *Emotion and Conduct in Adolescence*. New York, D. Appleton-Century Co., 1940, pp. 173, 200, 306.
20. Zachry, C. B.: Problems of adolescents. *In* Seidman, J. ed.: *The Adolescent*. New York, The Dryden Press, 1953, p. 80.

Section One

CHARACTERISTIC BEHAVIOR

Chapter 36

Early Adolescent Years

The early adolescent years are a conglomerate of odd sizes, old habits, self-doubts, thrills, battles, and boredom. The junior high school pupil differs from the elementary school child because of the unaccustomed demands made on him by physical changes, social needs, and emerging independence from his family. His school life imposes new experiences and requirements. His social acceptability becomes critical. He directs his own behavior in many areas of living, and he subjects himself to reëvaluation. His relationships with his parents sustain significant alterations, and conflict and disappointment are more common for both parent and child.

SCHOOL

The adolescent's introduction to junior high school can be a painful experience. Gullible and lowly, he is beginning again, and his awe and fear of older students is real. He must travel a different and lengthier route to school and familiarize himself with a new building in which he is certain he will be hopelessly lost, and he must mingle with boys and girls who are strangers to him. He must study under many teachers, eat lunch in public, and remain away from home nearly all day. Regular physical education classes are new to him, and the necessity of changing clothes and taking showers with his classmates seems a devastating invasion of privacy to some girls and boys.

The young adolescent no longer seeks or needs the personal approval of his teachers. He respects them if they are knowledgeable, fair, and relaxed;[16] he scorns them if they bungle and scold. Whether

310

he likes them or not, he cannot help implying that he is indifferent to them in the presence of his classmates, whom he joins in talking and passing notes. He irritates his teachers by slouching in his chair and offering clever comments unrelated to the discussion.

His schoolwork is more demanding than previously and he cannot succeed without increased effort. Homework is intensified, and if the young adolescent is unaccustomed to self-discipline or if he is uninterested in academic superiority, his grades plunge downward. Many girls are willing to devote the extra effort necessary to meet their teachers' demands, but most boys are less concerned with scholarship than with the new ideas they encounter. They become rocket experimenters with the information they acquire in science class; they argue political viewpoints presented by a civics teacher; and they ponder the merits of becoming a secret agent, an atomic scientist, or a naval officer. A boy dismisses his current unsatisfactory grades with an airy prophecy about the excellent marks he will obtain next semester.

Besides these academic interests, the junior high school student involves himself in extracurricular activities of his own choosing. He may try his skills in cheer-leading, team athletics, publications, politics, chess competition, language club, chorus, or orchestra. Because he selects activities in which he is interested and able, he gains both satisfaction and status.

By the time he reaches his last year at junior high school, self-assurance has replaced his initial anxiety.[16] He knows school customs, many of the teachers, and most of his classmates, and he is a member of the highest class. He has established himself as an individual of characteristic talents, and he has created a place for himself at school.

SOCIAL CONTACTS

There are few concerns more critical to adolescence than identification with the peer group.[26] School loyalty soars,[15] and the young person displays a blind devotion to the group and makes personal sacrifices for its members—sacrifices which baffle adults.[1] The standards of peers consistently are held more valid than those of the family.[27]

The strong positive feelings of the young person toward his peers no longer are solely a reflection of his desire to be accepted by them and included in their activities; he must also emancipate himself from his family without undue fear or loneliness, and both his desire for independence and his acquistion of methods for achieving it are enhanced by association with peers who set the example.

Social classification begins and is emphasized in some schools by sororities and fraternities which ape the membership bids and formal parties of college groups. Even without organized selection, social groups form. The well-dressed, dating, handsome, vivacious boys and girls are known as "soc"; the less well-endowed—financially, intellectually, and morally—are "hoods"; the studious, quiet boy or girl who does not mix with the crowd is a "square"; and the lone student who fails academically and socially and who looks and acts differently from everyone else is a "fruit" or a "dip." Most young adolescents prefer to be accepted by any group rather than left out, and it is for this reason that a boy or girl who identifies himself with the "hoods" cannot be convinced that he courts trouble for himself.

Unfortunately for the adolescent, at the time when he most needs to associate with his age-mates, their circles shrink, and many are excluded.[24] Keenly aware of social distinctions and concerned about others' opinions, girls dread exclusion much more than boys, who continue to rely on their own efforts to draw attention. Even boys, however, no longer tolerate and forgive a classmate's deficiencies and peculiarities,[20] and they ridicule his deviation with a scorn based on their own fear of being in his position. Adolescents believe that they maintain a precarious acceptance only by alertness in forestalling criticism, and this conviction contributes to their demands for excellence in clothing, homes, and parental behavior.[7]

Fears related to their families are unfounded, however, because if they are acceptable themselves, they are welcomed into both formal and informal groups regardless of their father's occupation or the family's social standing.[6, 23] Concepts of acceptability change even during this three-year period; and the quiet, demure girl, liked best by seventh graders, loses her popularity to the active, talkative girl during the next two years.[21] Junior high school boys who are acceptable are those considered neat, attractive, outgoing, and interested in sports. Socially neglected young people are nonassertive, and socially rejected boys and girls are those considered unattractive in personal appearance, untidy, restless, and talkative.[17]

Regardless of group affiliation, the adolescent tends to acquire the values of his peers and to give these values precedence over parental opinions. He proudly identifies himself as a teen-ager, dressing in the current mode, talking the current idiom, enthusing over the current crushes—knowing he is different from his elders and from children and being extraordinarily pleased about it.[2, 15] His appearance is of the utmost importance to him. Girls demand quantities of clothes, and boys are adamant about the length of their trousers and the type of shirts they must wear. Girls laboriously put up their hair in curlers every night; and boys, assisted by hair oil and exasperated foot-stamping, carefully comb in waves at precise spots on their heads. That the appearance of beauty is sought, rather than beauty itself, seems evident from the young adolescent's tendency to combine a carefully tended coiffure with an obviously dirty neck.

Identification with his own sex is relatively complete and permanent in the young adolescent.[14] A boy thinks about success and earning power in his future vocation, and a girl thinks about being ideally feminine in both charm and beneficence.[8]

Musing about future adulthood, both boys and girls are more aware of each other as possible marital partners than they were previously, although their thoughts are fleeting and nurtured more by talk with friends than by action. Most boys still arrange to meet girls inside the theater, unwilling to use their own limited supply of money to entertain them. The transfer of the young person's general interest in members of the opposite sex to restricted attention for a single boy or girl may take place either gradually or suddenly.[5, 32] Few younger adolescents are closely attached to each other except for reasons of prestige and dating convenience. Those who are, however, think and talk about marriage and, despairing of parental understanding, sometimes run away and try to marry. Most boys of this age are far from ready for such a step. Because of enlarging sex organs and nocturnal emissions, they are increasingly aware of sexual feeling, and they engage in masturbation and stock a supply of pornographic magazines, but this leads not to serious courtship but to worry about their preoccupation with sex.

Crushes and hero worship are common among younger adolescents. Girls become attached to older girls, admiring them for their competence, which occasionally has a masculine tinge; and boys idealize a high school or college boy who is athletic and self-confident. Crushes are also heterosexual, bestowed with devoted enthusiasm and rapt imitation on older young people or on entertainers. The adolescent walks and talks like his idol, savoring any contact and pretending the admired one is with him continually. Crushes can motivate the adolescent to behave more maturely as he tries to conduct himself in ways he believes would bring him admiration from the object of his attachment, and this purposeful effort toward pleasing another helps to give certainty to the establishment of his own personality and to prepare him for later courtship.

SELF-DIRECTION

The young adolescent delights in his new feeling of independence and experiments with satisfying his own desires. He becomes more casually disobedient and thereby invites conflict with his parents and sometimes endangers his health, safety, or reputation. Formerly reliable, he now wanders home from school just before dinner time, and he leaves the house without obtaining permission or even informing his parents that he is going. His whereabouts are unpredictable, and although he may have permission to go to the movies, he stops en route at a friend's house and spends the evening playing records instead. He does not think of his easy departure from understood policies as disobedience: He merely is assuming the privilege of freedom which coincides with maturation. His parents, however, worrying about where he is and what he is doing, consider him deceptive and defiant, and they are concerned over their rapidly disappearing control.

The adolescent's health can deteriorate undetected as he assumes greater freedom to eat and sleep as he chooses, and his ill-advised decisions combine with multiple body changes to create physical stress and susceptibility to disease. Jones[21] observed that the morbidity rate increases during adolescence. Posture is poor, skin color is pasty, and problems with skin pimples and boils are common. Growth is disproportionate, and anemic conditions appear, increasing susceptibility to disease. The heart grows larger and the blood vessels smaller. The tuberculosis rate increases, and hereditary defects, such as previously unevidenced epilepsy, become obvious.[22] Sexual promiscuity leads to gonorrhea and syphilis, now increasing with less vigilant attention to treatment.

The adolescent skips breakfast, lunches on a hamburger and coke, and may miss dinner if his mother works and meal arrangements are haphazard. Failure to obtain the food he requires to sustain his rapidly growing body keeps him tired, irritable, and prey to colds and infection.

He complains of not getting enough sleep,[31] and because he manages his time poorly and is not self-disciplined, he does stay up late. Missing the rest he needs, he is inattentive and bored in school, his frustration-tolerance is low, his appetite is poor, and he is susceptible to illness. A few adolescents sleep whenever they are home during the day and with no apparent disturbance of their ability to sleep at night. Warm temperatures and continuous medication, such as the use of bromides and barbiturates, induce drowiness, but sometimes habitual napping is adopted as a way to use up time.[22]

The adolescent's desire to direct himself, regardless of the deleterious effect of his decisions, is nowhere more apparent than in his rejection of his parents in favor of his peers as companions, managers, and recipients of his fealty. He dabbles in the lives of his peers and is persuaded by them into experiences which shake his moral standards. To a peer's complaints of mistreatment and misunderstanding, he responds by assuming the role of confessor and counselor, forgiving all violations of legal and moral codes and empathizing with his friend in accusations and self-recrimination.[16] He can and does get himself into trouble by his sympathy. He sneaks out at night to talk, or he accompanies a friend on a stealing foray in the belief that his influence and loyalty will deter him. Girls permit sexual intimacy in affectionate solace to a boy who claims to be abused at home, and the adolescent's experiments with drugs are initiated by the urging of friends he does not wish to offend.

His ill-advised actions reflect his belief that adults are lacking in generosity and that they regard all adolescents as children with insignificant problems.[18] His sharing of others' burdens makes him feel more mature.

SELF-EVALUATION

The younger adolescent is noted for his extreme emotional displays, his unfairness to less favored peers, his resentment of his younger siblings, and his criticism of his parents. Although he wants to go where he pleases and do what he likes with the freedom of an adult, he is childishly unreasonable in many of his relationships. He appears to be more selfish than formerly,[32] and he seeks special favors at home to compensate for the embarrassment and rejection he suffers at school.

His belligerency confirms his strong negative feelings about himself. He is an odd mixture of child and adult, and he is dissatisfied with himself because he is uncomfortable in the role of either. He evaluates himself as he believes his peers do, sometimes considering himself to be a complete fool. At home, he prefers to stay by himself in his room, listening to a radio and thinking, or writing in a diary.[16]

Physical changes are responsible for some of his feelings of dissatisfaction with himself. In every classroom throughout the three years of early adolescence, there are girls and boys in both pre- and post-pubertal stages of growth. Among 12-year-olds, most girls are taller than boys,[19] but many boys start growing rapidly when they are 13 years old, and by 14 years they have surpassed the girls. Until they do so, however, they retain childish characteristics and interests outgrown by girls of the same age. The incongruity in size of boys and girls who are partners in dancing class adds to the boys' awkwardness and uneasiness.

The physically retarded boy tends to be of slender build and is relatively weak. He is regarded as less masculine and more animated, attention-seeking, affected, and tense than the early maturing boy.[25] He cannot keep up in athletics, and he is treated as a younger child by peers and parents alike.[11, 13, 21, 31] Sometimes a physically retarded boy, in vigorous rejection of classification as a child, reacts aggressively in an effort to command respect. One diminutive 13-year-old, who looked two years younger, embarked on a series of auto and truck thefts during which he traveled some distance from home. The publicity given his exploits provided him with ample notoriety. Other small boys attach themselves to a gang of older boys, serving as willing dupes in illegal activities in exchange for the satisfaction of associating with apparently mature boys. A few late-maturing boys withdraw from all contacts, and others seek prestige through romantic overtures toward girls.

Other aspects of physical development embarrass the young adolescent. Some boys grow tall but retain a childish face. Their hands and feet are proportionately huge, and they clumsily knock things over or stumble. Their newly-acquired strength produces jerky, uncoördinated movements.[33] Vocal cords lengthen and the size of the larynx increases. During the months these changes are occurring, the pitch of a boy's voice frequently changes in mid-sentence, and to everyone but the boy, his unexpected squeaks are hilariously funny.

A girl taller than her friends stoops and shuffles to hide her height. A too-ample bosom greatly discomfits her, and the boys do not hesitate to refer publicly to her endowment. If she is flat chested, she wears padded bras and worries about being found out. Girls unaccustomed to regular menstruation manage their protection poorly and are embarrassed by stains or protruding pads. Both boys and girls are harassed by unsightly pimples, the combined result of overindulgence in sweets and the clogging of skin pores with secretions from now overactive glands.[33]

The young adolescent's struggles with his new life and his unsatisfying attempts to identify himself as worthy of a new respect are clearly evident in his divergent interests. The girl who argues in the morning about her need to wear lipstick plays contentedly with paper dolls after school is over. The boy who masterfully teases the girls at school returns to wrestling with neighborhood friends when he gets home. Enticing the opposite sex is more effort than fun, and old ways of amusement are more relaxing.

His vacillating behavior reminds him of his immaturity, however, and judging himself only by the actions of his peers to which he is witness, he is certain that they are much more mature, independent, and self-assured than he, and he broods over his deficiencies.

Uncertainty and self-vilification are more prevalent at the beginning of this period than at the end because after three years of practice the young adolescent can maintain forms of mature behavior more consistently and for longer periods of time. His sense of humor works well for him, and as he greets both peers and parents with a lordly "Hi, fans!" or a solemn "All rise!" he demonstrates a confidence which is reënforced by his dramatization of it. Age and experience also eliminate early uncertainties and enable him to achieve in areas which satisfy him.

RELATIONSHIPS WITH PARENTS

All of the aspects of the young adolescent's life which influence his behavior affect his relationships with his parents. He also is capable at this age of judging adult behavior critically, and he repudiates his parents if their actions degrade him.

School

Parents become alarmed when the young adolescent does poor work in junior high school, especially if he is a boy and they plan a vocation for him which requires college. There is less contact between school and home than formerly, both because the child no longer has a single teacher with whom parents can confer and because each teacher, instructing several hundred students daily, is not personally concerned with individual laxity in learning.

The courteous, respectful attitude accorded teachers and principals by the elementary school child is replaced with negative appraisals and uncomplimentary labels by the young adolescent, and this attitude may cause his parents concern. He further resists adult direction by failing to conform to school rules regarding dress and conduct, and if he persists, he is subjected to disciplinary action. When his misbehavior is reported to his parents, they may respond with anger and increased penalties, and the young person, unconvinced that his offenses are serious, classes all adults as enemies. If the child's nonconformity is condoned and defended by parents, his rebellion at school intensifies, and the subsequent punishment or suspension he receives leads him eventually to blame his parents for their failure to require acceptable behavior of him.

Social Contacts

The social contacts of the young adolescent, which alternately buoy and discourage him, create similar reactions in his parents. They use their influence to make certain he is included in formal social groups and they send him to dancing school each week. During the early adolescent years, girls welcome this kind of assistance more than boys. Parental concern with the adolescent's social acceptability deepens his own concern.

Suggestions about friends the adolescent should cultivate or groups he should join are adopted only if the adults' ideas coincide with his own.[28] He resents their arrangements and promotions of associations, not only because he differs with their judgment but also because he wants to end their domination. Both parents interfere more with their daughters' social lives than with their sons',[1] partly to protect a girl's reputation and to ward off potential harm and partly in their continued recognition of a boy's greater need to achieve independence by freedom of action and choice. Conflict between parents and daughters about social behavior is common because of adult interference.

The child who associates with peers who lead him into delinquency is in constant strife with his parents, who urge him to divest himself of his friends or forbid him to associate with them. Their criticism of the behavior of his friends leads him to defend them more vigorously and to unite with them in complete rejection of all adults. The young adolescent considers his parents hypocritical to denounce his peers, because in his rearing they have stressed loyalty and understanding of others.

Parental ridicule of the adolescent's weird dress and verbal expressions also tends to divide them because parental criticism emphasizes differences in attitude of the two generations. On the other hand, a parent who imitates the adolescent's mannerisms and his enthusiasm for current songs and popular idols is resented for his intrusion into a generation to which he does not belong.

Parents also must combat the child's desire for a more distracting and mature social life than is suitable. He is ready and eager to accompany his friends anywhere at any time,[30] and the adults hesitate to restrict him, fearing his anger and concerned that he will be considered different from his peers. They tolerate, but resent, his appropriation of the telephone and of the house for continuous contact with his friends. They wonder about allowing a son to spend hours at a girl's home or permitting a daughter to go steady, and their uncertainty about establishing regulations for social behavior resembles the adolescent's own groping maneuvers.

Self-direction

The decisions the adolescent makes about his physical habits have far-reaching consequences to his health, but parents believe that he now is too old to be guarded and directed as he once was. When he insists that he must stay up late to finish his homework, they do not object, and when he misses breakfast, they conclude that sleep is more important because he chooses it. Noting his size and energy, they reassure themselves that he must be in good health.

They are confused about how to handle his casual attitude toward obedience. He remains indifferent to their exhortations or pleas and, certain that he is entitled to more freedom than when he was younger, they do not know whether to establish any rules for behavior. If they believe restrictions are necessary, they are doubtful about which are important and how compliance should be assured.

His loyalty to his friends, which can result in deterioration of his moral standards, causes parental anxiety, and the adults worry about his experimenting with behavior condoned by peers but patently unwise or unethical.

Self-evaluation

When the young adolescent feels uncertain of himself and discouraged with his standing among his peers, he shows his unhappiness at home. He is moody and and easily angered, and he abuses his siblings and criticizes his parents. He is unpleasant to live with, and it is difficult to alter his feelings of dissatisfaction and discouragement.

He not only broods over his own defects but also is conscious of the status of the family,[9] and his moral standards for adults are high and rigid. He feels that his father's drinking and his mother's chain-smoking are improper. If he must face the dissolution of his parents' marriage, he is disturbed by this public admission of adult failure and the repudiation of serious obligations; and if a third person is involved in the divorce, the adolescent is appalled and disgusted.[20] He cannot reconcile self-centered or improper behavior with his concept of adulthood, and he is ashamed when his parents act irresponsibly.

PARENTAL RESPONSIBILITIES

Despite appearances, parental direction is mandatory in establishing a structure of order for the young adolescent, whose daily living is being subjected to so many new and difficult adjustments. Parents who are prepared for the child to be unpredictable and variously mature or childish can aid him in stabilizing his behavior and can protect him in areas in which his inadequate judgment harms him. It is their obligation to teach him responsibility, to grant him increasing independence,[7] and to provide control which reminds him that basic codes of behavior may not be abandoned.

Daily chores arranged to fit his schedule should permit the young person to earn enough for his own entertainment, for part of his clothing, and also for giving and saving.

The amount of time permitted him for recreation and social activities should be based on his school performance. As long as he is conscientious about his studies, he merits freedom for television, parties, visiting, and sports. If he is indifferent to school requirements, the rewards of pleasure must be reserved until he exercises greater self-discipline, although a minimum amount of freedom should be granted on weekends to relieve pressure.

Rules should be established coöperatively with regard for the rights of all members of the family, and reasonable penalities should be set in advance and uniformly imposed for violations. Rules should specify visiting hours for friends, use of the telephone, the time at which the adolescent is expected home after school and at night, the hour at which he should be in bed, the activities for which he must have permission, and the extent of care required by him of his room and clothing.

Family recreation should continue because the young adolescent is not as dedicated to isolating himself from his parents as he implies, but he no longer need be required to accompany his parents on visits to their friends. Individual contacts and private conversation with each parent are important in assuring him of parental interest in his activities, ideas, and problems. Because the mother represents dependency, the father is the most favored and respected parent, and the mother must be ready to delegate authority to him and to absent herself when there are opportunities for father and child to be alone together.

Parents should continue to praise the young person for responsible or thoughtful acts and should avoid making fun of him or placing him in social situations for which he is unprepared. Although they can absorb a modicum of criticism from him, they need to be ready with an able defense occasionally, and they should request an apology when he is rude. Parents who believe they are rearing the adolescent well and that their guidance is essential to his development will be able to appreciate his increasing intellect and social skill and will tolerate better the strains his behavior imposes on them.

REFERENCES

1. Ausubel, D. P.: *Theory and Problems of Adolescent Development.* New York, Grune and Stratton, Inc., 1954, pp. 224, 226–227, 229.
2. Bernard, H. W.: *Adolescent Development in American Culture.* Yonkers-on-Hudson, New York, The World Book Co., 1957, pp. 72–78.
3. Bordis, P. D.: Attitudes toward dating among the students of a Michigan high school. *Sociol. Soc. Res.,* 1958, *42,* 274–277.
4. Christensen, H. T.: Dating behavior as evaluated by high school students. *Amer. J. Sociol.,* 1952, *57,* 580–586.
5. Cole, L.: *Psychology of Adolescence.* New York, Farrar and Rinehart, 1936, pp. 101, 105.
6. Congalton, A. A.: Social class consciousness in adolescents. *Victoria Univ. Coll. Publ. Psychol.,* 1952, No. 3.
7. Conklin, E. S.: *Principles of Adolescent Psychology.* New York, Henry Holt and Co., 1935, pp. 247, 272.
8. Crane, A. R.: Stereotypes of the adults held by early adolescents. *J. Educ. Res.,* 1956, *50,* 227–230.
9. Davis, J. A.: Correlates of sociometric status among peers. *J. Educ. Res.,* 1957, *50,* 561–569.
10. Davis, K.: Adolescence and the social structure. *In* Seidman, J. M., ed.: *The Adolescent.* New York, The Dryden Press, 1953, pp. 42–48.
11. Dimock, H. S.: *Rediscovering the Adolescent.* New York, Association Press, 1937, p. 151.
12. Farnham, M.: *The Adolescent.* New York, Harper and Bros., 1952.
13. Frazier, A., and Lisonbee, L. K.: Emotional development. *In* Seidman, J. M., ed.: *The Adolescent.* New York, The Dryden Press, 1953, p. 166.
14. Gardner, G. E.: Psychiatric problems of adolescence. *In* Arieti, S., ed.: *American Handbook of Psychiatry.* New York, Basic Books, Inc., 1959, vol. 1, pp. 871.
15. Garrison, K. C.: *The Psychology of Adolescence.* New York, Prentice-Hall, Inc., 1934, pp. 101, 138, 165.
16. Gesell, A., Ilg., F. L., and Ames, L. B.: *Youth, the Years From Ten to Sixteen.* New York, Harper and Bros., 1956, pp. 104–110, 139–145, 148, 160, 175–182.
17. Gronlund, N., and Anderson, L.: Personality characteristics of socially accepted, socially neglected, and socially rejected junior high school pupils. *Educ. Adm. Superv.,* 1957, *43,* 329–339.

18. Hess, R. D., and Goldblatt, I.: The status of adolescents in American society: A problem in social identity. *Child Developm.*, 1957, *28*, 459–468.
19. Hollingworth, L. A.: *The Psychology of the Adolescent.* New York, D. Appleton-Century Co., 1928, pp. 6–7, 93.
20. Horrocks, J. E.: *The Psychology of Adolescence,* Ed. 2. Boston, Houghton Mifflin Co., 1962, pp. 25–26, 96–97, 104–105.
21. Jones, H. E.: Adolescence in our society. *In* Seidman, J. M., ed.: *The Adolescent.* New York, The Dryden Press, 1953, pp. 58–60.
22. Kanner, L.: *Child Psychiatry,* Ed. 3. Springfield, Ill., Charles C Thomas, 1957, pp. 323, 477–483, 505–506.
23. Keislar, E. R.: Differences among adolescent social clubs in terms of members' characteristics. *J. Educ. Res.*, 1954, *48*, 297–303.
24. Khanna, A.: A study of friendship in adolescent boys and girls. *Manas (Delhi)*, 1960, *7* (1), 3–18.
25. McCandless, B. R.: *Children and Adolescents.* New York, Holt, Rinehart and Winston, 1961, pp. 295–305.
26. Midcentury White House Conference on Children and Youth: The course of healthy personality development. *In* Seidman, J. M., ed.: *The Adolescent.* New York, The Dryden Press, 1953, pp. 204–218.
27. Neiman, L. J.: The influence of peer groups upon attitudes toward the feminine role. *Soc. Probl.*, 1954, *2*, 104–111.
28. Remmers, H. H., and Radoler, D. H.: *The American Teen-Ager.* Indianapolis, Bobbs-Merrill, 1957.
29. Solomon, D.: Influences on the decisions of adolescents. *Hum. Relat.*, 1963, *16* (1), 45–60.
30. Staton, T. F.: *Dynamics of Adolescent Adjustment.* New York, The Macmillan Co., 1963, pp. 76, 242, 256.
31. Strang, R.: *An Introduction to Child Study.* New York, The Macmillan Co., 1938, pp. 585, 615.
32. Symonds, P.: Development of the ego and of the self. *In* Seidman, J. M., ed.: *The Adolescent.* New York, The Dryden Press, 1953.
33. Thom, D. A.: *Normal Youth and Its Everyday Problems.* New York, D. Appleton-Century Co., 1932, pp. 26–32, 56–57.
34. Zachry, C. B.: *Emotion and Conduct in Adolescence.* New York, D. Appleton-Century Co., 1940, pp. 285–295.

Chapter 37

Later Adolescent Years

The older adolescent crowds a lifetime of activity, decisions, and emotional commotion into his last three years at home. He is on the run seven days a week, plowing through heavy school assignments, attending club meetings, working on plans for parties and the yearbook, and involving himself in school athletics or dramatics either as a participant or a spectator. One third of all high school students hold part-time jobs,[10] and many complain of too little leisure and not enough sleep.[2, 34]

The decisions he is forced to make are crucial and enduringly characterizing. They include the degree to which he permits others to influence his behavior, the selection of endeavors to which he commits himself most completely, the methods he chooses to ensure his emancipation from home, and the specific and critical judgments he formulates concerning marriage and vocation.

He is exhilarated by conquest, success, and freedom.[20] He is depressed by the knowledge that most of his experiences are entirely real and their effect is lasting: No longer is he imitating his elders, nor can he retreat from the results of his actions. Often he is disappointed in himself and sometimes he becomes frantic because he considers himself unequal to his rapidly approaching, independent life. He blames his parents for rearing him inadequately, and at the same time he fights their continued attempts to control and teach him. He tells them it is too late; he believes this and is sorry about it, and in a precipitous short cut, he sometimes repudiates childhood by leaving school and home before he is prepared to do so.

SCHOOL

Even though the tenth grade student relinquishes his old place of leadership and must leave the junior high school of which he has become fond, he does not consider himself completely inexperienced and insignificant when he enters senior high school. He is more aware of himself as a person who has capabilities and resources,[13] and he is proud to have arrived at the highest public school level.

His ability to achieve academically becomes important to him,[24] and consistent failure impels him to compensate with aggressive delinquencies or to leave school altogether. The high school population is split between the college-bound students and those who plan to find employment or obtain vocational training after graduation, and the two groups maintain mutual aloofness.

The adolescent who focuses his attention on academic success devotes most of his time to it. He is thorough in completing assignments, diligent in preparing for tests, willing to undertake complex projects, and thinking seriously about possible vocations. Boys are concerned about being accepted by prestige universities, and their grades, as well as their rating on college entrance examinations, assume new and vast significance. The adolescent who needs financial support to continue his education also pressures himself to earn high grades in order to qualify for financial aid, and some students take college entrance examinations two or three times in order to improve their scores.

School loyalty reaches a peak during the senior year[12] and expresses the adolescent's strong tie to the familiar. Even though he anticipates and demands his freedom from old customs and control, he is aware that his future holds moments of loneliness, and he cherishes the setting in which he has grown to feel appreciated and competent.

SOCIAL CONTACTS

The older adolescent contrasts himself not only academically but also socially with others, and cliques are well defined. If his social position is subordinate, he resents the small group of students "who run everything,"[25, 34] and he anticipates that his social inferiority will endure throughout his life.[1] Personal traits still are the basic consideration in obtaining group approval, and the talkative, active adolescent is the one who not only is included in plans but initiates many of them.[17] Coöperative, considerate, honest and self-controlled boys are more popular than those who show off, quarrel, and bully others,[9] and academic competence correlates with social acceptability.[31] Informal groups often are formed by individuals behaving in similar ways because of similar training or pressures. Adolescents who easily assume independence, who resist authority, or who exhibit conforming behavior tend to associate with one another.[28]

Conversation among adolescents is dominated by evaluations and reports on members of the opposite sex, and the adolescent who does not date gains the impression that everyone is besieged with dating opportunities and that these are the prime interest and occupation of everyone but himself. Actually, however, 48 per cent of high school boys seldom date, and 30 per cent of the girls have no boy friend.[29]

Early dates are unpleasant affairs, marked by diffidence on the part of both boy and girl,[4] and dating is engaged in initially not because of any strong desire of the adolescent, but because it is expected by the group.[8] Any date is an unknown quantity, which may involve a boy's exploration of sexual possibilities and a girl's uncertainty about how she should respond.[36] Drinking may be urged, and wild automobile races or impulsive trips to distant places may occur. Many adolescents feel more fright than gaiety during such events, and they are distressed by their awareness of helplessness and conflict.

Normal heterosexual contacts at school suffice to satisfy some of an adolescent's interest in associating with the opposite sex. Lapkowska[21, 22] found that high school boys and girls who attended sexually segregated schools showed a high content of erotic interest in essays they wrote about their future plans and their own personal characteristics, in contrast to the low erotic interest expressed by adolescents attending co-educational high schools.

The adolescent whose social contacts are severely limited loses opportunities for new experiences, which he not only desires but needs.[33] He arrives at adulthood somewhat retarded in social development, unaccustomed to camaraderie, and unfamiliar with social practices. He may be miserable without friends,[25] or he may be content to occupy his time as he prefers and not endure the limitations of freedom which conformity to the ideas and actions of his peers imposes. If he has no skill at repartee and is a poor dancer and swimmer, he is not averse to missing social gatherings, although he does feel sorry for himself. He believes that he alone is uneasy in social gatherings and also that he inevitably impresses others unfavorably. Many college students report social awkwardness as a major problem,[30] however; and it seems probable that few young people consistently feel assured socially.

SELF-DIRECTION

The older adolescent has greater freedom to direct his own actions, and the decisions he makes have lasting consequences for him. Moral choices confront him constantly. He experiments with part-time employment in anticipation of his imminent need to provide for himself and to choose a vocation. Some adolescents select a marital partner during these years.

Moral Decisions

The adolescent faces a dilemma as he tries to be a credit to his peers and yet not suffer total disruption of his relationship with his parents.[12] His friends admire courage and daring,[20] talk expansively about the fun and freedom they have, and insist on everyone's right to both. He feels guilty of violating group mores if he does not demand from his parents complete freedom to do as he wishes, but if he has it, he is uneasy and afraid.

Choices between right and wrong must constantly be made. If he is dating, he must make difficult decisions about physical intimacy. In driving, he chooses either to use a car for pleasure and power or to obey the law and exhibit courtesy to other drivers and to pedestrians. He has opportunities to smoke and drink and must decide whether to do so. When his decisions are self-centered, they are unsatisfying and unsettling to him because he has certain concepts of altruism and idealism, appropriate for his age. Usurpation of others' rights and defiance of society's codes of conduct, even when these actions are supported by his peers, are forms of behavior inharmonious with his steadily-developing maturity.

Vocational Planning

Few decisions are as vital to a boy as his choice of vocation.[1, 5, 11, 15, 25] Financial security, pride, social status, and personal happiness depend on the wisdom with which he selects the work he will do throughout his life. Too often, chance determines the choice.[39]

An adolescent often chooses work for which he does not have the requisite physical strength, personality characteristics, intelligence, or academic skill.[5] Many young people believe that being a surgeon, a minister, or a teacher automatically assures them of others' respect, and they are unaware of the drudgery, disappointment, and even public vilification associated with these professions. Some adolescents choose a vocation solely because it pays well, forgetting that years spent in distasteful work are long and burdensome.

Other adolescents have been committed since infancy by their parents to the pursuit of careers in business, medicine, politics, or military service.[7] Deviation from a father's dream causes trouble, and a boy without a settled interest in another field or one who fears parental disappointment or wrath may accede discontentedly to his family's plans for him.

For most girls, a vocational choice is not the pressing decision that it must be for boys, and girls not planning to attend college usually enroll in business or beauty school and acquire technical training with which they can earn their own living. They rarely consider that they may spend a lifetime at a certain kind of work, and usually they do not need to do so. A girl who has worked hard and successfully at her studies may receive no encouragement to attend college, especially not from her father, who sees her role as that of wife and mother and who cannot comprehend any need for heavy financial sacrifices to provide further education. Without monetary aid and parental interest, few girls attempt college, but the intelligent girl confined to dull work is unhappy and lonesome and may marry hastily to escape her unpleasant life.

Adolescents receive better vocational guidance now than did earlier generations. Vocational interest tests (such as the Kuder Preference Record, the Strong Vocational Interest Test, and the Thurstone Interest Schedule) identify work areas which the student would find compatible with his current interests. Guidance counselors have information about the educational requirements, employment opportunities, and working conditions of many vocations, and they sponsor vocational seminars at which persons engaged in a variety of occupations discuss them with senior students and their parents. Part-time work familiarizes an adolescent with vocational possibilities in a given setting, and volunteer work as a hospital aide or a recreation assistant defines job requirements in these broad areas. Courses in shop, agriculture, business, and home economics provide students with elementary skills in several possible vocations.

Boys must arrange to discharge their military obligations,[2, 30] and an individual who has no clear vocational goals and who is disinclined toward college after high school graduation finds entrance into the military service a useful step for gaining trade skills, a broader knowledge of people, and time to stabilize his thinking about work he wishes to do.

Marital Choice

Anticipating the demise of childhood, the adolescent is increasingly serious about everything he does.[15] If he dates, he evaluates his companions as future marital partners, and he may select one, whom he courts assiduously and plans to marry. Older adolescent girls who are not college bound actively seek husbands, and even those who intend to continue their education. sometimes become attached to a steady boy friend whom they eventually marry.

SELF-EVALUATION

Most older adolescents have a sufficient store of self-confidence. They have recognized achievements to their credit in academic, social, or athletic spheres, and they have successfully discharged numerous and varied responsibilities. They are familiar with a wide variety of events and human reactions, and they have weathered disappointments and failure. They are self-respecting, and they know how to behave in most situations common to their daily lives.

Yet, the nearer the adolescent approaches adulthood and the more frequently he considers himself to be an equal of the adult, the more he also recognizes the hurdles yet to be overcome before his maturity is a fact. A girl, wondering whether anyone will ever want to marry her, is deeply concerned about the mysteries of sexual relations and childbirth. A boy, aware that he must be responsible not only for himself but for a wife and children, feels unequal to assuming the role of protector and provider. In the final semester of their senior year, both boys and girls suddenly realize that there are significant decisions to be made. School no longer is available, expected, or required. If education is desired, it must be sought, and the kind of education selected is now the adolescent's decision.

His self-esteem is enhanced as he flaunts his independence, but because he usually is satisfied with himself, he becomes overly disturbed by events which suggest that he is inflating his real worth.[7] When inadequacy and failure are embarrassingly evident, the adolescent reacts with self-defense, excusing his actions and complaining of unfair treatment.[12] In these ways, then, he advertises his need to appear competent at all times.

RELATIONSHIPS WITH PARENTS

Parents engaged in running battles with their children throughout the high school years find each day long and difficult. Those whose conflicts and anxieties are sporadic, however, discover that these three years speed by with inexorable finality. Both parent and child, by this time, have had numerous contacts with different kinds of people and have lived through demanding, humiliating, perplexing, and proud occasions. There is a basis for greater facility in communication between them, and the adolescent's academic knowledge and ability to reason, as well as his skill in areas unfamiliar to his parents, combine to produce a new respect for him as a capable, mature individual.

On the other hand, in preparation for his imminent departure and in his need for status, the adolescent resists direction more than ever and seems less accessible to counsel and less amenable to parental wishes. Antagonistic feelings develop between parent and child as each insists on having his own way. Each takes a last, desperate stand in the relationship—the parent trying to crowd years of guidance and training into the final few months and the adolescent trying to practice the independence which soon will be forced upon him.

There are specific disagreements about the hours he is to keep, about smoking and drinking, and about laxity in completing school assignments and home chores. Use of the car is a subject of constant argument and concern. If he does not date at all, his parents, especially his mother, become worried about his disinterest in or inability to attract members of the opposite sex, and they pressure him to alter matters. Or they may feel that he devotes excessive time to dating and neglects his studies. They may disapprove of his choice of dates and correctly foresee trouble ahead.

The adolescent's rejection of his parents may appear extreme during these years,[1, 39] and he is especially determined to divest himself of his mother's interference with his life.[20] He finds it infinitely easier to leave home when he can convince himself that he has outgrown his need for his parents, but in convincing himself he causes pain by his aversion to them.

An adolescent also resents his parents because he envies them. Although he considers them uninformed, stodgy, and rigid, he also believes them to be exceedingly fortunate in having arrived at their present level of competence and financial security, and he unhappily anticipates the struggles facing him in reaching their settled state.

Both parent and child suffer doubts and recriminations. Parents note the adolescent's immaturity, and blaming themselves, they are concerned for his future. The adolescent worries about his deficiencies and wishes he had studied more and heeded his parents' counsel. His happy childhood is over, and he does not remember that it was happy.

Parents recognize that they are losing their source of reflected pride and that no longer will they have someone on whom to bestow direction, training, affection, and care. In the future, the young person's achievements will be credited to him alone, and soon he will find a mate with whom he will share affection and from whom he will seek help.

For all of these reasons, the older adolescent's last years at home are excitable and exciting but studded with moments of depression, regrets, and wishful thinking. Attempts on the part of both parent and child to use each other for the last time disturb their contacts and distort their decisions. The adolescent and his parents, as the end of their relationship approaches, occasionally are distressed by the short time remaining to them and disappointed at the way their life together is ending.

PARENTAL RESPONSIBILITIES

Problems are not insoluble. Fairness, compromise, and steady progress in fostering the older adolescent's ability to fend for himself minimize both conflict and anxiety for parents. Their assistance to him in maturing will consist of providing increasing practice in independence, filling in gaps in his knowledge, identifying discrepancies in his thinking, and suggesting alternatives in his planning.

All of the suggestions appropriate for the junior high school student are applicable to the older adolescent, but continuing changes are needed in recognition of his age. By chores and outside work he should earn increasingly greater amounts of money, and by the time he reaches his senior year he should be responsible for all of his expenses except board, room, and medical bills. Rules should be liberalized regularly,[5] and some should be abandoned each year by joint agreement. Until the adolescent has reached 18 years of age and completed high school, however, a few rules are needed and are helpful in avoiding misunderstandings and in providing guidance and support, and parents have an obligation to limit the adolescent's nights out in accordance with his school performance and conscientious discharge of other responsibilities.

He needs practice in living away from home and managing by himself. He should travel without his parents occasionally, and during the summer he can visit relatives, attend camp, or find work away from home.

The adolescent does not want his parents to usurp his privacy with trifling, prying questions, nor does he appreciate ultimatums and warnings, but he is involved in making crucial decisions and he needs and wants his parents' opinions. Although adults quickly discover that their condemnation of a friend or their adamant statements about post-high school plans result only in the adolescent's rebellion and evasion,[12] this does not mean that their reasonably expressed opinions and suggestions are not valued. When their opinions are sought, they should be given, accompanied with reasons. The adolescent is fortified by knowing what parental standards are and that his parents care about what he does,[20] and even though he will not always follow their advice, at least he does not decide blindly as he must without their counsel.

Parents who anticipate danger for their adolescent because of his romantic attachment to a much older person or to one who has a long record of failure and instability should not neglect to express their concern. A girl or boy who rarely dates often overvalues the attention of anyone who shows an interest in him and marries for fear he will not have another opportunity. Failure to discuss the relationship is equivalent to approval, leaving the young person alone to analyze and manage unfamiliar experiences and pressures.

High school boys and girls who are determined to marry sometimes are convinced to delay by being given experience in the trials of marriage. One set of parents succeeded in postponing the strongly desired marriage of their adolescent children by assigning to them the roles they would have if they married. For several months, the girl was given complete charge of the family household: She did all the cleaning, washing, ironing, cooking, and shopping. The boy made out checks (for his father's signature) in payment of all the bills which arrived. Astonished at the work and expense associated with marriage, they independently decided to wait until they were older.

The young person who does not have plans for himself when his public schooling is completed tends to prolong dependent attitudes and behavior, and discussions concerning possible vocations and alternative post-high school plans should occur regularly throughout the later adolescent years. He should not be pressured to make a specific vocational choice, however, nor should he be held to parental plans. His own desire to continue, postpone, or cease formal education should be respected, providing he has arrived at a definite procedure to follow, and this procedure should be approved prior to his graduation from high school.

The father holds a unique position of influence, wisdom, and authority for the older adolescent. Contacts between them need to be increased because a boy must learn to imitate his father and a girl must select a mate capable of competent manhood. The adolescent succeeds better in adult living if he is fully aware of the strength and responsibility required of a mature man and if he recognizes clearly how he differs in role and attitude from a woman. With appropriate and adequate attention from his parent, the older adolescent can emancipate himself from them with reasonable certainty that he will be able to manage his freedom well.

REFERENCES

1. Ausubel, D. P.: *Theory and Problems of Adolescent Development.* New York, Grune and Stratton, Inc., 1954, pp. 226–227, 229.
2. Bernard, H. W.: *Adolescent Development in American Culture.* Yonkers-on-Hudson, N. Y., The World Book Co., 1957, pp. 110, 124–125, 188–189.
3. Bordis, P. D.: Attitudes toward dating among the students of a Michigan high school. *Sociol. Soc. Res.,* 1958, *42,* 274–277.

4. Christensen, H. T.: Dating behavior as evaluated by high school students. *Amer. J. Sociol.*, 1952, 57, 580–586.
5. Cole, L.: *Psychology of Adolescence.* New York, Farrar and Rinehart, 1936, p. 388, Chapter 11.
6. Congalton, A. A.: Social class consciousness in adolescents. *Victoria Univ. Coll. Publ. Psychol.*, 1952, No. 3.
7. Conklin, E. S.: *Principles of Adolescent Psychology.* New York, Henry Holt and Co., 1935, pp. 250, 253, 272–273.
8. Crist, J. R.: High school dating as a behavior system. *Marriage Fam. Liv.*, 1953, 15, 23–28.
9. Dimock, H. S.: *Rediscovering the Adolescent.* New York, Association Press, 1937, p. 137.
10. Franklin, R. D., and Remmers, H. H.: Report of Poll 57 of the Purdue Opinion Panel: *Youths' Attitudes Re Elections, Competition, Discipline, Status, Spare Time, Driving, Grandparents, and Health.* Lafayette, Ind., Purdue University, Division of Educational Reference, 1960.
11. Gardner, G. E.: Psychiatric problems of adolescence. *In* Arieti, S., ed.: *American Handbook of Psychiatry.* New York, Basic Books, Inc., 1959, vol. 1, p. 871.
12. Garrison, K. C.: *The Psychology of Adolescence.* New York, Prentice-Hall, Inc., 1934, pp. 101, 113, 138, 165.
13. Gesell, A., Ilg, F. L., and Ames, L. B.: *Youth, the Years From Ten to Sixteen.* New York, Harper and Bros., 1956, pp. 214–222, 250–255.
14. Hess, R. D., and Goldblatt, I.: The status of adolescents in American society: A problem in social identity. *Child Developm.*, 1957, 28, 459–486.
15. Hollingworth, L. A.: *The Psychology of the Adolescent.* New York, D. Appleton-Century Co., 1928, pp. 44, 85, 93, 191.
16. Horrocks, J. E.: *The Psychology of Adolescence,* Ed. 2. Boston, Houghton Mifflin Co., 1962, pp. 123–124, 166.
17. Jones, H. E.: Adolescence in our society. *In* Seidman, J. M., ed.: *The Adolescent.* New York, The Dryden Press, 1953, p. 60.
18. Keislar, E. R.: Differences among adolescent social clubs in terms of members' characteristics. *J. Educ. Res.*, 1954, 48, 297–303.
19. Khanna, A.: A study of friendship in adolescent boys and girls. *Manas (Delhi)*, 1960, 7 (1), 3–18.
20. Landis, P. H.: *Adolescence and Youth.* New York, McGraw-Hill Book Co., 1945, pp. 164, 177, 179, 236, 335.
21. Lapkowska, S.: Wplyw w koedukacji na zainteresowania erotyczne uczennic (The influence of coeducation on the erotic interest of schoolgirls). *Psychol. Wych.*, 1959, 16, 50–63.
22. Lapkowska, S.: Wplyw koedukacji nad zainteresowania erotyczne uczniow (The influence of coeducation on erotic interests of adolescent boys). *Psychol. Wych.*, 1960, 17, 419–431.
23. Lowrie, S. H.: Factors involved in the frequency of dating. *Marriage Fam. Liv.*, 1956, 18, 46–51.
24. Lucas, C. M., and Horrocks, J. E.: An experimental approach to the analysis of adolescent needs. *Child Developm.*, 1960, 31, 479–487.
25. Malm, M., and Jamison, O. G.: *Adolescence.* New York, McGraw-Hill Book Co., 1952, pp. 121, 160, 332–333.
26. Midcentury White House Conference on Children and Youth: The course of healthy personality development. *In* Seidman, J. M., ed.: *The Adolescent.* New York, The Dryden Press, 1953, pp. 204–218.
27. Neiman, L. J.: The influence of peer groups upon attitudes toward the feminine role. *Soc. Probl.*, 1954, 2, 104–111.
28. Phelps, H. R., and Horrocks, J. E.: Factors influencing informal groups of adolescents. *Child Developm.*, 1958, 29, 68–86.
29. Remmers, H. H., and Radoler, D. H.: *The American Teen-Ager.* Indianapolis, Bobbs-Merrill, 1957.
30. Rogers, D.: *The Psychology of Adolescence.* New York, Appleton-Century-Crofts, 1962, p. 116.

31. Ryan, F. R., and Davis, J. S.: Social acceptance, academic achievement, and aptitude among high school students. *J. Educ. Res.*, 1958, *52*, 101–106.
32. Solomon, D.: Influences on the decisions of adolescents. *Hum. Relat.*, 1963, *16* (1), 45–60.
33. Staton, T. F.: *Dynamics of Adolescent Adjustment*. New York, The Macmillan Co., 1963, pp. 76, 183, 417.
34. Strang, R.: *An Introduction to Child Study*. New York, The Macmillan Co., 1938, pp. 597, 600–601, 616.
35. Thakar, R. S.: Social acceptability among school-going adolescents. *Educ. Psychol. Rev. (Baroda)*, 1961, *1*, 29–31.
36. Thom, D. A.: *Normal Youth and Its Everyday Problems*. New York, D. Appleton-Century Co., 1940, pp. 108, 269.
37. Thrasher, F. M.: The gang as a symptom of community disorganization. *J. Correct. Wk.*, 1957, *4*, 54–56.
38. Wolman, B.: Spontaneous groups of children and adolescents in Israel. *J. Soc. Psychol.*, 1951, *34*, 171–182.
39. Zachry, C. B.: *Emotion and Conduct in Adolescence*. New York, D. Appleton-Century Co., 1940, pp. 285–295.

Section Two

BEHAVIOR PROBLEMS

Chapter 38

Psychophysiological Disturbances

Psychophysiological disturbances are defined as adjustive reactions of the body to emotional tension and strain,[34] either precipitated by a single disturbing situation in an individual easily incapacitated or else adopted as habitual manifestations of a self-concept of inadequacy. The adolescent's use or misuse of the needs or function of his body as an expression of disturbed feelings is also included in this discussion.

Many psychophysiological symptoms are distressing to the individual and some are painful or frightening. Some are more satisfying than others in providing solicitous attention or are more useful in excusing him from unpleasantries or affording a means of indirect aggression and control of others. Such reactions, however, can limit the child's ability to function and can lead to critical withdrawal behavior.

Hypochondriasis and conversion reactions are psychoneurotic symptoms by which the adolescent indicates that he is physically incapacitated. Anorexia, obesity, and enuresis are habit disturbances involving the use or abuse of the body by a distraught, immature individual. Headaches, stomach aches, and vomiting result from experiences of tension and strain which directly produce organ malfunction. Stuttering is a symptom reaction perpetuated by habitual imperfect control of the speaking mechanisms.

HYPOCHONDRIASIS

Hypochondriasis is a chronic complaint habit in which the individual is preoccupied with health, reporting organ malfunction when none

333

exists or exaggerating the effect of minor physical disorders.[20, 32, 35] Cameron[8] indicated that hypochondriasis originates in and is perpetuated by the child's imitation of a family pattern of overattention to illness or to health, and Kanner[20] reported that 53 per cent of the 145 hypochondriacal children he studied were found to have hypochondriacal parents. Parents not only complain of their own ailments but also attribute the source of a child's malaise to an inherited weak heart or delicate stomach. If they make a fetish of good health by launching on soy bean, yoghurt, and wheat germ diets, by exercising vigorously, and by checking daily on digestion and bowel functions, they alert the child to slight indications of illness which are greeted with alarm by all members of the family. Prompt attention to a child's complaints is considered a sign of conscientious mothering, and the high price of medication is a favorite conversational topic among adults.[10]

Parental oversolicitude encourages hypochondriasis. A mother who provides her child with daily transportation to school is informing him that he is incapable of walking this distance. A parent who indignantly objects to exercise assigned by a gym instructor as too strenuous focuses the adolescent's attention on fatigue symptoms and encourages him to retreat from ordinary physical exertion.

Actual illness or injury and repeated or prolonged hospitalization oversensitizes the young person to indications of illness. When he notices signs of physical malfunction, he anticipates the worst and relives the helpless feeling he experienced during previous illness.

Hypochondriasis serves as an adjustive technique in many ways. An adolescent may use his illness aggressively to control or punish his parents. He excuses his bad temper and his excessive demands as the fruits of malaise, rather than acknowledging them to be self-indulgence. He may use illness to gain and hold the attention of parents otherwise too busy to be interested in him, or he may use it as a special device to ensure him solicitude when his siblings are more accomplished than he.*

Many adolescents develop hypochondriacal complaints identical with those of their parents in identification with them and in an inappropriate attempt to acquire the trappings of maturity. The young person who finds life dull or disappointing may focus on body symptoms as a compensatory interest, and illness always provides a satisfactory rationalization for social and school failure.[8] When the adolescent's attention is channeled toward the functioning of his body, however, he is distracted from considering and overcoming serious interpersonal difficulties.[10]

Hypochondriasis in children and adolescents has an 85 per cent recovery rate if it is managed wisely.[20] A thorough physical examination is necessary for an adolescent complaining of illness, and sometimes

---

* See Case 33, Grace E., p. 521.

an accurate diagnosis of hypochondriasis is difficult to make. The physician who finds most complaints to be exaggerated can help by remedying all significant physical ailments and instituting a normal health program of adequate nutrition and rest for the patient. These steps not only make the young person feel better but give his family an opportunity to take definite action toward ensuring his good health, and he welcomes this attention. Parents of hypochondriacal children tend to ignore their real medical needs, such as treatment for dental caries or infected tonsils, yet continue to show great concern over nonexistent physical ills.[20] Medication, including placebos, for nonexistent illness should not be prescribed, nor should the physician recommend removing the adolescent from school in order to rest. This treatment confirms the family's belief that he is ill and entrenches hypochondriacal complaining.

The adolescent overattentive to physical malfunction is signalling his need for sympathetic contact with his parents, and they should provide this, as well as aid him in altering situations which trouble him and in developing needed skills. He should be encouraged to engage in hobbies, conversation, and social activities that he enjoys to divert his attention from the functioning of his body. To revise attitudes of dependence, he needs the responsibility of daily chores and the freedom to manage his own money. In the absence of fever, the young person should attend school and should be expected to continue his usual duties. When he is ill, he should be isolated in bed and should not be permitted to enjoy a reprieve from his obligations by wandering around the house or watching television.

CONVERSION REACTIONS

Cameron[8] defined conversion reactions (hysteria) as being "characterized by the development of persistent inactivation, or persistent autonomy, which resembles superficially the inactivation or autonomy produced by neurological damage or disease but lacks an adequate basis in organ or tissue pathology." Conversion reactions are confused easily with neurological disturbances; and if these disturbances are ruled out, conversion reactions often are interpreted by physicians, family, and peers as malingering. The individual appears unconcerned by the limitations the symptom imposes on him, and his disability is never so complete that he is in real physical danger: He sees, hears, and moves when he must do so to protect himself.

Inactivation

Conversion symptoms of inactivation involve a loss of normal function, which can assume any of several forms. The individual may experience anesthesia or analgesia, in which he is insensitive to touch or pain in circumscribed areas. The disturbance can be recognized readily as a conversion symptom when the patient reports insensitivity only for a part of the body which corresponds to his concept of anatomy and reflects ignorance of nerve and muscle systems. Insensitivity to stimulation of the hand alone has been designated "glove anesthesia" and to the leg alone as "stocking anesthesia" because these areas are identical with those covered by clothing and are regarded by the layman as independent in function. Paralysis of arms or legs also occurs in discrete body areas inconsistent with actual anatomical divisions. The inability to walk or stand, because of paralysis, spasticity, or trembling of the legs, is termed *astasia-abasia*.

Conversion blindness or deafness may be either partial and selective or complete. The sight may be blurred, or "tunnel vision" may occur, in which peripheral stimulation is screened out. Selective deafness is apparent when the adolescent fails to hear the speech of certain persons but not of others or when he loses his hearing only during certain times of the day.

Aphonia is a limitation of the ability to speak. The patient cannot talk above a whisper, although he still may be able to sing loudly or whistle. He may become mute or stutter, but in stuttering he distorts the usual pattern by repeating the first word of a sentence several times and then completing the sentence fluently.

Autonomy

Autonomous conversion symptoms are exaggerated, inappropriate part-reactions which block out other responses. They include muscle tremors, cramps, tics, seizures, and amnesia.*

The individual maintains environmental contact during the appearance of a circumscribed motor reaction, such as a tremor, cramp, or tic, but a conversion seizure resembles an epileptic attack in that there is no awareness of others during the seizure and it is followed by amnesia for its occurrence. A seizure may last from a few minutes to several hours, and recovery from it may be immediate or may require several days.

Conversion reactions appear to be inexplicable or premeditated, and yet their prototypes can be observed in normal, daily behavior. Inactivation symptoms seem less mysterious if it is remembered that everyone experiences temporary losses of function. Absorbed in an activity or preoccupied with worry or grief, a person fails to hear, see, or feel what is happening near him. Cramped arms and legs, deprived of circulation, become temporarily paralyzed. Fear of speaking in public

---

* See Case 34, Winifred A., p. 522.

or awe of a companion causes an individual's speech to become tentative and confused or to fail completely.

Autonomous functioning has antecedents in many normal actions. Everyone experiences involuntary tremors and cramps after muscle fatigue or irritation. The ability to respond appropriately to stimulation even though attention is minimal resembles the autonomy of conversion part-responses, and this is practiced daily in carrying on a variety of activities simultaneously. A mother talks on the telephone, motions to a child to shut the door, and scribbles out a grocery list; a man lights a cigarette while he adds a column of figures and estimates the time remaining before he must leave for a meeting. The individual's attention shifts momentarily from one action to another, and an action already initiated can be continued without concentrated attention to it.

Conversion symptoms differ from these identical forms of inactivation and autonomy because they persist without adequate reason. Cameron[8] ascribed their perpetuation to overcomplete repression, disuse, and role-taking. When a distressed individual reacts to tension by repressing his response to disturbing stimuli, he is overly thorough in his repression, enlarging it to include entire groups of biosocial stimuli only casually related to those causing him anxiety. In this way he guards against any possibility of becoming disturbed, and he also emphasizes the totality of his functional loss. Disuse contributes to perpetuation of a conversion symptom because when the individual fails to respond to stimulation and part of his body remains inactive, atrophy or contractures may develop which cause normal functioning to become progressively more difficult. The individual with a conversion symptom has adopted a pose of incapacity which excuses his inability to achieve. He cannot allow a cure of his symptom, unless it is discreetly or miraculously accomplished, because this subjects him to the possibility of being named a fraud or a coward.

Conversion reactions are precipitated by distress which cannot be borne or by conflict which cannot be resolved. Extreme fear, during which body functioning is disturbed, can initiate an enduring conversion symptom. Severely neglected or abused children gain both sympathy and fascinated attention with conversion symptoms. The adolescent who expects constant approval and applause becomes uneasy if he is ignored or criticized and may respond with a conversion symptom. An illness or injury draws the individual's attention to a specific symptom which is later utilized at a time of distress, especially if the original disability brought solicitude.

Many clinicians have been unable to restrain a feeling of aversion toward the individual who develops conversion symptoms. He has been labelled excitable, moody, selfish,[12] lying, domineering, and insincere,[13] and his symptoms have been called a "spoiled child reaction."[28] More objective investigations of the attitudes and characteristics of persons developing conversion symptoms suggest a multiplicity of contributing personality components. Eysenck et al.[17] factor analyzed psychological tests administered to neurotic, psychotic, and normal persons, and they found a high degree of extraversion among those with conversion reactions. Fulkerson[19] stated, however, that personality tests completed by hysterics have low validity, a fact which he attributed to carelessness in responding. These two conclusions do not necessarily neutralize each other because both suggest that indifference and purposelessness are characteristic of hysterics.

Stukat[43] intensively investigated suggestibility but did not find hysterics more suggestible than other subjects on any of his tests. Suggestibility was found to be related to ease of conditioning, however, and Pervov[29] reported that hysterics find it difficult to form new conditioned responses, particularly inhibitory ones. These findings indicate that the person developing conversion symptoms is tied rigidly to previously learned reactions which are not subject to alteration by thoughtful control or intent, especially in unstructured situations. That conversion symptoms are automatic, overlearned responses is implied by Rosen's[31] designating them "physiological negativism" and by Walton and Black's[44] description of a case of chronic conversion aphonia as a conditioned avoidance response.

These studies all discredit the belief that conversion reactions are contrived. Instead of using purposeful logic in selecting his responses, the hysteric appears to have limited ability to master crises cognitively, great reluctance to maintain contact with those who demand more of him than he is willing or able to produce, and a resultant directing of attention toward bodily malfunction during emotional stress. This response is appropriate for him because it combines self-preoccupation with a conviction of incapability.

With adequate treatment, recovery from conversion reactions is possible and can be maintained. Clark,[11] in a follow-up study of adolescent girls one to six years after treatment, found that two thirds either held or improved on the gains they had made. They had formed better relations with girls of similar age, achieved a better vocational adjustment, and felt less hostility toward their parents than previously.

Removal of the conversion symptom is not a complete solution to the problem; nevertheless, it is a necessary step in restoring the individual to adequate function and in returning him to the environment he has forsaken. It is possible to remove a conversion symptom by shock or scare tactics; and the recovery of lost function common to religious pilgrimages and exhortations is well known. Even though function is restored temporarily or permanently, however, there is danger in jeopardizing the patient's trust if he is tricked into discarding his symptom.

Relearning procedures are more satisfactory because they are logical techniques which are not emotionally disturbing. Malmo *et al.*[25] restored hearing in an hysterically deaf girl by conditioned response procedures. Shaffer[35] reported curative effects in hysterical soldiers who were required to attempt daily to use nonfunctioning arms, legs, or eyes. Brown and Pisetsky[7] found that hysterical paraplegics who resisted psychotherapy responded to physical therapy. Treatment directed toward restoration or inhibition of responses need not be deceptive because associative learning, practice, and exercise contribute to the retraining of function which has been temporarily forgotten and further entrenched by disuse. Participation and effort by the patient are required for successful restoration of function, and these attributes are needed also if his ability to cope with problems is to be improved.

An adolescent with conversion symptoms recovers more readily if his symptom does not relieve him of most of his usual duties or bring him too much notoriety.[20] Undue attention should not be paid to the disability nor should special sympathy be offered. He should not have the privileges of illness but should be expected to continue as usual with his daily obligations. A program of requiring the adolescent to practice responsibility and earn privileges increases his self-confidence and self-discipline. Usually he has had inadequate and inconsistent training, and a stricter regime of regular daily routines is needed not only to provide him with direction he has not had before but also to demonstrate parental concern for his welfare. The adolescent's need to attract attention can be averted if his parents spontaneously initiate conversation with him and invite him to share their activities, but they must also make it possible for him to shift from dependence on them for companionship to identification with his peers.

ANOREXIA NERVOSA

Deliberate self-starvation, termed *anorexia nervosa*, occurs in some adolescents, usually girls, who are emotionally distressed. Lesser *et al.*[23] studied 15 girls who refused to eat, 11 of whom were hospitalized for treatment. Self-imposed dieting, originating from concern about weight or height, initiated anorexia in 40 per cent of the cases. For another 40 per cent, a competitive situation existed with which the girl could not cope satisfactorily and to which she responded by ceasing to eat. Compulsive characteristics are evident in anorexia nervosa when a girl refuses to eat in self-punishment or atonement for real or imagined unworthy thoughts or actions.

Kanner[20] recommended hospitalization for treatment of anorexia nervosa, but Lesser reported that hospital management of the girls he studied was difficult. Eventually, however, seven adjusted well, and six made a fair adjustment. None died from starvation. Prognosis was better for girls with personalities containing hysterical components than for those with schizoid or compulsive traits.

More attention for the former and affectionate reassurance for the latter encourages the adolescent to abandon her hunger strike. She should be placed under a physician's care for a planned, gradual return to normal eating, after being given factual explanations about the dependence of body function on food and after the removal of its connotation as a device for gaining attention or as a weapon for self-punishment or revenge.

OBESITY

Obesity may be a holdover from elementary school practices,* or it may appear for the first time during adolescence, as the young person becomes acutely aware of his limitations and greatly concerned by the imminence of his departure from home. Contrary to popular opinion, he is not jovially unconcerned about his weight, although adults admit that as overweight adolescents they pretended to be flattered by the nicknames and comments their size elicited. Far from being indifferent to his condition, the adolescent is humiliated by the difficulties he encounters in fitting into school chair-desks and theater seats, in climbing stairs, and in buying extra large clothing. His bulk adds reality to his feeling of being an outcast, and often he overeats in self-indulgence to assuage his loneliness.[2] His heaviness limits his participation in social and athletic activities, at which he is awkward and self-conscious, and his failure to utilize the food he consumes in energy-demanding activity compounds the problem.[41]

Obese adolescents can reduce their weight, but they must be detemined to do so in spite of the pressures and habits impelling them to continue overeating. Older adolescents can muster this degree of self-control with a physician's help. Group reducing is more successful than lone effort, and such weight-reducing organizations as TOPS† are open to adolescents. Oversolicitous parents need to revise their management of the young person and to provide experiences which enable him to mature.

ENURESIS

The incidence of enuresis drops during adolescence. Kanner[20] reported that only 1 to 4 per cent of the younger adolescents seen at

---

* See Chapter 27, "Habit Problems: Eating and Sleeping," pp. 220–221.
† "Take Off Pounds Sensibly"

his clinic were enuretic. Perpetuation of enuresis into adolescence can be a contributing or concomitant factor in serious behavior problems, as evidenced by the findings of Michaels and Steinberg,[26] who reported that 19 per cent of 200 delinquents they studied were enuretic. Boys still wetting their beds at adolescence consider themselves immature and dependent; yet they strongly object to such a self-concept, and they act defensively and aggressively to convince themselves that it is incorrect.

Some enuretic adolescents are successful athletically or scholastically and dependable at outside work, but at home they persevere in long-held attitudes of self-pity and dependency. Others extend these attitudes to all of their relationships and activities, and they continue to regard themselves as too helpless either to work or to conform.

Enduring enuresis results from inattention to and irresponsibility for the habit. An enuretic adolescent will be helped by talking with a physician who can reassure him that there is nothing wrong physically, give him facts concerning the incidence of enuresis at his age, and assign him the obligation of exercising self-control over bladder function. With the shifting of responsibility for controlling enuresis to the young person, parents must abandon their concern and cease to excuse, explain, or inquire about its occurrence.

HEADACHES

Headache can be an associated symptom of illness ranging from the common cold to meningitis, and it also is related to physiological changes in the adolescent.[20] Other causes of headaches include prolonged fatigue and inadequate nourishment, a particularly disturbing event which results in tension, and a consistent pattern of strong emotion combined with excessive work.[42] Sometimes the need for sympathy or for an excuse to escape onerous duties or dreaded social events also will lead to headache complaints.

The adolescent with frequent headaches needs a thorough physical examination, including a vision check. In the absence of illness or physical disability, the daily pressures he endures should be identified and unnecessary stress should be eliminated. If the young person is taking college preparatory work but does not learn easily or like to study, he should be allowed to abandon plans for college and change to a general or vocational course. If he is involved in too many activities or required to participate in those considered important by his parents but which he dislikes, changes are needed.

All stress cannot be removed by avoiding tension-producing situations, however. If the adolescent is under strain because he is inadequate in a subject which is not beyond his ability to master, he can be given tutoring or direction in study so that he can perform better. Increasing his skill in any academic, social, or athletic area in which he feels deficient decreases his tension. The use of analgesics to reduce headache pain enables the young person to continue necessary work,[18] and parents can see that he has sufficient rest and some recreation daily to permit relaxation.

STOMACH ACHE AND VOMITING

The effect of emotional tension on the stomach is known to everyone who has lost his appetite or his dinner from excitement, dread, or anger. Saul[34] stated that the physiological bases of stomach distress, which include disturbances of both secretion and motility, are as varied as the symptoms.

Stomach pain and vomiting have been traced to both aggressive and self-punitive attitudes, and a specific disturbing incident usually can be identified as triggering temporary malfunction of the stomach.

Eichhorn and Tracktir[15] induced emotions hypnotically in a study of the relationship between emotion and gastric secretion. Dividing their subjects into groups characterized by tendencies toward high or low anxiety, they found that under fear conditions the high anxiety group secreted more gastric acid than did the low anxiety group, but the results were reversed under anger conditions. They concluded that stomach disorders are a conjoint product of personality and the kind of precipitating event operating.

Ulcers occur in even young children, and the adolescent who complains of stomach ache or who is vomiting frequently needs to be examined by a physician. Even without demonstrable organ defect or disease, physical symptoms justify the institution of an ordered regime of rest and adequate nutrition. Emotionally induced pain and the disruption of body function are as exhausting as that resulting from disease or injury.

Because gastric disorders frequently are a direct response to a fearful or anger-producing event, the incident should be identified so that parents can talk over with the adolescent what happened and how he felt. Without depreciating his feeling as being unwarranted, they can give him information about their own similar experiences, suggest a variety of techniques for meeting problem situations, and encourage him to rely more on himself. If the home atmosphere is one of continual turmoil and anger, this condition should be revised, and if tension is related to outside demands, a reduction in these provides relief from strain.

STUTTERING*

Speech is a complex activity which demands unfaltering coördination between muscles and nerves and requires a smooth flow of nervous impulses between stimulation and response.[1] It is particularly susceptible to disruption during emotional stress, and everyone has experienced speech blockage, has used word approximations, and has found himself unable to communicate his ideas at times of overconcern.

The adolescent who stutters regards himself as being shut off from contact with others. Inasmuch as 90 per cent of stuttering originates during the first ten years of life,[1] a young person who has failed to overcome his speech defect has lived with it over a lengthy span of time and has acquired major fears and apprehensions about speaking which haunt every contact he has with other people. Although most investigators have concluded that there is no single personality peculiar to the stutterer, some studies have uncovered attitude and behavior trends which are consistent with the embarrassment of a continuous and prominently displayed defect.

Guilt feelings during stuttering and dejection aftewards are reported by stutterers,[39] and they consistently set low standards of achievement for themselves.[40] Stutterers appear to be both more hostile and more anxious than nonstutterers, and their emotional reactions interfere significantly with both the expression and the recall of ideas.[27, 33] Bluemel,[6] after reviewing the studies of stutterers which have been made during the past century, concluded that speech disturbance develops in a poorly integrated person, one who is easily confused and inwardly excitable and who does not think with verbal clarity.

Although many clinicians believe that psychotherapy should accompany speech therapy, they agree that active work with the speech problem itself is basic for permanent improvement.[38] Studies have confirmed the favorable prognosis for stutterers who develop confidence in their ability to overcome stuttering and who work at doing so.

Speech therapy teaches the stutterer how to relax oral and neck muscles, how to coördinate his breathing with the production of sounds, and how to speak firmly with normal inflection and modulation,[20] thus bringing speech under voluntary control. Practice in reading, speaking, and also stuttering aids the individual by helping him to achieve a more relaxed and casual attitude toward his speech by speaking deliberately and frequently, rather than by fearfully avoiding speech.[6] Rousey[32] found a general decrement in the stuttering of 18 adolescents who talked ten hours daily for five consecutive days. Shames,[36] in discussing the efficacy of negative practice, warned of the need to minimize involuntary stuttering before voluntary stuttering is practiced,

---

* See Chapter 30, "Speech Disorders," pp. 248–250.

and he suggested adaptation to troublesome sounds by concentrated practice prior to attempting voluntary stuttering. Knoblochova[22] worked directly toward physical relaxation by prescribing therapeutic sleep sessions. This benefited all of the stutterers with whom he worked in their mastery of voice exercises and aided others in directly improving speech.

REFERENCES

1. Barabara, D.: Stuttering. *In* Arieti, S., ed.: *American Handbook of Psychiatry.* New York, Basic Books, Inc., 1959, vol. 1, pp. 950–952.
2. Bayles, S., and Ebaugh, F. G.: Emotional factors in eating and obesity. *J. Amer. Diet. Assoc.*, 1950, *26*, 430–434.
3. Bloodstein, O.: The development of stuttering: I. Changes in nine basic features. *J. Speech Hear. Dis.*, 1960, *25*, 219–237.
4. Bloodstein, O.: The development of stuttering: II. Development phases. *J. Speech Hear. Dis.*, 1960, *25*, 366–376.
5. Bloodstein, O.: The development of stuttering: III. Theoretical and clinical implications. *J. Speech Hear. Dis.*, 1961, *26*, 67–82.
6. Bluemel, C. S.: Concepts of stammering: A century in review. *J. Speech Hear. Dis.*, 1960, *25*, 24–32.
7. Brown, W., and Pisetsky, J. M.: Sociopsychologic factors in hysterical paraplegia. *J. Nerv. Ment. Dis.*, 1954, *119*, 283–298.
8. Cameron, N.: *The Psychology of Behavior Disorders*. Cambridge, Mass., Houghton Mifflin Co., 1947, Chapters 7, 11, 12.
9. Cherry, C., and Sayers, B. McA.: Experiments upon the total inhibition of stammering by external control, and some clinical results. *J. Psychosom. Res.*, 1956, *1*, 233–246.
10. Chrzanowski, G.: Neurasthenia and hypochondriasis. *In* Arieti, S., ed.: *American Handbook of Psychiatry*. New York, Basic Books, Inc., 1959, vol. 1, pp. 260, 266.
11. Clark, E.: A follow-up study of adolescent girls treated for hysteria. *Smith Coll. Stud. Soc. Wk.*, 1952, *22*, 91–111.
12. Cole, L.: *Psychology of Adolescence*. New York, Farrar and Rinehart, 1936, p. 294.
13. Detmar, B.: *Nervous Disorders and Hysteria: Disease or Character Defect? Their Nature, Cause, Symptoms, Consequences, and Treatment*. London, Thorsons Publishers Ltd., 1951.
14. Diatkine, R.: Le bégaiement (Stuttering). *Évolut. Psychiat. (Paris)*, 1951, *4*, 525–544.
15. Eichhorn, R., and Tracktir, J.: The relationship between anxiety, hypnotically induced emotions and gastric secretion. *Gastroenterology*, 1955, *29*, 422–431.
16. Emonds, P. L. F.: Het stotteren (Stuttering). *Gawein*, 1953–1954, *2*, 1–17, 43–47.
17. Eysenck, S. B. G., Eysenck, H. J., and Claridge, G.: Dimensions of personality, psychiatric syndromes, and mathematical models. *J. Ment. Sci.*, 1960, *106*, 581–589.
18. Friedman, A. P., and von Storch, T. J. C.: Tension headache. *J. Amer. Med. Assn.*, 1953, *151*, 174–177.
19. Fulkerson, S. C.: Individual differences in response validity. *J. Clin. Psychol.*, 1959, *15*, 169–173,
20. Kanner, L.: *Child Psychiatry*, Ed. 3. Springfield, Ill. Charles C Thomas, 1957, pp. 323, 373–376, 404–406, 440, 477–483, 505–506, 520–531, 627–637, 649–675.
21. Kent, L. R.: A retraining program for the adult who stutters. *J. Speech Hear. Dis.*, 1961, *26*, 141–144.
22. Knoblochova, J.: Léčeni koktavosti trvalým spánkem (The treatment of stuttering with the prolonged sleep). *Neurol. Psychiat. Českoslov.*, 1951, *14*, 223–231.

23. Lesser, L. L., Ashenden, B. J., Debuskey, M., and Eisenberg, L.: Anorexia nervosa in children. *Amer. J. Orthopsychiat.*, 1960, *30*, 572–580.
24. Majerus, P. W., Guze, S. B., Delong, W. B., and Robins, E.: Psychologic factors and psychiatric disease in hyperemesis gravidarum. *Amer. J. Psychiat.*, 1960, *117*, 421–428.
25. Malmo, R. B., Davis, J. F., and Barza, S.: Total hysterical deafness: an experimental case study. *J. Pers.*, 1952, *21*, 188–204.
26. Michaels, J. J., and Steinberg, A.: Persistent enuresis and juvenile delinquency. *Brit. J. Delinq.*, 1952, *3*, 114–123.
27. Moore, W. E.: Relations of stuttering in spontaneous speech to speech content and to adaptation. *J. Speech Hear. Dis.*, 1954, *19*, 208–216.
28. Morgan, J. J. B.: *The Psychology of Abnormal People*. New York, Longmans, Green and Co., 1937, p. 475.
29. Pervov, L. G.: Osobennosti narusheniia vyssheĭ nervnoĭ deiatel'nosti u bol'nykh isterieĭ (Features of higher nervous activity in hysterics). *Zh. Vyssh. Nervn. Deiatel'.*, 1958, *8* (5), 654–658.
30. Proctor, J. T.: Hysteria in childhood. *Amer. J. Orthopsychiat.*, 1958, *28*, 394–407.
31. Rosen, S. R.: Vasomotor response in hysteria. *J. Mt. Sinai Hospital* (*N.Y.*), 1951, *18*, 179–190.
32. Rousey, C.: Stuttering severity during prolonged spontaneous speech. *J. Speech Res.*, 1958, *1*, 40–47.
33. Santostefano, S.: Anxiety and hostility in stuttering. *J. Speech Hear. Res.*, 1960, *3*, 337–347.
34. Saul, L. J.: Physiological effects of emotional tension. *In* Hunt, J. McV., ed.: *Personality and the Behavior Disorders*. New York, The Ronald Press Co., 1944, vol. 1, pp. 270, 275.
35. Shaffer, L. F.: *The Psychology of Adjustment*. Cambridge, Mass., Houghton Mifflin Co., 1936, pp. 236–243, 252.
36. Shames, G. H.: A utilization of adaptation phenomena in therapy for stuttering. *J. Speech Hear. Dis.*, 1953, *18*, 256–257.
37. Shearer, W. M.: A theoretical consideration of the self-concept and body image in stuttering therapy. *ASHA*, 1961, *3*, 115–116.
38. Sheehan, J. G.: An integration of psychotherapy and speech therapy through a conflict theory of stuttering. *J. Speech Hear. Dis.*, 1954, *19*, 474–482.
39. Sheehan, J. G., Cortese, P. A., and Hadley, R. G.: Guilt, shame and tension in graphic projections of stuttering. *J. Speech Hear. Dis.*, 1962, *27* (2), 129–139.
40. Sheehan, J. G., and Zelen, S. L.: Level of aspiration in stutterers and non-stutterers. *J. Abnorm. Soc. Psychol.*, 1955, *51*, 83–86.
41. Stefanik, P. A., Heald, F. P., and Mayer, J.: Caloric intake in relation to energy output of obese and non-obese adolescent boys. *Amer. J. Clin. Nutr.*, 1959, *7*, 55–62.
42. Stenbäck, A.: Headache and life stress: a psychosomatic study of headache. *Acta Psychiat.* (*Kbh.*), 1954, (92).
43. Stukat, K.: *Suggestibility: A Factorial and Experimental Analysis*. Stockholm, Sweden, Almqvist and Wiksells, 1958.
44. Walton, D., and Black, D. A.: The application of modern learning theory to the treatment of chronic hysterical aphonia. *J. Psychosom. Res.*, 1959, *3*, 303–311.

Chapter 39

Social Deviations

Social deviations in the adolescent herald the insidious development of serious asocial and antisocial attitudes and behavior. The individual who sets himself apart from his fellows gradually comes to distrust them and then becomes deceptive or revengeful in his social relationships.

Social deviations occur when the child experiences humiliation, rather than pleasure, in his contacts with others. His most significant contacts are those with his parents, and he acquires from his relationship with them and from their techniques of rearing him the attitudes about himself and the expectations associated with others which govern his approach to his peers. His attitudes toward people become distorted when he experiences violations of his trust of parents; when he is unable to acquire consistent, sex-appropriate, acceptable behavior; and when he is taught to consider himself privileged to indulge his own desires.

Seidman[21] noted that gross inconsistency exists between the ethical values taught by adults and their own behavior, which is often prejudiced, unfair, dictatorial, disloyal, selfish, or immoral. This discrepancy serves to confuse and disillusion adolescents attempting to establish values which they can use in self-direction. Contradictions between precept and example lead the adolescent to attitudes of scorn and contempt for adults' exhortations and commands, and he imitates the worst of parental behavior in disdainful rejection of his parents as unfit to direct him.

A child subjected to the unpredictable, senseless, and impulsive behavior of immature, psychotic, or alcoholic parents suffers anxiety,

346

and his own actions become inconsistent. He is unable to learn with any certainty which kinds of behavior will result in just reward or punishment, and he approaches others in a trial and error fashion, using inept and unsuccessful techniques for seeking their acceptance. He fails to acquire behavior appropriate for his sex because he has no admired model to imitate, and this also makes him a misfit.

The child who is reared without penalty for misbehavior or who is shielded by his parents from unpleasant obligations regards himself as entitled to special privileges and exempt from ordinary responsibilities. He holds others in contempt and considers them gullible and foolish for working conscientiously and for behaving honorably, and he takes advantage of their trust of him.

The adolescent social deviate may join a gang or he may pair with another maladjusted young person for companionship and support in antisocial activities. Some cannot achieve even this degree of joint effort and remain isolated from their peers, unable to identify or emphathize with them. The adolescent with a psychopathic personality disorder neither isolates himself nor seeks companions in revenge. He mingles with others superficially, indifferent to them as persons, and satisfies his own inclinations while acting the part of a reasonable, moral individual.

GANG ASSOCIATIONS

Gangs are typically preadolescent phenomena, according to Wolman,[24] who stated that those formed during the adolescent years consist of maladjusted young persons. Thrasher[23] believed that an adolescent joins a gang when he is thwarted in one or more of four basic desires: fun and excitement, security, recognition, and response. Gang membership offers all of these, as does association with only one other companion who has a propensity for aggressive or spectacular behavior.

Gangs are more prevalent in economically deprived neighborhoods, but they also originate among middle- and upper-class adolescents. Lower class gangs are created by a need for union of adolescents who suffer status frustration and loss of self-esteem in comparing their rearing, their parents, their possessions, and their opportunities with the middle-class standards they encounter daily in school.[6] Gang violence is common when members are angry at being deprived of success and of authority and when they are certain that the future will find their situation unimproved.[20] Coincident with unfavorable class comparison, however, are the individual's problems of adjustment, and these are the true instigators to gang association. Neglect, cruelty, rejection, and inconsistent supervision and discipline cause the adolescent to be sensitive to class distinctions, to be dissatisfied with himself, and to be driven to express resentment.[12]

By identifying himself with the outcasts, the adolescent confirms his negative and hopeless opinion of himself. He revenges himself on parents whom he believes have failed him, achieves a degree of status and acceptance in his group, and acquires a feeling of superiority when he engages in prohibited antisocial behavior.[22] Pearl J., Madge R., and Warren M. were three adolescents who considered themselves as rejects and who sought companionship in their rebellion.

Pearl, 13 years old, held open house for her friends after school while her mother was working and no one was home. Despite average intelligence, her grades were low. She smoked, lied about where she was going or where she had been, and once stayed out all night on a double date. Pearl was the youngest of four children and the only girl. All of her brothers were married or away from home. The parents had been divorced recently, and the father had married a woman he had dated for some time previously. The mother, now working to support herself and Pearl, went out often at night with both women and men friends. She alternated between extreme laxity with Pearl and violent abuse of her.

Madge was 14 years old and had three times run away from home, always in the company of a friend. She was gone for several days at a time, sleeping in cars and being protected by her friends who knew where she was but did not tell. At school she had been suspended several times for rudeness to teachers and for refusal to obey rules. Unaccepted by other girls in her class, she considered them above her socially and had felt this distinction since she entered junior high school. The second of five children, Madge formerly had been companionable with her mother, who often sided with her in difficulties she had with teachers. The mother permitted Madge to evade chores expected of her, but she upbraided her loudly and lengthily and had slapped her for lying. The girl often screamed that she did not want to live with her mother and claimed she ran away to spite her.

Warren was 17 years old and had been involved since he was in junior high school with a gang of boys engaged in stealing. He had never been apprehended, however, and his parents were unaware of his activities. He was the oldest of three boys and had superior intelligence, which he exhibited only rarely at school. From an early age, he had succeeded in avoiding work by such methods as truanting from school or dumping papers he was supposed to deliver. His mother required nothing of him, but scolded him continually for his thoughtlessness and irresponsibility. Warren strongly resented boys from families better endowed financially and socially than his own, and he felt ostracized at school.

Both Madge and Warren eventually were committed to state industrial schools where each responded to the control given them there. Pearl's mother, deeply concerned, agreed to revise her own entertainment habits, maintain a strict chore schedule for Pearl, enable her to entertain friends when she was at home, and refrain from both violent action against her and allowing the girl to abuse her verbally or physically. Mother and daughter moved to a new neighborhood and a new school.

Prohibiting the adolescent's association with undesirable friends is not always successful, especially if he is accustomed to coming and going as he pleases. Trouble can be averted by close supervision and parental insistence on meeting the young person's companions and their spending some time at home. When the adolescent lies about where he goes and what he does when with these friends, he should be temporarily grounded, a penalty which curtails the association and forestalls further difficulties.

A three-pronged approach is needed to rid the adolescent of his need to associate with peers who defy authority. First, he must be more strictly supervised so that he has less opportunity to get into trouble. Many adolescents who attach themselves to gangs are left alone for hours every day because both parents work, and experimenting with their freedom is inevitable. Second, he needs to be held with complete firmness to home and school responsibilities. Usually he is accustomed to procrastinating or arguing his way out of work, and this has taught him that he can resist direction and evade responsibility. Finally, in recognition of his rightful resentment of verbal tirades and nagging about his deficiencies, these should cease, and parents should begin to talk over with him his ideas on all disputed subjects. Compromises can be made, but these should not involve major matters until the adolescent has earned trust by demonstrating greater responsibility and obedience. As he grows in dependability and self-control, he gains pride in himself and no longer needs to find companions among rebellious classmates.

THE ISOLATE

The social isolate is an individual who is ridiculed by his peers because of his inept methods of approaching others or because of his deviation from accepted standards of dress and appearance. He attracts unfavorable attention because he does not fit in with the group, and he is rejected contemptuously as a poor representative of the youth subculture. He is not belligerently offensive, but he does not possess the composure counted essential by his peers, and they snicker at him and imitate him, disgustedly labelling him "queer," "fruit," "odd-ball," "mental case," or "dip-head." Sometimes they pretend to be interested in him, asking personal questions of him or baiting him with insincere compliments.

Often the isolate is physically ungainly or unattractive. A boy may be tall and thin, or fat, weak, and awkward. A girl may be exceptionally heavy or tall, unusually plain, unkempt in grooming, and unstylish in the clothes she wears.

In addition to obvious physical oddities, the isolate is an atypical representative of his sex. A boy may attempt to demonstrate masculinity by adopting supposed male characteristics, such as talking rudely to teachers or smoking ostentatiously. Or, in a caricature of camaraderie and self-possession, he calls attention to himself by effusively greeting his peers, singing to himself, and urging others to join him in the numerous pursuits or causes which are his current enthusiasms.

A girl may try to appear more self-sufficient than she is by using exaggerated make-up and behaving in a coy and seductive manner with boys or by flaunting school authority. Or she may retreat completely, skittering through the halls with eyes averted, speaking to no one, and responding to a rare greeting with a brief, frightened echo.

The isolate's inability to look and act as a typical member of his own sex is basic to feelings of personal inadequacy and emotional instability,[16] and this is true even though he does not have marked characteristics of the opposite sex. His amorphous sex-role concepts may have originated from confusion in the sex-role of his parents or from exposure to severe criticism and excessive control. These experiences lead to decreased initiative and limited self-confidence or to rejection of the like-sexed parent as a model for his own behavior. Early and prolonged isolation from contact with his peers also causes strained and ineffectual social relationships.

Adolescents believing themselves to be socially undesirable have been described as schizoid and anxious[11] and as sensitive to any occurrence which appears to be threatening or rejecting. The social isolate, because of his seclusiveness and his ready misinterpretation of events, may develop delusional attitudes. To interpret any incident correctly, an individual must be able to shift his perspectives, even under stress, and he cannot do this if he is burdened with excessive needs or anxiety. Delusions which persist may develop into paranoid disorders. The adolescent may become convinced that others are not only against him but are plotting to harm him, and because he does not share his conclusions with others, he fails to evaluate them objectively. As he continues to ruminate about these convictions, they become strengthened and he believes them to be completely valid.[4]

As the young person rationalizes his belief that others desire to harm or eliminate him, his delusions of persecution may lead to delusions of grandeur. He attributes others' ill will to envy of his wisdom and power, and he structures an elaborate system of delusions which establish him as the savior of his country, his race, or his religion. Believing in his power and prominence, he then needs to have his superiority acknowledged and confirmed by others, and he seeks to call their attention to his unusual eminence and special status. The performance of deeds intended to demonstrate his superior position and discredit or destroy his imagined enemies becomes his consuming preoccupation and results in slanderous or murderous attacks on others.

The isolate must be guided from his lonely path and aided in finding a normal place among his peers. A single concerned, cheerful, but critical friend, well accepted by others and well versed in adolescent norms, can encourage and instruct the isolate in more acceptable forms of behavior and appearance. Teachers who publicly praise his work and give him opportunities to perform when he can do so capably set an example of commendation and acceptance which has an effect on his peers.

At home, the isolate of either sex should be given more attention by his father. He needs praise and the assignment of responsibility from this parent, who symbolizes the world outside the home. He can be encouraged to experiment with new activities, unsupervised by his parents. He needs to acquire real skills in at least one area and in several, if possible. His physical appearance and awkwardness can be altered by assisting him with dress, grooming, and weight reduction, if necessary. A dance instructor can train him not only in dancing, a major adolescent activity, but also in the social proprieties and in appropriate approaches to others. He should not return home to a silent household or to one in which everyone is preoccupied with his own activities and problems and has no time to talk. His opportunities to share recreation, experiences, and ideas should be increased both at home and through church and school organizations.

PSYCHOPATHIC PERSONALITY DISORDER

The individual with psychopathic personality disorder is aggressive and impulsive. He is unable to form a satisfying relationship with other people, and he feels no guilt over his misbehavior or his violation of others' trust. He presents no outward appearance of abnormality in his attitudes, conversation, or expression of emotion. He reasons well, demonstrates insight into and remorse for his behavior, and convinces listeners of his sincere intention to reform. He has normal or superior intelligence and is aware of social amenities and the requirements of society's moral code. He appears to condone and support these, and his purported aspirations for achievement and honorable behavior are in complete accord with those held by others. His earnest pronouncements are merely parroted expressions, however, and repeatedly he fails in his assigned responsibilities and is banished from school or from his job; or he engages in antisocial acts which include theft, swindling, forgery, bigamy, public sexual misbehavior, and murder.[5]

Bender[2] described the psychopath's behavior during childhood. As a pre-school child, the psychopath abuses children who approach him, and he displays neither anxiety nor neurotic defense mechanisms in doing so. He is attention seeking, clinging, dependent, seductive, and amiable with adults; but he can stand no separation, disappointment, or demand from them, and he quickly abandons his allegiance at such times. He is hyperkinetic, distractable, and has a short attention span. He is alternately moody and excitable, and he has frequent temper tantrums. As he becomes older, he tends to observe and copy the behavior of other children. He is unable either to remember the past or to profit from previous experiences. Language development is deficient and is observable in adolescent psychopaths as a significant decrement in verbal ability as compared to performance ability.[7]

The psychopath's meaningless mimicry of idealistic concepts and values and his bland untruthfulness suggest that he is continually dramatizing. Unable to maintain relationships of sincerity and trust and feeling no obligation to others, the psychopath follows his avowals of repentance and reform not with expected conformity but with his habitual self-centered, impulsive, and hurtful actions.

The development of psychopathic personality disorder has been attributed to one or more of three sources: early emotional deprivation, resulting in destruction of trust; persistent indulgence of the child's wishes; or organic defect, which produces peculiarities of response inaccessible to ordinary training.

Early neglect of the infant and his isolation, confinement, or limited contact with humans acclimates him to solitude and self-dependence. Denied affection and care, the small child continues to seek it, but he has no faith that he will find it permanently.[2, 3, 14] In the histories of some psychopaths there is evidence of early sadistic treatment from adults, and this severe break in trust of the parent by the child results in his fearing close, dependent relationships.[1, 10] Left to fend for himself, the child learns to wheedle or deceive sympathetic adults and also to help himself to what he needs. As an adolescent, he maintains his social attitudes, in imitation of the indifference and disregard he has experienced, and he continues his habit of acquiring what he wants in any way possible. Literally unable to communicate with others, he makes his way alone.

The indulged child, intimidating his parents and appealing successfully to their sympathy with exaggerations and falsifications, learns early to scorn both honor and others' concern.[14] He is taught by his parents that he can do no wrong. They are quick to defend him when he is abusive or lazy; instead of requiring him to make restitution when he steals or vandalizes, they do it for him; they apologize for him, weep over him, and excuse his self-centered, bullying behavior. Accustomed to deceiving adults with promises and flattery, he continues to use this technique whenever he is apprehended, and he finds satisfaction in shocking or hurting those closest to him.

There are indications that organic damage plays an important role in the behavior of the psychopath. Bender's[2] description of him as a child who is hyperkinetic, beset with language difficulties, and unable to develop a close personal relationship suggests the inconsistencies and perplexities in response of the brain-damaged child. Other investigators[10, 15, 22] have stated that brain damage, either congenital or acquired during the first decade of life from infection or disease, is the reason that the psychopathic child cannot learn from past experience or acquire any measure of self-control. Because his impulsive, undirected behavior so often is purposeless or self-destructive, it seems probable that he is impelled by impulses beyond his control.

Treatment of the adult psychopath has long been considered difficult, if not hopeless, but adolescent psychopaths are being assisted in altering their behavior. A necessary first step is strong and consistent control of behavior by adults, who closely supervise, limit, and direct the adolescent's actions. Because he is supervised, he no longer is permitted to behave in socially disapproved ways or to involve himself in activities which lead to trouble for himself. As his antisocial behavior gradually decreases, anxiety and guilt may replace it, and he then must learn to tolerate and manage these emotions. Treatment of this nature is being conducted in psychiatric hospitals, where the accomplishment of permanent change is anticipated to require a stay of several years.[9, 17, 19]

Hospitalization of the adolescent with psychopathic personality disorder is not always possible. Indeed, his difficulties may never be diagnosed correctly at this age because of his parents' protection. Parents who are dissatisfied with the child's behavior, however, and desire to alter it can achieve some success by revising their own habits of reacting to him. They must supervise him closely, enforce rules strictly, assign and insist on his discharge of responsibilities, and require him to apologize and make restitution for all misbehavior. They will need to question his statements, refrain from his defense, yet still convince him that his welfare is their concern.

Parents who have been neglectful or brutal can sometimes change their ways with encouragement and motivation to do so. If not, institutionalization is preferable to the adolescent's remaining at home. Although he will not develop close relationships in an institution, the psychopath is offered more normal models for mature behavior and held to stricter standards for his own actions, and this serves to teach him consistency of behavior and greater conformity to society's requirements.

The psychopath who is influenced primarily by organic malfunction needs practice in communication, close supervision, an orderly daily regime, and training in the acquisition of skills. He benefits by praise of actions which are desirable and by frequent friendly contacts with others.

REFERENCES

1. Bandura, A., and Walters, R. H.: Dependency conflicts in aggressive adolescents. *J. Soc. Issues*, 1958, *14*, 52–65.
2. Bender, L.: *Aggression, Hostility, and Anxiety in Children*. Springfield, Ill., Charles C Thomas, 1953, pp. 152–157.
3. Bender, L.: Psychopathic personality disorders in childhood and adolescence. *Arch. Crim. Psychodyn.*, 1961, *4*, 412–415.
4. Cameron, N.: *The Psychology of Behavior Disorders*. Boston, Houghton Mifflin Co., 1947, Chapter 14.
5. Cleckley, H. M.: Psychopathic states. *In* Arieti, S., ed.: *American Handbook of Psychiatry*. New York, Basic Books, Inc., 1959, vol. 1, pp. 567–588.
6. Cohen, A. K.: *Delinquent Boys: the Culture of the Gang*. Glencoe, Ill., The Free Press, 1955.
7. Fisher, G. M.: Discrepancy in verbal and performance IQ in adolescent sociopaths. *J. Clin. Psychol.*, 1961, *17*, 60.
8. Garrison, K. C.: *The Psychology of Adolescence*. New York, Prentice-Hall, Inc., 1934, pp. 101, 138, 165.
9. Gordon, S.: A psychotherapeutic approach to adolescents with character disorders. *Amer. J. Orthopsychiat.*, 1960, *30*, 757–766.
10. Guttmacher, M. S.: Diagnosis and etiology of psychopathic personalities as perceived in our time. *In* Hoch, P. H., and Zubin, J.: *Current Problems in Psychiatric Diagnosis*. New York, Grune and Stratton, Inc., 1953, pp. 139–155.
11. Heilburn, A. B., Jr.: Social value: Social behavior inconsistency and early signs of psychopathology in adolescence. *Child Developm.*, 1963, *34*, 187–194.
12. Johnson, A. M.: Juvenile delinquency. *In* Arieti, S., ed.: *American Handbook of Psychiatry*. New York, Basic Books, Inc., 1959, vol. 1, pp. 853.
13. Landis, P. H.: *Adolescence and Youth*. New York, McGraw-Hill Book Co., 1945, pp. 164–179.
14. Levy, D.: Psychopathic behavior in infants and children: a critical survey of the existing concepts. Round Table, 1950. The deprived and the indulged forms of psychopathic personality. *Amer. J. Orthopsychiat.*, 1951, *21*, 250–254.
15. Lurie, L. A.: Psychopathic behavior in infants and children: a critical survey of the existing concepts. Round Table, 1950. Psychopathic behavior of little known or idiopathic origin. *Amer. J. Orthopsychiat.*, 1951, *21*, 224–226.
16. Mussen, P.: Some antecedents and consequents of masculine sex-typing in adolescent boys. *Psychol. Monogr.*, 1961, *75*, (506).
17. Noshpitz, J. D.: Opening phase in the psychotherapy of adolescents with character disorders. *Bull. Menninger Clin.*, 1957, *21*, 153–164.
18. Nyman, G. E., and Smith, G. J. W.: A contribution to the definition of psychopathic personality. *Lunds U. Arsskr.*, *Avd. 2*, 1959, 55 (10).
19. Rapaport, D.: Treatment of psychopathic delinquents. *J. Soc. Ther.*, 1956, *2*, 166–170.
20. Scharr, J. H.: Violence in juvenile gangs: Some notes and a few analogies. *Amer. J. Orthopsychiat.*, 1963, *33*, 29–37.
21. Seidman, J. M.: Psychological roots of moral development in adolescence. *The Catholic Psychological Record*, 1963, *1*, 19–27.
22. Teagarden, F. M.: *Child Psychology for Professional Workers*. New York, Prentice-Hall, Inc., 1940, pp. 473, 487.
23. Thrasher, F. M.: The gang as a symptom of community disorganization. *J. Correct. Wk.*, 1957, *4*, 54–56.
24. Wolman, B.: Spontaneous groups of children and adolescents in Israel. *J. Soc. Psychol.*, 1951, *34*, 171–182.

Chapter **40**

School Problems

The adolescent's strong desire to achieve is inextricably bound to his school performance, which can provide him with evidence of superiority that gives substance to his confidence.[3, 40] Parental clamor for excellent school standing increases as adults worry about their child's imminent entry into competitive job-seeking and hope for him a higher status than they achieved.[18] They no longer blame teachers and school for a child's educational difficulty: They scold the adolescent for laziness and purposelessness, finding his effort incongruous with his demands for adult privileges.

Scholastic excellence is far from universal among high school students, however, and those who do not attain it minimize its importance, criticize their school and teachers, and find excuses for their failures. In a study of 8000 high school students' attitudes toward school, Coleman[8] found a nonchalant or negative attitude; and Scarborough[36] reported that 50 per cent of the students he questioned were dissatisfied with their teachers and believed their school programs inadequate for their needs, whether or not they planned to attend college. Boys' earlier casual work habits shadow them into high school, and despite their equal standing with girls on achievement and intelligence tests, their grades are lower, and the percentage of girls in the top decile of graduating classes is more than twice that of boys.[29]

Although some of a student's disparagement of the school can be attributed to his own lack of diligence, there is also justified criticism of the school's failure to meet the needs of its older students. School boards, composed of well-educated citizens, think in terms of standards for the college-bound and have little or no awareness of the needs of a large segment of high school students. Although 40 per cent of all high school graduates continue their education, this still leaves over half of the members of every graduating class who must find employment at the termination of high school.

When the school fails to offer useful education to these pupils, it shares responsibility with the home for early dropping out and increased delinquency, and its unsuitable program expands the daily problems of discipline and competitive grading.[7, 39, 41] Inflexible teaching methods and an inadequate understanding of the reasons for pupil failure have also been cited by school personnel for the wasted days of high school.[28] Emphasizing that discipline, school work, and status are interrelated, Allen[1] suggested that school for adolescents should be as little like elementary school as possible and should enable students to earn the rewards of learning in areas which are personally important to them.

Brown[5] proposed that junior and senior high school instruction be given in three-grade units to permit division of the students according to their individual capabilities in each subject, with five levels of instruction available: (1) remedial work; (2) practice with basic skills; (3) studies intended for the student of average ability; (4) instruction in depth; and (5) individual exploration of a field by a student who wishes to exceed the informational boundaries of a single course.

To permit greater individual initiative and participation in learning, as well as to utilize facilities more adequately, he suggested that students spend 10 per cent of their time in class units of 100 or more for lectures, demonstrations, and testing. Students would spend 45 per cent of their time in small discussion groups, consisting of five to 15 members, for the purpose of examining information and problems associated with the course and concurrently improving their communication skills and personal relationships. They would spend the remaining 45 per cent of their time in individual study, with traditional group seating in libraries abandoned in favor of individual study carrels. An approach of this kind ensures individualization of the student's work, instruction at a level appropriate to his interest and current ability, and freedom to broaden learning to any degree he himself desires.

School problems encountered during adolescence are similar to those of the elementary years, but they are more serious in their confirmation of personal maladjustment or their cementing of attitudes of defeat and failure. Reading disability, underachievement and failure, discipline problems, school phobia, and truancy and dropping out of school all appear during the junior and senior high school years.

READING DISABILITY

The adolescent who enters junior high school reading at a third grade level is ashamed of himself and is totally incapable of succeeding with seventh grade work. Inaccurately diagnosed and insufficiently aided as an elementary school child, he has long believed that he is stupid and that he cannot learn to read. He tries to hide his inadequacy by distracting trouble-making, refusal to participate in academic activities, and aggressive behavior both in and out of school. Ten times as many boys as girls are deficient in reading ability,[33] and their failure results from one or several physical or emotional causes.*

Remedial reading classes for adolescents should be conducted daily and should occupy the major share of school time until the pupil is able to read well enough to manage the reading required to learn other subjects. Classes should be small and should consist of students with similar ability. Individual instruction is necessary, and diversification of assignments and the use of reading material consistent with adolescent interests is helpful in motivating effort.[6] Training of adolescents with organic defects is slow, and a final achievement of only fourth or fifth grade reading ability is frequently all that can be predicted. This level, however, is considered adequate for many adult occupations and reading needs.

UNDERACHIEVEMENT AND FAILURE

The underachieving or failing adolescent with average or superior intelligence may be continuing a pattern he has followed ever since he started school, or his failures may appear for the first time after he enters junior high school.

Habitual underachievement is characteristic of children of all ages who do not master basic language skills. Without these, the adolescent cannot do well in junior and senior high school where his learning depends on his ability to read well, to organize ideas and express them in writing, and to reason with both concrete facts and abstract concepts.[12]

Poor performance in the advanced grades can result from a child's never having disciplined himself to devote the time and effort required to master schoolwork, now steadily increasing in quantity and complexity.† Impulsiveness and lack of goal-orientation characterizes underachievers with superior intelligence and contrasts with the persistence and ability of superior students to make long-range plans.[11] Limited interests and inadequate self-discipline are indicated by the finding that excessive television watching, which is more common in boys than in girls and which averages 28 hours weekly for high school students, is associated with slightly lower grades.[46]

---

* See Chapter 31, "School Problems," pp. 258–260.
† See Case 35, Lester M., p. 523.

School failure which appears for the first time during early adolescence indicates the presence of stress and unresolved emotional conflict.[12] Some adolescents deliberately refuse to study to spite their parents,[13] and on hostility tests intelligent male underachievers were found to score significantly higher than successful students.[38] Other comparison studies have described the intelligent underachiever as rigid and tactless,[2] anxious,[31] passive, feminine, and antagonistic toward his father.[25]

As the child reaches adolescence, he becomes fully aware of his own insufficiencies and he also is critical of the inconsistencies in his parents' lives. Discouraged and lonely, he rejects parental counsel and direction, and he ceases trying to achieve, concluding that standards are meaningless and effort unrewarding.

The underachieving or failing adolescent needs assistance from both school and home. At school, necessary remedial instruction should be available, and the student's program should be tailored to fit his interests and current abilities.[20] A teacher of underachievers needs to be aware of both their academic deficiencies and their feelings of insufficiency and irresponsibility and must treat them with respect and firmness. Assignments should be completed at school to enable the student to receive the special help he needs and to establish consistent work habits. Time and privacy for individual study should be provided, and levels of achievement should be established as interim goals for the student to attain.

Parents need to teach the indifferent adolescent to respond to adult direction and to meet home requirements satisfactorily, with the father assuming the major role in control and companionship for the adolescent. Parents whose behavior is immature, immoral, or threatening to the adolescent's security must revise their actions before he will be able to divert his attention from antagonism and worry to study.

DISCIPLINE PROBLEMS

Discipline problems appear more reprehensible in the adolescent than in the elementary school child because at his age he is expected to inhibit aggressive actions. Nonconforming, belligerent behavior in the adolescent is a signal that prompt and continuous joint action by school and parents is needed.

Phillips, Wiener, and Haring[32] attributed discipline problems in the younger adolescent to the rapid changes in social status, sexual awareness, class structure, and independence experienced simultaneously by the beginning junior high school student. These substitutions in his way of life suggest that he is more mature, and he attempts to live up to the implications of this advancement by divesting himself of the younger child's conforming nature. In asserting himself, however, he often clashes with adult authority.

Zeitlin[48] reported that 41 per cent of the students in seven high schools were cited during one year for disciplinary problems, most of which consisted of behavior disruptive to orderly classroom procedure. Teachers have indicated that problem behavior among girls reaches a peak in junior high school, and among boys in senior high school.[16] Junior high school girls suddenly become aware of distinctions in social status, and their standing is of critical concern to them; high school boys who are failing in their studies become worried about the future, and the disturbance of both is expressed in rebellion at school. Girls dissatisfied with school admit that they feel personally inadequate, but boys do not subject themselves to this self-analysis and blame their unhappiness on school authorities.[22] The adolescent who consistently defies school rules, disturbs classroom activities, and is insolent with teachers has little self-respect. Lonely and unsure of himself both at school and at home, he tries to achieve status and defend his integrity in any way he can.

Tempting as it is for school authorities to wash their hands of the refractory adolescent, this is a poor answer for the problems with which he clearly is struggling. Traditional penalties for recalcitrant students— detention after school, paddling, and suspension—seldom have any effect on the habitual offender. Students themselves suggest as more suitable punishment the cleaning up of school grounds or doing other kinds of work under the direction of custodians or teachers. School boards should be concerned with the vital need for special facilities and for more teachers to reclaim the potentially useless or dangerous young people over whom supervision will be possible for only a few more years.

Miller[26] stated that the school could make a major contribution to the lessening of behavior problems by revising its curricula and classification procedures. He recommended a smaller pupil-teacher ratio and special groupings for nonadjusting adolescents; supervised work-and-school programs for slow learners unable to profit from a full-time, regular academic schedule; and experimental schools combining working, learning, and outdoor experience for adolescents presenting serious behavior problems in the usual school setting. Vocational courses offering direct training in a marketable skill give the frustrated adolescent a new sense of his own worth and lessen his apprehension about his future. All of these revisions afford personal attention to the individual and relief from steady academic pressure, as well as providing him with the high status and broadened confidence which result from work and accomplishment.

Adequate discipline and order at home, combined with parental acknowledgement of the adolescent's achievements and recognition of his rights, increase his self-control.[32] As the young person is held to more responsibility, he begins to feel more competent and less childish, and his need to assert himself in public in inappropriate, aggressive ways decreases.

SCHOOL PHOBIA

School phobia in the adolescent causes parents to feel helpless, and school officials become disgusted with both child and parents. The adolescent is too large to carry bodily into a classroom, and his adamant refusals and copious tears imply a depth of fear which is incongruous and incomprehensible.

The adolescent afraid of school is a child who has remained infantile and dependent, and he avoids unpleasantries because he has no skill at coping with them.[10] He tends to be demanding and self-righteous, pouting when he cannot have his own way and accusing others of selfishness when they disappoint him. He is negativistic, and he seeks attention by annoying and intruding on others. These characteristics are displayed predominantly at home, however. When his parents are not with him, he is shy, aloof, fearful, and uncommunicative. He refuses to associate with his peers, and he is ready game for their teasing because he will not defend himself.

His unhappy personal traits are caused most often by a mutually demanding and controlling relationship with his mother, who dramatizes her own problems and who tries to move the child by emotional punishment and pleas. She habitually permits his wishes to dominate her, however, after her frantic attempts to control his responses prove unsuccessful. She convinces him that he is helpless by interceding for him in every difficult situation; she teaches him that he is better than others by insisting on special treatment for him; she preaches that other people are selfish and inept, and she prevents him from establishing friendships. She resents the trouble he causes her, just as he resents her smothering dominance, but he enjoys the protection and admiration she gives him, and neither can relinquish the emotional dependence to which he is accustomed.

The adolescent's refusal to go to school can often be traced to one or a series of precipitating incidents. If he is treated roughly by classmates or has suffered disappointment or embarrassment at school, the limit of his endurance is reached so quickly that he cannot face a return to the difficulties of school. He prefers to remain at home, where he can enjoy himself and do as he likes.[17]*

---

* See Case 36, Steven G., p. 524.

Slow progress is reported by most clinicians who work with the adolescent afraid to attend school. His self-confidence and adaptability are grossly deficient in meeting the challenges of peers who continually practice their independence, and he feels totally overwhelmed.

As is true with the younger child, it is important not to delay the adolescent's return to school. He should attend, but he may sit in the principal's or counselor's office if he chooses, completing his school assignments during the regular hours. He should return to classes gradually, perhaps to only one at a time, and he should decide the order of return himself. He is in real need of a compatible friend, and a classmate with whom he can talk between classes and at lunchtime can make the difference between his acceptance or refusal of school attendance.

His fear of being separated from his mother reflects his own belief that he cannot get along alone and shows his concern that his mother will be able to get along without him. The push-and-pull of their relationship can be altered if the father assumes control of the adolescent, providing him with favorable attention, interest in his achievements, and instruction in specific skills. The mother must learn to withhold suggestions, sympathy, indignation at others, and criticism of the adolescent's solutions to his problems.

TRUANCY AND DROPPING OUT OF SCHOOL

Truancy in junior and senior high school presages eventual dropping out of school. The truant is expressing his dissatisfaction with the school, and as he attends less, his interest in and involvement with school decrease. As soon as he is legally able to do so or as soon as he can succeed in having himself expelled, he ceases attending altogether. Most drop-outs leave school during the tenth grade.

No state has been able to hold more than 75 per cent of its eligible students in high school until graduation day,[19] and it has been estimated that nearly 20 per cent of the 26 million youth who will enter the labor force between 1960 and 1970 will have failed to complete high school, with an additional 9 per cent having completed only elementary school. Although employment needs for unskilled workers will remain about the same during this time, there will be a 20 per cent drop in the demand for farm workers, a source of employment heavily used by uneducated youth. Automation, mechanization, and scientific developments demand greater maturity, knowledge, and judgment in workers than formerly was needed. Graduation from high school increases a young man's income by an average of $2000 annually.[45]

The adolescent who truants and eventually drops out of school usually is continuing a pattern of absenting himself from school which was established years earlier.[27] If he has missed school frequently, he is at a disadvantage academically and truants to escape comparison, finally giving up completely.[34] A drop-out rate of 14.5 per cent has been noted among good readers, but it rises to 50 per cent among poor readers.[30] Frequent school transfers, entailing different curricula and standards, also contribute to the student's problem of keeping up with classwork.[9]

Parental attitude about the importance of school is a major influence on the child's school attendance.[4] Lower income families maintain poor liaison between home and school, and parents fail to communicate with the school when their children are absent for illness or when the family is moving.[37] Parents of middle and higher income status minimize the need for school attendance when they are overly ready to permit the child to miss school when he wishes to do so. Rural children have been influenced to remain in school by parent-fostered goals directed toward leadership positions and professional work and a general family attitude of attention to the children and to study.[44]

Overcrowded, noisy homes may be a factor in a young person's dropping out of school.[35] He cannot escape from unpleasant home conditions as long as he remains in school and cannot earn his own livelihood.

Inadequate intelligence is a principal cause for leaving school.[9] Although many school systems provide special classrooms for slow learners during the elementary years, only a few recognize the need for continued special training for the dull or retarded adolescent. Frequently these children are placed in regular high schools and given token classwork in physical education, home economics, music, and shop. They attend school with children of normal intelligence, keeping occupied for at least part of the day but failing to receive the training they must have in order to support themselves and suffering from being ignored or ridiculed by the other students.

Some adolescents leave school against the wishes of their parents and contrary to the educational emphases in their rearing, and personal discontent and emotional disturbance are motivating factors. Cook[9] found that on the Bell Adjustment Inventory high school drop-outs scored high on personal maladjustment, and drop-outs have been described as deficient both in social aggressiveness and in the need to achieve.[35] Sometimes an adolescent is in serious conflict with a parent or is preoccupied with a real or exaggerated defect in himself which keeps him tense and distractable, and his resulting inability to learn convinces him that school is disagreeable and a waste of time. In retaliation for real or imagined grievances at home, the adolescent may leave school as an assertion of independence or in order to disconcert and anger parents whose social position demands his continuance. The young person who has never learned to work finds school irksome and embarrassing, and if he is accustomed to doing as he chooses, leaving school is a logical outcome of well-established attitudes and habits of self-indulgence.

Prevention of truancy and dropping out of school should begin years before the day the adolescent announces that he is quitting.[15] Children with limited capacity to learn or those achieving inadequately should be identified and aided promptly.[45] Those with a pattern of poor attendance should be singled out and contacts between home and school should be strengthened.

The greatest attraction of the high school for many potential dropouts is its extracurricular activities,[30, 47] and there is merit in suggestions that these be diversified and available to all students. The real need for education and training of adolescents is not met, however, when the primary goal is merely to keep them attending and they do so only because school is pleasant and exciting.

More realistic and productive are schools which conduct extensive programs of vocational information and evaluation for all students and which offer a wide variety of course work, including vocational training.[43, 45] Combined work and school programs are of value for restless adolescents who seek early independence and financial gain. Part-time work supplies young people with a sample of the life they believe they so strongly desire and provides a comparison which may result in their setting higher goals. Combined programs also help the dull or retarded adolescent, who profits more from his work experience than from academic study and who can find better employment later because of his work record. Such programs offer a compromise between total school attendance or none at all. When the adolescent chooses to drop out, his resultant failure to find employment and his inevitable disappointment with himself and his future prospects can lead to delinquencies or idleness which permanently curtail any potential contribution.

Adolescents dropping out because of personality or emotional difficulties are also assisted by combined programs. These adolescents acquire a feeling of importance as they work with adults and earn a pay check, and they have less time for brooding and anger. Inevitably, they rank for themselves the relative values of unskilled work and of continuing their education in order to assure wider employment opportunity for themselves.

REFERENCES

1. Allen, E. A.: Attitudes of children and adolescents in school. *Educ. Res.*, 1960, 3, 65–80.
2. Angelino, H., and Hall, R. L.: Temperament factors in high- and low-achieving high school seniors. *Psychol. Rep.*, 1960, 7, 518.

3. Bernard, H. W.: *Adolescent Development in American Culture.* Yonkers-on-Hudson, N. Y., The World Book Co., 1957, pp. 72–78.
4. Brooks, E. E., Buri, J., Byrne, E. A., and Hudson, M. C.: Socioeconomic factors, parental attitudes and school attendance. *Soc. Wk.,* 1962, 7, 103–108.
5. Brown, B. F.: *The Nongraded High School.* Englewood Cliffs, N. J., Prentice-Hall, Inc., 1963, pp. 70–72, 104–106, 136–137.
6. Bullock, H.: *Helping the Non-reading Pupil in the Secondary School.* New York, Teachers College, Columbia University, 1956.
7. Byrne, R. H.: Beware the stay-in-school band-wagon! *Personnel Guid. J.,* 1958, 36, 493–496.
8. Coleman, J. S.: Academic achievement and the structure of competition. *Harv. Educ. Rev.,* 1959, 29, 330–351.
9. Cook, E. S., Jr.: An analysis of factors related to withdrawal from high school prior to graduation. *J. Educ. Res.,* 1956, 50, 191–196.
10. Coolidge, J. C., Willer, M. L., Tessman, E., and Waldfogel, S.: School phobia in adolescence: A manifestation of severe character disturbance. *Amer. J. Orthopsychiat.,* 1960, 30, 599–607.
11. Davids, A., and Sidman, J.: A pilot study: Impulsivity, time orientation, and delayed gratification in future scientists and in underachieving high school students. *Except. Children,* 1962, 29, 170–174.
12. DeHirsch, K.: Two categories of learning difficulties in adolescents. *Amer. J. Orthopsychiat.,* 1963, 33, 87–91.
13. D'Evelyn, K. E.: *Meeting Children's Emotional Needs.* Englewood Cliffs, N. J., Prentice-Hall, Inc., 1957, pp. 94–95.
14. Dimock, H. S.: *Rediscovering the Adolescent.* New York, Association Press, 1937, p. 137.
15. Dresher, R. H.: Factors in voluntary drop-outs. *Personnel Guid. J.,* 1954, 32, 287–289.
16. Eaton, M. T., D'Amico, L. A., and Phillips, B. N.: Problem behavior in school. *J. Educ. Psychol.,* 1956, 47, 350–357.
17. Eisenberg, L.: School phobia: A study in the communication of anxiety. *Amer. J. Psychiatr.,* 1958, 114, 712–718.
18. Gardner, G. E.: Psychiatric problems of adolescence. *In* Arieti, S., ed.: *American Handbook of Psychiatry.* New York, Basic Books, Inc., 1959, vol. 1, p. 884.
19. Gaumnitz, W. H., and Tompkins, E. E.: *Holding Power and Size of High School.* Circular No. 322, Washington, D. C., U.S. Office of Education, 1950.
20. Goldberg, M. L., and associates: A three-year experimental program at DeWitt Clinton High School to help bright underachievers. *In* Trapp, E. P., and Himelstein, P., eds.: *Readings on the Exceptional Child.* New York, Appleton-Century-Crofts, 1962, p. 317.
21. Horrocks, J. E.: *The Psychology of Adolescence,* Ed. 2. Boston, Houghton Mifflin Co., 1962, p. 298.
22. Jackson, P. W., and Getzels, J. W.: Psychological health and classroom functioning: A study of dissatisfaction with school among adolescents. *J. Educ. Psychol.,* 1959, 50, 295–300.
23. Kagan, J., and Moss, H. A.: *Birth to Maturity.* New York, John Wiley and Sons, 1962, p. 123.
24. Kanner, L.: *Child Psychiatry,* Ed. 3. Springfield, Ill., Charles C Thomas, 1957, pp. 568–574.
25. Kimball, B.: Case studies in educational failure during adolescence. *Amer. J. Orthopsychiat.,* 1953, 23, 406–415.
26. Miller, L. M.: Schools—our nation's first line of defense against juvenile delinquency. *Sch. Life,* 1954, 37, 21–22.
27. Mullin, M. M.: Personal and situational factors associated with perfect attendance. *Personnel Guid. J.,* 1955, 33, 438–443.
28. Nolan, E. G.: *School Factors Related to Delinquency.* Los Angeles, Office of the County Superintendent of Schools, Division of Research and Guidance, 1951.
29. Northby, A. A.: Sex differences in high school scholarship. *Sch. Soc.,* 1958, 86, 63–64.

30. Penty, R. C.: *Reading Ability and High School Drop-outs*. New York, Teachers College, Columbia University, 1956.
31. Phillips, B. N.: Sex, social class, and anxiety as sources of variation in school achievement. *J. Educ. Psychol.*, 1962, *53*, 316–322.
32. Phillips, E. L., Wiener, D. N., and Haring, N. G.: *Discipline, Achievement, and Mental Health*. Englewood Cliffs, N. J., Prentice-Hall, Inc., 1960, pp. 156–161.
33. Rabinovitch, R. D.: Reading and learning disabilities. *In* Arieti, S., ed.: *American Handbook of Psychiatry*. New York, Basic Books, Inc., 1959, vol. 1, pp. 864–867.
34. Roberts, J. L.: Factors associated with truancy. *Personnel Guid. J.*, 1956, *34*, 431–436.
35. Rousselet, J.: Quelques aspects des ambitions sociales des adolescents (Some aspects of the social ambitions of adolescents). *Enfance*, 1962, (3) 291–301.
36. Scarborough, B. B.: Parents for an hour. *Purdue Univ. Stud. Higher Educ.*, 1953, (80) 55–60.
37. Sexton, P. C.: Social class and pupil turnover rates. *J. Educ. Sociol.*, 1959, *33*, 131–134.
38. Shaw, M. C., and Grubb, J.: Hostility and able high school underachievers. *J. Counsel. Psychol.*, 1958, *5*, 263–266.
39. Smith, P. M.: The schools and juvenile delinquency. *Sociol. Soc. Res.*, 1952, *37*, 85–91.
40. Staton, T. F.: *Dynamics of Adolescent Adjustment*. New York, The Macmillan Co., 1963, p. 81.
41. Strang, R.: *An Introduction to Child Study*. New York, The Macmillan Co., 1938, p. 597.
42. The Initial Teaching Alphabet. *Time*, 1964, *83*(4), 52.
43. Wetzel, P. W.: What are we doing for school drop-outs? *Amer. Sch. Bd. J.*, 1955, *131*, 29–31.
44. Wilson, P. B., and Buck, R. C.: The educational ladder. *Rural Social.*, 1960, *25*, 404–413.
45. Wirtz, W. W.: *The Challenge of Jobless Youth*. Washington, D. C., President's Committee on Youth Employment, 1963.
46. Witty, P.: Television and the high school student. *In* Seidman, J. M., ed.: *The Adolescent*. New York, The Dryden Press, 1953, pp. 231–234.
47. Youmans, E. G.: Factors in educational attainment. *Rural Sociol.*, 1959, *24*, 21–28.
48. Zeitlin, H.: Phoenix reports on high school misbehavior. *Personnel Guid. J.*, 1957, *35*, 384–387.

Chapter 41

Sex Problems
and Deviations

Sex to the adolescent is a stimulus, a curiosity, a challenge, and a weapon. His own changing body, with the appearance of pubic hair, genital growth, seminal emissions for the boy, and breast development and mentstruation for the girl, inexorably directs attention toward the assumption of a mature sex role. Sex glands produce new sensations and impulses. His friends talk continually about their conquests or aspirations for conquest of members of the opposite sex, and he sees hand-holding, kissing, and caressing all around him. His parents elevate him to a new status by permitting him to listen to their conversations about adult indiscretions, their veiled references to sexual attractiveness, their off-color jokes, and their use of common terms for sex functions; and they urge him toward acquisition of a girl or boy friend of his own.

Despite this excessive stimulation toward sex activity, the adolescent is restrained from uninhibited indulgence because of guilt feelings implanted by earlier taboos surrounding sex interest and behavior. The American adolescent is confronted by a peculiar divergence of social reactions to sex: He is encouraged to early and promiscuous sex activity by the overattention to sex of both peers and adults, but he reaps censure and ostracism if his behavior leads to venereal infection or pregnancy, and the standards of society condemn broad premarital sex participation. In a comparative study, Christensen and Carpenter[9] reported that permissiveness for premarital coitus is greater in Denmark

366

than in the United States, but the incidence of sexual activity is less in that country.

The adolescent who does engage in premarital sex activities not only is concerned by his violation of conscience but also is anxious about his ability to perform sexually, and the contingencies of pregnancy and infection worry him. The actual occurrence of such disasters precipitates desperate measures, and unwanted pregnancy in an adolescent girl has led to suicide or murder. Because sexual behavior normally involves another person, other emotional elements are introduced in addition to fear and guilt. The sex act itself is observed, evaluated, and shared by another; and the degree to which it enhances or deflates self-esteem differs for the partners. Girls find it almost impossible not to become involved emotionally with a sex partner, and subsequent contacts of any kind are disturbing.

Abnormal sexual activity occurs in an adolescent whose rearing has included severe punishment, failure to identify with the like-sexed parent, or unusual encouragement toward sexual expression.[44]

Brutal, unwarranted, unpredictable punishment can impel an adolescent to use sexual activity to hurt others and to achieve feelings of power. Hartogs[29] studied the early life of sex-delinquents and sex-criminals, most of whom were seriously disturbed males. Of these sex offenders, 92 per cent had been frequently or severely beaten between the ages of two and 17 years by one or both parents. They had been whipped with razor straps, electric cords, broom sticks, and iron bars, sometimes while tied to a bed. Food, liberty, money, and friends were concurrently withdrawn as punishment. Some children were completely undressed before being beaten; some were kicked or knocked unconscious. Most of these individuals accepted the beatings as deserved.

Extreme censure or punishment associated with a child's normal heterosexual interests or urges results in their repression and the substitution of deviate behavior. When the like-sexed parent is absent or abusive or when the opposite-sexed parent teaches the child to regard the like-sexed parent as inferior, normal sexual identity is not acquired and the child imitates the opposite-sexed parent in attitudes and behavior.

Some parents, by the example of their own promiscuity or by refusing the child privacy and giving inordinate attention to his body, focus his attention on sex. The child understands sex activity to be both interesting and pleasing to his parent, and in his tentative sex explorations he is attempting to imitate and to satisfy the adult.[21]

Public and judicial disapproval of the sex offender is harsher than for other law violators, but ordinarily he is neither vicious nor aggressive. He tends to be inoffensive and immature[49] and to be limited in judgment and self-control by emotional disturbance and below average intelligence.[14] Sex offenders are considered treatable by some investigators,[10] and Bromberg,[8] in discussing the rehabilitation of hospitalized deviates, emphasized the need to retrain the offender in his relationship and obligation to society, rather than to attempt the "disposition of instinctive forces within the ego of the individual patient." Ellis et al.,[15] however, stated that sex offenders tend to be recidivists, to be severely disturbed emotionally, and to offer a poor prognosis. Prognosis is more favorable for younger sex offenders who are without emotional disorder.

Sexual problems encountered among adolescents are masturbation, pornographic interest, and premarital pregnancy and early marriage. Deviate behavior includes promiscuity and sexual aggressiveness, incest, prostitution, homosexuality, fetishism, exhibitionism, and rape.

MASTURBATION

Masturbation is universal among adolescent boys, and its occurrence must be considered normal.[36] It is much less common among girls. Kinsey[38, 39] reported that 99 per cent of the adolescent boys he questioned achieved orgasm by masturbation, and 25 per cent of the girls did so.

Even though advances have been made in educating adults to the knowledge that neither insanity nor criminality is caused by masturbation, there are still many parents who vigorously campaign to frighten the masturbating adolescent with dire predictions of the results of his action. Many boys are anxious about the effects of masturbation and are afraid that others can tell that they indulge in it.[57, 58] When a boy's knowledge of his sexual anatomy is incomplete, he may be concerned about injuring himself physically.

Preoccupation with and overindulgence in masturbation carries with it a propensity for solitude and fantasy. Fantasy which accompanies masturbation represents the wish-fulfillment of the individual, and it varies from imagining a specific heterosexual partner to envisioning an animal partner or attachment to a fetish.[43] When indulgence in masturbation and its accompanying fantasy is excessive, attention to sex permeates the adolescent's life, with resultant avoidance and rejection of personal relationships[36] and isolation which is stunting to normal adolescent development.

Adequate sex instruction on physical changes and the function of glands and sex organs ought to be given the masturbating adolescent as reassurance that he cannot harm himself. He is entitled to know that his experimentation is normal, rather than perverted. Aware of these facts, however, he then should be encouraged to control his desire to overindulge in masturbation. Parents can assist him in keeping occupied with work, study, projects of his own, and recreation with friends.

PORNOGRAPHIC INTEREST

The ready availability of pornographic materials is the subject of annual clean-up campaigns by parent-teacher associations and church groups, but regardless of these efforts, few adolescent boys do not see pornographic literature or pictures. They exchange pornographic materials as they once exchanged comic books. To the majority of boys, joint perusal of pornography is merely another way to impress others and to appear sophisticated. A boy may become so fascinated with lewd pictures and descriptions, however, that vicarious erotic experiences replace normal interests and activities. If he is unable to divert his attention from engrossment with sex, ill-advised sexual experimentation may be precipitated.

Adequate sex information and reassurance concerning the naturalness of his interest can be offered to the boy by his father, along with suggestions that other interests are more desirable. A father can introduce his son to new, more mature activities which provide self-satisfaction and shared companionship.

PREMARITAL PREGNANCY AND EARLY MARRIAGE

With greater indulgence by adolescents in premarital sexual relationships, pregnancy prior to marriage is increasing. Fleck *et al.*[18] studied 100 unwed pregnant girls and found them to be immature and rebellious, in part because of their rejection by family, peers, friends, and society. Premarital pregnancy sometimes occurs in reaction to the loss of a loved one through separation or death,[31] and at such times a dependent relation with a man is sought. Some girls desire pregnancy in order to make secure a threatened relationship with a boy friend.[42]

Early marriage is not always associated with premarital pregnancy, but it often is. In a study of brides under 21 years of age, it was found that 43 per cent gave birth to their first child in less than eight months after marriage. Girls marrying at early ages are more unstable emotionally than those marrying later and also have poorer relationships with their parents.[50] Inadequate emotional adjustment has also been noted in boys who marry early.[48] There appears to be no connection between socioeconomic status and early marriage.[50]

Early and steady dating leads to early marriage. Constant companionship with one member of the opposite sex ceases to be exciting unless the relationship progressively becomes more intimate. As intimacy increases and the adolescents' families accept them as a couple, their speech and behavior become less guarded, and unanticipated sexual intercourse results.[55]

A family pattern of premarital pregnancy and early marriage funnels the adolescent's attention to early sex activity as being appropriate and approved behavior, as well as offering a reasonable means of attaining early independence.

Premarital sexual relations between steady daters of the middle or upper economic class often are based on mutual affection—or at least take place with no desire to harm or exploit the partner. A girl accedes to her boy friend's advances because she does not wish to offend him, she wants to please, and she has allowed herself to become sexually aroused by his caresses. A lower-class boy, however, uses sexual conquest as evidence of mastery over girls and prestige among peers. He makes a distinction between the girls who participate in his promiscuous adventures and the girl he intends to marry, insisting that he would not engage in premarital intercourse with her nor would he marry a girl with premarital sexual experience.[2]

As Landis[40] emphasized, the risk of premarital sex is the risk to a future marriage relationship. Adolescents forced into marriage because of a pregnancy feel trapped and unwillingly bound, and they make little effort to enjoy their marriage and each other. Because each knows the other to have been willing to engage in extramarital relations, neither fully trusts the other not to do so again. The unwanted child is often the focus for divisive marital battles.

Adolescents with broad sexual experience prior to marriage find it difficult to alter habitual attitudes associated with coitus. A boy accustomed to using girls for his own sexual pleasure cannot show the patience and tenderness needed in a marital relationship, and he may be dissatisfied with monogamy. A girl who has been sexually promiscuous may have felt such revulsion or guilt over her experiences that she cannot welcome sexual relations with her husband. She, too, may reach the point where she seeks extensive extramarital contacts to heighten sex feeling which has proved inadequate in marriage.

Later ages for beginning dating and parental encouragement to broaden heterosexual contacts are needed to prevent premature, intimate relationships. Thorough sex instruction should be given, including a discussion of the impetus which petting gives to completion of the sex act. Group discussion among adolescents, led by knowledgeable and respected adults, aids a wavering young person by convincing him that his standards of chastity are not unique.

If premarital pregnancy occurs, there should be a careful weighing of all the economic and personal factors involved in marriage of the couple. The decision to marry or not to do so should not be based on either social pressure or moral obligation.

PROMISCUITY AND SEXUAL AGGRESSIVENESS

Approximately 12,500 boys and girls under 18 years of age were arrested in 1965 for sexual offenses other than forcible rape and prostitution. Almost two thirds of these were boys. However, this proportion reflects the greater incidence of male arrests for all crimes, because of the cases reaching juvenile court, 9 per cent of all girls were charged with sexual offenses, compared to only 2 per cent of all boys.[33, 34]

Stockwell[56] reported that 85 per cent of the 12- to 18-year-old residents of a girls' industrial school had had sexual experience prior to commitment. Kinsey et al.[38, 39] stated that from 66 to 98 per cent of all males have premarital intercourse, with the greater incidence occurring among the less educated, and that 26 per cent of all females under 20 years have premarital intercourse. Venereal disease is spreading rapidly and is a major medical problem among older adolescents, with one state reporting that one of every 50 adolescents was infected in a single year.

Many sexual delinquents come from homes in which the promiscuity, drinking, and law violations of the parents set an example which inevitably is imitated by the child.[36] Some young girls without this precedent succumb readily to the urging of their companions because of their desire to do something daring. Many sexually promiscuous adolescent girls feel inferior intellectually, socially, or in physical attractiveness, and sexual relationships help them to feel that they are valued and desirable. A conviction that others consider them bad and worthless has spurred some girls into sexual promiscuity. They act on the premise that if they are held in disrepute, they are entitled to the excitement associated with it. Confusing sexual intercourse with love and affection is a common reason for an adolescent girl to begin promiscuous relations, which substitute for missing parental love. In a similar attempt to recreate lost parental love and demonstrate filial loyalty, an unhappy adopted girl identifies with her natural mother by engaging in sexual misconduct after she becomes aware of the fact that she is illegitimate. Sexual involvement with strangers or with several men or boys successively can be deliberate actions of a girl angry with her parents and attempting to worry and provoke them.*

Although girls desiring sexual contacts entice boys, it is the male who is expected to be the aggressor, and a boy may attempt to prove his manliness to himself by seductive advances which he does not wish to have accepted. He attempts sexual approaches only in situations

---

* See Case 37, Belle Y., p. 525.

where he is certain he will be refused, and his behavior is akin to the abortive approach of the exhibitionist.

The adolescent who uses sexual experiences to prove himself or to antagonize his parents involves himself in intimate relationships which are not based on affection and lasting concern, and in doing so he increases his anxiety and rootlessness. Attempts should be made to help him understand that he jeopardizes his own emotional well-being when he adopts this method of reacting to his problems, and he should be assisted in finding other ways of adaptation.

Different modes of interaction between parent and child should be tried, but if these cannot be maintained, the promiscuous adolescent will do better with a complete change of environment. Sometimes this will be an institutional setting where he can have supervision and useful guidance. Older adolescents may need to live and work alone, and even though they occasionally will make unwise decisions and revert to earlier ways, the constant pressure to do so because of disturbed home relationships is gone.

INCEST

Incestuous sexual relations are indulged in by less than one in every million people in English-speaking countries. Father-daughter incest is much more common than that between mothers and sons.[52]

Intellectual inadequacy on the part of both participants is a common finding,[36] and emotional dependency and immaturity are also characteristic.[32, 52] Father and brother aggressors are negativistic and hostile,[54] and severe emotional disturbances are common in both partners of an incestuous relationship.[32]

Fox[20] found an inverse relationship between prepubertal shared activities of brothers and sisters and postpubertal sexual attraction, and suggested that because no communicative relationship existed between the siblings during their early years, they were less hindered in regarding each other as sexual objects during adolescence.

Kaufman[37] traced the initial act of incest between father and daughter to a time at which both felt the mother had abandoned them by giving birth and attention to a new child, by finding interests of her own outside the family, or by seeking solace from the maternal grandmother.

An adolescent participating in incestuous relationships must be removed to a more favorable and better supervised environment. Adequate sex instruction, as well as social and moral training, is needed. Stable adults who can offer some of the affection and acceptance he requires should be available to him.[32]

PROSTITUTION

About 825 persons under 18 years of age were arrested in 1965 for prostitution or commercialized vice, 98 per cent of whom lived in cities or towns with a population of 2500 or more. Of these 825 persons, 223 were male, either involved with girl friends whom they prostituted and on whose earnings they lived or engaged in prostitution themselves, usually with homosexuals.[33]

Girl prostitutes come from broken homes, in which alcoholism and paternal instability are common features.[13] Financial gain, without the necessity of working hard and regularly for an employer, is the prime motivator for a girl's entering into prostitution. Durban[12] reported that immediately before becoming prostitutes, all the girls he studied were in severe economic need. Although half of them originally came from homes of at least moderate economic status, a break with their parents and their subsequent departure from home created the destitution which necessitated their earning money.

Girls who adopt prostitution as a profession are those who have been exposed to sexual promiscuity as a way of life, either by the behavior of their parents or friends, or by their own previous undiscriminating sex habits. Not infrequently, there is a history of a parent's forcing the girl to have sexual intercourse with an adult friend. A prostitute does not become emotionally involved with her patrons, and sexual activity has neither personal nor moral connotations for her.

A girl just beginning to prostitute herself may not have acquired the casual indifference to intimate relationships which is necessary for preservation of emotional stability, and sometimes she can be directed away from continuing her activities by institutionalization. In such a setting she can be supervised, and her need for food, clothing and shelter can be met. She can be taught work which will enable her to support herself. If she can also acquire respect for men by associating with some who are different from those she has known, her desire for a normal marriage and family may be reawakened. Gibbens,[23] after studying 18 girl prostitutes under 17 years of age, reported that the outlook for their rehabilitation was no worse than that for girls engaged in other kinds of disapproved behavior.

HOMOSEXUALITY

Estimates of the percentage of male adolescents who participate in homosexual activities with either adults or peers range from 11 per cent[40] to as high as 50 per cent.[38] Many of these involvements are short lived, however, and do not result in enduring homosexual activity. Some adolescent boys with persisting connections with adult homosexuals are not true homosexuals themselves but utilize the relationship for purposes of threat or blackmail.[46, 51]

The true homosexual is characterized by feelings of inadequacy and is preoccupied with problems of femininity and masculinity. He is tense, restless, bewildered, and immature.[4] He dislikes heterosexual contacts, but he is not always impotent.[46] Giese,[24] in a five-year study of 2000 adult male homosexuals and 100 adult female homosexuals, reported that the male is incapable of a stable relationship with one partner, but female homosexuals remain loyal to a single partner.

Sometimes a male homosexual can be identified by his posturing and mannerisms, but this is the exception rather than the rule, and most homosexuals do not betray their confused sexuality by outward appearance or behavior. Homosexual partners exchange roles and do not consistently assume either the male or female role. Sexual gratification is a less prominent motivating factor in homosexual activities than are generalized attitudes of spite and aggression.[21]

Homosexual experience frequently is initiated by an adult preying on a minor[46] or by peers in institutional settings,[28] but such contacts do not result in permanent homosexuality unless the individual has failed to acquire the identity of his own sex and actively avoids the opposite sex.

Lack of heterosexual companionship during childhood and adolescence creates feelings of uneasiness in the individual during any association with members of the opposite sex. Unskilled in approaching or pleasing them, he protects himself from potential rejection by avoiding them altogether.[6]

If the normal heterosexual drive is inhibited because of negative and forbidding attitudes toward sex taught by parents or church, the adolescent may turn to masturbation or homosexuality as a compromise for the satisfaction of his sexual impulses.[6] Sexual awareness is intense during adolescence, but heterosexual intercourse must be postponed because a boy cannot marry and support a family, and sexual activities with a member of his own sex offer substitute satisfaction.[30]

Identification with a domineering, homosexual parent of the same sex may occur, especially if the opposite-sexed parent is inadequate. The child learns to spurn all members of the opposite sex as insignificant and he clings to his own sex as superior.[36] Identification with the parent of the opposite sex, who assumes importance either by dominating or rewarding the child, produces sexual confusion and a vacillating valuation of his own sex. This is a frequent occurrence when the like-sexed parent is feared or hated, is ineffectual, or is absent altogether.[36] A boy often is the victim of this situation, with his mother adding to his confusion and inadequacy by protecting him from harm, refusing him contacts with other people, catering to his whims, and placing him romantically and preferentially above his father.[30, 46]

Other forces directing the adolescent toward solace with his own sex are experiences of sexual brutality; parental disparagement of and unhappiness with their own sex roles; prolongation of crushes or hero-worship;[6] and rearing which permits or requires adoption of the interests, dress, and manners appropriate to the opposite sex.[11]

Acceptance of his own sex role should be encouraged by stressing its advantages to the child and by assuring the development of appropriate play interests, and this can be achieved even at the pre-school level.[35] When a child has reached the later elementary years, clothing consistent with his sex should be worn regularly, and boys should not be permitted to wear girls' clothing in dramatic productions or casual play. Contacts with children and adults of both sexes are needed throughout the child's life, and coeducational schooling supports easier adjustment to heterosexual relationships than does that which divides and isolates the sexes. Training in social skills eases the way for the boy or girl who feels that he is a social failure with members of the opposite sex and who turns to his own sex for this reason.[17, 57]

McLeish[46] considered the adolescent homosexual to be curable because he is in an experimental stage and heterosexual impulses have not been completely stifled by prolonged avoidance of the opposite sex. Teaching the homosexual boy or girl to value his own sex and also to gain skill in social contacts with members of the opposite sex strengthens his normal tendencies toward heterosexual association.

FETISHISM

Fetishism is the use of an object for sexual satisfaction in substitution for a partner of the opposite sex. Sexual pleasure is elicited by viewing or fondling a part of the body or an article of clothing associated with the opposite sex.[21] The perversion is rare among adolescents, but it occurs more frequently in boys than in girls.

Salfield[53] reported the case of a 14-year-old boy who stole women's undergarments. Because of conflict with his parents, he had failed to identify with either, and his attachment to female underwear was interpreted as a rudimentary attempt to assume the male role and to avert homosexuality. A relationship between fetishism and dependency was suggested by Wulff,[60] who stated that the fetish is an object associated by sight or smell with a loved person. Aspects of magical power and of aggression appear to be included in the practice of fetishism.[21]

Closer identification with his father is needed by the adolescent male fetishist, in order that he can assume an appropriate male role. Diverting attention to other satisfying sex-role activities is helpful, and the child's needs for affection and acceptance should be met. He can be deterred from preoccupation with a fetish by emphasizing the social prohibitions attendant on his actions.

EXHIBITIONISM

Exhibitionism is the compulsive display of the genital organs, an act accompanied by great anxiety and performed only in the presence of strangers. It is rare in girls and women. The guilt experienced by the exhibitionist is evident in his return to the scene of his act and in his reporting other exhibitionists to the police.[21] Landis[40] noted that one sixth of the college women he questioned about early sex experiences reported episodes with exhibitionists.

The exhibitionist is an infantile person, usually with potency disturbances and little interest in normal heterosexual acts.[21, 45] Hartogs[29] stated that exhibitionists have been subjected to severe discipline. Their mothers typically are sadistic, domineering, and frigid, and their fathers are harsh, embittered, and unstable, often indulging in countersadism against wife and child.

Exhibitionism sometimes is considered an abortive sexual advance.[27, 47] Although it may be aggressive,[21] more often it appears to be an expression of the individual's fear of completion of the sex act. His fear may be based on an aversion to being unfaithful to his own wife or girl friend, or it may be related to concern about causing pregnancy or infection.[3]

Exhibitionism also is regarded as an act intended to gain recognition and acceptance from others. Gerson and Heigl[22] described a 16-year-old boy who exposed himself only to middle-aged women. He derived no sexual satisfaction from his behavior and sought only attention and approval from them. Bejke[3] believed that an exhibitionist is strongly tied to his mother and that his victim is often a mother-image. McLeish[45] concluded that the exhibitionist is reared with little sympathy or understanding and therefore continues his habit of seeking these. Lefevre[41] interpreted exhibitionism as a compulsive, magic-tinged attempt of the individual to break out of his loneliness and force another person to notice him.*

Guttmann[27] and Teagarden[57] noted that exhibitionism occurs as a postencephalitic symptom and is associated with deteriorating psychoses and intellectual deficiency.

---

* See Case 38, Louis M., p. 526.

The adolescent who exposes himself to girls or women is a bewildered and lonely young person in need of accurate sex instruction and counsel. Revision of the rejecting and punitive attitudes and behavior of parents is needed, and the father or a father-substitute, if necessary, should provide previously lacking acceptance and support.

RAPE

One in every 500 boys appearing in juvenile court in 1965 was charged with rape;[34] 2076 under the age of 18 were arrested for rape during that year.[33]

Fontanesi and Zilli[19] described adolescent rapists as members of families with a history of law violation and delinquency. In general, they are of low social, economic, intellectual, and educational status; they are emotionally immature; and many have abnormal electroencephalograms. There are adolescent rapists whose environmental and personal background does not fit this description, however. A boy may be of average or better intelligence, come from a family with a good reputation, and be known for his industry and reliability. Never in trouble before, suddenly he is the confessed rapist-killer of a neighbor woman, girl schoolmate, or small girl with whom he was on good terms. Such a boy is found to be emotionally immature, with a low opinion of his own worth and manliness. He has heard other boys tell of their sexual prowess, and he believes himself to be abnormal because he has had no sex experience. He attempts to gain experience with someone he knows, vaguely anticipating the understanding he has always had. With no concept of enticement, however, he forces compliance with a knife or gun and kills impulsively when his victim startles him with resistance and fear, and he realizes that he risks exposure and punishment.

Rearing practices conducive to criminal sex behavior are listed by Hartogs[29] as (1) marked inconsistency of parental disciplinary attitudes; (2) rigid protection of the child from sexual knowledge or early play; (3) disproportionate punishment and the withholding of affection; (4) periods of overly strict discipline alternated with periods of complete neglect; (5) parental example of sex unreliability and maladjustment; (6) parental example of criminal behavior; and (7) sexual overstimulation through parental fondling or bed-sharing. He also stated that rapists typically have dominating, sadistic mothers and have fathers who are meek or absent from the home. The child is thwarted and abused and never acquires self-discipline or concepts of moral or social responsibility. He develops intense feelings of masochistic passivity and dependence on his parents—feelings which are repugnant to him and which he refutes with aggressive attack.

Gang rape is instigated by a leader who needs to demonstrate his sexual ability to the group. He directs the thinking of the others toward sexual activity and leads them into abduction and rape.[7]

Prevention of rape must include adequate instruction in sexual anatomy and function. Boys should be taught moral responsibility, which they will be able to demonstrate consistently if they are held to normal obligations of work and permitted increasing freedom appropriate for their age. The immature boy needs to know that most adolescent sex talk is empty boasting, and there is no need for sexual testing. Adolescent boys benefit from being treated as maturing individuals who are entitled to respect and trust, and they learn in this way to respect others. Frequent heterosexual group contacts aid a diffident boy to feel less ill-at-ease with girls and teach him how to communicate with them on bases other than sex.

REFERENCES

1. Allen, C.: The meaning of homosexuality. *Int. J. Sexol.*, 1954, 7, 207–212.
2. Bandura, A., and Walters, R. H.: *Adolescent Aggression.* New York, The Ronald Press Co., 1959, p. 175.
3. Bejke, R.: A contribution to the theory of exhibitionism. *Acta Psychiat. (Kbh.),* 1953, *80,* 233–243.
4. Bender, L., and Paster, S.: Homosexual trends in children. *Amer. J. Orthopsychiat.,* 1941, *11,* 730–744.
5. Bennett, I.: *Delinquent and Neurotic Children.* New York, Basic Books, Inc., 1960, p. 93.
6. Bernard, H. W.: *Adolescent Development in American Culture.* Yonkers-on-Hudson, New York, The World Book Co., 1957, pp. 423–425.
7. Blanchard, W. H.: The group process in gang rape. *J. Soc. Psychol.,* 1959, *49,* 259–266.
8. Bromberg, W.: Sex deviation and therapy. *J. Soc. Ther.,* 1955, *1,* 203–210.
9. Christensen, H. T., and Carpenter, G. R.: Value-behavior discrepancies regarding premarital coitus in three western cultures. *Amer. Sociol. Rev.,* 1962, *27,* 66–74.
10. Coogan, M. J.: Wisconsin's experience in treating psychiatrically-deviated sexual offenders. *J. Soc. Ther.,* 1955, *1,* 3–6.
11. Curti, M. W.: *Child Psychology.* New York, Longmans, Green and Co., 1938, pp. 367–368.
12. Durban, P.: Facteurs sociaux et atmosphère étiologique de la prostitution (Social factors and etiological atmosphere of prostitution). *Hyg. Ment.,* 1951, *2,* 48–54.
13. Durban, P., and Durban.: La prostitution féminine à Toulouse (Female prostitution in Toulouse). *Toulouse Méd.,* 1951, *52,* 524–547.
14. Ellis, A.: A study of 300 sex offenders. *Int. J. Sexol.,* 1951, *4,* 127–134.
15. Ellis, A., Doorbar, R. R., and Johnston, R.: Characteristics of convicted sex offenders. *J. Soc. Psychol.,* 1954, *40,* 3–15.
16. Epstein, A. W.: Fetishism: A study of its psychopathology with particular reference to a proposed disorder in brain mechanisms as an etiological factor. *J. Nerv. Ment. Dis.,* 1960, *130,* 107–119.
17. Farnham, M.: *The Adolescent.* New York, Harper and Bros., 1952.
18. Fleck, S., Devanna, A. W., Hagerty, M., and Rekate, J.: Pregnancy as a symptom of adolescent maladjustment. *Int. J. Soc. Psychiat.,* 1956, *2,* 118–131.

19. Fontanesi, M., and Zilli, E.: Les 17-chetostéroids urinaires dans un groupe de delinquants auteurs de viol avec violence (Urinary 17-ketosteroids in a group of delinquents guilty of rape with violence). *Arch. Psicol. Neurol. Psichiat.,* 1961, *22,* 147–153.
20. Fox, J. R.: Sibling incest. *Brit. J. Sociol.,* 1962, *13,* 128–150.
21. Friedman, P.: Sexual deviations. *In* Arieti, S., ed.: *American Handbook of Psychiatry.* New York, Basic Books, Inc., 1959, vol. 1, pp. 596–599, 605–606.
22. Gerson, W., and Heigl, F.: Über einen jugendlichen Exhibitionisten (Of a juvenile exhibitionist). *Prax. Kinderpsychol., Kinderpsychiat.,* 1954, *3,* 249–257.
23. Gibbens, T. C. N.: Juvenile prostitution. *Brit. J. Delinq.,* 1957, *8,* 3–12.
24. Giese, H.: Zur Psychopathologie der homosexuellen Partnerwahl (Psychopathology of homosexual partner-choice). *Jb. Psychol. Psychother.,* 1953, *1,* 223–225.
25. Gray, H.: Marriage and premarital conception. *J. Psychol.,* 1960, *50,* 383–397.
26. Gross, A. A.: The persistent problem of the homosexual—a social approach. *Psychol. Serv. Cent. J.,* 1956, *9,* 25–36.
27. Guttmann, O.: Exhibitionism: a contribution to sexual psychopathology based on twelve cases of exhibitionism. *J. Clin. Exp. Psychopath.,* 1953, *14,* 13–51.
28. Halleck, S., and Hersko, M.: Homosexual behavior in a correctional institution for adolescent girls. *Amer. J. Orthopsychiat.,* 1962, *32,* 911–917.
29. Hartogs, R.: Discipline in the early life of sex-delinquents and sex criminals. *Nerv. Child,* 1951, *9,* 167–173.
30. Havemann, E.: Why? *Life, 56*(26), 76–80.
31. Heiman, M., and Levitt, E. G.: The role of separation and depression in out-of-wedlock pregnancy. *Amer. J. Orthopsychiat.,* 1960, *30,* 166–174.
32. Hersko, M., Halleck, S., Rosenberg, M., and Pacht, A. R.: Incest: A three-way process. *J. Soc. Ther.,* 1961, *7,* 22–31.
33. Hoover, J. E.: *Uniform Crime Reports—1965.* Washington, D. C., United States Department of Justice, pp. 116–121.
34. *Juvenile Court Statistics—1964.* U.S. Department of Health, Education, and Welfare, 1963, No. 83.
35. Kagan, J., and Moss, H. A.: *Birth to Maturity.* New York, John Wiley and Sons, 1962, p. 169.
36. Kanner, L.: *Child Psychiatry,* Ed. 3. Springfield, Ill., Charles C Thomas, 1957, pp. 578–593.
37. Kaufman, I., Peck, A. L., and Tagiuri, C.: The family constellation and overt incestuous relations between father and daughter. *Amer. J. Orthopsychiat.,* 1954, *24,* 266–279.
38. Kinsey, A. C., Pomeroy, W. B., and Martin, C. E.: *Sexual Behavior in the Human Male.* Philadelphia, W. B. Saunders Co., 1948.
39. Kinsey, A. C., Pomeroy, W. B., Martin, C. E., and Gebhard, P. H.: *Sexual Behavior in the Human Female.* Philadelphia, W. B. Saunders Co., 1953.
40. Landis, J. T.: Experiences of 500 children with adult sexual deviation. *Psychiat. Quart. Suppl.,* 1956, *30,* 91–109.
41. Lefevre, J.: La personalité de l'exhibitionniste (The personality of the exhibitionist). *Acta Neurol. Psychiat.* (*Belg.*), 1959, *59,* 253–267.
42. Loesch, J. G., and Greenberg, N. H.: Some specific areas of conflicts observed during pregnancy: A comparative study of married and unmarried pregnant women. *Amer. J. Orthopsychiat.,* 1962, *32,* 624–636.
43. Lukianowicz, N.: Imaginary sexual partner. *Arch. Gen. Psychiat.,* 1960, *3,* 429–499.
44. McCord, W., McCord, J., and Verden, P.: Family relationships and sexual deviance in lower class adolescents. *Int. J. Soc. Psychiat.,* 1962, *8,* 165–179.
45. McLeish, J.: Exhibitionism. *Med. World* (*Lond.*), 1960, *93,* 126–128.
46. McLeish, J.: The homosexual. *Med. World* (*Lond.*), 1960, *93,* 237–239.
47. Maclay, D. T.: The diagnosis and treatment of compensatory types of indecent exposures. *Brit. J. Delinq.,* 1952, *3,* 34–45.
48. Martinson, F. M.: Ego deficiency as a factor in marriage: A male sample. *Marriage Fam. Liv.,* 1959, *21,* 48–52.
49. *Michigan. Governor's Study Commission on the Deviated Criminal Sex Offender.* Detroit, Mich., The Commission, 1951.

50. Moss, J. J., and Gingles, R.: The relationship of personality to the incidence of early marriage. *Marriage Fam. Liv.*, 1959, *21*, 373–377.
51. Reiss, A. J., Jr.: The social integration of queers and peers. *Soc. Probl.*, 1961, *9*, 102–120.
52. Rhinehart, J. W.: Genesis of overt incest. *Comprehen. Psychiat.*, 1961, *2*, 338–349.
53. Salfield, D. F.: Juvenile fetishism. *Z. Kinderpsychiat.*, 1957, *24*, 183–196.
54. Schachter, M., and Cotte, S.: Étude medico-psychologique et sociale de l'inceste, dans la perspective pédo-psychiatrique (Medical-social-psychological study of incest, from the pedo-psychiatric point of view). *Acta paedopsychiat.*, 1960, *27*, 139–146.
55. Staton, T. F.: *Dynamics of Adolescent Adjustment.* New York, The Macmillan Co., 1963, pp. 372–373, 394–397.
56. Stockwell, S. L.: Sexual experience of adolescent delinquent girls. *Int. J. Sexol.*, 1953, *7*, 25–27.
57. Teagarden, F. M.: *Child Psychology for Professional Workers.* New York, Prentice-Hall, Inc., 1940, pp. 373, 379.
58. Thom, D. A.: *Normal Youth and Its Everyday Problems.* New York, D. Appleton-Century Co., 1932, pp. 56–57, 63, 70–71.
59. Welch, P.: The "gay" world takes to the city streets. *Life*, *56*(26), 68–74.
60. Wulff, M.: On fetishism. *Int. J. Sexol.*, 1951, *4*, 224–227.

Chapter 42

Withdrawal Reactions

Worry and depression, anxiety, daydreaming, drug addiction, compulsions, schizophrenia, and suicide are withdrawal reactions which in varying degrees permit the individual to avoid contact with others and prevent adequate resolution of his problems. A withdrawal reaction can be an expression of feelings of inadequacy or a retreat from reality; or it can combine retreat with an inappropriate, ineffective, and self-destructive solution to difficulties.

The withdrawing adolescent's behavior is created by feelings of helplessness,[52] as evidenced in worry, depression, and anxiety. His expressing concern in these ways may be superseded by the averting of attention to problems with excessive daydreaming or drug addiction. If these means of avoidance are inadequate to quell anxiety and if the adolescent takes no useful steps toward reversing his withdrawal tendencies, he may attempt to reason away, explain, or control his feelings of inadequacy by developing compulsive rituals or schizophrenic symptoms, solutions which are ineffectual and distressing. Attempted suicide represents the individual's effort to rid himself finally of conflict or distress.

Shaffer[56] attributed the development of withdrawal reactions to fear-conditioning, frustration of other defenses, or habit formation. The most serious and detrimental withdrawal is that based on guilt, which appears when the child has become conditioned to persistent fearfulness as a result of severe and repeated physical punishment or angry threats and scoldings. In a constant state of anxiety and tension, he responds with withdrawal to minor or even nonexistent menace. Fear-conditioning also develops if a child is overprotected and learns from parental solicitude to mistrust his own abilities and to consider himself incompetent.[41] Feeling this way, he tends to avoid competition at school and play, and he begins to isolate himself from his peers at an early age.

If parents frustrate a child's attempts to utilize defenses other than withdrawal, they succeed in restricting him to this single method of reacting to all problems. When his attempts to stand up for himself or to act aggressively are punished, he learns to avoid punishment by withdrawing at times of conflict with others or at times of challenge. Habits of repressing anger and inhibiting aggression, well-learned during the elementary school years, persist through adolescence and early adulthood, especially for girls.[41]

Withdrawal reactions can be acquired without attendant emotional components. A child reared without playmates or brought up in a family which has few social contacts receives no experience in associating with others, and he is hindered in developing social techniques. A child who is less able than his peers in learning ability, speech, play skills, or physique hesitates to expose himself to comparison, and he remains aloof from others to protect himself from ridicule or the awareness of inferiority. A child who has had a prolonged, isolating illness becomes so accustomed to spending his time alone that he does not need friends for stimulation or entertainment. In all of these situations, the child feels more comfortable by himself than he does with others, and the longer contacts are postponed, the more he is habituated to isolation and withdrawal. Garrison[29] noted that a child who fails to become socialized eventually faces conflict between his own personal interests and preference for solitude and his developing social consciousness.

WORRY AND DEPRESSION

Scattered through the ebullience of youth are episodes of deep unhappiness and discouragement. Few adolescents, feeling forsaken over a repulse of the moment or because of the great uncertainties of the future, have not thought that life was too difficult to bear longer. Girls' helpless sobbing and boys' remarkable regressions, even to thumbsucking, attest to their feelings of hopelessness. Despert[20] considered depression among young people to be more common than is indicated by the literature, and other studies have confirmed the sadness and despair of adolescence.

Worry is manifested principally by verbal contemplation, which ordinarily occurs in solitude. It is perpetuated when the individual fails to seek information and resists advice because he believes that he ought to be able to find his own solutions to his problems. Meissner[47] reported that adolescent boys indicated on a questionnaire that they experienced a marked increase in depression, sadness, dissatisfaction with life, feelings of being misunderstood, and feelings of loneliness as they grew older. More than 50 per cent were moody, depressed, and worried about their studies; many of them felt that they were not understood by adults or peers.

Angelino et al.[1] found that socioeconomic background affected the kinds of worries reported by children and adolescents. Upper-class boys and girls worried about the possibility of accidents and that world tragedies might affect them personally, but lower-class children were no longer concerned with personal harm by the time they reached the age of 12. At 15 years of age, lower-class boys worried about finishing high school and being able to go to college, but upper-class boys were concerned only about whether they would be able to enter the college of their choice. Worries related to economics and politics showed a sharp increase for lower-class boys at 16 years and were more acute than those of upper-class boys in this area, although these boys had been concerned about such matters two years earlier.

Meissner,[46, 48] in a comparison study of worry among adolescent boys now and 20 years ago, reported greater complacency at the present time than previously. He found significant differences in the numbers of boys in the two generations who indicated that they became discouraged easily, were excessively conscious of faults, felt sad and depressed, were worried about finding jobs later, were disturbed by low grades, and were worried about being normal and understood. Major sources of concern remained the same, however, and centered on school, sex, unpopularity, immoral activities, religion, vocation, and the future.

Labile in mood and temperament, adolescents are susceptible to extreme reactions when faced with disappointment, failure, or crisis.[34] Their own generosity and altruism increase as they grow older,[63] and because they now are more understanding and restrained, others' rebuffs and rejections hurt when they are unprovoked.

The adolescent's contradictory desires to become independent and to remain irresponsible clash constantly during his high school years,[72] and he is dispirited by his clearly evident unpreparedness for the imminent changes in his life. Boys are more severely distressed by the approaching demands of maturity than are girls because the concept of maleness embraces strength, aggression, effectiveness, and interpersonal dominance[41]—qualities which few adolescent boys display consistently.

Cameron[16] described states of depression as being characterized either by agitation or by retardation of response. Agitated depression is related to the anxiety disorders and is typified by restlessness, inability to sleep or to concentrate, and preoccupation with feelings of worthlessness and self-blame. The individual reproaches and condemns himself unceasingly for the difficulties he is experiencing, and eventually he may broaden self-accusation to consider himself responsible for social and world ills. Retarded depression is a fatigue reaction to anxiety, in which the individual withdraws and insulates himself from contact with others. He tensely but passively anticipates punishment or disaster, which he believes he deserves because of his inadequacies and failures.

Gutheil[34] identified reactive depression as manifestly prevalent during adolescence and defined it as a state of prolonged disappointment or sadness related to a specific event or a series of events which the individual can readily identify as precipitating his unhappiness. Complaints of fatigue and pain often are somatic equivalents of reactive depression.

Depressed reactions are tinged with hostility directed against persons who have disappointed or disparaged the adolescent, but because his attitude is ambivalent, he feels guilty about blaming others for his failures and his guilt deepens his conviction of unworthiness and prolongs his sadness.[16]

A worried or depressed adolescent needs to talk about events which distress him. He can be reassured about the normality of his feelings of hopelessness, and he can be guided toward accurately evaluating situations so that their significance can be appraised correctly.

Helping him plan realistically and definitely for his immediate future provides him with a modicum of security and minimizes his worries about a bridgeless leap from dependency to self-reliance. The adolescent needs to have a solid foundation of tested abilities in many areas: educational, financial, creative, and social. He should have years of experience in self-care and in acquiring skill with everyday tasks. These abilities increase his confidence and aid him in conquering the worry and depression he experiences.

ANXIETY

Anxiety reactions are manifestations of generalized fear, and they include chronic anxiety, anxiety attacks, panic reactions, and phobias.[16] They are adjustive reactions which fail to reduce the self-concern and tension which produce them.[56]

The chronically anxious person experiences aching from taut muscles in his head, neck, or back. His fingers or tongue tremble, and his walking and even his sitting are strained. He has little appetite, he cannot concentrate or remember efficiently, and he finds it difficult to sleep or relax. Irritable and tired, his self-motivation vanishes as he ponders decisions in a state of morbid dread.[56]

To protect himself from anxiety, he begins to avoid the people and situations which increase it, and eventually he gives up most contacts with others and focuses completely on himself and his worries. In his struggle to avoid pain, he succeeds only in intensifying it as he concentrates on his fears and inadequacies.

An anxiety attack occurs in a setting of chronic anxiety as an acute episode which resembles great fright. The individual becomes agitated, sweats, breathes rapidly, and complains of choking or suffocating. His heart beats rapidly, he is unsteady on his feet, and he feels dizzy or faint. He believes that he is going to die or that he is going insane. The attack may last from a few minutes to an hour.[16, 21]

A panic reaction is an extreme anxiety attack and may include aggressive assault, flight, or suicide. The individual may be disoriented, not knowing where he is or who his companions are. He may feel trapped and suffer from delusions of persecution, or he may hallucinate taunting voices. The panic may be brief, or it may last for several months with fluctuating intensity. Eventually it may be replaced by a chronic paranoid reaction or schizophrenic disorganization.[16]

A phobia is an anxiety disorder in which the fear is specific for an object or event which can be identified by the individual. Neither he nor others can explain his fear, which is irrational, unwarranted, and embarrassing. Although the person tries to avoid placing himself in circumstances in which his phobia is evident, this is difficult because the feared object ordinarily is commonplace. Frequent phobias are of animals, germs, dirt, small rooms, open parks, high places, storms, or the dark. Talking, reading, or thinking about the feared object may elicit an anxiety attack. Development of a phobia is evidence of general, long-standing anxiety, now funneled onto a specific scapegoat which is related only distantly, if at all, to the multiple factors responsible for the individual's living in uncertainty and dread.

Portnoy[52] distinguished between anxiety and fear in terms of the fearful person's ability to react with either fight or flight when a feared object is encountered. He believed that the individual with a specific fear is conscious of himself, his surroundings, and his resources and that this is not true of the person suffering from generalized anxiety or from anxiety attacks. Under these conditions of persistent or acute anxiety, the responses of the individual are compulsive, and he makes no attempt to control his reactions. Generalization of anxiety results in the adolescent's concealing his real fears from himself and thus avoiding his responsibility to solve his problems.

Anxiety reactions develop from a variety of backgrounds. A child who has been the recipient of parental oversolicitude worries about being harmed by others and about his inability to take care of himself.[16, 42] If he is forced by his parents toward attainment of perfectionistic standards of behavior and performance, he will fail repeatedly and will be informed constantly that he is inadequate. This causes him to become highly self-critical, and subsequently he becomes anxious, insecure, and depressed.[45] The belief that he is a disappointment to his parents is particularly disturbing to an adolescent, and he experiences conflict as he simultaneously tries to satisfy his parents and to divest himself of his need for them.[16]

The adolescent who must bear burdens for which he is unprepared may develop anxiety. If he is exposed continually to the worries of his elders, he not only empathizes with them but he also feels guilty because he cannot alleviate their problems. A single traumatic event, such as the death of a near relative, an emergency operation, a fire, a car accident, or disillusionment over the unexpected immoral action of a relative or friend, can precipitate anxiety which lasts for several months.[42]

There are several ways in which pressure can be removed and tension lessened for the anxious and fearful adolescent. A physician's reassurance concerning his health, especially if he fears death or insanity, is usually of immediate efficacy.[42, 52] The young person who is tense about school grades should be assisted in doing better; if he worries about social contacts, he needs more of them. He should reverse his practice of avoiding problems and begin to master situations which trouble him.[56]

He can be encouraged to talk about his worries. Many problems lose significance as they are verbalized, and some vanish entirely when the adolescent gains previously lacking knowledge which enables him to understand or explain experiences which have caused him concern. His tendency to keep his worries to himself and to devote great amounts of time to dwelling on his deficiencies needs to be halted.[52, 56]

He should have the respect appropriate for his age; and therefore he needs the responsibility for completing school work and chores and the freedom to do what he likes, away from adult supervision or correction, when his work is finished. Pleasurable activity relieves his tension and allows him independence of choice, and these permit him to discover that his gloomy life can be colored with greater attractiveness. When it is, he can sustain effort more consistently and banish feelings of anxiety more quickly.

DAYDREAMING

For the adolescent, daydreaming is a normal activity. At no other period of his life are so many major decisions required of him. Within a few years' time he must find a mate and prepare for a vocation, and how he is to take these steps and what they will mean in the way he lives for years to come are subjects about which he constantly speculates. Later adolescence is the peak period for daydreaming.[58]

Daydreams are always satisfying and usually pleasant because they fulfill wishes for love, achievement, and security.[37] They provide the dreamer with the gratification of romantic conquests, exhibitions of bravery, and the possession of superior knowledge, power, wealth, and importance. Daydreams may be sad, as the adolescent envisions himself as injured or lost or ill, but these daydreams also afford satisfaction in the contemplation of sympathy and guilt felt by others over the dreamer's misfortunes. Sometimes an adolescent daydreams of the death of a relative or acquaintance who is especially annoying to him, and he manages in this way to achieve revenge without taking direct action.[56]

Zachry[71] pointed out that the daydreamer shifts between imagination and reality, unable to decide whether he can settle for plans for flight or must establish a feasible program of action. He is indecisive because he hesitates to shape his own future by arriving at final conclusions, and he procrastinates by daydreaming unless he is forced to take action.

There are values associated with daydreaming, particularly for the adolescent who now must think of himself more as adult than child. His daydreams help him sort out varying pictures of himself as an adult, and they aid him in planning as he assesses different roles and eventually discards those which are impossible or unsatisfying. In testing reality against his inner wishes, the adolescent reëvaluates himself as a maturing person.[53] Daydreaming is beneficial also in providing relief from daily pressures and in creating feelings of success and self-admiration which are conducive to optimism and self-assurance.

Daydreaming is detrimental, however, when disproportionate amounts of time are devoted to it and the individual is deprived of needed contacts with other people and of other kinds of activity and when actual achievement is replaced with fantasied success.[56] Excessive indulgence in daydreaming can lead to disorganization of thought and action, as prolonged withdrawal causes loss of contact with reality.*

Daydreaming can be moderated by identifying those areas in which it substitutes overcompletely for action and making it possible for the adolescent to find pleasure in real achievement.[56] To guard against severe withdrawal, the adolescent's parents should take every opportunity to talk with him about his experiences, his plans, and his thoughts and to assist him in making definite arrangements for the future. Inviting families with adolescent children to the home provides personal contacts which the withdrawing young person cannot easily escape.

---

* See Case 39, Helen J., p. 527.

DRUG ADDICTION

In 1965 there were 4350 arrests of persons under 18 years of age for violation of narcotics laws.[38] Measured by the number of addicted persons, however, the problem is less severe at present than it was in 1900. Addiction reached an all-time low during World War II, when it was difficult to obtain and smuggle in narcotics.[70] One in every 3000 to 5000 high school students is an addict, and approximately 440 adolescents are patients in the two federal hospitals at Lexington, Kentucky, and Ft. Worth, Texas, which specialize in curing addiction.[13] Although the proportionate number of addicts has decreased, the effects of addiction may be more serious: The average adolescent addict spends $40 a week on drugs.[70]

Heroin is the only opiate available to most addicts and is preferred to morphine because it is three times more powerful and can be diluted easily. The addict takes heroin intravenously, and within a few seconds his face flushes, his pupils constrict, and he feels a tingling sensation, particularly in his abdomen. The tingling soon gives way to a feeling of euphoria, and later the addict drifts into somnolence. Effects of the drug wear off in three or four hours. Addicts are uninterested in activity, become increasingly careless about their living habits, and spend most of their time in bed.

As the addict continues to take the drug, his body develops tolerance and he must increase the dosage to produce the same effect. A few hours after his last dose, he becomes anxious and develops withdrawal sickness. He perspires, feels chilled, and tosses restlessly. His eyes water and his nose runs. His arms and legs begin to ache and twitch; and he becomes nauseated, vomits, and suffers diarrhea. Abstinence symptoms for heroin reach a peak in 24 hours, and for morphine in from 36 to 48 hours. Within a week the addict has lived through the worst of withdrawal sickness; he is weak and nervous but he has lost his physical dependence on the drug, although complete recovery requires from two to six months.[70] There is evidence that drug addiction causes permanent damage to the blood, the liver, and the nervous system.[51]

In the last 12 years, newer drugs not controlled by narcotics laws, readily available and relatively inexpensive, have been used by adolescents. Barbiturates taken in quantity are habit-forming and are used by some addicts to maintain continuous intoxication, during which they are depressed and irritable and show poor judgment. Sudden withdrawal of barbiturates usually causes convulsions and may cause death, and medically supervised, gradual withdrawal requires from ten days to two months.[70] Amphetamines also are widely used by adolescents. Sniffing vapors of airplane glue, gasoline, paint thinner, and nasal inhalers or injecting the toxic ingredients of these products are increasing practices of young people.[7, 51]

Studies of drug addicts confirm the impression that addiction is an instrument of withdrawal. The addict, without attempting to solve his problems or to acquire a new outlook by communicating with his fellows, disappears into another world where problems do not exist. Gang membership contraindicates addiction because most gangs recognize the addict as an isolate.[69] They approve of taking heroin occasionally, provided it does not lead to addiction. In a few gangs, the principal activity is drug-taking, but boys in these groups do not engage in typical gang aggression, and even within the gang, the act itself is solitary.[17]

Toolan et al.[65] compared 36 adolescent heroin addicts with a control group and concluded that they were essentially nonaggressive and passive, although they gave an impression of social ease. Empathizing with their mothers, they formed superficial relationships with everyone else; and as the addiction progressed they became increasingly withdrawn, renounced their friends, and turned away from athletic and scholastic interests. Finally, reality was vested only in the effects provided by the drug. Laskowitz[44] considered the adolescent addict as socially distant, lacking in courage, suffering from strong feelings of inadequacy, and preferring to be shielded and pampered. Gold[32] described the addict as "geared for failure rather than success" and as a withdrawn, isolated observer of life rather than a participant in it. Yahraes[70] reported that eighth grade boys using drugs were pessimistic, distrusted authority, lived with a sense of futility, and found it difficult to assume the masculine role.

There are large numbers of addicts among underprivileged minority ethnic groups.[4, 26] In New York City, 75 per cent of adolescent addicts live in the poorest, most crowded, and most dilapidated areas of the city.[70] Addicts often come from large families, in which parental control is minimal and inconsistent—sometimes because of the actual or effective absence of one parent as the result of divorce or alcoholism.[7] Gerard and Kornetsky,[31] however, in a study of 32 adolescent opium addicts, found that the majority came from middle-class homes but that they presented a background of limited contact with both peers and adults and a history of avoidance or denial of personal problems.

Although Jaeger[40] considered drug addiction in adolescents to be a flexible and reversible process, other investigators are less optimistic.[32] Of 1900 New York City residents discharged from the Lexington federal hospital between 1952 and 1955, over 90 per cent became readdicted, most of them within six months; and more readdiction occurs in persons under 30 years of age than in older individuals.[70] Work experience has proved beneficial to hospitalized addicts because it involves action rather than verbal communication, which patients find difficult, and also because it provides the adolescent with practical skills to use upon his return to the community.[33]

COMPULSIONS

Compulsive behavior represents the individual's solution to unresolved conflict. He is afraid to make a decision because it may be wrong, and compulsive actions serve as rituals with magical power to protect him from error. If the adolescent fails to perform the compulsive act, he suffers severe anxiety and the conviction of impending disaster.[16]

There are various kinds of compulsive behaviors, and an individual may engage in several of them during the same period of time. A common compulsion is the need to repeat the same action, even though it serves no purpose. An individual may feel compelled to wash his hands repeatedly, and he continues to do so even after they become cracked and begin to bleed.

Serial compulsions require the individual to perform a group of actions, such as dressing, in a prescribed order. If he inadvertently forgets whether he has followed the correct routine or perhaps has mistakenly put on his left shoe before his right, he must undress completely and start all over again.

Compulsive orderliness forces the young person to maintain absolute neatness. Buttons must be in a precise line, and a broken shoelace or a run in a stocking causes great alarm. Shoes, drawers, closets, books, and knickknacks are carefully arranged and meticulously kept in place.

Compulsive punishment requires the adolescent to impose restrictions and penalties on himself for deviations from his own prescribed rules and procedures. Sometimes he punishes himself physically; at other times he denies himself coveted recreation or penalizes himself with physical exertion or tedious study.

Compulsive belief in the power of magic to ward off the evil which may follow erroneous decisions or actions causes the individual to practice rituals he believes will guarantee him freedom from anxiety. One young person obtained relief for the day from the anxieties related to his compulsions and indecisiveness by standing behind a certain door early in the morning and repeating a four-line doggerel.

Compulsive thinking is uncontrollable pondering about hurting someone, stealing, or committing suicide, and it usually includes the need to weigh alternative actions endlessly. Sometimes compulsive thinking results in completion of the fantasied action, and it cannot be assumed that compulsive ideas will never lead to harm for the individual or for others.[16]

Behavior of a compulsive nature develops in a person who is

vacillating between fear of and desire for an object or activity.[21] Many compulsive reactions have been linked with the individual's contemplation of sexual contact, evolving from an experience as innocuous as participating in a group discussion of sex or from one which was threatening and immediate, such as solicitation or attempted rape. If the adolescent rejects sexual interest and behavior as immoral and yet finds himself attracted sexually, he cannot reconcile his opposing attitudes, and he avoids acknowledging the existence of feelings and thoughts he considers indecent or unworthy. His indecision becomes intolerable, and he introduces self-controlling actions of many kinds as demonstrative evidence that order and discipline are paramount in his life. His compulsions also serve as hampering, time-consuming devices which curtail his freedom of action and freedom of choice, and these are freedoms he wishes to avoid.

An adolescent tends to be susceptible to the development of adient-avoidant conflicts if he has been reared by adults who are precise and proper in their habits and who permit him no deviation from impeccable behavior. When a child's ordinary anger and justified tears are considered inappropriate or degrading and when right and wrong are absolutes determined by parental edict, the child learns to fear making decisions and to be intolerant of normal emotions. Children subjected to warnings about sinfulness and eternal punishment in hell are guarded, anxious, and guilty. They may acquire these feelings from the teachings of a fundamentalist church and have them reënforced by parental injunctions to pray for forgiveness for their transgressions.

A compulsive adolescent resents the domination his compulsions exert over him, just as he resents the unyielding domination of the rearing under which he suffers but does not resist. He shows his resentment with attacks on others, both verbal and physical, especially if he is in a position of authority. He belittles others' achievements and questions their motives, and he guards carefully against others' taking advantage of what he considers to be his own good nature. He mistrusts other people and hurts them when he can, and he finds no comfort or kindness in others because he has not known these himself.*

The first step in ridding an adolescent of compulsions is to enable him to talk about them with a therapist who does not ridicule him or laugh at his behavior. Many young people have never discussed their compulsions with anyone, and this seclusiveness has contributed to perpetuation of the actions.[42] Parents need assistance in loosening the strings which bind the child to them and in acquiring a less rigid attitude themselves. An expression of confidence in the child's innate capacity to achieve and to cope with his own problems needs to replace their

---

* See Case 40, Simon C., p. 528.

assumption that he must be protected and directed all his life. A tolerant attitude toward others teaches the young person to respond to them, and also to himself, in less critical and rigid ways.

The adolescent should practice making decisions for himself. He can begin by deciding when, during the day, he will comply with his compulsion, thus placing it more under self-control, limiting its occurrence, and emphasizing its nuisance value and irrationality. As he progresses in deciding for himself the details of his daily life, he should be permitted and encouraged to decide and act on other more important matters, including which subjects he wishes to study and which hobbies and recreation he prefers. Short trips away from home give him practice in independence and convince him that he can manage adequately without adult direction. Discussion of conflicts, particularly in the sexual sphere, helps him accept his feelings without guilt.

SCHIZOPHRENIA

The accurate diagnosis of schizophrenia is as difficult to make in adolescents as it is in children. Bender[11] observed that the behavior of the schizophrenic, the psychopathic, the brain damaged, and the emotionally deprived adolescent are similar in so many respects that distinguishing among them creates many problems. Stern[61] believed that early schizophrenia is often confused with the violent reactions common to adolescent crisis, and among adolescents discharged from the New York State Psychiatric Institute as neurotic, 50 per cent had developed signs of schizophrenia when a follow-up study was made later.[49]

Relatively few cases of schizophrenia are diagnosed in children under 15 years of age, but less than 1 per cent of the admissions to state hospitals are of children below this age. Of all admissions to state hospitals, 16 per cent are of adolescents and young adults between the ages of 15 and 29; and schizophrenia has been well established as a disorder of youth and early adulthood.[49] A variety of symptoms, mild and transient, can be interpreted as signalling incipient schizophrenia, but the totally disintegrating withdrawal of psychosis ordinarily is precipitated by the inexorable march of time, which forces an inadequate and lonely young person into the demands of work and marriage he is unprepared to meet. Extreme withdrawal occurs more commonly in boys than in girls, at a ratio of ten to three.[15]

Stern[61] stated that adolescent behavior which could be considered prodromal to schizophrenia includes (1) difficulty in interpersonal relationships; (2) seclusiveness and daydreaming; (3) withdrawal from work; (4) personal neglect; and (5) a tendency toward delinquency.

Previously unevidenced hypochondriacal complaining also is a common precursor of schizophrenic disorganization.[3]

The adolescent who devotes inordinate amounts of time to secluded daydreaming finds it increasingly difficult to return to ordinary activities.[21] Gradually, his private thinking leads to persistent delusions, and when he finally expresses these to parents or peers, they may be aware for the first time that something is seriously wrong. The schizophrenic's delusions may bring him pleasure or cause him fear. He may believe that others wish to persecute him or that they are influencing his behavior and thinking. He may believe that he is a member of a royal family or has great wealth; or he may hold the opposite conviction and be convinced that he is worthless, sinful, and responsible for all the evil which besets the world. Associated with his hypochondria may be the belief that parts of his body have changed or vanished; or, steadily more unobservant and more frightened, he believes that his surroundings have been altered: Buildings, trees, and streets are in new places, and he is certain that these changes were planned deliberately to confuse him.

In the early stages of psychosis, delusions are more logically founded in reality than they are later. They also are more restricted in content and better supported by congruent emotion. As time progresses, however, the delusions envelop unrelated aspects of the patient's environment, and to a listener they seem entirely bizarre and unreasonable. With progressive disorganization, the emotional reaction appropriate to the delusions disappears and the delusions themselves remain only as fragments which are no longer traceable to the events from which they originated. Sometimes the delusions themselves vanish, or at least are unexpressed, and only the emotional component which accompanied them remains: suspicion, aloofness, condescension, or depression.[16]

The extreme withdrawal of the schizophrenic is responsible for most of the other symptoms observed in his behavior. As he ceases his contacts with people, he loses the need to communicate effectively. His thinking, and subsequently his speech, takes shortcuts, and although he understands the intended meaning of his incomplete, vague verbalizations, others do not. He loses the attentiveness and self-control necessary for precise thought and expression, and therefore he uses word approximations, voicing a word which is related by sound or meaning to the one he intends but one which is inexact. He creates new words, *neologisms,* from parts of words or parts of the object or event of which he is thinking. Sentences and paragraphs are rambling and meaningless to a listener because he mixes up his word sequences and rarely uses connectives, a mode of speech called *scatter.* Some patients cannot make the effort to communicate even to this extent, and they block when trying to talk, hesitating for long periods before they can say anything at all. In total withdrawal from communication, the schizophrenic becomes mute.[16]

As he withdraws, his interest in both his own and others' lives wanes, and he becomes increasingly inactive. His solitude makes him indifferent to his appearance and to his behavior. He is slovenly in personal care and uninterested in maintaining even minimum cleanliness. He dances and sings, grimaces, asks inappropriate questions and makes fatuous comments without awareness or concern that he is making a spectacle of himself.[3]

Although he is indifferent to what others think of him, he is not unaware of their efforts to communicate with him. Whitman[68] found that schizophrenics in a learning situation responded to behavioral cues of the experimenter, although they did not realize that they were doing so. Their verbalization was more noticeably impaired when they were absorbing stimulation from another person and reacting appropriately to it.

The extreme variability and complete unpredictability of the schizophrenic's behavioral and emotional reactions are factors which make it difficult to list characteristic symptoms. The schizophrenic may be excited or stuporous, resistive or cataleptic, overtalkative or mute, hostile or erotic, indifferent or ecstatic, aggressive or submissive. Cameron[16] suggested that sudden shifts in the schizophrenic's attitude and behavior result from the intervention of auditory or visual hallucinations. The patient hears voices which dictate to him, warn, or threaten; he hears sounds which are mystifying and frightening; or he sees a nonexistent person or scene which excites him or makes him anxious.

Emotional incongruity or flattening is characteristic of schizophrenics. The individual appears to be emotionally unaffected as he recites fearful and strange events, describes his own vicious behavior, or hears of tragedy occurring to members of his family. Cameron[16] cited three reasons for the schizophrenic's lack of appropriate emotional response. It may be the end result of prolonged withdrawal and hopelessness, with the individual expressing less emotion as part of a generalized, decreased response to stimulation of all kinds. This interpretation is supported by the fact that emotional distortion or apathy seldom are seen in the early stages of illness. Apathy may also result from the patient's having learned earlier to conceal all evidence of emotional feeling in order to protect himself against scornful and abusive treatment from other people. Or, the emotion may appear inappropriate to an observer because he does not understand the meaning of the patient's verbalizations or actions. To the schizophrenic, his own statements and actions appear logical and reasonable, and marked emotional expression is unwarranted.

Personal characteristics of the adolescent prior to the development of psychosis have been studied. Male high school students who later developed schizophrenia were found to be less interested in girls, group activities, and sports than most boys their age. Their general mental health and school adjustment were poor, and they tended to be seclusive.[14] Arieti[3] described the potential schizophrenic as an aloof, nonemotional person who severely limits both his social contacts and his activities. By needing to protect himself this way, he indicates his real dependence on others and his fear that they are unaccepting of him. He is inept at managing by himself, and he dreads being forced into any demanding situation. Sometimes a dependent adolescent does not withdraw but instead energetically casts about for different ways of making contact with others. He tries submission, aggression, and detachment; and he is highly vulnerable and easily hurt. Life for him is a series of crises, often created by his own poor judgment. His behavior recalls the brain-damaged child, with his bewildered, erratic eagerness to sample and participate in life.

The family background of schizophrenic patients often consists of extreme marital disharmony between the parents and an enduring atmosphere of unhappiness, tension,[3] immaturity, and defensiveness.[9] Several studies have disclosed that the mothers of schizophrenics are overcontrolling in extreme and emotional ways, and they inspire pity, shame, and guilt in their children.[28] In contrast to the mothers' aggressive domination, the fathers are weak and ineffectual.[3, 43]

Fleck et al.[27] observed a difference in family background between male and female patients. Male schizophrenics had dominant mothers and ineffectual fathers, but females had paranoid, seductive fathers and indifferent mothers. Arieti[3] noted that mothers who were indifferent and nonaccepting of the child sometimes were the victims of tyrannical, insecure husbands, whose orders and abuse they accepted passively in complete renunciation of emotional sharing. The family setting in which schizophrenia develops appears to be that of self-centered, violent abuse of others by one parent and the avoidance of protest by the other, who absents himself from all involvement with the family. The withdrawing child, therefore, has a model to imitate and a reason to be afraid.*

Prognosis for adolescent schizophrenics has been estimated by several investigators. Symonds and Herman[62] classified 50 schizophrenic girls between the ages of 12 and 18 into three groups: (1) girls who had made an adequate adjustment previously and showed serious disturbance only with the onset of schizophrenic symptoms; (2) those who had histories of many serious personality and behavior problems in childhood; and (3) childhood schizophrenics who had now reached

---

* See Case 41, Gerald G., p. 529.

adolescence. As might be expected, they considered prognosis most promising for the first group and least hopeful for the third.

Colbert and Koegler[18] compared 40 adolescent schizophrenics whose symptoms had appeared in childhood with 20 whose symptoms had not developed until adolescence. The former showed marked physiological disturbances, thought poverty, and spatial disorientation. The authors suggested that early remedial reading, speech, and visual-motor training would have lessened the effect of these perceptual disturbances and altered the course of development.

Eisenberg[23] evaluated 63 autistic children when they reached the age of 15 years, and he found that their prognosis was related to the degree of useful speech they had at the age of five years, a finding which confirms the importance of communicative ability in ensuring that a child matures at a steady rate.

A follow-up study conducted by Errera[24] of 54 adolescent schizophrenics seen in an outpatient clinic 16 years earlier indicated that 25 per cent had made a good adjustment but that the others remained severely handicapped. Hamilton et al.[35] reported that two thirds of hospitalized boys aged 14 to 19 years improved with a program which emphasized dynamic psychotherapy, socialization, and group participation.

The potentially schizophrenic adolescent, alone and afraid, needs practice in many areas of living and of endeavor, and he needs to obtain this practice in situations where he is encouraged and praised, not severely criticized. Attempts should be made to help his parents alter their attitudes and treatment of him. If they can curtail their emotional displays, their use of the child, or their indifference to him and if they can treat him consistently and fairly, he will lose his fear. He should be subject to less direction from the dominant parent and should be encouraged to use his own judgment on minor matters. Evidence of family solidarity, with cessation of parental antipathy and more experiences of united activity, must replace individual isolation and self-centeredness.

The school can help a withdrawn and anxious young person by using him as an assistant to a teacher or an administrator. He gains work experience, confidence, and even prestige in this way. In his classes he can be assigned to work with one other student on a report or project, and this provides opportunities for communication and coöperation as well as achievement. Contacts with a guidance counselor or teacher-advisor should be well designed to help him plan realistically for his future and prepare for it in easy stages.

Working with young children can convince the withdrawn and fearful adolescent that he has some superior abilities, but he should have such contacts only in a supervised nursery where he is taught skills in dealing with children. Unsupervised baby-sitting by a disturbed adolescent has led to neglect or to physical or sexual abuse of his charges.

A withdrawing adolescent needs the opportunity to share his ideas and feelings with an impartial outsider who can halt his progressive seclusiveness by supporting him and by initiating environmental and familial changes. Prolonged spells of brooding should be interrupted and the young person should be encouraged to talk, both about personal worries or beliefs and also about more objective occurrences. Communication can also be maintained in other ways. Reading biographies and history enlarges the adolescent's viewpoint, and writing about subjects which are important to him diverts him from thinking only of his own hopeless situation and personal inadequacies.

SUICIDE

Suicide among adolescents is responsible for approximately 3 per cent of all deaths in the ten-to-19-year age range, and four times as many boys as girls are successful at killing themselves. In 1964, 81 boys and ten girls between the ages of ten and 14 years and 516 boys and 136 girls betwen the ages of 15 and 19 years committed suicide.[67] Bakwin[5] reported that the peak month for suicide is May, which suggests a relationship between the ending of the organized activity of school and an individual's feelings of hopelessness.

Statistics concerning successful suicide do not indicate the extent of attempted suicide, which appears to be widespread and includes a greater proportion of girls. Gaultier et al.[30] studied 47 cases of attempted suicide among adolescents, and 40 of this group were girls. Toolan[64] studied 102 children and adolescents with suicidal thoughts and actions, the majority of whom were girls. These patients accounted for 11 per cent of all hospital admissions under the age of 16 years.

Although both schizophrenic and depressive symptoms have been observed in adolescents attempting suicide,[6] psychosis rarely is associated with it.[30, 36, 42] A history of previous attempts at suicide is common among hospitalized patients.[25, 30] Despert[20] pointed out that attempted suicide by children is ordinarily an impulsive act. Seldom do young people have a realistic concept of death or expect to succeed in killing themselves, and even adults who attempt suicide do so with an attitude of gambling with fate and a belief that their effort will be thwarted.[59, 60]

Although a suicide attempt is precipitated by a specific problem, usually the individual has previously and for some time considered killing himself. Finally, he reaches the point at which he feels completely helpless to alter a situation which he can no longer tolerate.[2, 12] His suicide attempt is a desperate appeal for love and help,[59, 60] and he seeks both pity and attention, hoping that his self-destruction will atone for his deficiencies and mistakes.

Some adolescents attempt suicide because they are convinced that they are inferior: A young person cannot face the reality of his defective intelligence, or he broods over epilepsy or paralysis or considers himself ugly.[10] He may no longer be able to endure the rigid direction forced on him by compulsions, or he may believe what he has been told about the inevitability of insanity caused by masturbation.[42] The suicide of one young girl followed her failure to be accepted into a social club, and other girls have attempted suicide when their boy friends left them. Inability to face failure at school and fear of punishment, degradation or ostracism for antisocial acts or because of pregnancy are common reasons for suicide attempts.[54]

Situations unbearable to the adolescent may be related to his family. Excessive restrictions on his freedom or severe and unwarranted punishment may become intolerable burdens. He may find it impossible to endure parental quarrels, alcoholism, or sexual promiscuity, and he attempts suicide as his solution for eradicating the problem.[10, 30]

Many attempted suicides are revengeful and represent an effort of the adolescent to influence others' actions and attitudes toward him.[59, 60] Rebellion against parents and the desire to make them suffer for their neglect and inconsiderate behavior are common facets of suicide attempts.[12, 42] Chaotic and broken homes, characterized by family delinquency and the absence of one or both parents, are typically a part of the background of many suicidal adolescents,[54, 64, 66] who react with self-pity and paranoid tendencies.[36]*

There is seldom a case of suicide in which the individual did not announce his intention to kill himself several times before actually trying to do so. Parents or teachers too often ignore the adolescent who talks of suicide, making no attempt to find out what is troubling him[64] and degrading him with their patent belief that young people have no serious problems. Clues forecasting imminent suicide to which adults should be alert are chronic sleeplessness, loss of appetite, and withdrawal.[57] An adolescent talking of suicide should be protected by close supervision, and every threat must be taken seriously. Suicidal impulses are temporary, and if protection can be given the young person during periods when he requires it, he may never attempt to take his life. Continued surveillance is needed, however, until his difficulties are resolved.[30]

An adolescent who has considered or attempted suicide is demonstrating a critical need for assistance in changing his ways of thinking and in finding solutions to his problems. Burdened with feelings of in-

---

* See Case 42, Dorothy B., p. 529.

feriority and habits of insufficient self-discipline, he needs large doses of reassurance and commendation for his achievements, as well as firm requirements which will enable him to accomplish more and regard himself with greater respect.

REFERENCES

1. Angelino, H., Dollins, J., and Mech, E. V.: Trends in the fears and worries of school children as related to socio-economic status and age. *J. Genet. Psychol.*, 1956, *89*, 263–276.
2. Appelbaum, S. A.: The problem solving aspect of suicide. *J. Proj. Tech. Pers. Assess.*, 1963, *27*, 259–268.
3. Arieti, S.: Schizophrenia: the manifest symptomatology, the psychodynamic and formal mechanisms. *In* Arieti, S., ed.: *American Handbook of Psychiatry.* New York, Basic Books, Inc., 1959, vol. 1, pp. 459, 467, 473.
4. Ausubel, D. P.: Causes and types of narcotic addiction: A psychosocial view. *Psychiat. Quart.*, 1961, *35*, 523–531.
5. Bakwin, H.: Suicide in children and adolescents. *J. Pediat.*, 1957, *50*, 749–769.
6. Balser, B. H., and Masterson, J. F., Jr.: Suicide in adolescents. *Amer. J. Psychiat.*, 1959, *116*, 400–404.
7. Barker, G. H., and Adams, W. T.: Glue sniffers. *Sociol. Soc. Res.*, 1963, *47*, 298–310.
8. Barschak, E.: A study of happiness and unhappiness in the childhood and adolescence of girls in different cultures. *J. Psychol.*, 1951, *32*, 173–215.
9. Baxter, J. C., Becker, J., and Hooks, W.: Defensive style in the families of schizophrenics and controls. *J. Abnorm. Soc. Psychol.*, 1963, *66*, 512–518.
10. Bender, L.: *Aggression, Hostility, and Anxiety in Children.* Springfield, Ill., Charles C Thomas, 1953, pp. 86–87.
11. Bender, L.: The concept of pseudopsychopathic schizophrenia in adolescents. *Amer J. Orthopsychiat.*, 1959, *29*, 491–512.
12. Bender, L., and Schilder, P.: Suicidal preoccupations and attempts in children. *Amer J. Orthopsychiat.*, 1937, *7*, 225–234.
13. Bernard, H. W.: *Adolescent Development in American Culture.* Yonkers-on-Hudson, N. Y., The World Book Co., 1957, pp. 419–420, 425–428.
14. Bower, E. M., Shellhamer, T. A., and Daily, J. M.: School characteristics of male adolescents who later became schizophrenic. *Amer. J. Orthopsychiat.*, 1960, *30*, 712–729.
15. Burns, C.: Pre-schizophrenic symptoms in pre-adolescents' withdrawal and sensitivity. *Nerv. Child*, 1952, *10*, 120–128.
16. Cameron, N.: *The Psychology of Behavior Disorders.* Cambridge, Mass., Houghton Mifflin Co., 1947, pp. 247–273, 281–315, 446–491, 497, 524–530.
17. Cloward, R. A., and Ohlin, L. E.: *Delinquency and Opportunity: A Theory of Delinquent Gangs.* Glencoe, Ill., The Free Press, 1960.
18. Colbert, E. G., and Koegler, R. R.: The childhood schizophrenic in adolescence. *Psychiat. Quart.*, 1961, *35*, 693–701.
19. Conklin, E. S.: *Principles of Adolescent Psychology.* New York, Henry Holt and Co., 1935, p. 272.
20. Despert, J. L.: Suicide and depression in children. *Nerv. Child*, 1952, *9*, 378–389.
21. Dorcus, R. M., and Shaffer, G. W.: *Textbook of Abnormal Psychology*, Ed. 3. Baltimore, The Williams and Wilkins Co., 1945, p. 362.
22. Durandin, G.: Recherches sur les motifs et circonstances du mensonge (Research on the motive and circumstances of lying). *Ann. Méd.-Psychol.*, 1957, *1*, 201–242.
23. Eisenberg, L.: The autistic child in adolescence. *Amer. J. Psychiatr.*, 1956, *112*, 607–612.

24. Errera, P.: A sixteen-year follow-up of schizophrenic patients seen in an outpatient clinic. *AMA Arch. Neurol. Psychiat.*, 1957, *78*, 84–87.
25. Ettlinger, R., and Flordh, P.: Attempted suicide. Experience of five hundred cases at a general hospital. *Acta Psychiat.* (*Kbh.*), 1956, *106*, 300–301.
26. Finestone, H.: Cats, kicks, and color. *Soc. Probl.*, 1957, *5*, 3–13.
27. Fleck, S., Lidz, T., and Cornelison, A.: Comparison of parent-child relationships of male and female schizophrenic patients. *Arch. Gen. Psychiat.*, 1963, *8*, 1–7.
28. Galvin, J.: Mothers of schizophrenics. *J. Nerv. Ment. Dis.*, 1956, *123*, 568–570.
29. Garrison, K. C.: *The Psychology of Adolescence.* New York, Prentice-Hall, Inc., 1934, p. 113.
30. Gaultier, M., Fournier, E., and Gorceix, A.: A propos de 47 cas de tentatives de suicides chez des adolescents (A study of 47 cases of attempted suicide in adolescence). *Hyg. Ment.*, 1961, *50*, 363–369.
31. Gerard, D., and Kornetsky, C.: A social and psychiatric study of adolescent opiate addicts. *Psychiat. Quart.*, 1954, *28*, 113–125.
32. Gold, L.: Toward an understanding of adolescent drug addiction. *Fed. Probation*, 1957, *22*, 42–48.
33. Gould, I. B., Smith, L., Barker, W., and Gamso, R. R.: A specific approach to the vocational needs of adolescent users of narcotics at Riverside Hospital. *Psychiat. Quart. Suppl.*, 1954, *28*, 199–208.
34. Gutheil, E. A.: Reactive depressions. *In* Arieti, S., ed.: *American Handbook of Psychiatry.* New York, Basic Books, Inc., 1959, vol. 1, p. 346.
35. Hamilton, D. M., McKinley, R. A., Moorhead, H. H., and Wall, J. H.: Results of mental hospital treatment of troubled youth. *Amer. J. Psychiatr.*, 1961, *117*, 811–816.
36. Hendin, H.: Suicide. *Psychiat. Quart.*, 1956, *30*, 267–282.
37. Hollingworth, L. A.: *The Psychology of the Adolescent.* New York, D. Appleton-Century Co., 1928, p. 191.
38. Hoover, J. E.: *Uniform Crime Reports—1965.* Washington, D. C., United States Department of Justice, pp. 116, 121.
39. Hurlock, E. B.: *Child Development.* New York, McGraw-Hill Book Co., 1950, p. 255.
40. Jaeger, J. O. S.: Teen-age drug addiction: some thoughts regarding therapy and prophylaxis. *Amer. J. Psychother.*, 1952, *6*, 293–297.
41. Kagan, J., and Moss, H.: *Birth to Maturity.* New York, John Wiley and Sons, 1962, pp. 134, 213, 226.
42. Kanner, L.: *Child Psychiatry*, Ed. 3. Springfield, Ill., Charles C Thomas, 1959, pp. 619–623, 641–645, 693, 730, 752–756.
43. Kohn, M. L., and Clausen, J. A.: Parental authority behavior and schizophrenia. *Amer. J. Orthopsychiat.*, 1956, *26*, 297–313.
44. Laskowitz, D.: The adolescent drug addict: an Adlerian view. *J. Individ. Psychol.*, 1961, *17*, 68–79.
45. McCandless, B. R.: *Children and Adolescents.* New York, Holt, Rinehart and Winston, 1961, p. 193.
46. Meissner, W. W.: Comparison of anxiety patterns in adolescent boys: 1939–1959. *J. Genet. Psychol.*, 1961, *99*, 323–329.
47. Meissner, W. W.: Some anxiety indications in the adolescent boy. *J. Genet. Psychol.*, 1961, *64*, 251–257.
48. Meissner, W. W.: Some indications of sources of anxiety in adolescent boys. *J. Genet. Psychol.*, 1961, *99*, 65–73.
49. Neubauer, P. B., and Steinert, J.: Schizophrenia in adolescence. *Nerv. Child*, 1952, *10*, 129–134.
50. Nickling, G., and Toolan, J. M.: 20-year follow-up of an adolescent service in a psychiatric hospital. *Psychiat. Quart. Suppl.*, 1959, *33*, 301–316.
51. Nylander, I.: "Thinner" addiction in children and adolescents. *Acta Paedopsychiat.* (*Basel*), 1962, *29*, 273–283.
52. Portnoy, I.: The anxiety states. *In* Arieti, S., ed.: *American Handbook of Psychiatry.* New York, Basic Books, Inc., 1959, vol. 1, pp. 307–323.

53. Rubé, P.: Adolescence: II. The inner world of adolescence. *Amer. J. Psychother.*, 1955, *9*, 673–691.
54. Schachter, M., and Cotte, S.: Tentatives, chantages et vélleités de suicide chez les jeunes (Attempts, simulations and obsessions of suicide in the young). *Criança Portug.*, 1951, *10*, 171–195.
55. Schneiderman, L.: Anxiety and social sensitivity. *J. Psychol.*, 1954, *37*, 271–277.
56. Shaffer, L. F.: *The Psychology of Adjustment.* Cambridge, Mass., Houghton Mifflin Co., 1936, pp. 166, 176–178 190–197, 207, 217, 263–271.
57. Shneidman, E. S., Farberow, N. L., and Leonard, C. V.: Some facts about suicide. Public Health Service Publication No. 852. Washington, D. C., United States Department of Health, Education, and Welfare, 1961.
58. Singer, J. L., and McCraven, V. G.: Some characteristics of adult daydreaming. *J. Psychol.*, 1961, *51*, 151–164.
59. Stengel, E.: Some unexplored aspects of suicide and attempted suicide. *Comprehen. Psychiat.*, 1960, *1*, 71–79.
60. Stengel, E.: The complexity of motivations to suicidal attempts. *J. Ment. Sci.*, 1960, *106*, 1388–1393.
61. Stern, E.: Praeschizophrene Zustände (Preschizophrenic states). *Prax. Kinderpsychol., Kinderpsychiat.*, 1956, *5*, 273–284.
62. Symonds, A., and Herman, M.: The patterns of schizophrenia in adolescence. *Psychiat. Quart.*, 1957, *31*, 521–530.
63. Symonds, P.: The development of the ego and of the self. *In* Seidman, J. M., ed.: *The Adolescent.* New York, The Dryden Press, 1953.
64. Toolan, J. M.: Suicide and suicidal attempts in children and adolescents. *Amer. J. Psychiatr.*, 1962, *118*, 719–724.
65. Toolan, J. M., Zimmering, P., and Wortis, S. B.: Adolescent drug addiction. *N.Y. St. J. Med.*, 1952, *52*, 72–74.
66. Tuckman, J., and Connon, H. E.: Attempted suicide in adolescents. *Amer. J. Psychiatr.*, 1962, *119*, 228–232.
67. *Vital Statistics of the United States, 1964.* Washington, D. C., Department of Health, Education, and Welfare, 1966, vol. 2, part A, tables 1–25.
68. Whitman, J. R.: Learning from social and nonsocial cues in schizophrenia. *J. Gen. Psychol.*, 1963, *68*, 307–315.
69. Wilner, D. M., Rosenfeld, E., Lee, R. S., Gerard, D. L., and Chein, I.: Heroin use and street gangs. *J. Crim. Law Criminol.*, 1957, *48*, 399–409.
70. Yahraes, H.: *Narcotic Drug Addiction.* Mental Health Monograph 2, Public Health Service Publication No. 1021. Bethseda, Md., United States Department of Health, Education, and Welfare, 1963.
71. Zachry, C. B.: *Emotion and Conduct in Adolescence.* New York, D. Appleton-Century Co., 1940, pp. 437–438.
72. Zachry, C. B.: Problems of adolescents. *In* Seidman, J. M., ed.: *The Adolescent.* New York, The Dryden Press, 1953, p. 80.
73. Zuckerman, M., Oltean, M., and Monashkin, I.: The parental attitudes of mothers of schizophrenics. *J. Consult. Psychol.*, 1958, *22*(4), 307–310.

Chapter 43

Aggressive Reactions

Aggressive behavior of the adolescent encompasses many forms and is motivated by many reasons. For any individual, it has different meanings and different results.[22] It may be group-determined; and smoking, driving violations, disobedience, drinking, and running away are more prevalent and are considered less reprehensible by young people than would be true without peer encouragement. Aggressive behavior may be personally aimed, with a direct intention to influence or harm another by lying, anger, assault, arson, or murder. It may represent neither group defiance nor personal vengeance but may reflect a faulty social conscience and a failure to respect the rights of others, as do some acts of stealing and vandalism.

Aggression which is partially the consequence of group pressure is common and is less often accompanied by overtones of violence than is aggressive action directed against individuals or society. Most susceptible to group influence are late-maturing boys, who have higher drives for both social acceptance and aggression than early-maturing boys.[24] The adolescent who engages regularly in aggressive behavior harms himself and others, isolates himself from his family, and subjects himself to judgment and punishment by society.

Most aggressive actions of adolescents are delinquencies under the law. There were 1.3 million children and youths between the ages of ten and 18 arrested in 1965. Of these, 384,000 were referred to juvenile courts. In the five years from 1960 to 1965, juvenile arrests increased 47 per cent, compared to an increase in the juvenile population of 17 per cent. The number arrested represents 4 per cent of the

402

total juvenile population but does not indicate the actual number involved in illegal actions, inasmuch as many violators remain undiscovered or are never arrested.[16]

There was a 14 per cent increase in delinquency cases in 1964 over 1963, although the child population increased by only 4 per cent. Rural courts experienced a 33 per cent increase over the preceding year, and the greatest increase in arrests was of girls in rural courts. The rate of delinquency cases is three times higher in urban areas than in rural, and four times as many boys as girls are referred to courts.[19]

Not all juvenile offenders reach the courtroom. Of the juveniles taken into custody in 1965, 47 per cent were handled within the police department and released, and 47 per cent were referred to juvenile court. Welfare agencies, criminal or adult court, or other police agencies received the remaining 6 per cent.[16] Juvenile courts disposed of cases in 1964 in these ways: 8 per cent were dismissed; 30 per cent were dismissed with warning; 22 per cent were placed on probation; 9 per cent were assigned informal supervision; 9 per cent were committed to institutions; and the remaining 22 per cent received a variety of dispositions.[19] The high rate of recidivism, which ranges from 55 to 68 per cent, indicates that the problems presented by juvenile law violators are not being solved.[20, 31]

Kvaraceus[21] described the delinquent as unstable and dependent, as well as restless, impulsive, and defiant. He is extroverted and active, showing fewer fears than a normal adolescent and therefore typically is daring and adventurous. He is egocentric and resentful of authority, but he has a strong urge for companionship. The companionship he seeks is limited to those boys who share his antisocial orientation, however, and with the majority of his peers, he is distant and aloof.[2] He is relatively noncommunicative with adults and seldom reveals his intimate feelings.[17]

Social factors contribute to the production of aggressive behavior. There is a population shift to urban centers, and individual families also are moving frequently, so that anonymity, which is conducive to delinquent actions, is maintained easily. Aggressive and delinquent children often are members of families broken by divorce or separation and reconstituted as mixtures with half-siblings and stepparents, and in these families there is divided authority and loyalty and little feeling of identification. Prestige is based increasingly on material possessions and economic status, and there is great dependence on commercial recreation. Associated with the family's desire for the pleasures money provides is the exodus of mothers from the home to work and the subsequent disappearance of the parent traditionally considered to be responsible for the child's rearing. Because earnings are poorly managed and a working mother is overtired, the homes of most delinquents are crowded, scantily furnished, and inefficiently kept.[5, 21] An adolescent living in such surroundings dislikes his home and spends little time there. He easily becomes involved in antisocial behavior because he is unsupervised for long periods of time.

An aggressive boy is one who has failed to identify with his father and has become indifferent or hostile to him. Critical, restrictive treatment of the boy by his father is common, as is brutal physical punishment.[12] Angered and affronted, the boy disdains his father as a model for his own thinking and behavior, and in rejecting his father, he simultaneously rejects all constituted authority. The mother of an aggressive boy tends to protect him and to support his resistance to his father, whom she considers overly harsh. She seldom demands obedience from her son and overlooks his failure to comply with her directions, thus strengthening his oppositional reaction to authority.[2, 33] Some parents tacitly encourage aggression against school or legal authorities by the interest, amusement, and support with which they respond to the adolescent's antisocial activities.[2, 18]

SMOKING

Smoking is not considered a legal delinquency, and its control is vested in parents and school officials. Smoking typifies adult status to the adolescent, and there are few young people who do not experiment with it. Less than 40 per cent smoke regularly, however, and only 24 per cent of the adolescents questioned by Remmers and Radoler[27] stated that they approve of smoking.

Adolescents who smoke persistently are those whose parents smoke and permit the young person to smoke at home, after an initial protest, with the rationalization that smoking is a lesser evil than lying. Soon they condone smoking openly by providing the adolescent with cigarettes. Some parents initiate their elementary school children into smoking, gaining pleasure from defying convention.

School administrations vary in their attitudes. Some refuse to permit access to washrooms during the noon hour to prevent smoking then, and others provide an area on the school grounds where students may smoke.

Parents who do not wish their adolescents to smoke will have most success if they not only discuss with them the detrimental effects on health and pocketbook but take pains not to make it easy for them to smoke. There is less frequent smoking by a young person who may not smoke at home, and there are deterrents to excessive smoking in the reasonably expressed attitude of his parents and the disapproval of some of his peers.

DRIVING VIOLATIONS

Staton[30] stated that the adolescent boy has a mania to drive, and certainly there is seldom one who does not demand the keys to the family car on the day he reaches legal driving age. Girls are nearly as swift as boys to exercise their legal rights, and at 15 or 16 years of age they drive themselves and their friends to school, games, meetings, and movies.

With the increase in the number of young persons who drive, there has been a steady rise in traffic offenses—so great in some states that half of all reported juvenile delinquencies consist of driving violations.[19] Juvenile courts handled 442,000 traffic cases in 1964.

Speeding, running stop lights, cutting in and out of traffic, racing, following too closely, and illegal passing are common offenses of the adolescent driver; and there are several reasons why he is an unsafe driver, even though he is well coördinated and reacts quickly. When he drives, he is on equal status with adults for the first time in his life, and he revels in the power and speed he commands. He is anonymous in a car and seldom needs to worry about being recognized when he sneaks through a four-way stop or screeches his brakes. He can and does rid himself of aggressive feelings by frightening other drivers, jeering their caution, or racing dangerously. If he has friends riding with him, and more often than not he has, he must show them how carelessly skillful he is in handling a car and how indifferent he is to driving regulations. Some of his violations originate in his lack of driving experience, which causes him to be inattentive to his own driving, to signals, and to other cars' movements. He is unable to anticipate trouble from conditions around him, and he is unfamiliar with what causes accidents. He misjudges the time required to stop and the leeway he needs to enter the traffic stream, and he is not always coördinated in his steering or knowledgeable about hazardous weather conditions and poor roads.

Even though many driving violations are not vicious in intent, they can be fatal in effect, and they should be promptly and effectively handled by the courts. Suspension of his driver's license is an impressive penalty for the adolescent, and his parents' pleas that he cannot get to school without the car should be ignored. Fines should be paid by the young person, not his parents, and some courts require fines to be worked out in clean-up projects for the city. One judge required adolescent violators to copy in full the state's voluminous traffic regulations and pass a test on the information, with failure necessitating repetition of the entire procedure. Several courts utilize adolescent advisory councils for traffic offenders, selecting members monthly from high schools in the city to hear cases along with the judge and to recommend penalties.

DISOBEDIENCE

The adolescent, unlike the usual younger child, disobeys deliberately. He is convinced that he has the right to do as he chooses and that any obligation to obey his parents and teachers is secondary to his own wishes. His attitude is an expression of his rejection of the ideas, decisions, and supervision of adults and of his need to use his own judgment in determining his behavior. Sometimes he regrets breaking with his parents, but he seldom feels that he is wrong or that they should interfere in his chosen course of action.

Disobedience in the adolescent is more likely to occur when parents fail to permit the independence, freedom, and privacy which maturation demands, trying to hold the young person to rules and procedures appropriate for a younger child. The adolescent also will disobey if rules are vague and unenforced by penalty. A girl will stay out until three o'clock in the morning if she knows she can expect a scolding but no restriction of her future activities. A boy will obtain and drink beer and liquor without fear or guilt if his funds are not curtailed nor his driving limited after such actions. An adolescent who becomes angry easily disobeys orders promptly and vengefully, sometimes frightening the adults into submission. Many parents capitulate at the first sign of resistance or angry rebellion, fearing the adolescent's displeasure or even an actual attack.

Parents can help the adolescent conform to necessary requirements if they assume that he has valid reasons for his viewpoints and are as willing to consider them as they are to propound their own. They need to note whether there are certain areas in which he is disobedient or whether he resists all directions. If the problem is restricted to a few specific acts of disobedience, such as staying out late or failing to complete chores, parents and adolescent should exchange opinions and arrive at reasonable compromises.

If disobedience is generalized and discussion ends always in an angry impasse, then rules covering the few most important areas of disobedience should be established and enforced by parents. Penalties which are effective with adolescents include extra work assignments, restriction of nights out, fines, and limitation of car use. Penalties should be counterbalanced with rewards so that increased freedom is regularly accumulated by the young person who operates within the expectations of adults. Immature, impulsive parents who do not merit the adolescent's respect need to revise their own behavior before they can expect compliance with their wishes.

DRINKING

Arrests for violation of the liquor laws are increasing steadily. In 1965, nearly 42,400 young people under the age of 18 years were arrested for such violations, and an additional 1,700 were arrested for driving while intoxicated.[16]

There is a sharp increase in the use of alcohol between the ages of 14 and 18 years, especially for boys. By the time they reach 18 years, 90 per cent of all adolescents have consumed some alcohol at social occasions, at home, or at religious ceremonies. Only 15 per cent of high school students who drink do not do so at home.[7] The incidence drops when a distinction is made between adolescents who have tasted alcohol and those who drink with some regularity. Sower[29] investigated the drinking patterns of 2000 junior and senior high school students, and he reported that only 10 per cent consider themselves to be persons who drink. There are more boys and more older students in this group, and they belong to either the highest or lowest social classes. Many of them have grandparents who speak a European language, and drinking is a well-established family and cultural custom. The adolescent's attitudes and actions in respect to alcohol consumption are nearly always similar to those of his parents, and drinking assumes significance as an adult activity. With few exceptions, the adolescent's drinking takes place in groups, where his need to conform or experiment is strong.[27]

The adolescent who drinks habitually often suffers personal conflict from doing so, and although 35 per cent of the adolescents questioned in one study indicated that they sometimes drank, only 11 per cent of them approved of drinking.[27] Disapproval or condemnation of the adolescent may result if he drinks frequently in opposition to the customs and mores of family, peer groups, and public opinion. Serious personal problems develop when the drinking adolescent is penalized by the law or expelled from school. Drinking serves as a catalyst to driving accidents, sexual promiscuity, group aggression, and rejection of responsibility—all of which involve the young person in behavior deviations of lasting detrimental effect.

MacKay[23] studied 20 adolescent problem drinkers and found that their drinking was well established at the onset of puberty. Their families were economically substandard and indifferent to their behavior. These boys were characterized by hostility and impulsiveness and were depressed and sexually confused. A domineering mother and a weak father who drinks heavily himself and is indifferent to his son will produce an adolescent who questions the value of being male and who cannot himself behave in a mature, dependable way. His drinking represents both rebellion and defeatism.*

If family relationships can be altered, the adolescent still can learn to respect his father and acquire a protective attitude toward his mother to replace his dependency and resentment. When parents cannot revise their behavior, an adolescent boy who drinks excessively needs to live in an institution or boarding school. There he will be supervised and will be able to develop his dormant, neglected abilities. Guided and taught by men who are more acceptable models than his father, he can correct his concepts of masculinity and eventually acquire self-respect.

RUNNING AWAY

It has been estimated that 200,000 to 300,000 children run away from home annually and that about 55,000 of these are brought before juvenile courts. Runaways comprise 8 per cent of the total number of offenses of juveniles, with girls contributing the larger share. Over 22 per cent of the girls appearing in juvenile court are charged with running away, and it is the most frequent of all girls' offenses.[19] Runaway younger children are included in the figures cited above; however, the excursions of the older children are more purposeful and of longer duration than those of the younger. Wattenberg[32] stated that among boys he studied the peak age for running away was 15 years.

Older children run away because of an accumulation of disappointments, a conviction of worthlessness, a feeling of not belonging anywhere, or a desire for distracting adventure and escape from obligations and worries. Some can no longer tolerate parental arguing or alcoholism. Adopted children, dissatisfied, lonely, and uneasy, may set out to find their natural parents.[6, 20, 31]

An adolescent runaway escapes distressing situations with little regard for his own safety and comfort, and with minimal planning he leaves home confident that he can get along by himself. Most runaways do manage to take care of themselves and do not complain when they become hungry or cold. Much of their bravado comes from being with peers, however. Many of them leave in pairs or small groups, making plans en route about what they will do next and encouraging each other by disdainful appraisals of adults.†

---

* See Case 43, Gilbert R., p. 530.
† See Case 44, Susan T., p. 531.

If the runaway adolescent, motivated essentially by problems of status and feelings of loneliness, has assets which can be utilized to ensure him greater pride at school, this helps to compensate for conflicts at home. Parents immersed in self-pity cause an adolescent to feel revulsion as well as loneliness, so that his feelings of loss are mixed and he believes that leaving home cannot worsen his situation. If the adults' concern can be shifted from themselves to the child, they not only can supply the attention and control he needs but can engender new respect for themselves and present a more stable family picture. Sometimes a runaway adolescent can live with relatives who are more responsible than his parents, and he is able to accept them as a substitute family.

LYING

Lying in the pre-school or elementary school child is criticized and punished, but few parents or teachers cannot acknowledge that it is natural for young children. An adolescent who lies, however, is severely condemned for resorting to deliberate falsification at an age when he is expected to demonstrate both courage and consistent truthfulness. The frequency and the character of lying determine the acuteness of the problem.

The adolescent lies for the same reasons that the child does: to escape punishment or to control others' attitudes or actions with false information. His lies may not be limited to expedient fabrications but also may include elaborate, complex tales of social contacts with distinguished companions, stories of noble birth, and claims of extraordinary achievements. Involved lying of this kind is considered pathological because it is inappropriate, unnecessary, and compulsive. The pathological liar reacts automatically to any situation in which he feels helpless or ineffective by producing a story which enhances his feeling of prestige. Durandin[8] noted that the absurdity of a lie identifies it as regressive and as an attempt on the part of the individual to retreat into a childish belief in the efficacy of magic and the primacy of fantasy. Truth, by contrast, is a slow conditioning process toward consistently objective and realistic thinking.

The pathological liar is an immature and self-centered person who believes he cannot influence and impress others in more conventional ways. Because he is insecure, he benefits from commendation for all accomplishments, even minor ones, and this provides him with satisfaction and recognition for what he does and lessens his need to make false claims. Requirements for acceptable performance need to be increased steadily until they are those appropriate for his age, and he

ıssisted in working out solutions for each of his problems
ıarns to manage reality instead of altering it. Whenever he
ınto a fantastic, complex fabrication, his listener will help him
ıf he seriously relates an even more elaborate tale. The pathological
liar challenged with his own weapon is startled into recognition of the
unnecessary dramatization in which he indulges, and his need to continue the habit diminishes.

ANGER AND ASSAULT

Anger

Anger in the adolescent usually terminates in action, either immediate or delayed. He may strike or curse the person with whom he
is angry, or as a substitute for direct attack, he may promptly commit
an illegal or aggressive act.* At times, however, there is no overt
expression of anger, and the adolescent does not appear to be upset
by a degrading or abusive incident. Actually, strong resentment not
only has occurred but lingers, and the young person secretly plans to
take revenge on the parent, teacher, or peer who has angered him. He
may confide his intentions to friends, and days or even weeks later,
he carries out planned retaliation.† Some young people are only moderately displeased at the time a disturbing incident occurs, but later,
as they review the experience, they become exceedingly angry. If their
anger is augmented by still other incidents, eventually there is a precipitous outbreak of violence or an episode of running away which
climaxes accumulated anger not previously expressed.

Anger in the adolescent originates from four sources. It can be
an habitual reaction to displeasure, learned earlier by imitating a quick-
tempered parent or adopted as an effective means of controlling parents. Because it is well established, it remains as an automatic response
long beyond the age when most young people control its overt expression and acquire some tolerance for disturbing experiences.

Anger may appear when the adolescent is thwarted. He is at an
age when his desires are numerous and imperative, and his dependence
on parental approval has decreased. His ideas about the clothes he
must have, the places he must go, the friends he must see, and the
hours he must keep are immutable, and when his parents differ with
him, he becomes enraged.

Many adolescents are angered by the belittling and nagging they
receive from parents and from some of their teachers. When adults
fail to require the young person to conform to their expectations but

---

* See Case 6, Albert B., p. 499.
† See Case 3, Neal R., p. 497.

scold and insult him for not doing so, he does not forgive and forget this insult to his dignity.*

The adolescent is angered by unfair punishment. If he is 15 minutes late getting home and his parents sentence him as severely as if he had stayed out all night, he resents their unyielding determination to control his behavior minutely. Young people similarly are angered by teachers who punish minor deviations from rules.

Occasional anger is unavoidable and often justified, but if anger dominates the adolescent's responses, it needs to be decreased before the young person's revengeful acts involve him or others in serious difficulty. Hidden anger can be prevented from accumulating to an explosive peak if communication is maintained. Parents need to talk with their adolescent more as an equal and to abandon old habits of quickly dismissing his ideas and attitudes as insignificant. The young person who can talk to his parents without fearing automatic disparagement loses his anger without needing to act upon it. Better emotional control is needed by the adolescent who is accustomed to using anger to have his own way. Parents should set an example by showing emotional restraint, and they should require an apology for rudeness.

Assault

Over 41,300 persons under 18 years of age were arrested for assault in 1965, and 6140 of these were girls.[16] Besides illegal assault, adolescents engage in many forms of personally-directed, violent aggression against others. Some of them curse or strike their parents or teachers, threaten each other, and engage in individual or gang fights, sometimes staged for peer audiences. In pairs or gangs, aggressive adolescents attack older people or the police with knives, blackjacks, and fists; and they also choke or torture animals.

With few exceptions, assaultive adolescents have been beaten and cursed by their parents or by other adults responsible for their care, and their own behavior is both imitative and retaliatory. Not only is assault practiced on them but they are encouraged to assault others. A parent who indulges in subversion of the authority and dignity of the other parent fosters the same attitude in the child. A parent who teaches the child that the courts and police are unfair and prejudiced and who labels all school and public officials as thieves and swindlers is demonstrating belligerence and suspicion toward society. The child absorbs these attitudes and acts accordingly.

Easson and Steinhilber[9] found that the encouragement of aggression in children is not limited to families of low socioeconomic status. Investigating seven boys between the ages of eight and 16 years who

---

* See Case 1, Wallace J., p. 495.

made murderous assaults on others, they found that all came from socially acceptable families. In each case, one or both parents had condoned or fostered the assault, and after its occurrence, they had not confiscated the weapon the boy had used.*

An adolescent who assaults others is dangerous, and permitting him to continue in habitual angry retaliation can lead only to injury or death for others in either the immediate or remote future. Institutionalization of an assaultive adolescent is necessary if changes cannot be achieved at home. In a group setting, he receives objective and impartial treatment most of the time, and he is not subjected to a barrage of extreme emotion, prejudice, and abuse from adults.

ARSON

Arson committed by an adolescent may be an expression of direct aggression against a parent, or it may be the result of generalized aggression developing from anger originally focused on a parent. Because of the absence of guilt feeling, arson committed against public or unknown owners of buildings appears to afford more lasting pleasure than that which is personally directed. Yarnell[35] stated that many adolescent fire-setters go in pairs consisting of one active and one passive member, and they claim that they set fires merely for excitement.

Kanner[20] found fairly consistent family patterns among arsonists he studied. Mothers were perfectionistic, and fathers were disappointing and actively rejected by the adolescents. Strong sibling rivalry was common. Arsonists appear to pity themselves excessively and to feel that any act which disturbs or harms others is justified because they themselves are unhappy.†

Schmideberg[28] considered the arsonist treatable but indicated that he must be made aware of the social significance of his crime. If the family setting is conducive to impulsive aggression, this concern for others' rights is not easy to instill in the adolescent and can be achieved only if the parents revise their own feelings of self-pity, indulgence, and helplessness. When they can manage their own lives and the life of the child with more authority, the adolescent gains self-confidence and better control of his behavior.

MURDER

There were 576 arrests by police of juveniles under 18 years of age

---

* See Case 45, Alan J., p. 532.
† See Case 46, Irma B., p. 533.

for murder and nonnegligent manslaughter in 1965, and 161 arrests were made for negligent manslaughter. Approximately 10 per cent of those involved were girls.[16] Children or adolescents who cause another's death often are found to be disturbed, impulsive, and unsupervised. They kill suddenly, following an incident which angers them and with a weapon readily available. Usual victims are playmates or siblings.

Bender[4] studied 33 boys and girls below the age of 16 years who caused or were blamed for the death of another person. Of these, 20 were boys between the ages of 11 and 15 years. They killed impulsively by stabbing, shooting, or repeated blows with a heavy object, and their action was triggered by rage or by fright following a robbery or sexual attack. The weapon was either handy or offered to the angered individual by another boy. These boys demonstrated pathological symptoms of schizophrenia, brain disease, or epilepsy; three developed epilepsy a few months following the killing.

Bender[4] observed that conditions conducive to imminent murderous attack are: organic brain damage with an impulse disorder, childhood schizophrenia accompanied by preoccupation with killing and death, compulsive fire-setting, defeating school retardation, unfavorable home experiences, and a personal experience with violent death. Indulged adolescents of either sex kill in anger when they are refused something they want or when they are criticized or punished. Sometimes an adolescent boy kills his father after the father's repeated abuse of members of the family.

Institutionalization of the adolescent who commits murder is necessary, with the hope that control, order, and supervision eventually will teach him restraint.

STEALING

Nearly 352,000 arrests of juveniles for stealing were made in 1965, and of all arrests for stealing, over half are of juveniles.[16] Stealing includes larceny, the appropriation of accessible articles; robbery, stealing from an individual by force or threat; burglary, entering a home or building and stealing; and automobile theft. Stealing is the chief offense for which boys are arrested,[31] and the rates of arrest are increasing steadily.[15]

There is little guilt feeling among those who steal, partly because stealing often develops as a group activity, occurring with increasing frequency and diminishing concomitant emotion. Ball[1] found that delinquent boys considered stealing to be much more prevalent than did nondelinquent boys, a reflection of their own habitual witness of and participation in stealing. Even adults categorize the seriousness of various kinds of stealing, with some considering car theft to be relatively inconsequential.[11, 31] Studies of persistent car-stealers, however, indicate that their motives are similar to those of adolescents engaging in theft of all kinds.

An adolescent steals for the same reasons an elementary school child steals: to obtain possessions for himself or to buy presents for and treat boy and girl friends; to revenge himself for rejection or punishment by parents; to compensate for neglect or lack of affection by parents; to imitate the low standards of morality and legal obedience practiced by parents; and to force greater parental control.* Adolescent gangs engaged in stealing often are composed of immature boys who seek some feeling of maturity by risk-taking.[20, 31] They enjoy the thrill of sneaking out at night and breaking into buildings, and although they have some awareness of eventual discovery, they give no serious thought to its consequences. They regard their activities as recreation, rather than as illegal usurpation of others' property, and they vaguely expect forgiveness, understanding, and protection from punishment. They take articles of considerable value, such as transistor radios, television sets, hi-fi equipment, automobile accessories, musical instruments, or cameras, most of which they store away and never attempt to dispose of or use.

The following descriptions of boys apprehended for stealing illustrate the background and motivations of adolescents who habitually violate the law in this way:

Will B., age 14, of dull intelligence, burglarized homes to obtain money, which he spent for candy and movies. He complained of frequent headaches, allergic reactions to some foods, leg pains, and nervousness. Tall for his age, he looked two years older than he was, but he did not get along well with boys his own age or older and preferred younger companions. Will was the fourth of four children, but only one older sister, now pregnant, still lived at home. There was also an eight-year-old half-brother, whom Will considered grouchy and spoiled. Will's parents were divorced, and he seldom saw his father. His stepfather had died five years earlier. All of Will's older siblings had had a hand in rearing him, but his mother was lax in attention to and discipline of him. He often stayed out late at night, and he did as he pleased most of the time. Will was institutionalized, and during his stay he was depressed and moody and sometimes refused to associate with the other boys. He was easily led, gave up quickly, and seemed inattentive and uninterested when adults tried to talk with him. His stealing was an outgrowth of his desire to find some pleasure for himself and also to occupy the hours he spent away from home. Because his mother was more concerned with the problems of the other two children, he was ignored, and he had few satisfactions in life except those he provided for himself by stealing.

Eugene S., age 15, of average intelligence, stole, drank, and truanted from school. He was the fifth of seven children and the oldest of three still at home. His older brothers had taken him along when they stole cars, and he had begun to steal at an early age to get food—taking ducks and then cooking them

---

* See Case 13, Randy J., p. 505.

himself. As a younger boy he had sold junk to a dealer, stolen it back, and resold it. Eugene's mother had deserted the family several years before and had been married four times since then. Sometimes when Eugene was angry with his father, he would think of living with his mother, but this was only a passing wish. For the past six years, a young woman and her illegitimate daughter had lived with the family. Although the father sometimes whipped Eugene, the boy defended him and praised him for his responsibility in building the family a house. In school, Eugene had failed two grades, and his marks were barely passing. He planned to quit school as soon as he legally could. Whenever he was out of school, he tried to earn money somehow, and he bought his own clothes and never requested money from his father. With other boys, Eugene was tolerant, generous, and understanding, although he believed that he was not well liked by them. Eugene had been forced to assume responsibility for himself, and furnished with repeated family models of stealing, he maintained this familiar way of meeting his needs. Although he responded to encouragement and friendliness, he was quick to believe that persons acting this way toward him were insincere.

Howard A., age 15, of superior intelligence, stole cars repeatedly, often taking other boys, who were unaware that the car was stolen, for rides. Once he left home for two weeks and slept in the cars he took. He stole his first car when he was with another boy, and they stayed up all night instead of going home. Howard was the oldest of three children. He was indifferent to his younger sister but very proud of his ten-year-old brother, to whom he acted as a father. The family lived in a run-down neighborhood in a large city, and Howard had to travel by both bus and streetcar to get to school. Often he walked six miles to a youth center, getting home late at night. His mother was grossly obese, slovenly at housekeeping, and often drank. The father drank heavily but was able to stop when Howard told police that he stole cars because of his father's drinking. The father had frequently whipped him when he was younger, and although the boy thought little of his father, he still sought evidence of his affection and wished he were different. Howard had always made excellent grades in school but quit two different schools when his car stealing became known and teachers and peers criticized this behavior. Serious and reserved, Howard was coöperative with adults and usually patient with younger boys, although occasionally he hit them to make them obey. His high standards for himself and his family made the contrast between what he wished were true and the actuality of inadequate parents and a miserable home too great for him to endure. Rigid and conscientious, he could not rebel directly, but the car stealing served as punishment for his family and for himself, even as it elevated him for a transient period to a higher status of economic and social acceptability.

John K., age 13, of average intelligence, was committed to the state industrial school for stealing. He was initiated into stealing by other boys and continued to steal for excitement and in order to obtain money and presents for other boys. John was the youngest of four children. An older brother, now married, had followed the same pattern of behavior, and two older sisters had had little to do with John. His mother called him her baby, complained that his trial was unfair, and sent him a letter or package daily while he was at the state school. The father was strict and had whipped John occasionally. He gave him money only when he approved of the use for which it was intended, and in general he had no contact with his son. Although John was well developed physically, his coördination was poor and his vision was defective. He complained that other boys jeered him because he was not athletic and that he had few friends. During the past two years he had attended four different schools, but he had had no great difficulty with schoolwork until recently. He had held summer jobs and enjoyed earning money, but he was required to turn it over to his mother and account for that which he needed. At the institution he worked well, volunteered for additional chores, and tried to please his supervisors. Overdependent and helpless, John reacted to the criticism of his peers with considerable disturbance, and much of his behavior was based on his desire to be acceptable to them. His stealing also reflected his need to be independent of his parents and to obtain money he could spend freely.

Assistance for the adolescent who steals needs to be based on the reason responsible for it, but restitution and penalties always should be imposed as deterrents to continued stealing. Sometimes parents can revise their behavior and their techniques of rearing the young person and can provide the attention he needs to overcome his inadequacies and dispel his worries.

VANDALISM

Headlined in newspapers a few years ago was the story of an expensive spree by the blue-blooded young scions of socially prominent families which resulted in thousands of dollars' worth of damage being done to a mansion rented for a party. No one wanted to press charges, and no one felt that a crime had been committed.

Most vandalism occurs under similar circumstances. A group of boys, wandering around at night looking for excitement, break into a school, a house under construction, or a home from which the owners are away; and once inside they can think of nothing to do but ruin it. Although the group seldom sets out deliberately to vandalize, each individual eagerly follows the lead of the first person who begins it, and none attaches great significance to his behavior or feels excessively guilty because of it.[34]

Sometimes vandalism is more specifically directed and committed in anger. Falstein et al.[10] reported the vandalism of a group of institutionalized boys and girls who rioted after an accumulation of grievances against their supervisors and instructors at a time when most of the professional staff members were out of town. A boy angered by punishment at school may break into the building at night and vandalize it, sometimes taking along a companion in an effort to disguise his basically aggressive motivation.

The adolescent who has engaged in vandalism must apologize to the owner and make restitution for the damage with money, work, or both. Often he is a young person who has had limited supervision and attention from his parents, who are themselves unconcerned with others' rights. An incident of vandalism should result in a reappraisal of their own and the adolescent's social values and moral codes, and they should give more careful attention to his rearing.

REFERENCES

1. Ball, J. C.: Delinquent and non-delinquent attitudes toward the prevalence of stealing. *J. Crim. Law Criminol.*, 1957, *48*, 259–274.
2. Bandura, A., and Walters, R. H.: *Adolescent Aggression.* New York, The Ronald Press Co., 1959, pp. 83, 131, 201, 205, 207, 279.
3. Bandura, A., and Walters, R. H.: Dependency conflicts in aggressive delinquents. *J. Soc. Issues*, 1958, *14*, 52–65.
4. Bender, L.: Children and adolescents who have killed. *Amer. J. Psychiatr.*, 1959, *116*, 510–513.
5. Bennett, I.: *Delinquent and Neurotic Children.* New York, Basic Books, Inc., 1960.
6. Berger, I., and Schmidt, R. M.: Kinder-psychiatrische und psychologische Untersuchungsergebnisse bei Spontan- und Reaktivfortläufern (Results of child psychiatric and psychological investigations of spontaneous and reactive runaways). *Prax. Kinderpsychol., Kinderpsychiat.*, 1958, *7*, 206–210.
7. Bernard, H. W.: *Adolescent Development in American Culture.* Yonkers-on-Hudson, New York, The World Book Co., 1957.
8. Durandin, G.: Recherches sur les motifs et circonstances du mensonge (Research on the motive and circumstances of lying). *Ann. Méd.-Psychol.*, 1957, *1*, 201–242.
9. Easson, W. M., and Steinhilber, R. M.: Murderous aggression by children and adolescents. *Arch. Gen. Psychiat.*, 1961, *4*, 1–9.
10. Falstein, E. I., Feinstein, S. C., Offer, D., and Fine, P.: Group dynamics: inpatient adolescents engage in an outbreak of vandalism. *Arch. Gen. Psychiat.*, 1963, *9*, 32–45.
11. Gibbens, T. C. N.: Car thieves. *Brit. J. Delinq.*, 1958, *8*, 257–265.
12. Glueck, S., and Glueck, E. T.: *Unraveling Juvenile Delinquency.* New York, Commonwealth Fund, 1950.
13. Häberlin, A.: Der Ungehorsam: seine Erscheinungsweisen, seine Ursachen, und seine Behandlungsmöglichkeiten (Disobedience: its incidence, causes, and treatment). *Beih. Schweiz. Z. Psychol. Anwend.*, 1953, No. 23.
14. Healy, W.: *The Individual Delinquent.* Boston, Little, Brown and Company, 1920.
15. Hoover, J. E.: *Preliminary Report of 1963 Crime Statistics.* Washington, D. C., United States Department of Justice, March 6, 1964.
16. Hoover, J. E.: *Uniform Crime Reports—1965.* Washington, D. C., United States Department of Justice, pp. 104, 116.
17. Jaffee, L. D., and Polansky, N. A.: Verbal inaccessibility in young adolescents showing delinquent trends. *J. Hlth. Hum. Behav.*, 1962, *3*, 105–111.
18. Johnson, A. M.: Juvenile delinquency. *In* Arieti, S., ed.: *American Handbook of Psychiatry.* New York, Basic Books, Inc., 1959, vol. 1. pp. 840–856.
19. *Juvenile Court Statistics—1964.* Washington, D. C., United States Department of Health, Education, and Welfare.
20. Kanner, L.: *Child Psychiatry*, Ed. 3. Springfield, Ill., Charles C Thomas, 1957, pp. 600, 682, 688, 701–702, 711, 719.
21. Kvaraceus, W. C.: *The Community and the Delinquent.* Yonkers-on-Hudson, New York, The World Book Co., 1954, pp. 95–100, 237.
22. Lansky, L. M., Crandall, V. J., Kagan, J., and Baker, C. T.: Sex differences in aggression and its correlates in middle-class adolescents. *Child Developm.*, 1961, *32*, 45–58.
23. MacKay, J. R.: Clinical observations on adolescent problem drinkers. *Quart. J. Stud. Alcohol*, 1961, *22*, 124–134.
24. Mussen, P. H., and Jones, M. C.: The behavior inferred motivations of late- and early-maturing boys. *Child Developm.*, 1958, *29*, 61–67.

25. Noshpitz, J. D.: A smoking episode in a residential treatment unit. *Amer. J. Ortho-psychiat.*, 1962, *32*, 669–681.
26. Perlman, I. R.: *Statistical Aspects of Antisocial Behavior of the Minor in the United States.* Washington, D. C., United States Department of Health, Education, and Welfare, December, 1963.
27. Remmers, H. H., and Radoler, D. H.: *The American Teen-Ager.* Indianapolis, Bobbs-Merrill, 1957, p. 252.
28. Schmideberg, M.: Pathological firesetters. *J. Crim. Law Criminol.*, 1953, *44*, 30–39.
29. Sower, C.: Teen-age drinking as group behavior. *Quart. J. Stud. Alcohol*, 1959, *20*, 655–668.
30. Staton, T. F.: *Dynamics of Adolescent Adjustment.* New York, The Macmillan Co., 1963, p. 181.
31. Teagarden, F. M.: *Child Psychology for Professional Workers.* New York, Prentice-Hall, Inc., 1940, pp. 467, 469, 487–488.
32. Wattenberg, W. W.: Boys who run away from home. *J. Educ. Psychol.*, 1956, *47*, 335–343.
33. Wylie, H. L., and Delgado, R. A.: A pattern of mother-son relationship involving the absence of the father. *Amer. J. Orthopsychiat.*, 1959, *29*, 644–649.
34. Wyss, R.: Zum kindlichen Vandalismus (Vandalism in children). *Z. Kinder-psychiat.*, 1954, *21*, 190–196.
35. Yarnell, H.: Fire setting in children. *Amer. J. Orthopsychiat.*, 1940, *10*, 272–286.

Part V

THE
HANDICAPPED
CHILD

Chapter 44

Introduction

Prospective parents proudly anticipate the birth of a child and delight in the promise he holds for winning esteem for himself and for the family. When the newborn child is physically or intellectually handicapped, their dreams are destroyed, and they feel deep disappointment and even shame. Some parents refuse to accept the irrevocability of the child's handicap. Some develop a continuing anger, in dread of the comments, stares, sympathy, and isolation they will encounter and in anticipation of the burden which the child's needs will impose on their freedom. They seek reasons for the handicap, and they blame themselves for transmitting genetic weaknesses. Many consider the child's handicap a visitation of deserved punishment upon themselves.[14] They fear the formidable responsibilities ahead, knowing they must provide for the child's training and physical care by extraordinary and unfamiliar means.

THE HANDICAPPED CHILD'S REARING

The distress parents feel is reflected in their rearing of the child, and the most common reaction is to overprotect him. Feeling sorry for the child and feeling guilty either about their role in causing his defect or their reaction to him because he is imperfect, they attempt to make amends. They placate him, hover over him, give him what he demands,

421

and never require acceptable behavior of him. He remains dependent on his parents for years and is demanding, dissatisfied, and immature. Kammerer[7] reported that overprotection was apparent in the rearing of 64 per cent of 80 orthopedically-handicapped children he studied and that their personal adjustment was significantly poorer than that of children similarly afflicted but not overprotected.

Other parents react in the opposite way, ignoring and neglecting the child. Concluding that his future is hopeless and that nothing can improve his situation, they abandon him and fail to provide the affection, stimulation, and special training he requires. The child becomes depressed, lonely, and resentful.

A few parents actively reject the handicapped child. They regard him as a disgraceful embarrassment, and they ridicule him, avoid associating with him, and punish him severely. The child treated this way becomes aggressive and anxious, and he is unable to develop a close relationship with anyone.

Some parents are determined to counteract or overcome the effects of the handicap by sheer force. They criticize the child constantly in an effort to improve him, and they authoritatively arrange his activities and make all decisions for him. They commit themselves to presenting him in as favorable a light as possible, but they consider him incompetent to assist in achieving this goal. The child is frustrated repeatedly and has limited self-confidence.[8]

THE HANDICAPPED CHILD'S SELF-CONCEPT

The child first becomes fully aware of his handicap and the liabilities it imposes during his elementary school years. He discovers that he is different from his peers, that special attention must be given to his education and training, that his choices and activities are restricted, and that his independence and social acceptability are impaired. Inevitably, he encounters more frustration and isolation than the normal child.[6] Nevertheless, he need not develop a deviate or maladjusted mode of response, and no typical "handicapped personality" exists.[7]

Certain attitudes are prevalent among many handicapped children, however. The child often is timid socially and feels inferior because he considers himself to be defective and because he repeatedly experiences isolation from peers and failure to compete adequately with them.[7] He is concerned about his physical and social limitations,[12] but if he accepts these and then sets attainable goals which he strongly desires to achieve, his personal adjustment improves. The child who remains dissatisfied with himself anxiously seeks social acceptance and busies himself with distracting activity to divert his attention from his unhappiness.[9] Sometimes the child assigns responsibility for his temper, selfishness, or aggression to his handicap.

Insecurity and depression may accompany the child's struggles to maintain his self-confidence despite his unhappy experiences with peers and with the members of his own family. He can reconcile himself to the limitations of his handicap without rancor or discouragement, however, if he is well accepted by parents and siblings, given the special assistance he needs, and permitted to formulate and attain reasonable goals of independence and achievement.

ASSISTANCE FOR PARENTS AND CHILD

Physicians, psychologists, social workers, and teachers concerned with the handicapped child need to be aware of the conflicting and painful feelings of parents, and they must avoid impersonal brusqueness in discussing the present and future problems the child presents.[4] When parents are as well informed about the nature and prognosis of the disability as the professional is, they can accept the reality of the handicap and refrain from years of fruitless search for nonexistent cures. Information about the disability, suggestions for managing the child, and referrals to community resources aid parents. Emotional reactions of guilt, withdrawal, anger, and resentment should be acknowledged as natural initial feelings.

Eventually, however, parents can learn to respect the child as an individual, possessing exactly the same human needs as every other child.[11] They can best assist him to develop self-respect from achievement and to win friends by exemplifying friendliness themselves to him and to others. Parent and child's joint effort to educate the curious, pitying, anxious, and rejecting persons whom they meet aids them in dispelling their own strong emotions.

A child's desire to be independent begins early in life and should not be hindered in the handicapped child, although attainable physical, intellectual, and social standards should be set. The child should not be placed in situations where he repeatedly fails or always is isolated by peers. His social contacts with nonhandicapped children should involve activities in which he can compete on a relatively equal basis and for which his experiential background is similar to that of the other children.[6]

The handicapped child's development toward competent maturity is thwarted when his physical movements and social contacts are restricted, when his dependency is prolonged, and when his parents are overanxious about the future. Parents and teachers need to respect the child and to provide him with the training and rearing necessary for full development of his inherent personal, intellectual, social, physical, and vocational capacities.

REFERENCES

1. Baum, M. H.: Some dynamic factors affecting family adjustment to the handicapped child. *Except. Childr.*, 1962, *28*, 387–392.
2. Blodgett, H.: A keystone in rehabilitation. *Crippled Child*, 1958, *35*, 14–15, 26–27.
3. Cook, J. J.: Dimensional analysis of child-rearing attitudes of parents of handicapped children. *Amer. J. Ment. Defic.*, 1963, *68*, 354–361.
4. Dembo, T.: Sensitivity of one person to another. *Rehabilit. Lit.*, 1964, *25*, 231–235.
5. Gibbs, N.: Zum Verständnis des gebrechlichen Kindes (Toward understanding the physically handicapped child). *Heilpädag. Werkbl.*, 1959, *28*, 50–54.
6. Johnson, G. O.: Guidance for exceptional children. *In* Cruickshank, W. M., and Johnson, G. O., eds.: *Education of Exceptional Children and Youth*. Englewood Cliffs, N. J., Prentice-Hall, Inc., 1958, pp. 611–647.
7. Kammerer, R. C.: An exploratory psychological study of crippled children. *Psych. Rec.*, 1940, *4*, 47–100.
8. Kanner, L.: *Child Psychiatry*, Ed. 3. Springfield, Ill., Charles C Thomas, 1957, pp. 117–132.
9. Mussen, P. H., and Newman, D. K.: Acceptance of handicap, motivation, and adjustment in physically disabled children. *Except. Childr.*, 1958, *24*, 255–260, 277–279.
10. Rawls, H. D.: Social factors in disability. *New Outlook for the Blind*, 1957, *51*, 231–236.
11. Reid, E. S.: Helping parents of handicapped children. *Children*, 1958, *5*, 15–19.
12. Richardson, S. A., Hastorf, A. H., and Dornbusch, S. M.: Effects of physical disability on a child's description of himself. *Child Developm.*, 1964, *35*, 893–907.
13. Saxer, G.: Emotionelle Schwierigkeiten des Körperbehinderten Kindes (Emotional difficulties of the physically handicapped child). *Heilpädag. Werkbl.*, 1958, *27*, 50–53.
14. Schechter, M. D.: The orthopedically handicapped child: Emotional reactions. *Arch. Gen. Psychiat.*, 1961, *4*, 247–253.

Chapter 45

The Mentally
Retarded Child

Mental retardation became evident as a national problem during the universal intelligence testing employed during World War II to screen and place men in military service. Not only was mental retardation widespread among the servicemen tested, but the complexity of the disability was apparent with the discovery that broad variability in skills, adaptability, personality characteristics, and accessibility to training existed among those classified as mentally retarded.[59]

In the ensuing 25 years, a new and continuing interest in mental retardation has developed. Knowledge of the etiology of mental retardation and steps to prevent its occurrence in the unborn child are increasing steadily. Research has produced significant findings related to the characteristics and capabilities of the retarded. Education and training of retarded children have broadened in scope and relevance, and parents of retarded children have united to provide and urge the community's provision of more educational facilities. Vocational training and supervised work experience have enabled the adolescent and young adult retardate to find employment in an industrialized society. The use of community resources for recreation and entertainment and membership in youth organizations are widening the experience and the social skills of retardates. Both parents and physicians have a more accurate understanding of the needs of the retarded child.

Incidence of Retardation

The incidence of retardation varies according to the kind of survey conducted and its location, as well as the age of the child. An accurate numerical count of pre-school retarded children and of older adolescents is seldom possible because at these ages children are not subject to the scrutiny of the schools' evaluation of their competence in academic learning.[33] It has been estimated, however, that three of every 100 persons are retarded.[16] Estimates of the numbers of retarded children in the school population range from 2 to 5 per cent and constitute some two million individuals.[17, 21, 36]

Diagnosis

Although diagnosis of the severely or moderately retarded child usually is not difficult, evaluation of the mildly retarded child is subject to many inaccuracies, and generalizations or judgments concerning his capacity cannot be made with certainty. Retardation sometimes is not suspected or diagnosed until after the child has started to school and his teacher finds that he does not learn at the same rate as his peers.

The individual tests of intelligence most widely used to identify the retarded child are the Revised Stanford-Binet Intelligence Scale and the Wechsler Intelligence Scale for Children. These tests consist of tasks for the child to perform, questions to answer, puzzles to solve, and directions to follow. Sometimes he must supply information; or he must imitate, create, or make a choice.

The tests indicate the child's ability on the specific tasks he is given, and what he is able to do is compared with the performance of the average child of his chronological age on the same tasks. A mental age is assigned on this basis, and the ratio between the child's chronological age and mental age establishes his intelligence quotient. Although it is often assumed that the child's performance on the tests measures his maximum capacity, this assumption is questionable,[22] and a diagnosis of mental retardation needs to be clarified by a description of the abilities being tested.[27]

The tests themselves, because they are constituted of different kinds of tasks and involve different methods of administration, do not produce identical results. Rohrs and Haworth[54] reported that retarded children earned higher intelligence quotients on the Stanford-Binet than on the full-scale Wechsler-Bellevue, and inconsistencies in ability to succeed with verbal tasks, as compared with performance tasks, on both tests have been observed repeatedly. A child with marked verbal difficulty or one handicapped by defective vision, hearing, or motor control cannot demonstrate his true capacity on the tests.[1] If he comes from a deprived or abusive social background or if he is fatigued,

afraid, or negativistic, he will fail test items he is capable of passing. Tests such as the Leiter International Performance Scale and Raven's Progressive Matrices can be given the child whose verbal or motor capabilities are limited, and the Vineland Social Maturity Scale provides supplementary information about the child's growth in independence and thus aids in the evaluation of his learning ability. Suspected retardation should be investigated at an early age, and examinations should be repeated regularly over a period of years. Specialists in pediatrics, speech, and social work should add the results of their observations to those of the educator and the psychologist.[1, 59]

ETIOLOGY

There are over 200 distinct causes for the occurrence of mental retardation in the child, and the significant determinants may appear during the prenatal, paranatal, or postnatal period.

Prenatal Period

Interference with the growth and development of the central nervous system during fetal life has far-reaching effects because of the rapid rate at which the unborn child is developing. At two months' gestation, the central nervous system comprises 50 per cent of fetal weight, but at birth it is only about 10 per cent of the total weight. Infection, metabolic defects, endocrine disorders, toxic agents, brain abnormalities, and trauma all can damage the fetus.[58]

Infection. Rubella infection in the mother during the first three months of pregnancy results in mental deficiency in 20 to 70 per cent of the children thus exposed. It is believed that the virus produces irreparable brain lesions in the fetus. There are also ocular and auditory nerve lesions and congenital anomalies of the heart, cranium, and teeth.

Syphilitic infection may be transmitted from mother to fetus, and infection at an early stage of pregnancy usually results in death of the child. At a later stage, diffuse or localized meningovascular lesions may result. The mental defect usually is mild, but irreversible.[33]

The parasite of toxoplasmosis, if transmitted from the placenta to the fetus, causes serious damage to the fetal brain with subsequent severe mental defect, hydrocephalus, and convulsions. Pneumonia and influenza in the mother sometimes also cause damage to the central nervous system of the fetus.

Metabolic Defects. Study of the chronology of the development of enzyme systems is aiding in understanding metabolic defects which cause fetal damage.[51]

Galactosemia is a disorder of carbohydrate metabolism, first evidenced shortly after birth and characterized by malnutrition, jaundice, liver enlargement, and mental retardation.[56] Galactose accumulates in the body fluids, where it serves as a toxic substance impairing tissues and organs. The elimination of milk and the substitution of lactose with other sugars aids the infant.[33]

Phenylketonuria is a disorder of protein metabolism, resulting in the accumulation of unmetabolized phenylalanine in the body fluids, and this is believed to interfere with the early normal development of the brain, possibly by inhibiting myelination. Mild to severe mental retardation occurs, and seizures are present in one third of the patients. Treatment by low phenylalanine diets in early infancy usually has proved successful in preventing the development of mental deficiency.[33]

Disorders of fat metabolism are apparent after birth, and with their onset the child shows progressive deterioration. Amaurotic family idiocy, or Tay-Sachs disease, has been reported in as many as three or four siblings in one family. There is conspicuous swelling of all neurons of the body, which are infiltrated with lipid material.[33] Vision is impaired and total blindness eventually results. Although reflexes are unaltered, there are often a spastic or flaccid paralysis, vasomotor disorders, and unusual sensitivity to sound; and death occurs before the end of the third year.[35] The disease is found predominantly in Jewish children. Fröhlich's syndrome (adiposogenital dystrophy) is also a disorder of fat metabolism which is characterized by hypogenitalism, marked obesity, and moderate mental retardation.[35]

Endocrine Disorders. Thyroid disease and diabetes of the mother may sometimes affect the developing fetus adversely.[58] Disturbances of endocrine function in the child also lead to retardation and other associated symptoms of maldevelopment.

Hypothyroidism, or cretinism, is caused by dysfunction of the thyroid gland, which is sometimes enlarged to form a goiter and sometimes atrophied. Insufficient iodine intake is related to the dysfunction, and endemic cretins are found in large numbers in certain areas of Europe and Asia where intake is limited. Growth is stunted, the head is enlarged, the neck is short and thick, and the hands are broad and short. Cretins typically have a low forehead, puffy eyelids, scanty eyebrows, a large depressed nose, thick lips, and a large and protruding tongue. The child is passive and appears stuporous. If desiccated thyroid is administered early, there are good results for physical growth and the intelligence level also can be improved.[33]

Toxic Agents. Exposure to radiation injures the developing nervous system of the fetus, and overexposure to x-ray has resulted in the production of a microcephalic child. Toxic substances ingested by the mother, such as alcohol or excessive amounts of vitamin D, may damage

the fetal brain; and abortifacients may also cause damage.

Immunological mechanisms act as toxic agents: Incompatibility in Rh factor of the blood systems of mother and child produces jaundice, anemia, paralysis, and convulsions at birth, and mental defect is apparent later. Lesions in the basal ganglia have been found. Prompt transfusions prevent the development of these symptoms.[33]

Jervis[33] tentatively classified mongolism (Down's syndrome) with the toxic mental deficiencies, observing that miscarriages, dysmenorrhea, and long periods of sterility are more characteristic of mothers of mongols than of normal children. Most studies indicate that the mothers of mongols are on the average five to ten years older than mothers of normal children, which suggests that senescence of the endocrine reproductive system or pathological lesions of the uterus may create a variety of toxic conditions in the mother. Extensive research has verified the presence of an extra chromosome, now considered responsible for producing a combination of defects in the child. The clinical syndrome is well defined and relatively common, occurring in approximately 20 per cent of moderately retarded children.[41] The mongoloid child has a small, round head which is flattened in back. The eyes have oblique palpebral fissures, they are closely spaced, and there is an epicanthal skin fold at the medial angle, giving the child an Oriental appearance. The hands are thick and stubby, the thumbs and toes are abducted, and the palm lines show no definite pattern. There are transverse fissures on the back of the tongue, which may be protruded. Dysfunction of the thyroid, adrenal, and pituitary glands, as well as metabolic abnormalities, have been observed. The child is characterized by placidity, good nature, affection, and obedience.[35]

Brain Abnormalities. Porencephaly is a lack of brain substance, usually in the anterior or middle parts. The child shows spastic paralysis, convulsions, defective speech, and mental retardation.

Microcephaly is disproportionate smallness of the brain and skull. The brain also may have a simplified convolutional pattern, islands of gray substance may be found within the white matter, and the corpus callosum may be absent. The head is cone shaped. Half of all microcephalic children suffer convulsions, and mental retardation varies from moderate to severe.

Hydrocephalus is an accumulation of an abnormal amount of cerebral spinal fluid (from one to five quarts) in the ventricles or subarachnoid space of the brain. Familial occurrence of the condition has been reported, and it also has been correlated with traumatic insults, infectious disease, maternal syphilis, tuberculosis, and alcoholism. The head shape shows prominent frontal and parietal protuberances, the skull is distended, and the fontanelles do not close for many years. The head enlargement is disproportionate to the facial size. Mental retardation varies from mild to severe. The hydrocephalic child usually is cheerful and affectionate, but he is awkward and has difficulty managing head movements.[35]

Trauma. Intrauterine trauma is considered rare, but if it is severe enough to cause uterine bleeding, anoxia may result.[33] Maternal convulsions may cause tears, and premature rupture of membranes or placental anomalies may occur.[58]

Familial Mental Retardation. Individuals are classified as familial retardates when they show no pathological condition which might interfere with normal brain function and no clinical manifestation other than intellectual deficit. Genetic factors are considered responsible for the retardation, and their significance is verified by the incidence of sibling retardation, which ranges from 24 to 51 per cent.[4]

Paranatal Period

During the birth of the infant, damage may occur from a variety of sources, and its usual effect is temporary asphyxia, which the infant cannot tolerate.[41] Among the conditions which can injure the infant at the time of delivery, Russell and Endres[58] listed anesthesia, gonorrheal infection, maternal hypertension and fetal hemorrhage, spasm or breech delivery, cephalopelvic disproportion, precipitate or prolonged delivery, and caesarean section. There are inherent dangers in prematurity or postmaturity.

Postnatal Period

Postnatal causes of mental retardation include brain damage resulting from encephalitis, toxicosis, and trauma. Emotional and environmental deprivation also are known to cause retardation in the young child.

Encephalitis. Encephalitis is responsible for the retardation of about 5 per cent of the institutionalized population. During the illness, the patient is in coma and there are convulsions, motility disturbances, and delirium, with mental defect apparent upon recovery. Encephalitis develops from a virus and may be a sequela of childhood diseases such as measles, scarlet fever, chickenpox, or influenza. Postencephalitic children are restless, impulsive, assaultive, and destructive; and defects are most severe in children suffering the disease during the first five years of life.[33]

Toxicosis. Most common of the toxic agents affecting infants and small children is lead. Lead-based paint is rarely used for children's toys at present because of its known danger, but the infant may ingest it from cosmetics or ointments applied to the mother's breasts, and toxic substances can be transmitted through the mother's milk. Because the poison accumulates in the child's system in small quantities over a period of time, the outward signs are delayed and often the condition is unrecognized until symptoms are severe. The symptoms vary from fretfulness and headache to manifestations of nervous system damage such as projectile vomiting, convulsions, paralysis, and delirium. Intellectual and behavioral retardation follow.[35]

Trauma. Many parents ascribe a child's behavioral and intellectual defects to falls suffered at an early age, but because of the frequency with which children fall, it is not always possible to assess the effect of a specific incident. Injury to the head may result in disturbed behavior which lasts from two to five weeks and which is followed by persisting irritability and unmanageability. Headaches occur, aphasia may develop, and there may be both paralysis and intellectual deterioration. Prognosis for the child is based in part on his pre-injury personality and his family's management of him.[35]

Emotional and Environmental Deprivation. The child who is deprived emotionally and environmentally during infancy and the preschool years performs poorly in school and earns low scores on standard intelligence tests. Children from homes of low socioeconomic status or isolated rural areas or children who have been residents of institutions most of their lives give minimal responses to stimulation and exhibit a low motivation to learn, to experiment, and to create.

Although pathological mothering cannot cause severe retardation, the child who is isolated from or abused by others often is mildly retarded.[67] Pasamanick[49] noted the higher rate of mental deficiency among Negroes and attributed it to their social and economic segregation, as well as to the lack of care during pregnancy, resulting in complications and prematurity. Zigler[70] found more social deprivation among familial retardates than among organic retardates, and he suggested that this accounts for motivational differences between them.

Culturally deprived children who are exposed in nursery schools to new experiences and increased personal contacts demonstrate accelerated intellectual activity and responsiveness.

CLASSIFICATION AND DESCRIPTION

For purposes of communication among adults responsible for his training, a child considered mentally retarded is classified at one of three levels. Over the years, the nomenclature designating these levels has changed, and at present several classification systems exist, some of which categorize into four or five levels. In general, however, the child with an intelligence quotient between 55 and 75 is considered mildly retarded; the child with an intelligence quotient between 25 and 50 is considered moderately retarded; and the child with an intelligence quotient below 25 is considered severely retarded. Mildly retarded (educable) children comprise 75 per cent of the total number of retardates; moderately retarded (trainable) children comprise 20 per cent; and only 5 per cent require custodial care throughout their lives.[62] The child with an intelligence quotient between 75 and 90 has difficulty learning in a regular classroom; yet there is almost never special provision made for his education.

Divisions of these kinds are far from absolute, and amorphous areas of accomplishment and potential exist for every child for several reasons. First, the obtained intelligence quotient is only an indication of capacity, and it may be revised according to the child's success or failure in acquiring the skills which the tests measure.[60] Second, the potential of two children earning identical scores on an intelligence test often is different because of accelerating or retarding personal factors. Depending on his language skill, his experience with success, his acceptance of himself, and the home training and attention he receives, one child's response to learning tasks will differ from another's. Finally, the chronological age, as well as the mental age, of the child is a factor in his educability. Intellectual growth is most rapid during the early years. In the retarded child, it not only develops at a slower rate than in the normal child, but it also reaches a final plateau at an earlier chronological age.

The Mildly Retarded Child

Physical Development. The mildly retarded child may be one to four months slower than the normal child in sitting, standing, or walking.[27] His movements may always remain deliberate because his control is uncertain, and awkwardness at physical sports or in manipulating a pencil may be apparent. He tends to be slight in build and shorter than the average child,[38] and he tires more readily.[1]

Physical distinctions of these kinds are not universal, however. The child whose retardation is undetected until he enters school often has a history of walking at the normal age, and he is reported to ride a tricycle, climb, and run as do children of similar age with whom he plays. He may be of normal height and weight, and in facial appearance he may be indistinguishable from his peers. This child, with the assets of normal appearance and physical coördination, is faced with problems unencountered by the physically deficient retardate. Parents and teachers react automatically with lower standards for the small and awkward child, but they expect normal performance from the physically adequate child. Acquaintances and strangers with whom he will have contact at various times throughout his life will expect good judgment and thoughtful performance from him because there is no obvious cue that he is incapable of them. His physical ability and normal appearance afford him the comfort of not having to endure the stares and pitying comments of others, however, and his self-esteem is enhanced because he looks like other people.

Learning Ability. Toward the end of the nineteenth century, the public schools began to provide classes for the mentally retarded child,[44] and today there are few school systems which do not attempt to segregate the slow learner and teach him in a small class geared to his own learning rate. There are insufficient numbers of these classes to provide for all of the children who require them, however, and smaller school systems cannot afford to maintain them. The mildly retarded child is taught basic reading, writing, spelling, and arithmetical skills, and he may attain a fourth or fifth grade level of achievement after nine or more years of instruction.

The slow learner has a short attention and interest span, limited creativity and imagination, a slow reaction time, low retentive power, an inability to think abstractly or utilize symbols, difficulty in transferring ideas, limited initiative and self-direction, low standards of workmanship, and defective ability in vocabulary acquisition, reasoning, defining, discriminating, and analyzing.[1] His teacher faces a complex task which tries her ingenuity and her patience. She must be aware that a pupil's unpleasant personality may result not from his retardation but from the reaction of his family and the neighbors to him. Many retarded children have multiple handicaps, and disturbances of perception, incoördination, and defective vision or hearing require that the teacher constantly adapt her techniques to the handicaps of individual children.

Even with effective teaching, the rewards of progress often are imperceptible, and teachers who work with the same children over a lengthy period of time record their achievements so that they can identify improvement which has occurred over a span of three or four years. Experienced teachers find that all activities should be short in duration and narrow in scope. Drill and practice are needed, but this should be meaningful. Concrete demonstrations, illustrations and other visual aids, field trips, and direct experiences should be extensively utilized. Expression by the child should be encouraged, and he should be included in plans made for some aspects of his work. Teaching should capitalize on the child's immediate experiences at school, at home, and in the community. Individual abilities need to be identified and developed, and creative ideas and interests should be encouraged. Games, flash cards, flannel boards, use of objects, and emphasis on oral methods produce learning which does not result from written work.

Frequent evaluation of work and reassurance help a child, but praise should be given only when it is earned. Pride in his class and school, in achievement, in his appearance, and in himself can be developed in the retarded child.

His education should include the opportunity to express himself in art and music, to learn basic scientific facts, and to acquire knowledge about the geography and social organization of the world in which he lives. He also needs a regular physical fitness program to improve his strength and coördination.[64]

His academic instruction suddenly is terminated when he reaches the age of 13 or 14 and is no longer considered eligible for the elementary special class. Few school systems provide continuing education for the older retarded child, and too often he is returned to regular classes and assigned an abbreviated schedule of physical education, home economics for girls, and shop for boys. At this age, his intellectual interests lag, and he prefers extracurricular and nonacademic activities to schoolwork. He has little knowledge of world affairs, and his reading consists of that available in mystery and movie magazines.[1] Feeling out of place and having time on his hands, usually he does not remain in school more than a year or two, but drops out and tries to find work.

A continued learning program is needed for the adolescent retarded child. He requires the protection and regulation of a systematic and supervised daily life, and he benefits from prolonged instruction of all kinds. He cannot teach himself, and if he is not occupied, he is likely to develop antisocial attitudes or to drift aimlessly. Inasmuch as only a few years remain during which he will be able to receive constructive help in preparation for adulthood, more precarious for him than for others, these years should not be wasted.

Although his limitations are real, it does not follow that his capacities are fully utilized.[59] His abilities should be evaluated thoroughly and his assets developed completely, because he almost certainly will become a wage earner. Studies have indicated that 75 to 90 per cent of the mildly retarded are self-supporting as adults.[60] Those who are not are found on the welfare rolls and in prisons, and rarely are they cared for in institutions for the mentally retarded.

Employers report that retardates learn more slowly than normal workers, but with instruction, they can acquire the skills necessary for jobs more complex than those at which they are started. They remain longer on the job than the average worker, but they show less judgment, are absent more often, and have a poorer relationship with their fellow workers.[60] Mildly retarded boys are employed in factories as assemblers, inspectors, helpers, or operators of simple machines. They also work as errand boys, porters, bus boys, dishwashers, and helpers on trucks. Retarded girls work in factories as assemblers, inspectors, packers, and sewing machine operators. They can work as hand sewers, messengers, and stock girls in stores; and they can do cleaning and kitchen work at hospitals. They serve as waitresses and bus girls in restaurants, or they can work in private homes under supervision.[19]

Speech Development. Speech is a symbolic process, and the retarded child cannot easily acquire it. He seldom begins to talk before the age of two years and often does not do so until even later.[27] Parents concerned about the possibility of retardation usually phrase their questions to physicians in terms of the child's slow acquisition of speech. Speech defects of all kinds are more common among the retarded than among normal children, and articulation frequently is imperfect. The vocabulary of the retarded child of all levels and at all ages remains inferior to that of the normal person.

Blanchard[8] stated that few retarded children progress beyond the communication level of the four-year-old child. The child whose mental retardation is functional or is the result of a postnatal cerebral accident is more likely to develop adequate speech. As long as the retarded child can communicate his needs, relate his experiences, and ask the questions to which he needs answers, his limited speech may not handicap him unduly. The retarded adolescent who restricts his speaking to those situations with which he is familiar sometimes cannot be distinguished from the normal child; and if he combines minimal verbal competency with a display of acquired social manners and considerate comments, he frequently is considered to be of average intelligence by those who listen to him.

The retarded child whose speech development does not permit communication with others is frustrated, embarrassed, and even endangered. Speech training in overcoming articulation defects and increasing vocabulary can be helpful to the older child.

Emotional and Social Reactions. The mildly retarded child often comes from a home devoid of both intellectual stimulation and affectionate concern. Benda *et al.*[4] studied 205 institutionalized children who were between five and 16 years of age and whose intelligence quotients were 50 and above. They found that 116 came from families in which one parent was permanently absent from the home, 129 were from families which could not provide for them, and 104 had been legally removed from their grossly inadequate homes.

Michal-Smith[44] described the retarded child as less able not only to care for himself but even to command attention for his needs from others. Because he himself is objective evidence of defect and inferiority, the child injures parental pride, and the adults indicate their disappointment in him in both overt and subtle ways. More often than not, he is the target of suspicion, fear, taunts, and rejection from others.[45]

Before he even begins school, he has learned that he cannot compete with his peers in many endeavors, and he has experienced failure many times.[59] His life consists of events characterized by inferior achievement, rejection, isolation, and degradation, and he approaches school apprehensively, expecting to face similar experiences publicly and daily. The child's attitude about himself significantly affects his ability to learn in school and later to conduct himself as an adult. Gorlow *et al.*[28] reported a correlation between the favorable self-attitude of retardates and their scores on reading and arithmetic achievement tests. Although this relationship may be the result of the better-achieving child's minimal intellectual difference between himself and average pupils, self-approval and confidence are known to improve achievement.

These investigators also found that young adult retardates paroled from institutions adapted successfully in direct relationship to their own expression of self-acceptance. Self-acceptance appeared to be associated with the stability of the individual's family during his early childhood. Retardates institutionalized before the age of five years reported themselves to be easily upset and angered and indicated that they cheated, swore, fought, and were selfish. Noninstitutionalized retardates evaluated themselves more favorably and tended to act in accordance with society's expectations.[29]

The needs of the retarded child to succeed and to be accepted are identical with those of the normal child, and their fulfillment affects his performance and his emotional control. Because of his limitations, he automatically is subjected to many debilitating and defeating experiences, and therefore arrangements should be made both at school and at home to ensure increased opportunities for success and earned approval.

The Moderately Retarded Child

Physical Development. Physical development usually is stunted in the moderately retarded child. Kugel and Mohr[38] reported that at the lower intellectual levels approximately two thirds of the children were below the seventeenth percentile in height and three fourths were below the seventeenth percentile in weight. Culley *et al.*[10] stated that institutionalized retarded children without motor dysfunction were similar to mongoloids in their short stature and body build; with motor dysfunction, the children were shorter and lighter in relationship to the severity of their motor handicap.

As mental retardation becomes more severe, not only motor incoördination but visual and hearing deficiencies are associated facets of generalized deficit. Results of tests designed to measure the extent of physical disability in a retarded child sometimes are distorted because of the child's inability or unwillingness to respond to stimulation or to follow directions. LaCrosse and Bidlake[39] conditioned retarded children to respond to an audiometer by using a candy reward, and they found that only 8 per cent had impaired hearing, with another 8 per cent considered to be giving unreliable responses. These percentages are in contrast with the more usual reports of a 30 to 60 per cent incidence of hearing loss among institution populations.

Learning Ability. Few public school systems have classes for the moderately retarded child, and often it is the parents who must unite to provide facilities and teachers on a private basis. Because the education of the moderately retarded child is a relatively new field, trained teachers are scarce, and the child's lack of communicative ability often is so great that consistent understanding between teacher and pupil is difficult. Speaking problems may be compounded for this child by sensory and perceptual deficiencies, and special techniques must be used to stimulate the nonverbal, nonresponding child.[53] Mecham and Jex[42] suggested that the teacher's techniques should include a stimulating and motivating psychological climate, the use of concrete experiences, the presentation of verbal symbols as labels for experiential concepts, and the use of standardized developmental schedules in verbal language to measure improvement.

Much of the moderately retarded child's school day is occupied with practicing social techniques, entertaining guests, learning to cook and iron, and using simple tools. Academically, the child cannot achieve beyond the kindergarten or first grade level.[5] With minimal reading ability, emphasis is placed on the recognition of words necessary for his direction or safety. He can also be taught thoughtfulness of others, obedience to authority, and helpfulness at home; and if he acquires these characteristics, the child earns acceptance from others.

The moderately retarded child who attains adolescence and young adulthood welcomes useful work, but he cannot achieve the competence at work or in self-management required for complete independence. Sheltered workshops are being developed in many cities to provide the moderately retarded young adult with work. This usually consists of manufacturing simple toys or household equipment or of packaging, and the work is contracted for by individual companies. The retarded worker begins in the sheltered workshop as a trainee without pay and later advances to an apprenticeship position and is paid a small stipend. Eventually he achieves the status of a full worker, and still later, if possible, he is placed in work in the regular job market.[5]

Institutionalized retardates similarly are taught work which they can perform for individuals in the community in which the institution is located. Jackson and Butler[32] evaluated girls aged 16 to 22 years, with intelligence quotients ranging from 40 to 80, six months after their parole from an institution. They found that those making the best adjustment were older and more intelligent, had achieved more academically, and had a better work record in the institution. They tended to come from rural areas, and they had remained longer at home with their parents before coming to the institution. Usually they were individuals who resolved conflicts by compliance with adult requirements but who remained assertive with their peers. Their history, therefore, was one of relative success at academic learning, working, accession to authority, and maintenance of self-respect—all characteristics required for independence. This degree of competence and success seldom is possible for the moderately retarded individual. Ordinarily he remains at the institution, and his work there or in the community is closely supervised. He is able to earn some money, and yet he need not be concerned about providing for his own food and shelter, and he always has the companionship of friends and the security of an established home.

Speech Development. Speech in the moderately retarded child usually is seriously deficient and may be absent altogether. His vocabulary is limited, his sentences are rare and short, and his articulation is so indistinct that often he cannot be understood. Memorizing and reproducing his name and address may be a real achievement for him. Ordinarily, he identifies what he sees with single words, and he avoids responding to questions. Blocked in communicating with others, he is frustrated at being unable to make his wants or needs known, to insist on his rights, or to share his experiences, and this frustration contributes to his feeling of isolation.

Verbal disability is not always present in the moderately retarded child, however, and sometimes he is able to report events occurring at home and school and give limited factual information about his family and classmates.

Rosenberg et al.[55] noted a relationship between the retarded individual's verbal facility and his social interaction. Institutionalized retardates of either high or low verbal facility interacted effectively with those of similar verbal competency; heterogeneous mixing of retardates of different levels of verbal facility resulted in diminished social interaction. These findings suggest that grouping children for instruction and activities in accordance with their verbal facility will ensure the greatest possible degree of participation and learning.

Emotional and Social Reactions. Disturbed family backgrounds are common in the history of the moderately retarded child, although perhaps with less frequency than for the mildly retarded child. Davies[11] reported that one fourth of the moderately retarded institutionalized children he studied came from broken homes. He also found that half of the mothers had problems with physical health which were related to their inability to keep the child at home.

Although the moderately retarded child does not always understand the verbal communications of others, he is aware of the meaning of a shove, an angry look, or an irritated tone of voice; and he is equally aware of the meaning of a smile, a hug, or the fact that he is being praised to others. He understands the pleasure expressed by those whom he assists in his class or at home, and he is proud when his work is commended.

In some ways, he has more opportunity for approval and affection than does the mildly retarded child, who is compared with normal children and expected eventually to maintain himself. The moderately retarded child, obviously ineffective and dependent, commands the attention, solicitude, and care needed by a small child, and his inadequacies excuse him from demands and criticism which are common occurrences in the life of a better-endowed child. Sometime he is treated as a pet at home, and often he is underestimated as an individual by the failure to understand his need to be useful.

The Severely Retarded Child

The severely retarded child must be cared for all of his life. He will not attain a mental age above three years, and often not above one year. He may never acquire the ability to sit, stand, or walk, and his vocabulary, if he speaks at all, is limited to two or three words. His responsiveness to stimulation is minimal,[65] and his life expectancy limited, although the effectiveness of modern antibiotics is prolonging life.

Because the physical care of the child is burdensome, especially as he grows older and becomes heavier, most families place him in an institution. Johnson *et al.*[34] found that nonambulatory, severely retarded children from six to 16 years of age could be trained in self-help to an extent previously considered impossible. These children learned to feed themselves from food containers with suction cup bases, using spoons with built-up handles; and they learned with training to transfer themselves from their beds or wheel chairs to the toilet. By rolling, crawling, hitching, scooting, and knee walking they were able to move themselves without help; and they practiced standing and walking using tilt boards, parallel bars, stand-up tables, walkers, carts, crutches, and canes. Their successful achievements in self-care not only reduced the heavy physical burden on attendants but also resulted in diminishing manipulative motor habits in the children, such as head-banging, masturbation, and sucking.

McKinney and Keele[40] reported that 24 severely retarded boys given increased physical attention by a group of mildly retarded women living in the same institution with them showed improvement in both purposive behavior and speech.

PARENTAL ATTITUDES

Few parents who are confronted with mental retardation in their child do not react with feelings of despair and self-pity. All of the challenges, disappointments, hurts, and perplexities of child rearing are magnified by the necessity to cope with the unknown complication of retardation. Parents often feel unequal to this added responsibility and dread their obligation to assume it. They also face problems of interminable care and the prospect of never being able to shed parental duties.[20]

They seldom escape guilt feelings, and they search their memories and their consciences to discover what they did to merit a defective child. They question their own hereditary background, and if they did not want the child or took active measures to abort him, they believe the child's defect is punishment for their feelings. Usually, guilty parents tend to overprotect the child, and their unnecessary help and concern keep the child immature and self-centered.[1] If the child's care is assigned to a housekeeper or regular sitter, he is even more likely to receive protection and assistance he does not require.[14] Sometimes parents attempt to compensate for their feelings of guilt by devoting themselves to the child, excluding every other obligation and need of their own and of other members of the family. They may move to another city and the father may accept work he dislikes in order to be near educational facilities for the child. The mother may refrain from participating in church or civic organizations or from assisting with her other children's activities, believing that she must remain near the retarded child at all times; and family vacations are considered an impossibility.

Parents sometimes refuse to accept the implications of retardation, and they spend unending amounts of time and money on diagnostic studies and constantly seek curative medications, operations, and new training techniques. They refuse to be convinced that the child cannot learn in a regular classroom, and they underscore their determination that the child be normal by enrolling him in dancing and swimming classes, youth organizations, and social clubs geared to the abilities of the average child. At home, they criticize him constantly, coach him incessantly, and clearly express their exasperation with his failure to learn what they try to teach him.[63] Their pushing, criticism, and unrealistic appraisal of the child make his life a succession of disappointments, and he is discouraged with himself and angry at his parents.*

If there is open parental hostility toward the child, he may suffer cruel treatment, including beatings, physical neglect, and abandonment. Institutionalized children often are those who have been forsaken

---

* See Case 47, Patricia C., p. 534.

permanently by their families. Of nearly 300 children who had lived in an institution for five years, one fourth had received neither visits nor gifts from their families during this time, and almost one half had never been visited.[60]

The presence of a retarded child in a family is an irritant which can succeed in disrupting it. Either parent may blame the other for the child's conception or heredity. The burden of care usually rests on the mother, and a father who appears unaware of the added fatigue and concern she bears and who makes no attempt to help is despised and resented. The parents may disagree about the rearing and education of the child, with one unwilling to accept the fact of retardation and the other weary of the struggle of pretense. Often there is conflict over the desirability of placing the child in an institution, and even parents who can agree that they are undecided about this must live with each other while weighing the alternatives and listening to the inevitable advice, or even ultimatums, of relatives. Sibling attitudes may be of concern to parents, although their feelings about the retarded child usually reflect those of the parents. Interviews with 21 adolescent siblings of retarded children indicated that the presence of the retardate in the home did not interfere with the siblings' leading a normal life, and they considered family relationships to be good.[31]

Special assistance for parents at the time they first learn that their child is retarded aids them in acceptance and in realistic planning. The first official confirmation of what they have suspected and dreaded can be a devastating calamity, leading to reactions which are harmful to themselves, the child, and the family as a whole.[61] In one study, it was found that 31 per cent of the parents were told of the child's retardation in the first year of his life, 32 per cent before the child was five years old, and 37 per cent after the child started school.[12] Mothers of severely retarded children recognize the atypical development of the child but relate it to a physical condition.[18] Fully half of the parents are dissatisfied with the manner in which they are informed of retardation and the advice they receive concerning the child.

There is a need not only to discuss the retardation compassionately but also to assist parents in learning to regard the child as possessing the same human needs that every child has.[3] Both parents should be included in a discussion of the findings so that the questions of each can be answered, distorted or incomplete reports are not relayed by one parent to the other, and the father's aid in caring for the retarded child is enlisted immediately.[60] Parental attitudes of guilt, withdrawal, anxiety, disbelief, and self-pity should be acknowledged as natural initial reactions.

Parents of retarded children who meet in groups to discuss their mutual problems or who work actively together to provide facilities for training their children are best able to accept the reality of retardation, to make suitable plans, and to rear the child sensibly.[7] Changes in parental attitude, in the management of the child, and in solving the question of institutionalization are reported by participants in regular group discussions.[25]

REFERENCES

1. Abraham, W.: *The Slow Learner*. New York, The Center for Applied Research in Education, Inc., 1964.
2. Allen, M., Shannon, G., and Rose, D.: Thioridazine hydrochloride in the behavior disturbance of retarded children. *Amer. J. Ment. Defic.*, 1963, *68*, 63–68.
3. Baum, M. H.: Some dynamic factors affecting family adjustment to the handicapped child. *Except. Childr.*, 1962, *28*, 387–392.
4. Benda, C. E., Squires, N. D., Ogonik, J., and Wise, R.: Personality factors in mild mental retardation: I. Family background and sociocultural patterns. *Amer. J. Ment. Defic.*, 1963, *68*, 24–40.
5. Benton, P. C., McHale, J., and Whitmore, L.: Habilitation of mentally retarded. *The Journal*, Oklahoma State Medical Association, June, 1958.
6. Berry, H. K., Rubenstein, J., and Simon, H. D.: Evaluation of screening tests for phenylketonuria in a diagnostic clinic for retarded children. *Amer. J. Ment. Defic.*, 1963, *68*, 49–53.
7. Bitter, J. A.: Attitude change by parents of trainable mentally retarded children as a result of group discussion. *Except. Childr.*, 1963, *30*, 173–177.
8. Blanchard, I.: Speech patterns and etiology in mental retardation. *Amer. J. Ment. Defic.*, 1963, *68*, 612–617.
9. Collmann, R. D., and Stoller, A.: Comparison of age distributions for mothers of mongols borns in high and low birth incidence areas and years in Victoria, 1942–1957. *J. Ment. Defic. Res.*, 1963, *7*, 79–83.
10. Culley, W. J., Jolly, D. H., and Mertz, E. T.: Heights and weights of mentally retarded children. *Amer. J. Ment. Defic.*, 1963, *68*, 203–210.
11. Davies, C. G.: Survey of problems of families of 168 mentally deficient children: The medical services. *Calif. J. Educ. Res.*, 1963, *14*, 153–163.
12. Davies, C. G.: The families of severely mentally retarded children: Family composition and health. *Calif. J. Educ. Res.*, 1963, *14*, 121–130.
13. Davy, R. A.: Adaptation of progressive-choice method for teaching reading to retarded children. *Amer. J. Ment. Defic.*, 1962, *67*, 274–280.
14. Dingman, H. F., Eyman, R. K., and Windle, C. D.: An investigation of some child-rearing attitudes of mothers with retarded children. *Amer. J. Ment. Defic.*, 1963, *67*, 899–908.
15. Dittmann, L. L.: The family of the child in an institution. *Amer. J. Ment. Defic.*, 1962, *66*, 759–765.
16. Doll, E. E.: A historical survey of research and management of mental retardation in the United States. *In* Trapp, E. P., and Himelstein, P., eds.: *Readings on the Exceptional Child*. New York, Appleton-Century-Crofts, 1962, pp. 21–22.
17. Doll, E. E.: The mentally deficient. *In* Trapp, E. P., and Himelstein, P., eds.: *Readings on the Exceptional Child*. New York, Appleton-Century-Crofts, 1962, pp. 55–57.
18. Ehlers, W. H.: The moderately and severely retarded child: Maternal perceptions of retardation and subsequent seeking and using services rendered by a community agency. *Amer. J. Ment. Defic.*, 1963, *68*, 660–668.
19. Engel, A. M.: Employment of the mentally retarded. *In* Frampton, M., and Gall, E. D., eds.: *Special Education for the Exceptional*. Boston, Porter Sargent, 1956, pp. 519–544.
20. Farber, B.: Effects of a severely mentally retarded child on the family. *In* Trapp, E. P., and Himelstein, P., eds.: *Readings on the Exceptional Child*. New York, Appleton-Century-Crofts, 1962, p. 232.

21. Farrell, M. J., Chipman, C. E., and Brazier, M. F.: Training and education of the mentally retarded. *In* Frampton, M., and Gall, E. D., eds.: *Special Education for the Exceptional*. Boston, Porter Sargent, 1956, pp. 465–477.

22. Freeman, F. N.: *Mental Tests*. Boston, Houghton Mifflin, 1939, pp. 18–20.

23. Fuller, R. W., Luce, M. W., and Mertz, E. T.: Serum uric acid in mongolism. *Science*, 1963, *137*(3533), 868–869.

24. Gelof, M.: Comparison of systems of classification relating degree of retardation to measured intelligence. *Amer. J. Ment. Defic.*, 1963, *68*, 297–317.

25. Giannini, M. J., and Goodman, L.: Counseling families during the crisis reaction to mongolism. *Amer. J. Ment. Defic.*, 1963, *67*, 740–747.

26. Glovsky, L., and Rigrodsky, S.: A classroom program for auditorially handicapped mentally deficient children. *Train. Sch. Bull.*, 1963, *60*, 56–69.

27. Goodenough, F. L.: *Developmental Psychology*, Ed. 2. New York, D. Appleton-Century Co., 1945, pp. 629–651.

28. Gorlow, L., Butler, A., and Guthrie, G. M.: Correlates of self-attitudes of retardates. *Amer. J. Ment. Defic.*, 1963, *67*, 549–555.

29. Gorlow, L., Butler, A., and Guthrie, G. M.: Personality differences between institutionalized and non-institutionalized retardate females. *Amer. J. Ment. Defic.*, 1963, *67*, 543–548.

30. Gragert, H. T.: Differential diagnosis, training, and job placement for the mentally retarded. *J. Rehabilit.*, 1962, *28*, 35–37.

31. Graliker, B. V., Fishler, K., and Koch, R.: Teenage reaction to a mentally retarded sibling. *Amer. J. Ment. Defic.*, 1962, *66*, 838–843.

32. Jackson, S. K., and Butler, A. J.: Prediction of successful community placement of institutionalized retardates. *Amer. J. Ment. Defic.*, 1963, *68*, 211–217.

33. Jervis, G. A.: The mental deficiencies. *In* Arieti, S., ed.: *American Handbook of Psychiatry*. New York, Basic Books, Inc., 1959, vol. 2, pp. 1289–1314.

34. Johnson, E. W., Gove, R., and Ostermeier, B.: The value of functional training in severely disabled institutionalized brain damaged children. *Amer. J. Ment. Defic.*, 1963, *67*, 860–864.

35. Kanner, L.: *Child Psychiatry*, Ed. 3. Springfield, Ill., Charles C Thomas, 1957, pp. 268–312.

36. Kastein, S.: The responsibility of the speech pathologist to the retarded child. *In* Michal-Smith, H., and Kastein, S.: *The Special Child*. Seattle, Washington, Bureau of Publications, 1962, pp. 17–25.

37. Kern, W. H., and Pfaeffle, H.: A comparison of social adjustment of mentally retarded children in various educational settings. *Amer. J. Ment. Defic.*, 1962, *67*, 407–413.

38. Kugel, R. B., and Mohr, J.: Mental retardation and physical growth. *Amer. J. Ment. Defic.*, 1963, *68*, 41–48.

39. LaCrosse, E. L., and Bidlake, H.: A method to test the hearing of mentally retarded children. *Volta Rev.*, 1964, *66*, 27–30.

40. McKinney, J. P., and Keele, T.: Effects of increased mothering on the behavior of severely retarded boys. *Amer. J. Ment. Defic.*, 1963, *67*, 556–562.

41. Masland, R. L., Sarason, S. B., and Gladwin, T.: *Mental Subnormality*. New York, Basic Books, Inc., 1958.

42. Mecham, M. J., and Jex, J. L.: Training mentally retarded children in oral communication. *ASHA*, 1962, *4*, 441–443.

43. Michal-Smith, H.: Psychotherapy for the mentally retarded. *In* Michal-Smith, H., and Kastein, S.: *The Special Child*. Seattle, Washington, New School for the Special Child, Inc., 1962, pp. 27–43.

44. Michal-Smith, H.: The mentally retarded and the slow-learning child. *In* Michal-Smith, H., and Kastein, S.: *The Special Child*. Seattle, Washington, New School for the Special Child, Inc., 1962, pp. 313–333.

45. Michal-Smith, H.: The psychologist's contribution to mental retardation. *In* Michal-Smith, H., and Kastein, S.: *The Special Child*. Seattle, Washington, New School for the Special Child, Inc., 1962, pp. 1–16.

46. Milgram, N. A., and Furth, H. G.: The influence of language on concept attainment in educable retarded children. *Amer. J. Ment. Defic.*, 1963, *67*, 733–739.

47. Mussen, P. H., and Conger, J. J.: *Child Development and Personality*. New York, Harper and Bros., 1956, pp. 61–70.

48. O'Connor, M., and Berkson, G.: Eye movements in normals and defectives. *Amer. J. Ment. Defic.*, 1963, *68,* 85–90.

49. Pasamanick, B.: Some misconceptions concerning differences in the racial prevalence of mental disease. *Amer. J. Orthopsychiat.*, 1963, *33,* 72–86.

50. Penrose, L. W.: *The Biology of Mental Defect*, Ed. 2. New York, Grune and Stratton, Inc., 1963.

51. Pfundt, T. R.: A consideration of the etiology of mental health retardation. *The Journal*, Oklahoma State Medical Association, June, 1958.

52. Prospo, C. J.: A suggested curriculum for the mentally handicapped. *In* Frampton, M., and Gall, E. D., eds.: *Special Education for the Exceptional*. Boston, Porter Sargent, 1956, pp. 478–487.

53. Rigrodsky, S.: Procedures for speech therapy with institutionalized mentally retarded children. *Train. Sch. Bull.*, 1962, *59,* 3–8.

54. Rohrs, F. W., and Haworth, M. R.: The 1960 Stanford-Binet, WISC, and Goodenough tests with mentally retarded children. *Amer. J. Ment. Defic.*, 1962, *66,* 853–859.

55. Rosenberg, S., Spradlin, J., and Mabel, S.: Interaction among retarded children as a function of their relative language skills. *J. Abnorm. Soc. Psychol.*, 1961, *63,* 402–410.

56. Rundle, A. T.: Etiological factors in mental retardation: I. Biochemical. *Amer. J. Ment. Defic.*, 1962, *67,* 61–68.

57. Rundle, A. T.: Etiological factors in mental retardation: II. Endocrine. *Amer. J. Ment. Defic.*, 1962, *67,* 69–77.

58. Russell, G. R., and Endres, R. K.: The physician's responsibility in mental retardation. *The Journal*, Oklahoma State Medical Association, June, 1958.

59. Sarason, S. B.: Mentally retarded and mentally defective children: Major psychosocial problems. *In* Cruickshank, W. M., ed.: *Psychology of Exceptional Children and Youth*. Englewood Cliffs, N. J., Prentice-Hall Inc., 1955, pp. 438–474.

60. Sarason, S. B., and Gladwin, T. B.: *Psychological Problems in Mental Deficiency*, Ed. 3. New York, Harper and Bros., 1959.

61. Schucman, H.: Further observations on the psychodynamics of parents of retarded children. *Train. Sch. Bull.*, 1963, *60,* 70–74.

62. Shackelford, J. W.: Mental retardation—the problem. *The Journal*, Oklahoma State Medical Association, June, 1958, 300–322.

63. Spock, B.: *Baby and Child Care*. New York, Pocket Books, Inc., 1957, pp. 587–591.

64. Stein, J. U.: Motor function and physical fitness of the mentally retarded. *Rehabilit. Lit.*, 1963, *24,* 230–242.

65. Sternlicht, M., and Wanderer, Z. W.: The flick-cry maturational scale for mentally defective youngsters. *Amer. J. Ment. Defic.*, 1963, *68,* 94–97.

66. Stevens, H. A., and Erdman, R. L.: Education of the mentally retarded child. *In* Frampton, M., and Gall, E. D., eds.: *Special Education for the Exceptional*. Boston, Porter Sargent, 1956, pp. 428–457.

67. Stott, D. H.: Abnormal mothering as a cause of mental subnormality: II. Case studies and conclusions. *J. Child Psychol. Psychiat.*, 1962, *3,* 133–148.

68. Warren, S. A.: Academic achievement of trainable pupils with five or more years of schooling. *Train. Sch. Bull.*, 1963, *60,* 75–88.

69. Weingold, J. T., and Hormuth, R. P.: Group guidance of parents of mentally retarded children. *In* Frampton, M., and Gall, E. D., eds.: *Special Education for the Exceptional*. Boston, Porter Sargent, 1956, pp. 511–518.

70. Zigler, E.: Social deprivation in familial and organic retardates. *Psychol. Rep.*, 1962, *10,* 370.

Chapter 46

Cerebral Dysfunction

Conditions of infection, radiation, toxemia, anoxia, metabolic disorder, dietary excess, and trauma which damage the central nervous system in the fetus or neonate can result in varying degrees of dysfunction.[5] Major impairment, either in scope or in specificity, can result in epilepsy or cerebral palsy; and minimal or diffuse impairment can create disturbance in all areas of psychological function.

EPILEPSY

Epilepsy in its various forms and in differing degrees of severity occurs in five of every 1000 individuals under 21 years of age. The epileptic seizure results from a disturbance in the electrochemical activity of the discharging cells of the brain and is produced by a variety of neurological disorders.[12]

In general, three types of seizures are recognizable. The *grand mal* seizure is characterized by a loss of consciousness and subsequent slumping or falling. The fall is followed by a tonic spasm involving the entire body, during which the head, and sometimes the trunk, is turned to one side. After 30 to 60 seconds, this rigidity is replaced with clonic convulsions lasting one to three minutes. These convulsions are jerking, kicking, irregular movements of the extremities and sometimes of the head and trunk, and they are accompanied by gasping or gargling noises and tongue movements. The eyes sometimes roll upward, and

445

the pupils do not react to light. The pulse rate and temperature may rise. Initial pallor changes to redness and then to cyanosis because of the spasms of respiratory muscles. Involuntary micturition or defecation may occur, and salivation increases. There is always amnesia for the attack, and when it is over, the child falls into a deep sleep. Grand mal attacks may take place while the child is asleep at night, and if so, their occurrence can be surmised from a bitten tongue, wet sheets, or confusion and headache in the morning. The frequency with which attacks occur varies with the individual and no set pattern exists.[30]

Onset of grand mal seizures may be preceded by an aura, or warning, consisting of sensations recognized as preliminary to an attack and usually remembered later. The aura is less common in children than in adults and may include such sensations as pain, numbness, hallucinations, temperature sensations, abdominal discomfort, tightness in the throat, tremulous movements, or automatic actions. Parents report that they sometimes know that an attack is imminent because of the child's changed behavior. An aura may occur only a few seconds before a seizure, or it may appear over the course of several days.

The *petit mal* attack is much less dramatic and frightening to observers and may even pass unwitnessed. There is a short, blank stare and a sudden cessation of both activity and awareness. Sometimes the attack is accompanied by rhythmic movements lasting only a few seconds. A child may have several petit mal attacks daily, and they are much more common in children than are grand mal attacks.

A *psychomotor seizure*, relatively rare in children, consists of inappropriate activity for which the child is amnesic. The behavior lasts for two or three minutes and may consist of such actions as making sucking noises, moving aimlessly, or tearing paper.[12] Adults usually consider such acts to be deliberate, and they scold the child for them.

Heredity contributes to the possibility of a child's developing epilepsy. Sustained epilepsy is three times more common among near relatives than among persons in the general population. The child of an epileptic has one chance in 70 of developing the disorder himself. Individuals whose seizures began in the first year of life have four times as many epileptic relatives as those whose attacks began after the age of 30.[39]

In addition to the predisposition afforded by heredity, acute infection which damages the nervous system is a common cause. Trauma, allergy, injurious prenatal conditions, malnutrition, fatigue, and emotional instability are all considered etiological factors.[12] Glandular disturbances, ingestion of certain drugs, and kidney disease also appear to be associated with convulsive disorders.[6]

The involvement of neural impulses is demonstrated by abnormal electroencephalograph tracings, which consist of waves of increased voltage occurring at either an unusually fast or an unusually slow rate. Slow waves are characteristic adjuncts of petit mal seizures, and fast waves of grand mal attacks. Psychomotor seizures are indicated by abnormally large voltage, slow waves occurring at twice the rate of waves typical of petit mal attacks. The electroencephalogram deviations are apparent in the intervals between seizures, as well as during the actual seizures. Specific lesions in the central nervous system are rarely found, although at times an area of degeneration is identifiable. Kanner[30] suggested that the essential etiological feature of epilepsy is a variation in the physiological processes of the body, which results in dysrhythmic, inadequate functioning in many vital areas.

Treatment

Epilepsy is controlled with drug administration. Originally, bromides were used, and later, phenobarbital, but the latter drug sometimes causes fatigue and drowsiness, and the child's initiative and energy are curtailed unduly. At present, dilantin is administered, usually with good results. Initially, medication must be given daily, but as control is established, the dosage can be reduced gradually and sometimes eliminated eventually.[39]

Difficulties in Management

The child's own understanding of the seizures, his family's attitude toward him, and the reaction of peers and teacher may make him feel guilty and peculiar. He must suffer repeated visits to the physician, lengthy and tedious examinations, and daily medication, as well as some restriction of his activity.[30] Some schools deny admission to the epileptic child. During adolescence, the epileptic becomes aware of the handicap his seizures impose on vocational choice. If they are controlled and there is little possibility of endangering himself at work, his chances for employment are improved, but public prejudice often closes many doors to him.[6]

At the time of his first attack, the child usually is anxious and fears that he will die, and he may become preoccupied in anticipation of recurring attacks. Inability to tolerate stress seems to be characteristic of the epileptic child, and conditions which create stress for him should be identified. Traumatic environmental incidents tend to precipitate seizures in some children, perhaps because the uncoördinated physiological attributes of emotion result in a diffuse neural discharge.

There appears to be no basis in fact for the popular concept of an "epileptic personality," and epileptic children demonstrate behavior and personality problems common to all children. The epileptic child sometimes is regarded as inevitably mentally retarded, and although studies of institutionalized epileptic children indicate inferior intelligence, such results are usual for long-term residents of institutions. Kanner[30] stated that in some children retardation and epilepsy are two facets of the same defect in functioning, and sometimes a retarded child does not have convulsions until he reaches puberty. Epilepsy occasionally is associated with intellectual deterioration in a child of normal intelligence, but many intellectually adequate children remain so throughout the course of the illness.

Parents' concepts of epilepsy need to be discussed. Usually adults are ashamed of the epilepsy and keep secret the existence of the condition, and during a seizure they may panic, believing the child is dying. They need to anticipate the occurrence of a seizure, understand its course and origin, and learn to protect the child by removing any nearby hard or sharp objects and by inserting a handkerchief between the child's teeth so that his involuntary thrashing and biting do not result in his harming himself. Prognosis should be evaluated realistically, but if the parents can learn to accept the epilepsy without unusual emotion, the child will remain secure and relaxed most of the time.[30]

CEREBRAL PALSY

Cerebral palsy is a condition of muscle function disturbances related to cerebral dysfunction. Over 31,000 cerebral palsied children were recipients of aid from crippled children's programs in 1962.

There are several forms which cerebral palsy can assume. *Flaccid paralysis* consists of complete lack of function. The muscle is flabby and does not respond to direct stimulation. *Congenital tremor* may be apparent early in life. *Ataxia* is loss of control of voluntary motion, either in speed or direction, and it is caused by disturbance in the cerebellum. If kinesthetic sense is lost, the child receives no sensation from movement of the joints and is unaware of the degree or direction of his motions. He can walk, reach, or write with greater success if he closely watches his movements. The child may lose control of his balance if disturbance in the inner ear or in the cerebellum results in suppression of the small muscle contractions which control position of the body.[52]

Most cerebral palsied children are victims either of *spastic paralysis* or of *athetosis*. Spastic paralysis results from hyperirritability to stimulation, and the resultant muscle contraction blocks purposive movement either partially or completely. Spasticity is caused by damage to the cortex or pyramidal system. Athetosis consists of an involuntary series of muscular contractions which appear as twisting, worm-like movements progressing in waves down the child's limb. Sometimes the amplitude of the motions is so small that they scarcely can be observed, or it may be so great that thrashing movements result. The trunk and extremities appear relaxed and are thrown about into all extremes of position. The condition is caused by damage to the basal ganglia.

Phelps[52] described the contrasting reactions of athetoid and spastic children to a doctor's request to present him with their hands. The athetoid does so immediately, having learned to attempt volitional movements quickly before they can be interrupted by the athetosis. His hand, once in the doctor's grasp, twists and pulls as the stream of athetoid movements appears. The same command to the spastic child results in a slower, stiffer, clawing motion, accompanied by contortions of the face or legs and sometimes by guttural sounds and labored breathing. Once grasped, the hand remains quiet unless it is stimulated in some way, such as by squeezing.

The cerebral palsied child often has multiple handicaps. The incidence of epilepsy among the cerebral palsied has been estimated variously at between 14 and 75 per cent. It is much more prevalent in spastic than in athetoid children.[42] Nielsen[50] found visual-motor impairment in 60 per cent of spastic children aged six to eight years, compared with 27 per cent impairment in normal children of the same age. Mental retardation occurs in 27 to 50 per cent of all cerebral palsied children,[9] and they are significantly below normal in body measurements and are retarded in motor development.[45] Speech problems and defective vision and hearing are common.

Birth injury accounts for less than half of the cerebral palsy cases. Midline defective development contributes to the damage, and vertex hemorrhage in premature infants because of rapid birth and sudden pressure changes has resulted in brain damage. Kernicterus, infection, and encephalitis also can cause impaired motor functioning.[52] Churchill,[8] in a review of the literature, reported that one third of the athetoid children he studied had jaundice at birth, and many others did not breathe for several minutes after birth. In 85 per cent of the spastic diplegia cases, prematurity was a contributing factor.

Education and Treatment

The cerebral palsied child must be assessed for educability, a difficult task inasmuch as standard intelligence tests require the child both to communicate and to manipulate objects. Williams[66] suggested that a year-long period of observation is required to determine the cerebral palsied child's educability, and this should include determination of the extent to which he can be helped to establish communication, his capacity and inventiveness for circumventing his physical handicap, and the degree to which his capacity for understanding improves during the assessment period. Regardless of the outcome of such evaluations, the cerebral palsied child should be given every opportunity to learn and to compensate for his handicap, inasmuch as his true capacity is obscured by multiple problems of sensation and expression.

The pre-school child should be in a nursery school, where he is subject to more stimulation than he often has at home. He will be able to play with clay and finger paint unaided, and he can learn to grasp and build with blocks. He can participate in a rhythm band, with bells strapped to his wrists if necessary. Although verbal communication is difficult and unrewarding for the cerebral palsied child, communication can be maintained and creativity can be developed through the use of drawings. The child learns also from listening to stories, and with help, he can begin to use scissors and to color. Holden[27] found that 74 per cent of a group of cerebral palsied children in nursery school were highly motivated to learn and that their motivation contributed to both their physical and their social improvement.

Kastein[31] described a home program for enticing and training the cerebral palsied pre-school child to speak. Exercises in sipping, blowing, sucking, and voluntary tongue movements are practiced first to strengthen and control speech muscles. As control develops, the child learns to pronounce the names of well-known pictured objects, and he progresses gradually to understanding and reproducing the stories in simple books. Because of their inept muscular control, many celebral palsied children will not attempt speech without special training of this kind.

The elementary school child often suffers from an interrupted school program, and he is subjected to many changes in location and teachers, depending on the available facilities. An increasing number of cerebral palsied children attend school in regular classrooms. Others attend special classes with a small group of similarly handicapped pupils, and individual learning programs are conducted for them.

In the special classes, such equipment as standing tables and parallel bars are available. Printing sets with knobs which can be grasped aid the child in coping with symbol reproduction. Automatic page turners and devices for holding pencils can be used by the child with limited or no manual control. Special typewriters are constructed so that the cerebral palsied child can operate them. The child without the use of his hands can learn facility with his toes, using his feet to type, to feed himself, and to dress.[9] For many cerebral palsied children, the instructional devices and techniques appropriate for the child with minimal brain damage will be helpful.

Better control over muscle movement is achieved by children given practical suggestions for the easier management of their bodies, as well as physical and occupational therapy. Glenting[21] reported on the progress of 60 young spastic hemiplegics, 50 of whom were seen over a three-year period. Two thirds of the children had improved in the ability to manage their legs, and one half improved in the ability to manage their arms.

Intellectual progress was satisfactory for 76 per cent of the children, and speech improvement occurred in 82 per cent. When intellectual retardation was present, motor progress was impeded.

Difficulties in Management

The cerebral palsied child must cope daily with the curious, rejecting, fearful, or pitying stares of others. He is left behind repeatedly because he cannot maneuver freely. He is unable to play as his peers do: He cannot skip rope, play jacks, climb trees, ride a bicycle, or throw a ball. He is unable to walk as fast or climb stairs as readily as his classmates, and he cannot participate in group sports of any kind.[9] He must devote years of effort to learning to feed and dress himself, and he experiences failure repeatedly. Because he cannot perform these needed functions readily, he remains dependent on his parents much longer than the normal child.

In school, he cannot control his movements sufficiently to enable him to reproduce symbols with facility, and unless he has special help, he learns little. If he cannot walk at all, he must be carried or supported; as he becomes older and heavier, this poses difficulties for his mother and women teachers, and he is confined to a wheel chair most of the time. Because he cannot manage his speech muscles, he is unable to communicate well. His attempts to do so result in sounds which are peculiar and misunderstood, and he is both embarrassed and rebuffed whenever he attempts to speak.

The usual problems of adolescence are appalling to the cerebral palsied child. His major difficulties with motor functioning restrict his employability and educational opportunities. His desire to be attractive to members of the opposite sex remains unfulfilled, and he anticipates a lonely, difficult adulthood. Constant attention to increasing the child's independence and self-sufficiency produces hopefulness for his eventual success as an adult and makes the daily difficulties of managing even the simplest tasks more bearable for both parents and child. The educability of the child must be considered carefully as he grows older, and the adolescent cerebral palsied child who is mentally retarded usually is better cared for and more content in an institutional setting than at home. If he is intellectually capable of college attendance, however, he should be assisted in acquiring all the education possible and in selecting attainable vocational goals.

MINIMAL BRAIN DAMAGE

When cerebral dysfunction causes mental retardation, paralysis, spasticity, blindness, or deafness, the child's handicap is apparent and he is treated accordingly. If damage to the brain is minimal, however, its effects on the sensory and motor abilities of the child and on his interpretative and integrative functioning are less readily detectable. Refined and extended examinataion and observation techniques confirm its influence in creating and prolonging learning and behavior problems in many children.

Improved prenatal care of mothers and better obstetrical procedures have increased the number of surviving mildly brain-damaged children, and the use of antibiotics to treat severe childhood diseases also has increased viability of damaged infants and children.[7] Studies of minimal brain damage place its incidence in clinic populations at 19 to 49 per cent, with more boys than girls affected.[10, 14, 40] Paine[51] reported that 31 of 41 children referred for poor school work, clumsiness, poor speech, or emotional problems showed abnormal neurological signs. Daryn[14] found diffuse brain damage in children in whom it had not been suspected previously and identified anomalies in skull x-rays as being similar to those found in mongoloid children. Most investigators believe that the minimally brain-injured child suffers from lesions or damage in cortical areas adjacent to those primarily responsible for vision, hearing, speech, or motor response and that the resultant disorders are caused by the blocking of pathways usually available for the passage of neural impulses and a subsequent faulty integration of stimulus and response.

More often than not, the existence of minimal brain damage remains undiscovered, and if it is diagnosed, its effects may not be understood nor accepted as valid by parents and teachers. When the child's intelligence is tested and found to be average or superior, his failure to learn is considered evidence that he is obstreperous and lazy. As the adults continually scold and punish the child for inadequate school achievement, he becomes increasingly bewildered, anxious, and uncontrolled. He cannot escape from his failures, nor can he find satisfactions to compensate for the disapproval and disappointment of parents and teachers.[47] Although maturation assists him in every way and in time his own behavior becomes more organized and regulated, the child who has endured a lengthy period of failure, anxiety, and rejection rarely recovers from the effects of these experiences. It is essential that the existence of minimal brain damage be detected so that special techniques can be used to educate the child and so that his parents can be aided in the difficult task of rearing him.

Characteristics of Minimal Brain Damage

Careful examination of the child is required to discover either a single sign or multiple symptoms of organic deficit.[44] There may be disability in one, several, or all of the psychological functions of perceptual-motor ability, abstraction, inhibition, and social response. Inadequate performance in any of these areas may be complicated or exaggerated by the child's self-concept.

Perceptual-motor Ability. The brain-injured child is plagued by an inability to organize the individual parts of what he perceives into meaningful wholes. He tends to separate letters, numbers, objects, pictures, and even social scenes into discrete parts, and he reacts to only one part at a time.[26, 61] This causes him to attend to what are considered insignificant details by others and to ignore associated and related stimuli of more pertinence.[5] Unable to utilize all of the stimulus clues available, he is puzzled or frightened by the fact that others respond with certainty and facility in situations which are meaningless to him. He does not understand how it is possible for his classmates to follow the teacher's instructions to reproduce from memory the letters of the alphabet. To him, the letter d is a vertical line and a circle, which he sees without connecting them, and he therefore does not distinguish between d and the letters b and p, which also consist of a vertical line and a circle.

All stimuli exert equal force in attracting his attention, and he cannot select a primary stimulus and ignore concurrent but nonessential stimuli.[26] The propensity of the brain-damaged child for attending equally to foreground and background is well known. Dolphin and Cruickshank,[16] testing cerebral palsied children with tachistoscopic materials, found that they had much more difficulty identifying foreground configurations embedded in a patterned background than did normal children. Vegas and Frye[65] tested retarded children, diagnosed as either familially or organically damaged, with pictures containing objects hidden in the backgrounds. Although the familial retardates named more objects altogether, the organically damaged children discovered more of the hidden objects.

Perceptual difficulties of these kinds seriously hinder the child's academic learning.[33] Unable to unify the parts of letters or numbers, he can neither remember nor reproduce them; and because he is attracted to numerous stimuli successively, such as a spot on the page of his book, a knife mark on his desk, a drawing on the blackboard, or a sound outside the door, he is inattentive more often than not to the letters and numbers he is supposed to be learning.

Poor motor coördination often is evident in the child with minimal brain damage and is demonstrated by his awkwardness in movement, his clumsiness at sports or exercises, and his inability to manage the fine muscle control required for writing.[10, 44] Eames[17] found that hyperopia, amblyopia, and muscle imbalance were more common in children with brain damage than in those without it and that the more severe the muscle imbalance and dominance variations, the greater the detrimental effect on the child's reading ability. Strabismus, mechanical speech imperfections, and adiadochokinesis (inability to perform rapidly alternating movements) have been noted in the brain-damaged child to a greater extent than in controls.[10] Tueber and Rudel[63] reported that early brain injury results in disturbance of the self-righting ability in children up to 11 years of age.

The disturbance in motor coördination causes the child to be uncertain of his movements, and this keeps him anxious. The younger brain-injured child shows his mistrust of his ability to manage physically by clinging to adults for physical support long after there would appear to be need for him to do so.[2]

The child's difficulties in coördinating stimulation and response successfully may be related to his tendency to perseverate. The child finds it difficult to stop one activity and begin another, and sometimes a period of rest must be interspersed to enable him to cease what he is doing and follow instructions to begin a new task. It seems to be easier for him to repeat a response once initiated than to attend carefully to a new stimulus and respond to it, and for this reason, some of his responses appear senseless. If he is asked to give the name of a circle and he replies "moon," he is likely to identify succeeding geometrical configurations as "moon" also, even though there is no resemblance. If he is asked to make five dots, he tends to cover his paper with them, unable to inhibit the response once it has been started.[60]

Brain-damaged adults who were assigned the task of reproducing designs could explain their incomplete, careless reproductions as being the result, in some degree, of a need to conserve energy. The child who finds that his responses are not facile, automatic, and correct, but are difficult to produce and often inappropriate, can be expected to repeat a given response rather than to exert the considerable effort required to assimilate, interpret, and react to a new stimulus.

Abstraction. Strauss and Lehtinen[60] required children to sort a variety of objects according to their concepts of which objects belonged together. They found that both brain-injured and normal children sorted objects according to color and form, but the brain-injured children tended to group objects because of an unessential detail or a vague function more than did the normal children. The brain-injured children also grouped objects in accordance with an imaginary or hypothetical situation, something which no normal child did.

The brain-damaged child can neither understand nor utilize abstract concepts applied to objects or situations with which he is not thoroughly familiar.[44] Because he cannot synthesize and generalize, his learning is piecemeal and slow, and often his attempts to find solutions to problems assigned him are desperate efforts to comply with instructions he cannot comprehend. His inefficient memory results partially from his inability to find meaning in what he experiences. He lives in a world of nonsense events, which occur unpredictably and without relationship to each other and which keep him constantly startled and confused. Stimulation, for him, is fractured into parts which vary with repetition and afford no consistent clue for discrimination and recall. There is no predictability in sensation for him, and therefore he cannot categorize or recall his impressions and associate them with similar events.

Inhibition. The brain-damaged child often is characterized by disinhibition. He is known in the classroom for his distractability and hyperactivity. He attends to multiple stimuli in rapid succession and thus cannot focus his attention on the teacher when she explains new work, nor on a written assignment he is expected to complete. He leaves his seat, crawls under the teacher's desk, climbs up on his own, interrupts others' work, talks, jokes, and is always on the move.[5] When there is group activity, he is even less able to inhibit his actions.

At home he is restless, disorganized, and wild. He does not obey parental instructions, and his headlong, constant activity exhausts the other members of his family. He behaves impulsively and uses poor judgment. He will ride his bicycle into heavy traffic, climb on rooftops, and use sharp tools awkwardly and carelessly. His practice of precipitating himself into dangerous situations, combined with his ineffectual motor control and his faulty interpretation of stimuli, make him accident-prone, and he is hurt often.

The child's inability to inhibit his responses is evidenced also by his sudden outbursts of violence at minor provocation. At such times he may seriously injure another child and be totally unable to explain his extreme anger. Episodes of unwarranted frenzy also occur.[4]

The tendency of the brain-damaged child to be unable to inhibit his behavior results partly from his failure to find meaning in stimuli and to make adequate responses when others can do so. Helpless, anxious, and bewildered, he reacts explosively or with a turmoil of motion to hide his awareness of his confusion and inadequacy. Greater disinhibition occurs under conditions of increased stimulation, and this suggests that nervous impulses are failing to flow smoothly along cortical pathways, with a resultant bombardment of unmodulated impulses which have not been assimilated and dispersed. Benton[5] believed that dysfunction of the diencephalon is immediately responsible for this failure. Strauss and Kephart[59] observed that the brain-injured child does not make as many responses as the ordinary child and suggested that he therefore stores energy which is released explosively by a minor stimulus.

A less anxious child, or one less inclined to respond with activity during stress, may be overinhibited. He avoids exposing himself to the unpleasantness of inept responses by refraining from both social contact and exploratory action. He appears apathetic, and he fails to respond to stimulation or to attempts to talk and play with him. He may protect himself from unfamiliar stimulation by restricting his playing to a few well-used toys, either repeating the same maneuvers with them or limiting his activity to placing them in formalistic arrangements. In self-protection from response, he shows anger when someone approaches him or disturbs his possessions.[55]

Social Response.   Newland[49] observed that the brain-injured child's social response is dependent on three factors: the characteristics he exhibits and his resultant social stimulus value; his choice of the individuals and groups with which he associates; and the total psychological structure in which these interactions take place.

The child's problems with inhibition contribute markedly to his own personality characteristics. If he is known for impulsivity and nonconformity or if he isolates himself and is compulsive in play, he is different from his peers and from adults, and he is avoided and rejected. If he hurts other children with explosive attacks, he will be feared and reviled. His obvious inadequacies at school compound his daily experiences of disapproval and failure. The futile attempts of his parents to control him cause them to express continually their exasperation and dislike.

Because he is isolated and rejected, the child's need for close personal contact is acute.[5] He seems immature because he seeks physical affection, comforting, and the support of his mother's presence in situations in which most children of his age are independent. As the child becomes older, he actively seeks acceptance from others, including strangers, by complimenting them on their appearance, possessions, or skills. A discussion of his teacher always includes his earnest assertion that she is the best teacher in the world, and he compliments and praises individuals whom he has just met. On many occasions, the child's acts of thoughtfulness, helpfulness, and unselfishness convince others that he is exceptionally mature.

Desirable kinds of behavior such as these, as well as the child's less amiable attempts to relate to others, result from his imitation of social mannerisms.[4] Unable to learn from experience, he manages to get along by adopting the phraseology and techniques of those who have gained acceptance and approval. The brain-damaged child has been described as pathetic in his eagerness to win friends. He uses such devices as offering help, boasting, clowning, gift-giving, and imitating currently popular modes of acting, speaking, and joking. His overeager efforts, repeated too often, seem unnatural, and he appears gullible and immature to his peers.

Because he cannot secure consistent acceptance and affection for himself, however, even a minor difficulty in a relationship with someone else causes him to feel seriously threatened and completely rejected. Lonely and left out from his earliest days, he has long believed that he must defend himself without help, and he procedes to do so, often by physically attacking anyone who corrects, directs, or criticizes him.

Self-concept. The normal child accepts his parents' opinion of him as a valid evaluation of his worth. If it is favorable, all of his other relationships and achievements are improved because of the confidence it creates. If it is unfavorable, the child seeks satisfactions to compensate for it. A good friend; special skill in academic work or athletics; or absorption in fantasy, reading, or a hobby all weaken the detrimental effect on his self-concept.

The brain-damaged child does not have the ability to circumvent others' unfavorable opinions of him in these ways. He leads a precarious existence, continually anticipating insurmountable difficulties, failure, censure, and trouble. He cannot rely on himself with certainty, and yet he is sure that there is no one else who will support or help him.*

His parents often dislike him and feel frustrated because of him.[35] He has successfully resisted all of their attempts to make him predictable and conforming, and they feel the effects of their failure. Benton[5] pointed out that the mother who is unable to satisfy her brain-damaged child's excessive demands for comforting and security, and who can neither control nor teach him, believes that she has failed in her function and develops strong feelings of hostility toward him. The father may blame the mother for spoiling the child, and he is ashamed of the child's undisciplined, immature behavior. He criticizes him severely for failure to learn and for misbehavior in school. His difficulties seem inexplicable, and the parents blame themselves.

At school, the brain-damaged child is heartily disliked by his teacher. She cannot cope with his constant activity, and he disrupts her instruction of the class. His failure to learn is discouraging to her, and if she conscientiously devotes hours of extra time to him and he still does not learn, she feels frustrated, helpless, and angry. She believes that he is deliberately inattentive and lazy, and he becomes an ever-present problem complicating her entire teaching effort.[5]

Tied to the criticisms and rejections of the adults most important in his life are the humiliations associated with his inability to keep up athletically, academically, or socially with his peers. The brain-damaged child is subjected to pressures and indignities which heighten his anxiety and lead to even greater difficulties in attention and inhibition. Because he has experienced failure so often, he is reluctant to attempt new tasks, and he remains guarded, self-protective, and alert to any possibility of danger from individuals or situations.[53] His loneliness, failures, and fearfulness increase his defensiveness, and the older child often seeks to prove that he is independent and needs no one. To demonstrate that

---

* See Case 48, Andrew D., p. 535.

he can care for himself, he may run away or, as an adolescent, move from his home to a rented room, leaving school and finding work wherever he can to support himself.

Diagnosis

Diagnosis of minimal cerebral dysfunction is not always easy, and a variety of observations and examinations must be made to determine its existence.[5] Seldom is the condition identified in the pre-school child. Although a distraught mother knows that the child does not respond to ordinary teaching methods; that he is hyperactive, unpredictable, or compulsive; and that he is immature emotionally and overdependent, these descriptions rarely hold significance for the pediatrician who has observed no gross physical or neurological malfunction. The pre-school child is not expected to have perfect fine muscle control or to display considerable ability in performing a variety of tasks, and therefore the standard tests which reveal perceptual and abstractive defects of the older child cannot be used with equivalent validity to examine the younger child.[19, 24]

After the child has entered school, however, and has demonstrated an inability to learn despite adequate intelligence, his difficulties are brought to the attention of professional children's workers, and careful and extensive examinations can be made. Examination of a child for minimal brain damage includes behavior observation; neurological examination; prenatal, paranatal, and postnatal history; psychological testing; and speech evaluation.

The child's behavior in various formal and informal situations should be observed, and an accurate description of problems encountered at home, at school, and with peers should be obtained. Parents may report hyperkinesis, distractability, attendance to minute stimuli, inexplicable fear and anger responses, and disruptive and unpredictable behavior which has occurred frequently and persisted through several developmental periods.[10] Bender[2] suggested that an aid to diagnosis of brain damage is the child's use of the adult's body for support and a facial expression which is anxious, vigilant, and mask-like.

Because neurological examinations consist of a gross sampling of central nervous system functioning,[5] sometimes no striking signs of impairment are revealed. The presence of strabismus and ineffectual visual-motor coördination are indicative, however, and mixed laterality, time and space disorientation, and adiadochokinesis may be apparent.[10] Anderson[1] reported that a neurological appraisal of 30 hyperkinetic children revealed abnormalities in all but one child, most often in perceptual or motor integration. Electroencephalographic tracings are abnormal in over 50 per cent of brain-damaged children, but a normal record is not proof that central nervous system pathology is nonexistent.

A history of prenatal, paranatal, infant and early childhood experience may give clues to the presence of minimal cerebral damage. Maternal eclampsia, infection, pelvic malformation, or hemorrhage prenatally; excessive anesthesia or trauma during delivery; infectious disease, toxicosis, or trauma in the neonate or young child all may cause central nervous system damage. Indications that the neonate has suffered asphyxia are a pallid or blue appearance during the first few days of life, increased somnolence, inability to swallow, listlessness, motor twitchings, or seizures. The second born of twins is more liable to birth injury.[60]

Psychological tests reveal minimal brain damage in the school-age child. Perception is examined by requesting the child to reproduce designs, either with objects or by drawing. The Kohs Block Designs Test requires the child to recreate designs pictured on cards by arranging bicolored blocks correctly. The Marble Board Test, used extensively in the study of brain-damaged children by Strauss and Werner,[61] requires the child to reproduce a design constructed of marbles against a background of small holes. The Ellis Visual Designs Test and the Bender Gestalt Test require the child to draw designs, each of which is pictured on a card. Failures in accurate reproduction of designs on such tests can sometimes be attributed to age, and discrepancies are more significant in a child of eight years or older.[36, 54]

Freehand drawing affords another test of visual-motor perception, and Bender[4] stated that a brain-damaged child's performance on the Goodenough Draw-a-Person test may be as much as two years below his performance on a standard intelligence scale. Distinguishing differences between weights and sizes, localizing sounds, and detecting brightness levels also are tests of perception. Frostig[20] suggested that five areas of perception should be evaluated in the child: eye-hand coördination, figure-ground perception, perception of form constancy, perception of position in space, and spatial relationships.

The child's ability to abstract common principles is examined by sorting, grouping, and matching tests. The Vigotski test[23] consists of blocks of varied colors, shapes, and sizes which the child is to sort according to a consistent attribute. Object sorting tests contain a wide variety of miniature or small, real objects, and the child must group these according to a characteristic which he must verbalize. Abstraction ability is evaluated by asking the child to match objects with pictures or words, to match forms, or to match or sort colors.[62] The way in which the child describes pictures or stories indicates whether he is responding to specific stimuli or is able to interpret indicated meanings.

The child's learning and memory abilities can be tested. Auditory memory tasks include such assignments as learning 15 orally presented words, and visual-verbal ability is evaluated by requiring the child to learn 15 pictures. Immediate recall is checked by requesting the child to repeat series of words or digits, both forward and backward; to repeat sentences from memory; or to learn a maze.

Ability to reason is checked by the child's recognition of similarities and differences between objects, words, or situations; his perception of absurdities in pictures or stories; and his skill with arithmetical puzzles. The minimally brain-damaged child shows disability in repeating serials, such as the months of the year or counting by two's. The child's ability to read and to write and spell from dictation, as well as the extent and usefulness of his vocabulary, all give clues to the existence of aphasic difficulties.[62]

A frequent finding is gross discrepancy between a child's ability with verbal items of a standard intelligence test and performance items. The discrepancy may favor either ability, and it is evidenced by a 15- or 20-point I.Q. difference between the two skills. A child defective in either verbal or performance skills tends to organize incoming impressions in terms of his superior function. Lehtinen[38] noted that the child whose discrepancy is in favor of language may develop a good vocabulary, become somewhat verbose, and utilize language in naming his perceptions and in constructing relationships. Perceptions are needed to structure the language, however, and without familiar, concrete objects to talk about, the child's verbal facility is turned into fluent but inaccurate reports of experiences. Although he can memorize well and learn arithmetic by rote, meanings escape him and he has no ability to organize and plan.

The child with more perceptual than verbal ability speaks incorrectly and finds it difficult to grasp shades of meaning or to express himself concisely. His vocabulary is limited, and he uses one word to designate a variety of objects or events. Verbal directions, given without demonstrations, confuse him. He simplifies all grammar, omitting articles and plurals, using the objective rather than the nominative case for pronouns, employing the present tense almost exclusively, and failing to invert sentences when he asks questions.[38]

Evaluation of speech may reveal mechanical difficulties in speaking, delayed onset, or echolalia—all of which may be symptoms of brain damage.[10]

Education and Rehabilitation

The child with minimal brain damage receives less assistance in adjusting to his handicap than does a child disabled in any other way. Usually this is because the difficulty remains undiagnosed, but sometimes even when an accurate diagnosis is made the child still receives no adequate treatment. Teachers do not know which methods are helpful, and small classes and individual instruction are unavailable. Moreover, the feeling of frustration and annoyance which teachers and parents experience in dealing with the child moves them to dispose of the problem he presents by ridding themselves of him. Even when they are aware that there is damage to the child's central nervous system which is affecting his reactions, they consider him obstreperous, defiant, self-centered, and lazy. Often he is relegated to a class for retarded children, excluded from school entirely, or placed in a military or correctional school. None of these solutions meets his special needs, and they serve only to convince him that he is stupid or bad—convictions to which he may react with hostile and violent behavior.

To assist the brain-damaged child, it is necessary to identify the specific deficiencies which handicap him and to assess his ability to compensate for or overcome these.[37] Although he suffers from a maturation lag which is self-correcting in time, it is important that acute anxiety or isolation do not become complicating components of his lengthened developmental period.[4] The child benefits from special instruction and practice in areas in which he is deficient; from reduced stimulation; and from order, firm discipline, and independence training in his daily life. Medication may reduce his hyperactivity, although the effect varies with the kind used and with the individual child.[5] Both amphetamines and dilantin are prescribed for the brain-damaged child.[10]

Academic Instruction. School systems seldom provide for the special instruction of the brain-damaged child because of prohibitive costs. Ideally, the child should receive instruction in a class consisting of not more than 12 students and preferably less. Seating arrangements should reduce distraction by other children, and this can be accomplished by facing desks to the wall or by providing individual study carrels. A windowless room, or one in which the bottom portion of the window is covered, reduces stimulation; and the practice of creating interest by covering walls and blackboards in a classroom with displays and instructions should be relinquished in favor of a single display, to be changed as needed. The brain-damaged child who must remain in a regular classroom should be able to work in a screened area whenever he wishes to do so or when his teacher considers it necessary.

Because of the child's difficulty with symbols, teaching techniques should utilize objects. Various materials can be used for demonstrations or to dramatize a fact or a process; and sorting, cutting, manipulating counters, and using printing and screening devices hold the child's attention and provide him with the skills required for reading and number work.[60]

Lehtinen[38] emphasized the importance of making certain that the child is aware of his errors. Repetition does not guarantee correct learning in the brain-damaged child, as many baffled teachers know. Repetition without correction of the child's perception consists only of rehearsing an incorrect and meaningless perception, and if the child attends to disparate parts of letters, words, numbers, or sentences, he forms no intelligible configuration and cannot recall what he has reviewed.

The child needs training in coördinating the separate parts of symbols, in generalizing accurately, and in interpreting what he experiences. He can be taught to sort objects according to function or can be required to look at and talk about a picture, answering questions about it until its meaning is clear. He can be trained to withhold verbal comment until a sentence or question has been completed, and then he can be asked questions about its intent. This technique assists him in delaying his response until he has focused on the entire series of words, instead of reacting thoughtlessly to a single word which has caught his attention.

The brain-damaged child seldom anticipates what the consequences of his actions will be. He can learn to restrain impetuosity by forced slowing of his completion of tasks assigned him, and this can be accomplished by using screening devices and requiring motor manipulations to accompany learning procedures. His teacher can ask questions about the results of various possible methods for completing an assignment before permitting him to begin it, and eventually the child learns to delay activity until some degree of attention has been paid to the requirements of the situation.

Arithmetic instruction must begin with accurate counting, and the child's movements must be slowed if this is to be possible. A deliberate pace can be set by having the child operate a screening device which exposes one dot at a time in a series to be counted or by requiring the child to screw or place a small peg in a board as he counts it. The use of various colors, in sequence, with the child pointing or touching as he counts, holds his attention to the task. Placing a block on top of each dot he counts helps him to stop when he has reached the correct number.

He also needs to recognize and be able to create groups, and he can learn this by matching cards with varying numbers of dots or circles printed on them. His reproduction of groups may be hindered by perseveration, which impels him to cover a page with circles when he has been instructed to draw just three. He can be assisted in mastering this kind of assignment by being given a stencil with the correct number of circles cut out. The result of his work is an accurate adherence to the instructions he was given, and he can see the correct reproduction he has created. Eventually he can work without the aid of the stencil.

Addition and subtraction can be taught by using a box containing beads on wires, with a movable metal strip as a divider, or small blocks can be used. After solving a problem in this way, the child can transfer his manipulations to paper, using written symbols.[60] Number symbols should not be taught until the child is able to count well, combine numbers up to six, and reproduce groups correctly. He can learn number symbols by tracing them with his finger, drawing them with stencils, or making the figure with dots and then connecting these with a line.

Reading instruction is often slow and discouraging, and its success is partially dependent on the extent and nature of cerebral dysfunction. The brain-damaged child may experience difficulty in the accurate perception of sounds, and therefore phonics practice will be less meaningful for him. Phonics instruction is needed, however, to provide the child with as many cues as possible in recognizing consistently the individual letters he must learn. Use of the Initial Teaching Alphabet simplifies his task.

The child's acquistion of the ability to reproduce letter symbols is aided by the use of individual letter cards with brightly colored letters against contrasting backgrounds. The child learns to combine the cards into words and later into sentences. Speaking the letter as he uses it reënforces its acquisition. Written reproduction may be complicated both by the child's attending to discrete parts of letters and by poor motor coördination. Both of these difficulties can be decreased by having the child trace lines and geometric forms, reproduce these with stencils, and then practice writing letters in the same way, in time progressing to copying the letter from a card. Later, he can practice correct writing by copying sentences.

Using one word in a variety of sentences aids the child in learning to generalize and also inhibits his tendency to respond to only one aspect of a sentence. Lehtinen[38] suggested posing riddles to the child to help him learn to delay his answers, respond to whole perceptions, and practice interpretation and analysis.

Motor Coördination. If the child's defective motor coördination can be improved, he will find much easier the daily tasks of handling his body, competing with peers athletically, and managing school materials.

Rhythm games and exercises should be a part of every school day, and similar physical activities can be carried out at home. Music accompanying the exercises aids in establishing rhythm.

The child can improve his balance and motor control by practicing walking on a straight line, then on a wide board, and then on one raised slightly off the ground. Jumping and hopping, once mastered, increase his physical security, and the child should practice ball handling. The older child can learn to swim, improving both his strength and coördination.

The child who is awkward at buttoning and tying shoe laces should practice these skills daily at times other than when he is trying to dress himself. Toy tools, pre-school screwdrivers, and peg sets, scissors, and crayons should be used daily.

Speech Training. If the child has difficulty in communicating, either because of muscular incoördination or distortion of word meanings, he should be under the regular tutelage of a speech therapist, who can also suggest exercises to be practiced at home. Parents assist the child in speaking when they devote time to him daily solely for conversation and thus encourage expression of his ideas and description of his experiences. When his phraseology is inappropriate, he should be questioned until he can state accurately what he intended to express, and mispronunciations or the use of nonexistent words should be corrected.

Social Experience. The brain-damaged child's natural tendency to adopt the social manners of his elders is evidence of his eagerness to learn how to get along with others, and he can be taught formal courtesies at an early age.

Adequate relationships with peers, however, will not be established by this kind of social knowledge. He needs frequent experience in playing with another child of his own age and sex. He should play with only one child at a time, preferably one who tends to be placid and nonirritating and one who likes him. Definite rules should be followed concerning the sharing of toys, just as is necessary for pre-school children, and some parental control of playing is helpful in curtailing excited, frenzied activity. Interspersing record playing or story reading with free play quiets the child, and play periods should be short. As the child grows older, it is increasingly difficult to manipulate his social experiences, but the amount of time he plays with others should be limited, and he should not be permitted to wander away from home and seek contacts by himself.

Prior instruction about what he is to say and do in any impending social situation guides him in responding adequately, and reminders at the time, if these are needed, will comfort rather than offend him.

If he hurts another child in impulsive anger, he must apologize and aid his victim in any way he can. To lessen his conviction that he must manage every situation by himself, he needs to be assured that adults will assist him in his dealings with other children, and he should be encouraged to report to parents or teachers when there are problems, rather than trying to settle matters himself. This procedure is a reversal of the training given the normal child, who is encouraged to fend for himself and not to tell tales, but the brain-damaged child needs to learn to rely on others for help and to inhibit impetuous actions.

Reduced Stimulation. Just as stimulation is reduced for the child in the classroom, it should be reduced at home. Television should be strictly limited, and exciting, frightening shows should be banned completely. Often the brain-damaged child is not interested in television because he finds it too difficult to remain quiet and does not understand what he sees and hears. The child needs time alone every day to play as he chooses in his own room. Dolls or toy animals with which he can act out various experiences help him in socialization,[4] but if his playing becomes destructive and aggressive, he should be diverted by questions and suggestions into more constructive and passive pursuits. Real-life toys, such as cars and trucks, play stores and gas stations, brooms, lawn mowers, and rakes help the younger child reënact the scenes around him in solitary play, and they thus become more familiar.

The child's day should be orderly so that he can predict its events reliably. Meals should be on time, and bedtime should be early and unvarying. Regular times for free play, physical exercise, and conversation with parents should be maintained daily, both to ensure time for these activities and to provide structure for the child's day.

Discipline. The brain-damaged child needs more control than the normal child, but usually he has less. His parents weary of the struggle to teach him conformity because he never remembers instructions, he disobeys continually, and he seems unable to learn. If they give up, however, he is left to do as he chooses, and his ill-considered behavior can endanger both himself and others.

Adults need to remember that he is not willfully disobedient and that severe punishment and constant criticism only make him miserable and lonely without improving his behavior. He needs firm direction from an early age,[10] and this must be continued long beyond the time when the normal child has learned to direct himself in many aspects of his life.

Instructions to the brain-damaged child must be detailed and explicit. Lehtinen[38] described the degree of specificity which is required: Telling the child to be quiet produces no change in his behavior, but explaining that being quiet means that his feet do not move, his hands do not move, and his mouth remains closed will result in compliance. Any direction given the child must be obeyed, and an adult who makes a request of the child should be prepared, if necessary, to remain with him and guide him through the completion of the requirement.

The brain-damaged child needs supervision of his outdoor play for a longer period of time than the normal child. Left unsupervised, he engages in experimentation which can result in his harming or even killing himself. He is also likely to disappear without warning, acting impulsively on an idea which occurs to him. Parents of the brain-damaged child cannot assume that repeated prohibitions of a given act, or even the experience of being harmed by it, will prevent the child's continuing it. He must be protected as a pre-school child is protected because he cannot anticipate danger, profit from earlier experiences, nor inhibit his impulsions to act.

Disobedience regarding rules about leaving home without permission or failing to return promptly from school should be followed with increased supervision which prevents the child from disobeying. Destructiveness, rudeness, and abuse of others should be handled as they are for the normal child, but parents need to be aware that such incidents will be more frequent and endure over a longer period of time, even with consistent training efforts. The child whose hyperactivity is annoying should be calmed by assigning him a specific task, to be completed alone or in conjunction with one of his parents away from the rest of the family.

Independence Training. The brain-damaged child needs a prolonged period of dependency, with physical affection and the understanding attention of his parents.[2, 10] Overstimulated, fatigued, and perplexed, he needs the reassurance that his parents will help him, and they often must protect and direct him as though he were a pre-school child. Because he is different from his peers and knows this, he is subjected to a constant, almost unavoidable loneliness which forces independence and self-reliance upon him.

Frequently, however, his conviction that he must manage alone results in aggressive attacks on others and in testing himself in a series of ill-advised adventures. His desire to be self-reliant is commendable, but it should be channeled into purposeful activity which will aid his maturation. Because he seems immature, is distractable, and performs assigned chores carelessly, he may not be asked to help at home. It is important that he do so in order to learn responsibility and to consider himself useful to his family, and he should be taught to do well several household chores. As basic tasks in self-care, he should also be expected to make his bed and care for his own possessions. He needs supervision in performing such work, and when he is learning, a parent should share it so that he can direct each step. The child can earn money by work which helps the family, and he can learn to use it wisely, with gradually increasing responsibility for meeting his own financial needs.

Puberty is a critical time for the brain-damaged child.[67] At his age, he is expected to direct himself, to learn adequately in school, to get along with other people, and to plan constructively for his future independence. He cannot do any of these things as capably as a normal child, and his deficiencies may appear more incongruous than before when he attains the physical appearance of maturity. If he has been fortunate enough to receive special academic training and wise management from his parents, as an adolescent he should be able to attend school in a regular classroom; associate with peers without excessive difficulty; and have some feeling of independence, achievement, and acceptance. His life should remain orderly, and continued planning of experiences and regular parental attention are necessary. If he is capable of college attendance, his ability to direct himself should be assessed, and practice should be given him in separation from his family, travelling alone, scheduling his study time, and managing money.

REFERENCES

1. Anderson, W. W.: The hyperkinetic child: A neurological appraisal. *Neurology*, 1963, *13*, 968–973.
2. Bender, L.: *Aggression, Hostility, and Anxiety in Children*. Springfield, Ill., Charles C Thomas, 1953, pp. 157–162.
3. Bender, L.: *Psychopathology of Children with Organic Brain Disorders*. Springfield, Ill., Charles C Thomas, 1956.
4. Bender, L.: The brain-damaged child. *In* Frampton, M., and Gall, E., eds.: *Special Education for the Exceptional*. Boston, Porter Sargent, 1956, vol. 3, pp. 48–61.
5. Benton, P.: Organic behavior disorders in children. *The Journal*, Oklahoma State Medical Association, 1961, pp. 581–585.
6. Broida, D. C.: Psychosocial aspects of epilepsy in children and youth. *In* Cruickshank, W. M., ed.: *Psychology of Exceptional Children and Youth*. Englewood Cliffs, N. J., Prentice-Hall, Inc., 1955, pp. 345–390.
7. Chess, S.: *An Introduction to Child Psychiatry*. New York, Grune and Stratton, Inc., 1959, pp. 94–100.
8. Churchill, J.: Current research in chronic neurologic diseases of children. *Merrill-Palmer Quart.*, 1963, *9*(2), 95–100.
9. Clements, S. D., and Peters, J. E.: Minimal brain dysfunction in the school age child: Diagnosis and treatment. *Arch. Gen. Psychiat.*, 1962, *6*, 185–197.
10. Clemmens, R. L.: Minimal brain damage in children. *Children*, U.S. Dept. of Health, Education, and Welfare, *8*(5) 179–183.
11. Colver, T., and Kerridge, D. F.: Birth order in epileptic children. *J. Neurol. Neurosurg. Psychiat.*, 1962, *25*, 59–62.
12. Connor, F. P.: The education of children with chronic medical problems. *In* Cruickshank, W. M., and Johnson, G. O., eds.: *Education of Exceptional Children and Youth*. Englewood Cliffs, N. J., Prentice-Hall, Inc., 1958, pp. 498–554.
13. Connor, F. P.: The education of crippled children. *In* Cruickshank, W. M., and Johnson, G. O., eds.: *Education of Exceptional Children and Youth*. Englewood Cliffs, N. J., Prentice-Hall, Inc., 1958, pp. 436, 461–497.
14. Daryn, E.: Problems of children with "diffuse brain damage": Clinical observations on a developmental disturbance. *Arch. Gen. Psychiat.*, 1961, *4*, 299–306.
15. Davis, H. B.: Factors rendering the cerebral palsied child capable or incapable of benefiting from formal education. *Cerebral Palsy Bull.*, 1960, *2*, 28–33.
16. Dolphin, J. E., and Cruickshank, W. M.: The figure-background relationship in children with cerebral palsy. *In* Trapp, E. P., and Himelstein, P., eds.: *Readings on the Exceptional Child*. New York, Appleton-Century-Crofts, 1962, pp. 508–513.
17. Eames, T. H.: Reading failures and nonfailures in children with brain damage. *Amer. J. Opthal.*, 1959, *47*, 74–77.
18. Eisenberg, L.: Psychiatric implications of brain damage in children. *Psychiat. Quart.*, 1957, *31*, 72–92.
19. Ernhart, C. B., Graham, F. K., Eichman, P. L., Marshall, J. M., and Thurston, D.: Brain injury in the preschool child. Some developmental considerations: II. Comparison of brain-injured and normal children. *Psychol. Monogr.*, 1963, 77(574).

20. Frostig, M.: Visual perception in the brain-injured child. *Amer. J. Orthopsychiat.,* 1963, *33,* 665-671.
21. Glenting, P.: Course and prognosis of congenital spastic hemiplegia. *Developm. Med. Child Neurol.,* 1963, *5*(3), 252-260.
22. Goldenberg, S.: Testing the brain-injured child with normal I.Q. *In* Strauss, A. A., and Kephart, N. C.: *Psychopathology and Education of the Brain-injured Child.* New York, Grune and Stratton, Inc., 1955, vol. 2, pp. 144-164.
23. Goldstein, K.: Functional disturbances in brain damage. *In* Arieti, S., ed.: *American Handbook of Psychiatry.* New York, Basic Books, Inc., 1959, vol. 1, pp. 770-796.
24. Graham, F. K., and Berman, P. W.: Current status of behavior tests for brain damage in infants and preschool children. *Amer. J. Orthopsychiat., 31*(4), 1961, 713-727.
25. Haring, N. G.: A review of research on cerebral palsy and emotional adjustment. *Except. Children,* 1959, *26,* 191-194.
26. Hawkins, V. T.: Educating the brain-injured child. *In* Frampton, M., and Gall, E., eds.: *Special Education for the Exceptional.* Boston, Porter Sargent, 1956, vol. 3, pp. 65-66.
27. Holden, R. H.: Motivation, adjustment, and anxiety of cerebral-palsied children. *In* Trapp, E. P., and Himelstein, P., eds.: *Readings on the Exceptional Child.* New York, Appleton-Century-Crofts, 1962, pp. 514-520.
28. Jones, V.: Character development in children—An objective approach. *In* Carmichael, L., ed.: *Manual of Child Psychology.* New York, John Wiley and Sons, 1946.
29. Kaliski, L.: The brain-injured child: Learning by living in a structured setting. *Amer. J. Ment. Defic.,* 1959, *63,* 688-695.
30. Kanner, L.: *Child Psychiatry,* Ed. 3. Springfield, Ill., Charles C Thomas, 1957, pp. 314-344.
31. Kastein, S.: Speech hygiene guidance for parents of children with cerebral palsy. *In* Michal-Smith, H., and Kastein, S.: *The Special Child.* Seattle, Washington, New School for the Special Child, Inc., 1962, pp. 129-153.
32. Kastein, S., and Klapper, Z.: Integrative therapy for the brain-injured child: A case study. *Except. Children,* 1957, *23,* 255-262.
33. Kaur, A. A., and Pasamanick, B.: Prenatal and paranatal factors in the development of childhood reading disorders. *Monogr. Soc. Res. Child Developm.,* 1959, *24* (73).
34. Keating, L. E.: A review of the literature on the relationship of epilepsy and intelligence in school children. *J. Ment. Sci.,* 1960, *106,* 1042-1059.
35. Klebanoff, L. B.: Parents of schizophrenic children: I. Parental attitudes of mothers of schizophrenic, brain-injured and retarded, and normal children. Workshop, 1958. *Amer. J. Orthopsychiat.,* 1959, *29,* 445-454.
36. Ko Y.: A study on figure rotation in the Bender-Gestalt Test. *Acta Psychol.* (*Taiwan*), 1961, (3) 94-195.
37. Lawrence, M. M.: Minimal brain injury in child psychiatry. *Comprehen. Psychiat.,* 1960, *1,* 360-369.
38. Lehtinen, L. E.: Preliminary conclusions affecting education of brain-injured children. *In* Strauss, A. A., and Kephart, N. C.: *Psychopathology and Education of the Brain-injured Child.* New York, Grune and Stratton, Inc., 1955, vol. 2, pp. 165-191.
39. Lennox, W. G.: The epileptic child. *In* Michal-Smith, H., ed.: *Pediatric Problems in Clinical Practice.* New York, Grune and Stratton, Inc., 1954, pp. 245-272.
40. Lezak, M. D., and Dixon, H. H.: The brain-injured child in a clinic population: A statistical description. *Except. Children,* 1964, *30,* 237-240.
41. Mayman, M., and Gardner, R.: The characteristic psychological disturbance in some cases of brain damage with mild deficit. *Bull. Menninger Clin.,* 1960, *24,* 26-36.
42. Melin, K.: EEG and epilepsy in cerebral palsy. *Developm. Med. Child Neurol.,* 1962, *4*(2), 180-183.
43. Michal-Smith, H.: Experiential programming for the cerebral palsied child: the

past as guide to the future. *In* Michal-Smith, H., and Kastein, S.: *The Special Child.* Seattle, Washington, New School for the Special Child, Inc., 1962, pp. 107–127.

44. Michal-Smith, H., and Morgenstern, M.: Psychodynamics of the brain-injured child and its implication in habilitation. *In* Michal-Smith, H., and Kastein, S.: *The Special Child.* Seattle, Washington, New School for the Special Child, Inc., 1962, pp. 45–64.

45. Mitchell, R. G.: The growth and development of children with cerebral palsy. *Cerebral Palsy Rev.,* 1961, *22,* 3–4, 17–19.

46. Moed, M., and Litwin, D.: The employability of the cerebral palsied: A summary of two related studies. *Rehabilit. Lit.,* 1963, *24* (9), 265–296.

47. Murphy, L. B.: Preventive implications of development in the preschool years. *In* Caplan, G., ed.: *Prevention of Mental Disorders in Children.* New York, Basic Books, Inc., 1961, p. 226.

48. Myklebust, H. R., and Johnson, D.: Dyslexia in children. *Except. Children,* 1962, *29,* 14–25.

49. Newland, T. E.: Psychosocial aspects of the adjustment of the brain-injured. *Except. Children,* 1957, *23,* 149–153.

50. Nielsen, H. H.: Visual-motor functioning of cerebral palsied and normal children. *Nord. Psykol.,* 1962, *14* (2), 43–103.

51. Paine, R. S.: Minimal chronic brain syndromes in children. *Developm. Med. Child Neurol.,* 1962, *4,* 21–27.

52. Phelps, W. M.: The cerebral palsy child. *In* Michal-Smith, H., ed.: *Pediatric Problems in Clinical Practice.* New York, Grune and Stratton, Inc., 1954, pp. 121–158.

53. Phillips, E. L., Wiener, D. N., and Haring, N. G.: *Discipline, Achievement, and Mental Health.* Englewood Cliffs, N. J., Prentice-Hall, Inc., 1960, pp. 94–95.

54. Quast, W.: The Bender-Gestalt: A clinical study of children's records. *J. Consult. Psychol.,* 1961, *25,* 405–408.

55. Rimland, B.: *Infantile Autism.* New York, Appleton-Century-Crofts, 1963.

56. Rosenblum, S.: Practices and problems in the use of tranquilizers with exceptional children. *In* Trapp, E. P., and Himelstein, P., eds.: *Readings on the Exceptional Child.* New York, Appleton-Century-Crofts, 1962, pp. 639–657.

57. Rowley, V. N.: Analysis of the WISC performance of brain-damaged and emotionally disturbed children. *J. Consult. Psychol.,* 1961, *25,* 553.

58. Small, J. G.: A psychiatric survey of brain injured children. *Arch. Gen. Psychiat.,* 1962, *7,* 120–124.

59. Strauss, A. A., and Kephart, N. C.: *Psychopathology and Education of the Brain-injured Child.* New York, Grune and Stratton, Inc., 1955, vol. 2.

60. Strauss, A. A., and Lehtinen, L. E.: *Psychopathology of the Brain-Injured Child.* New York, Grune and Stratton, Inc., 1950.

61. Strauss, A. A., and Werner, H.: Disorders in conceptual thinking in the brain-injured child. *In* Trapp, E. P., and Himelstein, P., ed.: *Readings on the Exceptional Child.* New York, Appleton-Century-Crofts, 1962, pp. 481–482.

62. Taylor, E. M.: *Psychological Appraisal of Children with Cerebral Defects.* Cambridge, Mass., Harvard University Press, 1959.

63. Teuber, H., and Rudel, R. G.: Behavior after cerebral lesions in children and adults. *Developm. Med. Child Neurol.,* 1962, *4,* 3–20.

64. Thurston, J. P.: Attitudes and emotional reactions of parents of institutionalized cerebral palsied, retarded patients. *Amer. J. Ment. Defic.,* 1960, *65,* 227–235.

65. Vegas, O. V., and Frye, R. L.: Effect of brain damage on perceptual performance. *Percept. and Motor Skills,* 1963, *17,* 662.

66. Williams, J. M.: When is a child with cerebral palsy ineducable? *Cerebral Palsy Bull.,* 1961, *3,* 453–457.

67. Winkler, W. T.: Die Beziehungen zwischen frühkindlicher Hirnschädigung und neurosen im Kindes und Jugendalter (Relations between brain damage in early childhood and neuroses in childhood and adolescence). *Z. Psychother. Med. Psychol.,* 1962, *12,* 1–10.

Chapter 47

The Visually
Handicapped Child

Educators and legislators neglected the needs of visually handicapped children for many years because the number of these children was so small that group training appeared impractical. In the early 1940's, however, an increase in the incidence of blindness in children made obvious the existence of deficiencies in provision of special assistance for their education. At this time, a condition known as retrolental fibroplasia blinded many prematurely-born infants, especially those whose birth weight was less than three pounds. During the next decade, research identified the major cause of the condition to be the administration of high concentrations of oxygen to these infants in an effort to preserve their lives. After adequate precautions were taken, retrolental fibroplasia nearly vanished, but many of its early victims still are attending school.

Legal blindness is commonly defined as central visual acuity of 20/200 or less in the better eye, after correction; and impairment severe enough to warrant a child's inclusion in a sight-saving class is defined as visual acuity of 20/70 or less in the better eye, after correction.[2] There are broad variations in visual acuity within these limits, and descriptive definitions of blindness have been devised by the Committee on Statistics of the Blind. Five categories of blindness are distinguished: (1) total blindness, or inability to perceive motion or hand movements at a distance of three feet; (2) inability to count fingers at a distance of three feet; (3) travel vision, but inability to read letters comparable in size to newspaper headlines; (4) ability to read headlines, but not 14-point or smaller type; and (5) inability to read 10-point type and insufficient vision for activities in which eyesight is essential.[1]

The estimated number of blind individuals is subject to error because the incidence at all age levels is incompletely reported. From the available information, it is believed that in 1957 there were 24,000 individuals under the age of 20 who were legally blind, a figure representing 7 per cent of the total number of blind persons.[10] One child in every 3500 or 4000 children in public elementary schools needs to learn braille; the rate in secondary schools is lower, and approximately 25 per cent of the total blind educable group attend secondary schools. It is believed that after the children blinded by retrolental fibroplasia have graduated from the schools, the incidence of blindness will drop to one child in every 7000 or 8000 of the school population.[18]

Retrolental fibroplasia has been considered responsible for blindness in 50 to 75 per cent of the affected age groups.[22] Other causes of visual handicapping are infectious diseases, injury, poisoning, tumor, and hereditary factors.[13]

Disease causes over 50 per cent of all blindness. General infectious diseases, such as measles, scarlet fever, typhoid fever, smallpox, diphtheria, and meningitis, which result in infections settling in the eyes cause 15 per cent of all blindness. Diseases of the eyes themselves are responsible for about 35 per cent of blindness. Ophthalmia neonatorum, resulting from venereal infection of the parents, has largely disappeared because of the legal requirement that the eyes of newborn infants be treated with silver nitrate solution. Interstitial keratitis is an affliction of the cornea associated with parental syphilis. Trachoma, also known as granulated eyelids, occurs under conditions of poor nutrition and sanitation and is especially prevalent among the Indian population. Cataract causes the lens to become opaque, and 15 per cent of one group of 2700 children in schools and classes for the blind were found to have cataracts.

Accidents are responsible for 15 to 25 per cent of blindness in both children and adults, with the incidence five times greater in males. Boys and men are blinded by explosions and flying objects, and girls and women by falls, burns, and cutting instruments. Poisoning or tumor can affect the optic nerve or the visual cortical centers and can damage or destroy vision. Hereditary factors are evident in blindness, and children born of parents who are closely related are ten times more liable to be blind than those born to unrelated parents. Census data indicate that 11 per cent of the blind have blind parents, siblings, or children.[2]

CHARACTERISTICS OF THE VISUALLY
HANDICAPPED CHILD

No distinctive personality is apparent in blind children, and the home environment of each child, his physical health, intelligence level, and the age at which sight was lost are all factors entering into his general adjustment.[12] His difficulties usually develop from the attitudes of his family and of neighbors and their children toward him. He requires continuous socialization, acceptance, and training, and without these, the child is frustrated and isolated and may acquire characteristics of intolerance or of helplessness.[1]*

Withdrawal and introversion may occur in the child. Because he does not participate in games with other children, he does not associate with them frequently or share their interests. He cannot understand completely what others are experiencing, and he feels isolated from them. They, in turn, believing that he cannot share their concepts, fail to communicate with him at all.[2]

The child who is isolated most of the time turns to fantasy. If he has some sight, his daydreams will include visual imagery; if not, his fantasy consists of sound and movement, and it serves as a substitute for broader and more realistic experience.[4] The child may also indulge in habits known as "blindisms," such as rocking, putting his fingers or fists into his eyes, whirling around rapidly, waving his fingers before his eyes, or nodding his head.[12] These movements provide stimulation for the child, who finds little else to entice or interest him. Speech disturbances are associated with withdrawal. The child may repeat, in a meaningless fashion, television commercials or phrases he has heard; or he may cease to speak entirely.[28]

Concomitant with withdrawal is the blind child's slow social adjustment. Without regular and natural contact with his peers, he has no opportunity to learn to fend for himself or to adapt to others.[30] He becomes self-conscious around people, and this feeling is heightened by a loss in self-esteem if he is convinced that his family and peers regard him as defective and different.[39]

His strong feeling of inferiority may cause him to behave aggressively, to lose his temper readily, to demand help, and to excuse himself from normal social and work obligations.[30] Some blind children resort to overtalkativeness to hide their anxiety and loneliness.[17] Lack of initiative is a common characteristic of the blind child,[26] who becomes accustomed to others' approaching him and fails to begin activities or solicit companionship independently. He is known for his suggestibility,

---

* See Case 49, Mary L., p. 536.

and he responds to encouragement. Often he has a good sense of humor and likes to play practical jokes.[4]

Differing conclusions about the personal adjustment of blind adolescents have been reported, with some investigators finding no significant distinctions between blind and sighted children[42] and others stating that inferiority feelings remain in the older child. Blind adolescents are concerned about physical defects, their personalities and abilities, and problems related to school and home life.[31] They experience difficulty in the areas of sex curiosity and dating, mobility, and concern for the future, and although these problems differ qualitatively from similar problems of sighted adolescents, they are no more severe.[23] Sakellariou[37] reported that blind adolescents demonstrate a strong desire to excel in their work, and as a group they are industrious, dependable, and conscientious. They are more anxious about external, uncontrollable events than are their peers, possibly because they feel more helpless and also because they are not familiar with all the facts surrounding natural or man-made disasters. Differences between adolescents born blind and those blinded later are observable, with the latter tending to refer to the past and to be less accepting of the finality of their condition. The young person who does accept his blindness as permanent, however, is quick to appreciate his remaining assets, and his self-confidence returns to a degree related to the importance of vision in his particular interests and skills.[39] The blind adolescent is not as unhappy as he generally is believed to be, and his basic goals are the same as his peers': to be self-supporting and to find an appropriate mate.[37]

EDUCATION, RECREATION, AND VOCATIONAL GUIDANCE

Education

Because the blind child's experience is restricted and his reading material is limited, an average educational retardation of three years is common.[13] Late school entry, personal maladjustment, the need to master new tools, faulty teaching, and unavailability of special equipment also are contributing factors in educational retardation.[12]

A normal range of intellectual competence exists among the blind. The Stanford-Binet Intelligence Scale has been adapted by Dr. Samuel Hayes for testing the intelligence of the blind child between the ages of six and 12 years, and verbal portions of the Wechsler Intelligence Scale for Children are used also.[26] Younger children can be examined with certain items from the Cattell Scale for Infants and the Merrill-Palmer Scale.[28] There appear to be unusually large numbers in the above-average and below-average intellectual groups, but whether this is a function of the test or of individual motivation and experience is unknown.[13]

Facilities. Massachusetts established the first state school for the blind in 1832, and by 1875 there were 35 states either administering or supporting schools for the blind. At present, every state provides such facilities or has arranged to use them in conjunction with a neighboring state. Chicago established the first public school class in 1896,[2] and in 1913 the first class for the partially sighted was formed in Boston. Classes for partially sighted children numbered 639 in 1955, and these provide for local education of visually defective children who formerly were sent to state residential schools.

In some cities, partially sighted and totally blind children meet in the same class and are taught in accordance with their specific needs. In others, the visually handicapped child spends most of his day in a regular class, participating in oral and group activities but attending a special class for work which requires specialized teaching and visual aids. Some children attend regular classes most of the time and receive their special instruction from an itinerant teacher who works for a limited time weekly with each child and also directs the regular teacher.[5, 6, 9] Educators cite three reasons for retaining the visually handicapped child in regular classes: (1) His similarity to other children, rather than his difference from them, is emphasized; (2) broad education and enriched facilities are available in regular classes; and (3) he is educated in a setting more nearly approximating that in which he must live as an adult.[19]

For some visually handicapped children, educational facilities are available only in state residential schools. Enrollment varies from 25, in sparsely populated states, to more than 300, and about 7000 children were registered in residential schools for the blind in 1960. In some areas, the residential school staff arranges with local school officials to include visually handicapped adolescents in the regular school program. In others, the state school is the only resource for the continued education of the older visually handicapped child who was able to obtain special instruction during his elementary years in his own city.[1]

A major problem in providing adequate facilities for blind and partially sighted children is the fact that their numbers are too few to justify employing full-time special teachers. When those children blinded by retrolental fibroplasia have been educated, most school districts will have no more than three to five blind children for whom to provide. Jones[18] suggested that future planning must take advantage of pooled resources and staffs of neighboring communities and combined instruction for blind and partially sighted children.

Academic Instruction. Blind children need many diversified experiences, both to familiarize them with objects and events they cannot see and to reduce their tendency to occupy themselves with fantasy, verbalism, and manipulative motor habits.[14] Taking them on short trips, making certain that they are able to identify many ordinary objects by touch, and talking about daily events aid their understanding of the academic materials they must master.

The kindergarten teacher of the blind or partially sighted child uses small objects, blocks, buttons, and sticks to teach counting, directions, and space orientation.[5] Large-type books are available for the partially sighted elementary school child, or if still larger print is needed, the teacher prepares materials by hand. Number concepts are learned by manipulating beads and blocks, and wire forms are used for geometry in high school.[22] Geography is taught with globes outlining land and sea areas in relief, and individual outline maps are used by the partially sighted child. The older elementary child can learn to type, and this saves him much time and effort.

It was once believed that the child with limited vision would lose it if he used his eyes, and for this reason many partially sighted children were instructed in reading braille instead of print. This concern is no longer considered valid, and any child who can read enlarged print with the aid of magnifying devices is taught to do so.[25] If he can read print, a much greater quantity of learning material is available to him, and Barraga[3] reported that adolescent girls reading both print and braille improved their speed in reading print with special training but did not increase their braille reading speed with similar training.

The partially sighted child uses telescopic lenses; a device known as the Megascope, which magnifies printed material;[36] or the Visagraph, which reproduces enlarged images of print and diagrams. The Optophone, a device still under development, is intended to translate ordinary print into sound, so that eventually blind individuals can dispense with braille and recorded books.[2]

The totally blind child learns to read and write braille, a coded system based on a cell containing six embossed dots, three high and two wide, which permits 63 possible combinations. Literary, musical, and mathematical codes have been developed from this cell. The braille system is based on a military code originally devised for communication at the front, and in 1834 it was adapted by Louis Braille for use. It was not widely adopted until 1860, however, and several competing systems have confused the instruction of the blind. In 1932, Standard English Braille Grade II was made uniform and is used universally in English-speaking countries.[12] Grade I braille requires full spelling of words, but Grade II braille permits contracted spelling, similar to shorthand. The braille student learns the 26 letters of the alphabet, numerals, special composition and punctuation marks, and 185 contractions which can be used to substitute for whole words or parts of words. Tactual perception varies with the child and contributes to or hinders his ability to read braille.[44]

The child learns to write braille by using a special slate or a braille-writer machine, which consists of three keys on either side of a space bar. With the machine a child can learn to write braille at the first grade level. A braille slate provides him with lighter writing equipment if he must change classrooms during the school day.[1]

Special Subjects. Music has long been emphasized in the curriculum of the blind child. Singing provides relief from tension, and the child can learn to play a musical instrument by reading the music in braille and memorizing it.

The partially sighted child often produces drawings or paintings containing fine detail, evidence that he observes carefully that which he can see. He also learns to use his hands in clay modeling, weaving, woodworking, leather work, and cooking.

Physical education is a regular part of the child's training. Rhythms and dancing are enjoyed by the blind child and give him practice in managing his body with ease. He can also engage in swimming, tumbling, wrestling, skating, and field sports.[22] In some gymnasiums used by the blind, balls and basketball backboards are equipped with sounding devices for better localization.[7]

Recreation

Withdrawal tendencies are averted in blind children who participate in dramatic and musical organizations and who join scouting programs. Combined day camps for sighted and blind children have been operated successfully without drastic program changes.[38] Bowling is a recently-acquired recreational pastime of the blind, and physical skills learned in school, such as dancing, swimming, field sports, and horseshoes, serve also as recreation. Adolescents play bridge with braille cards.

Vocational Guidance

The employment of the blind individual is not yet a matter of common acceptance and pertinent planning, but the contributions of distinguished blind persons in the fields of education, law, politics, and the arts indicate that blindness in itself is no deterrent to success in many fields.

Most of the blind, however, are employed in manufacturing workshops especially established for them.[13] They sometimes fill orders of the government or of large business concerns, or they sell their products from door to door or through mail advertising. Agriculture, trade, and the professions are other common areas in which blind persons work. A smaller number is engaged in domestic or clerical work or in teaching.

To insure employment for the blind, vocational counselors advocate legally restricting certain areas of work, such as newsstand-keeping, broom making, weaving, poultry raising, and radio mechanics.[12] Special arrangements sometimes are made with employers willing to guarantee the hiring of a given number of blind persons who can be trained to perform certain work competently. The blind individual's vocational handicap is caused less by his visual disability than by the belief of employers that he cannot work effectively.

Employment presupposes the blind person's ability to travel alone. When he can do so, he is no longer dependent on other people to escort him at their convenience, and therefore he can contract for regular work. Independent travel requires special sensory training, including the ability to localize sound, to interpret auditory and olfactory cues, to develop kinesthetic memory, to discriminate texture and contour of terrain, and to detect pressure and temperature changes resulting from the presence or absence of large obstacles which affect wind and sun action. The blind person also must develop the coördination essential to good equilibrium and learn to respond promptly to all signs of danger.[39]

PARENTAL ATTITUDES AND RESPONSIBILITIES

Most parents are shocked by the realization that their child will never see, and they envision a lonely, poverty-stricken adulthood for him. Mothers react with confused and contradictory feelings, and fathers feel inadequate to communicate with the child. If parents isolate or reject the child, he becomes frustrated, anxious, and bitter.[1, 28] Group discussions aid parents to respond more naturally to the child and to rear him appropriately.

Misconceptions about the child are based on adults' inadequate knowledge of the abilities of blind persons. Parents who immediately begin to familiarize themselves with blind children and their activities can evaluate correctly their own child's future and avoid both overprotection and despair. They should visit classes for blind and partially sighted children and observe them as they learn and carry on their daily activities. They need to begin to make plans for the child's academic education and to investigate the opportunities for recreation, social participation, and vocational training. If they do this while he is still young, they not only ensure his receiving all the assistance available to him but also reassure themselves that he can attain self-sufficient maturity.

Before he is ready for training by others, however, he needs home tutelage, affection, and stimulation. Expecting too little of him is a common error.[32] As an infant, he needs to be moved from place to place more frequently than the sighted baby, and it is important that he hear conversation and be spoken to often. When he is old enough to be propped up with pillows, toys can be tied on a string near him and his hands directed toward reaching and hitting them. Although the blind baby should not be picked up without warning, he enjoys being played with and fondled.

The older baby should not be kept too long in a play pen but should be encouraged to make side trips and to feel the floor, the rug, and the grass outdoors. He can be enticed to move by the sound of a bell or by being guided with a light touch. Because spatial orientation develops slowly and unpredictably, forcing him to move tends to increase his dependency and fearfulness,[8] but with support and encouragement, he learns to explore and move about independently. Insufficient practice of movement produces a tense, awkward gait, sometimes with toe-walking or foot-stamping.[28]

The young blind child needs many opportunities to use his other senses. He should be helped to feel and listen, and he needs to be taken many places, with his parents explaining his surroundings and what is happening. Everything done with the child should be accompanied by descriptions and by assisting him to use his other senses for gaining knowledge.

Training him in independence and self-care is essential. At about the same age as the sighted child he can learn to feed and dress himself and to attend to his toileting. He can help with chores such as setting the table and making his bed. He can acquire play independence by learning to use a tricycle, skates, and a wagon.

Enrolling him in nursery school provides him with both playmates and protection and guarantees him experiences in socialization which are of inestimable importance to him.[28] It may be necessary to exert special effort to find playmates in the neighborhood, but these contacts should be made, and they are not difficult to arrange at the pre-school age when mothers can be invited to visit with their children.[41] Norris et al.[33] reported in a five-year study of 259 blind pre-school children and concluded that the blind child can develop into an independent and freely functioning individual who compares favorably with sighted children.

In many smaller communities there are no educational facilities for blind or partially sighted children. Parental contacts with state agencies may lead to information about other blind children, and the joint efforts of all the families concerned can result in the provision of local instruction. If this is not possible and the child must attend a residential school, parents will find the separation less difficult if they involve themselves with the school and assist in its work.

REFERENCES

1. Abel, G.: The education of blind children. *In* Cruickshank, W., and Johnson, G. O., eds.: *Education of Exceptional Children and Youth.* Englewood Cliffs, N. J., Prentice-Hall, Inc., 1958, pp. 295–338.
2. Baker, H. J.: *Introduction to Exceptional Children.* New York, The Macmillan Co., 1953.
3. Barraga, N.: Mode of reading for low vision students. *Int. J. Educ. Blind.* 1963, *12,* 103–107.
4. Benton, P. C.: The emotional aspects of visual handicaps. *The Sight-Saving Review,* 1951, *21* (1),·23–26.
5. Bertram, F. M.: The education of partially sighted children. *In* Cruickshank, W., and Johnson, G. O., eds.: *Education of Exceptional Children and Youth.* Englewood Cliffs, N. J., Prentice-Hall, Inc., 1958, pp. 265–294.
6. Bryan, D.: The itinerant teacher plan for the education of partially seeing children in Illinois. *In* Frampton, M. E., and Gall, E. D.: *Special Education for the Exceptional.* Boston, Porter Sargent, 1955, pp. 129–133.
7. Buell, C.: Development in physical education for blind children. *The New Outlook for the Blind,* 1964,58.
8. Burlingham, D.: Some notes on the development of the blind. *Psychoanal. Stud. Child.,* 1961, *16,* 121–145.
9. Burrell, C.: The partially seeing. *In* Frampton, M. A., and Gall, E. D., eds.: *Special Education for the Exceptional.* Boston, Porter Sargent, 1955, pp. 114–128.
10. *Facts on Blindness in the United States.* U.S. Department of Health, Education, and Welfare, Public Health Service Publication No. 706.
11. Ferson, R. F.: Vocational guidance at the Western Pennsylvania School. *The New Outlook for the Blind,* 1955, *49,* 6–15.
12. Frampton, M., Hoard, S., Kerney, E., and Mitchell, P.: The blind. *In* Frampton, M., and Gall, E. D., eds.: *Special Education for the Exceptional.* Boston, Porter Sargent, 1955, pp. 2–34.
13. Garrison, K. C., and Force, D. G., Jr.: *The Psychology of Exceptional Children.* New York, The Ronald Press Co., 1959.
14. Harley, R. K., Jr.: Verbalism among blind children: An investigation and analysis. New York, American Foundation for the Blind, 1963.
15. Hepfinger, L. M.: Psychological evaluation of young blind children. *The New Outlook for the Blind,* 1962, 56, 309–315.
16. Hoshikawa, M.: Ichi nichi nyūgaku no kōka ni tsuite—Sutoshite futsū gakkō seito no taido no henka ni tsuite (Effect of one day's life in a school for the blind upon normal children). *Psychol. Blind,* 1962, *11,* 25–42.
17. Jervis, F. M., and Haslerud, G. M.: Quantitative and qualitative differences in frustration between blind and sighted adolescents. *In* Trapp, E. P., and Himelstein, P.: *Readings on the Exceptional Child.* New York, Appleton-Century-Crofts, 1962, p. 358.
18. Jones, J. W.: The blind child in school. *School Life,* February-March, 1961.
19. Jones, J. W.: *The Visually Handicapped Child.* U.S. Department of Health, Education, and Welfare, Bulletin No. 39, 1963.
20. Laufman, M.: Blind children in integrated recreation. *The New Outlook for the Blind,* 1962, *56,* 81–84.
21. Lesser, A.: *Health of Children of School Age.* U.S. Department of Health, Education, and Welfare, Children's Bureau Publication No. 427, 1964.
22. Lowenfeld, B.: If he is blind. *In* Frampton, M., and Gall, E., eds.: *Special Education for the Exceptional.* Boston, Porter Sargent, 1955, pp. 48–52.

23. Lowenfeld, B.: The blind adolescent in a seeing world. *Except. Child,* 1959, *25,* 310–315.
24. Lowenfeld, B.: The role of the residential school in the education of blind children. *In* Abel, G. L., ed.: *Concerning the Education of Blind Children.* New York, American Foundation for the Blind, 1959, pp. 23–31.
25. Lowenfeld, B.: The visually handicapped. *Rev. Educ. Res.,* 1963, *33,* 38–47.
26. McAndrew, H.: Rigidity and isolation. A study of the deaf and the blind. *In* Trapp, E. P., and Himelstein, P.: *Readings on the Exceptional Child.* New York, Appleton-Century-Crofts, 1962, pp. 369–370.
27. Manshardt, C. E.: The role of the public school system in the education of blind with sighted children. *In* Abel, G. L., ed.: *Concerning the Education of Blind Children.* New York, American Foundation for the Blind, 1959, pp. 33–41.
28. Moor, P. M.: Blind children with developmental problems. *Children,* 8 (1), 9–13.
29. Moor, P. M.: The preschool blind child, his needs and resources. *In* Abel, G. L., ed.: *Concerning the Education of Blind Children.* New York, American Foundation for the Blind, 1959, pp. 7–21.
30. Nakaya, H.: Mōji ni okonatta P.F.T. no kekka (Results of P.F.T. in elementary schools for the blind). *Psychol. Blind,* 1962, *11,* 1-10.
31. Nemoto, H. Mō seito no retto ishki ni tsuite (Inferiority complex of blind pupils). *Psychol. Blind,* 1963, *12,* 23–30.
32. Norris, M.: What affects blind children's development. *Children,* 1956, 3(4).
33. Norris, M., Spaulding, P. J., and Brodie, F. H.: *Blindness in Children.* Chicago, University of Chicago Press, 1957.
34. Pringle, M. L.: The emotional and social adjustment of blind children. *Educ. Res.,* 1964, *6, 129–138.*
35. Reese, A. B.: Retrolental fibroplasia. *The Sight-Saving Review,* 1951, *21*(1), 36.
36. Richardson, E. C.: Visual instruction of the partially sighted. *In* Frampton, M.. and Gall, E. D., eds.: *Special Education for the Exceptional.* Boston, Porter Sargent, 1955, pp. 138–146.
37. Sakellariou, G.: *An Explorative Study of the Personality of the Blind.* Athens, Greece, Hellenic Psychol. Assn., 1964.
38. Saul, S. R.: Serving the blind child in the neighborhood community center: a professional challenge. *J. Jewish Communal Serv.,* 1959, *35,* 285–292.
39. Spar, H. J.: Some special aspects of an adequate vocational training and employment program for the blind. *In* Frampton, M., and Gall, E., eds.: *Special Education for the Exceptional,* Boston, Porter Sargent, 1955, pp. 64–74.
40. Taber, M.: The preschool child who is visually handicapped. *In* Frampton, M., and Gall, E., eds.: *Special Education for the Exceptional.* Boston, Porter Sargent, 1955, pp. 44–47.
41. *The Preschool Child Who Is Blind.* U.S. Department of Health, Education, and Welfare, Children's Bureau, Folder No. 39, 1953.
42. Underberg, R. P., Berham, F. G., Verillo, R. T., and Cowen, E. L.: Factors relating to adjustment to visual disability in adolescence. *The New Outlook for the Blind,* 1961, *55,* 253–259.
43. Weiner, L. H.: Educating the emotionally disturbed blind child. *Int. J. Educ. Blind,* 1962, *11,* 77–79.
44. Weiner, L. H.: The performance of good and poor braille readers on certain tests involving tactual perception. *Int. J. Educ. Blind,* 1963, *12,* 72–77.
45. Wolman, M. J.: Preschool and kindergarten child attitudes toward the blind in an integrated program. *The New Outlook for the Blind,* 1958, *52,* 128–133.

Chapter 48

Auditory Impairment

Early detection of auditory impairment is crucial, because after the first three or four months of life the infant's vocalizations no longer are appropriate for his age, and his hampered communicative ability impedes both his socialization and his learning ability.

A few children are totally unable to hear sound. For others, auditory impairment ranges from those considered profoundly deaf, with a hearing loss exceeding 60 decibels, to those whose hearing is imperfect but who can function either with or without a hearing aid. It is estimated that .1 per cent of the school population has impaired hearing and that there are approximately 32,000 children handicapped in this way.

It is not always possible to determine the cause for deafness in the individual child. In a study of 2500 children attending a school for the deaf, 50 per cent of the hearing disturbances were considered to be inherited; 17 per cent to be due to prenatal and paranatal factors, such as rubella, kernicterus, and asphyxia; and 33 per cent to be the result of infantile infectious diseases, particularly meningitis. There is evidence that premature infants are highly susceptible to infections of the middle ear and that metabolic disorders, especially of the thyroid gland, exist in children who are congenitally deaf.[39] Postnatally, meningitis is the most frequent cause of deafness during the first five years of life. Scarlet fever, measles, whooping cough, typhoid, and influenza also cause deafness during this period, as do abscesses of the ear or head. Middle ear infection is a common cause of deafness among elementary school children.[22]

Screening checks of hearing ability in young children will identify those whose hearing is impaired. Under three months of age, the hearing infant responds reflexly to loud sounds. Between three and six months, he moves his eyes or body in response to the sound of his mother's voice, and by the fourth month, the child indicates in this way that he is attempting to localize other sounds which interest him. Between six and nine months, the baby gives evidence of trying to localize quiet sounds, such as rustling paper or voices other than his mother's, although by this age he may ignore loud sounds. Children between nine and 15 months of age can locate automatically quiet sounds which interest them at a distance of three or four feet from either ear. Children between 16 and 30 months are able to locate automatically any sound which attracts their attention, and they also can obey commands spoken quietly at a distance of three feet. Between two and a half and five years, the normally hearing child can understand simple speech spoken quietly or whispered from a distance of three feet, and he can respond to it in words.

Hearing in the older pre-school child is tested with an audiometer, which permits presentation of sound frequencies ranging between 250 and 6000 cycles per second. The screening examination is termed a sweep-frequency test and requires the child to respond when each of seven pitches (300, 500, 1000, 2000, 4000, 6000, and 8000 cycles per second) is presented to him at an intensity of 10 or 15 decibels. Failure to hear at least five of the seven tones indicates the need for more thorough testing.[35]

Other tests which are used include evaluation of the child's speaking adequacy in describing pictures and measurement of the galvanic skin response to auditory stimulation. Neural activity during sound stimulation is indicated by the electroencephalograph. Older children can be tested in a group with the gramophone audiometer test, in which they are required to write numbers they hear as they are played on a record.[19]

Kastein and Fowler[24] emphasized the subtle distinction between functional and physiological hearing thresholds. They reported that of 156 children referred for examinations for deafness, 54 had a peripheral hearing loss; 27 had a peripheral hearing loss accompanied by brain injury, mental retardation, or emotional disturbance; and 75 had no detectable hearing loss. Perceptual difficulties, acquired aphasia, mental retardation, or emotional disturbance were responsible for these children's failure to respond to sound. Results obtained from the initial audiometric tests differed from both the diagnostic impression of speech pathologists and of the child audiologist, and after auditory training, the hearing thresholds for these children were lowered. The child's qualitative language is considered by these investigators a reliably differentiating diagnostic method for the evaluation of hearing loss. Some children, however, whose auditory impairment has not been diagnosed have been considered retarded or emotionally disturbed, and their treatment and training have been established on the basis of these faulty impressions.

CHARACTERISTICS OF THE CHILD WITH AUDITORY IMPAIRMENT

The deaf infant feels but does not hear his own vocalizations. He cannot hear the sounds which other people make, and he is aware only of loud sounds as he senses their vibrations. He cannot discriminate between different sounds, and he associates meaning only by observation of others' facial expressions and gestures. The casual glimpses he has of words on the lips of others are too few to enable him to acquire meanings, and he ·learns to think without using words. As he grows older and needs to communicate more, he uses gestures to express his wants and looks for gestures from others to discover what they are attempting to convey to him. His communications necessarily are limited in both number and variety of ideas, and he accompanies his gestures with cries and shouts, the only vocalizations he knows. Rarely is he understand by outsiders, and his intellectual and social development is hindered because he cannot use and understand words.

As times goes on, the child with impaired hearing suffers from his inability to follow group conversation or conversation at a distance, and both his information and his social contacts are limited for this reason. He feels insecure about contributing to conversation. He must strain to hear, and often he is unwilling to exert the effort required to interpret sounds and he learns to ignore them.[10] * Because he has insufficient cues about what is occurring and what response is required and because he often finds his efforts to communicate rebuffed and misunderstood, he ceases trying to make his speech comprehensible, and social contacts become less important to him.

Myklebust[33] observed that because it is difficult for the deaf child to feel that he is a part of his environment, he tends to withdraw, and this can lead to his living in a fantasy world of his own. He remains socially immature and is dependent on his parents for assistance of all kinds longer than the hearing child is. A greater frequency of persisting sleeping and feeding problems, temper tantrums, and enuresis is re-

---

* See Case 50, Leonard M., p. 537.

ported among deaf children than among hearing children of comparable age.[9]

Bindon[2] compared hearing and nonhearing 15-year-olds, and she concluded that the rigid personality pattern of deaf adolescents appeared to be related to their retarded socialization, caused by communication failure resulting in prolonged immaturity and a paucity of shared experiences.

As the child grows older and becomes more aware of his difference from others, he often feels inferior and becomes depressed. Withdrawing from social contacts, especially with hearing persons, leads to attitudes of suspiciousness toward others, and the deaf person may choose to live as a privileged member of a relatively segregated group of deaf individuals.[6] He tends to feel cheated and to believe that his deafness deprives him of love, friends, achievement, and security.[29]

Adolescent and young adult deaf persons have been described as unwilling to coöperate with others, expecting others' assistance and having narrow interests and attitudes. They tend to be self-centered and do not adhere to the usual social courtesies. On the other hand, they are known to be law-abiding citizens, prompt and conscientious about work obligations and free from racial and religious intolerance. Few neuroses or psychoses are reported among the deaf.[14]

EDUCATION

Deaf and hard-of-hearing children almost invariably are retarded academically. Education depends essentially upon the use of verbal symbols, and it is in the understanding, fixation, and use of verbal symbols that the deaf child is defective. Kodman[26] studied 100 hard-of-hearing children between seven and 17 years of age, only 35 of whom wore hearing aids. Their mean educational achievement was at the 3.8 grade level, in contrast to an expected mean placement at the beginning sixth grade level. The abandonment of hearing aids by older children undoubtedly is a contributing factor to academic difficulties.

The deaf child's motivation to learn is related to many personal factors in his life. His greater dependency and his inclination to withdraw from contacts hinder natural curiosity and interest in learning, as well as his willingness to devote effort to learning. The best students in one residential school were children whose parents had a higher socioeconomic status and who themselves had superior intelligence and visual perception, experienced few serious illnesses and accidents and were considered mature in personality.[13] A deaf adolescent must be within the average range of intelligence to obtain a vocational diploma, and he must be well above average to obtain an academic diploma from high school.[3]

The slow and discouraging progress of many deaf children leads to their abandoning school before their education is complete, and only a small proportion of those who start school remain to finish high school. The drop-out rate is as high as 80 per cent in some residential schools.[14]

Facilities

The Reverend Thomas Hopkins Gallaudet, with the help of friends, succeeded in establishing a state school for the deaf in Hartford, Connecticut, in 1817. New York and Pennsylvania followed suit in 1818 and 1820, and 24 state residential schools were established in the succeeding 50 years. Every other state, with the exception of Delaware, Nevada, New Hampshire, and Wyoming, had an established residential school by 1914, and these states provided funds for educating their deaf children at neighboring state schools and in public school classes. The Wyoming school, established in 1957, is the only state school which utilizes the oral method of instruction exclusively.*

The first public day school for deaf children was established in Boston in 1869, and ten such schools now exist. The number of day school classes operating within the framework of the public school system is steadily increasing, although varying needs in specific locations have caused the abandonment of these special classes in some cities after periods of nine or ten years. There are 19 denominational and private schools for the deaf, most of which are supported by the Catholic and Lutheran churches.[22] Approximately 69 per cent of all deaf children are educated in state residential schools, 17 per cent attend day classes in the public school system, and 6 per cent attend the large public day schools for the deaf. Private schools educate the remaining 8 per cent.[1]

Attempts to integrate deaf children into hearing groups at an early age are being made in some cities. Ewing and Ewing[10] reported on the transfer of selected deaf pupils, at the age of eight or nine years, from a day school for the deaf to a regular elementary classroom. A teacher of the deaf accompanied them, and with her assistance they became part of a class consisting largely of hearing children. In other cities, deaf children are included in physical education and other special classes with hearing children.

The only college for the deaf in the world is Gallaudet College in

---

* Personal communication from Mrs. Berneice Fort, Wyoming State School for the Deaf, Casper, Wyoming.

Washington, D. C. Many educators of the deaf believe that if a high school graduate has been well trained orally and is intellectually competent to master college work, he should be in a college for hearing individuals. Many deaf adolescents are most familiar with manual communication, however, and cannot function in an ordinary college setting.

Methods of Communication

Two methods of communication are employed in the instruction of deaf children, the manual and the oral, and although there are strong advocates of the superiority of one method over the other, in practice the methods are used in combination.

In the manual method, the hands are used to convey meaning. Certain finger and hand combinations represent each letter of the alphabet, and words and sentences are spelled out. Sign language of the deaf consists of a pictured representation of what the individual is attempting to convey, and it is expressed not only with hand movements but also by pantomime and gestures. Sign language is discouraged in schools, and the child is expected to express himself by spelling manually, rather than by pantomiming or using signs. The exclusive use of manual methods of communication restricts the deaf child to contacts with other deaf individuals who understand what he is expressing and who can communicate with him in the same way.

The oral method of communication, strongly advocated by many teachers of the deaf as mandatory for adequate communication with hearing individuals and for attainment of the broadest possible education, was originally given impetus by Alexander Graham Bell and Edward Gallaudet, both of whom urged that every deaf child be taught to read the speech of others and to speak himself. Communication is successfully achieved when the child can learn to lip read and can produce word sounds which are meaningful to others. Teachers of the method use neither the manual alphabet nor sign language, and the children are discouraged from resorting to them. Pintner and Brunschwig,[34] in a study of 1300 deaf adolescents, found that those taught by the oral method were better adjusted than those taught manually.

In actual practice, both methods are used. The oral method is followed in the classroom, but signs and the manual alphabet are utilized in group meetings and in casual contacts between individuals when the communicants are deaf and facile understanding is needed.[22]

Hearing Aids

Most deaf children have some residual hearing, and children with hearing losses up to 95 decibels are able to benefit from wearing hearing aids. Some children with hearing losses up to 80 decibels have been able to discriminate sounds and comprehend speech, as well as to lip read more adequately, because they could hear the speech of their teachers. Using a hearing aid, they also can hear their own sound productions and modify them accordingly.

At least 75 per cent of the hearing handicapped benefit from using a hearing aid, especially those who are conduction-deafened rather than nerve-deafened.[35] Parents of young deaf children reported that 80 per cent of them had been fitted with at least one hearing aid, and 60 per cent had their first aid before they were six years old. About 46 per cent of the children made maximum use of their aids, wearing them as casually as clothing, and 53 per cent of the parents considered their child's present hearing aid to be satisfactory in function.[37]

Hearing aids can be uncomfortable to wear, however, and if the adjustment is poor and extraneous noises are excessive, the resulting confusion of sounds is annoying and distracting. As children grow older, they frequently avoid the use of a hearing aid. They leave them at home when they come to school and rarely wear them when playing. A child can be taught that listening is enjoyable if he wears an aid when drum beats and music are used for marching, skipping, and dancing and if intriguing stories are read to him and conversation is that which he wants to hear. The child who expects frequent scoldings regularly misplaces his hearing aid.

Intelligence

Intellectually, the deaf child is not inferior to the hearing child, although there may be qualitative differences in learning capacity. Nonverbal tests such as the Pintner-Patterson, the Leiter International Performance Scale, the Arthur Performance Scale, the Cornell-Coxe, and the performance scales of the Wechsler Intelligence tests are used to evaluate the intelligence of deaf children. Raven's Progressive Matrices also is used, and the Ontario School Ability Examination was designed especially for deaf children. Some dissatisfaction has been expressed with the use of nonlanguage tests alone for measuring intelligence because of the belief that performance ability does not always indicate accurately basic intellectual capacity and also because the validity of performance tests decreases as the child becomes older.[30]

Some investigators have compared intellectual and integrative abilities of hearing and nonhearing children. Rosenstein[36] examined 60 deaf and 60 hearing children with a perceptual discrimination task, a modified Wisconsin Card Sorting task, and a concept attainment and usage task. Each test was presented visually and nonverbally. There was no significant difference between the groups in ability to perceive, abstract, or generalize, and he concluded that when the language involved in the test is within the capacity of the deaf child, no differences in ability exist.

Larr,[28] however, reported retardation among deaf children in conceptual capacity, and Kates *et al.*[25] noted that deaf children are hesitant to begin problem-solving tasks. Farraut[12] stated that deaf children aged eight to 12 years were retarded on tests of verbal comprehension and abstract reasoning in comparison with hearing children, and he suggested that auditory impairment might distort certain intellectual abilities and hamper their integration.

Individual differences are more significant than group differences, however. Goda[18] found that among profoundly deaf adolescents those who were skilled in one area—such as writing, speaking, lip reading, or reading—were equally skilled in all areas and that those who were deficient in any ability were consistently inferior.

Educational Techniques and Problems

The Pre-school Child. Early identification of deafness should be followed by training of the young child to listen and to speak. Hearing aids have been fitted on infants under one year of age, thus enabling them to hear and respond to sounds at the age when speech mechanisms and speech skills normally develop.

Correspondence courses in the instruction of the pre-school deaf child are available to parents. One of the most widely used is distributed by the John Tracy Clinic, and it includes exercises the parent can use with the child to develop his understanding of language and speech; methods of training him in listening, lip reading, and the use of other senses; and suggestions for creative activity and preparation for learning to read. Pre-school behavior problems also are discussed.*

Parents working with a child whose hearing is impaired must expect that progress will be slow. The child cannot acquire understanding instantaneously, and he needs extensive experience with words and sounds. Making certain that there are many opportunities for speech and communication, including the child in all family activities, providing him with the usual pre-school toys, and arranging contacts with hearing playmates are necessary prerequisites to formal education.

The Elementary School Child. The deaf child's classroom is much like that of the hearing child except that it is equipped with sound-absorbing walls and furnishings, such as carpets and drapes. A group hearing aid supplements individual aids, and a large mirror placed near the area used for group work makes possible the observation of lip

---

* This course is obtainable on request from the clinic, located at 924 W. 37th St., Los Angeles, California.

movements of both teacher and students. Special training aids utilize the reënforcement provided by sight, and real objects for demonstrations and explanations, visible projects in science and geography, and films and slides are important. A phonograph can be utilized in association with explanatory pictures.[1]

Lip Reading. Reading the speech of others from observing their lip movements begins at home during the pre-school years, but it is a skill which must be practiced constantly. The difficulties associated with acquiring meaning from watching lip movements are great, and some educators state that lip reading is essentially skilled guessing. Although the ear can detect even slight variations in sound, the eye cannot detect these variations from lip movements because differences are indistinguishable. The letters *p, b,* and *m* are identical to the lip reader; *t, d,* and *n* are also identical in appearance.[22] The child must learn to interpret meaning from the situation as well as from lip movements, and he can do this most readily if he is accustomed to watching the lip movements of his parents and teachers whenever he is with them. His lip reading vocabulary grows as his teacher trains him to observe her lip movements while following directions she gives to match objects by color or size, to match pictures, or to identify objects with pictures.[29]

Speech Training. The use of speech involves close control over fine muscle movements and is aided by accurate hearing and coördinated neuromuscular skill. Speaking is a natural accomplishment of the hearing child, who is exposed daily to inflections and variations in the speech of others and who practices making sounds himself continually, gradually learning to imitate correctly what he hears. The child with impaired audition has no opportunity for multiple stimulation and repeated practice, and his attempts to speak, even with encouragement and instruction, will barely resemble the words he is trying to say.

All beginning speech of the deaf child should be accepted as adequate, for improvement comes only with practice. Like the hearing child, the deaf child will understand meanings of words long before he can say them; and also like the hearing child, he will omit connectives, adjectives, and adverbs when he first begins to talk. He cannot remember any word which has no meaning for him, so that repeating words he does not understand, even though these consist of a gramatically correct sentence, is of little value to him. Increasing a meaningful vocabulary is basic to adequate speech.

He can learn to control the volume and pitch of his voice by amplification of its sound and by experiencing the difference between the vibrations of a tense and a relaxed voice quality by feeling his own and his teacher's throats as each reproduces the same sound.[1]

Vermeulen[40] described a wind instrument which permits the child to control the intensity, start, duration, and rhythm of notes with his own breath. The use of this instrument enables the child to acquire breath control, which is basic to speech development, and formerly deaf-mute children improved in their speech after working with the instrument.

Reading.   There is a tendency on the part of parents and pre-school teachers to introduce reading to the young deaf child before it normally would be presented if he could hear. When the child is too young to learn to read, he becomes bored, fatigued, and indifferent to reading. Eye-hand coördination must be developed before adequate reading is possible, and the visual acuity required for focusing on printed symbols develops at different rates in children.

When reading instruction is given the deaf child, however, it is important to identify the printed word with the action or object it represents so that its meaning is clarified, inasmuch as auditory reënforcement is slight. Demonstration, visualization, and dramatizing words are valuable aids in fixating their meaning.

Writing.   To the extent that the deaf child finds it difficult to express himself clearly, completely, and grammatically in speech, he also finds it difficult to express himself in writing. Grammatical distinctions are a problem to him, as are abstract concepts. His vocabulary and his ability to think verbally are restricted, and his lack of skill with words is reflected in his writing.[17] He learns first by tracing, then by copying, and finally he is able to write from memory.

Supplemental Instruction.   Formal academic instruction of the deaf child should be supplemented with learning recreational skills, acquiring hobbies, participating in group activities of all kinds, reading for pleasure and current information, and training in conversational speech patterns. All of these endeavors result in useful diversions and skills and relieve the tedious struggle with academic learning.[27]

Vocational Training

It is estimated that fully 95 per cent of all deaf persons support themselves with work they do.[7] Surveys of working adults with auditory impairment indicate that they are employed in every field. The deaf are ministers, x-ray technicians, waiters, taxi drivers, clerks, dentists, engineers, salesmen, and machine operators.

Vocational education first was introduced for the deaf in 1817 at the American School for the Deaf in Connecticut. At present, state vocational counselors help adolescents who are no longer attending school to plan for vocational training and to find work for which they are qualified. A 1965 legislative act provides for the establishment of a technological school for the deaf, to be associated with a recognized college or university for a renewable 20-year period. The school will grant a B.S. degree in technology to graduates, and research projects will be conducted which relate to problems encountered in training.

PARENTAL ATTITUDES AND RESPONSIBILITIES

Parents of the deaf child may resist acknowledging that the deafness exists, or they may feel bitter at being forced to bear this unusual burden in child rearing. They are bewildered about how to establish contact with the child, and they are concerned for his future.[8]

The parents need to give the deaf child every opportunity to learn and to communicate. The infant deaf child develops differently from the hearing child almost from the beginning, and it is important that he is not isolated and disregarded because he makes no contribution. He should be included in family activities and receive the special attention and instruction necessary to familiarize him with common objects and varied social situations. In one study of parental attitudes about prognosis for the deaf child, it was reported that 28 per cent of the hearing parents of deaf children did not believe the child ever could communicate orally, and they made no effort to supply the training which would enable him to do so.

An infant should be equipped with a hearing aid to enable him to develop more normally, to respond to sounds, and to communicate with understanding.[1] The child can be taught to look and listen at an early age if his parents frequently speak directly to him, name objects, name pictures, use words to identify his possessions and his activities, and constantly relate words to his experiences.

The deaf child should associate with other children during his pre-school years, and he gains social skill by attending a nursery school for hearing children. Although communication with his peers is limited, it will be understood because of the mutuality of children's interests.

Parents should visit classes for the deaf to observe the methods used by teachers and the success attained by pupils. A counselor from the special services division of the state board of education can give them continuing guidance during the child's pre-school years, as well as assist them in contacting teachers and schools as they plan for the child's academic education.

Group discussions with parents of other deaf children enable all of the adults to recognize that others face similar problems, and both techniques and attitudes which ease the task of rearing the child can be learned from other parents. Extreme attitudes of overprotection or rejection are softened by group discussion of common problems.[19] Membership in organizations serving the deaf and subscribing to magazines dealing with the programs for and achievements of the deaf help parents to adopt a more natural and optimistic attitude toward the child.* Their feelings about him contribute to his ability to respond to others and to exert the effort needed to learn.

REFERENCES

1. Avery, C. B.: The education of children with impaired hearing. *In* Cruickshank, W. M., and Johnson, G. O., eds.: *Education of Exceptional Children and Youth.* Englewood Cliffs, N. J., Prentice-Hall, Inc., 1958, pp. 339–385.
2. Bindon, D. M.: Rubella deaf children: A Rorschach study employing Munroe Inspection Technique. *Brit. J. Psychol.,* 1957, *48,* 249–258.
3. Brill, R. G.: The relationship of Wechsler I.Q.'s to academic achievement among deaf students. *Except. Children,* 1962, *28,* 315–321.
4. Craig, W. N.: Effects of preschool training on the development of reading and lip-reading skills of deaf children. *Amer. Annals Deaf,* 1964, *109,* 280–296.
5. Davis, H., and Silverman, S. R.: *Hearing and Deafness.* New York, Holt, Rinehart and Winston, 1960.
6. DiCarlo, L. M., and Dolphin, J. E.: Social adjustment and personality development of deaf children; A review of literature. *In* Trapp, E. P., and Himelstein, P.: *Readings on the Exceptional Child.* New York, Appleton-Century-Crofts, 1962, pp. 360–361.
7. Doctor, P. V.: Challenges of the present time to the educators of the deaf. *In* Frampton, M., and Gall, E. D., eds.: *Special Education for the Exceptional.* Boston, Porter Sargent, 1955, vol. 2, pp. 169–175.
8. Elstad, L. M.: The deaf. *In* Frampton, M., and Gall, E. D., eds.: *Special Education for the Exceptional.* Boston, Porter Sargent, 1955, vol. 2, pp. 148–168.
9. Ewing, A. W. G.: *Educational Guidance and the Deaf Child.* Manchester, Great Britain, Manchester University Press, 1957.
10. Ewing, I. R., and Ewing, A. W. G.: *New Opportunities for Deaf Children.* London, Great Britain, University of London Press, 1958.
11. Falconer, G. A.: Teaching machines for the deaf. *Volta Rev.,* 1960, *62,* 59–62, 76.
12. Farraut, R. H.: The intellective abilities of deaf and hearing children compared by factor analysis. *Amer. Annals Deaf,* 1964, *109,* 306–325.
13. Fielder, M. F.: Good and poor learners in an oral school for the deaf. *Except. Children,* 1957, *23,* 291–295.
14. Fusfield, I. S.: Counseling the deafened. *In* Frampton, M., and Gall, E. D., eds.: *Special Education for the Exceptional.* Boston, Porter Sargent, 1955, vol. 2, pp. 209–218.
15. Fusfield, I. S.: How the deaf communicate: Manual language. *Amer. Annals Deaf,* 1958, *103,* 264–282.
16. Fusfield, I. S.: How the deaf communicate: Speech. *Amer. Annals Deaf,* 1958, *103,* 264–282.
17. Fusfield, I. S.: How the deaf communicate: Written language. *Amer. Annals Deaf,* 1958, *103,* 255–263.
18. Goda, S.: Language skills of profoundly deaf adolescent children. *J. Speech Hear. Res.,* 1959, *2,* 369–376.
19. Gordon, J. E.: Relationships among mothers' n achievement, independence training, attitudes, and handicapped children's performance. *J. Consult. Psychl.,* 1959, *23,* 207–212.

---

* The Volta Bureau, 1537 35th St. N.W., Washington, D. C., publishes the *Volta Review,* which contains articles about the deaf and also has information available about facilities in all parts of the country.

20. Hardy, W. G.: Hearing aids for deaf children. *In* Frampton, M., and Gall, E. D., eds.: *Special Education for the Exceptional.* Boston, Porter Sargent, 1955, vol. 2, pp. 234–238.
21. *Hearing Loss.* United States Department of Health, Education, and Welfare, Public Health Service Publication No. 207, Health Information Series No. 53, 1964.
22. Heck, A. O.: *The Education of Exceptional Children.* New York, McGraw-Hill Book Co., 1953, pp. 224–281.
23. Hoag, R. L.: Role of the U.S. Office of Education in the preparation of teachers of the deaf. *Amer. Annals Deaf,* 1963, *108,* 408–413.
24. Kastein, S., and Fowler, E. P., Jr.: Differential diagnosis of communication disorders in children referred for hearing tests. *In* Michal-Smith, H., and Kastein, S.: *The Special Child.* Seattle, Washington, New School for the Special Child, Inc., 1962, pp. 173–192.
25. Kates, S. L., Yudin, L., and Tiffany, R. K.: Concept attainment by deaf and hearing adolescents. *J. Educ. Psychol.,* 1962, *53,* 119–126.
26. Kodman, F., Jr.: Educational status of hard-of-hearing children in the classroom. *J. Speech Hear. Dis.,* 1963, *28,* 297–299.
27. Lane, H. S.: Extracurricular activities of deaf children. *Volta Rev.,* 1960, *62,* 172–173.
28. Larr, A. L.: Perceptual and conceptual abilities of residential school deaf children. *Except. Child,* 1956, *23,* 63–66, 88.
29. Lassman, G. H.: *Language for the Preschool Deaf Child.* New York, Grune and Stratton, Inc., 1950.
30. Lavos, G.: Evaluating the intelligence of the deaf. *In* Frampton, M., and Gall, E. D., eds.: *Special Education for the Exceptional.* Boston, Porter Sargent, 1955, vol. 2, pp. 185–199.
31. McLaughlin, H. S.: A modern day school program for teachers of the deaf. *In* Frampton, M., and Gall, E. D., eds.: *Special Education for the Exceptional.* Boston, Porter Sargent, 1955, vol. 2, pp. 200–208.
32. Mira, M. P.: The use of the Arthur Adaptation of the Leiter International Performance Scale and the Nebraska Test of Learning Aptitude with preschool deaf children. *Amer. Annals Deaf,* 1962, *107,* 224–228.
33. Myklebust, H. R.: Towards a new understanding of the deaf child. *In* Frampton, M., and Gall, E. D., eds.: *Special Education for the Exceptional.* Boston, Porter Sargent, 1955, vol. 2, pp. 176–184.
34. Pintner, R., and Brunschwig, L.: Some personality adjustments of deaf children in relation to two different factors. *J. Genet. Psychol.,* 1936, *49,* 377–388.
35. Ronnei, E. C.: The hard of hearing. *In* Frampton, M., and Gall, E. D., eds.: *Special Education for the Exceptional.* Boston, Porter Sargent, 1955, vol. 2, pp. 260–284.
36. Rosenstein, J.: Cognitive abilities of deaf children. *J. Speech Hear. Res.,* 1960, *3,* 108–119.
37. Rushford, G., and Lowell, E. L.: Use of hearing aids by young children. *J. Speech Hear. Res.,* 1960, *3,* 354–360.
38. Stone, J., Fielder, M. F., and Fine, C. O.: Preschool education of deaf children. *J. Speech Hear. Dis.,* 1961, *26,* 45–60.
39. *Summary of Progress in Hearing and Speech Disorders.* Research Profile No. 4, U.S. Department of Health, Education, and Welfare, Public Health Service Publication No. 1156, 1963.
40. Vermeulen, R.: A musical instrument for deaf-mute children. *Philips Tech. Rev.,* 1957, *18,* 276–278.

Part VI

CASE
HISTORIES

Although there are limitations for growth in some children and for adaptability in some parents which presage a dim outlook for improved behavior, nevertheless pessimism is never indicated until the adults responsible for the child have been encouraged to institute new and pertinent management methods. Even a minimum of constructive training of the child has produced improvement in behavior. When adults are concerned intellectually rather than emotionally with a child's deviate behavior, their objectivity engenders increased thoughtfulness in the child.

The following case histories are descriptions of children with behavior problems for whom assistance was sought by parents, welfare agencies, schools, or courts. Their names have been changed, as well as all other identifying characteristics of their families. Assembled over a period of 20 years, many of the histories are the stories of children who now are adults, and with the concern attendant on familiarity with others' problems, the writer trusts that the lives of these individuals are less troubled than they were at one time. The histories are condensations of detailed diagnostic studies which combined information and observations obtained from many sources. Although numerous details of experiences and test performance are omitted, the significant contributing factors related to the problems of each child are retained.

The case descriptions indicate that no symptom occurs in isolation: Each child displays several handicapping forms of behavior. Nor can behaviors be categorized to a degree which implies that there are limitations in the manner of expressing disturbance. The history of a child cited in the discussion of withdrawal reactions will indicate that his difficulties also include school problems, psychophysiological symptoms, and even aggressive reactions. Distress manifests itself in every facet of a child's life.

Multiple factors are indicated or identified as causative agents in every case, and suggested procedures for retraining the child are included in the history, except for institutionalized children with whose parents no continuing contact could be maintained.

Case 1

Wallace J., age 13, with dull intelligence, teased other children and threw rocks at them, was belligerent with his mother, and had to be prodded continually to do what he should. He daydreamed excessively. He had no friends and cried when sent to the principal's office for misbehavior. Achievement tests placed him at a third grade level.

Wallace was the second of two children. His older sister was capable and reliable but aggressive toward Wallace. He teased her often but cried when she hit him in retaliation. The mother, pleasant and intelligent, was resentful of Wallace's pugnacious attitude toward her. She still supervised his eating closely and required him to clean his plate at every meal. She reminded him before school to comb his hair and brush his teeth, and she saw to it that he left on time. She and the boy's sister usually finished his uncompleted chores. For punishment, he was spanked. Mr. J. was weak in manner and seemed dependent on his wife. There was much arguing in the family about the father's drinking, with both mother and daughter severely critical of him. At such times, Wallace would try to take his father's part and was speedily rebuffed for his pains. On group hunting trips with other men, father and son got along well, and the boy was completely reliable then. Wallace had been a blue baby, and a heart operation was performed when he was six years old. There was hemorrhaging, a slow recovery, and a hint from the surgeon that the child nearly died. From his earliest days, Wallace had tired easily, and at present he seldom engaged in group sports.

Wallace was a tall, slightly-built boy who talked softly and deferentially, and this was his usual manner with adults. At times he used odd expressions, and he seemed to show little real emotion. He evidenced no guilt about any of his behavior. Tests indicated deep feelings of fear, aggression, loneliness, and inferiority. Poor judgment, limited intellectual control, and childish emotion were revealed. Perhaps because of his poor health, the marital difficulty, or his being the younger child, Wallace was treated as though he were incompetent and needed continual care. He accepted his mother's concept of his ability but bitterly resented her supervision. He could not hold his own with other boys, either at play or in schoolwork, and so he attacked them.

A reading tutor was obtained for Wallace and he was able to raise his reading level from second to sixth grade within five months. No emphasis was placed on his succeeding in schoolwork during this time. The mother was able to relax her habit of prodding the boy, leaving it to him to get himself ready for school and to eat or refrain from eating at meals. He soon developed an enormous appetite, something he had never had. He was assigned regular chores for which he was paid, and he began to save his money to buy a rifle. He joined a group of boys and girls meeting after school at the drug store. Although the mother regarded these contacts with some apprehension, she was encouraged to permit this freedom. Weathering a sudden financial reverse together, husband and wife developed a closer relationship.

Case 2

Bill C., age 12, of superior intelligence, was unable to make friends, demanded many privileges, and teased and fought with his younger siblings. After quarreling with another boy, he would refuse to make up, and he repulsed boys who came to the house to ask him to play. He seldom completed his schoolwork and always excused his failure to do so. Called "Fatty" by other boys, Bill often complained of being tired and of having severe headaches. These complaints disappeared when school was out for the summer. If his father scolded or punished him, he cried and remained disturbed for several days. Recently he had been apprehended for stealing.

Bill was the oldest of four children, and he reserved his most intense hatred for his nine-year-old sister, the only girl. Mrs. C. was tense and near tears during interviews, but her greatest concern was her relationship with her husband. He travelled much of the time and wanted her exclusive attention when he was home. They disagreed constantly about money, and both had expensive tastes. Mr. C. teased his wife and ridiculed her, and when he had been drinking, he abused her physically. The family had moved 20 different times, usually because of financial difficulty. Bill often succeeded in postponing his scheduled bedtime for an hour or more, and his mother urged rich foods on him, despite his weight. After he was dressed in pajamas for the night, he sometimes sat on his mother's lap. He had few chores, and though he did not resist these, he always had to be reminded of them.

Bill was tall and heavy but did not appear overweight. He tried to maintain a mature, casual relationship with the examiner, characterized by witty comments which he delivered unsmilingly. He tended to protect and excuse his parents and their actions, claiming that they were not well. Tests showed that he performed indifferently, his standards were low, and he had regressed intellectually. He thought of his mother as protecting and close, and he regarded his father as angry and punishing. Undisciplined and witnessing much immature behavior and violence on the part of his parents, including quarrels over him, this boy played the part of an infant. He consistently took the easy way out and exerted no effort either to achieve or to please others because he had never been expected to behave responsibly or to comply with rules.

The mother failed to keep regular appointments. In time, however, she was able both to refrain from petty needling of her husband and to defend herself when she needed to do so. All of the children were required to do more chores. She made an effort to give Bill more space for his possessions and to protect him from the marauding of his younger brothers, but he was no longer permitted to sit on her lap. She was encouraged to convince him that his parents would not intercede for him when he got into trouble and that he would have to accept deserved punishment. He was permitted to drop league baseball, which had interfered with his joining Scouts and going on trips with his father, two activities in which he had long wished to engage. Within a year, his schoolwork had improved to such a degree that he made the honor roll.

Case 3

Neal R., age 15, of average intelligence, complained repeatedly of feeling ill and often stayed in bed instead of attending school. He became exhausted easily and never finished anything he started. Reserved and mannerly away from home, he was belligerent with his mother and sister, and he once attacked his sister with a belt. After one fight he had with her, he destroyed all of his own model airplanes. Several months earlier he had shot a water pistol at a toy store clerk who accused him of stealing. The clerk claimed that the pistol was filled with gasoline. He told his mother that he hated her and described himself as "a big, fat slob who will never amount to anything." He sometimes stayed up until 2 or 3 A.M. baby-sitting, and he hit the children in his care to make them mind.

Mrs. R. worked full time to provide for Neal and his younger sister. The father was working in another state in an effort to get money to pay business debts. He was described as perfectionistic and grim prior to his business breakdown, and the mother vacillated between rejoining or divorcing him. Although the mother ordered the children to do various chores, they would not, and she did them herself. Because she habitually began her housework late in the evening, often she had only three hours' sleep at night, and after exhausting herself physically, she took several days off to rest. When she did not like what Neal did, she kicked him, and for punishment, she sent him to bed. She spoke of his acquaintances as his "little friends." She gave him a great deal of money to buy gasoline-powered model airplanes and expensive cameras, despite the family's heavy indebtedness and the fact that she herself wore ragged clothes.

Neal was a tall, heavy boy who wore glasses. His face was round and babyish, and his manner almost completely expressionless. He rarely smiled, and he discussed personal matters with the same dispassion with which he described his political theories. He seemed uninterested in doing well on tests, and he cancelled, failed, or was tardy for appointments. Tests indicated feelings of self-pity and little sense of conscience. Thinking disturbance was acute, and the possibility of criminal violence was indicated. Emotionally inhibited, physically overconcerned, and somewhat feminine in his interests, Neal directed aggression against himself as well as against others. His problems could be ascribed to the immature, conceding, and disorganized behavior of his mother, which he imitated, and to his fear of the demands and cold punishment of his father. The mother treated him as an emotional football for her own distraught feelings, and his infantile behavior was not only permitted but encouraged and excused.

The mother could not follow through on specific recommendations made to her, but she did decide to rejoin her husband. After the family moved, Neal found work in a drug store, but nothing else is known of his subsequent behavior.

Case 4

Harriet L., age 15, of high average intelligence, cried almost hysterically at any indication that other girls rejected her. Each Friday night she frantically telephoned acquaintances to ask if she might accompany them to the movies. In a crowd or with strangers, Harriet was shy, self-conscious, and unable to carry on conversation. Although she was sensitive to others' feelings, she was also quick to assume that any chance negative remark was intended for her. Her schoolwork was deteriorating, and at home she was demanding, selfish, and dictatorial with a younger sister.

Harriet was the second of three children. Her older brother, a boy of superior intelligence, withdrew from the family and was failing his senior year at high school. The younger sister was lazy, careless, and envious of Harriet's greater freedom. Mrs. L. felt sorry for herself, managed poorly, and alternately pleaded with and screamed at the children. Devoted to her son, she had not wanted Harriet and had turned her care over to a servant girl, who was very fond of her. The mother had always felt that she ran a poor third in the girl's affections, after the maid and Harriet's father, and that the child had never liked her. She bestowed all of her love on her son, and Mr. L. was antagonistic toward both his wife and the boy. He enjoyed Harriet's companionship and was proud of her insistence on earning money she needed for extras. The family income was limited, but the home was elaborate and had been built in the best residential area. The children were provided with all of the expensive clothing they requested. The family's social acceptability was of great importance to Mrs. L., although she continually scorned and criticized other people. As a pre-schooler, Harriet had been preoccupied with cleanliness; and during her elementary years, she had few friends and she cried constantly in dissatisfaction with her school achievements.

Harriet was a girl of average size for her age and pleasing appearance, except for skin problems. She was able to talk with relative freedom and she could describe accurately those incidents which disturbed her. She was convinced that there was something seriously wrong with herself, and she seemed unable to think of herself as entitled to ideas and feelings of her own. Tests produced an occasional odd response, and she resisted free expression on tests. She pictured her mother as an unpredictable, complaining person with whom she had no sound relationship. Association between men and women was emphasized in projective stories, and there were indications that Harriet had thought of running away. She had always believed that her mother disliked and disapproved of her, particularly for her lack of popularity, and she was still trying to win approval by frenzied efforts toward social acceptance. The mother's devotion to her son and exclusion of other members of the family had produced an atmosphere of bitterness. Harriet's belligerence at home, as well as her school failures, stemmed from the fright she felt at her parents' interpersonal difficulties, her failure to assert herself with her peers, and her conviction that she was unimportant to her mother.

The parents began to assume more appropriate marital roles, and audibly discounted the need for popularity. After her considerable assets were reviewed with her, Harriet was able to stop begging others to permit her to associate with them. At last report, she was choosing those peer activities in which she wanted to participate, she had entered a school election as a contestant, and she was seeking her father's advice on how to rid herself of an unwanted boy friend.

Case 5

Eddie A., age 15, of average intelligence, was rude and disrespectful to teachers and had dropped out of school several times during the previous three years. He complained of headaches and fatigue, and he had missed school frequently when he was younger because of illness. His grades always had been below average, and he failed ninth grade because of prolonged absence. Eddie associated with boys and girls who were 20 years old, joining them in drinking and petting, and staying out until early morning. He was with them nearly every night.

Eddie was the second of two sons, and his parents were divorced when he was six months old. The mother remarried, and although Eddie got along well with his four half-siblings, he resented his older brother, who was conscientious and had always been successful in school. Mrs. G., talkative and ineffectual, waited on all of the children and was careless and disorganized with her own housework. She had interfered when her father (with whom she and the boys lived after the divorce) and then her second husband had attempted to punish Eddie. After several such incidents, Mr. G. never again tried to discipline the boy and developed an intense dislike for him.

Eddie was tall and thin, and he had many skin eruptions. He was overly courteous toward the examiner and expressed concern about how well he was doing on tests. These indicated that his vocabulary was below average, that it was difficult for him to learn new subjects, and that he was unable to make careful observations. He tended to avoid other people and, according to projective studies, had no close relationship with members of his own family. His intellectual deterioration and anxiety resulted from the freedom he had been allowed. Because his parents paid no attention to his late hours and inappropriate social life, he was lonely and knew he could depend only on himself. His school rebellion was understandable because of his educational inadequacies and his conviction that he was undesirably different from his classmates.

Although Mrs. G. could see that her docile serving of the children only made them irresponsible, she could not alter her habits, and both parents and son failed appointments. After a week's absence from school for illness, Eddie joined a work crew which was leaving the state.

Case 6

Albert B., age 16, of average intelligence, was sent to the clinic by the court after being put on probation for stealing and wrecking a car. He was failing in high school and sometimes created a disturbance in class. At home, he refused to do chores, bullied the younger children, and complained constantly.

Albert was the second of five children. His 17-year-old sister, married to a serviceman stationed overseas, lived at home with her baby son. The three younger siblings were so annoying to Albert that he began eating by himself rather than sit at the same table with them. Mrs. B. looked older than she was and seemed discouraged and tired. Living under crowded conditions, the family had little money and occasionally was on relief. Mr. B., who worked all night as a janitor in an office building, went to bed as soon as he came home. The children seldom saw him except when he emerged from the bedroom to roar for quiet. Because the father had punished Albert severely when he was small, the mother felt sorry for him and never enforced any request she made of the boy. She had always waited on him and dressed him until he was seven. When asked to help with heavy work, his unfailing comment was, "Why should I?" He sat idle while his mother chopped wood and tended the stove used for heating. The stealing incident had followed his parents' refusal to permit him a second can of beer on New Year's Eve. He repeated the same act several weeks later when chastised by a relative for criticizing his mother. Shortly thereafter, a grandmother with whom he had lived at times suddenly died, and during the gathering of the family preceding the funeral, Albert began to sing and dance and finally refused to attend the service.

Albert was a tall, thin, pimply-faced boy who at first would not look at the interviewer. He was excessively polite, was eager to gain sympathy, and talked steadily about how he had been mistreated. He excused his own misbehavior. Tests showed odd thinking, inability to concentrate, and unhappy awareness of being the center of parental battles. He thought of himself as being infantile, helpless, and useless, which he was because of his mother's failure to require anything of him. Completely self-centered and ineffectual, he was easily frustrated, irritated, angered, or overwhelmed by unpleasant or demanding situations.

Placed on probation by the court after his second offense and permitted to leave school to take a job so that he could pay for the damage he had done, Albert worked briefly but was then laid off. He spent the pay he received on entertainment. He could not find work, and he refused to do more than dally at yard jobs given him by relatives. His father lost a new daytime job which he had taken in order to be home in the evening with his family. Father and son searched for work together, and Albert's desire to be accepted by his father, as well as to play more of a man's role, was evidenced by his hope that they might find jobs in the same place. He still refused most chores, but he enjoyed the complete attention of both parents while the younger children were in school and his sister was at work. Parental attitudes seemed to be reversing, with the father more understanding and the mother more critical of Albert. Clinic contacts were broken by the parents.

Case 7

Irene B., age seven, of dull intelligence, showed little emotion, was vague in her speech, could not concentrate, did poorly in school, and blamed others for her difficulties. When spanked, she never cried, and she played by herself for long periods of time. Her teacher reported that she sometimes wept for no apparent reason and that she needed constant attention and affection. A year ago, she was refusing to play with other children, lied, and stole both money and toys. These latter problems had diminished during the previous year, after her father's remarriage.

Irene was the second of three children. Her mother had attempted to abort her and after her birth had left her alone in her crib for hours at a time. The mother finally deserted the family. Irene then lived with a constantly changing series of sitters and relatives, and at times her mother would appear and reclaim the children. Mr. B. felt his responsibility to his children, but he had little to do with their direct care, and eventually he married again. Mrs. B., the stepmother, had two children older than Irene, and when the mother

first began caring for all five children, she was impatient with Irene's unresponsiveness and somewhat desperate about her inability to cope with the
child's disturbing behavior. Her educational standards for all of the children
were high, and she was disgusted with Irene for her limited interest in and
success with learning.

Irene was a pale, thin little girl, who was unresponsive at the clinic. Even
answering simple questions seemed to necessitate extraordinary effort on her
part. Although tests showed limited intelligence, it could not be determined
whether this finding accurately represented learning capacity or reflected the
child's disrupted life and early neglect. Projective tests indicated that she
felt isolated and angry because of her school failures and that she tended to
reject the feminine role. Her early and prolonged isolation from affectionate
human contacts, as well as the outright rejection by her mother and the need
to adjust to new and continually changing caretakers produced her physical
and emotional withdrawal. Stealing was a simple method of getting what she
wanted, inasmuch as she had no adult on whom she could rely to meet her
needs or desires. School difficulties were to be expected in a child as uprooted
and alone as Irene had been, especially with her limited learning ability.
Under the most stable living conditions she had ever experienced, those
following her father's remarriage, her problems had decreased despite the
inability of stepmother and child to feel relaxed with each other.

The stepmother attended a class on child management and was able to
give Irene more individual attention and praise. She accepted the interpretation of the reasons for school problems and refrained from emphasizing
school achievement or drilling the child in schoolwork. Irene found a girl
friend in the neighborhood and began to play regularly with her. Her schoolwork began to improve.

Case 8

Milton R., age 12, of average intelligence, had a violent temper, attacked
his younger brothers and sister, was insolent with his mother, and did not get
along well with classmates. His school grades were variable.

The oldest of four children, Milton was born when his parents were quite
young, and it was seven years before the next child arrived. Mrs. R. had
chronic severe abdominal pain resulting from emotional tension. She was
harried and tired from the many volunteer responsibilities she assumed in the
community and from her habit of staying up late every night. She was severely critical of all aspects of her husband's behavior. Mr. R. was an immature man who found it difficult to accept the responsibilities of caring for a
family. Spending money freely, he counted on rent money from his brother-in-
law, who lived with them, to supplement his own earnings. He had a violent
temper, and during an outburst he sometimes smashed furniture and
threatened members of his family. He was critical of all recognized authority
and angered by notes from school requesting money for the children's books
or activities. He felt that Milton was born before he was ready for fatherhood,
and he was jealous of the attention his wife had given the boy. He was impatient and critical toward him and had threatened several times to have him
committed to the state industrial school.

Milton was short for his age but attractive in appearance, neat, and clean.
He talked constantly, usually to avoid the introduction of distressing topics,
but he was able to talk about these when asked to do so. Projective tests indicated that he rejected unpleasantries and tried to give the impression that he

was more capable and important than he was. He was conscious of his small size, felt that other boys were against him, disliked his father, and was jealous of his younger siblings. He did not feel close to anyone, and he believed that most people are antagonistic toward one another. He had considered running away, something his father had done as a boy.

The mother was persuaded to have her younger brother move out of the home, where he had acted as a supplementary father not only by his financial contributions but also in his relationship with both the children and his sister. Mrs. R. acquired greater understanding of typical male characteristics and was better able to refrain from criticizing her husband for speech and behavior which she felt was undesirable, ill-mannered, or even immoral. She was also able to keep out of disagreements occurring between father and son. Mr. R., discouraged with his past relationship with the boy, found it hard to start over, but he did make some attempt to take a more active part in planning and setting rules for him, and he was encouraged not to express his negative attitude toward others in the child's presence. He found a new job which gave him more status but less money, and he began to take charge of the family bookkeeping, a task his wife had handled previously. He continued to feel somewhat abandoned by his wife and to drink too much at times. Mrs. R. attended a class on child management and succeeded in becoming much closer to her son, although she still was hesitant about asserting herself when he became angry with her.

Case 9

Bernard K., age 11, was a boy of superior intelligence. He was enuretic and had tics of head-jerking and eye-blinking. He had no real friends and was domineering with the few boys who did play with him, believing they considered him a sissy.

An only child, he received continuous attention and criticism from his mother. Mrs. K., a domineering woman, was aggressive and abusive with the interviewer and highly critical in her evaluation of other people. With Bernard, she was effusively insincere, often failed to keep her promises to him, and interfered in his relationships with other children. Her attitude toward her husband was one of constant devaluation and she resented his not taking a more active part in disciplining the boy. When he presumed to criticize her actions, she slapped him. Mr. K. was smaller physically than his wife, and when both were interviewed together, he deferred to her opinions. Privately, he admitted that he had given up long ago trying to change the home situation.

Bernard was a stocky boy, who tried to maintain an adult relationship with the examiner by commenting jokingly about test items. He was over-conscientious and meticulous in his answers. Tests showed feelings of inadequacy, an overactive conscience, poor judgment, and guilt feelings. Aggressive feelings existed, but were disguised and well submerged. The mother's belittling of the father made Bernard uncertain of the desirability of identifying with him as a male figure, and his own feminine characteristics made him uncertain also in his approach to other boys. Failure to give him freedom and responsibility at home and with his friends resulted in his playing the assigned role of baby, evidenced by his enuresis. The continual criticism, high standards, and strict control imposed on him by his mother, along with her own expression of a belligerence toward others which he was not allowed to show toward her, produced the acute tension and fear associated with his tics. The mother did not return for appointments.

Case 10

Tony J., age 16, of average intelligence, came to the clinic because of his poor grades and his occasional truancy from high school. Severe headaches, reported first to the school nurse, were increasing in frequency.

Tony was an only child. Mr. J., forced unwillingly into marriage, doubted his paternity of the boy. He often cursed him, sometimes in the presence of his friends; accused him of lying; and made telephone calls to his friends, teachers, and coaches to check on his whereabouts and his veracity. A heavy drinker, the father for some time had picked up girls in bars, and a year ago had an affair with the mother of a girl Tony dated steadily. Discovery of the father's affair, along with his insistence that Tony stop dating the girl because she was "no good," precipitated the final disintegration of the family. Mrs. J. admitted having a quick temper and said that she and her husband quarreled constantly. When Tony reported his father's affair to her, she threatened divorce, and this produced temporary sobriety in Mr. J., but his antagonism toward the boy increased.

Tony, short but husky, talked eagerly and openly to the examiner and neither hid nor excused his own misdeeds. He empathized with peers who were having problems and tried to assist them any way he could. Tests indicated little drive, low self-confidence, depression, confusion, and poor memory and judgment. Because many of the parental arguments were based on the father's treatment of him and also because his reporting of his father's affair caused even more serious trouble, Tony felt directly responsible for the adults' failure to reconcile their differences. After a final argument with his father, Tony was ordered to leave the house, and he moved in with his maternal grandmother. His mother soon followed him. During this period, Tony began to lose his temper frequently and he refused to do chores requested of him by his grandmother and mother. His headaches decreased in intensity, however, and he attended school regularly.

An attempt was made to reassure him that he was by no means the sole cause of the difficulty between his parents, and he was given specific instructions in behavior to assist him in regaining self-control and to enable him to replace his anxiety over past events with constructive action. At the time of the last contact, he seemed more alert, relaxed, and confident. The mother had decided on divorce and had rented an apartment for herself and Tony.

Case 11

Ruth M., age nine, with low average intelligence, was referred to the clinic after a physician's examination revealed no physical basis for her severe headaches and frequent vomiting in school. She daydreamed a great deal, and although it was difficult to gain her attention, she was obedient when aware of requests. She had not learned to read. As a small child, she had few friends, and her older sister appropriated for herself the children who were Ruth's age.

Ruth was the second of four girls, ranging in age from five to ten years. The oldest sister, with whom Ruth shared a room, was belligerent toward her, and Ruth often cried over her treatment. Mrs. M. was pale and underweight, sometimes vague and hesitant in her speech. She seemed unable to remember details, she appeared depressed, and she was greatly concerned with her own health. Mr. M. was gone frequently because of his work, and the mother felt unfairly burdened in having to care for the children without him. The four pregnancies had occurred in rapid succession, and Mrs. M. had been ill throughout each. When the girls were babies, she had worked hard and often was weary and discouraged. She had screamed constantly at Ruth and her older sister from their earliest years, and she admitted that she still did so and whipped all of the children for misbehavior. Continually exhausted, Mrs. M. often went to bed with the children and did not get up in the morning to prepare their breakfast. If she did not nap during the day, she could scarcely last through the supper hour.

When seen for psychological testing, Ruth talked and smiled easily, but often she did not finish what she had started to say because her thoughts wandered in midsentence. Tests showed that Ruth was frightened and also that she had strong feelings of injustice and rebellion related both to her mother and to school. Characters in stories she told used sickness, sleep, and forgetting to avoid duties or unpleasantries. Finding her own mother impossible to please, Ruth tried to feel close to her by imitating almost exactly her techniques of evading responsibility. She resented the greater independence and apparent competence of her older sister, but she did not believe that it was possible for her to behave the same way.

Despite poor prognosis, Mrs. M. understood the interpretation of Ruth's problems, and while attending a class in child management, she completely reversed her former habits and attitudes. She accepted the responsibility of caring for the children and no longer considered her husband neglectful of the family. She was able to organize her work better and to stop her tirades against the children. Eventually she began to participate in community activities. Ruth was given a room with her next younger sister, and she joined a Scout group separate from that of her older sister. Her physical complaints disappeared, and she showed an independence in associating with others and in self-management which had never been evident previously.

Case 12

Doris F., age eight, of superior intelligence, had a violent temper, called names, hit her mother, and was disliked by other children. She sucked her thumb constantly, and from an early age had pulled out her hair in handfuls. She had nightmares and was afraid of the dark. In school, however, where her educational achievement was a grade higher than her placement, she was considered obedient and self-reliant.

Doris' parents were middle-aged, and she was their only child. Mrs. F. was a small, plain woman who told of being a poor manager at home and admitted that she herself had a severe temper. She was protective of Doris and critical of other children who rejected her. She accepted the child's abuse without real protest and seldom asked her to help around the house because she dreaded Doris' violent objections. Mr. F., who was partially paralyzed, did some travelling alone in connection with his work, but when he was home, his wife chauffeured him everywhere and made most of the family decisions. She resented this responsibility, however, and considered herself both burdened and unappreciated. Mr. F. appeared to be better controlled emotionally than his wife, and he was interested in Doris in a detached sort of way. Doris' playmates were almost entirely smaller children, usually pre-schoolers, whom she could dominate without opposition.

When she was seen at the clinic, Doris, who was an unattractive, thin child, talked constantly and loudly, expressed herself dramatically, and laughed in a high-pitched voice. As she became more restless, she kicked the wall, and hit and pulled at her parents in semi-playfulness. During testing, she attempted to dominate the examiner, and anxiety and antagonism were evident in both her behavior and her test responses. Without adult controls, Doris had had to rear herself, and she had done so in an atmosphere of emotional turmoil. She reflected her mother's insecurity and anger, and she was unable to face the challenge offered by children her own age.

The mother was able to follow many suggestions made in a class in child management. She learned to treat Doris' temper with consistent firmness, and the child was paid for regular, required chores. As more contact with children her own age was initiated, Doris' association with smaller children tapered off. The mother was urged to find interests of her own and also some which she and Mr. F. could share without the child. Mrs. F. undertook part-time secretarial work and seemed calmer and better able to permit the father to assume more responsibility for family decisions.

Case 13

Randy J., age 13, with high average intelligence, was sent to the clinic by the court after he shot a rifle bullet at a school building, injuring a boy inside. A year earlier, he had made darts from pins and shot them at his classmates in school, and he experimented frequently with explosives, over the neighbors' protests. Two years ago, he and a friend had vandalized another school building.

Randy, the fourth of five children (all boys except for the youngest child), had an older brother who was his constant companion and mentor. The two oldest brothers were married. Mrs. J., a tired woman in poor health, listened to the problems of her neighbors and shouldered some of their burdens, but she left Randy's guidance to her older son. Mr. J. encouraged the boy to ignore his mother's directions to help with chores and finish his schoolwork, and he minimized and excused his every misbehavior. His sole attempt to discipline Randy was made after repeated conferences with school authorities about his low grades. The father finally told him that he must spend two hours in his room each evening, preferably for the purpose of studying, but the decision concerning use of the time was his to make. Supplied with a tape recorder and radio, plus his father's tacit consent, Randy spent his evenings amusing himself.

Randy was an attractive, wholesome-looking boy of average physical build, who paid careful attention to his dress and appearance. He talked freely about numerous infractions of rules, dismissing them laughingly as unimportant. He resented any reference to the shooting incident, however, and refused to discuss it. Tests showed childish fear and egotism and strong feelings of revenge and of guilt. Randy was fascinated with the forbidden and dangerous, and although he wanted the power to hurt others, he himself was fearful of being physically harmed. Whenever he was belittled in any way, he became aggressive. The shooting episode had followed his dismissal from the school football team and had occurred when the team was assembled after school for practice. All of his life Randy had been forced to feel devotion for a brother who protected but dominated him and who impressed him with tales of his own daring. With no identity of his own and no responsibility for himself, Randy retained infantile ways of responding to rebuffs, and he considered these justified because of his well-learned habit of resisting conformity and obedience. His feelings of inadequacy were acute, however, and these were intensified by the rejection or criticism of those he knew to be more capable than he.

It was recommended that Randy perform regular chores in order to earn money to meet his own needs and that he be required to complete schoolwork. The tie between the brothers was to be loosened, with Randy encouraged to associate with boys his own age. The parents were to take over the control exercised by the brother. Even though the brother eventually moved away from the family, no control was given Randy by his parents. Although at first he was obedient to the curfew terms of his probation, once he had broken them and had not been punished by his parents, he continued to do so. His parents bought corsages for his girl friends and a motor scooter for him at his request. He continued to evade successfully all assigned chores and schoolwork. Twice he involved his father in difficulty by appropriating equipment belonging to his firm. Even with the constant pressure Randy exerted on his parents to force them to control him, there was no significant response. Eventually he became involved in a series of gang stealing episodes, and when caught, he was sent to the state industrial school, despite his father's efforts to substitute military school for the correctional institution.

Case 14

Bobby R., age 10, with dull normal intelligence, was referred by a physician who believed he might be brain damaged and retarded. The boy was repeating the third grade; and he also had repeated the first grade. He sucked his thumb constantly, chattered to himself, and became confused and fearful when taken to a doctor. His memory was poor and his vocabulary limited, and the mother thought of him as a retarded child.

Bobby was the fourth of four boys. His older brothers had been solicitous of him and cared for him at school and in other public places. Mr. R., whose work took him out of town frequently, was described as a conscientious man but critical of his sons. As an infant, Bobby had a kidney infection, and at 11 months he had severe diarrhea and nearly died. Although he was in the hospital only one night, the illness so frightened his mother that she was unable to help Bobby learn to eat normally. The child existed on strained foods and milk until he was seven years old. During his first year at school, he slept much of the time there and at home; he was anemic and complained of stomach pain; his coördination was poor; and he was so weak that he could not keep up with the other children. The mother, still fearful about diet because of the early diarrhea, was told by pediatricians to let Bobby decide what he wanted to eat. Nearly starved, physically tiny, and with everyone in the family overprotective of him, this child remained infantile and unable to develop. When he was seven, the mother finally told him there were no more strained foods. Gradually he began eating table food, and a growth hormone increased his height four inches and his weight 15 pounds in a single year.

Bobby could talk adequately with the examiner and showed no fear during testing. Although reading errors occurred at the first grade level, Bobby was able to read some fifth grade material. His measured intelligence was dull normal, and school staff members believed that his learning ability potentially was average. There was no evidence of brain damage on psychological tests.

Mrs. R. was reassured concerning Bobby's intellectual ability. It was suggested that his brothers work with him in developing strength and skill in physical games, something he had shown interest in only during the previous three months. His habit of staying up late at night to watch television was stopped so that he could get more rest and avoid the overstimulation which contributed to his fearfulness. The mother made plans to spend 30 minutes each evening working with Bobby on reading, spelling, and arithmetic and to give him more responsibility, including sending him on errands without his brothers. His teacher agreed to insist on completion of assignments, rather than to permit his usual erratic performance, and the mother attended a class in child management and acquired greater objectivity toward him.

Case 15

Ralph T., age five, of high average intelligence, retreated fearfully from his classmates at kindergarten and often hid behind the piano. For the past two years he had been enuretic diurnally, and after school started, he wet his bed each night. He had violent temper tantrums several times a day.

Ralph was the second of four children, the two youngest of whom were girls. Neither parent was able to handle Ralph when he kicked and screamed, and each tried instead to reason with and placate him. He stayed near his own home, and he had only one playmate, a boy who always played at Ralph's house.

Fearful and rebellious on his first visit to the clinic, Ralph was able to stay without his parents and talk freely with the examiner the next time he came. His conversation was wild and dramatic, and he covered his face and laughed irrationally while telling stories about test pictures. These confirmed his extreme anxiety, as well as his jealousy of his sisters. Left to manage himself because his parents feared opposing him and because his mother's time was limited by the demands of caring for a large family, Ralph was aware of his inadequacy and helplessness. He feared new situations because he had learned he could not count on parental support and direction, and his fear was enhanced by his inexperience with children his own age away from home.

Mrs. T. put into practice the suggestions given in a class on child management. She played alone with Ralph daily, managed his temper tantrums consistently and effectively, required him to perform small chores, and arranged for him to play at other children's homes. Although he had used the excuse of wet sheets to leave his bed and join his parents in theirs every night, Ralph was no longer permitted this reward but was expected to change his sheets if he wanted a dry bed. Retraining for day wetting was started. The extreme temper displays disappeared within a few weeks, and it was not long before Ralph was playing normally with his classmates at school.

Case 16

Loretta K., 12 years old, of average intelligence, was abusive toward her mother, calling her names, pulling her hair, and stepping on her feet. Sometimes, when she was angry, she beat her dog severely. Loretta was domineering with friends, who usually were younger than she, and at school she was left out of games and committees. She habitually reported this to her mother, who then complained to the principal and teacher. Mrs. K's response to the girl's attacks on her was either to pretend indifference or to protest mildly.

Loretta was an only child whose parents were divorced about the time she started school. The father had requested the divorce in order to marry a younger woman, and he had remained indifferent to Loretta during most of the following six years, although the child paid him short visits during summer vacations. Mrs. K., a nurse, felt acutely her own loneliness and the burden of caring for Loretta, and she still resented her husband's abandonment. Although the mother's working schedule would have permitted her to be home most of the afternoon, she did not come home, nor did she eat breakfast or lunch with Loretta in order to avoid the child's unpleasantness. The house was always in turmoil, and the mother made little effort to keep either it or Loretta clean and neat. Loretta frequently cooked the evening meal. She belonged to Girl Scouts and the church choir; and she was enrolled in weekly swimming lessons, music lessons, and sewing lessons. When she was alone at home, she usually read, and she could not have friends in because her mother was not home.

During psychological examination, Loretta's emotional control was rigid, and she found it difficult at first to give even tentative responses to the friendliness offered her. Tests suggested that she identified with the male sex, was concerned about financial security, and had marked negativistic feelings—traits related to her mother's assumption of the role of financial provider and her identification with the mother's own feeling of being abused. Resentful of her mother's outright avoidance and convinced that her mother did not love her, Loretta attacked her verbally and physically. She gained attention and support from her only when she complained of mistreatment, and her mother's reaction also provided her with the satisfaction of vicariously attacking those who did not accept her.

Mrs. K. began to reserve specific times to spend with Loretta. She managed to eat breakfast with her, to get home earlier in the afternoon, and to have friends of Loretta's age come to the house. Some of the girl's outside activities were given up. Although the mother could not physically control Loretta when she was angry, she began to leave the house at such times, a practice which resulted in quick cessation of the temper and attempts on Loretta's part to atone for her behavior. The mother also ceased complaining to school authorities about difficulties Loretta reported and instead began to help her accept rebuffs. Although the tantrums did not cease, they decreased, and Loretta used milder methods in continued attempts to dominate her mother. She became better able to accept explanation of the reasons for many of the troublesome situations in which she found herself, and gradually she acquired some skill in both self-control and defending herself with others.

Case 17

Paul G., nine years old, with superior intelligence, was fearful, hyperactive, and masochistic. His attention span was short and he was unable to concentrate long enough to finish schoolwork. He never became angry or cried when he was hurt or when his younger brother annoyed or hit him, which was often, and he resisted any offer of affection from his mother.

Mrs. G. was an attractive but tense young woman, who was ashamed of having only a high school education. She was overtalkative and blamed herself for the boy's problems. The father, a university professor, was disgusted with Paul and was overly severe in his criticism and punishment of him. Paul was born while his father was in the army, and he and his mother lived with the maternal grandparents for 18 months. Often he was left alone in his crib, and a radio substituted for his mother when he fussed. Whenever he was out of his crib, the three adults required him to perform for them, and they succeeded in teaching him the alphabet before he was two years old. When the father returned and the family was reunited, he entered a university to study and there were slim financial resources for several years. Paul, though walking, was kept in his crib for hours at a time, and when let out, he would huddle in a corner. As a small child, he was turned out to play with older children who abused him, and he was required to remain with them.

Paul was slight and pale, and during psychological testing he tended to panic when he did not know an answer immediately. He was acutely critical of himself, and he was unable to utilize his intelligence efficiently. He attempted to mask or disown every emotion, and his approach with adults was to fool, control, or ignore them. He felt unwanted, alone, and falsely accused, feelings he tried to joke away. He believed himself to be completely worthless and blamed himself for every personal, family, or public crisis.

The mother attended a class in child management and began to give Paul daily attention and praise, as well as better training in independence and responsibility. Despite the father's continued disinterest in his son and even though some of his tension and hyperactivity remained, Paul gradually became better able to function at school, and his emotional reactions became more normal. He cried when he received a poor grade, and he began to show more anger and jealousy toward his younger brother. The mother acquired more confidence in her ability to rear Paul, although she needed periodic reassurance that his changed behavior represented improvement.

Case 18

Henry P., age nine, with superior intelligence, was overweight and often indulged in huge eating jags, consuming as much as an entire bag of cookies or a jar of jam at one time. He sucked his thumb constantly, wandered off in the neighborhood to visit adults, took small amounts of money from his mother's purse, and was careless with chores. He seldom acceded to teachers' instructions, and though his teachers liked him, he exhausted them. He was accepted by most of the children but spent his play time with the girls.

Henry was the second of three boys, and a 17-year-old stepsister, his father's child by a previous marriage, also lived at home. The oldest boy was reliable and helped his mother repair the effects of Henry's indifferently-executed chores. Mrs. P., 20 years younger than her husband, was intelligent and talkative. Although she felt that Mr. P. punished Henry excessively, she admitted becoming so exasperated with the child that she had to leave the house to restrain herself from seriously hurting him.

Henry, who was so fat that he waddled, had a high voice and was overly courteous with the examiner. His verbal intelligence was high, but there was marked variation in his performance throughout the tests. Projective studies showed that he felt that his mother scorned him, which he resented, and there were indications that he had sudden impulses to attack women in authority. The disapproval of his father was as difficult for him to bear as the scorn of his mother, and the obvious preference of both for the reliable older brother was painful. Henry retreated into childish, attention-getting behavior, acting in unorthodox and disapproved ways as often as possible, convincing himself that he was blameless in everything and solacing himself with food.

It was recommended that the father spend some time alone with him, and he was able to do this and combine it with some sports training. The mother instructed neighbors to send Henry home promptly whenever he came visiting, and she made herself available to play games and talk with him as soon as he arrived from school. She became more insistent on his satisfactorily completing chores, and she paid him for his work and for refraining from thumb-sucking. With some difficulty, Mrs. P. became convinced that the child did not need the huge quantities of food she served him at meals, and she began to help him keep a calorie-count chart, which restricted only his total caloric intake each day. As the parents spent more time with him, they began to appreciate his sage observations, and as he started to behave more responsibly because they required him to do so, their annoyance with him decreased. It was hoped that the gradual weight reduction, combined with greater pride in himself and the belief that his parents were interested in and approved of him, would make it possible eventually for him to find a place among the boys in his class.

Case 19

Barbara N., age eight, of average intelligence, resisted going to bed every night and got up repeatedly for every kind of reason. She was put to bed by her father because her mother worked as a waitress at night. After the mother came home and went to bed, Barbara would waken during the night and call to her, and sometimes the mother slept with her. She had a violent temper, sucked her thumb, abused her dog, and said she wished she were dead. At school, she daydreamed and was slow and unreliable about following instructions.

Barbara was the only child of middle-aged parents, and Mrs. N. had always worked. The maternal grandmother cared for her as an infant, training her to use a cup by the age of five months and to use the toilet by the age of one year. Mrs. N. was rigid in manner, but greatly disturbed by the child's problems. She was belligerent with a teacher who gave Barbara low grades, but she constantly told the child that she could do better. Her response to the child's anger and misbehavior varied from giving her a severe whipping for a minor offense to mere head-shaking. Mr. N. related better to Barbara, but he was strict with her and was also the target of her accusations that neither parent loved her.

A tall, blonde, attractive child, Barbara's voice was high and uncertain. She laughed often and seemed to be trying to elicit disapproval from the examiner by reciting incidents of her own misbehavior and anger. Projective tests indicated her feeling of being continually punished and trying to behave as though this were unimportant to her. She felt that she did not have the support of her parents in her relations with others and that purported friendly gestures were insincere. Barbara dominated her parents by screaming, name-calling, and telling them they did not love her. They were uncertain in their management and unhappy with themselves as the child resisted and defied them. The adult standards set for her had always been excessive and had resulted in constant disapproval and criticism. The child's anxiety and loneliness were expressed most clearly at night, when her fear was evident.

It was suggested that the severe punishment and constant criticism be stopped and that Barbara be praised regularly for desirable behavior and be given more physical affection. She was required to do simple chores regularly and to go to bed at a set time each night. She understood that if she left her bed, she would have to go to bed earlier the next night to make up the time lost in stalling. Her father enforced the new rule strictly, and within two weeks Barbara was staying in bed and dropping off to sleep quickly. Mrs. N. became better able to withstand Barbara's defiance and to insist on compliance with her orders, and both parents achieved a new understanding of the child's needs.

Case 20

Betty R., age nine, of low average intelligence, called other children names, pushed and slapped them, and told tales about them. At school she did her work poorly and annoyed the other children when they did theirs. She resisted directions at home, sucked her thumb, cried easily, and was careless with possessions. She was overweight, and sometimes ate steadily for an entire day.

An only child, Betty was born 12 years after the parents were married. The mother cried often, was extremely conscious of others' opinions, and seemed lonely. The father also tried hard to please others but occasionally rebelled against people who took advantage of him. He had instructed Betty to fight the other children when they teased her. The maternal grandmother lived with the family, and Mrs. R. was fearful of her mother's criticism of the child. Whenever the grandmother corrected Betty, Mrs. R. added another scolding. She constantly gave Betty instructions and warnings which the child ignored, and eventually she became furious with her after the disobedience had lasted over several days. When she was angry, she both slapped and spanked Betty, but she was highly sympathetic toward her when she had trouble with other children and defended her as being the victim rather than the aggressor. Most of her difficulty with children occurred at school.

Betty was obviously overweight, but she was a pretty child and exceptionally neat and clean. She maintained a calm, mature manner with the examiner and was coöperative and friendly. During tests she was unaware of her errors and she quickly reached the limit of her capacity, with performance ability at the level of only borderline intelligence. She seemed unable to concentrate or to think independently. Projective studies suggested that she did not feel close to her parents. She saw her father as unhappy and disapproving and her mother only as someone on whom to lean when she was hurt. She expressed a strong desire for closer family ties and for brothers and sisters "who would stick up for me." Betty had been infantilized by her mother, whose behavior standards for her were perfectionistic but who never enforced requirements. Her own attitude toward Betty was unpredictable, critical, emotional, and competitive, and the child imitated this behavior in situations where she was insecure. This was particularly common at school, where she did not learn easily. Her self-control was insufficient to permit her to work steadily, and she resented the other children's better adjustment.

Mrs. R. attended a class on child management and began to pay more consistent attention to Betty and to have some fun with her. She also required regular chores of her and agreed to stop all violent punishment. She tried to express greater indifference when Betty reported trouble with other children at school, rather than to respond with tears and dire predictions or to blame Betty's classmates. A weight reduction program was started, and Betty joined a Brownie group and had no difficulty with the other girls. The teacher began to insist on Betty's completing her work, and she also interested some of the other children in showing friendliness toward her. There was an immediate improvement in Betty's schoolwork and a gradual improvement in her relationships with her classmates. It was necessary to emphasize repeatedly to the mother that Betty had many fine qualities, and progress was erratic.

Case 21

Nelson P., 11 years old, of superior intelligence, was being treated for ulcers. He had a violent temper, screamed and cried often, defied his mother's orders, tormented animals, swore at adults, threw rocks at other children, and rolled on the ground, crying and kicking, when other boys teased him. He talked continuously at school, and played only with girls.

Nelson was the younger of two children. His older sister, domineering and critical, took care of him for many years while both parents worked. The father ignored Nelson, preferring the girl; and the mother was flighty, anxious, and had a violent temper. The father died suddenly, and after his death Nelson's aunt and older girl cousins came to live with the family. All of the women and girls corrected Nelson and told him how to behave. Eventually the mother remarried, and the stepfather brought his 14-year-old son to live with the family. This boy shared a room with Nelson and was superior to him in athletic ability, scholarship, and responsibility. The mother resented the stepson, protected Nelson from him whenever she could, and gave her own children expensive gifts bought with money left by their father.

Nelson was a boy of slight build, who talked easily but rarely smiled. Much of his work was done on a trial and error basis. Tests verified poor judgment and indicated that he regarded his mother as denying and punishing. Although he admired his stepfather, he found closeness to anyone difficult to maintain. Abandoned by both parents at an early age, Nelson was left to the immature and erratic handling of his sister. He was never taught self-control or required to accomplish what he could. Because he was always with women and girls, he felt awkward and different from boys and he avoided them. Nelson followed his mother's example of abrupt, violent verbal and physical aggression, and his uncertainty and dissatisfaction with himself was apparent in his limited use of his intellectual capacity, his overtalkativeness, and the development of ulcers.

The mother observed that her own flare-ups were echoed immediately by Nelson and she managed to gain better control of herself. She was encouraged to require chores and the earning of money and privileges by both of her children. She attended a class on child management and this helped her to handle difficulties with Nelson with greater confidence than before, but she reported variable progress. The boy's schoolwork improved temporarily, and he began to take more responsibility for completing his homework than ever before. He still resisted his mother's instructions, which she continued to give belligerently, and eventually she sent him to a military school.

Case 22

Kenneth J., age ten, of average intelligence, soiled himself occasionally and wet his bed about twice monthly. Two years earlier, he had also been enuretic during the day. He refused to study at school or to talk to his mother, and sometimes he lied. He hit and threatened his younger siblings whenever his mother was not watching. At school Kenneth was sarcastic with both classmates and teachers, complained that the other children tormented him, and rushed carelessly through his assignments so that he could return to reading.

Kenneth was the oldest of three children. When he was eight years old, his parents were divorced, and his incontinence had begun at that time. The mother went to work and gave the children considerable responsibility for home chores. She usually absented herself in the evening with numerous activities. An elderly woman served as baby-sitter and considered Kenneth unmanageable.

Small for his age, Kenneth was precise in speech, serious in manner, and excessively courteous with the examiner. Tests indicated that he was able to do careful work, and he did so when his mother was not present. He felt that he was being continually punished, and he resented anyone in authority. He could talk about his mother's anger toward him and his toward her, and he showed little tolerance for any disappointment or disagreeable experience. Wanting to remain a child, he had been given extra responsibility during the past two years and he felt the burden of being the oldest male in the family. He seemed to feel guilty about still loving his father, although the father had remarried and had nothing to do with his children. He believed his parents had betrayed him because each apparently was going his own way, having abandoned him to replace them in supervising the younger children. His wetting and soiling represented both his wish to be cared for himself and a deliberate attack on adults, whom he always disturbed greatly in this way. He behaved as he chose at school, assuming the rights of adulthood which he believed had been thrust upon him.

The mother attended a class on child management and was able to give Kenneth much more time than before. They had several long talks together, and she told the boy the reasons for the divorce, something she had not done previously in an effort to avoid criticizing his father. The child's ignorance that there were sound reasons for the breakdown of the marriage had contributed to his belief that his parents were selfish and irresponsible. The mother curtailed her evening activities and stayed home more with the children, and she helped Kenneth establish regular habits of completing his schoolwork and his chores. This had not been done earlier because she was seldom home, and when she was there she was too tired to enforce requirements. She encouraged Kenneth to invite boys home to play. Although he remained sensitive to even implied criticism at school, the soiling ceased, he was able to confide in his mother, and he showed more initiative in completing assigned tasks.

Case 23

Charles S., age nine, with superior intelligence, stuttered and had many head and facial tics. He could not sit still, cried when he did not do things perfectly, was depressed and worried, and had both headaches and stomach aches at school.

Charles was the older of two boys. The younger brother was relaxed and friendly. Mr. S. travelled in his work, often being gone for weeks at a time, and the family had moved frequently because of the father's work assignments, sometimes remaining in one place for only a few months. Mrs. S. had adjusted to the frequent moves but felt a heavy responsibility for bringing up the boys alone. Overconcerned about their welfare, she usually denied Charles' requests to visit other boys or to go exploring with them. She, too, stuttered occasionally. She felt that Charles tended to be dictatorial with other boys and that he always waited for them to approach him. He spent hours perfecting models, was a good swimmer, and played baseball in Little League, although he was not well coördinated. He often asked his mother for suggestions about what to do in his spare time. He had a 25 cent weekly allowance, which he could not spend without permission. Mrs. S. reported that he talked unceasingly, especially at dinner time, and often her patience was exhausted from listening to him. Charles' teacher reported that he often stuttered through the first sentence when called on to read and that he would choke up on or skip the letters *p*, *b*, and *s*. She believed his classmates did not ridicule his stuttering but said they would "laugh him out of it." He cried if he had a paper with a poor grade, and he complained of not being able to see the board and of having stomach pain. Usually his mother would come to get him at such times, but occasionally he was sent to lie down. The teacher associated his tics of nose or brow wrinkling with his glasses, believing that he often tried to shift them to a different position in these ways. She noted no tics on days he forgot to wear the glasses.

Charles was a boy of average size, who was serious and intent. He explained in considerable detail about the work he was doing with models. During testing, he stuttered and sighed occasionally, sometimes blinked his eyes, and at times he was inattentive and preoccupied. Tests suggested that mother and son protected each other, and the boy felt that his father did not like him. He expressed a need for relaxation, and he had thought of running away.

It was recommended that Charles' stuttering be treated with attentive listening from his parents but without corrections or suggestions for improvement. His torrent of speaking was to be curtailed, with his mother requesting him to take his turn at talking during meals. The father agreed to devote more time to the boy when he was home and to express his approval of him directly. The mother was persuaded that more contacts with other boys and greater freedom in activities with them would be helpful. Charles was to be allowed to earn money and spend it with less supervision. The mother began to refrain from paying undue attention to Charles' complaints of illness and to avoid giving suggestions for activities when Charles asked for these. He was permitted to leave his glasses off when he did not need them, and he was taught to move them manually when they were uncomfortable. The family moved again shortly after the study was completed, and it is not known if the parents succeeded in easing the pressures on Charles.

Case 24

Leo P., age ten, with dull intelligence, was failing in school and had been for the past two years. Teachers reported that he was poor in spelling and phonics, could not work alone, would talk only in a small group, and failed to pay attention in reading class. He did not work at school, and his homework was done incorrectly. His stepmother reported that he seldom talked and had difficulty expressing himself when he did. He was enuretic and lied when accused of this. He seemed to be in a daze but was obedient and quiet both at school and at home.

Leo lived with his father, stepmother, and 20-month-old half-brother, with whom he was patient and generous. Leo had been born prematurely, and as a pre-schooler he was badly neglected by his mother, who frequently locked him out of the house all day. The parents had been divorced for several years, but Leo had been sent to his father only a year earlier after a court ruling that the mother was too emotionally disturbed to care for him. The father and stepmother often lied to Leo, and they failed to keep promises they made him. The stepmother considered the child to be queer and dangerous, interpreting his silence as an indication that he was angry and plotting revenge.

Leo was short for his age, and although he sometimes laughed, usually he appeared sad and burdened. Subtest scores on the Wechsler Intelligence Scale for Children were erratic, and the scatter was such that it seemed probable that intelligence was potentially average but was depressed because of the neglect, emotional trauma, and communication difficulties which always had been a part of his life. Stories he told were confused and rambling, and ideas were unrelated. Word substitution occurred: *e.g.*, *grass* for *floor*. While reading for the examiner, he often commented, "That doesn't make sense," and "I don't get that." Leo was highly dependent on his father and feared his displeasure because the final custody placement had not been made and he did not know how long he would remain with him. Badly frightened most of his life, he had never been able to trust adults to be honest with him. Besides his destructive personal experiences, he was aphasic and could neither understand others nor express himself adequately, and the inability to communicate made his life at home lonely and confusing, and his years at school a succession of bewildering failures.

It was suggested to the parents that they give Leo physical affection, praise, and attention and that they temporarily overlook his enuresis and lying. When Leo was given a task to do, they should make their instructions explicit and detailed so that he understood what was expected of him. The need for them to keep their promises and refrain from deception was stressed. The teacher was informed about the child's special difficulties with verbal usage, and she agreed to make certain that Leo understood his assignments, to limit the length of assignments, but to require him to complete them. The teacher did succeed in helping Leo succeed more often with his schoolwork, but the parents broke contacts with the clinic. A year later, the child had reverted to his old pattern of nonparticipation at school.

Case 25

Willard K., age 11, with superior intelligence, was dismissed from his class for constant talking, mumbling, and wisecracking to the teacher. He did no schoolwork of any kind.

Willard was the oldest of three children and had a brother five years old and a baby sister who was six months. Mr. K. drank excessively. One or another of Mrs. K.'s relatives had lived with the family throughout the marriage, and the father resented this, as well as his wife's attempts to improve his behavior. She had worked continually until the birth of the last child, and the maternal grandmother had reared Willard and his brother. Every member of the family tended to pity himself and complain constantly. Willard had attended three different schools, earning average and poor grades in each of them. As a small child he had no playmates, and he spent his time with adults in the neighborhood and with the three adults in his own family. He antagonized other children with his superciliousness, and they taunted him for his poor athletic ability. He believed himself to be right about everything and never hesitated to criticize others, but he disputed the justification for any correction of his own behavior.

Willard was short for his age and appeared awkward. His voice was high and feminine. During testing, he talked to himself, dramatized, noticed every sound, and could not relax. Tests indicated that Willard felt abandoned by both parents because of the mother's working and the father's indifference and self-centeredness; and he was highly anxious because of the atmosphere of tension, disapproval, and self-righteousness in which he lived. He was accustomed to gaining the attention and approval of adults by clever comments, but this social technique was inappropriate for and unacceptable to teachers and peers. He had feelings of self-pity and resentment, in imitation of the adults in his family, but usually he pretended his problems were non-existent and he avoided thinking of them by constant talk and dramatization. Having no skill in maintaining friendships with other children, he was lonesome, and his failure to complete his schoolwork isolated him even more.

An understanding principal permitted him to attend a class of high achievers as an auditor. He sat in the back of the room and was not permitted to talk at any time. The teacher, a man, checked his work in individual conferences and gradually began to call on him to answer questions. Within a few weeks, he was doing good work in class and obeying the injunction not to talk. The parents arranged for him to start swimming lessons, and he rode his bicycle and got himself to the pool daily. A real effort was made to help him find friends. The parents began to enforce each order they gave him and ceased their usual screaming and complaining about his behavior. The grandmother left the home, and for the first time the family was alone. The father took a new job which required some travel but which gave him more prestige and responsibility. Willard began to get along better with other boys and did well with his swimming.

Case 26

Laura K., age 11, of low average intelligence, was known to have had intercourse with three different boys. She had run away from home and from a children's home and had stolen money from her mother.

Laura's parents were divorced when she was three years old. Her mother placed her in a series of children's homes for a few months at a time and occasionally took her out to live with her, an aunt, and a cousin. The cousin was a boy two years younger than Laura, and he was favored by both women. Laura's mother remarried but later separated from this husband and then entertained a series of boy friends at home. Laura reported that she was disliked by girls and that she preferred boys as friends. She thought of them romantically, however, and talked of being in love with them. She claimed that an eight-year-old had intercourse with her when she was six years old and that then she was passed on to his friends. In school, Laura was deficient in reading and spelling, and the first time she returned to live with her mother, she would not speak or participate in group activities at school for six weeks. She began to do so only after the principal spanked her.

Laura, small for her age, presented a picture of childishness, anxiety, and disorganization. She wore short dresses, deliberately lisped, and spent most of her time playing with paper dolls to whom she assigned romantic roles. She was slow at eating and at working, and she was indifferent to her personal appearance. She reacted inappropriately in emotional situations; giggled constantly; and was extremely restless, fingering her lips, sucking her finger, pounding her hands, and biting her nails. Thinking was confused and she had difficulty remembering. She admitted that she daydreamed constantly about her boy friends. Rejected by her mother and shifted from place to place with dizzying speed, Laura never was able to develop affectional ties. As a substitute and in direct identification with her promiscuous mother, she occupied herself with fantasies of romantic love and acted out her part with sexual intercourse. A permanent foster home was recommended, but her eventual adjustment is unknown.

Case 27

Raymond K., age eight, with superior intelligence, was referred by the school for daydreaming and listlessness. At home he needed constant reminders to get dressed and he seldom finished anything he started. He objected to chores and schoolwork, and he was irresponsible about any task he was given. He sometimes was asthmatic, and he was a poor sleeper and had nightmares. He was enuretic and was wakened each night by his mother and taken to the bathroom.

The oldest of five children, Raymond especially disliked his four-year-old brother, who destroyed his belongings, but he was dictatorial with all his siblings. Mrs. K., exhausted from bearing and caring for so many children, sometimes screamed at them and whipped them. She gave in easily to their demands, however, finding little energy to oppose them. She diverted herself from the pressure of their needs by having guests in often and going on trips with her husband, practices which increased the inconsistency of the children's care and training. The father travelled most of the time, and he was busy, tense, and inattentive to the children. He was displeased with Raymond's irresponsibility and tended to push him to greater intellectual achievement, including the selection of difficult books at the library which he was to read. Raymond had not talked until he was two-and-a-half years old. At the present time, he stayed indoors most of the time, usually reading, and he rarely played with other children. During school recesses, he stayed by himself and did nothing, and he preferred to remain in the classroom and not go outside at all. He did not demand affection, seldom showed enthusiasm, and laughed without comprehension whenever his mother laughed. Both parents had shown great anger and disgust with him.

Raymond was small and frail. He talked slowly, showed little emotion, occasionally misunderstood questions, and seemed to think carefully before answering. He continually asked for directions and tried to make certain that he did what was requested. Tests showed that he felt pressured toward mature behavior and that he resisted by attempts to escape from action. He wished that he might be able to change himself into another person or animal so that "I could hide from anyone who tried to get me." Raymond was overwhelmed by the noise, confusion, and lack of direction at home. He was convinced that he did not measure up to his parents' expectations, and he avoided testing this belief by refraining from any action. Tired from frightening dreams and worry over bed-wetting, he arrived at school ready only to rest. He had been supported in his own devices for escaping involvement with others by being allowed to stay indoors when the other children were sent out to play; and he had evaded responsibility for schoolwork by gaining his mother's concurrence in the validity of his claim that he knew everything the teacher was teaching and did not need to complete assignments.

The mother attended a class in child management and was able to give Raymond more individual, friendly attention. She no longer let him avoid doing schoolwork, nor did his teacher, but both parents refrained from choosing his library books or otherwise pushing him into extra learning effort. She required him to play outside daily and began to regularize previously haphazard mealtime and bedtime hours. She stopped rousing him at night, and she tried to protect his belongings and his playing from the younger children. His father was to begin playing ball with him, but he did not manage to do so. Raymond's grades improved quickly, and the teacher reported considerable change in his ability to get started with his work.

Case 28

Calvin M., age seven, with average intelligence, was afraid of fire drills at school and worried about a fire occurring there. He was terrified at any noise and frightened by television scenes. In school, he watched the other children, daydreamed, was silent and withdrawn, but showed restlessness and a short attention span. It took him a long time each day to travel the few short blocks between school and home, and on three separate occasions he had ridden his bicycle several miles away from home without permission.

Calvin was the older of two adopted children. His parents were intelligent, patient, but baffled by his conduct. They acceded to the demands and conditions he imposed for compliance with their wishes, and little was expected of him in either responsibility or self-control. He went to bed late, often after wrestling with his father. He belittled his small sister and was rough when he played with her. His playmates were restricted to children younger than he.

Calvin was a child of average size who at first resisted the examiner's overtures. Later he began to talk more freely and he obviously was proud of the work he had done on the tests. His fine motor coördination was poor, and his thinking sometimes was confused. Calvin was worried about himself and was excited and frightened by many things he did not understand. With his poor coördination, he could not do as well as other children in school, and he did not try. His parents had failed to direct him firmly enough, and his anxiety increased as he continued to dominate them. Tired and excited at bedtime, he did not sleep well, and in school he was both preoccupied and fatigued. His resentment of his younger sister stabilized as he succeeded in his aggressiveness toward her, but his guilt over his behavior and his certainty that she was preferred by the parents complicated his family relationships. His fears reflected his feelings of inadequacy and helplessness.

Mrs. M. attended a class on child management and learned to use reward and punishment in teaching Calvin what he must do. She also gave him more time herself and arranged for boys in his class to come to play. He was no longer allowed to abuse his sister physically, and the parents insisted on completion of tasks they gave him without prior concessions on their part. He was put to bed earlier, and the wrestling was assigned to an earlier time in the day. To encourage him to come home from school promptly, Mrs. M. had a snack ready for him each day, and she was waiting to sit and talk with him when he arrived. The teacher began to insist on his completing his schoolwork, and instead of his failing the grade, which she had predicted at the start of the year, he passed with average marks. There were still unexpected spurts of rebellious behavior, but in general Calvin became more responsive and responsible.

Case 29

Catherine P., six years old, of average intelligence, was defiant and stubborn at home. She hit and kicked her mother when she tried to punish her, and she cried for more than an hour when sent to her room. She was rude to playmates, masturbated frequently, and often said she wished she were a boy.

Catherine was the oldest of three children, and she was jealous of her two younger brothers, aged four and two-and-a-half years. Much of the difficulty among the children arose because the boys played with Catherine's toys without her consent, and often she hit them in retaliation. For three years after her next younger brother was born, Catherine had insisted on wearing diapers and drinking from a baby bottle. Mrs. P., pregnant with her fourth child, blamed herself for her daughter's behavior and felt rejected by both her husband and the child. Mr. P. had directed his wife to be more patient with Catherine, and he showed no sympathy toward his wife. The father managed the child better, inviting her confidence when she cried but spanking her when she was angry and out of control. During the first two months of her life, Catherine had cried steadily for 12 hours each day. Her freedom of movement was severely restricted as an infant because she was required to wear foot casts to correct pronation. The mother had attempted to toilet train her too soon and had interpreted her failures as deliberate rebellion.

Catherine, slight in build, bore a strong facial resemblance to her mother. She talked easily with the examiner, followed directions, and was well controlled. Tests indicated a mild tendency to reverse sexual roles, strained emotional expression, annoyance with her younger brothers, a need for recognition and prestige, and loneliness. The antagonism between mother and child had become acute because the mother felt uncertain and unsuccessful in rearing Catherine. She had attributed attitudes and emotional needs to Catherine which did not exist, and she had permitted the child to retain behavior which was unsatisfying and inappropriate, even while she disapproved of it.

The mother attended a class in child management and was able to give Catherine both approval and special attention. She also protected her playthings and playtime from the marauding of the boys. She was encouraged to show strong disapproval at any attack Catherine made on her but to take the initiative in restoring friendly relations after an argument with her. The father refrained from criticizing the mother's handling in front of Catherine. Both parents emphasized that masturbating was impolite behavior and was not to be continued. Catherine's temper tantrums became much less frequent, and both the masturbation and her talk of wanting to be a boy decreased. The mother acquired confidence in her ability to handle the child and began to understand that Catherine did need her affection, approval, and protection.

Case 30

Gregory L., age ten, of superior intelligence, was jealous of his seven-year-old brother Joe, even to the extent of pouting and complaining when Joe was given birthday presents. Gregory also refused to work in school, exploded when asked to do anything, and screamed and shouted at home. He lost expensive clothing and made no effort to find it, picked up toys he found in other people's yards, and twice had run away from home. Gregory cried when his classmates teased him or played tricks on him.

Gregory was the oldest of three boys, the youngest of whom was still a pre-schooler. Joe, the middle son, did good work in school and was popular with other children. Mrs. L. was tense and talked rapidly and loudly. Her husband was restrained in manner and speech and appeared dependent on her. Both agreed that they criticized Gregory constantly but rarely followed through on instructions they gave him. They chose books for him at the library, forced him to clean his plate, enrolled him in numerous extra classes and activities, and considered him a brilliant individualist who did not need to conform.

Gregory was a slight, small boy wearing glasses. He talked freely with the examiner and joked on an adult level. He performed erratically on tests, and his dependence on parental affection and intercession was apparent. His extreme jealousy of Joe was a natural result of comparing his own school and social failures to the younger boy's successes. He worried his parents deliberately in a vain attempt to get them to control his infantile behavior and to keep them attentive to him. They ensured his dependency and irresponsibility by pushing and overcontrolling on nonessentials, while overlooking his temper and sympathizing with his complaints about school and peers.

Mrs. L. attended a class in child management and began to give Gregory both more favorable attention and more freedom to direct his own life. She and the father agreed to curtail general criticism but to follow through on every request they made of him. Gregory continued to set himself apart from other boys, but he did begin to do better in school. He was overheard advising Joe not to envy their four-year-old brother his birthday presents, telling him that he had felt foolish when he did the same thing. His uncontrollable behavior and aggression at home decreased.

Case 31

Rex A., age 11, of average intelligence, took money from his parents and walked off with food at the grocery store and toys at the dime store.

He was the second of five children. Mrs. A. was a patient and subservient person who worked hard to care for her family and required little of the children. She was most concerned about and involved with the oldest boy, who suffered from asthma. Mr. A. paid little attention to the children and seemed to resent the fact that his wife's interests were centered in the children, rather than in him. Both parents devoted considerable amounts of time to church work, and the family attended services four times weekly. Rex was considered a responsible boy by his teacher, although he had demonstrated immaturity when he first started to school.

Rex was a boy of average size for his age, who appeared passive and expressionless. He readily admitted his stealing but disclaimed responsibility for his acts, indicating that he was unfairly treated by his parents and that his rights and needs were ignored. He resented his older brother and admitted that he was angry when he stole. Although the parents had scolded Rex and questioned him about his reasons for stealing, they had not required retribution of him and had felt completely helpless in dealing with the problem.

They agreed to keep money at home out of sight and to supervise Rex closely when he was with them in stores. He was to return anything he did manage to take and confess what he had done to the salesperson. He was to be given an opportunity to earn regular sums of money at home. The parents were encouraged to heed his complaints and to subordinate some of their activities and plans to his, so that he could have friends at home to play and more free time. The father began to spend some time alone with each child every week, and he rearranged the room space to provide more privacy and greater congeniality of roommates for the members of his large family.

Case 32

Peter C., age six, with average intelligence, would not come home after school. He detoured far out of his way, often stopping at strangers' houses and asking them to take him home. He screamed frantically whenever his mother left the house or even if he thought she had left.

Peter was the oldest of three children. Mr. C. worked out of town, and when he was home, he was impatient and angry with the children. The mother, unkempt, immature, and emotional, constantly quarreled with her husband. She liked to visit friends and relatives during the day, taking the younger children with her, and sometimes she had not returned when Peter's school day was over. Meals were hastily assembled at odd hours, and bedtime for the children was erratic. After repeated remonstrations with Peter about coming home promptly had proved useless, she once beat him severely when he arrived late, and his extreme fear followed this episode. Peter's teacher reported that he was immature and was careless about looking after his possessions and completing his work. His physician stated that he had periods of severe vomiting and that he sometimes slept all afternoon. He had poor eye-hand coördination, he lisped, and he had a slight hearing loss.

Peter showed great fear when first seen at the clinic, and he needed to check repeatedly to assure himself that his mother was waiting for him. When she was talking in an inner office and he could watch the door, he played quietly and happily by himself. Tests suggested that he enjoyed his mother's concern over him. Burdened with physical handicaps and uncertain care, Peter also had listened to angry quarrels between his parents and to threats of leaving. He could not trust his mother to keep her promises, and he feared her threats and punishment. He was afraid that she would be home and would punish him, but feared also that she might not be home and would never return.

Mrs. C. could readily understand the boy's fears, and she agreed to send the other children to neighbors to play during the first 30 minutes Peter was home after school. At first she met him at school and walked home with him; later, she met him half-way; and finally, she waited for him at home, where she had a snack prepared and talked or played with him alone. She learned to revise her habit of perpetual visiting, and she stayed home and finished her housework. She had meals on time and prepared them better, and she got the children to bed early, even when visitors were there. The parents began to work out some of their difficulties and to curtail their impulsive punishment of the children. Peter soon was doing much better work in school, and his fear of going home vanished within a few weeks.

Case 33

Grace E., age 13, of average intelligence, complained of pains in her chest and a sore throat, and her complaints occurred so frequently that she missed many days of school. In insisting that she was too ill to attend school, she sometimes vomited, cried, and screamed. Her mother had taken her to four different physicians, none of whom could discover any serious physical difficulty.

Grace was the youngest of four children. An older brother was a senior in high school, and two older sisters were married. The parents were in their late fifties and both were working. They were protective of Grace, worrying about her health and accompanying her to school or taking her in the car. The older brother had missed school often with similar complaints, and the two older sisters, who were exceptionally tiny as children, had been ill frequently. Grace was born by Caesarean section and was kept in the hospital for three weeks after her birth. As a young child, she had been hospitalized twice with a high fever. At the present time, she weighed 148 pounds and was awkward in her movements. She could ride a bicycle, skate, and dance, however, and enjoyed all of these activities. She stayed up late at night watching horror shows on television, and although she had a room of her own, she preferred to sleep in her parents' bedroom on a cot. She was given few chores and did not do these unless she was forced.

Grace was distant and defensive with the examiner at first, but gradually she came to enjoy her visits to the clinic. Tests showed poor ability to concentrate and to organize, and her verbal ability was superior to her performance ability. Her scores on achievement tests were consistently higher than her grade placement. Projective tests indicated that Grace was afraid that her parents might die and that she would be left alone. Their age, and illnesses they had had, contributed to this fear. Despite her worry, Grace tended to be an optimistic person, and she envisioned herself as able to overcome all difficulties and to be of service to others. Her goals for herself were high, but not unrealistic. Her hypochondriasis was based on her discomfort over the social contacts of school, her inept study habits, and her fear that she might return home from school to find her parents permanently gone. The family habit of attention to illness encouraged this method of self-protection. As the youngest child, she was accustomed to avoiding responsibility and receiving special consideration, and she had little reason to feel confident of her ability to manage independently. She actually did not feel completely well much of the time because of her excessive weight, the tension of the television horror shows, and the fatigue resulting from insufficient sleep.

The parents were encouraged to see that Grace went to bed earlier, and with her coöperation, they started her on a reducing program under medical supervision. When she complained of illness before school in the morning, she was required to go to school, with the understanding that if she continued to feel badly she should report to the school nurse. She was paid for regular chores at home, where her help was needed because of her mother's working. The parents deliberately talked about their own complete recovery from their former illnesses. Grace's school attendance became regular, and her grades were above average. She assumed responsibility for preparing the evening meal and was praised by her father for her skill as a cook. She welcomed the opportunity to have her own money and buy her own clothes, and she was faithful in trying to reduce her weight. Although the parents failed to alter the girl's sleeping habits, they did their best to lessen her fears.

Case 34

Winifred A., age 14, with average intelligence, trembled uncontrollably at times, but only in her mother's presence. Sometimes only one hand trembled. She became angry and cried easily, she could not sit still, and she was unable to concentrate. Her rages were so severe that they frightened her older brother. Two weeks prior to coming to the clinic she had tried to run away. In school, she could not remember what she studied, and she sometimes argued with teachers. Often there was an outburst when she received a low grade.

Mrs. A., a beautiful and capable woman, had worked since Winifred was in fourth grade, and she resented the girl's ability to obtain anything she wanted from her father. Mr. A. was irresponsible financially, and he depended on his wife to manage family affairs. Because he worked nights, he and Winifred prepared dinner each evening for the family, although the girl's help was erratic. He also drove her to school each morning, although the family lived within walking distance. Winifred's grades had been below average since she started junior high school, and achievement tests indicated that she was 18 months retarded educationally. Her physical health had always been poor.

It was suspected that she had polio within a week after birth; at two years, she was burned so badly that she had to learn to walk again. She had had festered boils, mosquito bite poisoning, an abscessed tooth, a broken collar bone, many attacks of croup, and a virus infection of the mouth. Her bedtime was erratic, and sometimes she was up and wandering around the house at two or three o'clock in the morning. She fell asleep while watching television, and her appetite was poor. A year ago, Winifred's friends had been considered undesirable by her mother, who finally refused her permission to associate with them. Occasionally, during this period, the girl lied about where she had been with them. At home she had few chores, kicked her clothing under the bed, and could obtain money whenever she asked.

Winifred was of average size for her age and variable in her attractiveness. She had many facial eruptions, but when she arranged her hair carefully, she looked older than she was. She cried easily during interviews and testing, usually when insisting that her mother was partial to her older brother, a studious, dependable boy. Tests indicated uncontrolled thinking and behavior, accompanied by fearfulness and distractibility. Winifred was concerned about having come between her parents by currying the favor of her father and angering her mother. She was envious, but admiring, of her mother's beauty and competence, and she felt helpless and inept in comparison. The mother, burdened and overworked, resented Winifred's easy life and was weary of her role as the responsible adult in the family. Never held to adequate standards of meeting obligations nor given sufficient physical care, Winifred was dissatisfied with herself and her abilities, discouraged by her frequent and severe physical troubles, and exhausted from lack of sleep and little food.

It was recommended that the parents assume their traditional sex roles, with the father to take over all authority for both children and the mother to work outside the home less but handle the domestic chores. Both Winifred and her brother were to be assigned regular work for which they were to be paid, thus enabling them to provide for some of their own needs. Mother and daughter were to spend time together regularly as companions. A strict bedtime was to be established and Winifred's eating watched. Both parents were to try to praise the girl daily, and she was to be given opportunities to invite friends home. Extreme temper was to be handled by isolating her, rather than by forcing her to remain and have the matter out, as had been her mother's practice. The father did become more dominant, but also more irritable in his unaccustomed role, and he witnessed his daughter's temper for the first time. The mother devoted time to her each evening to do whatever she wished, and she also arranged an out-of-town shopping trip for the two of them. With an early bedtime, Winifred soon was sleeping soundly all night, and her appetite improved. The trembling decreased, and gradually she was able to concentrate and remain calm for longer periods of time.

Case 35

Lester M., age 14, of average intelligence, had been retained in eighth grade but was still doing failing work in that grade. He always found excuses for not doing his homework, and when his parents helped him, he attempted to have them do the work for him. He had been enuretic until a year ago, had been in several fights at school, and had helped himself to money left around the house. He blamed others for his own mistakes, complained frequently, and became sullen or belligerent when criticized or caught lying by his parents.

Lester was the third of four children. An older sister lived at home and worked, and an 18-year-old brother shared a room with him and treated him solicitously. A 12-year-old brother was the same size physically as Lester. Mr. M. was gone frequently from home because of his work, but when there, he was overly generous with money, gifts, and freedom for Lester; and he waited on him and acceded to his wishes. Mrs. M. found it almost impossible to control Lester and his younger brother; and the boys paid no attention to her requests or rules. Lester had had poliomyelitis when he was 18 months old, and he had been strapped in bed for three weeks at that time. After this he tired easily, slept a great deal, and was slightly paralyzed in one foot for several years. Although he liked sports, he was not skilled at them. During his pre-school years he had no playmates and spent hours alone amusing himself. Later, his friends were all either taller or more intellectually inclined than he, and often he deserted a group of boys with whom he had started to associate. Frequently he bought treats for other boys, however. His failure to complete his assigned school work was apparent first in fifth and sixth grade, and his present written work was studded with misspelled words. In class, he did not seem to understand or listen to directions.

Lester was small physically and emotionally expressionless. When he first came to the clinic, he found it difficult to use words, either conversationally or on tests, but the difficulty did not persist during succeeding interviews and tests. He stated firmly that he did not want to learn to read, and he had truanted from an after-school remedial reading class. Tests demonstrated poor verbal and arithmetic skills, and his oral reading was slow and labored. Projective tests indicated his consistent ability to control his parents with emotional outbursts and his awareness of the overprotection his father gave him. He felt worthless, and he mistrusted the reliability and good intentions of others. Both parents had been greatly concerned about Lester when he had polio, and this illness and its after-effects set a pattern of lassitude and loneliness for him. The isolation, combined with failure on the part of the parents to require responsible behavior, produced a child who regarded himself as infantile and indulged himself accordingly, assisted by both his father and his brother. His severe educational handicaps, added to his disinclination to work, ensured his complete disinterest in improving matters.

It was recommended that the father listen to Lester read for 15 minutes each day and that the boy read another 15 minutes to himself from material of his own choosing. He was to be required to complete one schoolwork assignment each night, and it was to be checked by his parents. He was to be given regular chores and paid for these, so that he could meet some of his own expenses from his earnings. Separating Lester from his older brother and assisting him in finding friends with whom he was compatible was urged. A school conference was held and communication between the school and parents established. The father began to assume more authority over the boy's behavior, but because Mr. M. became seriously ill shortly after the clinic study, many of the suggestions were not followed and Lester's progress is unknown.

Case 36

Steven G., age 13, of average intelligence, within a month of starting junior high school, refused to go to school, crying hysterically when his parents questioned him about his reasons or threatened to make him go. Transferred to another school, he continued to cry in the principal's office and begged his mother to stay with him. During this period, he vomited repeatedly.

The oldest of three children, Steven fought with his sister, age 11, a less attractive and intelligent child than he; and he was jealous of his six-year-old brother. Mr. G. was a quiet man, who paced the house restlessly when the children argued and who was unable to express his own views at the clinic because of his wife's constant interruptions. He appeared to be patient and helpless, and he had become greatly disturbed after he punished Steven in a vain effort to get him back in school. The mother talked constantly, cried, earnestly requested help, but ignored suggestions. She believed that Steven was a brilliant child and claimed that he did everything well. She especially appreciated his thoughtful, courteous treatment of her in public. He still called out at night for his mother to bring him drinks of water, however, and she complained about his pestering, whining, crying, and laziness. Teachers reported that the mother had always interfered in any relationship between themselves and Steven, and consequently he was distant in his attitude toward them. Mrs. G. was seldom home, occupying herself with a variety of activities, and she remained in bed while the children prepared their own breakfast. Steven had been born two months prematurely and had had difficulty taking milk during his first year. As an infant, he had been held almost constantly. Throughout his life considerable attention had been paid to his health; he had a low pain threshold; he was a finicky eater; and he was troubled with constipation. In kindergarten, Steven had not known how to play with other children. He responded with an automatic refusal whenever he was asked to do anything, and he was afraid of making mistakes. Later on, he worked very little at his studies and procrastinated unless forced to complete the work.

He had been ill with flu a few days before the fall semester had started, and he had worried about vomiting at school. A few weeks later, after a slight roughing up from another boy and threats from a group of boys, he asked his mother to pick him up in the car after school, which she did. When the other boys taunted Steven about needing his mother's protection, Mrs. G. became enraged, grabbed one of the boys, and ordered Steven to hit him. He did so, and it was after this incident that he could not be persuaded to return to school.

Steven was an attractive, rather short boy, who sat with his head bowed during interviews and who gave minimal answers to questions. He was more productive during testing, however, and occasionally smiled. He would not talk about his refusal to attend school, merely shaking his head when questioned. Mistrustful and fearful of others, unsure of himself, feeling ill and lonely, Steven could not tolerate the accumulated events which had resulted in his humiliation and fear. Before the study had been completed, Mrs. G. took the boy to live with a relative in another state, where at last report he still had not reëntered school.

Case 37

Belle Y., age 15, of dull intelligence, was referred to the clinic after running away and being found in the company of a soldier with whom she had lived for several days. She had also run away from home a year previously, and at that time had had sexual intercourse with a carnival worker. She had been apprehended several times for theft.

Belle was the younger of two children. The mother preferred Belle's older brother to her, and in fact had arranged before her birth for her adoption. Her imminent arrival had precipitated the departure of Mr. Y. The mother remarried when Belle was four years old, but the stepfather had stated recently that he would leave the family if Belle's behavior did not improve. The mother was a rigid, unforgiving woman who quarreled constantly with Belle and who seemed to enjoy talking about her misdeeds. She complained that since the age of four years, Belle had cheated in games and schoolwork, lied, stolen, and during the past few years had had a bad temper. Belle had attended six different schools and had been retained one year. During the previous year, she had been unable to concentrate in school and was failing. The family had lived in a small town for one year, where Belle had many friends, and during this period she had done no stealing.

Belle weighed nearly 200 pounds. She also had a 40 per cent visual loss, and she reported difficulty with hearing and sleeping. She was uneasy during interviews, and when talking about her experiences with the soldier, she wrung her hands and twisted and tore paper. Both of her sexual adventures had followed episodes of quarreling with her mother which had made her extremely angry. She admitted taking underclothing, a coat, jewelry, money, and bicycles from stores, and she could explain her actions only by saying that she wanted or needed these things. She was reported to have burned candles several times inexplicably, and to have believed that the air register in a physician's office was a device wired to permit eavesdropping on her conversation. Tests indicated her extreme anxiety and inability to utilize her intelligence. Experiencing rejection and disapproval all of her life, and held responsible for the mother's loss of marital partners, Belle retaliated with behavior highly inconsistent with her mother's rigid rearing, although perhaps subtly encouraged by her attention to it. The conflict between her actions and her conscience overwhelmed Belle, and her loneliness was not appeased by her casual acquaintances. It was recommended that she be retained in the state industrial school for her own self-protection, with the hope that she might in time acquire greater emotional stability in a setting away from her mother.

Case 38

Louis M., age 14, was referred to a diagnostic center for evaluation as a dependent child. He had a history of having exhibited himself to girls.

Louis was the second of three brothers, all of whom had spent some time in an orphanage and who were fond of each other. Prior to entering the orphanage at the age of nine, Louis had lived with his maternal grandparents, both of whom had since died. The grandfather, sexually promiscuous, senile, and mentally defective, was believed to have fathered Louis and his younger brother. His daughter, the boys' mother, had been committed to a state hospital as psychotic eight years earlier. Louis was highly concerned about his mother and planned to "rescue" her from the hospital when he became older. He had been told by a physician that insanity is inherited.

On intelligence tests, Louis' performance ranged from superior to borderline, but on achievement tests, he was consistently above average. He had never been a behavior problem in school, and his attitude there always had been favorable and his attendance good. Louis was bothered with asthma, especially during the winter, and he was hard of hearing. At the orphanage, his friends had been younger than he. His interest in girls had been recent but energetic: He hugged and kissed them, and wrote many amorous notes. When Louis talked about girls, he lost all emotional restraint, laughing inappropriately and speaking and thinking illogically. He reported that he masturbated alone and with other boys and that he could not control erections induced by seeing scantily clad women in movies. Louis had been told that it was wrong to exhibit himself, and he was worried about losing all self-control. He believed that his sexual actions would harm him both physically and mentally and that he would "go insane" and be sent to a state hospital like his mother. Tests showed strong inferiority feelings, a tendency to disintegrate under threat, aggressive feelings directed against himself, physical concern, and childish emotion. His excessive attention to sex stemmed from the promiscuity of the adult members of his own family, recalled when his own sex interest was aroused by his adolescence, and also from sex misinformation which added to his guilt feelings, his fear of insanity, and his conviction that his behavior was inevitable and uncontrollable. His anxiety was so profound that intellectual functioning was seriously disturbed.

Louis was given reassurance about the normality of erections and masturbation, and thorough information about the anatomy and functioning of his body. The obligation of a man to be able to provide for a wife and family before undertaking sexual activity was also discussed with him. This explanation and reassurance produced an immediate acceleration of performance on intelligence tests, which now confirmed his superior ability. He was placed with a rural foster family, and at last report he was working conscientiously at school and on the farm, and had been elected to a class office by his schoolmates.

Case 39

Helen J., age 16, of average intelligence, was failing in school, had no friends, showed poor judgment, and daydreamed excessively. She had formed the habit of sitting in a rocker looking out the window for lengthy periods, and she could not remember what she read from her texts because she reverted to daydreaming after the first few sentences.

Helen lived with her maternal grandparents, to whom she was sent after the death of her mother, a veteran of five marriages. As a young girl, Helen was permitted to run the streets, was encouraged to solicit attention from men and boys, and at her mother's instigation had intercourse with one of her mother's boy friends. She was put in charge of three younger half-siblings, one of whom suffered a permanent injury while under her care. The grandmother had high standards for Helen, exerted strong control, and criticized her continually. The grandfather compared her to her mother whenever he was displeased with her, although both were trying to do what they believed was best and had taken her into their home at the sacrifice of their own comfort and convenience. Her teachers thought well of her and believed that she tried hard, but was overambitious for the ability she had.

Helen was a tall girl, with a wistful expression and a rare smile. She appeared to be completely discouraged, and she arrived for each appointment with a new problem and the announcement that suggestions for solutions to prior problems had not worked. Projective tests indicated that Helen could not share emotionally and that she felt others were insincere. Intelligence had deteriorated and judgment was poor. She resisted authority and solved her problems by fantasy. She withdrew from others because she could neither give nor receive affection, but she indulged in self-pity and dramatization, quietly enjoying the trouble she caused her grandparents.

Helen was permitted to join a girls' social club which had been ruled out because meetings were held on school nights, and she was given more responsibility at home and greater freedom of choice in buying her own clothes. She had planned to attend college, and this was discussed realistically with her and she was discouraged from attending. The grandparents were instructed to interrupt any prolonged daydreaming and to talk with her whenever she wanted to converse or ask questions.

She could not follow study suggestions given her, but she did begin to talk at length with her grandmother about her ideas and feelings. She decided that she would join the Women's Army Corps when she graduated from high school, but failed the entrance examination twice. Soon after her graduation, she moved out of her grandparents' home and lived in rented rooms or apartments. She held various jobs for short periods of time. Twice, after becoming drunk, she had intercourse with men she met at bars. Periodically, she talked about going to college and occasionally she asked her grandparents for permission to return to their home. Nothing is known of her after this time.

Case 40

Simon C., age 14, of low average intelligence, was a compulsive hand-washer and was afraid to enter closets, open windows, or ride over bridges. He walked in his sleep and claimed that he had a weak nervous system just like his mother's.

Simon was the younger of two children, but his older sister was married and living away from home. Mrs. C. worried and cried about Simon's compulsions and fears, and she herself was known as an exceptionally conscientious housekeeper. She severely criticized her husband for neglecting Simon, and the boy parroted her scorn, stating that his father had not gone far in school and could not do anything right. Simon dwelt at length on the sensitivity of his nerves and the pain he had suffered during various illnesses and accidents. Several times, to escape the tormenting of other boys, he had changed schools. His only friends were younger boys, whom he criticized and disparaged. He never tried to defend himself from the physical attacks of much smaller boys, and he cried over what he considered mistreatment by them.

Simon was solemn and rarely smiled or relaxed. He moved his hands constantly as he talked. He was belligerent in attitude and expressed no feeling of responsibility for any of his own behavior. He attributed his hand-washing to wanting to keep clean, and said he had not tried to break the habit, nor had his mother helped him to do so. Although there were indications that the hand-washing was associated with masturbation, Simon denied this contemptuously. Wanting to remain protected and irresponsible, he wished to control others and have them defer to him.

Overprotected by a compulsive, tearful mother who destroyed the worth of maleness by her attacks on his father, Simon was anxious, ineffective, and helpless in his relationships with both children and adults. He imitated his mother's actions and thinking because he was afraid to initiate his own, and he feared she would transfer her criticism of his father to himself. His over-concern about being proper was evidenced both in his compulsions and in his conversation, as was his resentment at being unable to free himself from his fear of his mother's rejection and displeasure.

Simon was evaluated at a residential diagnostic center, and nothing is known of his eventual progress.

Case 41

Gerald G., age 17, of average intelligence, was developing systematic paranoid delusions when seen at the clinic. He truanted from school, complained of mistreatment by everyone, could not be trusted with work or to keep promises, and was enuretic. He had run away three times. At school he withdrew from classmates, clowned to attract attention, and was considered by male instructors to be both shiftless and arrogant. Women instructors had no problem with him.

Gerald was the oldest of three children, and bitterly resented the youngest, a girl. His severe criticism of her frequently made her cry. Mrs. G. was a large woman, mannish in appearance, who, at her husband's insistence, had worked since Gerald was a small child. The father, a salesman, was gone most of the time, and when he was home he treated Gerald as a not-too-bright child. Gerald's allowance had been granted and withdrawn erratically without reason through the years. He had had a paper route when he was 11 years old, and soon managed to abandon it by leaving his papers in a ditch rather than delivering them. He had always avoided boys and never had been interested in girls. He used the family car for speeding and racing.

A slender boy with wavy hair and a flushed face. Gerald was expressionless and sullen during interviews, and resentful and suspicious during testing. He was uninterested in planning for his future, and he talked only of his hatred of his family and the unfair treatment he had had. Projective tests indicated regression, negativism, and extreme defensiveness. Any connotations of sex or implications of violence in the test materials were disturbing to him. Confused, distractible, and cynical, Gerald did not want to grow up; yet he was aware of and disgusted by his infantile characteristics. His need to gain attention from his busy and usually absent parents contributed to his early irresponsibility, and his rearing had been neglected and inconsistent. Sexual roles were indistinct for Gerald, who disliked his father for his contemptuous treatment and resented his mother for her apparent indifference to him. He could see little difference in their functions.

Warned that Gerald's strong hate might erupt into violence, the mother quit working, over the father's protests. She also talked with the father about minimizing his criticism of Gerald and his direction of him in such matters as bathing, smoking, and occasional beer-drinking. Gerald was permitted to quit school, and found work in a two-man garage. He did some carpentry work around the house, and completed a room for himself in the basement, after which his enuresis ceased. He began to date a girl who had exhibited much troublesome behavior, saying he felt sorry for her. There were occasional flare-ups, and once he quit his job, but within a few days he returned and apologized. His conflicts with his sister decreased.

Case 42

Dorothy B., age 18, of dull intelligence, had attempted suicide twice, and several other times had talked about it. She cried easily, sometimes without apparent reason, but laughed whenever she hurt someone else. She exaggerated tales of where she went and what she did, and even created glamorous imaginary experiences to impress friends. She often lied to her parents, was rude to her mother, and admitted that she wanted to hurt her.

The second of three children, Dorothy resented both her older brother, who had more freedom than she and some authority over her, and her younger sister, whom she considered spoiled. Mrs. B. was talkative and somewhat resentful of Dorothy. She had never required any regular chores of the girl, and when Dorothy did cook or iron, the mother criticized her work and often did it over. Mr. B. was a quiet man who was oversolicitous with the children, and when Dorothy, as a child, had complained of having her feelings hurt, her father had talked to her by the hour in attempting to console her. At present, however, he was disgusted with her excessive emotional displays and her unreliability, and once he had not spoken to her for a week. It was after a serious argument with her parents that her first suicide attempt took place. Although she ranked below the fiftieth percentile on achievement tests, Dorothy nevertheless had earned average grades during most of her school career, and teachers considered her conscientious and considerate. She had dated since she was 13 years old, and was reported to require circumspect behavior from her boy friends. She was restricted by her parents in her associations, and she seemed proud when she reported to friends that she had been grounded temporarily by her parents for misbehavior. She had been disturbed when a boy friend was ordered by his parents not to date her any more because of her religion, and she talked often about the onus of being a member of a minority religious group, sometimes mentioning suicide when she discussed this problem.

Dorothy was heavy, short, and rather unattractive. She talked and cried easily during interviews and described herself as "lazy, inconsiderate, spoiled, with a bad disposition: gets hurt easily and good at hurting other people." Projective tests indicated strong feelings of self-concern and inadequacy, preoccupation with running away and suicide, lying as the result of fearfulness, and worries related to boy friends and to her family. Dorothy had learned at an early age that she received her father's solicitous attention when she announced that her feelings were hurt. Accustomed to quick sympathy, she constantly sought it; and added to her practice of overdramatization of her problems was the conviction that she was incapable of achievement and inferior both for this reason and because of her religion. Dashing through life with constant attention to her own feelings and to the reaction of others toward her, Dorothy could take no rebuffs or unpleasantries, and her own dissatisfaction with her lack of direction and self-control was evident in her conscientious school performance, her high standards for others, and her pleasure at parental restrictions. Her suicide attempts were a crowning effort to hold the attention she had always had from increasingly unsympathetic parents, whom she wished to force into feeling guilty for their criticism of her.

The parents began to require regular housework from Dorothy, and her mother agreed to train her to work well, to praise her for her efforts, and to refrain from doing over what she did poorly. The father was to assume complete authority over the girl; recognize her truthfulness when it occurred; and in talking with her, encourage her to use her judgment in handling problems rather than to look for sympathy from others. Definite arrangements were made for her to continue her training at a business college after graduation from high school, and the arrival of a new boy friend on the scene distracted Dorothy from her usual problems. At last report, she was reacting with anger, rather than tears, to frustrations, and was displaying her newly acquired cooking skill with some pride.

Case 43

Gilbert R., age 17, of average intelligence, was arrested for drunken driving, resisting arrest, and damaging property while drunk. He had been involved with the court for similar offenses during the past two years. He was often absent from school during this period, sometimes truanting and sometimes staying away with his parents' knowledge, and recently he had been dismissed for failure to attend. When he had been drinking, Gilbert was belligerent, and he had been involved in many fights.

Gilbert was the second of four children. His older brother had followed a similar pattern of behavior, but had been able to gain control of himself when he left home to attend college. He had been domineering and supercilious with Gilbert. The family was relatively prosperous, and Mr. R. had given Gilbert all the money he requested, and when he obtained his driver's license at 15 years, his father gave him a car. He considered the boy hopeless, however, often cursed him, and had whipped him severely when he was younger. The father himself had been drinking heavily and associating with other women for many years. Mrs. R. was a suspicious, confused, vague, supercilious woman, who was critical of authorities, defensive of Gilbert, and unable to follow through on any plans to control him. Although Gilbert once had been popular, his friends now complained that he became angry easily, used vile language, and went off alone to drink when he did not like their plans. When he began junior high school, he was considered a quiet boy, but he did little schoolwork, and by the time he was 13, he appeared bored both with his friends and with school. He was smoking at that age, and neighbors considered him a pest. He failed two subjects in tenth grade, and was failing all of them during the first few months of eleventh grade, at which time he was dropped from school.

Gilbert was a tall, attractive-appearing boy who was quiet and serious in manner. He indicated that he had first truanted in company with other boys and that they had spent their time riding around town and getting drunk. He blamed no one for his difficulties, but he could not predict that he would be able to avoid them in the future. Tests suggested that in general his judgment was good and his emotion controlled; but he was anxious, depressed, and worried about homosexuality. Imitating his father and brother in their behavior, he still rejected both of them as persons. Without an adequate male model, he was sexually confused. Neither parent provided him with discipline or constructive attention, and he was permitted to do as he pleased, with both parents gaining some emotional satisfaction from pampering, castigating, and identifying with him. Living under confusion, violence, and strong emotion, he missed the protection and attention his parents should have given him.

The parents were able to exercise greater control for a short period of time, and Gilbert was readmitted to school on probation, revokable at the first offense. The mother soon became involved in further planning with other agencies and dropped her contacts with the clinic. Nothing is known of Gilbert's eventual progress.

Case 44

Susan T., age 14, of superior intelligence, had run away from home and truanted from school during the past two years. Once she was with four older boys at 3 A.M., and another time she and another girl ran off with two boys in a stolen car. They were several hundred miles from home when they were apprehended. Susan also had been in a number of fights with girls.

Susan was the only child of a marriage which ended in divorce when she was two years old. Her father was an alcoholic, of which she was ashamed, although she rarely admitted it and sometimes talked of going to live with him. Susan had lived with her grandmother until she was seven years old, at which time the mother remarried. At the time Susan was seen at the clinic, the home was in an uproar because of the adults' continual quarreling. The mother seemed completely out of contact with Susan, and the stepfather drank excessively. Both parents worked, and Susan had chores to do, which she always protested. The mother substituted threats and name-calling for control of her daughter, and Susan argued angrily with her and called her names, for which she was slapped. At school, Susan's teachers recognized her superior intelligence, but the girl broke most of the school rules and no punishment effected any change in her behavior. She was unaccepted by her classmates and had few friends. When teachers criticized her, she remained silent; and she showed little initiative in study.

Susan's elaborate hair arrangement and heavy make-up made her appear much older than she was. Her conversation consisted of critical descriptions of the behavior of adults, and she believed that she and her companions were justified in any kind of behavior because of the attitudes and actions of their parents. She described herself as stupid and as having a bad temper. Projective tests indicated that she wished to be protected and free from problems. Susan had always wondered if her mother really wanted her, and she had become convinced that her mother was concerned only with her own problems and not with Susan. The girl imitated her parents in her uncontrolled behavior and identified with them in the same way. She also tried to divert the attention of each of them from the other by her tantrums and misbehavior, and she felt completely isolated both at home and school.

The mother did take control of Susan for a brief period of time, arranging for her supervision during one summer and also spending more time discussing their differing viewpoints. Soon after school started in the fall, however, Susan ran away again, and she was sent to the state industrial school.

Case 45

Alan J., age 15, of above average intelligence, criticized and cursed his mother, and fought her with his fists. His parents described him as stubborn and claimed that they always had to force him to obedience. He never admitted being wrong, and he was failing in school, which had been true most of his life.

The oldest of three children, Alan had a 14-year-old brother who was in the same grade because Alan had been retained in fourth grade. A 12-year-old sister, conscientious about her schoolwork and her father's favorite, was a special target for Alan's resentment. Mrs. J., a hard-working, determined woman who slept little and talked constantly, had used extreme methods to teach Alan since he was a small child. She hit his hand with a ruler when he made an error at piano practice, fought hand-to-hand with him when he attacked her, and still was forcing him to clean his plate at mealtime. She also overmanaged her husband, considered him weak and unmanly, and at times had taken over the support of the family. Mr. J. secretly enjoyed Alan's criticism of and rebellion against his mother and never corrected him for it. He made no objection to Alan's spending the evening watching television and starting his homework at ten o'clock each night. He acceded to the boy's demands and defended his irresponsibility, but he alternated this protection with occasional severe castigation and beatings. As a small child, Alan had played with younger children most of the time. At present, he had a girl friend with whom he spent much of his time. None of the children had regular chores and none had regular earnings or allowances.

Alan was a short, sturdy boy with a pleasant manner, but he could not talk freely and he was quick to misinterpret the interviewer's comments. He planned revenge against teachers he felt were unfair, admitted his need to impress others with his importance, and said that he would never forgive his mother for having him repeat a grade. Projective tests indicated aggressive feelings toward the father, a strong belief that a mother should not take charge of a family, and a concept of himself as spoiled and unhappy. There was perseverative and unrealistic thinking, indecision, and blocking in communication. Alan had never been held to consistent achievement, and violence was the only method ever used to motivate him. He felt himself the least able and favored of the children, and he resented his father's failure to take firmer control of the entire family. He was well aware of the charged, negative relationship existing between his parents, who seldom spoke to each other.

In time, the parents were able to assign regular chores for the children and to permit them to earn their own money; in addition, Alan found work after school. The mother agreed not to strike Alan and to prevent his hitting her. She was to require an apology from him each time he was verbally abusive, and the father was to see that this was given if the boy did not accede to his mother's demand. The father was to spend some time with Alan and to cease providing him with daily taxi service to school. Study hours were to be established, and he was to be limited to one hour of television daily. The parents did support each other more in handling the boy, although the father could not bring himself to enforce study hours. The mother tried to leave most of the boy's management to the father, but repeatedly expressed her certainty that he would do nothing about him. The home atmosphere remained taut and explosive, although Alan's cursing of his mother decreased sharply after he was required to apologize, and there were no more physical attacks. He still refused to follow her orders, however, and the general picture for all members of the family remained the same.

Case 46

Irma B., age 14, of average intelligence, had set 14 fires in the month prior to her commitment to a state industrial school. She had also stolen frequently, once had nearly killed her adoptive mother, and had run away from home several times.

Irma was adopted at 18 months, but she was not told of her adoption until she was nine years old. Her adoptive father died when she was three years old, and the mother, who had taken Irma only to hold her marriage together, was left with a child she did not want. Several months before the outbreak of the girl's fire-setting, the mother had married a man who had been courting her for nine years, but who still continued to work on his mother's farm and live there some of the time because of his mother's refusal to accept her son's wife and daughter. The stepfather refused to adopt Irma, and when the girl tried to use his name as her own, her mother told her that she could not do so. Irma often had been in trouble at school, and at such times her mother would upbraid the teachers, defending the child and ordering them to treat her in prescribed ways. In discussing Irma, the mother often cried and expressed her helplessness. She ascribed Irma's difficulties, which she considered grossly abnormal, to heredity. Irma's only friends were boys, one of whom was only nine years old, and her mother often criticized her boisterous play, telling her she should be more lady-like.

Irma was overweight, but she resented being put on a diet by her mother. Much of her stealing was of food or of money with which she bought food. She also stole cosmetics, and was sensitive about her appearance. Her fire-setting had started when, as a small child, she had torn up paper, set it afire, and thrown it into the toilet. Two years prior to her recent fire-setting spree, she had set the kitchen curtains afire. One of her recent fires was set after she was embarrassed at being beaten in a fight with a five-year-old girl—a fight to which she had invited several boys because she was certain she would win. She complained that other children at school tormented her. She could not explain the attack on her mother and claimed that she had not been angry with her, although she would have succeeded in killing her had she not been interrupted. Projective tests showed confused, illogical thinking, and preoccupation with aggression, deceit, jealousy, and killing. She had many fears associated with her appearance, family, school, and sex. Reared by a mother who felt unjustly burdened and confined by her, Irma had known only strong and conflicting emotion. The mother criticized the girl severely, punished her, and expressed her belief that Irma was hopeless; but nevertheless she excused and defended every aggressive act the child directed against others. Unable to find a reasonable and self-respecting relationship with anyone, Irma was unable to accept the final rejection of her mother's remarriage, which refused her a place in the newly constituted family. Prognosis for Irma was considered poor.

Case 47

Patricia C., age 18, was brought to the clinic because of a tendency to "freeze in her speech." The mother was unable at first to admit the child's long history of school failure, and she resented the need to discuss this. The girl was reported to tremble in social situations where conversation was expected of her, and often she could say nothing at all.

Patricia was the older of two girls. Her younger sister, age seven, was alert and active, but so fearful at night she insisted on sleeping with Patricia, which the older girl did not welcome. Mrs. C. criticized Patricia constantly and refused to permit her in the kitchen to cook because she was so inept. She never accepted the diagnosis of retardation and would not enroll her daughter in a special class. The child had been kept in the regular public school classes and had been sent to dancing, dramatics, music, and baton twirling lessons with children of normal intelligence. Mr. C. admitted that he had criticized Patricia for carelessness but he considered his wife's domination of the girl to be extreme. Patricia had suffered a series of physical disabilities. She was troubled by allergy as a small child and often was held by her parents during this period; and she had difficulty with hearing. She was underweight, ate poorly, was ill frequently, and had little strength in her hands. She was worn out by six o'clock in the evening. As a small child, she never showed anger; but at present, she sometimes expressed anger toward her mother when she pushed her. When she was seen, she was taking a few classes at the high school and was being tutored regularly. She had a few friends, her own telephone, and enjoyed playing records. She had attended community dances a year earlier. In the evening, she retired to her room and spent some time looking out the window and practicing talking to herself before her mirror.

Patricia was small for her age. She wore heavy glasses and walked with a slight limp, but she was pleasant and friendly and did not immediately present a picture of retardation. She was overtalkative and appeared to be under great pressure to talk. Occasionally she mispronounced or slurred words, and she tried to use an impressive vocabulary in her speech. Educational achievement tests placed her at the third grade level, and her teacher reported that until recently her sentences were incoherent, but within the past 18 months there had been considerable improvement. For years, she rarely spoke when with her tutor, and a former teacher believed that the child had vegetated during the year she was in her classroom. Intelligence tests showed mild retardation, with an intelligence quotient of 64; and earlier tests had placed her intelligence quotient ten points lower. Projective tests indicated that Patricia felt lonely and ashamed of herself, but that she wanted to act responsibly. She saw her mother as emotional and changeable, with the children triggering emotion but actually assuming no importance in her life. Patricia showed considerable interest in dating and in marriage.

The parents could understand that their demands and dissatisfaction with Patricia had only hindered her using the abilities she had. They agreed to praise her regularly, accept academic work as adequate, and dispense with all extra lessons. The mother planned to train her thoroughly in cooking and housework, so that she not only would feel more helpful at home, but also would be more competent to find employment. Encouraging Patricia's association with girls who accepted her and with whom she felt comfortable was suggested, with the caution that these would usually be those younger than herself. Within a few months, the parents reported that Patricia was not showing as much temper as formerly and that her speaking ability had improved. They were attempting to restrain their criticism, had eliminated piano and ballet lessons, and stated that Patricia was remaining with the family in the evening rather than retreating to her room. She was teaching herself to play the piano and was much less antagonistic toward her sister. The mother planned to assign her regular household duties and investigate the possibility of her working part time in a children's nursery.

Case 48

Andrew D., age 12, of average intelligence, was referred to the clinic by his junior high school principal because he was reading at the fourth grade level. His teacher reported that the boy seemed near panic when he thought he might be required to read aloud in class and that it was necessary to give him detailed directions about assignments in order for him to understand what was expected of him.

Andy was the second of two children, and he and his older sister were on friendly terms. Mrs. D. was bland and expressionless. She seemed unable to communicate either intellectually or emotionally. Mr. D. had told his son, often and disgustedly, that he would never learn to read. He was proud of the boy's athletic ability and his eagerness to fight, however, and sometimes he read Andy stories from sport magazines. Andy's scores on achievement and reading tests had always been at least two grades below his placement, and he had been retained in second grade because of poor reading. He had had both tutoring and summer school work, all with limited results, and books he brought home from the library were never read. His birth had been precipitous, and as a small child Andy fell often and once was knocked unconscious. The parents assigned him no regular chores and did for him the occasional work they requested and which he rarely completed. They gave him money whenever he asked for it. He kept busy most of the time attending movies, going to the junior high canteen, or playing at school gyms or athletic fields. His parents reported that he rarely became angry with them and never talked back, but he cried when he could not do as he wished. Once he became so angry with another boy he planned to kill him and had to be restrained, and with children at school, especially younger ones, he was aggressive and abusive.

Andy was of average size for his age and was excessively polite during interviews. He talked very little about his troubles and was unable to feel at ease. Tests showed low average verbal ability; odd, inattentive thinking; and evidence of brain damage in perceptual distortions and verbal confusion. He made errors in reading passages scaled for the first grade. Projective tests suggested his known irresponsibility and a tendency to excuse his own undesirable behavior. He was afraid for his physical safety and worried about his intellectual ability, and there were indications that he was lonesome and led a life quite separated from that of his family. The brain damage, combined with his unwillingness to work and the anxiety caused by his loneliness and immaturity, resulted in the inattention and impulsive responses which prevented his learning to read adequately even with extra instruction. His abuse of younger children reflected his own feelings of worthlessness and burden, and his need to protect himself from embarrassment was apparent in his excessive fear of public exposure of his deficiencies in the classroom.

Concentrated reading tutoring was recommended for Andy. It was suggested that he choose simple books and each evening read alternate pages with his father. Regular home study hours were to be established, and the father was to assume more control of the boy and give him more attention. Andy was to be assigned regular chores and to be permitted to earn his own money. The parents began some of these programs, but terminated their contact with the clinic before results could be evaluated.

Case 49

Mary L., age six, had been blind since birth. She had never been toilet trained, her temper tantrums were daily events, and she talked less now than she had as a younger child. She often sat in a corner, rocking and banging her head against the wall.

Mary was an only child, and her distraught parents had had little guidance in caring for her. Mrs. L. had carried the child in her arms everywhere until she was in her third year, and when questioned, she had cried, "She's blind!" She rocked Mary to sleep nightly and comforted her immediately whenever she cried. Attempts at toilet training had been half-hearted, and the parents still dressed and fed her. Mr. L. was as distressed over his wife's unhappiness as with the lack of progress in the child. Both thought of her as helpless, unable to learn, and dependent on them for the duration of her life.

Mary was a small, thin child, who interrupted the conversation between the parents and the interviewer with complaints and demands to go home.

Minimal examination of her learning ability suggested that intelligence was normal, and the parents were urged to enroll her in the special class for visually handicapped children maintained by the public schools. They were reassured about her potential abilities, and a more accurate picture of her probable future was sketched. They could understand that in pitying Mary and believing her incapable of caring for herself, they had prolonged her dependency and inhibited her initiative so that she was dissatisfied both with herself and with them. They began to encourage her to feed and dress herself, and they regularized toilet training. Mary's teacher was a forthright person who permitted no displays of temper to go uncorrected and who identified each learning error a pupil made and insisted on accurate work. During her first year at school, Mary learned to use a braille-writer, and she proudly answered her teacher's questions and exhibited her skill for visitors. Although she occasionally was enuretic during the school day, this was becoming less frequent, and her pleasure over the activity of school and the association with other children was obvious.

Case 50

Leonard M., age 13, with high average intelligence, was evaluated in connection with the possibility of his return from a residential state school for the deaf to his own home and entrance into the public schools.

Leonard was the oldest of three children. He was profoundly deaf, with a binaural loss of 80 decibels for pure tones. A new hearing aid recently had reduced his loss to 29 decibels for individual speech sounds, within the range of normal conversation.

He was sent to a state residential school for the deaf at the age of three years and had been taught there for ten years. As a young child, he did not try to talk, it was impossible to gain his attention, and he acquired no concept of language. He read lips poorly. Finally, by using a multi-sensory, analytical method designed for aphasic children, he began to respond. When he was eight years old, he was placed in a foster home where a hearing boy about his own age was a member of the family, and he participated in Scouting and other activities with hearing children, while still receiving training at the school for the deaf. During the past six months, Leonard was assigned to a sixth grade class in a public school in the same city in which the deaf school was located, and he won an award for language achievement. He returned daily to the deaf school for special help.

Leonard was a friendly child, interested in everyone and in everything about him. He constantly asked questions and was honest in admitting his failure to understand, rather than resorting to nodding and smiling in pretense. It was believed that he would be able to return home and enter the public school program with some regular help from a speech therapist.

AUTHOR INDEX

539

SUBJECT INDEX

Problem behavior (*Continued*)
  and excessive punishment, 90, 94–95
  and fatigue, 56, 59–61
  and freedom to defy and attack, 98,
    102–103
  and immaturity, 34, 37–40
  and neglect, 42, 45–46
  persistence of, 132
  and responsibility, rejection of, 62–63,
    66–68
  rewards of, 9–10
  and self-respect, damaged, 83, 86–88
  and sex differences, 15
  and unbalanced social experience, 48–
    49, 52–54
Procrastination, 99
Professional workers. See also *Child
    guidance clinic, Guidance counselor,*
    and *Teachers.*
  and handicapped child, 423
  and school problems, 254
  and theory, 1, 4, 5–6, 110, 337
  and therapy, 287
Prostitution, 373
Protection
  of adolescent, 308, 334
  and aggression, 404
  and anxiety, 385–386
  of feelings, 3, 101
  of handicapped child, 421–422
  and immaturity, 34–40
  and lying in elementary child, 291
  of mentally retarded child, 440
  and obesity, 221
  rejection of, in elementary child, 215
  and school phobia, 264
  and social deviations, 347
  unnecessary, 51, 84, 99, 164, 198, 276,
    308, 421–422
Provocation
  by adolescent, 305–308, 371
  by elementary child, 199
  by pre-school child, 110–115, 121–125,
    136
Psychiatrist. See *Professional workers.*
Psychoanalytic theory, 5
Psychologist. See *Professional workers.*
Psychomotor seizure, 446
Psychopathic personality disorder, 347,
    351–353
Psychophysiological problems. See also
    specific problems.
  in adolescent, 333–345
  in elementary child, 234–246
  and fatigue, 61
  in immature child, 38
  and self-respect, 87, 333
  and social isolation, 54, 393

Psychosis. See also *Schizophrenia.*
  in childhood, 281–284
  in immature adolescent, 40
  with parental role distortion, 80
  and social isolation, 54
Punishment
  of adolescent, 411
  and aggression, 163, 228, 296, 411
  and behavior revision, 10
  excessive, 90–97, 198, 237, 411
  insufficient, 2, 98–108
  of like-sexed child, 93
  of pre-school child, 122, 131, 133, 163
  and psychosis, 283
  self-punishment, 222, 235, 298, 339
  and sexual deviations, 367, 376, 377

Questions, of pre-school child, 127

Race, 23–24
  and drug addiction, 389
Rape, 377–378
Raven's Progessive Matrices, 427, 487
Reading disability
  in adolescent, 356–357
  and aphasia, 251
  in elementary child, 258–260
Rebellion, 199, 305, 308, 313, 315, 328.
    See also *Aggression, Negativism,* and
    Resistance.
Recreation
  adolescent, and parent attitude, 307,
    318
  family, 23, 319
  of handicapped, 476, 490
Regression
  and fatigue, 61
  in pre-school child, 127, 150, 178–179
  and worry, in adolescent, 382
Rejection. See *Parent.*
Relatives, 22–23, 132
Religion. See *Church.*
Resentment
  of neglect, 45–46
  and rejection of responsibility, 67
  of social isolation, 54
Resistance, 120–121. See also *Aggression,
    Negativism,* and *Rebellion.*
Respect, for child's feelings, 3. See also
    Self-respect.
Responsibility
  acquisition of, 62
  failure in and neglect, 46
  rejection of, 62–70